Dictionary of Trade Policy Terms
Fifth Edition

This is an accessible guide to the vocabulary used in trade negotiations. It explains about 2,500 terms and concepts in simple language. Its main emphasis is on the multilateral trading system represented by the agreements under the World Trade Organization (WTO). In addition it covers many of the trade-related activities, outcomes and terms used in other international organizations, such as the United Nations Conference on Trade and Development (UNCTAD), the World Intellectual Property Organization (WIPO), the Food and Agriculture Organization (FAO) and the OECD. The last five years have seen a rapid spread in the formation of free-trade areas in all parts of the world. This dictionary allocates generous space to the vocabulary associated with such agreements. It offers clear explanations, for example, of the concepts used in the administration of preferential rules of origin. Additional areas covered include emerging trade issues and issues based particularly on developing-country concerns.

WALTER GOODE has worked on international economic relations since the late 1970s. He has wide experience in bilateral and multilateral trade negotiations, and has represented Australia in negotiations and meetings in the GATT, WTO, UNCTAD and OECD. His publications include *Australian Traded Services* (1987), *Uruguay Round Outcomes: Services* (1994) and *Negotiating Free-trade Agreements: A Guide.*

WORLD TRADE ORGANIZATION

Dictionary of Trade Policy Terms

Fifth Edition

Walter Goode

HF
1373
.G66
2007

CAMBRIDGE UNIVERSITY PRESS
Cambridge, New York, Melbourne, Madrid, Cape Town, Singapore, São Paulo

CAMBRIDGE UNIVERSITY PRESS
The Edinburgh Building, Cambridge, CB2 8RU, UK
Published in the United States of America by Cambridge University Press, New York

www.cambridge.org   Cam
Information on this title: www.cambridge.org/9780521712064

Printed in the United Kingdom at the University Press, Cambridge

A catalogue record for this publication is available from the British Library

ISBN 978-0-521-88506-5 hardback
ISBN 978-0-521-71206-4 paperback

Dedicated to
Elizabeth and Siegfried

CONTENTS

Disclaimer   *page* viii

Preface   ix

Dictionary   1

Acronyms used in international trade relations   493

Bibliography   510

DISCLAIMER

Dr Walter Goode is an officer of the Australian Department of Foreign Affairs and Trade (DFAT). The explanations, definitions and comments expressed in this volume do not reflect the views of DFAT or those of the Australian Government. These may be found in departmental and Australian Government statements and publications.

Any views given in this dictionary on WTO agreements, provisions, panel and Appellate Body reports, or any other information provided by the WTO, are the sole responsibility of the author, and do not necessarily represent the views of WTO Members, the WTO Secretariat, or the Appellate Body Secretariat. As such, the definitions in this dictionary do not constitute authoritative interpretations of the legal texts of the WTO and are presented for illustrative purposes only.

PREFACE

This *Dictionary of Trade Policy Terms* is now in its fifth edition. It contains about 600 new entries, and it is substantially different from the previous edition. I also have rewritten, either completely or substantively, about 120 entries. For various reasons many other entries have had to be updated. New expressions are being formed all the time, and at times it has been difficult to decide whether a term should have its own entry. On these occasions I have sought to form a judgement whether the term is likely to endure, at least for some years. No doubt I have committed errors both in including and omitting entries.

The WTO Doha Development Agenda (DDA) negotiations have produced new words and concepts. Progress in these negotiations has been accompanied by a rapid spread of free-trade agreement negotiations. This edition reflects this development. One example is that the dictionary now offers a fairly complete coverage of terms arising from the use of preferential rules of origin. As in past editions, I have sought to explain these terms in a form accessible to people who are not in the thick of negotiations. This means that I sometimes have had to neglect some details and nuances the negotiator cannot live without, but I hope that the result is still satisfactory for the reader.

I should stress that this dictionary concerns itself with words and topics routinely used with by trade officials in trade negotiations. It is not a dictionary of international economic relations. The areas of the two disciplines overlap in some cases, but the distinction between them is clear. Trade policy consists of a mixture of economics, law and politics, with the latter two often the dominating influence. International economics in comparison is much more rigorous. Even a brief look at textbooks of international economics suggests that economists are not always convinced of the validity of concepts used by trade negotiators or, indeed, their achievements. Obviously I have benefited from the work being done by the WTO, but the contents of this dictionary are naturally independent of it.

This dictionary has now been translated into the Chinese, Korean, Romanian, Vietnamese and Serbian languages. This is a pleasing development which, I hope, underlines its usefulness. I therefore take satisfaction from having been able to contribute to making the world of trade policy more accessible to a broad public.

Entries are in alphabetical order, usually in their most common form. Examples are *Kyoto Convention* for the *International Convention on the Simplification and Harmonization of Customs Procedures*, *UNCTAD* for the *United Nations Conference on Trade and Development* and *CITES* for the *Convention on International*

Trade in Endangered Species of Wild Fauna and Flora. In each case I have also included the formal version of the entry, with a referral to the main entry.

Entries are mostly self-contained, but in a few cases I thought it useful to duplicate partly an explanation under a different entry. Many entries contain referrals in *italic bold* to other entries. Readers should use these referrals as they like. Occasionally they may find something in this way that they had forgotten or didn't know. References to the WTO are so frequent that there seemed little need to provide a cross-reference when they occur.

Some entries are longer than is customary in dictionaries. Some are unquestionably longer than they should be. Still, I think that the reader should be offered, for example, a small historical survey of important concepts like the most-favoured-nation principle, the place of developing countries in the multilateral trading system or major events like the Kennedy or the Tokyo Rounds. Some entries are idiosyncratic, or at least the reader will think, with a deal of justification no doubt, that they are. That, I am afraid, is in the nature of books.

Other entries are of historical significance only. Among these are the Atlantic Charter, the Havana Charter, the Global Negotiations, the Marshall Plan, the Haberler Report and the United Nations Conference on Trade and Employment. One thing these entries do, however, is to show how persistent some of the problems of international trade policy are, and how hard it can be to find solutions for them.

This dictionary contains a few greatly abbreviated accounts of disputes brought before the GATT. No dictionary of trade policy could be complete without a mention of *hatters' fur* or *Belgian family allowances*. Those seeking further details on these and other disputes should consult the GATT and WTO *Basic Instruments and Selected Documents* (the BISD). I have not included any abstracts of disputes brought before the WTO. These are available in full in the *Dispute Settlement Reports* published by Cambridge University Press or the relevant WTO documents on www.wto.org. The reader seeking brief summaries of WTO disputes may also wish to turn to the one-page summaries now available from the WTO Secretariat.

One change from the last edition is that I have cited references for some of the entries. Some of them guide the reader to the source material I have used. In other cases they point to interesting material that could not possibly have been reflected here. I have also given a few Internet addresses, but some of these are likely to change over the years. The bibliography gives more information on the books and articles I have consulted.

I am again indebted to many people, and I cannot mention them all here. Among them are the participants in the trade policy workshops I have conducted in the past three years in Bandar Seri Begawan, Beijing, Jakarta, Kuala Lumpur and Manila. I relied heavily on Peter Gallagher of Inquit Communications in Melbourne and Andy Stoler of the Institute of International Trade at Adelaide University as presenters in these workshops.

I would like to thank Dr Felix Addor from the Swiss Intellectual Property Office for his kind help particularly in matters concerning of geographical indications. His assistance has allowed me to produce what I believe is a balanced treatment of this still controversial area.

My thanks are also due to Dr Geoffrey Bannister of the World Bank who generously gave me his advice on the item covering trade and poverty, a subject drawing increasing attention. I was able to benefit both from his published material and his personal advice on my proposed entry.

I am especially obliged to Finola O'Sullivan of Cambridge University Press who has once more given me much good advice and who has managed this project with great efficiency. Wendy Gater and Richard Woodham have also made sure that this dictionary would be published on time and to their standards.

Jean-Guy Carrier of the World Trade Organization has once more done everything to ensure speedy publication. I would like to thank him for that.

Professor Kym Anderson of the Centre for International Economics at the University of Adelaide has continued to support my work on this dictionary.

I again would like to acknowledge the support I have had from my colleagues. Justin Brown, Chris DeCure, Michael Mugliston, Milton Churche, Ric Wells and John Larkin, all from the Department of Foreign Affairs and Trade, in particular have helped me, sometimes inadvertently, to clarify my thinking on certain issues through debate and discussion. Roy Nixon from the Australian Treasury has clarified my thinking on several aspects of investment. I am grateful for their interest in this book.

It is obvious that I have benefited from the efforts of many, but the responsibility for any errors of fact, inadequate interpretation or infelicitous expressions is, as authors are wont to say, entirely mine.

WG
April 2007

A

Absolute advantage: an idea described by Adam Smith in his *Inquiry into the Nature and Causes of the Wealth of Nations*, and developed further by others, that countries engage in international trade to obtain goods more cheaply from abroad than they could make them themselves at home. Smith argued that international trade allows a greater specialization than would be possible in an autarkic system, thereby permitting resources to be used more efficiently. Writing about the reasons why families buy things rather than making them themselves, he said: "[w]hat is prudence in the conduct of every private family can scarce be folly in that of a great kingdom. If a foreign country can supply us with a commodity cheaper than we ourselves can make it, better buy it with some part of the produce of our own industry employed in a way in which we have some advantage." See also *autarky*, *comparative advantage*, *gains-from-trade theory*, *Heckscher-Ohlin theorem*, *self-reliance* and *self-sufficiency*. [Smith 1991 (1776)]

Absolute standard: see *minimum standard of treatment*.

Absorption: countering the higher tariffs resulting from *anti-dumping measures* through lowering the price of the good. In other words, the producer or exporter of the good absorbs the additional cost caused by higher tariffs to preserve his place in the market. See also *anti-absorption* and *circumvention*.

Absorption principle: also known as "roll-up" principle, used in the administration of *preferential rules of origin* under *free-trade agreements*. It means that in defined cases, usually after they have undergone specific processing requirements in the territory of a free-trade partner, the *non-originating materials* forming part of a good to be imported will not be included in the calculation of the *regional value content* of that good. In other words, although the materials are in strict terms non-originating and thus not eligible for preferential treatment, they are in fact deemed to be *originating materials*. See also *substantial transformation*.

Accelerated tariff liberalization: ATL. A later stage of the *APEC* initiative for *early voluntary sectoral liberalization*. APEC ministers decided in Kuala Lumpur in November 1998 to transfer the tariff elements of the first nine sectors of this initiative to the WTO. The nine sectors are forest products, fish and fish products, toys, gems and jewellery, chemicals, medical equipment and instruments, environmental goods and services, energy, and a telecommunications mutual recognition agreement. In the *Auckland Challenge* APEC members agreed to pursue the initiative until the end of 2000. ATL then became part of the negotiations under the *Doha Development Agenda*.

Acceptable level of risk: defined in the WTO *Agreement on the Application of Sanitary and Phytosanitary Measures* as "the level of protection deemed appropriate by the Member establishing a sanitary or phytosanitary measure to protect human, animal or plant life or health within its territory". The level varies according to country, but it is meant to be based on scientific principles. The *precautionary principle* may also apply. This concept is also known as the "appropriate level of sanitary or phytosanitary protection". See also *sanitary and phytosanitary measures*.

Accession: the act of becoming a member of the WTO (World Trade Organization), or another international organization or agreement. Negotiations are limited to ensuring that the acceding country can meet its membership obligations. Accession to the WTO thus requires negotiations between the applicant and the existing members to ensure that the applicant's trade regime will be in harmony with WTO rules, and that the applicant is able to observe these rules. On accession, the schedules of tariffs and services commitments the new member offers should be broadly comparable to those of existing members which have participated in successive rounds of *multilateral trade negotiations* and reduced their trade barriers over the years. In other words, a country has to be prepared to offer roughly the same as it will enjoy from membership. Accession to the *OECD* requires new members to show that their economic regime is broadly in tune with those of existing members. Membership of *UNCTAD* or other United Nations bodies does not entail this sort of obligation. Accession to the *European Union* is known as *enlargement*. See also *schedules of commitments on services* and *schedules of concessions*.

Access to Medicines: an aspect of the work on *intellectual property rights* in the WTO. It deals with the balance between obligations under the *Agreement on Trade-Related Aspects of Intellectual Property Rights* (TRIPS) and the expectations of developing countries for affordable medicines. Developing countries claim that *compulsory licences* and *parallel imports* are essential for their governments to carry out effective health policies through affordable medicines. In their view, the TRIPS agreement is biased in favour of pharmaceutical companies residing in developed countries. The differing views on access to medicines show the inherent tension between intellectual property rights (a form of monopoly rights) and public expectations of vigorous competition between companies. The *Doha Declaration on the TRIPS Agreement and Public Health* was aimed at reducing this tension. It aims to make it easier for some developing countries seeking the required authorization to grant a compulsory licence for the purpose of making a pharmaceutical product and exporting it to *least developed countries* and other developing countries which are also members of the WTO. This is subject to the condition that the system will only be used in case of a national emergency or in cases of public non-commercial use.

Accordion of likeness: an expression used by the *Appellate Body* in *Japan – Taxes on Alcoholic Beverages*. It holds that the meaning of the term *"like product"* has to be interpreted more or less generously according the nature of the product itself. It says that there can be no precise and absolute definition of what is "like". In its words, "[t]he accordion of 'likeness' stretches and squeezes in different places as the provisions of the *WTO Agreement* are applied". [WT/DS8/AB/R]

Accounting rate: the charge made by one country's telephone network operator for transporting calls originating in another network to their final destinations within the second network. See also *telecommunications termination services*.

ACP–EC Partnership Agreement: a framework for trade and economic cooperation between the *ACP states* (except Cuba) and the *European Community*, signed on 23 June 2000 as the successor to the *Lomé Convention*. On 1 April 2003 it entered into force for twenty years. It has five pillars: (a) a comprehensive political dimension, (b) participatory approaches to ensure the involvement of civil society in beneficiary countries, (c) a strengthened focus on poverty reduction, (d) a framework for economic and trade cooperation and (e) reform of financial cooperation. The Agreement has several review mechanisms. Its trade aspects will be renegotiated after eight years to make them fully compatible with WTO obligations. During this time (called the preparatory period) the European Community will give non-reciprocal preferential access free of duty and charges to products from ACP states. Special provisions apply to some agricultural products, especially sugar. Support for national budgets in countries highly dependent on agriculture and/or mineral exports is available to ACP states if losses from export earnings jeopardize overall macroeconomic stability. The Agreement entails wide-ranging cooperation in trade-related areas including, among others, *trade in services, competition policy, trade and environment* and *trade and labour standards*. The parties have also undertaken to use the preparatory period to remove progressively barriers to trade between them and to pursue cooperation in all areas relevant to trade. See also *ACP–EC Protocol on Sugar* and *Special Preferential Sugar Agreements*.

ACP–EC Sugar Protocol: first concluded in 1975 as Protocol 3 to the *Lomé Convention*. It is an instrument of indefinite duration. The Protocol is now part of the *ACP–EC Partnership Agreement*. Through this Protocol the *European Community* undertakes to purchase, at guaranteed prices, specific quantities of cane sugar, raw or white, originating in *ACP states*. The following annual quantities apply: Barbados (49,300 tonnes), Fiji (163,000 tonnes), Guyana (157,000 tonnes), Jamaica (118,300 tonnes), Kenya (5,000 tonnes), Madagascar (10,000 tonnes), Malawi (20,000 tonnes), Mauritius (487,200 tonnes), Swaziland (116,400 tonnes) and Tanzania (10,000 tonnes). See also *Special Preferential Sugar Agreement*.

ACP states: The African, Caribbean and Pacific states associated with the *European Community* through the *ACP–EC Partnership Agreement* which gives them *preferential market access* to the European Community and other benefits. The group of ACP states was established on 6 June 1975 through the *Georgetown Agreement*. It now operates under a revised agreement adopted in November 1992. Its General Secretariat is located in Brussels. The members of the group are Angola, Antigua and Barbuda, Bahamas, Barbados,

Belize, Benin, Botswana, Burkina Faso, Burundi, Cabo Verde, Cameroon, Central African Republic, Chad, Comoros, Republic of Congo, Democratic Republic of Congo, Cook Islands, Côte d'Ivoire, Cuba, Djibouti, Dominica, Dominican Republic, Eritrea, Ethiopia, Fiji, Gabon, The Gambia, Ghana, Grenada, Equatorial Guinea, Guinea-Bissau, Guinea, Guyana, Haiti, Jamaica, Kenya, Kiribati, Lesotho, Liberia, Madagascar, Malawi, Mali, Marshall Islands, Mauritania, Mauritius, Federated States of Micronesia, Mozambique, Namibia, Nauru, Niger, Nigeria, Niue, Palau, Papua New Guinea, Rwanda, Saint Kitts and Nevis, Saint Lucia, Saint Vincent and the Grenadines, Samoa, Sao Tome and Principe, Senegal, Seychelles, Sierra Leone, Solomon Islands, Somalia, South Africa, Sudan, Suriname, Swaziland, Tanzania, Togo, Tonga, Trinidad and Tobago, Tuvalu, Uganda, Vanuatu, Zambia and Zimbabwe. Cuba is not a party to the ACP–EC Partnership Agreement.

Acquis communautaire: all legislation adopted under the treaties establishing the *European Community*, including *regulations*, *directives*, *decisions*, *recommendations* and *opinions*, as well as the judgments handed down by the *European Court of Justice* and international agreements concluded by the European Community. It consists of about 80,000 pages and is ever-changing. Before a country accedes to the *European Union*, its national legislation needs to be harmonized with the *acquis communautaire*. This can mean revising hundreds of parliamentary acts. No member state may derogate permanently from the *acquis*. *See* also *enlargement* and *European Community legislation*.

Action plan: often the outcome of last resort. It once really had the meaning of planning something and then doing it, and it sometimes even does so today. More often, however, an action plan is no more than a catalogue of things that could be done if anyone was interested.

Actionable subsidies: a category of subsidies described in the WTO *Agreement on Subsidies and Countervailing Measures*. Subsidies may be actionable, and therefore illegal, if they cause *injury* to the domestic industry of another member, negate other commitments made under the GATT, or cause *serious prejudice* to the interests of another member. If such adverse effects exist, the country maintaining the subsidy must withdraw it or remove its adverse effects. See also *countervailing duties*, *non-actionable subsidies*, *prohibited subsidies* and *subsidies*.

Act of state doctrine: the principle, as expressed in a United States Supreme Court judgment of 1897, that "every sovereign State is bound to respect the independence of every other sovereign State, and the courts of one country will not sit in judgment on the acts of the government of another, done within its own territory". Other jurisdictions of course also use this doctrine.

Adding-up problem: see *fallacy of composition*.

Additional commitments: the *General Agreement on Trade in Services* permits WTO members to make *commitments* on trade in services that are additional to those made under *market access* and *national treatment*. Qualifications, standards and licensing matters are mentioned specifically, but additional commitments need not be confined to these areas. See also *schedules of commitments on services*.

Additive regionalism: describes the concurrent membership of several *free-trade agreements* by one country. See also *spaghetti-bowl effect*. [Schiff and Winters 2003]

Adjusted value: see *build-down method* and *build-up method*.

Adjustment costs: the economic and social costs arising from *structural adjustment*.

Administered protection: see *contingent protection* and *non-tariff measures*.

Administered trade: see *managed trade*.

Administrative guidance: the practice of influencing the activities of an industry by government ministries through formal or informal measures. Guidance may simply consist of advice on how to interpret a government act or decision. It may also be a method of enforcing, for example, *voluntary export restraints* through the publication of indicative production and export forecasts. Industries are then supposed to work out among themselves how to divide the export cake. Administrative guidance of the second kind probably works best in countries where the enforcement of *competition policy* is weak.

Administrative international commodity agreements: these are *international commodity agreements* that do not operate a *buffer stock*, *export quotas* or other mechanisms designed to influence the price of a commodity through manipulating the amount coming on the market. This type of agreement is concerned with matters such as *market transparency*, more efficient production, processing and distribution, consumer information, and the collection and dissemination of statistical information. See also *economic international commodity agreements*.

Administrative protection: see *contingent protection* and *non-tariff measures*.

Administrative regulation: see *regulation*.

Administrative ruling of general application: defined in the *APEC principles on transparency standards* and some *free-trade agreements*, such as *NAFTA*, as "an administrative ruling or interpretation that applies to all persons and fact situations that fall generally within its ambit and that establishes a norm of conduct, but does not include: (a) a determination or ruling made in an administrative or quasi-judicial proceeding that applies to a particular person, good or service of another economy in a specific case, or (b) a ruling that adjudicates with respect to a particular act or practice". In other words, an administrative ruling of general application establishes a norm of conduct applying to all persons, goods, services and practices, as the case may be, in a given economy.

Ad **notes:** the notes and explanatory provisions contained in Annex I to the **GATT**. They amplify and interpret some of the GATT articles proper. They always have to be read together with the relevant article.

Ad referendum **agreement:** provisional acceptance of the outcome of a set of negotiations. Definitive acceptance may depend on the results of related negotiations, approval by the government or the fulfilment of some other condition. See also *bracketed language* and *without prejudice*.

Ad valorem: a proportion of the value of a good or a transaction. See *ad valorem tariff*.

Ad valorem equivalent: a calculation of the level of a *specific tariff*, which converts a rate expressed as a fixed monetary value per product into a value expressed as a percentage of the value of the product. This gives the *ad valorem tariff* rate. For example, a specific tariff of one dollar levied on a compact disc worth ten dollars would give an *ad valorem* equivalent of 10%. On a disc worth twenty dollars, a tariff of one dollar would amount to 5%. See also *compound tariff*.

Ad valorem tariff: a *tariff* rate expressed as a percentage of the value of the goods to be imported or exported. Most tariffs are now expressed in this form. See also *customs valuation* and *specific tariff*.

Advance deposit: the requirement to lodge all or part of the cost of the imported good with a government authority, usually at the time it is ordered. See also *non-tariff measures*.

Advance informed consent: an obligation embodied in the *Cartagena Protocol on Biosafety*. It establishes the need for an exporter to seek consent from an importing country before the first shipment of a *living modified organism* intended for intentional release into the environment. See also *prior informed consent*.

Advance rulings: an aspect of customs procedures. Many customs authorities provide advice on request, normally in writing, on how they will treat a good to be imported. Such advice may include the tariff classification, the applicable tariff rate and whether a good qualifies for *preferential market access*. Such advice is not always legally binding, but customs authorities usually honour it unless it was based on false information or an error of law. Advance rulings therefore are an important way to bring predictability into the trading system. Importers and exporters alike may apply for them.

Advisory Centre on WTO Law: established on 17 July 2001 in Geneva as an independent *intergovernmental organization* with funding from nine developed countries and more than 25 developing countries and economies in transition. The Centre provides legal services and training to developing countries and economies in transition that have contributed to its endowment fund. *Least developed countries* can use the Centre's services without contributing funds.

A fortiori: Lat. with stronger reason; much more so.

African Economic Community: AEC. An organization aiming to promote the economic, social and cultural development of Africa. It was established on 12 May 1994 through the Treaty of Abuja. Membership, which now exceeds fifty, is open to all members of the Organization of African Unity, now the *African Union*. The AEC will aim in the long term to form an African Common Market. In the medium term it will concentrate on trade cooperation and *trade facilitation*. Its secretariat is located in Addis Ababa.

African Group: a group of 41 countries active in the WTO. Its members are Angola, Benin, Botswana, Burkina Faso, Burundi, Cameroon, Central African Republic, Chad, Congo, Democratic Republic of Congo, Côte d'Ivoire, Djibouti,

Egypt, Gabon, The Gambia, Ghana, Guinea, Guinea-Bissau, Kenya, Lesotho, Madagascar, Malawi, Mali, Mauritania, Mauritius, Morocco, Mozambique, Namibia, Niger, Nigeria, Rwanda, Senegal, Sierra Leone, South Africa, Swaziland, Tanzania, Togo, Tunisia, Uganda, Zambia and Zimbabwe.

African Growth and Opportunity Act: AGOA. Part of the United States *Trade and Development Act of 2000*, valid until 30 September 2008. The Act is based on a congressional finding that it is in the mutual interest of the United States and the countries of *sub-Saharan Africa* to promote stable and sustainable economic growth and development in sub-Saharan Africa. It gives eligible sub-Saharan countries duty-free access to the United States for most products. Provisions for textile products are more restrictive. AGOA also promotes the negotiation of *free-trade agreements* between the United States and sub-Saharan countries. Countries must meet certain eligibility requirements to benefit from this Act. Among these are that the country (a) has established, or is making progress towards, a market-based economy, (b) enjoys the rule of law and political pluralism, (c) is eliminating barriers to United States trade and investment, (d) has economic policies to reduce poverty, (e) has a system to combat corruption and bribery and (f) protects internationally recognized *workers rights*. Activities undermining United States national security or foreign policy interests and engaging in gross human rights violations or international terrorism make a country ineligible for the benefits of this Act. Countries must also have implemented commitments to eliminate the *worst forms of child labour*. *AGOA II*, passed in 2002, extended the benefits of the Act, especially for some textile imports from certain African countries into the United States.

African regional integration arrangements: this entry summarizes the main *regional integration arrangements* concluded by African countries since the 1950s. It only lists *free-trade areas*, *customs unions*, *common markets* and *economic unions* having at least three members. *A. West Africa.* Benin, Côte d'Ivoire, Niger, Togo and Upper Volta (now Burkina Faso) formed in 1959 the *Council of the Entente* to promote regional economic development and integration. The West African Customs Union (Union Douanière de l'Afrique Occidentale or UDAO) was also formed in 1959 by Dahomey (now Benin), Côte d'Ivoire, Mauretania, Niger, Senegal, Soudan (now Mali) and Upper Volta. It was succeeded in 1966 by the *West African Economic Community* which had the same membership. The *Mano River Union* was established in 1973 by Liberia and Sierra Leone. Guinea joined it in 1980. The West African Economic Community and the Mano River Union, together with Cape Verde, The Gambia, Ghana, Guinea-Bissau, Nigeria and Togo now form *ECOWAS* (Economic Community of West African States) which was established in 1975 and relaunched in 1993. *B. Central Africa.* The Equatorial Customs Union (Union Douanière Equatoriale or UDE) was formed in 1960. Its members were Chad, Central African Republic, Congo and Gabon. UDE was succeeded in 1964 by the *Central African Customs and Economic Union* (Union Douanière et Economique de l'Afrique Centrale or UDEAC). Its members were Cameroon, Central African

Republic, Chad, Congo, Equatorial Guinea and Gabon. UDEAC was succeeded in 1999 by the *Communauté Economique et Monétaire de l'Afrique Centrale* (CEMAC). The *Communauté Economique des Pays des Grands Lacs* (CEPGL or Economic Community of the Great Lakes) was founded in 1976. Its members are Burundi, Rwanda and Congo. The Economic Community of Central African States (Communauté Economique des Etats de l'Afrique Centrale or CEEAC) was established by the members of UDEAC and those of CEPGL in 1983. It became inactive in 1992. *C. Eastern and Southern Africa.* Kenya, Tanganyika and Uganda formed an *East African Community* (EAC) and an East African Common Market in 1967, but it collapsed in 1977. The EAC was was re-established in 2000. The Preferential Trade Area for Eastern and Southern African States (PTA) was formed in 1981 and superseded by the *Common Market for Eastern and Southern Africa* (COMESA) in 1993. Its members are Angola, Burundi, Comoros, Democratic Republic of Congo, Djibouti, Egypt, Eritrea, Ethiopia, Kenya, Lesotho, Madagascar, Malawi, Mauritius, Namibia, Rwanda, Seychelles, Sudan, Swaziland, Uganda, Zambia and Zimbabwe. *D. Southern Africa.* The South African Customs Union (SACU) was established in 1969 as the successor to the Southern African Customs Union of 1910. SACU's members are Botswana, Lesotho, Namibia (since 1990), South Africa and Swaziland. The Southern African Development Coordination Conference (SADCC) was formed in 1980 by Angola, Botswana, Lesotho, Malawi, Mozambique, Swaziland, Tanzania, Zambia and Zimbabwe. In 1992, it became the *Southern African Decelopment Community* (SADC). South Africa joined in 1994. *E. Africa-wide integration arrangements.* The Lagos Plan of Action, adopted by the *Organization of African Unity* in 1980, called for the creation of five Regional Economic Communities (RECS): North Africa, West Africa, Central Africa, Eastern Africa and southern Africa. The following are in existence: *Arab Maghreb Union* (AMU), Economic Community of Central African States (ECCAS, now inactive), Southern African Development Community (SADC) and the Economic Community of West African States (ECOWAS). A continent-wide arrangement, the *African Economic Community*, was established in 1994. It now has more than 50 members. Any member of the *African Union* can join it. [Bhalla and Bhalla 1997, Crawford and Fiorentino 2003, De la Torre and Kelly 1992, Ndlela 1992, Okigbo 1967, Robson 1968]

African Union: established in July 2001 at a meeting in Lusaka of African heads of government as the successor to the *Organization of African Unity*.

African Union Convention on Preventing and Combating Corruption: see *corruption*.

AFTA: *ASEAN Free Trade Area*. Established through the *Agreement on the Common Effective Preferential Tariff Scheme for the ASEAN Free Trade Area* on 1 January 1993. The main mechanism for the tariff reductions under AFTA is *CEPT* (Common External Preferential Tariff). Goods traded preferentially are covered by the *Inclusion List*. The ASEAN-6 (Brunei Darussalam, Indonesia, Malaysia, Philippines, Singapore and Thailand) will eliminate their tariffs by

2010 and the newer ASEAN members (Cambodia, Laos, Myanmar and Vietnam) in the main by 2015. Vietnam took on the full obligations in 2006. Sensitive products (all of these are agricultural) will have final rates of 0–5%. Final rates for highly sensitive products (various types of rice) for Indonesia and Malaysia will be 20%. The ASEAN-6 extend tariff preferences to Cambodia, Laos, Myanmar and Vietnam through the *ASEAN Integration System of Preferences*. AFTA has a work program for eliminating *non-tariff measures*. See also *ASEAN Economic Community*, *ASEAN Framework Agreement on Services*, *ASEAN Investment Area* and *Initiative for ASEAN Integration*.

Agadir Agreement: the *free-trade agreement* between Egypt, Jordan, Morocco and Tunisia signed on 11 January 2003 in Amman. It derives its name from the launch of the project in Agadir, Morocco, in 2001.

Agency for international trade information and cooperation: see *AITIC*.

Agenda 2000: the *European Community* financial reform plan for 2000–06 aimed at strengthening the union among European countries to get ready for the new members. The strategy identifies three main challenges: (a) how to strengthen and reform the *European Union*'s policies so that they can deal with *enlargement* and deliver sustainable growth, higher employment and improved living conditions for Europe's citizens, (b) how to negotiate enlargement while at the same time vigorously preparing all applicant countries for the moment of accession, and (c) how to finance enlargement, the advance preparations and the development of the Union's internal policies. Major changes to the *Common Agricultural Policy* have been made as result. See also *Europe Agreements* and *Treaty of Nice*.

Agenda 21: The Agenda for the twenty-first Century. This is a program of principles and actions relevant to *trade and environment* adopted on 14 June 1992 by *UNCED* (United Nations Conference on Environment and Development) in Rio de Janeiro. Program area A seeks to promote *sustainable development* through trade. Its objectives are (a) to promote an open, non-discriminatory and equitable trading system that will enable all countries to improve their economic structures and improve the standards of living of their populations through sustained economic development, (b) to improve access to markets for exports of developing countries, (c) to improve the functioning of commodity markets and achieve sound, compatible and consistent commodity policies at national and international levels with a view to optimizing the contribution of the commodity sector to *sustainable development*, taking into account environmental considerations, and (d) to promote and support domestic and international policies that make economic growth and environmental protection mutually supportive. Program area B aims (a) at making trade and environment mutually supportive in favour of sustainable development, (b) to clarify the role of *GATT*, *UNCTAD* and other international organizations in dealing with trade and environment-related issues, including, where relevant, conciliation procedure and *dispute settlement*, and (c) to encourage international productivity and competitiveness and encourage a constructive role on the part of industry in dealing with environment and development issues. See also *commodity policy*, *Rio Declaration on Environment and Development* and *World Summit on Sustainable Development*.

Aggregate measurement of support: a term used in agricultural negotiations. It is the annual level of support expressed in monetary terms for all domestic support measures where government funds are used to subsidize farm production and incomes. It includes product-specific support and support given to agricultural producers in general. The annual level of support has to be reduced as a result of the *Uruguay Round* negotiations. Domestic support measures with minimal impact on trade do not have to be reduced. See also *Agreement on Agriculture*, *amber box*, *blue box*, *equivalent measure of support*, *green box*, *subsidies* and *total aggregate measurement of support*.

Aggressive multilateralism: usually describes the option available to the United States of using the WTO dispute settlement mechanism vigorously, backed up by *Section 301* to the extent that that would be legal and desirable.

Aggressive reciprocity: the unilateral action of an economy which seeks to force a trading partner to change its **trade policy**. Measures used include *retaliation* in response to perceived unfair actions, the use of domestic trade legislation, etc. Aggressive reciprocity is capable of solving some trade issues, but often at the expense of considerable political ill-will. It has also been described as the "crow-bar theory of trade policy". See also *bilateralism*, *passive reciprocity*, *Section 301*, *Special 301*, *unfair trading practices* and *unilateralism*.

Aggressive unilateralism: see *unilateralism*.

AGOA: see *African Growth and Opportunity Act*.

AGOA II: improvements made to the *African Growth and Opportunity Act* as part of the United States Trade Act of 2002. Most of the improvements relate to preferential treatment of textile imports.

Agreement Concerning the International Registration of Marks: see *Madrid Agreement Concerning the International Registration of Marks*.

Agreement for Facilitating the International Circulation of Visual and Auditory Materials of an Educational, Scientific and Cultural Character: see *Beirut Agreement*.

Agreement for the Protection of Appellations of Origin and their International Registration: see *Lisbon Agreement*.

Agreement for the Repression of False or Deceptive Indications of Source on Goods: see *Madrid Agreement for the Repression of False or Deceptive Indications of Source on Goods*.

Agreement on Agriculture: one of the outcomes of the *Uruguay Round*. It is administered by the WTO. The Agreement provides the first effective multilateral framework for the long-term reform and liberalization of agricultural trade. The Agreement establishes new rules and commitments in *market access*, *domestic support* and *export competition* (i.e. the handling of *subsidies*). It encourages the adoption of domestic support policies that are less trade-distorting, and it allows actions aimed at easing domestic adjustment burdens. Some of the measures required by the Agreement are (a) a reduction by developed countries in export subsidy expenditures by 36% over six years in equal instalments, and a 24% reduction over ten years for developing countries; (b) a cut by developed countries in the volume of subsidized exports by 21% over six years, 14% for developing countries over ten years; domestic subsidies, as calculated through the *aggregate measure of support*, have to be cut by 20% over six years, calculated from 1986–88 as the *base period*; and (d) all *existing non-tariff measures* have to be converted into tariffs and bound, followed by a reduction by an unweighted average of 36% over six years in equal tranches, again with 1986–88 as the base period. For developing countries the cut is 24% over ten years. The Agreement entails *minimum access commitments* where markets were closed before, and *special safeguards* under strictly defined conditions to deal with import surges after *tariffication*. Negotiations aimed at further liberalization of agricultural trade resumed in 2000. They are now part of the negotiations under the *Doha Development Agenda*. See also *agriculture and the multilateral trading system*, *amber box*, *blue box*, *green box*, *continuation clause* and *peace clause*.

Agreement on Basic Telecommunications Services: WTO agreement first envisaged in the *Uruguay Round* outcome on *trade in services* and concluded on 15 February 1997. It contains *market access* commitments made by 69 members covering cross-border trade and supply through a *commercial presence*. The Agreement entered into force on 1 January 1998 through the *Fourth Protocol to the General Agreement on Trade in Services*. See also *cross-border trade in services*, *International Telecommunication Union* and *reference paper on telecommunications services*.

Agreement on counterfeiting and piracy: see *counterfeiting and piracy agreement*.

Agreement on Customs Valuation: formally the WTO *Agreement on Implementation of Article VII of the General Agreement on Tariffs and Trade 1994*. It sets out a system of non-discriminatory rules to be followed by customs authorities when they assess the value of imports for the levying of *customs duties*. See *customs valuation* and *customs valuation agreement*.

Agreement on Government Procurement: one of the WTO *plurilateral agreements*. It contains rules for the purchase by governments of goods and services for their own use. Such purchases are not covered either by the rules of the *General Agreement on Trade in Services* or the *GATT*. The agreement covers government purchasing contracts for goods, services and construction at the level of central government, state or provincial governments and utilities above a certain size. The agreement aims to ensure that, subject to legitimate border measures (e.g. health and safety standards, *intellectual property protection*, etc.), foreign suppliers receive no less favourable treatment than domestic suppliers for relevant government purchasing contracts, i.e. they give each other *national treatment*. It also stipulates that the parties accord each other *most-favoured-nation treatment* regarding government procurement covered by the

Agreement, but there is an element of direct reciprocity in the extent to which members allow firms from other members to compete in their government procurement. This applies particularly to purchases at the sub-federal or sub-central levels. The agreement also seeks transparent government purchasing procedures and practices. In late 2006 the parties to the agreement agreed provisionally on a revised version which reflects current procurement practices and is easier to read. See also *APEC Non-Binding Principles on Government Procurement*, *second-level obligations* and *Working Party on Transparency in Government Procurement*. [Arrowsmith 2003]

Agreement on Implementation of Article VI of the General Agreement on Tariffs and Trade 1994: the WTO *Anti-Dumping Agreement*. See also *anti-dumping measures* and *dumping*.

Agreement on Implementation of Article VII of the General Agreement on Tariffs and Trade 1994: the *customs valuation agreement*. It sets out the principles and procedures to be followed by WTO members in their assessment of the value of imported goods for the purpose of levying the appropriate amount of *customs duties*. The primary base for assessing the customs value is the *transaction value*. Broadly, this is the price actually paid or payable for the goods for export under conditions of competition. See also *customs valuation*, *identical goods* and *similar goods*.

Agreement on Import Licensing Procedures: the agreement setting out the procedures to be followed by WTO members in their administration of *import licensing* regimes. It defines import licensing as "administrative procedures used for the operation of import licensing régimes requiring the submission of an application or other documentation (other than that required for customs purposes) to the relevant administrative body as a prior condition for importation into the customs territory of the importing Member". The Agreement has provisions on automatic import licensing (i.e. approval of the application is always granted) and non-automatic import licensing (i.e. all cases where licensing is not automatic). The Agreement also establishes a system for notifying import licensing procedures to the WTO.

Agreement on Mutual Acceptance of Oenological Practices: see *World Wine Trade Group*.

Agreement on Preshipment Inspection: a WTO agreement setting out the conditions and procedures under which members may carry out *pre-shipment inspections* to ensure that the cost of goods shipped corresponds to the invoiced cost. Such inspections are used mainly by developing countries to prevent capital flight, commercial fraud, evasion of *customs duties* and other similar practices. The Agreement requires user members to apply *GATT* principles and obligations to the conduct of inspections. These include *non-discrimination*, *transparency*, protection of confidential business information, avoidance of unreasonable delay, the use of specific guidelines for conducting price verification and the avoidance of conflicts of interest by preshipment inspection agencies. Exporting members must apply their laws and regulations concerning preshipment activities in a non-discriminatory way. They must publish promptly all applicable laws and regulations and, if requested, they must afford user members technical assistance. In the case of disputes, the parties have access to independent review procedures mandated by the Agreement. These procedures should be administered by an independent body made up of an organization representing preshipment inspection agencies and an organization representing exporters. The decision of the three-member review panel is binding on all parties to the dispute. [Rome 1998]

Agreement on Rules of Origin: an agreement administered by the WTO. It sets out a program of work by the Committee on Rules of Origin for the long-term harmonization of *rules of origin*. Rules of origin are defined as laws, regulations and administrative determinations applied by members to determine the country of origin of goods admitted under *most-favoured-nation* conditions. The country of origin of the goods is either the country where the good has been wholly obtained or, if more than one country is involved, the country where the last *substantial transformation* was carried out. The Agreement stipulates that rules of origin should be administered in a consistent, uniform, impartial and reasonable manner. They should not themselves create restrictive, distorting or disruptive effects on international trade. Rules of origin must state what does confer origin rather than what does not. The Agreement contains an annex in the form of a declaration dealing with the administration of rules of origin admitted under preferential conditions. See also *change in tariff heading* and *preferential rules of origin*.

Agreement on Safeguards: a WTO agreement setting out and clarifying when and how members may resort to action under *GATT* Article XIX, also called *escape clause*. This Article deals with the possibility of emergency action to protect domestic industry from an unforeseen increase in imports which is causing, or likely to cause, serious *injury* to the industry. "Serious injury" is defined as a significant overall impairment in the position of a domestic industry, and "threat of serious injury" means that such injury is clearly imminent. The Agreement notes that a finding of a threat of serious injury must be based on facts, not merely an allegation, conjecture or remote possibility. The Agreement sets out criteria for safeguards investigation which include public notice for hearings and other appropriate means for *interested parties* to present evidence. The criteria may include whether a safeguard measure would be in the public interest. If a delay in taking safeguard action would cause damage difficult to repair, *provisional safeguard measures* not exceeding 200 days may be taken. Safeguards action must be non-discriminatory. It must be imposed against the product and not against the source of the product. In other words, even though products from country X might be perceived to be the main problem, country X may not be singled out for import reductions. *Selectivity* is possible only if (i) if it is clear that imports from certain countries have increased disproportionately in the period under consideration, (ii) all the other conditions for taking safeguard action have been satisfied, and (iii) if this would be equitable to other suppliers.

Generally, the duration of a safeguards measure should not exceed four years, though this may in some circumstances be extended to a maximum of eight years. Any measure imposed for more than one year must be accompanied by *structural adjustment* aimed at liberalizing access. Members taking safeguards action may have to offer *compensation*. The Agreement prohibits so-called *grey-area measures*, including *voluntary restraint arrangements*. All safeguards measures in force on 1 January 1995 had to be phased out within five years. See also *de minimis safeguards rule*, *Transitional Product-Specific Safeguard Mechanism* and *transitional safeguards mechanism*.

Agreement on Subsidies and Countervailing Measures: a WTO agreement which establishes three categories of subsidies and the procedures to be followed in dealing with them. The categories are *prohibited subsidies* (subsidies contingent on export performance or the use of domestic rather than imported goods), *actionable subsidies* (subsidies which may only be maintained if they do not injure the domestic industry of another member, do not cause *nullification or impairment* of benefits, or do not cause *serious prejudice* to the interests of another member) and *non-actionable subsidies* (subsidies which may be maintained by members). The Agreement details an accelerated timetable for *dispute settlement* cases arising from the application of the Agreement. It also sets out the conditions under which *countervailing duties* may be imposed. It does not apply to *agricultural subsidies*. See also *Agreement on Agriculture*, *amber box*, *blue box*, *green box*, *Permanent Group of Experts* and *provisional countervailing duties*.

Agreement on Technical Barriers to Trade: the TBT agreement. A WTO agreement aimed at ensuring that technical regulations and standards, including packaging, marking and labelling requirements, and procedures for assessment of conformity with technical regulations and standards do not create unnecessary obstacles to international trade. It is the successor to the *Tokyo Round* Standards Code. The Agreement encourages members to use appropriate international standards, but it does not require them to change levels of protection because of standardization. It covers not only the standards applicable to a product itself, but also related *processes and production methods*. Prescribed *notification* procedures apply. An annex to the Agreement contains a *Code of Good Practice for the Preparation, Adoption and Application of Standards*. Central government standardizing bodies have to comply with it. Local government and non-government bodies may choose to do so. See also *conformity assessment*, *International Electrotechnical Commission* and *International Organization for Standardization*. [Marceau and Trachtman 2002]

Agreement on Textiles and Clothing: a WTO agreement succeeding the *Multi-Fibre Arrangement* (MFA). It differed from the MFA in that it brought international trade in textiles and clothing again under the normal liberalizing and non-discriminatory WTO trade rules by 1 January 2005. This is also the date when the Agreement itself expired. The Agreement was supervised by the *Textiles Monitoring Body*.

Agreement on the Application of Sanitary and Phytosanitary Measures: the SPS Agreement. A WTO agreement aiming to ensure that food safety and animal and plant health regulations are not used as disguised barriers to international trade. The Agreement preserves the right of governments to take *sanitary and phytosanitary measures*, but they must not be used to discriminate arbitrarily or unjustifiably between WTO members that apply identical or similar measures. It encourages members to base their domestic measures on international standards, guidelines and recommendations where these exist. Members may introduce or maintain higher standards if there is scientific justification, or if a *risk assessment* has shown that this is appropriate. An importing country must consider the standards applied by an exporting country as equivalent to its own standards if the exporting country can demonstrate that this is the case. The Agreement sets out detailed procedures governing the *transparency* of regulations, *notifications* and the establishment of national *enquiry points*. See also *acceptable level of risk*, *appropriate level of sanitary or phytosanitary protection*, *equivalence*, *International Office of Epizootics* and *International Plant Protection Convention*. [Anderson, McRae and Wilson 2001, Marceau and Trachtman 2002, Peel 2004]

Agreement on the Common Effective Preferential Tariff Scheme for the ASEAN Free Trade Area: see **AFTA**.

Agreement on the Importation of Educational, Scientific and Cultural Agreements: see *Florence Agreement*.

Agreement on Trade in Civil Aircraft: one of the *WTO plurilateral agreements*, originally concluded as part of the *Tokyo Round*. Members of the Agreement undertake to eliminate all customs duties and other charges on (a) civil aircraft, (b) civil aircraft engines, parts and components, (c) other parts, components and sub-assemblies of civil aircraft and (d) ground flight simulators. The Agreement requires that purchasers should be free to select suppliers on the basis of commercial and technological factors, and without *quantitative restrictions*. WTO rules on *subsidies* apply. See also *EU–US aircraft agreement* and *Large Aircraft Sector Understanding*.

Agreement on Trade in Large Aircraft: see *EU–US aircraft agreement*.

Agreement on Trade-Related Aspects of Intellectual Property Rights: TRIPS. A WTO agreement concluded during the *Uruguay Round*. It was negotiated to deal with a growing tension in international trade arising from widely varying standards in the protection and enforcement of *intellectual property rights* and the lack of multilateral rules on international trade in counterfeit goods. Part I of the Agreement deals with general provisions and basic principles. It states that the Agreement applies to *copyright* and related rights, *trademarks*, *geographical indications*, *industrial designs*, *patents*, *layout-design of integrated circuits* and protection of *trade secrets*. Standards of protection to be applied are those of the *Paris Convention* (1967 revision), the *Berne Convention* (1971 revision), the *Rome Convention* and the *Treaty on Intellectual Property in Respect of Integrated Circuits*, but there is no need to accede to these instruments to satisfy the Agreement. Members are free to determine the appropriate method to implement the provisions of the Agreement within their own legal system and practice. Part II covers the standards to be applied to the availability, scope and use of intellectual property rights. Among these are that copyright protection must be for at least 50 years. Initial registration of trademarks must be for at least seven years, followed by an indefinite number of renewals also of at least seven years. Members have to protect geographical indications, and additional protection is available for geographical indications for wines and spirits. Protection must be given for independently created industrial designs that are new and original. Patents must be "available for any inventions, whether products or processes, in all fields of technology, provided that they are new, involve an inventive step, and are capable of industrial application". The term of protection for patents is at least 20 years from the date of filing. The term of protection for lay-out designs (topographies) of integrated circuits is ten years from the date of filing or the date of the first commercial application. Undisclosed information must be protected against unfair competition as provided in the Paris Convention. Special mention is made of undisclosed test or other data submitted as a condition of approving the marketing of pharmaceutical or agricultural chemical products which utilize new chemical entities. The Agreement recognizes that "some licensing practices or conditions pertaining to intellectual property rights which restrain competition may have adverse effects on trade and may impede the transfer and dissemination of technology", and it seeks to minimize such problems through a right to consultations. The means of enforcement of intellectual property rights outlined in Part III of the Agreement include administrative, civil and criminal remedies. Detailed provisions apply to preventing trade in counterfeit or pirated goods. The normal WTO procedures apply to the settlement of disputes. *Least developed countries* had until the end of 2005 to meet the obligations of the Agreement. Finally, the Agreement establishes the *Council for TRIPS*. See also *access to medicines*, *industrial property* and *intellectual property*. [Gervais 2003, World Trade Organization 1999a]

Agreement on Trade-Related Investment Measures: TRIMS. A WTO agreement concluded during the *Uruguay Round*. It aims to eliminate conditions attaching to permission to invest that may distort or restrict trade in goods. The annex to the Agreement contains an illustrative list of TRIMS deemed inconsistent with Article III (National Treatment) and Article XI (General Elimination of Quantitative Restrictions) of the *GATT*. These are (a) requirements that an enterprise must use a defined amount of products of domestic origin, (b) permission to import related to export performance, and (c) any requirements related to *quantitative restrictions* of imports. The Agreement also raises in Article 9 the possibility that at a later stage it might include provisions on *investment* and *competition policy*. See also *foreign direct investment*, *local content requirements*, *Singapore issues* and *trade-balancing requirement*.

Agreement Regarding International Trade in Textiles: see *Multi-Fibre Arrangement*.

Agreement Respecting Normal Competitive Conditions in the Commercial Shipbuilding and Repair Industry: see *OECD shipbuilding agreement*.

Agricultural export subsidies: a benefit paid by governments to producers or exporter of agricultural commodities to ensure that their surpluses, usually produced at costs above world market prices, find a market somewhere. This happens, for example, under the *Common Agricultural Policy*. Agreement was reached in 2006 in the *Doha Development Agenda* negotiations to eliminate agricultural export subsidies by 2013, but the temprorary suspension of the negotiations led to some uncertainty about this commitment. See also *agricultural subsidies*, *agriculture and the multilateral trading system* and *subsidy*.

Agricultural Market Access Database: AMAD. Contains information on *tariff* and *non-tariff measures* for more than fifty countries. The database is hosted by the *OECD*. It uses material supplied by Agriculture and AgriFood Canada, the Directorate-General of Agriculture in the *European Commission*, the *Food and Agriculture Organization*, the *OECD*, the *World Bank*, *UNCTAD* and the Economic Research Service of the United States Department of Agriculture. [www.amad.org]

Agricultural products: these are defined in Annex 1 to the WTO *Agreement on Agriculture* as mainly the products listed in chapters 1 to 24 of the *Harmonized System*. The group includes both raw and processed products, but it excludes forestry and fishery products.

Agricultural subsidies: assistance given to farmers governments, mostly through monetary payments, but sometimes in kind, such as favourable freight rates. Agricultural subsidies typically include (a) incentives to keep growing a product, grow more of it or switch to producing another, (b) income support to ensure that the standard of living of farmers is comparable to that of city dwellers, and (c) payments to ensure that the farming produce finds a market, either at home or abroad. Thus the main forms of agricultural subsidies are production subsidies, income-support payments and marketing and/or export subsidies. All of them are funded through national treasuries and therefore the tax payer. Income equalization sometimes also is a disguised subsidy. As the incomes of farmers can vary greatly from year to year, income tax payable may be low in some years, but high in others. Income equalization schemes allow farmers to even out their incomes over several years and in this way minimize their taxes. Agricultural subsidies are necessary where the farming sector cannot compete against the imported product. Reasons for this may be inefficiency, an inability to compete with subsidized imports or consumer preferences for an imported product. Hence subsidies related to production are often accompanied by *import restrictions*, such as *quotas*, *tariff rate quotas*, high tariffs generally and *seasonal tariffs*. Some say that *sanitary and phytosanitary measures* are being used for this purpose also. Agricultural subsidies tend to be expensive. This is the main reason why some countries have started to reform their support regimes. *Decoupling* can be an important step. The farmer still receives a subsidy, but the amount is no longer linked to production quantities or acreages. The WTO *Agreement on*

Agriculture seeks to deal with agricultural subsidies through classifying them into "boxes" according to their purpose and impact. Those falling into the *green box* are permitted without limit. Subsidies belonging to the *blue box* are considered minimally trade-distorting because they are related to the imposition of production limits. *Amber box* subsidies must be reduced in accordance with commitments made during the *Uruguay Round*.

Agriculture and the multilateral trading system: the rules of the GATT do not distinguish between agricultural and other products except in minor ways. Article XI requires the general elimination of all *quantitative restrictions*, but Article XI:2 permits some import and export restrictions on agricultural products under closely defined conditions. Article XVI (Subsidies) enjoins parties to avoid the use of subsidies on the export of *primary products*, and Article XX (General Exceptions) allows members to suspend some of their obligations to comply with measures they have accepted as part of their membership of *international commodity agreements*. Trade under these agreements was effectively not subject to GATT rules. For the first few years of the GATT's existence agricultural production and trade in agricultural products did not cause any real difficulties. Western Europe was still recovering from the effects of the late war, and there were as yet few hints of the persistent surpluses that were to be a feature of world agricultural trade a decade later. In particular, there seemed to be markets for United States domestic surpluses, except for dairy products. By the time of the 1955 *GATT review session*, there was a feeling among members that the time had come also to bring commodity arrangements under the supervision of the GATT. The United States, however, had run into a problem. Domestic production ran persistently ahead of consumption, and its import market was attractive to foreign suppliers. The 1951 Trade Act specifically held that new trade agreements could not be made in contravention of existing United States agricultural programs. The *import restrictions* permitted under GATT Article XI:2 appeared insufficient to deal with this problem. In 1951 the United States had been granted a *waiver* from the GATT rules to impose import restrictions on dairy products. This was superseded by a request in 1954, and granted in 1955, for a waiver without a time-limit until it would be able to bring the provisions of the *Agricultural Adjustment Act* into line with GATT obligations. This was the *Section 22 waiver*. The United States was now permitted to impose import restrictions on agricultural products as it deemed necessary. This action created a precedent for the treatment of agriculture under GATT rules. For example, when Switzerland acceded provisionally to the GATT in 1958, it obtained a *carve-out* for its entire agricultural sector. Nevertheless, the remainder of the GATT membership continued its search for an international regime for trade in commodities. A proposal had emerged in early 1955 for a *Special Agreement on Commodity Arrangements* (SACA). It contained a mechanism for dealing with disequilibria between production and consumption of primary commodities, including the possibility of commodity arrangements. Whether this arrangement would have existed side by side with the GATT, or whether it would have been subordinate to it, was never made clear. In any case, whatever the merits of the proposal, this did not matter, since it did not enter into force. There were those who considered that they would fare better under the existing GATT provisions. Others saw no point in proceeding once the United States made it clear that it was not interested in becoming a member of SACA. Attempts over the next three decades to impose GATT disciplines on agricultural trade fell well short of this proposal. An initiative later in 1955 to deal with the problem of surplus disposal, particularly under United States acts such as *PL 480*, petered out after several years of discussion. The next attempt to deal with the problem of agricultural trade came with the commissioning of the *Haberler Report* in 1957. It was aimed particularly at analysing the failure of the trade of developing countries to develop as rapidly as that of industrialized countries, excessive short-term fluctuations in the price of primary products and widespread resort to agricultural protection. The panel report, titled *Trends in International Trade*, was issued in October 1958. It argued, among other things, for a moderation of agricultural protectionism in North America and Western Europe, and its overall tenor was in favour of *trade liberalization*. Though the Report was universally welcomed, its influence turned out to be quite small. A committee was indeed established to consider the Report's recommendations in detail, and this led some to believe that a solution was nearer. Analysis and discussion there were, but the most that can be said about the longer-term effect of the Haberler Report is that it can be regarded as the first step towards the launch of the *Dillon Round* in 1960. In any case, by that time Western Europe's complete recovery from the effects of the war and the establishment of the *European Economic Community* had led to a new situation in global agricultural trade. The introduction of the *Common Agricultural Policy* with its *variable levies* and domestic support measures meant that the Community joined the United States in contributing to global trade distortions. Next, the *Kennedy Round*, launched in 1963, appeared to offer another opportunity to sort out agriculture. One of its objectives was the adoption of measures for access to markets for agricultural and primary products. It began badly with the outbreak of the *Chicken War*, a dispute between the United States and the European Economic Community over the sudden closure of German and other European markets for poultry through the operation of variable levies. The outcome on agriculture of the Kennedy Round was poor. Its main achievement was creating the impetus for the eventual conclusion of a new *International Grains Arrangement*. The mandate for the *Tokyo Round* (1973–1979) included negotiations on agriculture, taking into account the special characteristics and problems in this sector. These negotiations again ended in failure. The conclusion of the *Agreement Regarding Bovine Meat* and the *International Dairy Arrangement* introduced a fragile peace into these trades, but they did not deal with the underlying problems of domestic over-production, *export subsidies*, import restrictions and other measures characterizing agricultural trade. The Tokyo Round ended with agreement that there should be continuing negotiations on the development of a *Multilateral*

Agricultural Framework aimed at avoiding endemic political and commercial confrontations in this area. Negotiations were rejoined, but not to any effect. As noted by Hudec, Kennedy and Sgarbossa, there had been 100 disputes in the GATT concerning agriculture between 1947 and the early 1980s, accounting for nearly 43% of all reported disputes. The United States and the European Economic Community had been involved either as a complainant or a respondent in 87 of them. A new start to finding a solution to the problems of agricultural trade was clearly necessary. The 1982 GATT Ministerial Meeting agreed on a work program for the examination of all matters affecting trade, market access, competition and supply in agriculture. A working party made recommendations in 1984 concerning better market access, greater export competition, clearer rules on quantitative restrictions and subsidies, and more effective special treatment for developing countries. The report containing these recommendations was adopted in the same year. These recommendations then receded into the background as negotiations began for what became the mandate of the *Uruguay Round*, but they provided in effect a draft set of negotiating objectives for the Round when it was launched in 1986. Ministers agreed at Punta del Este that negotiations should aim to achieve greater liberalization of trade in agriculture and to bring all measures affecting import access and export competition under strengthened and more operationally effective GATT rules and disciplines. Attention would be given to the reduction of import barriers, a better competitive environment and the effects of *sanitary and phytosanitary measures*. Another new factor now entered into play. In the Kennedy and Tokyo Rounds the negotiations on agriculture were conducted mainly between the European Economic Community and the United States. Other agricultural traders existed very much at the margin of these negotiations. The formation immediately before the launch of the Uruguay Round of the *Cairns Group*, a group then consisting of fourteen agricultural producers and exporters, ensured that there would be an influential and moderating third voice. Agriculture was one of the most difficult negotiating subjects during the Uruguay Round. The issues were well understood, but no real progress was made until the European Community had accepted that changes to the Common Agricultural Policy were necessary for internal budgetary reasons alone, and that reductions in price supports were possible without tearing the Community's social fabric apart. Even then, the *European Commission* had great difficulty obtaining a negotiating mandate from the member states. Its difficulties in participating meaningfully in the agricultural negotiations led to the collapse of the Brussels Ministerial Meeting in December 1990. Matters were not helped by adherence by the United States to its objective of zero subsidies, something that observers doubted it would be able to deliver even in respect of its own practices. The Round then effectively marked time until the *Blair House Accord* in November 1992. Negotiations remained difficult, and some changes in favour of the European Community were made to this accord in December 1993. This allowed concluding the Round within a few days. Trade in all agricultural products is now covered by GATT rules, but extensive further negotiations will be required to achieve a trade regime resembling that for industrial products. Negotiations on agriculture resumed on 1 January 2000 under *Article 20* (the *continuation clause*) of the WTO *Agreement on Agriculture*. These negotiations are now part of the *Doha Development Agenda*. See also *Baumgartner proposals*, *Mansholt proposals* and *Ploughshares War*. [Hudec, Kennedy and Sgarbossa 1993, Ingco, Nash and Cleaver 2004, Josling, Tangermann and Warley 1996, Croome 1995, Melaku Geboye Desta 2002, Preeg 1970, GATT 1959]

Aid for Trade Initiative: an outcome of the WTO *Hong Kong Ministerial Conference*. Paragraph 57 of the ministerial declaration states that "Aid for Trade should aim to help developing countries, particularly LDCs, to build the supply-side capacity and trade-related infrastructure that they need to assist them to implement and benefit from WTO Agreements and more broadly to expand their trade". See also *developing countries and the multilateral trading system*.

Aim and effect: a test used in some GATT dispute settlement proceedings to ascertain whether there is possible *de facto national treatment* discrimination. For example, a measure might have the aim of affording protection, but its effect may be to discriminate in favour of the domestic product. [Cossy 2006]

AITIC: Agency for international trade information and cooperation. A Swiss-financed agency based in Geneva which aims to assist *less-advantaged countries* to play a more active role in the work of the WTO and other trade-related organizations. AITIC became an *intergovernmental organization* in December 2002.

ALADI: Asociación Latinoamericana de Integración. The Latin American Integration Association (LAIA). Formed in 1980 by Argentina, Bolivia, Brazil, Chile, Colombia, Ecuador, Mexico, Paraguay, Peru, Uruguay and Venezuela following the collapse of *LAFTA* (Latin-American Free-Trade Association). The objective of ALADI, as set out in the Treaty of Montevideo, is to pursue the gradual and progressive establishment of a Latin-American *common market*. *Mercosur* is seen as a step towards achieving this objective. ALADI's secretariat is located at Montevideo. See also *South American Free Trade Agreement*.

Alliance for Progress: initially a ten-year development plan for Latin America containing economic and social objectives. It was launched by President Kennedy in 1961. Among other aims, it was to find "a rapid and lasting solution to the grave problem created by excessive price fluctuations in the basic exports of Latin American countries" and to accelerate the economic integration of Latin America. Some progress was made over the years, but when the Alliance for Progress was formally ended in 1980, many thought that its achievements fell short of its aims. See also *Andean Trade Preference Act*, *Andean Trade Promotion and Drug Eradication Act*, *Caribbean Basin Initiative*, *Enterprise for the Americas Initiative* and *FTAA*.

Alliance for Strategic Products and Special Safeguard Mechanism: a group of developing countries formed at the *Cancún Ministerial Conference*. It is now known as the G-33, but it has more than forty members. The Alliance has three main aims. First, developing countries should be able to nominate a certain number of agricultural *tariff lines* as special products. These would not be subject to tariff reductions. Nor would there be any new commitments to liberalize *tariff rate quotas* for these products. Second, *special agricultural safeguards for developing countries* should be created to protect their markets against cheap and subsidized agricultural imports. Third, products designated as special products should have access to the special safeguard mechanism. See also *Doha Development Agenda*.

Alliance of Small Island States: AOSIS. See *small island developing states*.

ALOP: see *appropriate level of sanitary and phytosanitary protection*. Also known as *acceptable level of risk*. See also *precautionary principle* and *sanitary and phytosanitary measures*.

Alternative dispute resolution: a method of settling disputes through *arbitration*, *consultation*, *dispute mediation*, etc., outside the formal framework of court proceedings. The parties to the dispute usually appoint a disinterested person who attempts to bring down an outcome based on fairness and equity. Alternative dispute resolution only works if the parties are genuinely committed to finding a solution and to accept a negotiated outcome since such awards are in most cases not enforceable through courts. One such mechanism is *SOLVIT* under which natural and legal persons residing in the *European Community* can seek redress against the misapplication of internal market rules by another member state. See also *dispute settlement* and *International Court of Arbitration*.

Alternative specific tariff: a tariff rate set either at an *ad valorem* rate, i.e. expressed as a percentage of the value of the product, or at a specific rate, i.e. set as a fixed monetary rate per article. The customs authorities then usually apply the higher of the two. See also *ad valorem tariff* and *specific tariff*.

Amber box: refers to domestic support measures for agriculture that distort production and trade, including price support and subsidies directly related to production quantities. They may have to be reduced through the *Total Aggregate Measurement of Support*. See also *blue box* and *green box*.

Amendments to WTO agreements: the following WTO provisions may only be amended by agreement of all members: Article IX (Decision-Making) of the *WTO Agreement*, Articles I (General Most-Favoured-Nation Treatment) and II (Schedules of Concessions) of the *GATT 1994*, Article II:1 (Most-Favoured-Nation Treatment) of the *General Agreement on Trade in Services*, and Article 4 (Most-Favoured-Nation Treatment) of the *Agreement on Trade-Related Aspects of Intellectual Property Rights*. Amendments to other provisions of the WTO multilateral agreements may be made by a two-thirds majority. Each member then has to conclude separate formalities to accept the amendment. The Marrakesh Agreement enables the *WTO Ministerial Conference* to decide by a three-fourths majority that any member not accepting an amendment within a certain time may be free to withdraw from the WTO or to remain a member anyway. All WTO members have one vote. The *European Communities* are entitled to a number of votes equalling the number of their member states. Amendments to the **WTO plurilateral agreements** are made under the provisions contained in these agreements. See also **decision-making in the WTO**.

American Selling Price: ASP. Until 1979 a method under the United States Fordney-McCumber Tariff Act of 1922, and carried over into the Tariff Act of 1930, for valuing some goods at the border for the purpose of levying customs duties. Duty assessments were based on the usual wholesale price, including preparation for shipping, at which an article manufactured in the United States was offered on the domestic market. The effect of this system could be a duty rate two to three times higher than if the method of valuation set out in GATT Article VII (Customs Valuation) had been chosen. The ASP was abolished through the *Trade Agreements Act* of 1979 by which the United States accepted the rules set out in the *Tokyo Round Agreement on Implementation of Article VII [customs valuation]*.

Amicus **brief:** an opinion offered to the court by a disinterested party (called *amicus curiae* or friend of the court) in the hope that this would assist the judges in arriving at the best possible outcomes. Courts don't always welcome being helped in this way. [Barfield 2001, Mavroidis 2001]

Amicus curiae: see *amicus brief*.

Analogue country: sometimes also called surrogate country. This describes the country selected by anti-dumping authorities for the purpose of price comparison when they consider that the price information available from the country of origin of the goods would not yield useful results. See *anti-dumping measures*.

Andean Community: the Cartagena Agreement of 26 May 1969 established the Andean Pact, sometimes known as Andean Group, as a sub-group of *LAFTA* (Latin American Free Trade Area). The Agreement aims to coordinate the industry and foreign investment policies of its members. Current members are Bolivia, Columbia, Ecuador, Peru and Venezuela. Chile was a member from 1969 to 1976. An Andean Free Trade Area was established on 1 January 1992, followed by the adoption of a *common external tariff* on 1 January 1995. On 1 January 1997 the arrangement evolved into the Andean Community. Its secretariat is located in Lima.

Andean Free Trade Area: see *Andean Community*.

Andean Integration System: an umbrella body established by the *Andean Community* in 1997 which covers all of the Community's institutions and mechanisms. Its aim is to intensify regional integration.

Andean Pact: see *Andean Community*.

Andean Trade Preference Act: ATPA. A United States act of 1991 which gave trade preferences for ten years to products from Bolivia, Colombia, Ecuador and Peru to encourage the development of licit trade. It was modelled on the *Caribbean Basin Initiative*. It was renewed and amended in 2002 as the *Andean Trade Promotion and Drug Eradication Act*.

Andean Trade Promotion and Drug Eradication Act: ATPDEA. Passed by the United States Congress in August 2002 to amend and renew the trade preferences given to Bolivia, Colombia, Ecuador and Peru under the *Andean Trade*

Preference Act (ATPA) until 31 December 2006. The Act distinguishes between ATPA and ATPDEA status. Separate criteria must be met to qualify for the latter. ATPDEA was extended in December 2006 for six months. A further extension of six months is possible if the United States and the other countries complete the legislative processes towards a *Trade Promotion Agreement*. This has happened so far in the case of Colombia and Peru.

Andriessen Assurance: an arrangement negotiated in 1985 between the *European Economic Community* (EEC) and Australia which keeps certain Asian beef markets free of *subsidies*. Named after Frans Andriessen who was EEC Commissioner for Agriculture at the time.

Animal welfare: a subject proposed by the *European Community* and Switzerland with the support of European *non-governmental organizations* for inclusion as a *non-trade concern* in the WTO negotiations on agriculture. Supporters of this proposal argue that the absence of a framework in the WTO for discussing farm animal welfare, the domestic animal welfare standards already achieved by them could be undermined by imports from countries where these standards are much lower. One of the solutions offered in response to criticism that such proposals may amount to hidden protectionism is to pay some sort of compensation to producers where these can show additional costs because of the need to maintain higher standards. This could be done through accommodating such payments in the *green box*.

Annecy Tariff Conference: the second of the nine rounds of *multilateral trade negotiations*. It was held at Annecy, France, from April to August 1949. It primarily aimed to facilitate accession to the GATT by ten countries (Denmark, Dominican Republic, Finland, Greece, Haiti, Italy, Liberia, Nicaragua, Sweden and Uruguay) which had not participated in the 1947 Geneva tariff negotiations. In the event, Uruguay did not accede until 1953. See also *Tariff Conference*.

Annex on Telecommunications: an annex to the *General Agreement on Trade in Services* which requires WTO members (a) to ensure *transparency* in their regulation of telecommunications, (b) give access to other members to public telecommunications transport networks and services on reasonable and non-discriminatory terms and conditions, and (c) to encourage and engage in technical cooperation.

Annexes to the General Agreement on Trade in Services: see *General Agreement on Trade in Services*.

Annex I countries: so named after their inclusion in Annex I of the *United Nations Framework Convention on Climate Change*. They are Australia, Austria, Belarus, Belgium, Bulgaria, Canada, Croatia, Czech Republic, Denmark, European Union, Estonia, Finland, France, Germany, Greece, Hungary, Iceland, Ireland, Italy, Japan, Latvia, Liechtenstein, Lithuania, Luxembourg, Monaco, Netherlands, New Zealand, Norway, Poland, Portugal, Romania, Russian Federation, Slovakia, Slovenia, Spain, Sweden, Switzerland, Turkey, Ukraine, United Kingdom and the United States.

Annex II countries: in the *United Nations Framework Convention on Climate Change* the *OECD* member countries.

Annex VII countries: refers to the countries listed in Annex VII to the WTO *Agreement on Subsidies and Countervailing Measures*. They are (a) the *least developed countries* so designated by the United Nations that are members of the WTO and (b) Bolivia, Cameroon, Congo, Côte d'Ivoire, Dominican Republic, Egypt, Ghana, Guatemala, Guyana, India, Indonesia, Kenya, Morocco, Nicaragua, Nigeria, Pakistan, Philippines, Senegal, Sri Lanka and Zimbabwe. The least developed countries are exempt from the prohibition on export subsidies. The others are exempt until their GNP per capita reaches $1,000 per year.

Anti-absorption: measures taken by the relevant authority to prevent perceived *absorption* of *anti-dumping measures* by the producers or exporters of the good in question. In other words, if the producer or exporter is thought to carry himself the burden of anti-dumping duties, the authorities may in some cases decide to increase these duties. See also *anti-circumvention*.

Anti-circumvention: measures by governments to prevent *circumvention* of measures they have imposed, such as definitive *anti-dumping duties*. Sometimes firms seek to avoid such duties through, for example, assembly of parts and components either in the importing country or a third country, or by shifting the source of manufacture and export to a third country. The term as used in the WTO does not refer to cases of fraud. These would be dealt with under normal legal procedures of the countries concerned. The *Agreement on Agriculture* contains an anti-circumvention provision. It stipulates that export subsidies not listed in the Agreement must not be used to circumvent export subsidy commitments. Nor must non-commercial transactions be used in this way. See also *anti-dumping measures*, *carousel effect*, *dumping* and *screwdriver operations*.

Anti-collusion duties: proposed by some as duties small developing countries could impose on developed-country suppliers found to engage in *price collusion*. Such duties would apparently be aimed at depriving colluding foreign suppliers of some unearned profits. The idea appears to be flawed. First, the proposed remedy would mainly be at the expense of users in the importing country and quite possibly to the benefit of other suppliers. Second, it is not clear how small developing countries, which often do not have adequate resources to fight collusion among domestic companies, could satisfactorily detect collusion among suppliers abroad. Price collusion is more likely to occur where there are substantial barriers to entry, where industries are protected or where markets are not transparent. Therefore, if collusion is suspected, the first step might usefully be to ascertain how the relevant market might be made more competitive and transparent. See also *antitrust laws* and *competition policy*.

Anti-competitive practices: often called *restrictive business practices* or unfair business practices. These are used by firms to limit their exposure to price mechanisms. This is possible when firms, or groups of firms, have *market dominance* or *market power*. In some cases, it may involve collusion among firms.

See also *antitrust*, *cartel*, *competition law*, *conduct* and *trade and competition policy*.

Anti-dilution doctrine: see *dilution doctrine*.

Anti-Dumping Act of 1916: enacted by the United States Congress under the heading of "Unfair Competition" in Title VIII of the Revenue Act of 1916. The Act makes unlawful the import into the United States of any article at a price substantially less than the actual market price, if this is done with the intent of destroying or injuring an industry, preventing the establishment of an industry or restraining or monopolizing any part of trade and commerce in such articles in the United States. The penalty can be a fine, imprisonment or both. Persons injured by such imports may sue for *treble damages*. The Act is drafted in the form of an *antitrust* law, but its intent is to permit the imposition of *anti-dumping measures* against a practice usually considered *dumping*. This question was considered by the *panel* in a dispute about the conformity of this Act with the WTO anti-dumping provisions. The panel found that the transnational price discrimination test met the GATT definition of dumping, but that its remedies violated the WTO rules. [WT/DS136/R, WT/DS136/AB/R, WT/DS136/ARB]

Anti-Dumping Agreement: the WTO *Agreement on Implementation of Article VI of the General Agreement on Tariffs and Trade 1994* which sets out the conditions under which *anti-dumping measures* may be imposed. See also *dumping*.

Anti-dumping duties: the duties imposed on a good following a determination that *dumping* has occurred and that this has led to *injury* or a threat of injury. Anti-dumping duties may be provisional or definitive. See also *determination of dumping*.

Anti-dumping measures: laws and regulations designed to counter *dumping*. In the United States anti-dumping laws originated as part of the early *antitrust* laws. One of these is the *Anti-Dumping Act of 1916*. These laws were aimed at pulling into line foreign firms perceived to be undercutting United States firms through anti-competitive practices described as *dumping*. Gradually, however, firms began to understand the value of anti-dumping measures in restricting imports, and the two regimes diverged. In other countries the main reason for enacting anti-dumping laws always was an intent to afford protection to domestic firms. Article VI of the GATT 1994 permits the imposition of anti-dumping duties against dumped goods, if dumping causes *material injury* to producers of competing products, described as *like products*, in the importing country. This is known as *causality*. The WTO *Anti-Dumping Agreement* (formally the *Agreement on Implementation of Article VI of the General Agreement on Tariffs and Trade 1994*) lays down precise and transparent procedures for the adoption of anti-dumping measures. Some sophisticated methods have been developed to measure alleged differences in prices and to determine injury. Anti-dumping measures may be instituted if the price charged to the importing country by a foreign firm is below *normal value* in its home country. Normal value is made up of fixed and variable costs of production, plus a range of other costs normally associated with production and trade. If there are too few domestic sales, normal value is to be taken to be the highest comparable charge in third markets or the exporting firm's estimated costs of production plus a reasonable amount to cover other expenses, as well as imputed profits. If there is no export price or if trade is between related parties and therefore considered unreliable as a price indicator, the export price may be constructed on the basis of what would have been charged to an independent buyer, or on some other reasonable basis. The scope for disputes about the right level of normal value is readily apparent. The concept of material injury to industries producing like products is equally fruitful of controversies. Neither the GATT nor the Anti-Dumping Agreement define material injury, but the latter contains an illustrative list of factors to be taken into account in an assessment of whether material injury has occurred. The list, which is not considered exhaustive, includes actual and potential decline in sales, profits, output, market share, productivity, return on investments, or utilization of capacity; factors affecting domestic prices; the magnitude of the *margin of dumping*; actual and potential negative effects on cash flow, inventories, employment, wages, growth, ability to raise capital or investments. Much has been written about the meaning of "like products", and whether it should be interpreted as the same product, a similar product or a different product put to the same use or achieving the same purpose. The Anti-Dumping Agreement now leaves no doubt on this point. The like product must be identical, i.e. alike in all respects. If there no such product, another may be chosen for comparison which, even though not alike in all respects, has characteristics closely resembling the product under consideration. Anti-dumping measures may only be taken to the extent that they cover the margin of dumping, i.e. the difference between normal value and the price at the border in the importing country, adjusted for specified normal costs associated with international trade. If the investigating authority finds that there has been dumping, the resulting protection for domestic industries on the basis of anti-dumping measures can be quite limited. Under the WTO rules, a good case for them has to be made, and there is provision for appeals by the affected parties. The Anti-Dumping Agreement stresses that an application for the imposition of anti-dumping measures must include evidence of dumping, injury and a causal link between the two. A simple assertion, unsubstantiated by relevant evidence, cannot be considered sufficient to meet the requirements. An application has to be made by domestic industry. No action may be taken if it is supported by firms representing less than 25% of total production of the like product. Under the rule on *de minimis dumping margins*, no action may be taken if the margin of dumping is less than 2%. Anti-dumping action remains controversial. Affected firms and their home countries sometimes see them mainly as a means to restrain unwelcome imports. Doubtless, there is some truth in this. Some petitions are frivolous and nothing more than *trade harassment*. As a form of *contingent protection*, they enable governments to restrict the flow of imports. This is understood clearly by petitioners. A particularly disliked practice is the *cumulative assessment of dumping*. This means that the country taking action may under defined conditions investigate alleged dumping by several countries at the same time. Hoekman, commenting on the detailed procedural requirements set out in the Anti-dumping Agreement, notes that this has become a lucrative area of specialization for the legal profession in territories that actively use anti-dumping measures. Anti-dumping enquiries can serve *transparency* by demonstrating to the exporting company suspected of dumping what its real cost structure is. This can lead to alternative approaches to production and trade regimes which might reduce or eliminate the need for anti-dumping measures. Marceau points out that dumping and anti-dumping laws are not just about price discrimination and predation. They are "buffers" between national systems of competition. Other analysts are more severe. J. Michael Finger says that "antidumping is ordinary protection with a grand public relations program", and that "antidumping is a trouble-making diplomacy, stupid economics and unprincipled law". That said, all mechanisms enabling governments to influence the flow of imports create ill-will. In the case of anti-dumping measures, exporters complain of their trade-restrictive impact, but industries in the importing country tend to see them as a cumbersome and onerous means to fix urgent problems. In some cases, a company asking for anti-dumping measures may at the same time be accused of dumping in another market. Consumers seldom call for anti-dumping measures. There will always be some contradictions inherent in the taking of anti-dumping measures. Today, there is a view among some trade policy makers that *competition policy* could be a better instrument to deal with dumping issues. This supposes that all WTO members would be willing to pursue effective competition policies, or that they would be willing to enforce each other's competition rulings. Reconciling the different outcomes caused by anti-dumping measures and competition enforcement is an argument for negotiations on *trade and competition*, but those who are comfortable with their anti-dumping regimes do not find the argument persuasive. In the United States anti-dumping laws and antitrust laws have a common origin. Many argue that until the two are re-united, the anti-dumping rules offer a somewhat transparent, if legalistic and sometimes flawed, mechanism to deal with some of the concerns raised by producers. The anti-dumping rules are to be clarified as part of the multilateral trade negotiations launched at Doha in November 2001. See also *accordion of likeness*, *Agreement on Safeguards*, *analogue country*, *boomerang clause*, *competition policy and anti-dumping measures*, *de minimis dumping margins*, *lesser duty principle*, *negligible imports* and *predatory pricing*. [Dam 2000, Didier 2001, Finger 1993, Hoekman 1995, Horlick and Sugarman 1999, Jackson and Vermulst 1990, Marceau 1994, Neufeld 2001, Sykes 1998]

Anti-globalization: a complex, often contradictory, view apparently based on the proposition that it is possible, through a combination of international economic cooperation and the pursuit of *autarky*, to assist the development of *developing countries* and to preserve jobs at home. Views abound on how this should be done, and there is no unanimity among its proponents on the best way to achieve this aim. Some see the matter mainly in terms of a *race to the bottom* as production of some goods moves to developing countries. In this sense anti-globalization is a type of *protectionism*. Others complain that not enough is done to help developing countries to promote their economic development. This view would appear to support *trade liberalisation*. Many adherents of anti-globalist views seem to be convinced that, but for the efforts of the WTO, the *IMF*, the *World Bank*, the *G-7*, *G-8* and other economic groupings, their aims, however defined, would be realized speedily. Anti-globalists also tend to overstate, intentionally or otherwise, the ability of *transational corporations* to influence public opinion. Some of these corporations, of course, are quite adept at influencing political power. See also *globalization*. [Deardorff 2003, Stiglitz 2002, Wolf 2004]

Antitrust Enforcement Guidelines for International Operations: a set of guidelines last reissued in April 1995 by the United States Department of Justice and the Federal Trade Commission. It gives guidance to businesses engaged in international operations on questions relating to the enforcement of *antitrust laws*. The guidelines cover areas such as jurisdiction over *conduct* and entities outside the United States, *comity*, mutual assistance in international antitrust enforcement and the effect of involvement by foreign governments on the antitrust liability of private entities. See also *effects doctrine*, *extraterritoriality*, *negative comity* and *positive comity*.

Antitrust laws: often known as *competition laws*. These laws are a subset of the rules making up *competition policy*. They aim to promote a competitive environment for firms through ensuring that they do not abuse *market power* in domestic markets. In some countries, especially the United States, antitrust laws have an extraterritorial dimension. The term "antitrust" derives its origin from a perception in the United States in the 1880s and 1890s that some industries, then organized into large-scale trusts with interlocking directorships, were undermining price mechanisms. The *Sherman Act*, passed in 1890, remains the cornerstone and symbol of United States antitrust laws. A 1994 House of Representative committee report notes that "first and foremost, antitrust is rooted in the distinctive American preference for pluralism, freedom of trade, access to markets, and – perhaps most important of all – freedom of choice". Penalties in proven cases of antitrust law infringement tend to be severe in many countries. In the United States, for example, the courts can impose *treble damages* on the offenders. See also *cartel*, *Clayton Act*, *essential services doctrine*, *extraterritoriality* and *Webb-Pomerene Act*. [Dabbah 2003, US House of Representatives 1994]

ANZCERTA: *Australia New Zealand Closer Economic Relations Trade Agreement*, usually referred to as CER. Entered into force on 1 January 1983. Trade in goods between the partners is free of *tariffs*, and there are no *quantitative restrictions*. The partners do not use *anti-dumping measures* against each other and rely on *competition laws* instead to the extent that dumping may be caused by anti-competitive behaviour. *Countervailing duties* may still be imposed. The parties accord each other *national treatment* in *government procurement*. Services were brought under the ambit of the free-trade agreement in 1988 through the *ANZCERTA Protocol on Trade in Services*.

ANZCERTA Protocol on Trade in Services: adopted in 1988 to bring *trade in services* within the *ANZCERTA* framework. The Protocol covers all services trade between Australia and New Zealand, except for a small number of specified activities listed in the two annexes where restrictions apply. No new activities may be added to the annexes. Periodic bilateral discussions have led to the removal or tightening of the inscriptions. See also *negative listing*.

APEC: Asia Pacific Economic Cooperation [forum]. Established in 1989. Its members are described as "economies". The objectives of APEC include (a) sustaining growth and development in the region, (b) strengthening an open *multilateral trading system* rather than the formation of a regional trading bloc, (c) a focus on economic rather than security issues and (d) to foster constructive interdependence by encouraging the flow of goods, services, capital and technology. APEC objectives are defined further in the *Seoul Declaration*. Following the terrorist attack on New York in 2001 APEC adopted a small security agenda and established a Counter-Terrorism Task Force. APEC's membership criteria adopted in 1997 are: (a) an applicant economy should be located in the Asia-Pacific region, (b) it should have substantial and broad-based economic linkages with the existing APEC members; in particular, the value of the applicant's trade with APEC members, as a percentage of its international trade, should be relatively high, (c) it should be pursuing externally oriented, market-driven economic policies, and (d) a successful applicant will be required to produce an *Individual Action Plan* (IAP) for implementation and to commence participation in the *Collective Action Plans* across the APEC work program from the time of its joining APEC. APEC's main agenda is to dismantle trade and investment barriers among all members by 2020. Developed economy members have undertaken to do so by 2010. Several working groups have also been established to advance cooperation across a range of issues, especially in the areas of business facilitation and information exchange. Members of APEC are Australia, Brunei Darussalam, Canada, Chile, China, Chinese Taipei (Taiwan), Hong Kong, Indonesia, Japan, Republic of Korea, Malaysia, Mexico, New Zealand, Papua New Guinea, Peru, Philippines, Russia, Singapore, Thailand, Vietnam and the United States. APEC Economic Leaders agreed at their meeting in Vancouver in November 1997 that no new members would be admitted until 2008. APEC is supported by a small secretariat based in Singapore. APEC's main meetings are hosted by one of the member economies for an entire year. This is APEC's main coordination mechanism. See also *Auckland Challenge*, *Bogor Declaration*, *Manila Action Plan for APEC*, *open regionalism*, *Osaka Action Agenda*, *Shanghai Accord* and other entries beginning with *APEC*.

APEC Blueprint for Action on Electronic Commerce: adopted in 1999. It established a detailed work program on electronic commerce based on the principle that governments, *inter alia*, would promote the development of electronic commerce by providing a favourable legal and regulatory environment. This environment is assumed to be predictable, transparent and consistent. The blueprint also contains the *APEC paperless trading initiative*.

APEC Business Advisory Council: ABAC. Established at the November 1995 *APEC* Ministerial Meeting in Osaka to ensure the continued cooperation and active involvement of the business and private sectors in all APEC activities. Each economy has three ABAC members.

APEC Business Travel Card: ABTC. A scheme enabling *bona fide* business people from participating *APEC* economies to travel to other participating economies without the need to obtain visas. Holders of the card are given preferential immigration clearance in the form of a separate gate.

APEC Economic and Technical Cooperation: ECOTECH. One of the three pillars of the *APEC* work agenda. It aims to support the achievement of the APEC goals by developing common policy concepts, implementing joint activities and engaging in policy dialogue. It was established at the November 1995 APEC Ministerial Meeting. Cooperation activities take place in the areas of human resources development, industrial science and technology, small and medium enterprises, economic infrastructure, energy, transportation, tourism, telecommunications and information, trade and investment data, *trade promotion*, marine resource conservation, fisheries, and agricultural technology. See also *APEC working groups*, *Bogor Declaration* and *Osaka Action Agenda*.

APEC Economic Leaders' Meetings: informal meetings of APEC leaders enabling them to share their visions for the Asia-Pacific region and provide directions for APEC's long-term development. Leaders' meetings have been held at Seattle (1993), Bogor (1994), Osaka (1995), Manila (1996), Vancouver (1997), Kuala Lumpur (1998), Auckland (1999), Brunei Darussalam (2000), Shanghai (2001), Mexico (2002), Bangkok (2003), Santiago (2004), Busan (2005) and Hanoi (2006). The 2007 meeting will be hosted by Australia, 2008 by Peru, 2009 Singapore and 2010 by Japan. See also *Bogor Declaration* and *Osaka Action Agenda*.

APEC framework for liberalization and facilitation: the APEC process of liberalization and facilitation is to achieve the goals set out in the *Bogor Declaration*, as described in the *Osaka Action Agenda*. It comprises (a) actions by individual APEC economies, (b) actions by APEC fora and APEC actions related to multilateral fora. See also *Manila Action Plan for APEC*.

APEC individual action plans: IAPs. These describe the voluntary actions by which APEC economies expect to reach the targets of the *Bogor Declaration*. IAPs contain each economy's proposed action and, where appropriate, proposed collective action on trade and investment liberalization and facilitation. They contain steps to be taken in seventeen areas: tariffs, non-tariff measures, services, investment, standards and conformance, customs procedures, intellectual property rights, competition policy, government procurement, deregulation, rules of origin, dispute mediation, mobility of business people, implementation of the *Uruguay Round* outcomes, transparency, free-trade agreements and information-gathering and analysis. IAPs contain more detail on near-term actions. They are less specific on policies or directions for the long term. They are updated regularly. See also *e-IAP* and *rolling specificity*.

APEC Information Notes on Good Practice for Technical Regulation: a compendium of resource and reference materials suitable for preparing, adopting or reviewing regimes for the regulation of products according to the *APEC Principles and Features of Good Practice for Technical Regulation*. It was first issued in September 2000. One of its aims is to help *APEC* economies in meeting their obligations under the WTO *Agreement on Technical Barriers to Trade*. [www.apecsec.org]

APEC model measures for RTAs/FTAs: see **model measures for RTAs/FTAs**.

APEC Mutual Recognition Arrangement for Conformity Assessment of Telecommunications Equipment: a non-binding arrangement which entered into force on 1 July 1999. It aims to streamline conformity assessment procedures for telecommunications and telecommunications-related equipment. It provides for the mutual recognition of conformity assessment bodies by the importing countries and mutual acceptance of testing and equipment certification procedures undertaken. APEC members can make the arrangement binding between themselves through an exchange of letters.

APEC Non-Binding Investment Principles: a voluntary code containing principles to be applied to investment flows, adopted in 1994. It aims to promote a policy environment characterized by increased confidence, reduced uncertainty and the liberalization and simplification of investment rules and policies. The principles include transparency, most-favoured-nation (MFN) treatment, establishment, national treatment, transfers, nationalization and compensation, performance requirements, taxation and investment incentives, dispute resolution, etc. See also *World Bank Guidelines on the Treatment of Foreign Direct Investment*.

APEC Non-Binding Principles on Government Procurement: adopted in 1999. The set consists of six main principles. 1. *Elements of transparency:* sufficient and relevant information should be made available to all interested parties consistently and in a timely manner through a readily accessible medium at no more than reasonable cost. 2. *Elements of value for money:* government procurement practices and procurement should achieve the best available value for money. The basis for comparison of offers should be benefits and costs on a whole-of-life basis, not simply the lowest price. 3. *Elements of open and effective competition:* the government procurement regime should be open, and procurement methods should suit market circumstances and facilitate levels of competition commensurate with the benefits received. 4. *Elements of fair dealing:* the design of the procurement system and the conduct of buyers should ensure that procurement is conducted in a fair, reasonable and equitable manner and with integrity. 5. *Elements of accountability and due process:* procuring (buying) agencies and individual procuring personnel should be accountable to their governments, the end users, the public and suppliers for the efficient, cost-effective and fair conduct of their procurement. Mechanisms for scrutiny of the procurement process and avenues for review of complaints should be available. 6. *Elements of non-discrimination:* procurement laws, rules and regulations should not be applied to favour the suppliers of any particular economy. See also *Agreement on Government Procurement*.

APEC paperless trading initiative: adopted in 1999 as part of the *APEC Blueprint for Action on Electronic Commerce*. Members agreed to endeavour to reduce or eliminate the requirement for paper documents needed for customs and other cross-border trade administration by 2005 for developed economies and 2010 for developing economies. This initiative applies to sea, air and land transport.

APEC Principles and Features of Good Practice for Technical Regulation: adopted in September 2000. This document contains two principles held to show good regulatory practice. First, economies should consider alternatives to mandatory requirements. Alternative mechanisms could include reliance on systems of legal recourse, liability laws and liability insurance schemes, taxes, fees and other charges, education programs, co-regulation, voluntary standards, self-regulation and codes of practice. Second, the least interventionist and least trade-restrictive compliance regime necessary should be used to achieve the regulatory objective. Good regulations are described as transparent and non-discriminatory, performance-based, reflecting international standards or internationally aligned standards, reflecting only the standards necessary to achieve the legitimate regulatory objective and being subject to review. [www.apecsec.org]

APEC Principles of Interconnection: adopted on 14 May 1999. This set of eight principles requires major suppliers of *basic telecommunications services* (i.e. those able to set prices and control facilities) to establish conditions enabling users of one public telecommunications transport network to communicate effectively with users of another. The first five principles govern the conditions applying to interconnection which is to be provided at any technically feasible point in the network, under non-discriminatory and transparent conditions, to non-affiliated service suppliers at non-discriminatory rates and of a quality no less favourable than that provided to its affiliates, in a timely fashion and negotiations in good faith, and at cost-oriented rates. The remaining principles are that a major supplier may not engage in anti-competitive practices, that all interconnection agreements must be published, and that a service supplier requesting interconnection with a major supplier may resort to applicable dispute settlement mechanisms regarding appropriate terms, conditions and rates for interconnection within a reasonable time. See also *reference paper on telecommunications services*. [www.apecsec.org]

APEC principles on transparency standards: formal name *Leaders' Statement to Implement APEC Transparency Standards*, adopted on 27 October 2002. The Statement commits APEC economies to the following principles on transparency in trade and investment liberalization and facilitation: (1) each economy will ensure that its laws, regulations, procedures and *administrative rulings of general application* will be published promptly either through official journals or the Internet, (2) each economy will publish relevant information in advance and give interested persons a reasonable opportunity to comment on them, (3) economies will endeavour to provide responses promptly to questions on its laws and regulations, (4) persons of another economy directly affected by administrative proceedings should be notified and given an opportunity to present facts and arguments concerning their positions, (5) each economy to ensure that domestic procedures are in place to enable prompt review and correction of final administrative matters, other than those taken for sensitive prudential reasons, and (6) "administrative rulings of general application" are defined as administrative rulings or interpretations that apply to all persons and situations that fall generally within their ambit and that establish a norm of conduct. Confidential information is exempt from action under the Statement.

APEC Principles on Trade Facilitation: a non-binding set of principles adopted in Shanghai in 2001. The principles are: (a) transparency (information on laws, rules, regulations, etc.), (b) communication and consultations, especially with the business and trading community, (c) simplification, practicability and efficiency by ensuring that rules and procedures are no more burdensome or restrictive than necessary to achieve their objectives, (d) non-discrimination, (e) consistency and predictability to minimize uncertainty to the trade and trade-related parties, (f) harmonization, standardization and recognition on the basis of international standards where possible, (g) modernization and the use of new technology, (h) access to due process to enable seeking redress with respect to the administration of rules, and (i) cooperation among government authorities and business and trading communities. See also *trade facilitation*.

APEC Principles to Enhance Competition and Regulatory Reform: a non-binding set of five principles adopted in Auckland in 1999. The principles are: *(1) non-discrimination* (competition and regulatory principles not to discriminate between economic entities, whether these are foreign or domestic), *(2) comprehensiveness* (broad application of the principles to goods and services, and private and public business activities), (3) *transparency* in policies and rules, (4) *accountability* (clear responsibility within domestic administrations for the implementation of the competition and efficiency dimension in the development and administration of policies and rules), and *(5) implementation* (take, *inter alia*, practical steps to promote consistent application of policies and rules, eliminate unnecessary rules and regulatory procedures, and improve the transparency of policy objectives). See also *competition policy*.

APEC Statement on Trade and the Digital Economy: adopted by APEC economic leaders on 27 October 2002. Its general objectives are (a) to have the digital economy continue to flourish in a liberal and open trade environment, (b) market access and national treatment commitments across a broad range of relevant goods and services, (c) transparent, non-discriminatory and least restrictive regulations, (d) a long-term *moratorium on customs duties on electronic transmissions*, and (e) economies to support demand-driven capacity-building projects to ensure that developing economies benefit fully from the *new economy*. Specific objectives are for APEC economies to encourage others to pursue the same degree of openness as they are aspiring to through (a) liberalization of trade in services, (b) enforcing the WTO *Agreement on Trade-Related Aspects of Intellectual Property Rights* and joining the *WIPO Copyright Treaty* and the *WIPO Performances and Phonograms Treaty* as soon as possible, and (c) to join the WTO *Information Technology Agreement*. [www.apecsec.org]

APEC Trade Facilitation Action Plan: a framework adopted in 2002 to reduce the cost of *trade facilitation* by 5% across the *APEC* region by the end of 2007. Actions and measures, which are voluntary, are to be taken under one of the following categories: movement of goods (includes customs, port, health and quarantine and similar procedures), standards, business mobility and e-commerce. The plan was extended for another five years in 2006 with a similar cost-cutting target.

APEC working groups: APEC has eleven working groups engaged in practical cooperation activities, such as preparation of technical manuals, information networks, training courses, etc. The eleven groups cover agricultural technical cooperation, energy, fisheries, human resources development, industrial science and technology, marine resource conservation, small and medium enterprises, telecommunications and information, tourism, trade promotion and transportation.

Appellate Body: an independent standing body of seven persons established under the WTO *Dispute Settlement Understanding* to hear appeals arising from *panel* decisions. The grounds for such appeals are confined to points of WTO law. The Appellate Body's members are persons of recognized authority with demonstrated expertise in law, international trade and relevant WTO agreements who are not affiliated with any government. When the Appellate Body was established, many thought that occasional cases only would be referred to it. That expectation was wrong. Today most WTO members tend to appeal against adverse panel decisions. See also *dispute settlement* and *Dispute Settlement Body*. [Sacerdoti, Yanovich and Bohanes 2006]

Appellation d'origine contrôlée: AOC. Under the French *Code Rural* and the *Code de la Consommation* an *appellation of origin* which has been given legal protection following an examination by the *Institut national des appellations d'origine*. "Appellation of origin" is defined as "denomination of a country, a region or a locality which serves to designate a product originating therein, the quality and characteristics of which are due to the geographical environment, including natural and human factors". An *appellation*, once granted, does not attest to the quality of the wine, but it emphasises the strong connection between the product and the locality in which it was grown. Once an AOC has been granted, it can never become generic and fall into the public domain. The labels of products granted this status must conform to prescribed legal requirements. See also *generic geographical indications* and *geographical indications*.

Appellations of origin: a category of *indications of source* which enjoys domestic protection under *intellectual property* laws. International protection can be achieved through multilateral treaties, such as the *Paris Convention* and the

Lisbon Agreement, or bilateral agreements. Protection in other countries is only available if the name is protected at home. Article 1 of the Paris Convention protects, among other types of industrial property, appellations of origin. It does not define the term, but it says that "industrial property shall be understood in the broadest sense ... and shall apply to agricultural and extraction industries, and to all manufactured or natural products, for example, wines, grain, tobacco leaf, fruit cattle minerals, mineral waters, beer, flowers and flour". Article 2(1) of the Lisbon Agreement defines an appellation of origin as "the geographical name of a country, region, or locality, which serves to designate a product originating therein, the quality and characteristics of which are due exclusively or essentially to the geographical environment, including natural and human factors". Article 2(2) defines the country of origin as "the country whose name, or the country in which is situated the region or locality whose name constitutes the appellation of origin which has given the product its reputation". In other words, protection for an appellation of origin is available under the Lisbon Agreement if the product bearing it has characteristics which can be ascribed exclusively or essentially to the place where it comes from. These characteristics may be due to natural and human factors. Article 3 of the Lisbon Agreement requires protection "against any usurpation or imitation, even if the true origin of the product is indicated or if the appellation is used in translated form or accompanied by terms such as 'kind', 'type', 'imitation' or the like". Expressions such as "konjak" or "Bordeaux-type wine" would therefore not be acceptable under this Agreement. Under United States law the appellations of origin available for wine are (a) the United States, (b) a state, (c) two or no more than three adjoining states, (d) a county, (e) two or no more than two or three adjoining counties in the same state, and (f) a wine-growing area which can be distinguished by geographical features and which has recognized and defined boundaries. Ownership of appellations of origin is collective, either through a private or a public body. All farmers belonging to the specified geographical area and respecting the applicable specifications have the right to use the geographical name recognized by the appellation of origin. See also *designation of origin* and *geographical indications*. [OECD COM/AGR/ APM/TD/WP(2000)15/FINAL]

Applied tariff rates: the tariff rates imposed by a customs administration when a good crosses the border. These rates are often considerably lower than the bound rates arrived at as a result of trade negotiations or the rates listed in national *tariff schedules*. See also *bindings* and *nominal tariff rates*.

Applied MFN tariff rate: the tariff rate actually used for imports from countries enjoying *most-favoured-nation treatment*, often the same as the *applied tariff rate*. Sometimes it is much lower than the *bound rate*.

Appropriate level of sanitary or phytosanitary protection: ALOP. Defined in the WTO *Agreement on the Application of Sanitary and Phytosanitary Measures* as the "level of protection deemed appropriate by the Member establishing a sanitary or phytosanitary measure to protect human, animal or plant life or health within its territory". Views on what constitutes an appropriate level of protection vary greatly. This concept is also known as the "acceptable level of risk".

A priori limitation: a quantitative ceiling on imports enjoying preferential treatment under a *GSP* scheme.

Arab Maghreb Union: consists of Algeria, Libya, Mauritania, Morocco and Tunisia. It was formed in 1989 with political, economic and social objectives, including the aim of achieving a Common Market. Its secretariat is located at Rabat. See also *Maghreb states*.

Arbitrary or unjustifiable discrimination: a term used in several of the agreements administered by the WTO where it is, however, not further defined. A hypothetical example of such discrimination would be where a country discriminates perfectly legally between trading partners that meet its *sanitary and phytosanitary measures* and those that cannot satisfy them. If it then discriminates further for whatever reason between those that meet the requirements, this could well be case of arbitrary or unjustifiable discrimination.

Arbitration: a way of settling disputes. It is more formal than *dispute mediation* which is aimed at bringing the parties together, and less legalistic than formal court proceedings which are adversarial. The parties agreeing to arbitration often bind themselves to well-defined rules of procedure. They also usually agree in advance that the award handed down by the arbitrator is binding on them. Arbitration proceedings are especially helpful when the parties to a dispute seek an equitable and definitive solution to a problem. They may also be cheaper to conduct because appeals to a higher authority are usually not possible. Article 25 of the WTO *Dispute Settlement Understanding* enables members to solve disputes by arbitration if that is their preference. They have to notify all other members before the start of the arbitration and also of the outcome. Other members may participate in the arbitration proceedings only with the agreement of the parties seeking arbitration. Many *free-trade agreements* contain arbitration rules. *NAFTA*, for example, contains two arbitration provisions. Article 20 establishes the procedures to be followed in the arbitration of disputes between the parties generally. Article 11 permits investors of a NAFTA party to seek arbitration in disputes with the NAFTA parties, but only concerning alleged breaches of some of the obligations set out in Chapters 11 and 15. See also *Article 22.6 arbitration, dispute settlement, Inter-American Convention on International Commercial Arbitration, International Court of Arbitration, Model Arbitration Clause, NAFTA Chapter 11, New York Convention* and *UNCITRAL Arbitration Rules*.

Area freedom: the concept of pest- or disease-free areas and areas of low pest or disease prevalence outlined in Article 6 of the WTO *Agreement on the Application of Sanitary and Phytosanitary Measures*. A determination of such areas has to take into account factors such as geography, ecosystems, epidemiological surveillance and the effectiveness of sanitary or phytosanitary controls. Exporting countries claiming that some areas within their territories fall into this category have to be able to provide the necessary evidence to the importing country. A demonstration of area freedom means that a country can export products from the area concerned even though the same product may be subject to disease in another area of the country.

Areeda-Turner test: a method proposed by Phillip Areeda and Donald Turner in 1975 "to examine the relationship between a firm's prices and its costs in order to define a rational dividing line between legitimately competitive prices and prices that are properly regarded as predatory". Areeda and Turner concluded that unless at or above average cost, a price below reasonably anticipated (1) shortrun marginal costs or (2) average variable costs should be deemed predatory, and the monopolist may not defend it on the grounds that his price was "promotional" or merely met an equally low price of a competitor. They say that although marginal cost data are nearly always unavailable, a price below reasonably anticipated average variable cost should conclusively presumed unlawful. This proposition by Areeda and Turner has spawned a considerable literature questioning and refining its assumptions, but the basic approach is considered to remain valid. See also *antitrust laws* and *predatory pricing*. [Areeda and Turner 1975]

Arguendo: Latin meaning "for the sake of argument", as in "assuming *arguendo* that the drafters of Article 12 intended it to mean . . . ".

Arm's-length pricing: a principle designed to assess whether the market price charged for goods and services traded internationally has been manipulated. The arm's-length price is usually defined as the price that would have been charged between independent firms dealing at arm's length in comparable circumstances. The methods to assess whether this criterion has been satisfied can be complex. See also *customs valuation* and *transfer pricing*.

Arrangements for Consultations on Restrictive Business Practices: a GATT mechanism adopted on 18 November 1960 aimed at ensuring that *restrictive business practices* do not frustrate the benefits of tariff reductions and the removal of *quantitative restrictions*. This mechanism lay dormant until 1996 when the United States invoked it in a dispute with Japan concerning photographic materials, the so-called *Kodak-Fuji case*.

Arrangement on Guidelines for Officially Supported Export Credits: a non-binding *OECD* arrangement concluded in 1978 and updated many times since. The OECD says that this is not an official instrument, but a "Gentlemen's Agreement" receiving administrative support from the OECD secretariat. The Arrangement aims to ensure an orderly *export credit* market and to avoid competition between countries for giving more favourable credit terms. It applies to export credits extended and supported directly by governments or on their behalf under a government guarantee. It also covers concessional financing under aid programs if the granting of a loan is tied to purchases from the donor country. See also *Large Aircraft Sector Understanding*, *mixed credits* and *tied aid*. [www.oecd.org]

Arrangement Regarding Bovine Meat: see *International Bovine Meat Agreement*.

Article V: the provision in the *General Agreement on Trade in Services* which establishes the conditions for *free-trade agreements* covering services.

Article XIX: the GATT article permitting the use of *safeguards* against import surges, but only if certain conditions have been met. It is better known as the *escape clause*. See also *Agreement on Safeguards*.

Article XX: the GATT article listing allowed *general exceptions* to the trade rules under defined conditions.

Article XXIV: the GATT describing the basic multilateral requirements for *customs unions*, *free-trade areas*, *free-trade agreements* and *regional trade agreements*.

Article 113 Committee: the predecessor of the *Article 133 Committee*. It took its name from Article 113 of the *Treaty of Rome*.

Article 133 Committee: often referred to as the 133 Committee. It takes its name from Article 133 of the *Treaty of Amsterdam*, one of the treaties amending the *Treaty of Rome*. It is the legal basis for the *European Community*'s *Common Commercial Policy*. This Article requires that the "common commercial policy shall be based on uniform principles, particularly in regard to changes in tariff rates, the conclusion of tariff and trade agreements, the achievement of uniformity in measures of liberalisation, export policy and measures to protect trade such as those to be taken in the event of dumping or subsidies". The *Treaty of Nice* made trade in services and the commercial aspects of intellectual property part of the common commercial policy if the action does not exceed the internal powers of the European Community. The *European Commission*, which speaks and negotiates on behalf of member states in the WTO, must conduct its trade negotiations in consultation with the 133 Committee. See also *competence* and *subsidiarity*.

Article 20 of the WTO *Agreement on Agriculture*: The clause authorizing the resumption of agricultural negotiations by 1 January 2000. See *continuation clause*.

Article 21.5 panel: a *panel* established under this article of the *Dispute Settlement Understanding* to rule on disagreements over the implementation of recommendations or rulings of a dispute settlement panel. Where possible, the panel hearing the original complaint will examine the disagreement over its ruling. It normally has 90 days to produce its report.

Article 22.6 arbitration: a procedure available under this article of the *Dispute Settlement Understanding*. When a WTO member refuses to comply with a *panel* ruling, the aggrieved party can ask for a new *panel* to rule on whether the original panel ruling has been implemented to satisfy the WTO rules. This is the *Article 21.5 panel*. If there is a new adverse ruling, the parties are then supposed to enter into discussion concerning mutually acceptable *compensation*. If this does not lead to any agreement, the complaining party may ask for authorization from the *Dispute Settlement Body* to suspend *concessions* or other obligations no later than the expiry of the *reasonable period of time* (usually a maximum of 15 months from the adoption of the panel or *Appellate Body* report). If the member which is the target of these actions complains about their level, the matter may be referred to *arbitration*. Generally, the original panel will act as arbitrator, but the WTO Director-General may decide to appoint a different arbitrator. Concessions or obligations may not be suspended during the course of the arbitration. The arbitrator's decision is final. See also *suspension of concessions or other obligations*.

Article 25 arbitration: see *arbitration*.

Arusha Declaration: adopted in July 1993 by the Customs Co-operation Council, now the *World Customs Organization* (WCO), to promote integrity in the delivery of customs services. The Declaration lists the following as key factors of integrity programs: (1) customs legislation should be clear and precise, (2) customs procedures should be simple, consistent and easily accessible, (3) automation of acts against corruption, (4) customs services should segregate functions, rotate staff and allocate examinations randomly, (5) line managers should have prime responsibility for identifying weaknesses, (6) internal and external auditing are essential, (7) managers should instil pride and loyalty in their officers, (8) recruitment and advancement procedures should be objective and free of interference, (9) customs officers should be given a code of conduct, (10) they should have adequate training, (11) their remuneration should be enough for a decent standard of living, and (12) customs administrations should foster an open and transparent relationship with brokers and the community. In the Maputo Declaration of 22 March 2002 WCO members committed themselves to an action plan to implement the elements of the Arusha Declaration.

ASEAN: Association of South-East Asian Nations. Formed in 1967 to promote economic progress and political stability in the region. It consists of Brunei, Burma, Cambodia, Indonesia, Laos, Malaysia, Philippines, Singapore, Thailand and Vietnam. Its main aims are (a) to accelerate economic growth, social progress and cultural development, (b) to promote regional peace and stability, and (c) to promote collaboration and mutual assistance in the economic, social, cultural, technical, scientific and administrative fields. See also *AFTA* and other entries beginning with ASEAN.

ASEAN Economic Community: an *ASEAN* organization which is to be established by 2020. Its proposed structure is said to be modelled on the early *European Economic Community*. See *Bali Concord II*.

ASEAN Framework Agreement on Intellectual Property Cooperation: concluded on 15 December 1995 in Bangkok. It aims to strengthen cooperation among *ASEAN* countries in *intellectual property* to promote regional and global trade liberalisation. It envisages the possibility of an ASEAN patent system and an ASEAN Patent Office, an ASEAN trademark system and an ASEAN Trademark Office as well as an ASEAN Intellectual Property Association (formed in 1996). The Agreement also establishes an extensive program of cooperative activities in all main areas of intellectual property.

ASEAN Framework Agreement on Services: adopted by *ASEAN* governments on 15 December 1995. The Agreement seeks (a) to enhance cooperation in services among member states to improve the efficiency and competitiveness of ASEAN services providers and to diversify production capacity and supply and distribution of services within and outside ASEAN, and (b) to eliminate substantially restrictions on trade in services among member states and to liberalize trade in services by expanding the depth and scope of liberalization beyond the commitments made under the *General Agreement on Trade in Services* (GATS) with the aim of realizing a *free-trade area* in services. Article II seeks cooperation through establishing or improving infrastructural facilities, joint production, marketing and purchasing arrangements, research and development, and exchange of information. Article III requires member states to liberalize trade in services in a substantial number of sectors within a reasonable timeframe through the removal of discriminatory measures and market access limitations and a prohibition of new restrictive measures. Under Article IV, member states are to enter into negotiations on measures affecting specific services sectors. Article V permits the *mutual recognition* of qualifications, education, experience and licences, but it does not require any member state to do so. The Agreement stipulates that the provisions of the GATS will apply on matters where it is silent. Three rounds of negotiations under this Agreement have been completed with modest results. A fourth round is to be completed in 2007. The target is a for a free flow of services by 2020. See also *AFTA* and *ASEAN Investment Area*.

ASEAN Free Trade Area: see *AFTA*.

ASEAN Industrial Cooperation Scheme: AICO. An industrial development program adopted in 1995 by the *ASEAN* countries to promote investment in technology-based industries and to enhance value-adding activities in goods and services production. It replaced the ASEAN Industrial Joint Venture Scheme. To be eligible for the benefits under AICO, a cooperative venture must consist of at least two companies located in different ASEAN countries, and the companies must have at least 30% of equity owned by ASEAN nationals. The approved output of AICO entities enjoys the preferential tariff rate for intra-ASEAN trade. All products except those falling under Article 9 (General Exceptions) of the *CEPT* arrangement may be produced under AICO.

ASEAN Industrial Joint Venture Scheme: see *ASEAN Industrial Cooperation Scheme*.

ASEAN Integration System of Preferences: entered into force on 1 January 2002. This scheme enables the six original members of *AFTA* (Brunei Darussalam, Indonesia, Malaysia, Philippines, Singapore and Thailand) to extend voluntary tariff preferences to the four newer members (Burma, Cambodia, Laos and Vietnam).

ASEAN Investment Area: AIA. Entered into force on 21 June 1999 and amended on 14 September 2001. It aims to establish a liberalized, transparent, competitive and dynamic environment for investment flows among *ASEAN* members. The AIA covers all direct investments other than portfolio investments and investment matters already covered by other ASEAN agreements. In principle, members give each other *national treatment*, except for investment in industries inscribed in the *temporary exclusion lists*, *sensitive lists* and *general exceptions list*. Services are covered to the extent that they are incidental to manufacturing, agriculture, forestry, fisheries and mining and quarrying. Temporary exclusion lists for the manufacturing sector were eliminated on 1 January 2003 by Brunei Darussalam, Indonesia, Malaysia, Myanmar, Philippines, Singapore and Thailand. Cambodia, Laos and Vietnam will eliminate them by 2010. The AIA is to form a building block for the *ASEAN Economic Community*. See also *AFTA*.

ASEAN-Japan Comprehensive Economic Partnership: an agreement signed on 8 October 2003 to strengthen economic integration between the *ASEAN* countries and Japan. It established the framework for the creation of a Comprehensive Economic Partnership (CEP), i.e. a *free-trade agreement* covering trade in goods, trade in services and investment. The CEP consists of separate agreements between Japan and individual ASEAN countries.

ASEAN Priority Integration Sectors: refers to eleven sectors identified by the *ASEAN* countries for early liberalization among themselves. They are wood-based and automotive products (coordinated by Indonesia), rubber-based products and textiles and apparels (Malaysia), agro-based products and fisheries (Myanmar), electronics (Philippines), e-ASEAN and healthcare (Singapore) and air travel and tourism (Thailand).

ASEAN Vision 2000: an action plan adopted by *ASEAN* governments on 15 December 1997 to realize fully the original aims of ASEAN. Many of these aims are economic, such as the full implementation of *AFTA* and the free flow of investment between the ASEAN members by 2020. See also *ASEAN Investment Area* and *Initiative for ASEAN Integration*.

ASEAN–x: a method used within *ASEAN* to indicate that not all of its members are participating in a program or activity. The magnitude of x varies.

ASEAN+3: the *ASEAN* countries plus China, Japan and the Republic of Korea. Its first summit meeting was held in Kuala Lumpur in December 1997. See also *East Asia Vision Group*.

ASEAN+3+2: the economies forming *ASEAN+3* plus Hong Kong and Taiwan.

ASEAN-5: Indonesia, Malaysia, Philippines, Singapore and Thailand. Used mainly for statistical purposes.

ASEAN+6: roughly equivalent to the participants in the *East Asia Summit*, i.e. the *ASEAN* members plus Australia, China, India, Japan, Republic of Korea and New Zealand. An informal study for a possible ASEAN+6 *free-trade agreement* was launched in 2006.

ASEAN-6: Brunei Darussalam, Indonesia, Malaysia, Philippines, Singapore and Thailand. Used mainly for statistical purposes.

ASEM: Asia-Europe Meeting. An informal process of dialogue and cooperation between 39 Asian and European countries. It consists, on the European side, of the 25 members of the *European Union*, Bulgaria, Romania and the *European Commission*, and on the Asian side of Brunei, Cambodia, China, India, Indonesia, Japan, Republic of Korea, Laos, Malaysia, Mongolia, Myanmar, Pakistan, Philippines, Singapore, Thailand and Vietnam and the *ASEAN* Secretariat.

ASEM's three main work areas are economic (reducing barriers to trade and investment, and financial and social policy reform), political, and cultural and intellectual. Summit meetings are held every two years. The first ASEM was held in Bangkok in March 1996, the second in London in 1998, the third in Seoul in 2000, the fourth in Copenhagen in 2002, the fifth in Hanoi in 2005 and the sixth in Helsinki in 2006. ASEM 7 will be held in Beijing in 2008. ASEM does not have a permanent secretariat. Coordination is done through foreign ministers and senior officials.

Asia-Europe Cooperation Framework 2000: adopted at the third *Asia-Europe Meeting* in Seoul in 2000. A rather tedious catalogue of principles and objectives as well as political and economic priorities to be undertaken by the ASEM members.

Asia-Pacific Trade Agreement: the name since December 2005 for the Bangkok Agreement (formally *First Agreement on Trade Negotiation Among Developing Countries of ESCAP*). It aims at trade expansion among developing country members of the *Economic and Social Commission for the Asia-Pacific* (ESCAP) through mutually beneficial trade measures. It was signed on 31 July 1975. Members are Bangladesh, China (since 2001), India, Laos, Republic of Korea and Sri Lanka.

Asset-based definition of investment: see *investment*.

Assistance: a more genteel term than *protection*, but it means the same and has the same effect.

Associated foreign direct investment: defined by *UNCTAD* as *foreign direct investment* triggered either by the establishment of an affiliate or the expansion of existing affiliates. See also *sequential foreign direct investment*.

Association Agreements: trade-related bilateral agreements concluded by the *European Community*. Some 70 *ACP states* are also separately associated with the European Community through the *ACP–EC Partnership Agreement*. See also *Agenda 2000*, *enlargement* and *Mediterranean Agreements*.

Association of Caribbean States: entered into force in August 1995. It consists of 25 Latin-American and Caribbean countries. They are Colombia, Costa Rica, Cuba, Dominican Republic, El Salvador, Guatemala, Haiti, Honduras, Mexico, Nicaragua, Surinam and Venezuela plus the members of *Caricom*. The Association's aim is to form the world's fourth-largest trading group. In December 1995 it adopted an action plan to achieve economic integration among members through liberalization of trade, investments, transport and other related areas; promotion and facilitation trade and investment; and promotion of the region's transport and tourism sectors. Its secretariat is located at Port-of-Spain, Trinidad and Tobago.

Association of Tin Producing Countries: ATPC. Established in 1983 with the objective of obtaining remunerative and equitable returns to tin producers and adequate to consumers at fair and stable prices. Disbanded in 2001. Members in the final years included Brazil, Bolivia, China, Democratic Republic of Congo,

Indonesia, Malaysia, Nigeria and Thailand. Its secretariat was in Kuala Lumpur until 1997, when it moved to Rio de Janeiro.

ASYCUDA: Automated System for Customs Data. A computerized management system developed by *UNCTAD* for handling freight manifestos, customs declarations, accounting requirements and other procedures related to foreign trade. It can be adapted to individual customs regimes. See also *paperless trading*.

Asymmetrical trade agreements: these are in the main bilateral trade agreements with unequal sets of obligations for the partners. This might mean different timetables for tariff reductions or the phasing out of *non-tariff measures*. In other cases, one party might give free entry to the products of the other party without expecting similar treatment in return. See also *Caribbean Basin Initiative*, *GSP*, *ACP–EC Partnership Agreement* and *SPARTECA* as examples of such agreements.

Asymmetrical preferences: an arrangement whereby a country gives trade preferences to another country without expecting reciprocity. See also *asymmetrical trade agreements*.

Asymmetrical price comparison: occurs, for example, when the investigators in an anti-dumping case use different methods to calculate the *normal value* and the *export price*. See also *dumping* and *anti-dumping measures*.

Asymmetrical trade openness: describes a situation in which an exporting country with relatively closed markets can take advantage of relatively open markets elsewhere. This proposition gained currency particularly in the United States in the 1980s as a reason for a growing trade deficit. It was based on the assumption that the United States offered the most open market, and that it adhered fully to the multilateral trade rules. Other countries were seen to be less open to varying degrees and adhering to *mercantilism*, but they benefited all the same from the United States openness. Some advocated market-opening measures as a remedy. See also *aggressive unilateralism*, *free and fair trade*, *Section 301* and *Super 301*.

ATA Carnet: see *Customs Convention on the ATA Carnet for the Temporary Admission of Goods*.

ATC: the WTO *Agreement on Textiles and Clothing* which integrated trade in this sector back to GATT rules within a ten-year period. It expired on 1 January 2005.

Atlantic Charter: agreed at the August 1941 Atlantic Conference between President Roosevelt and Prime Minister Churchill. The Charter set out in paragraphs four and five an early definition of the *multilateralism* that was to guide post-war reconstruction. It expressed the wish of the United States and the United Kingdom "with due respect for their existing obligations, to further the enjoyment by all States, great or small, victor or vanquished, of access, on equal terms, to the trade and the raw materials of the world which are needed for their prosperity". The words "existing obligations" were meant to give comfort to the United Kingdom regarding the *imperial preferences arrangement*. Paragraph five read "... they desire to bring about the fullest collaboration between all nations in the economic field with the objective of ensuring, for all, improved labour standards, economic development and social security". In time, these sentiments led to the *Bretton Woods agreements* and, ultimately, the *GATT*.

At-the-border barriers: these consist in the main of *tariffs* and *non-tariff measures*, including *import quotas*. Some add exchange rates to this category, but these are not usually the responsibility of trade ministries. See also *behind-the-border issues*.

Attraction-aversion dilemma: defined by William A. Stoever as "the dilemma of desiring the benefits that foreign investors could bring while wanting to limit the intrusion of foreign entities". See also *foreign direct investment*, *globalization* and *anti-globalization*. [Stoever 2002]

Auckland Challenge: the long declaration issued at the *APEC Economic Leaders' Meeting* at Auckland in September 1999. The *APEC Principles to Enhance Competition and Regulatory Reform* seem to be its only noteworthy part.

Audiovisual services: the production, distribution and exhibition of films and video tapes. Some sensitive policy areas converge on this sector. They include claims of *cultural identity*, the protection of *intellectual property rights* and the aim to liberalize trade. These competing claims play themselves out against the broader canvas of rapid technological change and the new possibilities for distribution of audiovisual services it offers. Governments sometimes apply screening quotas and cross-ownership limitations on newspapers, radio and television stations in an attempt to preserve the local cultural characteristics. See also *broadcasting directive*, *local content rules in broadcasting* and *trade and culture*.

Australia and the third world: see *Harries Report*.

Australian subsidy on ammonium sulphate: a *non-violation* case brought by Chile against Australia under the GATT in 1950. It resulted from the discontinuation by Australia of its war-time subsidy for the sale of imported nitrate of soda of which Chile was a major supplier. A similar subsidy for ammonium sulphate was continued. The subsidy in both cases had been intended to balance war-time shortages of nitrogenous fertilizers, but it was continued for several years after the war because of a continuing shortage. The working party established to look at this case found that the value of a *concession* granted to Chile at the time of the 1947 tariff negotiations had been impaired as the result of a measure which did not otherwise conflict with the provisions of the GATT. This happened because ammonium sulphate and nitrate of soda had for a long time been treated in the same way. Chile therefore had reasonable expectations that the war-time subsidy would be applied to both fertilizers as long as there was a local shortage of nitrogenous fertilizer.

Australian argument for protection: the conclusion drawn in the *Brigden Report* that the "evidence available does not support the contention that Australia could have maintained its present population at a higher standard of living under free trade". It continued that "the same average income for the same population could not have been obtained without protection". The Brigden Report did not claim that protection would increase aggregate national income, and therefore it did not undermine the argument for free trade.

Australia New Zealand Closer Economic Relations Trade Agreement: see *ANZCERTA*.

Autarky: national self-sufficiency in production. Pure autarky is a theoretical construct. It is not attainable in the modern world. Where it has been tried, it has led to misery. The pretended policy of autarky in some countries has only been possible through substantial assistance from friendly countries and humanitarian help from others. The term is now also used loosely for economies that seek to produce the bulk of their requirements at home regardless of the cost through policies aimed at *self-reliance*, *self-sufficiency* and *techno-nationalism*. Some texts use *autarchy* when they mean *autarky*. That is wrong. *Autarchy*, according to the *Shorter Oxford English Dictionary*, means absolute sovereignty.

Automatic import licensing: an *import licensing* system where applications are always approved. See *Agreement on Import Licensing Procedures*.

Automaticity: the "automatic" chronological progression in the WTO for settling trade disputes in regard to panel establishment, terms of reference, composition and adoption procedures. See also *dispute settlement* and *Dispute Settlement Understanding*.

Automatic termination: see *sunset clause*.

Autonomous liberalization: countries often lower their **tariffs** or remove other market access restrictions without being asked by others. They do so because they envisage a flow of benefits for their economies. The extent to which they should be able to claim payment for their autonomous liberalization in *multilateral trade negotiations* then becomes an issue for negotiators. A notional credit is created to exact payment from others, sometimes with the use of complicated formulas. The logic of using negotiating credit in this way is not always clear since the country benefiting most from autonomous trade liberalization is the country doing it in the first place.

Autonomous preferential rules of origin: refers to *rules of origin* applied, for example, under *GSP* schemes to enable the *donor country* to determine whether goods imported from a *beneficiary country* qualify for *preferential tariff treatment*. The donor country has no contractual obligation to consult beneficiary countries when it establishes or amends these rules. [Inama 2000]

Autonomous tariff quota: when a component or a finished good is not produced within the *European Community*, manufacturers or importers may apply for duty-free entry of that good. If the application is granted in the form of an autonomous quota, the good may be imported duty-free within the quota limit. Other importers may then also make use of the quota. Other customs authorities have similar mechanisms. See also *tariff quota* and *temporary tariff suspension*.

Auto pact: see *Canada–United States Automotive Products Agreement*.

Averaging: a method of inventory management which uses the average cost of goods bought over a given period as the valuation basis. Its main relevance to trade policy stems from the need to calculate a *regional value content* under the *rules of origin* adopted in some *free-trade agreements*. See also *first-in, first-out* and *last-in, first-out*.

Average tariff: a device used to give an informative picture at a glance of a complete tariff schedule, which will usually have troughs and peaks, in a single average rate. It is the unweighted mean of either all applied or all bound rates. Such rates are also used for comparing the treatment of product sectors in different countries. See also *applied tariff rates*, *bindings*, *peak tariffs* and *trade-weighted average tariff*.

Aviation rights: see *freedoms of the air* and *open skies*.

B

Backdoor protectionism: the use of measures such as unreasonable product standards or excessively stringent quarantine rules to reduce the flow of imports. Ostensibly, such requirements are imposed to protect the public interest and, sometimes to their surprise, the consumers. See also *protectionism*, *sanitary and phytosanitary measures* and *technical barriers to trade*.

Backloading: the practice of ensuring that liberalizing commitments do not fall due until late in whatever phase-in period has been agreed in trade negotiations. It may also refer to deferring mandatory trade liberalization under an agreement or arrangement until the last possible legally acceptable moment. See also *frontloading*.

Back-to-back investigation: sometimes used to describe the initiation of an anti-dumping or countervailing investigation immediately after another investigation involving the same product has been terminated. See also *anti-dumping measures* and *countervailing duties*.

Balance of advantages: a principle sometimes used in *multilateral trade negotiations* which holds that advantages derived from the *exchange of concessions* in trade negotiations should be broadly balanced among participants. The balance is usually achieved through the *requests-and-offers* technique. This principle is not based on economic theory. Its ultimate basis is the fallacious assumption that *trade liberalization* entails a cost to the liberalizing country. See also *mercantilism*.

Balance of concessions: a judgement WTO members make in the course of negotiations and on their conclusion about the relative value of what they sought and were given. They usually try to ensure that the two are about equal. See also *balance of advantages*.

Balance of payments: BOP. A statistical summary of a country's total trade, other economic transactions and financial inflows and outflows at a given time. The BOP is made up of current account (current transactions), capital account (capital transactions) and a balancing item to even out difficulties in recording international transactions. The current and capital account components of the BOP may each either be in surplus or deficit, but the BOP itself must always show a balance. The current account is the component of the BOP showing trade in goods and services, income and unrequited transfers (e.g. foreign aid payments, workers remittances, etc.) over a specified period. The capital account records currency inflows and outflows due to international dealings in financial assets, such as investments and loans.

Balance-of-payments consultations: WTO members may use GATT Article XII (Restrictions to Safeguard the Balance of Payments) in the case of developed countries, Article XVIII:B (Governmental Assistance to Economic Development) in the case of developing countries in some circumstances and Article XII of the *General Agreement on Trade in Services* to impose import restrictions to shore up deteriorating foreign exchange reserves. The basic conditions under which restrictions may be taken are almost the same under these articles: the measures taken must be no more than is necessary (i) to forestall the imminent threat of, or to stop, a serious decline in monetary reserves, or (ii) in the case of very low monetary reserves, to achieve a reasonable rate of increase in these reserves. Any WTO member taking this step has to consult the WTO membership, either before or immediately after doing so, on the nature of its balance of payments difficulties, alternative corrective measures that may be available to it and the possible effect of restrictions on other members. Once restrictions have been imposed, they are subject to reviews. Reviews normally use the "full consultation procedures", but the "simplified consultation procedures" apply in the case of *least developed countries* or when developing countries have adopted liberalization programs in response to earlier consultations and when, in the case of developing countries, the consultations would occur in the same year as a *trade policy review*.

Balance of trade: in standard usage, this is the balance between exports and imports in an economy. In some countries it refers to the *balance on merchandise trade* only. In others it is the *balance on goods and services trade*. The concept conveys few analytical insights. The term also refers to attempts, rooted deeply in *mercantilism*, to ensure that the value of imports does not exceed that of exports. Bhagwati has described this attitude as "trade is good, but imports are bad". Adam Smith wrote that "[n]othing, however, can be more absurd than this doctrine of the balance of trade, upon which not only these restraints, but almost all the other regulations of commerce are founded. When two places trade with one another, this doctrine supposes that, if the balance be even, neither of them either loses or gains; but if it leans in any degree to one side, that one of them loses and the other gains in proportion to its declension from the exact equilibrium." Where countries have applied *import restrictions* to balance their trade, they have usually only succeeded in reducing the overall amount of trade and thus in reducing welfare. Whether a country imports more goods than it exports depends on many factors, including its stage of economic development and the structure of its economy. Balanced merchandise trade is not in itself an indicator of successful economic policies. As Schumpeter noted in his *History of Economic Analysis*, "an 'unfavorable' balance may be the symptom of increasing wealth, but also of a process of impoverishment; a 'favorable' one may mean prosperity and employment, but just as well the reverse". See also *beggar-thy-neighbour policies*, *mercantilism*, *trade deficit* and *trade surplus*.
[Smith 1991 [1776], Schumpeter 1982 [1954], Bhagwati 2002]

Balance on goods and services trade: the difference between exports and imports of goods and services, measured over a given period.

Balance on merchandise trade: the difference between exports and imports of goods, measured over a given period.

Bali Concord II: the declaration issued by a meeting of *ASEAN* members in Bali on 7 October 2003. It envisages the establishment of an ASEAN Security Community, an *ASEAN Economic Community* and an ASEAN Socio-cultural Community. The Economic Community is to result in the free flow of goods, services and investment and a freer flow of capital by 2020. It will build on *AFTA*, the *ASEAN Framework Agreement on Services* and the *ASEAN investment area*.

Baltic states: Estonia, Latvia and Lithuania.

Banana cases: this refers to two trade disputes brought for adjudication in the GATT and the WTO. The first was a case launched in 1993 in the GATT by Colombia, Costa Rica, Guatemala, Nicaragua and Venezuela against the European Economic Community (EEC) and decided in early 1994. It arose from a change in the EEC import regime for bananas which resulted in differing *market access* depending on whether they originated within the EEC, traditional *ACP states*, non-traditional ACP states or third countries. The complainants charged that this violated the non-discrimination provisions of the GATT, and that the EEC also had broken its *tariff bindings*. Altogether, the *panel* was asked to find on the consistency of the import regime with about ten GATT articles. On many of them it found that the EEC had no case to answer. Importantly, however, it decided that the manner of EEC's preferential tariff treatment of banana imports was contrary to the *most-favoured-nation treatment* required by GATT Article I. The second case had a wider ambit. It was initiated in early 1996 in the WTO by Ecuador, Guatemala, Honduras, Mexico and the United States concerning the European Community (EC) regime for the import, sale and distribution of bananas. The complainants alleged that the EC was in contravention of its obligations under the *GATT*, the *General Agreement on Trade in Services* (GATS), the *Agreement on Trade-Related Investment Measures*, the *Agreement on Agriculture* and the *Agreement on Import Licensing Procedures*. The panel found that the EC had breached its commitments under the GATT, GATS and the import licensing provisions. One point of particular interest arising from this panel finding is that it applies aspects of the provisions relating to *trade in services* to trade in goods. The European Community lodged an appeal against the decision, but the *Appellate Body* upheld most of the contested findings.

Banded formula: a method for reducing tariffs proposed during the *Doha Development Agenda* negotiations. It divides tariff levels into three bands which could be described roughly as high, medium and low, and it suggests tariff reductions for each band. The biggest reductions would occur at the high level. See also *blended formula*.

Bangkok Agreement: see *Asia-Pacific Trade Agreement*.

Bangkok Declaration: part of the final report adopted at UNCTAD X in Bangkok on 19 February 2000. Its focus is on *globalization* and *UNCTAD*'s contribution to the international debate on development-related global issues. The declaration is supplemented by a plan of action.

Bangkok Declaration on Partnership for the Future: the declaration adopted on 21 October 2003 at the *APEC Economic Leaders' Meeting*. It consists of three parts. The first part is a list of actions in support of trade and investment liberalization. The second part is concerned with fighting terrorism and resisting the proliferation of weapons of mass destruction. The third part deals with using *APEC* to help people and societies benefit from globalization.

Barbie doll case: refers to a newspaper report in 1996 which claimed that the economic benefit to China of a Barbie doll made there, bearing its *mark of origin* and selling in the United States for $9.99, was only 35 cents. Most of the remainder could be allocated to shipping, ground transport, wholesaling costs, retailing costs and profit. Whatever else the example may demonstrate, it shows clearly the degree to which even the production of relatively simple articles has now been internationalized. See also *globalization*. [UNCTAD/ITCD/TSB/2]

Barcelona Process: a program of trade and development cooperation between the *European Union* and originally twelve Mediterranean countries which was initiated in 1995 in Barcelona. The twelve were Algeria, Cyprus, Egypt, Israel, Jordan, Lebanon, Malta, Morocco, Palestinian Authority, Syria, Tunisia and Turkey. Libya is an observer. Cyprus and Malta have now joined the European Union. See *Euro-Mediterranean Association Agreements* and *Euro-Mediterranean Economic Area*.

Bargaining tariff: the name accorded in popular parlance to the United States tariff once it could be used to bargain down the tariffs of others following the adoption of the *United States Reciprocal Trade Agreements Program* in 1934. The tariff then in force was the *Smoot-Hawley tariff* which was unalterable except through congressional amendment. The term is now used more commonly to refer to the practice of keeping an obsolete tariff in the hope that it may be used to exact a tariff reduction from others. Sometimes it works, but it is a poor negotiating tool. See also *autonomous tariff*, *conventional tariff*, *multi-column tariff* and *single-column tariff*.

Barriers to trade: any measures that in some way influence, limit or deny *market access* for goods or services. Such measures come in several categories, and many are in place for good reasons. Thus the word "barrier" is not always appropriate, and it might be better to talk of impediments to trade because trade under them is possible, though possibly at less than optimal flows. The main categories of barriers can be listed as (a) governmental measures, (b) *restrictive business practices* and (c) barriers facing goods and services because they not meet the needs of the market for reasons of price, quality, shipping costs, delivery times, etc. The remainder of this entry is not concerned with the third category. The main trade barriers imposed by governments are obviously *tariffs* and *non-tariff measures*. Tariffs are transparent, well understood, and their level clearly determines the extent to which they act as a barrier. *Tariff quotas* are intended to be barriers even if imports outside the quota are in theory possible. Other measures usually based on tariff increases are *trade remedies*, i.e. *safeguards*, *anti-dumping measures* and *countervailing measures*. Then there is the category of non-tariff measures that can act as trade barriers or impediments. Examples of them are *import quotas* and *export quotas*, foreign exchange restrictions, *import licensing* and onerous customs procedures, but this list is by no means complete. Other important measures are *technical barriers to trade* (standards) and *sanitary and phytosanitary measures*. Obviously, the justification for the use of such measures varies greatly, but few would argue that measures to protect health and safety are not needed. A test in these cases is whether a measure is a *disguised restriction on trade*. Finally, governments can use the *general exceptions* and the *security exceptions* as trade barriers under certain conditions. Actions by business can also result in barriers to trade through, for example, *import cartels* and other *anti-competitive practices*. The *UNCTAD Coding System for Trade Control Measures* offers a comprehensive overview of measures that might be called barriers to trade.

Barter trade: an exchange of goods or services estimated to have the same value. Each party's contribution may be valued for accounting purposes in terms of a third-country currency, but the principal trait of barter trade is that no money changes hand between the parties to the transaction. See also *compensation trade* and *countertrade*.

Basel Convention: *Basel Convention on the Control of Transboundary Movements of Hazardous Wastes and Their Disposal*. Adopted on 22 March 1989 under the auspices of the United Nations Environment Program (UNEP). It entered into force on 5 May 1992. The Convention aims to reduce and control the international movement of hazardous waste and to ensure that these wastes are disposed of in an environmentally sound manner. Its two trade-related provisions state that (a) the parties have the right to ban the import of hazardous wastes, and (b) they may not export to or import hazardous wastes from non-members of the Convention. In September 1995 the parties decided to amend the Convention to include a ban on the movement of hazardous waste for recycling from developed to developing countries starting on 1 January 1998. See also *multilateral environment agreements* and *trade and environment*.

Base period: the time period, rather like a snapshot, agreed during the *Uruguay Round* agricultural negotiations as the basis on which all reductions and commitments were to be made. For market access and domestic support commitments, the base period was 1986–88. For export subsidy commitments, it was 1986–90. See also *Agreement on Agriculture*.

Base rate: a term often used to describe the tariff levels that form the starting point for reductions to be made through tariff negotiations. The levels concerned are those in force on a certain date. A decision whether to use *bound tariff rates* or *applied tariff rates* is necessary. In *free-trade agreement* negotiations it is usually the latter.

Basic agricultural products: defined in the WTO *Agreement on Agriculture* as "the product as close as practicable to the first sale". This definition leaves room for dispute. If one were to follow it strictly, cheese made on the farm would be a basic agricultural product, but if it was made in an industrial dairy it would be a processed product.

Basic Instruments and Selected Documents: see *GATT Basic Instruments and Selected Documents* and *WTO Basic Instruments and Selected Documents*.

Basic telecommunication services: includes voice telephony, telex, facsimile and data transmission. See also *Agreement on Basic Telecommunications Services, International Telecommunication Union, Negotiating Group on Basic Telecommunications, reference paper on telecommunications services* and *value-added telecommunications services*.

Basket tariff quota: a *tariff quota* covering a range of closely related internationally traded products. If a tariff quota is applied at the four-digit level under the *Harmonized System* (HS), it would still be possible to give additional protection to sensitive products by splitting the four-digit level into six digits or more. *Quota rights* could then be allocated selectively within the entire four-digit range. In this way, a tariff quota can be used as a protectionist measure even when it is allocated fully to importers.

Baumgartner proposals: a set of ideas suggested for action in the GATT in 1961 by the then French Minister for Finance and Economic Affairs, M Baumgartner, for the management of world trade in agricultural products. The essence of the proposals was an extension of the *Common Agricultural Policy* model to global markets, supplemented by the United States *Food for Peace program*, to dispose of surplus production. The cost of this plan would have been met by the importing countries. The key component of the pricing mechanism was the "normal price" which would have been set at a level well above what then was the price on the open market. See also *agriculture and the multilateral trading system* and *PL 480*.

Beggar-thy-neighbour policies: also beggar-my-neighbour policies.Trade or economic measures, such as export subsidies, import quotas and tariffs, taken with the aim of improving domestic economic conditions, e.g. raising employment, and the intention of making them a cost to other countries. Such policies may lead to similar measures by others in response. Beggar-thy-neighbour policies are considered to have been a major factor in deepening and prolonging the Great Depression of the 1930s. See also *balance of trade*, *mercantilism* and *Smoot-Hawley tariff*. [Robinson 1947]

Behaviour: a term used in the administration of *antitrust laws* or *competition laws*. It is virtually the same as *conduct*, and it describes the actions of firms that may fall within the ambit of the applicable laws.

Behind-the-border issues: policies and measures adopted by governments which are aimed primarily at the domestic economy, but which may have an impact on imports and exports. These include domestic *subsidies*, *competition policy*, *standards*, labour conditions, and many others. See also *at-the-border barriers*.

Beirut Agreement: *Agreement for Facilitating the International Circulation of Visual and Auditory Materials of an Educational, Scientific and Cultural*

Character. Adopted under the auspices of the **United Nations Educational, Scientific and Cultural Organization** (UNESCO) in 1948. The agreement provides that the parties do not levy import duties or impose *quantitative restrictions* on the import of defined materials.

Belgian family allowances: a case brought against Belgium by Norway and Denmark in 1952 under the GATT. It concerned the imposition of a levy on foreign goods purchased by Belgian public bodies when these goods came from a country whose system of family allowances did not meet specific Belgian requirements. The *panel* concluded that, as the levy was charged at the time the purchase was paid by the public body rather than when it was imported, the point at issue was *national treatment*. It considered, however, that arriving at a very definite ruling would be difficult, partly because it found the concept of a levy to offset the absence of family allowance payments in other countries difficult to reconcile with the spirit of the GATT. It noted with evident relief that in the meantime the Belgian Government had decided to make its measures consistent with the GATT. *Japanese measures on leather* deals with another attempt in the GATT to defend a restrictive trade measure through reference to a social policy. See also *social clause* and *trade and labour standards*.

Beneficiary countries: a term often used to describe the countries receiving preferential treatment under *GSP* schemes. It serves to emphasize the unilateral nature of GSP schemes. See also *donor countries*.

Benefit: under the WTO *Agreement on Subsidies and Countervailing Measures* this is a criterion necessary to establish whether a *subsidy* exists. The Agreement describes six categories of governmental measures that may satisfy the criterion if they confer a benefit. These are (a) a financial contribution by a government or public body, (b) a government practice involving a direct transfer of funds, (c) government revenue foregone or not collected, (d) provision by a government of goods and services other than infrastructure, (e) payments made by a government through a funding mechanism, (f) payments made through a private body on behalf of a government, and (g) any form of income or price support in the sense of GATT Article XVI (subsidies) which confers a benefit.

Benefits of trade: refers to benefits different to the ones postulated in the *gains-from-trade theory* which states that two countries with different price structures will get better economic returns if they trade with each other than if they adhere to *autarky*. The theory of *comparative advantage* also points to the benefits of international specialization. There are some other benefits. Trade gives access to capital goods, machinery and raw materials. It leads to the *transfer of technology* through the commercial and cooperative spread of new techniques, ideas and skills. Trade promotes the transfer of capital as firms seek to produce in the country best suited to their needs. Trade also brings about an additional benefit not always seen as that: anti-monopolist policies and an environment of competition.

Benelux: a *customs union* formed in 1948 between Belgium, the Netherlands and Luxembourg. Plans for the three to enter into an economic union were superseded by their founding membership of the *European Economic Community* on 1 January 1958.

Benign mercantilism: see *mercantilism*.

Berne Convention: the *Berne Convention for the Protection of Literary and Artistic Works* protects the rights of authors of literary and artistic works. It was concluded in 1886 and revised several times since, the last time in 1971. The main aim of the latest revisions was to move the convention towards according substantially uniform protection in all member countries. It is administered by *WIPO*. The 1971 revision of the Berne Convention is one of the standards to be observed under the WTO *Agreement on Trade-Related Aspects of Intellectual Property Rights*. See also *intellectual property*.

Best-endeavour undertakings: conditional promises to take certain actions, or to consider the possibility of taking certain action. If they are part of a trade agreement, they are an aspect of *soft law*. In trade negotiations best-endeavour undertakings are often the first step towards more binding obligations. See also *nagging rights*.

Best information available: a concept used in the administration of *anti-dumping measures*. The WTO *Anti-Dumping Agreement* states that even though the information provided by a party to a dumping investigation may not be ideal in all respects, this is not a reason for disregarding it, as long as the other party has acted to the best of its ability. If the evidence or information is not accepted, the supplying party should be given the reasons for it. It should also be given an opportunity to supply further explanations, taking account of the time-limits for the investigation.

Best practice for RTAs/FTAs in APEC: a set of twelve non-binding principles adopted in November 2004 to assist *APEC* economies negotiating *preferential trade arrangements*. The principles are (1) *consistency with APEC principles and goals*, (2) *consistency with the WTO*, (3) *go beyond WTO commitments*, both in terms of existing obligations and areas covered by the WTO, (4) *comprehensiveness* to deliver maximum economic benefits to all sectors of the economy, (5) *transparency* by ensuring that texts are readily available, in English where possible, on official websites, (6) practical measures in *trade facilitation* to reduce transaction costs, (7) *mechanisms for consultation and dispute settlement* to reduce uncertainty and prevent and resolve disagreements quickly, (8) *simple rules of origin that facilitate trade* by recognizing the increasingly globalized nature of production, (9) commitments on economic and technical *cooperation*, (10) *sustainable development* by recognizing that economic development, social development and environmental protection are mutually supportive, (11) openness to *accession by third parties*, and (12) *provision for periodic review* to ensure full implementation of the terms of the agreement. [www.apecsec.org]

Bicycle theory: the proposition that the *multilateral trading system* must keep moving forward through successive liberalizing rounds and agreements if it is to remain liberal. On this analogy, the system would fall over like a bicycle if long gaps between liberalizing moves were to permit protectionist sentiments and actions to become dominant. See also *protectionism*.

Bid challenge: in *government procurement* a complaint by one party that the other party has not followed the agreed rules in awarding a contract. A challenge usually has to be made within a specified period. The parties normally also agree that challenges should be heard by an impartial and independent tribunal, and that the challenger can attend all hearings.

Bilateral air services agreements: air traffic agreements concluded between governments in accordance with Article 6 of the *Chicago Convention*. They specify, sometimes in great detail, matters such as names of the carriers, the number of scheduled flights and the maximum number of passengers the other country may direct to one's own country. They also list the airports that may be used. See also *freedoms of the air* and *open-skies arrangements*.

Bilateral aviation rights: the rights specified in *bilateral air services agreements* for airlines to carry passengers and freight between the two countries. See also *open-skies arrangements*.

Bilateral cumulation: used in the administration of *preferential rules of origin*. For example, the rules may permit country A to use materials imported from country B and, after they have been processed, to re-export them to country B. Such goods are then admitted in country B under its *preferential tariff*, assuming that any other applicable conditions have been met.

Bilateral investment treaties: BITs. A name given by many countries to their *investment promotion and protection agreements*. The model United States agreement contains rights and obligations concerning the application of *most-favoured-nation treatment* and *national treatment*, whichever is the better; fair and equitable treatment more generally; permission for aliens to enter the other party's territory to establish, develop, administer and advise on an investment and to engage top managerial personnel regardless of nationality; an undertaking not to impose performance requirements; the provision of effective means for asserting claims and enforcing rights; transparency of regulation; procedures to be followed in case of expropriation; and freedom to transfer funds. See also *international investment agreements*.

Bilateralism: a preference for conducting international trade policy mainly through bilateral negotiations, sometimes through *free-trade agreements*. Bilateralism assumes that results are more easily obtained if only two parties are involved, partly because available economic or political pressure would be less diluted. In principle, fewer diverting factors are involved. This is true in cases where it is possible to isolate the purely bilateral dimension. Often this cannot be done since at least one of the parties may have obligations in the same matter towards third parties. Some advocates of bilateral negotiations see them as the only valid way for achieving results. The history of bilateral negotiations since the mid-1980s casts doubt on the general validity of this proposition, but bilateralism has been used with success for the resolution of some selected issues. The effectiveness of bilateral approaches depends on the amount of *negotiating coin* a country has to influence the behaviour of the other. It is largely an approach which works more in favour of the strong and against the interests of small and medium-sized countries. Bilateralism can also introduce additional tensions into the multilateral system. One form of bilateralism is used in the *multilateral trade negotiations*. WTO members often negotiate tariff *concessions* bilaterally, but they apply the results multilaterally in accordance with the *most-favoured-nation* obligation. See also *aggressive reciprocity*, *Section 301*, *Special 301* and *Super 301*.

Bilateral restraint agreement: see *voluntary restraint arrangement*.

Bilateral safeguards: see *bilateral transitional safeguards*.

Bilateral trade agreement: an agreement between two countries setting out the conditions under which trade between them will be conducted. If both parties are already WTO members enjoying the attendant *non-discrimination*, *market access* and other benefits, the main additional reason for a bilateral agreement may be a program of bilateral *trade facilitation* and *trade promotion* activities. Sometimes it may be a *free-trade agreement*. If one party is not a member of the WTO, the agreement will normally provide for *most-favoured nation treatment* and *national treatment*, protection of *intellectual property rights*, *consultation* and *dispute settlement*, and other principles and mechanisms necessary for ensuring smooth trade flows and the speedy resolution of problems. Bilateral trade agreements usually contain a provision for periodic reviews of trade developments at ministerial or officials level, such as a *Joint Trade Committee* or a *Mixed Commission*. See also *Trade and Investment Facilitation Agreement* and *Trade and Investment Framework Agreement*.

Bilateral transitional safeguards: a means available under many *free-trade agreements* measures to restrain surges in imports of *originating goods*, i.e. goods eligible for preferential tariff treatment. These safeguards mechanisms, sometimes simply called bilateral safeguards, are usually modelled on the *global safeguards* (safeguards imposed under Article XIX of the GATT), but they can only be used for goods still subject to tariffs. In time the need for the mechanism should disappear. They usually require that a safeguard can only be imposed if (a) the import surge causes, or threatens to cause, *serious injury* to domestic industry and (b) the surge in imports has been caused by a tariff reduction under the terms of the agreement. An investigation also has to be conducted to ensure that the safeguard is warranted. Agreements usually set a ceiling for any safeguard tariff. The measure also is time-bound. Compensation in the form of lower tariffs for other goods may be payable. See also *safeguards*.

BIMP-EAGA: Brunei–Indonesia–Malaysia–Philippines East ASEAN Economic Growth Area, proposed at a meeting of *ASEAN* economic ministers in October 1993. It covers Labuan, Sabah, Sarawak (Malaysia), North, Central, South and South-East Sulawesi, Maluku, Irian Jaya and East, West and Central Kalimantan (Indonesia), Mindanao and Palawan (Philippines) and all of Brunei. BIMP-EAGA is aimed at developing trade and investment between contiguous underdeveloped areas of separate countries. See also *AFTA*.

BIMST-EC: Bangladesh India Myanmar Sri Lanka Thailand Economic Cooperation. A group established in Bangkok in June 1996 to promote economic cooperation among its members. Myanmar (Burma) joined in December 1997. Nepal is
an observer. A framework agreement enabling the creation of a *free-trade area*
entered into force on 30 June 2004. Negotiations for a *free-trade agreement*
are continuing. Thailand provides a secretariat for BIMST-EC. [www.bimstec.org]

Binding: also called *concession*. A legal obligation not to raise tariffs on particular
products above the specified rate agreed in *WTO* negotiations and incorporated
in a country's *schedule of concessions*. Bindings are enforceable through the
WTO. Their purpose is to provide greater commercial certainty through a ceiling
on tariffs which cannot be breached without an offer of *compensation* to affected
trading partners. These ceilings are often higher than the *applied tariff rates*.

Binding commitments: binding or bound commitments are a legal obligation not
to make *market access* conditions for services more restrictive than described
in a country's *schedule of commitments on services* submitted to the WTO.
Bindings are enforceable under WTO rules and may only be breached through
negotiation with affected trading partners. A country breaching a binding may
have to offer *compensation* to other trading partners in the form of *commitments*
in other services.

Binding overhang: situations where *bound tariffs* in a country's tariff system as
a whole are significantly higher than *applied tariffs*. [Francois and Martin 2003]

Binding ratio: the proportion of *bound tariffs* to unbound ones in a given customs
territory.

Biochemical prospecting: see *UNCTAD-BIOTRADE initiative*.

Biopiracy: the unauthorized search in the wild by biotechnology companies for
plants or genes that may be useful for the development of, for example, new
pharmaceuticals or improved strains of commercial crops. Some developing
countries in particular consider that they are disadvantaged by this practice
because they may not receive proper compensation for the use of plants that
occur naturally in their territories. The biotechnology companies, on the other
hand, are seen by them as benefiting commercially through their application for
patents for discoveries made in this way. This is the basis for the argument that
there should be a new class of *intellectual property rights* to curb biopiracy. The
entire concept remains contentious.

Bioprospecting: the search for plants or genes that may be useful for the development of, for example, new pharmaceuticals or improved strains of commercial
crops. Bioprospecting differs from other branches of biotechnology in that it
is looking for as yet undiscovered applications. See also *biopiracy*. [Ministry of
Economic Development 2002]

Bipartisan Trade Promotion Authority Act of 2002: see *Trade Promotion
Authority*.

Black Sea Economic Cooperation Organization: BSEC. Established on 1 May
1999 as the successor to the Economic Cooperation Area of Black Sea Countries. Its members are Albania, Armenia, Azerbaijan, Bulgaria, Georgia, Greece,

Moldova, Romania, Russia, Turkey and Ukraine. BSEC runs an extensive intergovernmental work program on trade cooperation. Its secretariat is located in Istanbul.

Blair House Accord: an agreement reached on 20 November 1992 between the United States and the *European Community* on three changes to the draft *Uruguay Round* outcome on agriculture. First, there would be a reduction in the cutback of the volume of subsidized exports from 24% to 21%. Second, some domestic subsidies paid directly by governments to producers would be exempt from the reduction commitment (see also *blue box*). Third, the *peace clause* giving immunity against complaints on subsidies being reduced was extended. These changes left intact the principles to govern trade in agriculture following the conclusion of the Round, but they gave participants greater flexibility in implementing them. The Blair House Accord enabled a restart of the multilateral negotiations, but its initial favourable reception faded away once it became clear that it had not resolved the fundamental differences on *market access* between the two parties. The Accord was revised in December 1993, and this removed the final difficulty standing in the way of the Uruguay Round outcome on agriculture. See also *Agreement on Agriculture, agriculture and the multilateral trading system* and *market access for agriculture*.

Blended formula: a method for reducing tariffs proposed during the *Doha Development Agenda* negotiations. It entails the use of the *Uruguay Round* tariff reduction formula for some tariffs, the *Swiss formula* for others, and eliminating tariffs altogether on some *tariff lines*. The formula used during the Uruguay Round combined an average reduction with a minimum reduction per tariff line, and it permitted some measures to protect *sensitive products* from increasing competition. See also *banded formula*.

Block exemptions: a term used to describe the practice of the *European Community* to exempt some *sensitive sectors*, most often agricultural and textile products, from the full application of the provisions of its *preferential trade arrangements*. Block exemptions may also be used in the administration of *competition policy* to exempt certain sectors or practices from the applicable laws. See also *Association Agreements* and *Europe Agreements*.

"Blocking" regulation: a *regulation* adopted by the *European Community* (EC) in 2003. It aims to protect "the interests of the natural and legal persons under the jurisdiction of Member States, in particular by removing, neutralising, blocking or otherwise counteracting the effects of the *Anti-Dumping Act of 1916*". Contravention of this Act may lead to the imposition by United States courts of fines, imprisonment and/or payment of *treble damages*. The EC blocking regulation provides that judgments made under this Act by United States courts cannot be recognized in the EC, and that costs or damages so incurred can be recovered from the assets in the EC of companies launching an action under the Anti-Dumping Act of 1916. [Council Regulation (EC) No 2238/2003]

Blocking statutes: national legislation aimed at countering the attempted extraterritorial use of *antitrust laws* by others. Such legislation typically forbids nationals of the country concerned to cooperate in antitrust investigations launched by a foreign country. See also *extraterritoriality*.

Blood diamonds: also known as conflict diamonds. See *Kimberley Process Certification Scheme*.

Blue box: agricultural supports linked to production, but subject to production limits and therefore minimally trade-distorting. The specific rules are: (a) payments are based on fixed area and yields; or (b) payments are made on 85% or less of the base level of production; or (c) livestock payments are made on a fixed number of head. These supports are exempt from the reduction commitments under the WTO *Agreement on Agriculture*. See also *amber box* and *green box*. [UNCTAD/DITC/COM/2003/6]

Bogor Declaration: adopted by the *APEC Economic Leaders' Meeting* on 15 November 1994 at Bogor (Indonesia) to achieve free trade in goods and services as well as free investment among APEC members. Developed economy members will achieve the target by 2010, developing economies by 2020. Leaders emphasized their strong opposition to the creation of an inward-looking bloc that would impair the pursuit of global free trade. Leaders also said that they would give particular attention to their trade with non-APEC developing countries to ensure that they would also benefit from APEC's trade and investment liberalization, in conformity with GATT/WTO provisions. See also *APEC* and *open regionalism*.

Bogor Goals: the aim of *APEC* members to achieve free trade and investment by 2010 for developed economies and 2020 by developing economies. See also *Bogor Declaration*.

Bolar exception: named after a case in 1983 in the United States District Court launched by Roche Products Inc., a research-oriented pharmaceuticals company, against Bolar Pharmaceutical Co., a manufacturer of generic products. The gist of the case was that Bolar had begun an effort to obtain federal approval for the marketing of a generic drug based on a patent held by Roche before that patent expired. Roche alleged that this violated United States patent law. The court held that Bolar's use of the patented compound federally mandated testing was not an infringement of the law because it was *de minimis* and experimental. An appeal by Roche, heard in 1984 by the Court of Appeals, was successful. Later that year the United States Congress passed the *Drug Price Competition and Patent Term Restoration Act* which gave backing to the practice at issue in the Bolar case. It stated that it was not an infringement to make, use, or sell a patented drug if that was done solely for uses reasonably related to the development and submission of information under a federal law regulating the manufacture, use, or sale of drugs. The thinking underlying this provision was that if a manufacturer of generic drugs had to wait until the expiry of a patent for a drug before being allowed to start developmental work, the patent term of the drug would be extended *de facto*, probably by several years, until approval could be obtained. See also *generic springboarding* and *intellectual property rights*.

Bona fides: *Lat. good faith*, often met as *bona fide* (in good faith). See also *mala fides*.

Bonus: see *Dairy Export Incentive Program* and *Export Enhancement Program*.

Boomerang clause: Article 91.2 of the *Treaty of Rome* deals with *dumping* practices by member states of the *European Economic Community* towards other member states during the 12-year transition period (1958–1970) leading to full implementation of the Treaty. Protective measures against dumping were possible during the transition period, but the *European Commission* decided what action to take. One of the possibilities open to companies found to have dumped products was to take them back. Article 91.2 made this possible with minimum friction. It states that products originating or having been entered for consumption in one member state that are exported to another member state had to be admitted free of all charges or *quantitative restrictions* when they were re-imported into the territory of the first member state. The Article did not prohibit dumping, but it reduced the incentive for doing so. In 1970 the members of the European Community stopped using anti-dumping action against each other. See also *competition policy and anti-dumping measures*.

Boomerang effect: the possibility that policies executed by a government may rebound on it. *Trade policy* generally seeks to avoid the boomerang effect by treating exporters from other jurisdictions and their products in a manner equivalent to that given to domestic producers and their products. The boomerang effect is more likely to occur under laws and regulations not subject to the *national treatment* provision. See also *beggar-thy-neighbour policies* and *retaliation*.

Bootlegging: the unauthorized recording of artistic performances for later broadcasting or other commercial gain. Such recordings are often cheap, and their quality inferior. See also *copyright*, *intellectual property* and *piracy*.

Borderless world: originally the title of a book written in 1990 by Kenichi Ohmae which is more concerned with ways in which a firm can make the best of competing in an interlinked global economy. It represents an aspect of the literature on *globalization* and *internationalization*. In the meantime, the idea of a world without national borders to trade has taken hold in some quarters. However, like the paperless office, this will take some time to achieve.

Border measures: see *tariff* and *non-tariff measures*.

Border prices: the price of goods when they arrive at the border and before they have gone through an assessment of any duty that may payable. The border price is therefore the equivalent of the *CIF* price.

Border protection: any measure which acts to restrain imports at the point of entry.

Border tax adjustments: refunds of, or additions to, indirect taxes (e.g. excise tax) or non-collection of dues borne by an article destined for domestic consumption if that article is exported. Such adjustments are sometimes also called *drawbacks* or remissions. Adjustment can also be a charge levied on an imported article that equals indirect taxes (e.g. sales tax) imposed on similar domestic products. Such adjustments are not illegal under the GATT. See also *export incentives*.

Border trade: see *frontier traffic*.

Bottleneck facilities: see *essential facilities doctrine*.

Bottom-up approach: preparing an agenda for trade negotiations by agreeing on negotiating subjects item by item. As agreement is reached on each item, the shape of the final agenda gradually becomes apparent. The term is also used to describe the use of *positive lists* for *schedules of commitments* in *free-trade agreements*. See also *top-down approach*.

Bottom-up multilateralism: a negotiating process resulting in bilateral and mini-lateral outcomes which are extended multilaterally from the bottom up. Cowhey and Aronson, proponents of this process, stress that such deals must encompass the basic principles of the multilateral trade regime, and they must be open to the scrutiny of third parties. They say that multilateral negotiations will only yield slow incremental progress towards liberalization, and that *regionalism*, and in some cases the sectoral approach, can provide a superior solution to many issues if appropriate consultative mechanisms between regions exist. See also *bilateralism*, *hub and spokes*, *minilateralism*, *multilateralism* and *sectoral trade negotiations*. [Cowhey and Aronson 1993]

Bound: see *concession*.

Bound tariff rate: sometimes bound rate or simply *binding*. The tariff a WTO member undertakes not to exceed. See also *applied tariff rate*.

Bounty: a subsidy available to domestic producers, usually to help an ailing industry. It can be aimed at bridging the gap between domestic and imported prices of a manufacture (e.g. shipbuilding), or the use of a specified input in a production process (i.e. superphosphate for agriculture). Many prefer bounties to tariffs as a method for supporting or protecting industries because the amount paid, and therefore the cost to other industries and consumers, is clearly evident. Budgetary pressures are likely to keep bounties in check. Another argument is that bounties can be targeted more accurately, and they do not become a charge on inputs to other industries except through the general taxation system. See also *protection* and *subsidies*.

Box: a form of domestic support for agriculture. See *amber box*, *blue box, green box* and *S&D box*.

Boycott: the refusal to supply a country or a firm, to import or buy from it, or to deal with it in other ways. This may in certain cases constitute an *anti-competitive practice* or a *restrictive business practice*.

Bracketed language: a section of a negotiating text put in square brackets either because the language is disputed or because its adoption will depend on agreement being achieved elsewhere in the text. See also *ad referendum agreement* and *without prejudice*.

Brain drain: see *reverse transfer of technology*.

Branch office economy: the proposition that modern communications technologies enable economic decision-making to be concentrated in a few financial centres, and that smaller economies are no longer their own masters. Holders of this view often expect their governments to take steps to prevent this. They fall into two main groups. The first advocates making the economy more competitive and therefore more attractive to foreign investors through trade and investment liberalization. The second calls for *protectionism*, though this is usually couched in words like positive intervention, the need for a more modern *industry policy* and other devices with this intent. See also *globalization* and *internationalization*.

Brandt Report: published in 1980 as *North-South: A Programme for Survival* by the Independent Commission on International Development Issues. This commission was convened in 1977 under the chairmanship of Mr Willy Brandt, a former chancellor of the Federal Republic of Germany. The report covered, among other topics, commodity trade and development, energy, industrialization and world trade, transnational corporations, investment and the sharing of technology, the world monetary order and development finance. It sought greater participation by developing countries in the processing, marketing and distribution of commodities, *compensatory financing arrangements* and the conclusion of *international commodity agreements*. It also advocated a *rollback* of *protectionism* by the industrialized countries, positive adjustment programs (*structural adjustment*), an easing of the rules of the *GSP*, and fair labour standards to prevent unfair competition and to facilitate *trade liberalization*. The quality of the report, its timeliness and the composition of the commission ensured wide coverage and public discussion of its proposals. Its proposals found their way into the agenda of all important conferences at the time, but the problems giving rise to them evaded a successful resolution. In 1983, the Brandt Commission published *Common Crisis: North-South: Co-operation for World Recovery* in response to what members of the commission saw as an inadequate response to the issues raised in its first report. The commission was formally disbanded in February 1983. See also *Cancun Summit* and *North-South dialogue*. [Brandt Commission 1980]

Brazilian unroasted coffee: a case brought before the GATT in 1980 which centred on the meaning of *like product*. Brazil complained that changes in the Spanish *tariff schedule* meant that Brazilian unroasted non-decaffeinated coffee was now treated less favourably than "mild coffee". The distinction between these coffee types was based on a statistical method used by the International Coffee Organization which broadly graded coffee into mild Arabicas, unwashed Arabicas and Robustas. Brazil claimed that Spain was contravening GATT Article I:1 (General Most-Favoured-Nation Treatment) in that it treated like products from different countries in a discriminatory way. Spain argued that "unwashed Arabica" and "mild coffee" were different products in terms of quality, taste and cultivation methods. The *panel* agreed with Brazil. It accepted the existence of different types of coffee, but it held that these differences were not enough to allow for a different tariff treatment. It also found that unroasted coffee was mostly sold in blends, and that "coffee, in its end-use, was universally regarded as a well-defined and single product for drinking". Accordingly, the panel suggested that Spain remove its discriminatory treatment of Brazilian coffee. [GATT BISD 28S]

Bretton Woods agreements: the United Nations Monetary and Financial Conference held at Bretton Woods, New Hampshire, in 1944 produced charters for the

World Bank (International Bank for Reconstruction and Development or IBRD) and the International Monetary Fund (*IMF*). It also proposed the establishment of the International Trade Organization (*ITO*) for which negotiations were held separately, but which ultimately resulted in a less ambitious outcome in the form of the *GATT*. The three are sometimes called the Bretton Woods institutions. See also *Havana Charter*.

Bribery: a form of *corruption*, usually entailing some payment either in money or kind or a favour. It is defined, for example, in the OECD *Convention on Combating Bribery of Foreign Public Officials in International Business Transactions* as "the promise or giving of any undue payment or other advantages, whether directly or through intermediaries to a public official, for himself or for a third party, to influence the official to act or refrain from acting in the performance of his or her official duties in order to obtain or retain business". The practice of paying or receiving bribes is not, of course, confined to international business transactions.

Bribery in international transactions: see *Convention on Combating Bribery of Foreign Public Officials in International Business Transactions*, *Draft International Agreement on Illicit Payments*, *trade and illicit payments* and *United Nations Convention Against Corruption*.

Brigden Report: commissioned in 1927 by the Australian Government to report on the effects of the tariff on the economy. It was named after Professor J B Brigden of the University of Tasmania who headed the enquiry. The report, published in 1929, recommended moderate levels of protection and warned that protection levels at the time had probably reached their economic limit. In the long run, the influence of the report was much greater on approaches to the assessment of protection levels than the making of tariff policy. See also *Australian argument for protection*.

Broadband services: communications services using still images, video, sound, text and data either separately or in combination. Broadband generally denotes the ability to communicate information at a high transmission rate. See also *audiovisual services*.

Broadcasting Directive: the *Television-Without-Frontiers directive*, issued by the *European Commission* in 1989 and amended in 1997. Its main aim is to create the conditions for the free movement of television broadcasts, i.e. European works, within the Community. The governing principle is that member states have to ensure freedom of reception, and they must not restrict retransmission of television programmes of other member states. Television broadcasting is defined as the initial transmission by wire or over the air, including that by satellite, in unencoded or encoded form, of television programs intended for reception by the public. European works are those originating from European Community member states, from European countries that are parties to the *European Convention on Transfrontier Television* and some co-productions involving Community producers and other European countries. Broadcasters must reserve, where practicable, a majority proportion of their transmission time for European works, but there are no numerical targets. This excludes time for news, sports events, games, advertising, teletext services and teleshopping. Member states may draw up a list of events considered of major importance for society that must be available for live or deferred free-to-air transmission. See also *audiovisual services* and *cultural identity*. [Council Directive 89/552/EEC, Council Directive 97/36/EEC]

Broader competition policy: see *competition policy* and *wider competition policy*.

Brundtland Commission: see *World Commission on Environment and Development*.

Brussels Convention: see *Convention Relating to the Distribution of Programme-Carrying Signals Transmitted by Satellite*.

Brussels Definition of Value: BDV. A standard for valuing goods at the border to fix the *customs duties* to be paid. It was developed under the auspices of the Customs Cooperation Council, now the *World Customs Organization*, located in Brussels. The BDV is the price goods would fetch on sale in the open market in the importing country at the time and in the place the import occurs. It sets out a number of considerations aimed at arriving at a decision on whether the actual sales price of the product corresponds with the notional standard of value. The BDV has now been superseded by the methods set out in the WTO *Agreement on Implementation of Article VII [customs valuation] of the General Agreement on Tariffs and Trade 1994*. See also *customs valuation*.

Brussels Ministerial Meeting: see *Uruguay Round*.

Brussels Tariff Nomenclature: BTN. A product classification for use in a national tariff. Developed by the Customs Cooperation Council, now the *World Customs Organization*, based in Brussels. This nomenclature was superseded by on 1 January 1988 by the *Harmonized System*.

BSE: bovine spongiform encephalopathy, or "mad cow disease".

BTA: see *border tax adjustments*.

Budapest Treaty on the International Recognition of the Deposit of Microorganisms for the Purposes of Patent Procedure: concluded on 28 April 1977. It aims to simplify patenting procedures for applicants whose invention involves a microorganism or the use of a microorganism not available to the public. In a growing number of countries, *patent* procedure not only requires the filing of a written description of the invention, but also a deposit, with a specialized institution, of a sample of the microorganism. This is complex and costly when it has to be repeated in several countries. Parties to this treaty agree that one deposit with any international depository authority is sufficient, regardless of the location of the authority. The Treaty is administered by *WIPO*. See also *intellectual property*.

Buffer stocks: holdings usually established under some *international commodity agreements* to influence and stabilize the price of *commodities*. Buffer stocks are sold when the price moves above a defined price band. They are accumulated when the price moves below a band reflecting current market prices. Buffer stocks can work when price fluctuations are short-term, and when high prices more or less cancel out low prices within a reasonable period. The price range covered by the agreement normally is structured so that the buffer stock manager must buy when the price is in the lowest band, assuming funds are left to do so. Then follows a band in which the manager may buy. That decision is based on the commercial outlook, available funds, the size of the existing buffer stock, etc. At yet a higher price level, the manager may sell. Once the commodity price enters the highest price band set out in the agreement, the manager must sell, assuming that there are stocks. Buffer stocks are intended to be self-financing. The maximum size of the stock and the method of financing it are usually contentious. Proponents of such mechanisms hold that a large buffer stock operation compared to the size of the market and endowed with strong financial resources can much more easily deal with market fluctuations than a smaller one. A larger stock also would be much more expensive to run. In the case of secular changes to demand and supply, large buffer stocks may hinder production adjustments. Sometimes producers seek to cope with long-term low prices through increasing their production. If the buffer stock continues to buy, it gives producers the wrong signal since at this time producers should be encouraged to limit production. Continued buying could send the operation out of business. If the price band for triggering buffer stock purchases or sales is too wide, the effectiveness of international commodity agreement as a tool for market intervention is greatly diminished. On the whole the record of buffer stocks has been disappointing. Their successes have tended to be temporary. The *IMF* maintains a Buffer Stock Financing Facility to assist the financing of member contributions to approved international buffer stocks, but it has not been used since 1984. See also *commodity policy*, *Common Fund for Commodities* and *Integrated Programme for Commodities*.

Build-down method: one of the methods used in the administration of *rules of origin* to establish whether a good imported from another party to a *free-trade agreement* qualifies for the *preferential tariff*. In the free-trade agreement between Singapore and the United States, and other free-trade agreements to which the United States is a party, the formula is:

$$RVC = \frac{AV - VNM}{AV} \times 100$$

where RVC is the *regional value content*, expressed as a percentage, AV is the adjusted value, and VNM is the value of *non-originating materials* that are acquired and used by the producer in the production of the good. The term "adjusted value" is defined in some detail in the agreement. In essence it means that the following have to be excluded from the customs value of the goods under consideration: any costs, charges or expenses incurred for transport, insurance and related services as part of the international shipment of the good from the country of export to the country of import. This method is a variation of the *FOB value method*.

Building-block approach: first, building blocks may be the elements ultimately making up a *free-trade agreement*. Some easy elements, such as *trade facilitation* activities, might be tackled first as confidence-building measures.

The more difficult trade-liberalizing provisions would come later. Second, *free-trade areas* are seen by some as the building blocks for a tariff-free *multilateral trading system*. Individual areas could ultimately be combined to bring down trade barriers between ever larger areas. See also *stumbling blocks*. [Bhagwati 1991]

Build-up method: one of the methods used in the administration of *rules of origin* to establish whether a good imported from another party to a *free-trade agreement* qualifies for the *preferential tariff*. In the free-trade agreement between Singapore and the United States, and other free-trade agreements to which the United States is a party, the formula is:

$$RVC = \frac{VOM}{AV} \times 100$$

where RVC is the *regional value content*, expressed as a percentage, AV is the adjusted value, and VOM is the value of *originating materials* that are acquired or self-produced, and used by the producer in the production of the good. The term "adjusted value" is defined in some detail in the agreement. In essence it means that the following have to be excluded from the customs value of the goods under consideration: any costs, charges or expenses incurred for transport, insurance and related services as part of the international shipment of the good from the country of export to the country of import.

Built-in Agenda: BIA. The extensive WTO work program resulting from the provisions contained in the instruments negotiated during the *Uruguay Round*. The BIA authorized or mandated new negotiations. These later became part of the *Doha Development Agenda*.

Bunching of tariffs: the practice of carrying out tariff reduction or elimination commitments in batches, often as close as possible to a deadline.

Burden of proof: the obligation of a plaintiff or a defendant to show that an alleged action has or has not occurred, as the case may be. The established procedure in the WTO for approaching burden of proof is described in *EC – Hormones (US) (Article 22.6 – EC)*. It states that "WTO members, as sovereign entities, can be *presumed* to act in conformity with their WTO obligations. A party claiming that a Member has acted *inconsistently* with WTO rules bears the burden of proving that inconsistency" [italics in the original]. The situation changes once the complainant has made a *prima facie case* or shown that an inconsistency has occurred. It is then up to the defendant to show that this is not the case. If the evidence were to show that claim and counterclaim are evenly balanced, the plaintiff would lose the case. [WT/DS26/ARB]

Burden-sharing: the idea that the cost of new trade measures should be borne by the widest possible group of affected countries. Some also use the term when they erroneously see *trade liberalization* as a cost to economies doing so. Burden-sharing is not the same as *reciprocity*, which demands roughly equivalent action from others. See also *balance of advantages*.

Business mobility: the ability of people to travel across borders to promote and undertake business activities. In the *GATS* this is known as the *movement of* *natural persons*. In a wider sense it also refers to the ability of natural and *juridi-cal persons* to establish businesses in other countries and to manage them. This is covered by the GATS under *commercial presence*. Many *free-trade agreements* have chapters covering business mobility to support the *cross-border supply of services* and investment chapters.

Business process outsourcing: BPO. See *outsourcing*.

But for **test:** a method adopted, for example, by the WTO *panel* in *Canada – measures affecting the export of civil aircraft* to establish whether a link existed between a governmental grant "to the Canadian regional aircraft industry and anticipated exportation or export earnings". The test in this case asks whether assistance would not have been given *but for* anticipated exportation or earnings. The panel found that assistance to the Canadian regional aircraft industry constituted *export subsidies* inconsistent with the *Agreement on Subsidies and Countervailing Measures*.

Butter mountain: the name given in common parlance to the dairy product surpluses caused by the *Common Agricultural Policy* of the *European Community*. See also *wine lake*.

Buy American Act: a United States act passed in 1933 to ensure (a) that only unmanufactured and manufactured articles, materials and supplies produced in the United States would be bought for public use and (b) that in the case of construction of public buildings and public works only articles, materials and supplies produced in the United States would be used at all construction stages. The Act does not apply to goods used outside the United States or not produced domestically. There are some other exceptions, including one where the public interest would demand otherwise or where the cost would be unreasonable if American materials were used. Members of the WTO *Agreement on Government Procurement* are exempt from significant aspects this Act. Many of the American states have their own Buy American law. See also *buy-local policies*.

Buy-local policies: a way of giving advantages to domestic producers of goods and services under the *government procurement* rules of some countries. Such policies are often expressed in terms of a preference margin favouring the home-grown product, but sometimes they may be limited to a decision to purchase locally if all other things are equal. Buy-local policies at times are used to promote the development of domestic industries.

Byrd Amendment: the *Continued Dumping and Subsidy Offset Act* passed by the United States Congress in October 2000. Named after Senator Robert Byrd who proposed it as an amendment to an appropriation bill for agriculture. The Act seeks to ensure that proceeds from anti-dumping and countervailing duty cases are paid to the United States companies that initiated the cases. Companies receiving such payments may use them for items such as plant modernization and pension expenditures.

C

Cabotage: reserving the provision of shipping or air services between domestic ports and airports, respectively, In most countries, to ships or aircraft owned and registered locally. Their crews must be hired under local employment conditions. In the United States ships providing cabotage services must also be built in domestic shipyards. See also *freedoms of the air* and *Jones Act*.

CAFTA: see *United States–Central America Free Trade Agreement*.

Cairns Group: a group of agricultural exporting nations lobbying for agricultural trade liberalization. It was formed in 1986 at a Ministerial Meeting in Cairns, Australia, just before the start of the *Uruguay Round*. Current members are Argentina, Australia, Bolivia, Brazil, Canada, Chile, Colombia, Costa Rica, Guatemala, Indonesia, Malaysia, New Zealand, Pakistan, Paraguay, Peru, Philippines, South Africa, Thailand and Uruguay. See also *Agreement on Agriculture* and *agriculture and the multilateral trading system*.

Calvo doctrine: a doctrine at one time prevalent in Latin American legal systems. It holds that foreign nationals, and particularly foreign investors, are not entitled to seek protection from their governments in excess of that available to nationals of host countries. In other words, it rejects any suggestion of privileged treatment for foreign investors. The doctrine in effect prevented countries adhering to it from concluding treaties for the protection of investment, and it therefore was seen as having a direct influence on investment flows. It is named after Dr Carlos Calvo, an Argentinian lawyer and diplomat, who enunciated it in 1885. [Seid 2002, Sornarajah 1994]

Canada – Measures affecting exports of unprocessed herring and salmon: see *herring and salmon*.

Canada–United States Automotive Products Agreement: entered into force in 1966. It permitted some motor vehicle manufacturers to bring vehicles, parts and accessories into Canada from the United States free of import duties. Some **performance requirements** had be met by companies participating in the scheme. The last time new applicants were given permission to participate in the scheme was on 31 July 1989. The Agreement became an irritant especially for Japanese car manufacturers who had begun operations in the United States in the 1980s. In 2000 a WTO *panel* ruled that certain elements of the agreement violated Canada's WTO obligations. The ensuing changes removed most of the reasons for the original agreement.

Canada–United States Free Trade Agreement: CUSFTA or CUSTA. Concluded on 2 January 1988. This Agreement has been superseded by *NAFTA*.

Canadian periodicals: a WTO case brought by the United States against Canada in 1996. Canada had maintained measures designed to prohibit the import of certain editions of foreign periodicals or to favour domestic periodicals through lower *excise duties* and postal rates. An important element of these measures was the aim of protecting Canadian *cultural identity*. In June 1997 the *panel* found against Canada on most counts, especially in relation to its obligations under GATT Article III (National Treatment) and Article XI (General Elimination of Quantitative Restrictions). This case is relevant to any work on *trade and culture*.

Cancún Ministerial Conference: the fifth *WTO Ministerial Conference* held at Cancún, Mexico, from 10 to 14 September 2003.

Cancún Summit: a meeting of 22 heads of state and heads of government held at Cancún, Mexico, in 1981. It aimed to find a way to restart the stalled *North-South dialogue*. It was organized in the favourable climate created by the first *Brandt Report*, issued in 1980. Although the meeting ended in an apparent consensus, it turned out to be a failure in bringing about its stated objective. Like all other North-South initiatives, it was not able to overcome the competing views of the main participants concerning the best way to implement any proposed measures.

Candidate countries: a name for countries that have applied to join the *European Union*. See also *Copenhagen criteria* and *enlargement*.

CAP: the *Common Agricultural Policy* which consists of a comprehensive system of production targets, marketing and support mechanisms designed to manage agricultural trade within the *European Union* and with the rest of the world.

Capacity-building: support for developing countries to improve their ability to implement and observe their international treaty obligations. Capacity-building programs are usually provided through multilateral and regional organizations, such as the WTO and *APEC*, the *multilateral development banks* or through bilateral programs. Various methods and principles have been devised to make capacity-building more effective. The OECD *Development Assistance Committee*, for example, has adopted the following principles: (a) coordinate trade capacity-building efforts among donors, both bilateral and multilateral, (b) ensure that trade capacity-building activities are comprehensive in scope and integrated in execution by going, for example, beyond trade ministries, (c) foster local ownership and participation in trade-related development cooperation activities, (d) devise and embrace approaches that will strengthen sustainability, (e) strengthen donors' own trade-related capacities through a systematic exchange of information on programs and experiences, and (f) commit greater financial and personnel resources to efforts to build trade policy frameworks in developing countries – with the prospect of substantial returns. See also *implementation*.

Caribbean Basin Initiative: CBI. Originally a United States 12-year plan which began on 1 January 1984 under the *Caribbean Basin Economic Recovery Act* of 1983 to promote the development of Caribbean Basin nations. It was made permanent in 1990. The CBI extends tariff-free treatment to all products from the Caribbean area, and reduced tariffs for textiles, some leather goods and petroleum products. Sugar imports are subject to *quotas*, but Caribbean sugar enters the United States free of tariffs. The 2000 *United States Caribbean Basin Trade Partnership Act* (CBTPA), part of the *Trade and Development Act of 2000*, offers Caribbean Basin beneficiary countries that are prepared to join *NAFTA* or another *free-trade agreement* tariff treatment roughly equal to that accorded to the NAFTA partners. CBTPA expires in 2008. See also *Alliance for Progress* and *Enterprise for the Americas Initiative*.

Caribbean Community and Common Market: CARICOM. Established on 1 August 1973 through the Treaty of Chaguaramas as the successor to the Caribbean Free Trade Association (CARIFTA). It consists of Antigua and Barbuda, Barbados, Belize, Dominica, Grenada, Guyana, Jamaica, Montserrat, St Christopher and Nevis, St Lucia, St Vincent and the Grenadines, Suriname, and Trinidad and Tobago. The Bahamas is a member of the Caribbean Community, but not of the Common Market. Anguilla, Bermuda, British Virgin Islands, Cayman Islands and the Turks and Caicos Islands are associates. Members have also agreed to a free internal market in air services. The Caribbean Common Market has now been superseded by the *CARICOM Single Market and Economy*. Its secretariat is located at Georgetown, Guyana.

Caribbean Common Market: Consists of all the members of *Caribbean Community and Common Market* except The Bahamas.

Caribbean Free Trade Association: see *Caribbean Common Market*.

Caricom: see *Caribbean Community and Common Market*.

CARICOM Single Market and Economy: CSME. Formed through the *Revised Treaty of Chaguaramas Establishing the Caribbean Community Including the CARICOM Single Market and Economy*, signed at Nassau, The Bahamas, on 5 July 2001 by Antigua and Barbuda, The Bahamas, Barbados, Belize, Dominica, Grenada, Guyana, Jamaica, Montserrat, St. Kitts and Nevis, Saint Lucia, St. Vincent and the Grenadines, Suriname, and Trinidad and Tobago. The CSME succeeded the *Caribbean Community* and CARICOM. The CSME permits the free movement of goods, services, capital and people among its members. The Single Market became effective on 1 January 2006, and the Single Economy is expected to follow in 2008. Its headquarters are in Georgetown, Guyana.

Carousel effect: used to describe some attempts to escape the effects of *anti-dumping* or *safeguards*. Some say that manufacturers or exporters will change periodically the make-up of a product subject to these measures to evade *retaliation*.

Carousel legislation: refers to Section 407 of the United States *Trade and Development Act* adopted on 18 May 2000 to encourage implementation by trading partners of the United States of WTO *dispute settlement* decisions that have gone against them. In such cases, the WTO rules permit the *suspension of concessions or other obligations*, though the procedures for doing so are carefully defined. A list of products is usually prepared and maintained for this purpose.

The United States has a different approach. The carousel legislation requires a mandatory and unilateral revision of this list of products 120 days after the application of the first suspension and then every 180 days after that. Many trading partners consider that doing so would go beyond the intentions of the *Dispute Settlement Understanding*.

Carry forward: under the *Agreement on Textiles and Clothing*, now expired, the use in the current year of part of next year's textiles and clothing export quota. See also *flexibility mechanism*.

Carry over: under the *Agreement on Textiles and Clothing*, now expired, the use in the current year of unused textiles and clothing export quota from the previous year. See also *flexibility mechanism*.

Cartagena Agreement: Agreement on Andean Subregional Integration. See *Andean Community*.

Cartagena Protocol on Biosafety: a protocol to the *Convention on Biological Diversity*, adopted 29 January 2000. The protocol seeks to protect biological diversity from the potential risks posed by living modified organisms resulting from modern biotechnology. It establishes a procedure for *advance informed agreement* and it refers to the *precautionary principle* (principle 15 of the *Rio Declaration on Environment and Development*). See also *multilateral environment agreements*.

Cartel: a formal or informal agreement between firms to manage domestic or international markets by lessening competition between the firms. Methods include agreement not to compete on price, limitations on the total output by the members to the agreement, market-sharing arrangements, etc. To what extent such activities are legal depends on a country's *competition policy*. Cartel arrangements work best when few firms dominate an activity. Agreements are divided into public and private cartels. A public cartel is one where the government forms and administers the rules for its own reasons. This may include acceptance of export cartels aimed at strengthening the competitiveness of domestic firms. An example of such rules is the United States *Webb-Pomerene Act*. *Pure export cartels*, directed exclusively at foreign markets, enjoy considerable freedom from the application of *competition laws*. *Mixed export cartels* affect domestic and export markets. *Import cartels* are much rarer. In many cases competition authorities do not approve their formation or operation. Public cartels might also be permitted to promote *structural adjustment*. Private cartels, or arrangements between firms, are usually kept secret, particularly if they are against the law or if they would lead to higher prices for consumers. See also *antitrust laws*, *rule of reason* and *trade and competition policy*.

Carve-out: an agreement among participants in negotiations to exempt for the time being a set of measures or a defined economic activity from the application of new or proposed trade rules. An example of a carve-out is the exemption from the *General Agreement on Trade in Services* rules of *bilateral aviation rights*.

Cascading tariffs: sometimes used instead of *tariff escalation*. It describes the practice of setting low tariffs on relatively simple components of a final product and to increase tariffs as the degree of processing increases. The aim is to add as much value as possible domestically.

Cassis de Dijon case: see *mutual recognition arrangements*.

Causality: the existence of a causal link between increased imports and serious *injury* or the *threat of serious injury* to domestic industry producing like or directly competitive products which can be used to impose *safeguards*. Likewise, members imposing *anti-dumping measures* must show that the harm to industry has been caused by *dumping* and not some other reason. See also *like products*.

Causal linkage: see *causality*.

CBD: see *Convention on Biological Diversity*.

CEFTA 2006: the free-trade agreement replacing the *South East Europe Free Trade Area* (SEEFTA) from 1 January 2007. Its members are Albania, Bosnia-Herzegovina, Croatia, Kosovo (as a territory administered by the United Nations) Moldova, Montenegro, Serbia and the Former Yugoslav Republic of Macedonia. See also *Stabilization and Association Agreements*.

Ceiling bindings: the practice in the WTO of binding all, or large sections, of a tariff at a specified level, often with a comfortable cushion above the *applied tariff rates*. Bindings are normally the result of negotiations. Countries that undertake to bind their tariffs are under a legal obligation not to increase these bound levels, but ceiling bindings allow them to make many desired increases. See also *bindings* and *peak tariffs*.

Ceiling duties: refers in most cases to the highest possible tariff rate in a national *tariff schedule*. Often these are the same as *ceiling bindings*.

Central African Customs and Economic Union: often referred to as UDEAC (Union douanière et économique de l'Afrique centrale). Established in 1964 with the ultimate aim of turning into a *common market*. Its members are Cameroon, Central African Republic, Chad, Congo, Equatorial Guinea and Gabon. UDEAC's secretariat is located at Bangui, Central African Republic. UDEAC was succeeded in June 1999 by the *Communauté Economique et Monétaire de l'Afrique Centrale*.

Central African Economic and Monetary Union: see *Communauté Economique et Monétaire de l'Afrique Centrale*.

Central American Common Market: CACM. One of the *preferential trade arrangements* of the *first regionalism*. The *General Treaty on Economic Integration* establishing it entered into force on 4 June 1961. Its members are Costa Rica, El Salvador, Guatemala, Honduras and Nicaragua. The task of promoting CACM has now been revitalized through the formation of *SIECA*.

Central American Free Trade Agreement: see *United States–Central American Free Trade Agreement*.

Central American Integration System: see *SICA*.

Central Asian Cooperation Organization: CACO. Established on 28 February 2002 as the successor to the Central Asian Economic Community. It consists of Kazakhstan, Kyrgyz Republic, Tajikistan and Uzbekistan. At the same time it widened its sphere of activity to include security and strategic issues in addition to economic matters.

Central Asian Economic Community: see *Central Asian Cooperation Organization*.

Central European Free Trade Agreement: CEFTA. An omnibus term for a complex structure of plurilateral and bilateral agreements which linked the Czech Republic, Hungary, Poland, Romania, Slovakia and Slovenia. CEFTA in its original form was largely redundant by the accession to the *European Community* of most of its participants. Its successor is *CEFTA 2006*.

Centrally-planned economies: CPE. A name until the late 1980s or early 1990s for the countries of Central and Eastern Europe, the USSR, China, Vietnam and some others in which economic activity was based on yearly plans usually elaborated by a body like the State Planning Commission. These countries were also known as non-market economies. Most CPEs have now turned into *market economies* or are on the way towards that goal. See also *economies in transition* and *Partners in Transition*.

CEPAL: Comisión Económica de las Naciones Unidas para América Latina y el Caribe. See *Economic Commission for Latin America and the Caribbean*.

CEPT: Common Effective Preferential Tariff. The mechanism established under *AFTA* for achieving the goal of reducing tariffs applicable to trade between the six original *ASEAN* members (Brunei Darussalam, Indonesia, Malaysia, Philippines, Singapore and Thailand) to between zero and 5%. Products traded in this way are entered into the *Inclusion List*. See also *ASEAN Integration System of Preferences*, *Sensitive List* and *Temporary Exclusion List*.

CER: closer economic relations. Originally this referred to the Australia New Zealand Closer Economic Relations Trade Agreement, or *ANZCERTA*, but it now has become one of the names used for trade and economic agreements.

CER Protocol on Trade in Services: see *ANZCERTA Protocol on Trade in Services*.

Certificate of origin: a document in paper or electronic form which states that the goods about to be imported are the product of a particular country. Such certificates are often used for goods imported under preferential conditions, such as the *GSP* or a *free-trade agreement*. The *GATT* membership agreed as early as 1953 that certificates of origin should only be used where they are strictly indispensable. See also *self-certification*.

Certificate of specific character: in the *European Community* a certificate which recognizes the specific character of an agricultural product or a foodstuff. "Specific character" is defined as "the feature or set of features which distinguishes an agricultural product or a foodstuff clearly from other similar products or foodstuffs belonging to the same category". Products covered include beer, chocolate, confectionery, bread, pastry, cakes, biscuits, pasta, pre-cooked meals, sauces, soups, beverages made from plant extracts, ice-cream and sorbets. The certificate cannot be given if the specific character of the product is due to its provenance, geographical origin or solely to the use of a technological innovation.

Only associations of producers and/or processors may apply for a certificate. The certificate is available to third countries that can meet the required standards and are willing to give equivalent protection to products imported from the European Community. [Council Regulation (EEC) 2082/92]

Certification mark: sometimes called a guarantee mark. A mark owned or administered by a public or private certifying body. It indicates that the product which bears it complies to certain standards, has specific qualities or originates in a certain geographical location. Prospective users of a certification mark have to apply for permission to do so. They usually have to demonstrate that they are able to meet the standards administered by the certifying body. See also *collective mark*, *geographical indications* and *trademark*. [WIPO SCT/8/4; SCT/9/4]

CGIAR: see *Consultative Group on International Agricultural Research*.

Chaebol **enterprises:** large Korean conglomerate firms of post-war origin. They are characterized by single-family ownership, and control remains concentrated even into the second or third generation of owners. They are prevalent particularly in manufacturing and construction. The share of total Korean economic output of *chaebol* firms appears to have been falling since the 1970s, but they remain significant economic actors. [Chang 2003]

Change in chapter heading: sometime used interchangeably with *change in tariff classification* or change in tariff heading. A method used in the application of *rules of origin* to ascertain whether *substantial transformation* has occurred. It is based on the *Harmonized System* which divides traded goods into 97 *chapters*. A chapter has two digits. According to this method an article produced in country A from materials originating in country B is considered a product of country A if it was made into a substantially different product there, i.e. it is now considered to fall under a different chapter of the Harmonized System. Such a system, if applied literally, would be highly restrictive. In practice, all such systems use changes in chapter headings (a change from one two-digit group to another), *headings* (four digits) and *sub-headings* (six digits), as the case may require it.

Change in tariff classification: CTC. Used in the administration of *rules of origin* to ascertain whether a good qualifies for entry under a *preferential tariff* through having undergone *substantial transformation*. The classification used is normally the *Harmonized System*. Some *free-trade agreements* specify that a change in tariff classification means that a product has undergone sufficient transformation in the exporting country to be moved from one 4-digit classification to another, but this is not a firm rule. See also *change in chapter heading*.

Change in tariff heading: see *change in chapter heading* and *change in tariff classification*.

Change in tariff lines: a concept used in the administration of *rules of origin* to determine where a good comes from. A change in tariff lines occurs when a material or good carrying a six-digit classification in the *Harmonized System* is transformed in a production process to a good carrying a different six-digit number. The two numbers may be consecutive, unless the particular regime precludes this, or they may be at some remove. See also *change in tariff classification*.

Chapter: one of the 97 two-digit entries in the *Harmonized System*. Examples are: 01 (live animals), 52 (cotton) and 72 (iron and steel). Many trade agreements are also divided into chapters. The parties to them name and number them as they deem best. See also *heading* and *sub-heading*.

Charter for an International Trade Organization: see *Havana Charter*.

Charter of Economic Rights and Duties of States: CERDS. An initiative launched at *UNCTAD* III (1972) ostensibly aimed at protecting the economic rights of all countries, but really promoting a change in what was seen as the entrenched lower status of *developing countries* in the international economic system. The draft Charter, originally intended to be binding on signatories and to become part of international law, was adopted by the United Nations General Assembly as Resolution 3281 (XXIX) on 12 December 1974. The Charter has 34 articles grouped in four chapters. Chapter I sets out fifteen principles that should govern the fundamentals of international economic relations among states. These are (a) sovereignty, territorial integrity and political independence of states, (b) sovereign equality of all states, (c) non-aggression, (d) non-intervention, (e) mutual and equitable benefit, (f) peaceful coexistence, (g) equal rights and self-determination of peoples, (h) peaceful settlement of disputes, (i) remedying of injustices which have been brought about by force and which deprive a nation of the natural means necessary for its normal development, (j) fulfilment in good faith of international obligations, (k) respect for human rights and fundamental freedoms, (l) no attempt to seek hegemony and spheres of influence, (m) promotion of international social justice, (n) international cooperation for development, and (o) free access to and from the sea by land-locked countries within the framework of these principles. Chapter II contains 28 articles describing the economic rights and duties of states. In abbreviated form they are (1) the right to choose economic, political, social and cultural systems in accordance with the will of the people, (2) full permanent sovereignty over all wealth, natural resources and economic activities, (3) if two or more countries share natural resources, they must cooperate in their exploitation, (4) the right to engage in international trade and other economic cooperation irrespective of political, economic or social systems, (5) the right to associate in organizations of primary commodity producers, (6) the duty to contribute to the development of international trade of goods, particularly through the conclusion of long-term multilateral commodity agreements, (7) responsibility of the state to promote the economic, social and cultural development of its people, (8) cooperation in achieving a more rational and equitable system of international economic relations, (9) responsibility to cooperate in the economic, social, cultural, scientific and technological fields, (10) the right to participate fully as equals in the international decision-making process to solve world economic, financial and monetary problems, (11) cooperation to improve the efficiency of international organizations, (12) the right to participate in subregional, regional and interregional cooperation in the pursuit of development, (13) the right to benefit from the advances in science and technology, (14) the duty to cooperate in promoting steady and increasing expansion and liberalization of world trade, (15) the duty to promote achievement of general and complete disarmament, (16) the right and duty to eliminate colonialism, racial discrimination, neo-colonialism and all forms of foreign aggression, (17) the duty to cooperate internationally for development, (18) developed countries to improve and enlarge the system of generalized non-reciprocal and non-discriminatory tariff preferences, (19) developed countries to grant generalized, preferential, non-reciprocal and non-discriminatory treatment in fields of international and economic cooperation where it may be feasible, (20) developing countries to increase their trade with socialist countries, (21) developing countries to promote the expansion of their mutual trade, (22) promotion of increased net flows of real resources to the developing countries, (23) developing countries to strengthen their economic cooperation and expand their mutual trade to accelerate their economic and social development, (24) the duty to conduct mutual economic relations through taking into account the interests of other countries, (25) special attention to be paid to the least developed countries, (26) the duty to coexist in tolerance and live together in peace, (27) the right to enjoy fully the benefits of world *invisible trade* and to engage in its expansion, and (28) the duty to cooperate in achieving adjustments in the prices of exports of developing countries compared to import prices. Chapter III details in two chapters the common responsibilities of states towards the international community, i.e. towards each other. Article 29 states that the seabed and ocean floor beyond the limits of national jurisdiction, as well as the resources of the area, are the common heritage of mankind. Article 30 makes the protection, preservation and enhancement of the environment for the present and future generations the responsibility of all states. Chapter IV observes, *inter alia*, that the prosperity of the international community as a whole depends upon the prosperity of its constituent parts. The majority of developed countries either abstained or voted against the Charter. The countries refusing to support the Charter were concerned that it did not contain a commitment to international law or a reference to the relevance of international law. Considerable debate developed over the legal standing of the Charter, but it slowly faded away as an international issue in any case. Some are of the view that although the Charter failed to bring about the intended changes in international economic relations, the controversy over it ensured that the concerns of developing countries would be given more attention in future. See also *Global Negotiations*, *New International Economic Order* and *North-South dialogue*.

Charter of the South Asian Association for Regional Cooperation: see *South Asian Association for Regional Cooperation*.

Chemicals: see *advance informed consent, Convention on Persistent Organic Pollutants, Convention on the Prior Informed Consent Procedure for Certain Hazardous Chemicals and Pesticides in International Trade, Global Classification and Labelling System for Chemicals, London Guidelines for the Exchange of Information on Chemicals in International Trade, prior informed consent* and *REACH*.

Cherry-picking: the attempt to choose from a menu of obligations or negotiating options only those likely to cause one the fewest difficulties. The vigilance of others often prevents this. See also *forum-shopping*.

Chiang Mai Initiative: adopted at a meeting of *ASEAN+3* finance ministers in Chiang Mai, Thailand, in May 2000. It created a network out of the currency swap arrangements then in existence among the ASEAN+3 members, with Japan at the centre. See also *New Miyazawa Initiative*.

Chicago Convention: the *Convention on International Civil Aviation*, concluded in 1944 with the aim of promoting a regime for safe and orderly international air services. Its provisions govern the methods of allocating bilateral air traffic rights, a basic feature of the global aviation system. The Convention is administered by the International Civil Aviation Organization (ICAO), located in Montreal. See also *bilateral air services agreements*, *freedoms of the air* and *open-skies agreements*.

Chicken War: a period of trade tension between the United States and the *European Economic Community* lasting from July 1962 to January 1964. It overshadowed the start of the *Kennedy Round*. It was triggered by the extension of *variable levies* under the *Common Agricultural Policy* to poultry which trebled German import charges. This led to an immediate and drastic decline in the export of United States poultry to Germany where up to that time United States exporters had been spectacularly successful. Claim and counterclaim for *compensation* followed. The establishment of a panel of experts by the GATT in November 1963 provided the basis of a solution. Both parties accepted that poultry trade worth $26 million was affected. To settle the score, the United States then imposed additional import duties affecting mainly French cognac, German trucks and Dutch dextrine and starch, thus ensuring that the United States retaliatory action would be noticed among members of the European Economic Community more broadly. The influence of the Chicken War on the remainder of the Kennedy Round is hard to judge, especially since it was followed by several other difficult periods. It provided a pointer, however, to the increasingly vexing problem of international agricultural trade facing exporters as the Common Agricultural Policy first led to European *self-sufficiency* and then to subsidized exports of many products. See also *agriculture and the multilateral trading system* and *Ploughshares War*.

Chief supplier provision: one of the main features of the *United States Reciprocal Trade Agreements Program*. It stipulated that no tariff concession would be made to any country unless it was the chief supplier of the product. The provision was intended to preserve United States bargaining power with countries yet to conclude a reciprocal trade agreement after earlier reductions had been applied to other trade agreement partners under the *most-favoured-nation* rule. The chief supplier provision was carried forward into the GATT in the form of the *principal supplier right*.

Child labour: Convention No 138 (Minimum Age Convention) of the *International Labour Organization* states that the minimum age of employment in acceding countries must not be less than fifteen years. This may be lowered to thirteen years for some forms of light work and twelve years for developing countries, provided that employment does not interfere with the child's education. Convention No 138 aims to raise the minimum age progressively, and ILO Recommendation No 146 suggests that the minimum age of employment should be sixteen years. See also *Convention Concerning the Prohibition and Immediate Action for the Elimination of the Worst Forms of Child Labour* and *core labour standards*.

China-ASEAN free-trade agreement: CAFTA. Proposed in November 2001 for conclusion within ten years. A framework agreement including an *early harvest* on tariff reductions was signed on 4 November 2002.

Chinese Taipei: the name for Taiwan in *APEC*, the *WTO* and some other international organizations. Taiwan joined the WTO as the Separate Customs Territory of Taiwan, Penghu, Kinmen and Matsu.

CHOGM: the *Commonwealth* Heads of Government Meeting, held every two years. *Trade policy* issues are usually on its agenda, but it does not make rules. CHOGRM (Commonwealth Heads of Government Regional Meeting), which meets infrequently, is composed of the Asia-Pacific Commonwealth members.

CIF: cost, insurance and freight. Denotes that the price of a good as quoted or invoiced consists of the cost of the good itself, plus the cost of insurance and freight by sea or inland waterway to the port of destination. See also *FOB.*

Circumvention: measures taken by exporters to evade *anti-dumping measures* or *countervailing duties*. It can refer also to the evasion of *rules of origin*, etc. Circumvention consists of disguising the true origin of the product, sometimes through manufacturing operations whose sole purpose it is to provide sufficient evidence to meet the requirements of an agreement. These sometimes fall into the category of *screwdriver operations*. The *Agreement on Agriculture* seeks to prevent circumvention of commitments to rein in export subsidies. Circumvention in the textile trade refers to avoiding quotas and other restrictions by altering the country of origin of a product. See also *anti-circumvention*.

CITES: *Convention on International Trade in Endangered Species of Wild Fauna and Flora*. Concluded in 1973 under the auspices of the International Union for the Conservation of Nature and Natural Resources (IUCN). The Convention entered into force on 1 July 1975. The IUCN is not part of the United Nations, but closely associated with it. CITES regulates international trade in wild animals and plants. It classifies threatened species into three categories: (i) those threatened with extinction that are or could be affected by trade, and it prohibits trade in these cases, (ii) species not necessarily threatened with extinction, but which could become so unless trade in them is strictly regulated, and (iii) species protected by states listing them and for which the cooperation of others is sought. Where trade is allowed under the Convention, it takes place through a permit system. See also *multilateral environment agreements* and *trade and environment*.

Civil aircraft code: see *Agreement on Trade in Civil Aircraft*.

Civil society: in the context of trade policy, those who are not directly involved in the discussions and negotiations in *intergovernmental organizations*, but who may be affected by their decisions or who may have points of view to put across. Most often *civil society* appears to refer to *non-governmental organizations* (NGOs), but it is also taken to mean, by *UNCTAD*, for example, parliamentarians, trade unions and academics. Most intergovernmental organizations now have a website aimed to meet the needs of civil society.

Classifications of goods, services and activities: see *Harmonized System*, *International Standard Industrial Classification of All Economic Activities*, *SITC* (Standard International Trade Classification) and *United Nations Central Product Classification*.

Clawback provisions: the ability of a foreign party ordered to pay *treble damages* in extraterritorial proceedings conducted under United States *antitrust laws* to recover through the national court system the amount in excess of actual damages. If the party ordered to pay treble damages is successful in its counterclaim, the party receiving the treble damages will be ordered to repay the amount deemed to be excessive. Recovery of damages really is only possible if the company receiving them in the first place has assets in the country conducting clawback proceedings. See also *extraterritoriality*.

Clayton Act: a United States *antitrust law* first passed in 1914. It seeks to prohibit a range of restrictive business practices and to "arrest the creation of trusts, conspiracies, and monopolies in their incipiency and before consummation". It also permits the imposition of *treble damages*. The Act in general applies to foreign trade, but some provisions are limited to interstate commerce. See also *competition policy*, *Robinson-Patman Act*, *Sherman Act* and *Webb-Pomerene Act*.

Clean Development Mechanism: see *Kyoto Protocol*.

Climate change: a term summarising the concern that increased concentrations of *greenhouse gases* in the atmosphere because of human interference will lead to accelerated changes in climate patterns. See also *trade and environment*, *Kyoto Protocol* and *United Nations Framework Convention on Climate Change*.

CLMV: Cambodia, Laos, Myanmar (Burma) and Vietnam. See *ASEAN*.

CNUCED: Conférence des Nations Unies sur le Commerce et le Développement. See *UNCTAD*.

Cobden-Chevalier Treaty: a commercial treaty concluded in 1860 between England and France. It brought **most-favoured-nation treatment** into general use within Europe for a few decades.

Cocktail approach: a term describing the concurrent use of several methods to achieve *tariff* reductions. A cocktail could include, for example, *item-by-item tariff negotiations*, *linear tariff cuts* and *zero-for-zero tariff reductions*. See also *blended formula*.

COCOM: Co-ordinating Committee for Multilateral Export Controls. It was formed in response to a 1951 *United Nations General Assembly* recommendation for an embargo on the shipment of "arms, ammunition and implements of war, atomic energy materials, petroleum and items useful in the production of implements of war" to communist countries. In 1958, the list of prohibited articles was reduced to strictly strategic goods, and there were several changes afterwards in the list of prohibited articles. COCOM's membership consisted of NATO (North Atlantic Treaty Organization) countries, except Iceland, plus Japan. The *Wassenaar Arrangement on Export Controls for Conventional Arms and Dual-Use Goods and Technologies*, effective from 1 November 1996, has superseded the COCOM arrangement.

Code-conditioned most-favoured-nation treatment: describes situations where *most-favoured-nation treatment* only has to be extended to members of the same GATT code or WTO agreement. An example of this is the WTO *Agreement on Government Procurement*. See also *conditional most-favoured-nation treatment*.

Code of conduct: usually a non-binding intergovernmental instrument that seeks to regulate certain types of behaviour of governments or private corporations. Codes of conduct are as difficult to negotiate as binding agreements since signatories normally expect to observe them in *good faith*. Sometimes, codes of conduct are in fact the first step towards a binding agreement.

Code of Good Practice for the Preparation, Adoption and Application of Standards: this is contained in Annex 3 to the WTO *Agreement on Technical Barriers to Trade*. Central government standardizing bodies must comply with its provisions, but it is open also to local government and non-government bodies. The Code contains fourteen substantive provisions aimed at the non-discriminatory and transparent preparation and administration of standards. See also *conformity assessment, International Electrotechnical Commission* and *International Organization for Standardization*.

***Codex Alimentarius*:** a program managed jointly by the *Food and Agricultural Organization* (FAO) and the World Health Organization for initiating, preparing, publishing and revising international food standards. These standards cover matters such as food labelling, food additives, contaminants, methods of analysis and sampling, food hygiene, nutrition and foods for special dietary uses, food import and export inspection and certification systems, residues of veterinary drugs in foods and pesticide residues in foods. In addition, there are standards applicable to particular commodities. The program is administered by the *Codex Alimentarius Commission*. [www.fao.org]

***Codex Alimentarius* Commission:** established in 1963. This is the body charged with developing food standards, guidelines, recommendations, etc., under the *Codex Alimentarius* program. The Commission's work on the harmonization of food standards supports aspects of the WTO work on *sanitary and phytosanitary measures* and *technical barriers to trade*. [www.fao.org]

Co-existence and diversity: a principle underlying the Japanese negotiating position in the WTO negotiations on agriculture. It means that the traditional social and community functions of agriculture should be allowed to co-exist with the function of agriculture as a provider of food and industrial raw materials. The implication is that a degree, but sometimes quite a lot, of agricultural *protec-tionism* will be necessary in some economies to ensure continuing diversity. See also *continuation clause*, *Friends of Multifunctionality*, *multifunctionality*, and *non-trade objectives*.

Collected tariff rate: the tariff rate actually levied and collected by customs authorities when a good is imported. See also *bound rate*.

Collective action: a term used in *APEC* to describe activities aimed at liberalizing or expanding trade that can, by definition, only be carried out jointly. This is done through the *Collective Action Plans*. These include *mutual recognition of qualifications and standards*, customs cooperation, etc. See also *concerted liberalization action*.

Collective Action Plans: used by the members of APEC to detail actions they have taken jointly under the *Osaka Action Agenda*. Their purpose is to make progress towards the *Bogor Goals*.

Collective mark: a mark owned by a cooperative, a trade association, an association of producers or manufacturers, etc. which indicates that the user of the mark is a member of that body. The mark is meant to assure clients of member firms or purchasers of the products made by them that they are dealing with a reputable firm or product. Permission to use a collective mark is usually dependent on compliance with rules concerning production standards or geographical location of the user of the mark. Article 7bis of the *Paris Convention* requires member countries to protect collective marks belonging to associations lawfully established in the country of origin. See also *certification mark*, *geographical indications* and *trademark*. [Paris Convention for the Protection of Industrial Property; WIPO SCT/8/4]

Collective preferences: a concept now slowly making its way into discussions of the aims and methods of *trade policy*. M Pascal Lamy, the then Commissioner for Trade in the *European Commission*, said on 15 September 2004 that collective preferences "synthesize the preferences of individuals through political debate and institutions", and that they are "the end result of choices made by human communities that apply to the community (i.e. any group of persons that have set up institutions capable of forging preferences) as a whole". Collective preferences, assuming the concept is valid, would therefore differ depending on the community looked at. Lamy thought that Europe's collective preferences, which might well be shared by others, could be summed up as *multilateralism*, environmental protection, food safety, cultural diversity, public provision of education and health care, *precautions* in the field of biotechnology and welfare rights.

Collective rights: see *community rights*.

Colorado Group: a group active in the WTO which seeks to develop multilateral principles for *trade facilitation*. It has Australia, Canada, Chile, Colombia, Costa Rica, European Community, Hong Kong-China, Israel, Japan, Korea, Morocco, New Zealand, Norway, Paraguay, Singapore, Switzerland and the United States as core members. See also *Trade Facilitation Alliance*.

Columbus Declaration: the ministerial declaration of 21 October 1994 launching the *Trade Efficiency Programme* administered by *UNCTAD*. Its appendix contains recommendations to governments for trade efficiency in banking and insurance, customs, business information for trade, transport, telecommunications and business practices.

Comecon: see *Council for Mutual Economic Assistance*.

COMESA: see *Common Market for Eastern and Southern Africa*.

Comité des Représentants Permanents: a *European Union* coordination mechanism. See *Coreper*.

Comity: a term used in international law to signify the reciprocal courtesy or mutual respect which one member of the family of nations owes to the others in considering the effects of its official acts. See also *negative comity* and *positive comity*.

Commerce: usually, but by no means exclusively, refers to activities related to the production, sale and distribution of goods and services within the *internal market*. See also *trade*.

Commercial defence mechanisms: see *contingent protection*.

Commercial displacement: the replacement of sales on commercial terms by gifts or subsidized sales. This occurs, for example, when the granting of food aid takes away opportunities for sales at market prices.

Commercial import: the *import* of a product into a *customs territory* for the purpose of sale, incorporation in a good for sale or for the production of goods for sale.

Commercial policy: a term now slowly disappearing and in general use being replaced by *trade policy* with which it has co-existed for decades. It covers governmental acts, policies and practices which influence trade in goods and services. The drafters of the *GATT* thought of commercial policy as the subjects covered in Part II of the GATT which includes, among others, *national treatment*, *anti-dumping* and *countervailing duties*, *customs valuation*, import and export fees and formalities, *marks of origin*, *quantitative restrictions*, *subsidies*, *state trading* enterprises, *safeguards*, and consultation and *dispute settlement*. Title VII of the *Treaty of Maastricht* retains the wording "common commercial policy" from the *Treaty of Rome* which defines it in Article 113 (Article 133 in the amended treaty) as "based on uniform principles, particularly in regard to changes in tariff rates, the conclusion of tariff and trade agreements, the achievement of uniformity in measures of liberalization, export policy and measures to protect trade, such as those to be taken in the event of dumping or subsidies". See also *Article 133 Committee* and *Common Commercial Policy*.

Commercial policy measurement: see *measurement of commercial policy* and *quantification of non-tariff measures*.

Commercial presence: any type of business or professional establishment within the territory of a member of the *General Agreement on Trade in Services* (GATS) for the purpose of supplying a service. This includes subsidiaries, branches and representative offices. See also *modes of services delivery*, *right of establishment* and *right of non-establishment*.

Commercial treaty: any agreement between two or more countries which is concerned mainly with the conduct of trade relations between them. For examples of commercial treaties see *bilateral trade agreement*, *economic framework agreement*, *free-trade agreement*, *trade and economic agreement* and *trade and investment facilitation agreement*.

Commission of the European Communities: see *European Commission*.

Commission on Enterprise, Business Facilitation and Development: established at UNCTAD IX. Its mandate covers assistance to developing countries on policy-related issues and training activities concerning the development of entrepreneurship, promoting the best use of the *Trade Efficiency Programme*, assessing the practical implications of the *Global Information Infrastructure*, examining successful development experiences and monitoring the implementation of the Programme of Action for the Least Developed Countries for the 1990s. The Commission meets once a year. See also *UNCTAD*.

Commission on Investment, Technology and Related Financial Issues: established at UNCTAD IX. Its mandate covers issues aimed at an improved ability of developing countries to attract and utilize *foreign direct investment*, examining issues related to *competition law* of particular relevance to development, undertaking analysis of science, technology and innovation policies as well as providing technical assistance in technology development, and examining specific development challenges regarding effective participation in international trade and investment. The Commission meets once a year. See also *UNCTAD*.

Commission on Phytosanitary Measures: established under the auspices of the *Food and Agricultural Organization* through the 1997 revision of the *International Plant Protection Convention* (IPPC). Its main functions are (a) to review the state of plant protection in the world and the need for action to control the international spread of pests and their introduction into endangered areas, (b) develop and adopt international standards, and (c) establish rules for the resolution of disputes concerning obligations under the IPPC. Until the entry into force of the revised IPPC, the Commission is known as the Interim Commission on Phytosanitary Measures.

Commission on Science and Technology for Development: a subsidiary body of *ECOSOC*, but serviced by *UNCTAD*. It has a work program with a strong development perspective covering technology for small-scale economic activities, gender implications of science and technology, science and technology and the environment, the contribution of technologies to industrialization in developing countries, and information technologies and their role in science and technology. The Commission meets every two years.

Commission on Trade in Goods and Services, and Commodities: established at UNCTAD IX. It has a wide mandate covering assistance to developing countries to enable them to benefit from and adjust to the *Uruguay Round* outcomes, assisting countries acceding to the WTO, identifying impediments to trading success, analysing issues related to trade preferences, assisting developing countries to strengthen their capacities in the services sector, work on *trade and environment* issues, and addressing issues of particular relevance to commodity-dependent countries. The Commission meets once a year. See also *UNCTAD*.

Commission on Transnational Corporations: previously a subsidiary body of *ECOSOC*, but now integrated into the *Commission on Investment, Technology and Related Financial Issues* of *UNCTAD*.

Commitment: a legally binding undertaking specific to a country under one of the agreements administered by the WTO. Examples of commitments are tariff *bindings* and inscriptions in the *schedules of commitments on services*. Such commitments usually stem from negotiations between two or more parties and are then made available in a non-discriminatory way to all parties of the agreement concerned. See also *additional commitments*.

Commitment mechanisms: as argued in the *Asian Development Outlook 2002* and elsewhere, *preferential trade agreements* can hasten or lock in economic policy reforms. Whether an agreement does this depends greatly on the robustness of its provisions, including the credibility of the applicable dispute settlement system. [Asian Development Bank 2002]

Committee of Permanent Representatives: a *European Union* coordination mechanism. See *Coreper*.

Committee on Regional Trade Agreements: the WTO body charged with examining *regional trade agreements*, sometimes called *preferential trade agreements*, concluded by WTO members, as well as developing policy towards such agreements. See *regional trade agreements*.

Committee on Rules of Origin: see *Agreement on Rules of Origin*.

Committee on Trade and Development: a WTO committee established on 26 November 1964. It is concerned with developing-country issues. One of its main tasks has long been the administration of *Part IV of the GATT* and the *Enabling Clause*. See also *developing countries and the multilateral trading system*.

Committee on Trade and Environment: a WTO committee established in response to the *Rio Declaration on Environment and Development* and *Agenda 21*. Its task is to identify the relationship between trade measures and environmental measures to promote *sustainable development* and to make recommendations on possible changes to the rules of the multilateral trading system concerning goods, services and *intellectual property rights*. According to the Committee's terms of reference, any suggested changes ought to be compatible with the open, equitable and non-discriminatory nature of the multilateral trading system. See also *multilateral environment agreements* and *trade and environment*.

Commodity: any article exchanged in trade, but commonly used to refer to raw materials. Examples are wheat, tin, copper, manganese, coffee, tea and rubber. See also *buffer stocks*, *commodity policy*, *commodity terms of trade* and *international commodity agreements*.

Commodity arrangements: a general term for schemes to manage the production and trade of commodities. See *administrative international commodity agreements*, *buffer stocks*, *commodity policy*, *economic international commodity agreements* and *Integrated Programme for Commodities*.

Commodity cartels: public or private *cartels* formed to maintain the price of a commodity above what it would fetch on open markets. The usual mechanisms are the imposition of *export quotas* and collusion to maintain prices above real market levels. Such cartels can only be successful if they include all of the important producers and if no commodity can be readily substituted. *OPEC* was a successful cartel for more than a decade, but its ability to keep prices up led to the entry of higher-cost producers into the market. The international diamond cartel based in South Africa also operated profitably for many years. See also *commodity policy*, *international commodity agreements*, *international steel cartel* and *resources diplomacy*.

Commodity Credit Corporation: CCC. A government corporation within the United States Department of Agriculture charged with stabilizing, supporting and protecting farm incomes. The main functions of the CCC are (a) to assist producers through loans, purchases and payments and through providing materials and facilities needed in the production and marketing of agricultural commodities, and (b) to permit the sale of agricultural commodities to other government agencies and foreign governments as well as to donate food to domestic and international relief agencies. The CCC also has a role in developing new domestic and international markets. Main commodities receiving CCC support are wheat, corn, oilseeds, cotton, rice, tobacco, milk and milk products, barley, oats, grain sorghum, mohair, honey, peanuts and sugar. Farmers can receive commodity loans in return for pledging and storing part of the commodity as a security. This mechanism is called the *loan rate*. Farmers may also be eligible for *deficiency payments*. CCC finances sales made under the *Export Enhancement Program* (EEP) and the *Dairy Export Incentive Program* (DEIP). See also *Food for Progress program* and *PL 480*.

Commodity policy: the part of *trade policy* dealing with governmental actions affecting international trade in commodities. Its principal objectives are to secure fair and remunerative returns to producers and reliable and competitive supplies to consumers. Neither of these aims can be defined objectively. Commodities have always been classified by some as needing special measures because of unpredictable supply and demand fluctuations and the attendant price changes and export income fluctuations. One reason for this is that in some commodities relatively small changes in supply and demand can lead to considerable price fluctuations. In other cases, particularly agricultural products, the livelihood of large population segments is to a greater or lesser extent influenced by developments in the market. Governments tend to be alert to such concerns and to seek ways and means to alleviate them. Modern international commodity policy began with the drafting of the *Havana Charter* which essentially favoured free-market principles. The draft Charter allowed the creation of *international* *commodity agreements* (ICAs) with price and trade controls, called intergovernmental control agreements, only if normal market forces were unable to deal rapidly with adjustments between production and consumption, and widespread unemployment in connection with a primary commodity was either happening or expected to happen. The free-market principle was, however, compromised in many ways as drafting proceeded to permit, for example, government planning by those who saw a need for it. Developing countries were allowed to maintain import restrictions to protect domestic industries. In the end, the Havana Charter did not enter into force. In 1947, *ECOSOC* established an Interim Co-ordinating Committee for International Commodity Arrangements (ICCICA) with a mandate to convene commodity study groups and to recommend calling conferences to negotiate commodity arrangements. Several ICAs with stabilization mechanisms were negotiated under its auspices. The *Haberler Report*, prepared under GATT auspices in 1958, cautiously supported the conclusion of international commodity agreements and limited *compensatory financing* schemes. When *UNCTAD* was established in 1964, ICCICA's functions were transferred to it. In the early 1970s proposals for a *New International Economic Order* were discussed without result. They envisaged a massive transfer of resources to developing countries, partly through commodity arrangements and schemes to deal with export earnings shortfalls. UNCTAD was from the beginning much more interventionist in its views of commodity policy, and at UNCTAD IV (1976) it developed the *Integrated Programme for Commodities* and the *Common Fund for Commodities*. These are mechanisms to regulate and stabilize international commodity trade through *buffer stocks* and compensatory financing. Sober assessments of the issues attaching to international commodities trade from the mid-1980s onwards, prompted to some extent by the collapse of the *International Tin Agreement*, cast increasing doubt on the merits of large-scale market intervention, both from the producer and consumer perspective. The consensus view appears to have returned to basically free-market principles which limit international cooperation to the promotion of *transparency* mechanisms and the financing of research and development to make commodities more attractive to manufacturers and users. See also *compensatory financing arrangements* and *single commodity producers*.

Commodity terms of trade: an index showing the ratio of commodity prices to prices for manufactured goods. Commodity terms of trade have improved if fewer commodities have to be sold to pay for a given amount of manufactures. They have deteriorated when more commodities have to be sold. See also *Singer-Prebisch thesis* and *terms of trade*.

Common Agricultural Policy: CAP. The *European Community*'s comprehensive system of production targets and marketing mechanisms designed to manage agricultural trade within the Community and with the rest of the world. The mechanism for financing the CAP is the *European Agricultural Guidance and Guarantee Fund*. The CAP's stated aim is to encourage stable agricultural market conditions, a fair standard of living for farmers, reasonable prices for consumers, increased agricultural yields and better labour productivity. Its implementation has always been difficult because of the attempt to mix social and economic policies. The CAP succeeded spectacularly in increasing yields and returns for many farmers, but it led to widespread disruption of global markets because the increased output, produced at high cost, could only be exported with the aid of massive *export subsidies*. It did little to stem the trend towards amalgamation of smaller farms. The CAP also led to high consumer prices in the European Union for agricultural products and has contributed to fiscal deficits there. On 1 January 2005 the European Union introduced substantial changes to the CAP. The most important of these are (a) a single payment for farmers, independent of production, (b) payments are linked to respect for environmental, food safety, animal and plant health and animal welfare standards, (c) a strengthened rural development policy with new measures to promote the environment and animal welfare, (d) reduction in direct payments for bigger farms, and (e) a mechanism for financial discipline to prevent over-expenditure until 2013 and revisions to the market policy for milk and cereals. See also *Agenda 2000*.

Common Arab Market: see *Greater Arab Free Trade Area*.

Common Commercial Policy: under Article 133 of the *Treaty of Amsterdam* (which amends Article 113 of the *Treaty of Rome*), the member states of the *European Community* conduct a common commercial policy based on uniform principles, particularly in regard to changes in tariff rates, the conclusion of tariff and trade agreements, the achievement of uniformity in measures of liberalization, export policy and measures to protect trade, such as those to be taken in the event of dumping or subsidies. Agreements on trade in services and the commercial aspects of intellectual property are subject to the common commercial policy, but only to the extent that they do not go beyond the Community's internal powers. This leaves a degree of uncertainty about the limits of the Common Commercial Policy. The policy is administered by the *European Commission*. Member states do not have the authority to change unilaterally the *common external tariff* or to enter into trade agreements with other countries. There are highly developed internal consultative mechanisms, such as the *Article 133 Committee*, under which member states may bring forward proposals for changes to the common commercial policy. See also *common agricultural policy*.

Common Crisis: *North South: Cooperation for World Recovery:* see *Brandt Report*.

Common customs tariff: see *common external tariff*.

Common economic space: an imprecise term which indicating that two or more countries have agreed to pursue some common economic policies and possibly form a *free-trade area*. In its most developed form it probably would be a *common market*. See also *single economic space*.

Common External Preferential Tariff: the mechanism for reducing tariffs under *AFTA*. See *CEPT*.

Common external tariff: the uniform tariff rates applied by the members of a *customs union* against non-members. Members of a customs union agree to eliminate or phase out all tariffs among themselves. At the same time, they replace their individual tariffs with a single tariff applied to third countries. Membership of a customs union may therefore entail an unchanged, higher or lower tariff by individual members on a given product. Under WTO rules, the resulting changes may not be used to increase the level of protection overall. *Free-trade areas* do not have a common external tariff.

Common Fund for Commodities: usually known as the Common Fund. It was originally proposed at UNCTAD IV in 1976 as the financing mechanism for the *Integrated Programme for Commodities*. Negotiations on its structure were completed in 1980. It entered into force in 1989 and now has 106 members, plus the *European Community*, the *African Union* and the *Common Market for Eastern and Southern Africa* as institutional members. The Common Fund has three main functions. The first is aimed at supporting the financing through the *First Account* of *buffer stock* operations and internationally coordinated national stocks. This function is not yet active. The second is aimed at financing of research and development in the commodities area, productivity improvements and the promotion of consumption through the *Second Account*. Its third function is to promote coordination and consultation in the field of commodities other than stocking and their financing. Funding is available for projects identified by *international commodity bodies*. Projects supported by the Common Fund are usually commodity-oriented rather than country-specific. Its secretariat is located in Amsterdam. See also *commodity policy*, *international commodity agreements* and *UNCTAD*.

Common market: a more developed type of *customs union* in which, in addition to the free movement of goods between member states, labour, capital and services can also move without restriction. Common markets lead to highly integrated economies. See also *four freedoms*.

Common Market: see *European Economic Community*.

Common Market for Eastern and Southern Africa: COMESA. The treaty establishing COMESA was signed at Kampala on 5 November 1993. It is the successor to the Preferential Trade Area for Eastern and Southern African States (PTA). Its members are Angola, Burundi, Comoros, Democratic Republic of Congo, Djibouti, Egypt, Eritrea, Ethiopia, Kenya, Lesotho, Madagascar, Malawi, Mauritius, Namibia, Rwanda, Seychelles, Sudan, Swaziland, Uganda, Zambia and Zimbabwe. The aims of COMESA are (a) to attain sustainable growth and development of member states by promoting a more balanced and harmonious development of its production and marketing structures, (b) to promote joint development in all fields of economic activity and the joint adoption of macroeconomic policies and programs to raise the standard of its peoples and to foster closer relations among members states, (c) to cooperate in the creation of an enabling environment for foreign, cross-border and domestic investment, including the joint promotion of research and adaptation of science and technology for development, (d) to cooperate in the promotion of peace, security and stability among the member states in order to enhance economic development in the region, (e) to cooperate in strengthening the relations between the Common Market and the rest of the world and the adoption of common positions in international fora, and (f) to contribute towards the establishment, progress and the realization of the objectives of the *African Economic Community*. In trade liberalization and customs cooperation, members undertake to (i) establish a *customs union*, abolish all *non-tariff barriers* to trade among themselves, establish a *common external tariff*, and cooperate in customs procedures and activities, (ii) adopt a common customs bond guarantee scheme, (iii) simplify and harmonize their trade documents and procedures, (iv) establish conditions regulating the re-export of goods from third countries within the Common Market, and (v) grant a temporary exemption to Lesotho, Namibia and Swaziland from the full application of some the provisions. COMESA's secretariat is located at Lusaka. See also *African regional integration arrangements*. [Murinde 2001]

Commonwealth: an association of 53 independent states established in its present form in 1949 through the London Declaration. Its members were at one time or another part of the British Empire. It is administered by the Commonwealth Secretariat located in London. Among its many functions, the Secretariat runs programs aimed at the economic and trade development particularly of developing members. The Commonwealth's current membership consists of Antigua and Barbuda, Australia, The Bahamas, Bangladesh, Barbados, Belize, Botswana, Britain, Brunei, Cameroon, Canada, Cyprus, Dominica, Fiji, The Gambia, Ghana, Grenada, Guyana, India, Jamaica, Kenya, Kiribati, Lesotho, Malawi, Malaysia, Maldives, Malta, Mauritius, Mozambique, Namibia, Nauru, New Zealand, Nigeria, Pakistan, Papua New Guinea, St Christopher and Nevis, St Lucia, St Vincent and The Grenadines, Samoa, Seychelles, Sierra Leone, Singapore, Solomon Islands, South Africa, Sri Lanka, Swaziland, Tanzania, Tonga, Trinidad and Tobago, Tuvalu, Uganda, Vanuatu and Zambia. See also *CHOGM* (Commonwealth Heads of Government Meeting) and *Trade and Investment Access Facility*.

Commonwealth of Independent States: CIS. Formed in December 1991 with many of the republics that had made up the Soviet Union. Its members are Armenia, Azerbaijan, Belarus, Georgia, Kazakhstan, Kyrgyz Republic, Moldova, Russia, Tajikistan, Turkmenistan, Ukraine and Uzbekistan. In September 1993 its members agreed on the creation of an economic union allowing the free movement of goods, services, labour and capital. This turned out to be more difficult than expected. CIS members then agreed in 1999 that the first stage towards an economic union should be a series of bilateral *free-trade agreements*. The CIS's secretariat is located in Minsk, Belarus. See also *Newly Independent States*.

Commonwealth preferences: the name for empire preferences (also known as imperial preferences) used especially in the post-war years, but it was already in use between the wars. See also *historical preferences* and *imperial preferences arrangements*.

Communauté Economique de l'Afrique de l'Ouest: see *West African Economic Community*.

Communauté Economique des Etats de l'Afrique de l'Ouest: Economic Community of West African States. See *ECOWAS*.

Communauté Economique des Pays des Grands Lacs: CEPGL. Established in 1976 to promote regional economic cooperation and integration. Its members are Burundi, Democratic Republic of Congo and Rwanda. Its secretariat is located in Gisenyi, Rwanda.

Communauté Economique et Monétaire de l'Afrique Centrale: CEMAC. Entered into force in June 1999 as the successor to the *Central African Customs and Economic Union* (UDEAC). Its members are Cameroon, Central African Republic, Chad, Congo, Equatorial Guinea and Gabon. Among its main objectives are (a) promotion of national markets through the abolition of intra-community obstacles to trade, (b) coordinated development programs, (c) harmonized industrial development and (d) creation of a true African common market. See also *African Economic Community* and *African regional integration arrangements*.

Community: often refers to the *European Community*, but it can mean any group of countries sharing common characteristics or working towards greater integration, usually under a framework agreement setting out its aims and likely shape.

Community Charter of Fundamental Social Rights for Workers: see *Social Charter*.

Community exhaustion: the doctrine that once a product embodying *intellectual property rights* (IPRs) has been lawfully placed on the market within the *European Community* (EC), it can be resold or transferred to any part of the EC without the further consent of the owner of these IPRs. See also *exhaustion doctrine* and *parallel import*. [Maskus 2000]

Community interest clause: this clause is part of a *regulation* issued in 1979 by the *European Community* which makes the imposition of anti-dumping or countervailing duties dependent on the existence of a Community interest in the matter. Importantly, "Community interest" includes the interests of consumers and processors of the imported product as well as the need for an internal competitive market. See also *anti-dumping measures* and *countervailing duties*.

Community of Andean Nations: see *Andean Community*.

Community rights: also known as collective rights. The terms describe the fact that communities may develop and/or own aspects of *traditional knowledge*. There is a view that these rights need new forms of *intellectual property protection*.

Comparability: a term used in the *APEC* discussions denoting arrangements which ensure a broad and perceived equivalence between individual APEC contributions towards the implementation of the *Bogor Declaration*. See also *comprehensiveness* and *Osaka Action Agenda*.

Comparative advantage: the theory first proposed by David Ricardo in 1817 that a country is more likely to export goods that it can produce relatively efficiently. The relative efficiency measure compares production costs of different goods in each country concerned, not the production cost of the same good in different countries. A country's comparative advantage is reflected in its unsubsidized exports to world markets which is then said to be a country's revealed comparative advantage. Comparative advantage is seldom static. Countries can acquire a comparative advantage through, for example, investing in the acquisition of skills by their workforces. Hence the concept of dynamic comparative advantage. See also *absolute advantage*, *competitive advantage*, *gains-from-trade theory*, *Heckscher-Ohlin theorem*, *kaleidoscopic comparative advantage* and *Stolper-Samuelson theorem*. [Brenton, Scott and Sinclair 1997, Krugman 1998, Maneschi 1998]

Compensation: a remedy available to members of the WTO in cases where another member breaks a bound commitment on services or imposes a tariff on a good above its bound rate. Such an action may be possible under the terms of the agreement, but the member taking it must then compensate others in some fashion, usually through making a tariff concession in another product or a commitment on another services activity. See also *binding commitments*, *bindings* and *safeguards*.

Compensation trade: a trading arrangement whereby the supplier of raw materials, manufactures or services to a foreign enterprise agrees to be paid in the form of part of the output of that enterprise. For the buyer enterprise, the advantages are that it does not need foreign exchange to import production components, that repayments are not due until the operation is up and running, and that it has a ready market for some of its products. A disadvantage may be that it will almost certainly have to sell its output at a discount. See also *barter trade* and *countertrade*.

Compensatory financing arrangements: intergovernmental schemes designed to minimize the effects of shortfalls in commodity export earnings and export earning fluctuations, particularly those of developing countries heavily dependent on commodity exports. Access to the main arrangement, the *IMF Compensatory and Contingency Financing Facility*, is subject to a range of conditions largely aimed at promoting *structural adjustment* and improvements in the *balance of payments*. The *STABEX* and *SYSMIN* schemes, which were available to *ACP states* under the *Lomé Convention*, have not been renewed in the *ACP-EC Partnership Agreement*. Some budgetary assistance is still available to ACP countries heavily dependent on export earnings from agricultural and mineral products if losses in earnings are likely to jeopardize macroeconomic stability. See also *Common Fund for Commodities*.

Competence: the constitutional empowerment given to governments to enact laws and enter into binding international commitments. In federated states, there is usually a division of power between the central government and the states or provinces, but in all cases the central government has control over foreign affairs and defence matters, including *international economic relations*. The *European Community* is a particularly interesting example of a division of power. It has explicit powers where these are specified in its treaties. Among these is the *common commercial policy*. It has implicit foreign relations powers where the treaties give it explicit powers in an area, and it can engage in negotiations with third countries. Transport is one of these areas. Where the Community has neither explicit nor implicit powers, the *European Council*, acting unanimously, may take the measures it deems necessary. See also *subsidiarity*. [Eeckhout 2004]

Competition: the way firms behave in the market place and how they respond to the actions of other suppliers and consumers. Underlying the idea of competition is the assumption that supply and demand are limited, at least in the short term, and that firms must strive obtain their share of the available resources. In ideal conditions, competition between firms would be based on price and the ability to innovate and respond to changes in the market. There would be no impediments to the operation of the price or market systems. In a real situation, human ingenuity, high entry barriers to some industries, efficiencies of scale obtainable from large-scale operations and other factors combine to impair competition in various ways. This may lead to economic rents being accorded to some firms, but without any obligation on their part to let the consumer benefit from this situation. Governments recognize this, and in many countries they seek to protect, where necessary, competition through *antitrust laws* and *competition policy*. Most economies are becoming internationalized, and government approaches to *trade policy*, i.e. their assessment of the extent to which foreign firms and their products should be allowed to compete in the market, therefore can be of critical importance to the level of competition prevailing in the market.

Competition law: rules and regulations, also known as *antitrust laws*, to foster the competitive environment in an economy, partly through the more efficient allocation of resources. The competition laws of most countries deal with four main groups of behaviour by firms: (a) horizontal arrangements (mainly arrangements between firms to maintain and control prices), (b) vertical arrangements (can include exclusive dealing, resale price maintenance, geographical limitations on activities and tied dealing), (c) misuse of market power by monopolies and large firms, and (d) control of mergers and acquisitions to ensure that they do not impair competitive overall conditions in the market. Measures dealing with horizontal and vertical restraints as well as the enforcement of laws concerning them are sometimes called *conduct* policies. Those dealing with mergers may be known as structural policies. Rules covering these matters are sometimes described as *narrow competition policy*. Many say that four variables affect the relative strength or weakness of competition laws: (a) scope of application to governmental entities and to government-encouraged or sanctioned conduct of state enterprises and private firms, (b) substantive rules governing specific business practices and arrangements, (c) scope of sectoral coverage and (d) enforcement. See also *wider competition policy*. [Dabbah 2003]

Competition policy: approaches of governments to the promotion and protection of competition. It consists of *competition laws* and policies achieving similar aims. Since the 1980s the term "competition policy" has broadened in scope in many industrial economies. It now may be concerned also with the welfare-enhancing effects of opening non-tradeable sectors to competition, the so-called *wider competition policy*. This includes gas, water and electricity utilities which once were considered natural monopolies. Competition policy is often seen as promoting especially the interests of the consumer, and comparisons are made with *trade policy* which, especially in the case of *trade remedies*, tends to favour the producer. See also *antitrust laws* and *trade and competition policy*.

Competition policy and anti-dumping measures: an issue relevant to a study of the feasibility of multilateral rules on *trade and competition*. Some say that there is a fundamental conflict between the concurrent administration by a government of anti-dumping laws and competition or *antitrust laws*. This view is based partly on the assumption that trade policy may confer benefits to domestic producers through *anti-dumping measures* that allow them to secure additional returns by enabling them to raise prices. Exporters who make price undertakings to evade the imposition of anti-dumping duties may in this way also be able to obtain economic rents. The contention is that such actions are legal under trade policy, but illegal under *competition policy*. Another conflict is seen as resulting from an underlying principle that anti-dumping laws are designed to protect domestic producers and sellers of goods, whereas competition laws are meant to protect consumers and importers. It really comes down to the question of what anti-dumping laws are meant to achieve. Some of the early anti-dumping laws, such as the *Anti-Dumping Act of 1916*, were intended to deal with *predatory pricing*, an anti-competitive practice banned by many competition laws. But current anti-dumping laws do no longer seem to have this motivation. They are seen rather as a means of promoting fairer trade, often in the sense of the *level playing field*. This apparent contradiction remains to be resolved. Countries and industries disadvantaged by anti-dumping measures tend to argue that such measures should be replaced by competition laws to the extent that they are actionable in this way. This has already happened in trade between Australia and New Zealand under *ANZCERTA*, between the members of the *European Community* and within the *European Economic Area*. These are special cases where the ground was carefully prepared over many years. There is widespread agreement among analysts that a measure of convergence in competition laws and their adequate enforcement will be necessary to achieve this goal more widely.

Competitive advantage: a contentious theory of industrial development popularized by Michael Porter and others in the *Competitive Advantage of Nations*. The origins of the theory itself appear to go back to the economist Alfred Marshall (1842–1924). It states that the success of a firm or an industry is based on cost advantages in the production of a relatively standardized product or product-based advantages related to the development of differentiated products. Firms with a competitive advantage are often concentrated geographically, which in turn assists the development of a workforce with the relevant skills. Critics of this theory have noted that through its emphasis on high-technology firms in advanced countries, and its devaluation of the importance of comparative costs, it appears to give legitimacy to public expenditure and protection policies designed to promote the premature development of high-technology industries. See also *comparative advantage* and *strategic trade theory*. [Porter 1990]

Competitive devaluation: a government-induced depreciation or *devaluation* of the *exchange rate* aimed at undercutting the competition from other countries. The risk in doing so is that one's competitors may retaliate with their own devaluations and leave everyone worse off. See also *beggar-thy-neighbour policies*.

Competitive hub-and-spoke bilateralism: describes a situation in which some countries in a given region try to conclude as many bilateral *free-trade agreements* as possible in an attempt to make themselves a regional economic hub.

Competitive liberalization: the idea, as described by Bergsten, that competing successfully in the global market place forces countries to liberalize their trade and investment regimes in response to liberalization by others. The term was adopted in 2002 by the United States to describe its policy of pursuing concurrently bilateral, regional and multilateral trade negotiations in the expectation that achievements in one of them would lead to further progress in another. [Bergsten 1996]

Competitive-need limitation: an aspect of the administration of the United States *GSP* scheme. If in any calendar year imports of a given product from a beneficiary country account for more than 50% of United States imports of that product, the exporting country's eligibility for benefits for that product is terminated. Similarly, once a country's share of exports to the United States of a given product exceeds a specified value, benefits will also be terminated. The specified value varies from year to year. The competitive-need limitation may be waived in certain circumstances, especially if the exporting country gives reasonable access to United States goods and services, and if it offers proper protection for United States-owned *intellectual property rights*. Most *least developed countries* enjoy automatic waivers from the limitation. See also *a priori limitation* and *graduation*.

Competitiveness: the ability of a firm, a production sector or even a country to hold its own in terms of economic efficiency against other firms, sectors or countries. Governments sometimes try to improve the competitiveness of a sector through the use of *export targeting*, *subsidies*, *protection*, creation of *national champions* or other measures. This can only be done at the expense of the remainder of the economy, and the longer-term effects of such practices is to reduce the economy's competitiveness overall.

Competitive neutrality: a concept relevant to the examination and administration of the nature of competition between private-sector firms and deregulated government monopolies. The need for competitive neutrality arises from the fact that removing barriers to market entry and ending government monopolies may not be enough to achieve genuine competition in that sector. In such a situation, the advantage may still lie with the enterprise that previously was a government monopoly or part of one. The remedy usually is some form of pro-competitive regulation. See also *deregulation* and *re-regulation*.

Competitive proliferation of FTAs: see *FTA syndrome*.

Compliance: observance of one's obligations under international agreements. See also *implementation*.

Compliance panel: a *panel* established under Article 21.5 of the *Dispute Settlement Understanding*. A WTO member may ask for the establishment of such a panel when a party to previous dispute settlement proceedings does not comply with the decision then made.

Composite tariff: see *compound tariff*.

Composition of trade: usually a statistical analysis of a country's trade in terms of product groups which shows what kinds of goods and services it imports from and exports to a given country.

Compound tariff: a rate of duty on a product which consists of two components. The first is an *ad valorem* rate, expressed as a percentage of the value of the product. The second component is a specific rate, expressed as a monetary value per article regardless of the value of the product. A hypothetical example would be one where each compact disc incurs a *specific tariff* of one dollar plus an *ad valorem tariff* set at 10%.

Comprehensiveness: a principle agreed by *APEC* leaders to signify that the commitment to free and open trade and investment by 2010/2020 will apply within the target dates and across all sectors and impediments. The principle allows for some flexibility on the timing of liberalizing across or within the different areas of an economy. See also *Bogor Declaration* and *Osaka Action Agenda*.

Compulsory licensing: a procedure for authorities to license companies or individuals other than the *patent* owner to use the rights of the patent – to make, use, sell or import a product under patent (i.e. a patented product or a product made by a patented process) – without the permission of the patent owner. Article 31 of the *Agreement on Trade-Related Aspects of Intellectual Property Rights* sets out the framework under which this may be done. Compulsory licensing may only be pursued if efforts to obtain the right to use the intellectual property on reasonable commercial terms have not been successful. See also *Access to medicines*, *Declaration on the TRIPS Agreement and Public Health*, *exhaustion doctrine* and *forced technology transfer*.

Computed value: one of the methods for *customs valuation* permitted by the WTO *Agreement on Customs Valuation* if no reliable price information is available. A computed value consists of the sum of (a) the cost or value of the materials and their processing, (b) a normal amount for profit and general expenses, and (c) the cost or value of all expenses necessary, such as transport, port handling charges and insurance.

COMTRADE database: its full name is United Nations Commodity Trade Statistics Database. This is a statistical database for the trade in goods of more than

130 countries. Goods are classified according to *SITC* and the *Harmonized System*. Data for many countries are available from 1962 to the present. The data can be interrogated on the COMTRADE website. [www.unstats.un.org/unsd/comtrade]

Concealed dumping: see *hidden dumping*.

Concerted liberalization action: sometimes also called concerted unilateralism. One of mechanisms devised by *APEC* economies to achieve the goal of free and open trade and investment by 2010/2020 as envisaged in the *Bogor Declaration*. Economies aim at roughly equal progress through the observance of *comparability*, and they seek to ensure that all sectors are included in the liberalization, as envisaged in the *comprehensiveness* principle. See also *APEC*, *APEC individual action plans*, *collective action* and *Osaka Action Agenda*.

Concerted unilateralism: see *concerted liberalization action*.

Concertina approach: describes a staged approach to *tariff* reductions. The highest rates are reduced first, then the second-highest, and so on until the target levels have been achieved across the board.

Concertina theorem: the theorem concerning *piecemeal tariff reform*, i.e. reductions on selected items only, postulated by James Meade that "[t]here is more likely to be a gain in economic welfare if the rate of duty is high on the primary imports which will come in increased volume and is low on the secondary imports which will come in reduced volume". The validity of the theorem was demonstrated by Bertrand and Vanek to the effect, as expressed by López and Panagaryia, that "in a small open economy, if the highest tariff is reduced to the next highest one, welfare will rise provided the import demand for the good with the highest tariff exhibits gross substitutability with respect to all other goods". [Bertrand and Vanek 1971, López and Panagaryia 1992, Meade 1955]

Concession: in the WTO, the lowering of a *tariff* or the removal of an impediment to *trade in services*, generally at the request of another party. In its narrowest sense, it may only cover the *binding* of a tariff item. Some commentators have suggested that this term should be replaced by *commitment* to remove the false impression that countries make a sacrifice by lowering tariff rates, and that *trade liberalization* is a cost on the economy. The *General Agreement on Trade in Services* already refers to commitments. See also *requests and offers*, *schedules of commitments on services* and *schedules of concessions*.

Conditional most-favoured-nation treatment: the granting of *most-favoured-nation treatment* (MFN) subject to conditions being met by the country receiving it. Membership of an agreement may be such a condition. In the case of the WTO *Agreement on Government Procurement*, for example, MFN on government purchases only has to be extended to the other members of the Agreement. This is also called *code-conditioned MFN treatment*. There are also cases where a country decides to grant MFN to another country only if some conditions unrelated to trade are met. Such a situation arose when the United States Congress adopted the *Jackson-Vanik Amendment* to the 1974 Trade Act which limited the granting of MFN to countries having a liberal emigration policy.

Conditional national treatment: the imposition of conditions on foreign-owned companies as part of giving them *national treatment* in other respects. For example, foreign-owned companies may have to comply with *performance requirements*, *reciprocity* conditions or *local content requirements* not applying to others.

Conditional offers: offers made in trade negotiations either in the expectation that others will make offers of equivalent value or on the assumption that one's own offer will be seen as matching those already on the table. Conditional offers may be withdrawn or modified at any time until a general settlement has been reached. See also *ad referendum agreement* and *without prejudice*.

Conduct: in *competition policy*, the behaviour of a firm in the market place, particularly in terms of the applicable *competition laws* or *antitrust laws*.

Conference on International Economic Cooperation: CIEC. A meeting of developed and developing countries convened by the French Government between December 1975 and June 1977 to discuss international economic issues, including energy, raw material prices, development, and finance. Some say that this was the true start of the *North-South dialogue*. France received much deserved praise for this initiative, but it is not possible to point to any concrete results from the conference.

Conflict diamonds: also known as "blood diamonds". Defined in the *Kimberley Process Certification Scheme* as "rough diamonds used by rebel movements or their allies to finance conflict aimed at undermining legitimate governments, as described in relevant *United Nations Security Council* (UNSC) resolutions, insofar as they remain in effect ... ".

Conflict of laws: see *private international law*.

Conformity assessment: includes, among other things, procedures for sampling, testing and inspection; evaluation, verification and assurance of conformity; and registration, accreditation and approval. The WTO *Agreement on Technical Barriers to Trade* sets out a *Code of Good Practice for the Preparation, Adoption and Application of Standards* which should be used by government and non-government bodies for framing and using technical regulations. It requires that procedures for determining conformity of products with national standards are fair and equitable, particularly where domestic and comparable imported products are involved. See also *International Electrotechnical Commission* and *International Organization for Standardization*.

Conscious parallelism: a form of *cartel* in which the competitors observe each other's behaviour and make decisions on output, prices, etc., accordingly. One difference with a normal cartel is that there is no express agreement between the firms to act in this way. [Pierce 2000]

Consensus: the usual method for taking decisions in the WTO. The *WTO Agreement* states in Article IX:1 that the "WTO shall continue the practice of decision-making by consensus followed under *GATT 1947*". It adds in a footnote that the "body concerned shall be deemed to have decided by consensus on a matter submitted for its consideration, if no member, present at the meeting when the decision is taken, formally objects to the proposed decision". Provision exists for formal voting, but such votes are rare or taken only when consensus has already been achieved. Consensus decisions reduce the scope for disputes arising from differing understandings of the rules. The search for consensus can, however, add to the negotiating period, and it can give rise to delays because of *foot drag-gers*. The *Doha Ministerial Declaration* refers several times to decisions having to be made by explicit consensus. It is not yet clear whether this will affect the way consensus is reached. See also *convoy problem*, *decision-making in the WTO* and *reverse consensus*.

Conservative social welfare function: one of the factors governing the actions of governments in their consideration of trade-liberalizing policies. It was first identified by Max Corden in *Trade Policy and Economic Welfare*. He says that, put in its simplest way, it means that governments feel that in an income distribution target any significant absolute reductions in real incomes should be avoided. In other words, he says, increases in incomes are given relatively low weights and decreases very high weights. The conservative social welfare function would therefore partly explain why governments sometimes are cautious about reducing tariffs or removing other trade measures which may affect adversely the operations of industries. [Corden 1974]

Consolidated Tariff Schedules: CTS. A database maintained by the WTO Secretariat. It contains the final *bound tariffs* of all members, as well as information on implementation periods, *initial negotiating rights* and other material relevant to a member's commitments. It is therefore an essential tool for tariff negotiations. See also *Integrated Data Base*. [WTO TN/MA/S/2]

Constructed value: a method available under the WTO *Anti-Dumping Agreement* to calculate the production cost of a product in the exporting country. This method may only be used if there is no export price or if the export price is considered to be unreliable because of doubts about the existence of *arm's-length pricing*. It is not normally used for *market economies*. See also *analogue country*, *anti-dumping measures* and *normal value*.

Consular formalities: the requirement that firms exporting goods to some countries obtain an endorsement by the consular representations of the importing country of invoices, *certificates of origin*, shipping manifests and other documents. Endorsement was subject to the payment of a fee often related to the value of the consignment. Fee structures and bureaucratic delays and procedures frequently became irritating factors in international trade relations. Most countries have now abolished consular formalities. See also *preshipment inspection*.

Consultation: the first stage in the WTO *dispute settlement* procedure, aimed at resolving issues cooperatively, sometimes through the *good offices* or *mediation* of a disinterested party. The fact-finding nature of consultation between parties often leads to a solution. If the consultations fail to settle a dispute within sixty days after a request has been made, the complaining party may request the *Dispute Settlement Body* to establish a dispute settlement *panel*. The parties may go to a panel earlier if they conclude that the consultations will not settle the dispute. WTO members receiving a request for such consultations must therefore treat them seriously. They cannot use them to gain extended breathing space. See also *Understanding on Rules* and *Procedures Governing the Settlement of Disputes*.

Consultative Sub-Committee on Surplus Disposal: CSSD. Established by the *Food and Agricultural Organization* in 1954 to monitor international shipments of surplus agricultural commodities. The aim of the monitoring was to "minimize the harmful effects of such shipments on commercial trade and agricultural production". The CSSD's activities have now evolved into a comprehensive set of rules and procedures to help aid donors account for and identify the flow of food aid shipments. [FAO document CCP 03/2]

Consultative Group of Eighteen: an informal mechanism within the GATT, established on 11 July 1975 with a membership of eighteen, broadly representing developed and developing countries. Initially, it was chaired by one of its members, but in 1979 the Director-General of the GATT was given that task. The CG18, as it was usually known, was meant to assist the GATT membership in carrying out its responsibilities through an early discussion of trade issues likely to cause difficulties. It had no decision-making responsibilities. Its membership was meant to rotate from time to time, but in practice there was hardly any movement once the initial slate had been agreed. Instead, the custom arose of admitting alternates to meetings also. The CG18 fell into disuse during the *Uruguay Round*. See also *Invisibles Group* for a more recent consultative mechanism in the WTO.

Consultative Group on International Agricultural Research: CGIAR. An informal network of public and private bodies that supports sixteen international agricultural research centres. CGIAR aims to further agriculture in developing countries to promote food security, to alleviate poverty and to preserve natural resources. Its secretariat is located within the *World Bank*.

Consumer subsidy equivalent: usually abbreviated to CSE. For an agricultural commodity, the CSE is defined as the amount that consumers would need to be paid to compensate them for the effect of removing agricultural support programs. Expressed as a percentage, it is the ratio of the total value of transfers received by consumers to total consumer expenditure on the product. When the consumer receives net assistance, CSEs are positive. When they are negative, the consumer is being taxed. See also *producer subsidy equivalent*.

Consumption abroad: one of the *modes of services delivery* defined in the *General Agreement on Trade in Services*. The consumer goes to the country of the producer to obtain the service, as is the case, for example, when one takes a holiday in another country.

Consumption tax: an *ad valorem* tax on goods and services, but not necessarily all of them, levied at the point where the consumer makes the purchase. For imported goods, this is after any customs duties have been paid on them. Common names for consumption taxes include value-added tax, goods and services tax, general sales tax, turnover tax, etc.

Contact points: see *enquiry points*.

Container Security Initiative: CSI. Launched by the United States Customs Service on 17 January 2002. CSI consists of four core elements: (a) establishing security criteria to identify high-risk containers, (b) screening containers deemed to have a high security risk before they arrive at United States ports, (c) using technology to do this quickly, and (d) developing and using smart and secure containers. CSI is aimed at seeking the cooperation in the first instance of the ports accounting for large shipments to the United States. Several of the world's largest ports now participate in this scheme.

Contestability of markets: see *international contestability of markets*.

Contingent multilateralism: an American term to mean that multilateral action should be taken whenever possible to improve *market access*, but sometimes preferential liberalization in the form of *free-trade agreements* and unilateral action would be better. See also *unilateralism*.

Contingent protection: protective mechanisms, also called commercial defence mechanisms, that are legal under the WTO agreements. They may be triggered to counter the effects of *dumping*, *subsidies* and unexpected import surges causing *injury* to domestic industry. Such mechanisms include *anti-dumping measures*, *countervailing duties* and *safeguards*.

Continuation clause: a provision contained in Article 20 of the WTO *Agreement on Agriculture* which calls for the resumption of multilateral negotiations on agriculture one year before the end of the agreed implementation period, i.e. by 1 January 2000. The long-term objective of the continuation clause is substantial progressive reductions in support and protection. The resumed negotiations, which became part of the *Doha Development Agenda*, also take into account (a) the experience up to then from implementing the reduction commitments, (b) the effects of the reduction commitments on world trade in agriculture, *non-trade concerns*, *special and differential treatment* to developing countries, (c) the objective to establish a fair and market-oriented agricultural trading system, and (d) other objectives needed to achieve the long-term objectives. See also *WTO built-in agenda*.

Continued Dumping and Subsidy Offset Act of 2000: see *Byrd Amendment*.

Contraband: refers to neutral cargo in times of war capable of being used to assist the military operations of an enemy. Rules concerning contraband have always been flexible and subject to interpretation on the spot, but in principle, upon interception goods found to be peacetime commodities would be allowed to continue. War material could be stopped. The elaboration and administration of rules on contraband has always been difficult because many goods and commodities are capable of either civilian or military goods. In popular parlance, contraband is often used where *smuggling* or smuggled goods would be the more appropriate term. See also *dual-use exports*.

Contracting party: the formal term for members of the *GATT 1947*. When the contracting parties acted jointly to adopt a decision, GATT documents denote this by the use of capital letters (the CONTRACTING PARTIES). GATT contracting parties are now WTO members.

Contractual non-reciprocal rules of origin: refers to *rules of origin* used under instruments such as the *ACP-EC Partnership Agreement* or *SPARTECA*. Agreements of this kind give defined developing countries preferential access to the developed partners. The reverse does not apply. All the parties to these agreements participate in negotiating the applicable rules of origin, but the developing country members are under no obligation to apply them to goods imported from the developed-country members. [Inama 2000]

Contractual reciprocal rules of origin: refers to *rules of origin* applied to goods traded under preferential conditions, such as a *free-trade agreement*. These rules are equally binding on all parties. [Inama 2000]

Contrary to honest commercial practice: see *in a manner contrary to honest commercial practice*.

Conventional international law: internationally applicable rights and obligations created through conventions, treaties, covenants, international agreements and other binding instruments. I Brownlie says that "Law-making treaties create *general* norms for the future conduct of the parties in terms of legal propositions, and the obligations are basically the same for all parties." Strictly speaking, treaties are only binding on the parties. However, as pointed out by M N Shaw, "where treaties reflect customary law then non-parties are bound, not because it is a treaty provision, but because it reaffirms a rule or rules of customary international law". See also *customary international law*. [Brownlie 1990; Shaw 1997; Starke 1989]

Conventional tariff: a tariff in which most or all duty rates are the result of negotiations under international conventions or treaties. This term is now largely forgotten. See also *maximum-minimum tariff*.

Conventional wisdom: words used by J K Galbraith in *The Affluent Society* to describe "beliefs that are at any time assiduously, solemnly and mindlessly traded between the pretentiously wise". He assesses the phrase as being nicely balanced between approval and ridicule. A description of the origin of this expression may be found in *A Life in our Times*, by the same author. See also *QWERTY principle* and *vestigial thought*. [Galbraith 1958, Galbraith 1981]

Convention Concerning the Prohibition and Immediate Action for the Elimination of the Worst Forms of Child Labour: ILO Convention No 182, adopted on 17 June 1999. It seeks to prohibit and eliminate the *worst forms of child labour* as a matter of urgency. The United States *Trade Promotion Authority* aims to promote universal ratification and full compliance with this Convention. See also *Declaration on Fundamental Principles and Rights at Work*.

Convention for the Protection of Producers of Phonograms Against Unauthorized Duplication of their Phonograms: see *Geneva Convention*.

Convention of Stockholm: see *EFTA*.

Convention on a Code of Conduct for Liner Conferences: sometimes known as the *UNCTAD* Liner Code. An intergovernmental agreement which entered into force on 6 October 1983. It seeks to develop the share of commodities and goods carried in developing country ships to improve their *balance of payments*. The Code's underlying principle is the 40-40-20 ratio which, although not specified in the Convention, allocates informally 40% of trade to shipping lines of the importing country, 40% to those of exporting country and 20% to third-country shipping lines. Liner code member countries have had difficulties achieving these figures in the face of commercial reality and changing directions of trade. See also *MFN exemptions*.

Convention on Biological Diversity: CBD. Entered into force on 29 December 1993. Its objectives are the conservation of biological diversity, the sustainable use of its components and the fair and equitable sharing of the benefits arising out of the utilization of genetic resources. It contains provisions concerning appropriate access to genetic resources and transfer of relevant technologies. The CBD's secretariat is in Montreal. See also *Cartagena Protocol on Biosafety*, *multilateral environment agreements* and *trade and environment*.

Convention on Combating Bribery of Foreign Public Officials in International Business Transactions: entered into force on 15 February 1999. All 29 *OECD* countries plus Argentina, Brazil, Bulgaria, Chile, the Slovak Republic and Slovenia have acceded to it. The Convention makes it a crime to offer, promise or give a bribe to a foreign public official to secure a business transaction. Separately, OECD members also agreed to end the tax deductibility of bribery payments. See also *Draft International Agreement on Illicit Payments*, *trade and illicit payments* and *United Nations Convention Against Corruption*.

Convention on International Civil Aviation: see *Chicago Convention*.

Convention on International Trade in Endangered Species of Wild Fauna and Flora: see *CITES*.

Convention on Persistent Organic Pollutants: adopted in Stockholm on 23 May 2001. It entered into force on 17 May 2004. Persistent organic pollutants are chemical substances that remain intact in the environment for a long time, become widely distributed geographically, accumulate in the fatty tissue of living organisms and are toxic to humans and wildlife. The Convention aims to eliminate or reduce the release of persistent organic pollutants into the environment. The Convention is administered by an Interim Secretariat located in Geneva. See also *dirty dozen substances* and *multilateral environment agreements*.

Convention on the Grant of European Patents: see *European Patent Convention*.

Convention on the Law of the Sea: see *United Nations Convention on the Law of the Sea*.

Convention on the Means of Prohibiting and Preventing the Illicit Import, Export and Transfer of Ownership of Cultural Property: a convention adopted by the *United Nations Educational, Scientific and Cultural Organization* (UNESCO) in 1970 in Nairobi. The parties designate the types of property, religious or secular, that are important for archaeology, prehistory, history, literature, art or science. They agree to oppose the illicit import, export or transfer of ownership of cultural property. Licit exports of cultural property are made under a system of certification. See also *UNIDROIT Convention on the International Return of Stolen and Illegally Exported Cultural Property*.

Convention on the Prior Informed Consent Procedure for Certain Hazardous Chemicals and Pesticides in International Trade: This Convention assists governments in preventing imports of chemicals that they cannot manage safely. If governments allow imports of a hazardous chemical or pesticide, exporters are obliged to provide extensive information on the chemical's possible health and environmental dangers. The Convention covers 22 pesticides and five industrial chemicals. This list can be extended through further negotiations. The convention entered into force on 24 February 2004. It is administered jointly by the *Food and Agricultural Organization* and the United Nations Environment Program (UNEP). See also *multilateral environment agreements* and *prior informed consent*.

Convention on the Settlement of Investment Disputes between States and Nationals of Other States: see *ICSID*.

Convention Relating to the Distribution of Programme-Carrying Signals Transmitted by Satellite: concluded at Brussels on 21 May 1974. It requires its members to make sure that any programme (pictures, sound, or both) emitted by satellite is only distributed by those who are authorised to do so. The Convention is administered by *WIPO*.

Convoy problem: this problem arises in *multilateral trade negotiations* when participants ready to move forward have to wait for the party least prepared or least willing to proceed. The slowest party, like the slowest ship in a convoy, then determines the pace of progress. See also *foot dragger* and *consensus*.

Cooperation Council of the Arab States of the Gulf: see *Gulf Cooperation Council*.

Copenhagen criteria: the standards, adopted in 1993, a *candidate country* must meet to qualify for membership of the *European Union.* They are (a) stability of institutions guaranteeing democracy, the rule of law, human rights and respect for and, protection of minorities, (b) existence of a functioning *market economy*, as well as the capacity to cope with competitive pressure and market forces within the Union; and (c) an ability to take on the obligations of membership, including adherence to the aims of political, economic and monetary union. See also *enlargement*.

Copenhagen Declaration and Programme of Action: a set of non-binding undertakings by the 117 countries that attended the World Summit for Social Development in March 1995 in Copenhagen. Some of its provisions draw attention to the role of trade and investment in promoting social development and have relevance to the debate on *trade and labour standards*.

Copyright: the exclusive right to do certain things with an original work, including the right to reproduce, publish, perform the work in public and to make adaptations of it. Copyright does not protect ideas themselves, but only the original expression of ideas. In literary, dramatic, musical or artistic works, it generally lasts for the lifetime of the author plus fifty years. See also *Agreement on Trade-Related Aspects of Intellectual Property Rights*, *Berne Convention*, *fair-use doctrine*, *intellectual property rights*, *neighbouring rights* and *Universal Copyright Convention*.

Core labour standards: minimum human rights standards applied to working conditions, but not defined as such in a single international instrument. The *ILO Declaration on Fundamental Principles and Rights at Work*, adopted by the *International Labour Organization* in 1998, states that all ILO members are obligated to promote, respect and realize the following principles: (a) freedom of association and the effective recognition of the right to collective bargaining, (b) the elimination of all forms of forced or compulsory labour, (c) the effective abolition of child labour, and (d) the elimination of discrimination in respect of employment and occupation. This list is now accepted by many as representative of core labour standards. The United States *Trade Promotion Authority* lists five core labour standards: (a) the right of association, (b) the right to organize and bargain collectively, (c) a prohibition on the use of any form of forced or compulsory labour, (d) a minimum age for the employment of children, and (e) acceptable conditions of work with respect to minimum wages, hours of work, and occupational safety and health. Proponents of multilateral rules on *trade and labour standards* tend to take core labour standards as their starting point. The *GSP* scheme of the *European Community* contains a special incentive arrangement for countries whose national legislation incorporates the conventions of the International Labour Organization covering core labour standards. See also *pauper-labour argument*, *race-to-the-bottom argument*, *social clause*, *social dumping*, *social labelling*, *social subsidies* and *wage-differential argument*.
[International Labour Office 2003, OECD 2000, World Commission on the Social Dimension of Globalization 2004]

Coreper: an abbreviation of Comité des Représentants Permanents. This is a *European Union* mechanism responsible for preparing meetings of the *Council of the European Union* (the Council of Ministers). Coreper I, which deals with social and economic issues, is made up of the Deputy Permanent Representatives. Coreper II, consisting of the Permanent Representatives (ambassadors) of the member states, deals with political, financial and foreign policy matters. Coreper often deals with contentious issues, but it has no power to make decisions. Although it became very early on one of the Community administrative mechanisms, it was only established formally by the *Treaty of Maastricht*.

Core-periphery thesis: a theory of *international economic relations* flourishing from about the 1950s to the 1980s. It postulates that the international economic system consists of an economically advanced core (the developed countries) and a less advanced periphery (the developing countries). It also assumes that the periphery is dependent on the core as markets for its products, especially primary commodities, and as a source of know-how. The theory is dynamic in that it assumes that in the long term the periphery itself may form new cores. Some have observed that the initial advantage of the core over the periphery may be whittled away. This process then creates new opportunities in the periphery which has become relatively more competitive. See also *dependence theory*, *North-South dialogue* and *Singer-Prebisch thesis*. [Prebisch 1963, Cohn 2003, Fieldhouse 1999]

Corn laws: a set of laws first enacted in England in the twelfth century to protect agricultural production. These laws were repealed in 1846. Their repeal, together with that of the equally protectionist Navigation Acts in 1849, marked the victory of the free-traders and the beginning of the liberal regime characterizing England's trade policy for the next fifty years or so. It also meant the final acceptance of economic "science" as an instrument of policy-making. See also *Cobden-Chevalier Treaty*.

Corporate dumping: refers to the alleged practice of companies to export to more accommodating markets products that may be out of date or no longer permitted to be sold in its usual markets. This is not a recognized trade policy concept.

Corruption: the abuse of power or influence to obtain a benefit through offering or accepting an inducement. A common form of corruption is *bribery*, but many other forms exist. Following are definitions in abbreviated form drawn from two conventions. The *Inter-American Convention Against Corruption* of 1996 lists (a) solicitation or acceptance, directly or indirectly, of any article of monetary value, or other benefit, such as gift, favour, promise or advantage, in exchange for performing a public function, (b) offering or granting, directly or indirectly, of any article of monetary value, etc., in exchange for performance of a public function, (c) any act or omission in the performance of one's duties to obtain a benefit illicitly, (d) fraudulent use of property, and (e) participation as a principal, co-principal, instigator, accessory, etc., after the fact. The *African Union Convention on Preventing and Combating Corruption* of 2003 lists in addition to these (a) diversion of any state property to anyone who is not the intended recipient, (b) offering or giving to, promising, soliciting or accepting from anyone in the private sector any undue advantage, (c) offering or soliciting, etc., an undue advantage to anyone claiming to be able to exert improper influence over another person, and (d) illicit enrichment. The *World Bank* attempts to say much of this with the phrase "abuse of public power for private benefit". See also *Convention on Combating Bribery of Foreign Public Officials in International Business Transactions*, *Draft International Agreement on Illicit Payments*, *trade and illicit payments* and *United Nations Convention Against Corruption*. [Tanzi 1998, Transparency International 2004]

Cotonou Agreement: see *ACP-ECPartnership Agreement*.

Cotton: see *International Cotton Advisory Committee* and *Sectoral Initiative in Favour of Cotton*.

Council for Mutual Economic Assistance: usually known as Comecon. Established in January 1949 with Bulgaria, Czechoslovakia, Hungary, Poland, Romania and the Soviet Union as members. They were joined later by Cuba, the German Democratic Republic, Mongolia and Vietnam. Albania was a member between 1949 and 1961. Yugoslavia was an associate member. The purpose of the Comecon was to facilitate the planned economic development of member country economies, acceleration of economic and technical progress, a rise in the level of industrialization in countries with less developed industries, uninterrupted growth of labour productivity, and a steady advance in the welfare of each member's people. The Comecon was dissolved in February 1991. See also *economies in transition*.

Council for Trade in Goods: the body supervising the operation of the 13 WTO multilateral agreements governing trade in goods included in Annex 1 to the *WTO Agreement*. The most important of these is the GATT. All WTO members are automatically members of this Council. It meets about once a month.

Council for Trade in Services: the body administering the *General Agreement on Trade in Services* (GATS). All members of the WTO are automatically members of the Council. It meets about once a month.

Council for TRIPS: the body administering the *Agreement on Trade-Related Aspects of Intellectual Property Rights* (TRIPS). Its role is to supervise the operation of the Agreement and members' compliance with it. All WTO members are automatically Council members. It meets about once a month.

Council of Arab Economic Unity: established in 1957 to promote regional economic integration through a framework of economic and social development. Members are Egypt, Iraq, Jordan, Kuwait, Libya, Mauritania, Palestine, Somalia, Sudan, Syria, United Arab Emirates and Yemen. Its secretariat is located in Cairo.

Council of Europe: established in 1949. It aims to strengthen democracy, human rights and the rule of law in member countries. It now has forty-six members. Its secretariat is located in Strasbourg. See also *Council of the European Union* from which it is organizationally distinct, though there is close cooperation between them.

Council of the Entente: an association with political and economic aims consisting of Benin, Burkina Faso, Côte d'Ivoire, Niger and Togo. It was established in 1959. One of the Council's main activities is the operation of the Mutual Aid and Loan Guarantee Fund which finances projects intended to promote regional economic development and integration. Its secretariat is located at Abidjan, Côte d'Ivoire.

Council of the European Union: a decision-making body, usually known as the Council of Ministers, which consists of representatives at ministerial level of all fifteen members of the *European Union*. The presidency of the Council rotates every six months among the member states. Meetings are held frequently. Participation depends on the subjects to be discussed. Foreign Ministers meet as the General Affairs Council. Decisions are made either by simple majority, qualified majority (majority of states and 72.3% of the total is cast in favour) or unanimity. Germany, France, Italy and the United Kingdom have 29 votes each, Spain and Poland 27 votes each, Netherlands thirteen votes, Belgium, Czech

Republic, Greece, Hungary, Portugal, Austria and Sweden have ten votes each, Denmark, Ireland, Lithuania, Slovakia and Finland seven votes each, Cyprus, Estonia, Latvia, Luxembourg and Slovenia have four votes each, and Malta has three votes. See also *European Commission*.

Counterfeiting: unauthorized representation of a registered trademark carried on goods identical or similar to goods for which the trademark is registered, with a view to deceiving the purchaser that he or she is buying the original goods. See also *Agreement on Trade-Related Aspects of Intellectual Property Rights*, *intellectual property* and *intellectual property rights infringements*.

Counterfeiting and piracy agreement: a Japanese proposal first made in late 2005 for an international treaty to limit *counterfeiting* and *piracy*. It would require, among other actions, exporting countries to take measures against pirated goods at the border. The proposal is not yet on the negotiating table.

Countermeasures: the means available to WTO members for dealing with exceptional circumstances and alleged breaches of the rules fall into two main categories. The first is made up of *trade remedies*, also known as trade defence mechanisms and contingent protection. They include *safeguards*, *anti-dumping measures* and *countervailing duties*. This group of measures can be initiated by any WTO member as long as it follows the relevant rules. The second group of countermeasures, i.e. the *suspension of concessions and obligations*, can only be taken with the authorization of the *Dispute Settlement Body*. In other words, to obtain redress for an alleged breach of the rules by another member one has to launch a case. As the *Appellate Body* observed in *Canada – measures affecting the export of civil aircraft* ". . . no member is free to determine whether a *prima facie* case or defence has been established by the other party. That competence is necessarily vested in the panel under the DSU, and not in the Members that are parties to the dispute".

Counter-notification: see *reverse notification*.

Countertrade: a more sophisticated and sometimes highly complex form of *barter trade*. For example, a country may export coal and accept mining equipment in payment. No money changes hands in this transaction. The buyer of the coal then seeks to place it in a third market in exchange for payment or some other product. Goods to be traded in this way are usually valued in a third-country currency, e.g. Swiss Francs, for accounting purposes. Countertrade is an inefficient way to trade, but it has sometimes been attractive to countries experiencing severe foreign exchange shortages. See also *compensation trade*.

Countervailable subsidy: refers to a *subsidy* against which, after an appropriate examination, *countervailing measures* may be taken.

Countervailing measures: action taken by the importing country, usually in the form of increased duties, to offset *subsidies* given to producers or exporters in the exporting country. GATT Article VI and the WTO *Agreement on Subsidies and Countervailing Measures* set out the rules for imposing such duties. Countervailing duties can be applied under certain restrictive conditions and subject to material *injury* being caused to a domestic industry. See also *anti-dumping* *measures* which are aimed at the actions of private firms rather than governments and *de minimis subsidies*.

Country-hopping: an informal name for the practice by importers currently subject to *anti-dumping measures* of changing their sources of supply of dumped products to a country or a company not under investigation. See also *carousel effect*, *circumvention* and *Persistent Dumping Clause*.

Country of origin: the country where a good or a service was produced or where, under applicable *rules of origin*, its last *substantial transformation* took place. In *intellectual property* "country of origin" can mean an *indication of source*, a *geographical indication* or an *appellation of origin*. In Article 2(2) of the *Lisbon Agreement* it is defined as "the country, or the country in which is situated the region or locality whose name, constitutes the appellation of origin which has given the product its reputation". In other words, in this sense the country of origin is more than simply the place where the product has been made. Here it has given the product some essential characteristic that would be absent from a similar product made in another country. See also *preferential rules of origin*.
[Lisbon Agreement on the Protection of Appellations of Origin and their International Registration; WIPO SCT/5/3]

Country-of-origin marking: an inscription on a product or the packaging material of a product that tells the end-user in what country the product was made.

Country risk: the odds that a country will not be able to meet its financial commitments. The odds are established through a risk assessment which takes into account economic, political and financial factors.

Court of International Trade: a United States tribunal established in 1980, but with functions dating back much earlier under different names, including the immediately preceding United States Customs Court. The Court has exclusive jurisdictional authority to decide any civil action against the United States, its officers, or its agencies arising out of any law pertaining to international trade. Its jurisdiction covers all of the United States, and it is authorized to hold hearings in other countries.

Covered agreements: the legal term for the agreements to which the WTO *Dispute Settlement Understanding* applies. These are (a) the *Marrakesh Agreement Establishing the World Trade Organization*, (b) the multilateral agreements on trade in goods consisting of the *GATT 1994*, the *Agreement on Agriculture*, the *Agreement on the Application of Sanitary and Phytosanitary Measures*, the *Agreement on Textiles and Clothing* (now expired), the *Agreement on Technical Barriers to Trade*, the *Agreement on Trade-Related Investment Measures*, the *Agreement on Implementation of Article VI of the General Agreement on Tariffs and Trade 1994* (the *Anti-Dumping Agreement*), the *Agreement on Implementation of Article VII of the General Agreement on Tariffs and Trade 1994* (the *Customs Valuation Agreement*), the *Agreement on Preshipment Inspection*, the *Agreement on Rules of Origin*, the *Agreement on Import Licensing Procedures,* the *Agreement on Subsidies and Countervailing Measures* and the

Agreement on Safeguards, (c) the *General Agreement on Trade in Services*, (d) the *Agreement on Trade-Related Aspects of Intellectual Property Rights*, (e) the *Understanding on Rules and Procedures Governing the Settlement of Disputes*, and (f) the plurilateral trade agreements consisting of the *Agreement on Trade in Civil Aircraft*, the *Agreement on Government Procurement*, the *International Dairy Agreement* (now terminated) and the *International Bovine Meat Agreement* (also terminated).

Cradle-to-grave assessment: see *life cycle assessment*.

Crawling peg system: a way to devalue or revalue a currency in stages in response to rapidly changing economic conditions. Each time the *exchange rate* is adjusted by the central bank, it remains fixed until the bank initiates the next change.

Creative ambiguity: used in the WTO, and probably elsewhere, to skirt around a difficult issue by leaving some aspect of it undefined. It normally leads to a compromise that leaves all more or less satisfied, at least at the time when the deal was made. The longer-term consequences can never be predicted.

Creative industries: describes occupations and industries deemed to entail a considerable degree of creativity or originality. Creative industries overlap to some extent with *cultural industries*, but they are much less rooted in tradition, much closer to commercial and marketing activities and probably less nationalistic. Some may be at the forefront of information technology. See also *knowledge-based economy*.

Creative minilateralism: a trade strategy for the opening of markets by the United States proposed by Thomas O Bayard and Kimberley Ann Elliott in *Reciprocity and Retaliation in U.S. Trade Policy*. It involves (a) bilateral talks, if necessary with the support of *Section 301* or the threat of antitrust action, (b) a much stronger analytical capacity for assessing structural and access impediments, and (c) the use of favourable constituencies in target markets. This would be combined with publicity campaigns and technical assistance to developing countries to allow them to design and implement more effective regulatory frameworks. See also *minilateralism*. [Bayard and Elliott 1994]

Credit for liberalization: see *negotiating credits*.

Creeping protectionism: developing a protectionist environment in small steps. See also *protectionism*.

Crisis cartel: also known as emergency cartel, rationalization cartel, depression cartel and similar names. This is a form of industry cooperation available in abnormal circumstances under some *antitrust laws*. Conditions for its use tend to include factors such as a permanent and severe decline of an industry, the promise of efficiency gains which are in the public interest and the assumption that the improvements would not be attainable through other means. See also *cartel* and *failing-firm doctrine*.

Critical mass: jargon probably borrowed inappropriately from nuclear physics. Its achievement is every trade negotiator's dream. It is the point at which support for negotiating proposition becomes so strong that indifference or opposition by others no longer matter much.

Cross-border alliances: see *strategic business alliances*.

Cross-border investment: see *foreign direct investment*.

Cross-border supply of services: see *cross-border trade in services* and *modes of services delivery*.

Cross-border trade: the movement of goods from one *customs territory* into another. See also *border trade*.

Cross-border trade in services: buying or selling services across borders without the need for the buyer or the seller to establish a *commercial presence* in the exporting or importing country. This can be done through, for example, conducting trade over the Internet where the buyer and the seller do not have to meet. In the language of the *General Agreement on Trade in Services* this would be mode 1. A second possibility is that of the consumer going abroad to purchase the service, as is the case in international tourism (mode 2). A third method is that of a person going abroad to sell services, for example an engineer providing on-site advice on a construction project (mode 4). See also *modes of service delivery*.

Cross-compensation: this can occur as part of *dispute settlement* when, for example, the WTO member found to be in breach of an undertaking does not withdraw the offending measure or practice, but offers *compensation* in some other area of trade instead. See also *suspension of concessions or other obligations*.

Cross-cumulation: the practice of considering concurrently the effects of *dumping* and *subsidies* to ascertain whether *injury* has occurred. See also *cumulative assessment of dumping*.

Cross-retaliation: an avenue open in certain circumstances to a WTO member whose rights under one agreement administered by the WTO have been infringed, to retaliate against the offending member under another agreement also administered by the WTO. The *Dispute Settlement Understanding* makes this possible.

Crow-bar theory of trade policy: see *aggressive reciprocity*.

CTD: see *Committee on Trade and Development*.

CTE: see *Committee on Trade and Environment*.

CTG: see *Council for Trade in Goods*.

Cuban Liberty and Democratic Solidarity (LIBERTAD) Act: see *Helms-Burton legislation*.

Cultural identity: the idea that countries have cultural characteristics that set them apart from other countries. There is nothing controversial about this, but it can become contentious in *trade policy* when countries seek trade rules to preserve or enhance their cultural traits. Many suspect that such rules would give countries the right to impose *import restrictions*, ostensibly for cultural reasons, but in reality to achieve other aims. For example, some may wish to protect a traditional production process and the workforce employed in this way even though more modern technology may produce an identical product more competitively. See also *Canadian periodicals*, *cultural industries*, *local content rules in broadcasting* and *trade and culture*.

Cultural industries: not an exact term. In the *United Nations Educational, Scientific and Cultural Organization* (UNESCO) it is taken to mean industries combining the creation, production and commercialization of contents that are cultural and intangible. These include printing, publishing and multimedia, audio-visual, phonographic and cinematographic productions as well as crafts and designs. This description is widely accepted. UNESCO notes, however, that in some countries architecture, visual and performing arts, sports, the manufacture of musical instruments, advertising and cultural tourism are also regarded as cultural industries. Article 2107 of *NAFTA* defines "cultural industries" as persons engaged in any of the following activities: (a) the publication, distribution, or sale of books, magazines, periodicals or newspapers in print or machine-readable form, but not including the sole activity of printing or typesetting any of the foregoing; (b) the production, distribution, sale or exhibition of film or video recordings; (c) the production, distribution, sale or exhibition of audio or video recordings; (d) the publication, distribution or sale of music in print or machine-readable form; or (e) radiocommunications in which the transmissions are intended for direct reception by the general public, and all radio, television and broadcasting undertakings and all satellite programmings and broadcast network services. See also *creative industries*. [www.unesco.org]

Cumulation: the ability under some systems of *rules of origin* to combine the value added by several preference-receiving countries to arrive at the *regional value content* of a good.

Cumulation zone: under some *preferential rules of origin* it is possible to combine, or cumulate, the contributions of several countries to the production of a good. This makes it easier for the exporting country to reach the *regional value content*. The countries from which inputs may be obtained in this way are known as the cumulation zone.

Cumulative assessment of dumping: the investigation by the importing country of alleged concurrent *dumping* by several countries of the same product. Under the WTO rules such an assessment is allowed only if (a) the *margin of dumping* for each country is more than *de minimis* and the imports from each are not negligible, and (b) the assessment would be appropriate in the light of competitive conditions between imported and domestic products. See also *anti-dumping measures*, *de-cumulation*, *de minimis dumping* and *negligible imports*.

Cumulative rules of origin: a system of *rules of origin* which permits the production or transformation of a product in two or more specified countries in order to satisfy the access rules of the importing country. This method is sometimes used under the *GSP* regimes to allow preferential treatment for developing countries that might not by themselves qualify for it because they have insufficient processing capacity. See also *substantial transformation*.

Cumulative subsidies: the WTO *Agreement on Subsidies and Countervailing Duties* provides that if imports of a product from more than one country are concurrently the subject of a *countervailing duty* investigation, authorities may assess the cumulative effect of these subsidies. However, they may only do this if (a) amounts greater than *de minimis subsidies* are involved and (b) if such an assessment is appropriate in the light of the competitive conditions in the import market.

Currency Board: pegging the value of a currency to that of another or a basket of currencies. This is usually done to stabilize a volatile currency and to give the government time to devise and institute macro-economic reforms. Argument continues among economists whether stabilization of a currency should come before or after the establishment of a currency board, or whether a currency board is needed at all.

Current access tariff quotas: access opportunities to be opened for agricultural products where *non-tariff measures* have been converted into *tariffs*. A formula was devised during the *Uruguay Round* negotiations whereby the level of access to be opened for a given product was determined through a comparison of the level of imports with consumption during the *base period*. Current access levels were adopted to ensure that imports represented at least 5% of domestic consumption applying in the Uruguay Round base period of 1986–88. See also *Agreement on Agriculture* and *minimum access tariff quotas*.

Current account: see *balance of payments*.

Current domestic value: a method for valuing goods to be imported for the assessment of *customs duties*. The value of the goods for duty purposes is the price at which goods comparable with those imported are sold under fully competitive conditions on the domestic markets of the country from which the goods were exported. This method has been superseded by the procedures contained in the WTO *Customs Valuation Agreement* (formally the *Agreement on Implementation of Article VII of the General Agreement on Tariffs and Trade 1994*). See also *customs valuation*

Customary international law: internationally accepted rules of conduct or obligations that derive their authority from the fact that (a) that they are customary among nations and (b) that there is an expectation by nations that in a given situation they will be obliged to follow a certain course of action (the *opinio juris* principle). Custom may be based on long traditions, or it may have arisen quite recently. What matters is that these two criteria must be satisfied in a claim invoking customary international law. J G Starke notes that custom is not the same as usage: "Usage may be conflicting, custom must be unified and self-consistent". See also *conventional international law*. [Aust 2000; Shaw 1997; Starke 1989]

Customs Convention on Temporary Admission: see *Istanbul Convention*.

Customs Convention on the ATA Carnet for the Temporary Admission of Goods: adopted by the Customs Cooperation Council, now the *World Customs Organization*, in 1961. It established the ATA Carnet, an international customs clearance document, which allows the temporary import of goods required for fairs and exhibitions, commercial samples, professional equipment, and sporting and musical equipment without the need to pay customs duties or the posting of a bond. The Carnet is normally valid for one year, and goods have to be re-exported within that time. The Convention was updated by the *Istanbul Convention* which entered into force in 1993.

Customs cooperation: cooperative activities between customs authorities, either bilaterally, regionally or through the *World Customs Organization*, to improve, *inter alia*, the efficiency of their operations and to make them easier to use by clients. Cooperation can include exchange of information and views on improvements of working methods such as *risk management*, exchange of officers, promotion of *paperless trading*, technical assistance programs and many other similar activities.

Customs Cooperation Council: the predecessor of the *World Customs Organization*.

Customs duties: charges levied at the border on goods entering or, much less often, leaving the country. These charges are specified in the national *tariff schedule*. They are usually based on the value of the goods, known as *ad valorem tariff* and sometimes as a cost per unit in the form of a *specific tariff*. See also *compound tariff*, *customs valuation*, *multi-column tariff* and *single-column tariff*.

Customs risk assessments: estimates made by the customs authorities of the extent to which consignments may contravene customs laws and regulations. Contravention may take many forms, such as duty evasion, *smuggling*, *trafficking* in prohibited substances and other articles, etc. Customs officers then pay extra attention to high-risk consignments.

Customs surcharge: a fee or a charge levied by customs authorities in addition to *customs duties*. Sometimes it simply means a charge for the handling of a consignment roughly equivalent to the cost of providing the service. At other times it can mean an *ad valorem* addition to the duty payable. See also *customs user fee*.

Customs territory: any state or territory with a *tariff* of its own and autonomy in the conduct of its international trade relations. Article XII of the *WTO Agreement* allows any state or separate customs territory to apply for membership of the WTO.

Customs union: an area consisting of two or more individual economies or *customs territories* which remove all tariffs and sometimes broader trade impediments between them. The members making up the area then apply a *common external tariff*. See also *common market* and *free-trade area*.

Customs user fee: an administrative charge levied by a customs authority to clear the import or export of goods. This fee should be based on the cost of providing the service. It should not be used to protect domestic products or as a source of revenue for the government.

Customs valuation: methods used by customs authorities to allocate a value to imported goods for the purpose of striking the correct import duty. The WTO *Customs Valuation Agreement* (formally the *Agreement on Implementation of Article VII of the General Agreement on Tariffs and Trade 1994*) aims to set out a fair, uniform and neutral system for the valuation of goods that precludes the use of arbitrary or fictitious customs values. The basic rule is that the customs value of imported goods in the case of unrelated parties is the *transaction value*, i.e. the price actually paid or payable for the goods when sold for export to the importing country. The buyer must be free to dispose of the goods as desired apart from legal restrictions imposed by the government, any limits on the geographical area in which the goods may be sold and any other restrictions that do not substantially affect the value of the goods. Additionally, the sale must not be subject to conditions for which a value cannot be determined, the buyer will not benefit directly or indirectly from a later resale, and the buyer and the seller must not be related. If they are related, the transaction value must be acceptable to the customs authorities. Freight, packaging, commissions, goods and services supplied to the buyer free of charge and some other costs may be added to the customs value. If there are suspicions that the transaction value is false, customs authorities may determine the value by going sequentially through five options: (a) the value of identical goods, (b) the value of *similar goods*, (c) the imported price of *identical goods* or similar goods minus applicable deductions for costs, (d) *computed value* and (e) if none of these methods work, other reasonable means may be used. Additional considerations apply where the importer and exporter are related entities. The Agreement also sets out the measures that may not be used to establish a value. These include, for example, *minimum customs values*, the price of goods on the domestic market of the exporting country, the selling price of goods produced in the importing country, a system which provides for the higher of two values, etc. See also *arm's-length pricing*.

Customs Valuation Agreement: formally the *Agreement on Implementation of Article VII of the General Agreement on Tariffs and Trade 1994*. It sets out a framework of procedures for the valuation of goods by customs authorities for the purpose of levying the correct **customs duty**. For most imports the basis for the valuation is the *transaction value*. That is the price actually paid or payable for the goods when sold for export to the importing country. In most cases the assumption is that the buyer and seller are not related. Moreover, apart from certain defined conditions, the importers must be free to dispose of the goods without restriction. If the transaction value cannot be determined properly, other methods may be chosen. See the entry on *customs valuation* for an outline of these methods.

Customs value: the value of a good as assessed by a customs administration. The term is sometimes defined legally as the value of a good determined in accordance with the WTO *Agreement on Customs Valuation*.

Cyclical dumping: see *dumping*.

DAC: see *Development Assistance Committee*.

DAC principles for developing the capacity for trade: see *capacity-building*.

Dairy Export Incentive Program: DEIP. A United States subsidy program first authorized by the 1985 Farm Act. Through this program, the United States Department of Agriculture pays a cash bonus to exporters of some dairy products to allow them to sell these products on world markets for less than they bought them. Payments are made by the *Commodity Credit Corporation*. Commodities able to benefit from DEIP are milk powder, butter fat, cheddar, mozzarella, Gouda, feta, cream, and processed American cheeses. See also *Export Enhancement Program* and *Farm Security and Rural Investment Act* of 2002 which extended the program to 2007.

Damage: see *injury* and *serious damage*.

D'Amato legislation: see *Iran and Libya Sanctions Act*.

Data protection in trade in services: the *General Agreement on Trade in Services* contains several provisions to ensure confidentiality of records and data. Article III *bis* suspends the *transparency* requirement if disclosure of information would impede law enforcement, otherwise contravene the public interest or prejudice the legitimate commercial interests of private or public enterprises. Article IX (Business Practices) only requires the supply of publicly available non-confidential information concerning anti-competitive business practices. Other information may be made available if the requesting member undertakes to safeguard its confidentiality. Article XIV (General Exceptions) permits the suspension of obligations under the Agreement to protect the privacy of individuals in relation to personal data and the confidentiality of individual records and accounts.

Davignon Plan: a plan adopted in 1978 by the *European Economic Community* to revitalize its steel industry. The plan was aimed mainly at putting a cap on production capacity. It also had a longer-term segment for restructuring and rationalizing the steel industry. *State aids* and *import restrictions* were an important factor in achieving the planned targets. The plan was named after Viscount Etienne Davignon, the then European Commissioner for Internal Market and Industrial Affairs.

Deceptive indications of source: see *indications of source*.

Decision: one of the means available to the *European Community* to enforce its mandate. A decision is binding only on those to whom it is addressed. This may be a member state, a single company or an individual. See also *European Community legislation*.

Decision in Favour of Least Developed Countries: see *least developed countries*.

Decision-making in the WTO: WTO members nearly always make their decisions by *consensus*, but they may vote if a consensus is not possible. The majority required for adoption of a measure varies with the subject. An interpretation of the agreements administered by the WTO, excepting the *plurilateral agreements*, requires a three-fourths majority of the *WTO Ministerial Conference* or the *General Council*, as does agreement to a *waiver*. Amendments to the *most-favoured-nation* articles in the *GATT*, the *General Agreement on Trade in Services* and the *Agreement on Trade-Related Aspects of Intellectual Property Rights* may only be made through unanimity. Each WTO member has one vote. The *European Communities* are entitled to a number of votes equalling the number of their member states. Interpretation of the plurilateral agreements is done according to the provisions contained in these agreements. See also *amendments to WTO agreements*. The *Doha Ministerial Declaration* has introduced the term "explicit consensus". It is not yet known what this means for achieving consensus.

Decision on Conflicting Requirements: taken by the *OECD* Ministerial Council in May 1984 to give effect to the *General Considerations and Practical Approaches Concerning Conflicting Requirements Imposed on Multinational Enterprises*. This instrument asks OECD members that may be contemplating legislative action which may conflict with the legal requirements of another member to endeavour to avoid or minimize such conflicts through moderation and restraint and respecting the interests of others. It asks members, *inter alia*, to be prepared to (a) develop mutually beneficial bilateral arrangements for notifying and consulting other members, (b) give prompt and sympathetic consideration to requests for notification and bilateral consultations, (c) inform other members as soon as practicable of new legislation or regulations, and (d) give full consideration to proposals made by others that would lessen or eliminate conflicts.

Decision on International Incentives and Disincentives: adopted by *OECD* members in 1984. It paves the way for consultations if a member country considers that its interests may be adversely affected by the impact on international investment flows of significant official incentives and disincentives to international direct investment by another member.

Declaration giving effect to the provisions of Article XVI:4: adopted in 1960. GATT members which acceded to the Declaration (all developed countries) agreed that from 1 January 1958 they would cease to grant, either directly or indirectly, any form of subsidy on the export of a product which would result in the sale of the exported product at a lower price than comparable prices charged for similar products in the domestic market. *Primary products* were exempted from this Declaration.

Declaration on Fundamental Principles and Rights at Work: adopted by the *International Labour Organization* (ILO) in June 1998. It holds that all members of the ILO have an obligation to promote and realize the following rights: (a) freedom of association and the effective recognition of the right to collective bargaining, (b) the elimination of all forms of forced or compulsory labour, (c) the effective abolition of child labour, and (d) the elimination of discrimination in respect of employment and occupation. Most of these are listed in the *Universal Declaration on Human Rights*. The Declaration offers a program of technical cooperation and advisory services to help countries to achieve these aims. It also stresses that labour standards should not be used for protectionist trade purposes. See also *Convention Concerning the Prohibition and Immediate Action for the Elimination of the Worst Forms of Child Labour*, *core labour standards* and *trade and labour standards*.

Declaration on Implementation-Related Issues and Concerns: one of the documents adopted on 14 November 2001 at the *Doha Ministerial Conference*. It identifies issues of concern to developing countries arising from the various agreements under the WTO and suggests how they should be dealt with in the negotiations. It also establishes a work program for the *Committee on Trade and Development* on cross-cutting issues.

Declaration on International Investment and Multinational Enterprises: adopted by the *OECD* Ministerial Council on 27 June 2000. It reaffirms the commitment of members to the *OECD Guidelines for Multinational Enterprises*, the *national treatment instrument*, the *Decision on Conflicting Requirements* and the *Decision on International Investment Incentives and Disincentives*.

Declaration on the Contribution of the World Trade Organization to Achieving Greater Coherence in Global Economic Policymaking: one of the outcomes of the Marrakesh Ministerial Meeting in April 1994 which formally ended the *Uruguay Round*. The Declaration says that the positive outcome of the Uruguay Round is to be seen as a major contribution towards more coherent international economic policies. It notes that difficulties originating outside the trade field cannot redressed through trade measures alone. The Declaration accordingly invites the Director-General of the WTO to discuss further with the *IMF* and the *World Bank* the possible forms of cooperation between the three with a view to achieving greater coherence in global economic policymaking.

Declaration on the Establishment of a New International Economic Order: see *New International Economic Order*.

Declaration on the Right to Development: see *Right to Development*.

Declaration on the TRIPS Agreement and Public Health: adopted at the *Doha Ministerial Conference* on 14 November 2001. The Declaration affirms that the TRIPS agreement can and should be interpreted flexibly to promote access to medicines for all. Key elements of the declaration are that each member has the right to grant *compulsory licences*, to determine what constitutes a national emergency or extreme urgency in public health, and to establish its own regime handling *exhaustion* of *intellectual property rights*. See also *access to medicines*.

Decompilation: the analysis of a computer program to discover the ideas or principles on which it operates. This normally involves a substantial recreation or reproduction of the program. National jurisdictions have differing views on its legality under *copyright* acts. The practice is accordingly controversial. A United States court held that *reverse engineering*, including decompilation of a program, to uncover its unprotected ideas and concepts was permissible under the relevant laws as "fair use", but in Australia decompilation may involve an infringement of the copyright owner's reproduction rights. See also *fair-use doctrine*.

Découpage: a procedure adopted during the *Kennedy Round* in the negotiations on tariff reductions on chemicals. It arose from the need to separate the concessions made under the existing United States negotiating authority (the *Trade Expansion Act* of 1962) from those that required additional congressional approval. The latter group was centred around the proposed abolition of the *American Selling Price* system, a method of valuing some chemicals at the border for the purpose of *customs duties*.

Decoupling: the separation of two or more actions, approaches or options that had previously been treated as a whole. For example, countries may decide to abolish the link between the amount of agricultural subsidies paid and the size of the planted acreage or the amount produced.

De-cumulation: when a petition for the imposition of *anti-dumping measures* against imports from several countries has been launched, the investigating authorities may decide to consider the combined impact of these products on the domestic market. This is called *cumulation*. When they decide to look at one or more supplier countries separately, possibly because their circumstances are quite different, it is called de-cumulation. [Vermulst 1990]

Deep integration: the integration by two or more countries of national policy frameworks that usually are the preserve of national governments. These include *competition policy*, technical standards, *subsidies*, monetary and fiscal policies, regulation and supervision of financial institutions, environmental issues, *government procurement* and more. The *European Community* has moved ahead farthest in deep integration, but *ANZCERTA* and *NAFTA* are also examples of deep integration. A contrast is usually drawn with shallow integration which may range from a preferential trade area to a *customs union* or *free-trade area*, but where each member retains a completely free hand concerning all other policies. Shallow integration also promotes a degree of harmonization of policies as has happened in the *multilateral trading system*. See also *European Community Single Market*, *negative integration* and *positive integration*.

De facto: existing, whether legally or not. See also *de jure*.

De facto discrimination: a term first used in the report by the WTO *Appellate Body* on the 1996 banana panel decision. The Appellate Body contrasts *de facto* discrimination with *de jure*, or formal, discrimination. Its meaning appears to be close to that of *implicit discrimination* in that it is based on practice rather than a legislative requirement. See also *banana cases*. [WT/DS27/AB/R]

De facto **GATT membership:** former colonies used to be able, upon independence, to participate in the GATT as *de facto* members if they agreed to administer their trade regimes in accordance with the GATT rules. This could only be done if the parent countries had been GATT members. *De facto* membership is not possible in the WTO.

Deficiency payment: a type of agricultural domestic support, paid by governments to producers of certain commodities and based on the difference between a target price and the domestic market price or *loan rate*, whichever is the less.

Definitive anti-dumping duties: the anti-dumping duties imposed once all the investigations have been completed. They have to be ended after five years unless a review initiated beforehand indicates that *dumping* would continue or recur. See also *anti-dumping measures* and *provisional anti-dumping duties*.

Definitive safeguard measures: refers to *safeguard measures* imposed after an investigation has shown a causal link between the difficulties experienced by domestic producers of a given good and an increase in imports of that good. See also *provisional safeguards*.

Degressivity: generally the principle that *protection* should be reduced over time. It has been an issue particularly in the administration of *safeguards* where governments were supposed to initiate *structural adjustment* policies resulting in lower protection in the sectors given safeguard protection. Often they preferred to continue *import restrictions* at the same level.

Deindustrialization: a phenomenon associated by many with *globalization* and seen as a negative development. Sometimes also called "hollowing-out". It is defined generally as the long-term decline in the share of manufacturing employment in the advanced or industrialized economies. In the view of many, the most important factor accounting for deindustrialization is the systematic tendency for productivity in manufacturing to grow faster than in services. In many countries, perceived deindustrialization is one of the important forces driving the formulation of *trade policy*, and governments often seek to stem its tide through imposing *protection* for *sensitive sectors*. See also *delocalization*, *internationalization* and *structural adjustment*.

Deip: see **Dairy Export Incentive Program**.

De jure: existing in law. See also *de facto*.

De jure **discrimination:** discrimination among trading partners formally embodied in legislation or regulations. See also *de facto discrimination*.

Délocalisant: a *semi-generic geographical indication*.

Delocalization: a term used by advocates of negotiations concerning *trade and labour standards*. It means that a company may decide to relocate its production facilities from a high-cost location to a low-cost country because it expects to save on expenses for the support of social conditions for the workforce. This claim is disputed. With the shift towards advanced, flexible production systems and the need to assure quality and reliability, increasing importance is attached to such factors as infrastructures, educational standards and skill levels. Relative wage levels then are a factor, but not the only important one, in the choice of location. See also *deindustrialization, globalization, internationalization, race-to-the-bottom argument* and *workers rights*.

***De minimis*:** a legal term describing that something is of little or no importance in the matter concerned.

***De minimis* dumping margins:** *dumping* margins of less than 2% expressed as a percentage of the export price in the country of origin. In the case of such margins, a country may not take *anti-dumping measures*. See also *negligible imports*.

***De minimis* imports:** the provisions of the WTO *Agreement on Trade-Related Aspects of Intellectual Property Rights* do not apply to small quantities of goods of a non-commercial nature contained in personal luggage or sent in small consignments.

***De minimis* in rules of origin:** a provision sometimes included in the *rules of origin* of *free-trade agreements*. It states that although a good may not have undergone a *change in tariff classification* sufficiently large in the partner country to enable it to qualify as an *originating good*, the importing country may accept it as such if the value of all *non-originating materials* is less than a stipulated percentage. A *de minimis* limit of 10% appears to be common.

***De minimis* safeguards rule:** safeguards action may not be taken against a developing country if its share of the imports of the product concerned is less than 3%. This rule only applies if the collective share of developing countries accounting for less than 3% each of imports of the product concerned is no more than 9%. See also *Agreement on Safeguards, safeguards* and *selectivity*.

***De minimis* subsidies:** the WTO *Agreement on Subsidies and Countervailing Measures* defines these as subsidies amounting to less than 1%. Authorities investigating the effect of an alleged subsidy are required to terminate their enquiries immediately if the volume of the subsidy falls into this category. If developing countries are involved, the *de minimis* level is set at 2% in the case of individual countries. This provision also applies if the volume of subsidized imports of the same product from developing countries does not exceed 4%, unless imports from developing countries with a share of less than 4% of imports exceed 9% of total imports of the same product by the country making the investigation.

Democracy clause: a provision in trade laws or international trade and investment treaties which promotes the observance of democratic freedoms. One example is the *ACP-EC Partnership Agreement*. Its members agree that respect for democratic principles and the rule of law is one of the essential elements of the Agreement. The *Mediterranean Agreements* concluded by the *European Community* also contain provisions requiring respect for human rights and democracy. See also *human rights clause* and *social clause*. [Petersmann 2001]

Denial of benefits: members of the *General Agreement on Trade in Services* (GATS) may deny the benefits of the Agreement to another member if they can show that a service does not originate in the territory of a GATS member or if a company supplying the service is not a national of a GATS member. See also *non-application*.

Denomination: see *appellation of origin*, *geographical indications*, *geographical names* and *Stresa Convention*.

Dependence theory: a theory much in vogue in the 1960s and 1970s holding that developing countries are economically, socially and politically dependent on power groups in developed countries, especially *transnational corporations*. The theory is now not considered to give a satisfactory account of the causes of development and underdevelopment and hence the policy choices available to developing countries. See also *core-periphery thesis* and *Singer-Prebisch thesis*. [Cohn 2003, Fieldhouse 1999]

Derbez text: the draft ministerial statement prepared for the WTO *Cancún Ministerial Conference* by Luis Ernesto Derbez, then Foreign Minister of Mexico. It outlined a plan for making progress in the negotiations under the *Doha Development Agenda*.

Deregulation: the process by which governments dismantle the regulatory structure of industries or professions to promote competition and hence improve the efficiency with which goods and services are delivered. See also *privatization*, *re-regulation* and *wider competition policy*.

Designation of origin: see *protected designation of origin*.

Determination of dumping: the process described in the WTO *Anti-Dumping Agreement* which leads to an assessment of whether *dumping* has occurred. This means determining whether the *export price* of the product concerned is lower than its *normal value*. Although an investigation may show that dumping has occurred, this does not necessarily mean that *anti-dumping measures* may be imposed. It still has to be shown that dumped product caused, or threatened to cause, material *injury* to an established industry or that it may have materially retarded the establishment of a domestic industry. This is known as *causality*.

Determination of origin: ascertaining where a good has come from, for example, for statistical purposes or to make sure that it qualifies for preferential tariff treatment under a *free-trade agreement*. This is an aspect of the administration of *rules of origin*.

Devaluation: a change in a country's *exchange rate* through a government decision with the result that more units of that country's currency are needed to buy the same amount of the foreign currency.

Developed country: a term usually applied to *OECD* member countries, though some of the more recent members might not consider themselves wholly so. The term "developed country" tends to convey a picture of an economically and socially advanced country, but the differences between the poorest and the wealthiest members of this group are great. Sometimes, developed countries are collectively referred to as the North because most of them are located in the northern hemisphere.

Developing country: an imprecise term based as much on economic and social foundations as on political perceptions and aspirations. It is applied to a country that does not consider itself, or is not considered by others, in some or many respects as matching the characteristics of a *developed country*. Developing-country status remains largely self-declared. No objective standard is available to judge whether a country is a developing country, except in the case of *least-developed countries*. *ECOSOC* uses agreed criteria to identify them. Often, developing countries are said to be those countries that are not *OECD* members. To others, developing-country status is the same as membership of the *Group of 77*. Sometimes, developing countries are referred to collectively as the South since many of them are located in the southern hemisphere. Various attempts have been made to put assessments of developing-country status on a firmer footing. The *World Bank*, for example, refers to *low-income economies* and *middle-income economies*. This is useful, but it leaves out indicators such as schooling, life expectancy, etc. See also *developing countries and the multilateral trading system*, *graduation* and *special and differential treatment*.

Developing countries and the multilateral trading system: when the text of the *GATT* was negotiated in 1947, there was an assumption among developed countries that on the whole it should apply equally to countries at different stages of development. At the same time, there was a strong developing-country view that they should not have to accord full *reciprocity* in *trade liberalization* to others, and that they should have preferential access to developed-country markets. In the end, provision was made in Article XVIII (Government Assistance to Economic Development) to facilitate the progressive development of developing country economies, especially the ones that could only support low standards of living and that were in the early stages of development. An interpretative note to the Article adds that the phrase "low standards of living" is to be taken to mean normal economic circumstances and not exceptionally favourable temporary conditions resulting from good export markets for primary commodities. The phrase "in the early stages of economic development" may apply not only to countries at the initial stages of economic development, but also to those which are undergoing a process of industrialization to correct an excessive dependence on primary production. Article XVIII permits developing countries to maintain tariff structures permitting the promotion of infant industries and to apply *quantitative restrictions* for *balance-of-payments* purposes. The administration of this provision has always been difficult because the criteria it uses are rather flexible. First, it assumes that countries will know when they are to be considered developing economies, and it does not contain a mechanism for them to graduate to developed-economy status. Second, the provisions relating to the development of infant industries can be quite complex in practice. Third, the criteria for *import restrictions* under the balance-of-payments provisions are not all that well defined. Restrictions may not be more severe than necessary (a) to forestall the threat of, or to stop, a serious decline in monetary reserves and (b) in the case of a member with inadequate monetary reserves, to achieve a reasonable rate of increase in its reserves. As the *Korean beef* case showed, however, the temptation exists to maintain balance-of-payments restrictions much longer than would objectively be necessary. In practice, developing countries have not found Article XVIII as useful to them as they had expected. Nor have developed countries viewed it as having great merit. A fundamental difficulty with the Article is in the eyes of some that it is based on the *import substitution* theory, the antithesis of the policies adopted by outward-looking, export-oriented economies. As economists have pointed out, the capital goods imports required by import substitution policies will invariably ensure a shortage of foreign exchange without an adequate balancing by export income. GATT articles are difficult to change, and the *GATT review session* of 1955 left this situation largely intact. Indeed, until the advent of the *Kennedy Round*, the developing countries as a whole played a minor role in major GATT negotiations. The years between 1948 and 1963 were dominated by tariff negotiations rather than the consideration of systemic issues. Some of the primary commodities developing countries produced and in which they were important traders faced few entry barriers to developed-country markets. Agricultural products, textiles and *tropical products* were, of course, a different matter. On the other hand, the system of *requests and offers*, used to bring down many of the high tariffs for manufactured articles, and the associated rule of *principal supplier rights*, meant that developing countries with their small market shares in most countries effectively were excluded from playing any role in the early tariff negotiating rounds. Despite their persistent efforts to show that they were not being drawn into the post-war trading system as had been expected, it was not until late 1957 that the GATT membership as a whole decided to study this problem more carefully. The result was the *Haberler Report*, issued in 1958, which concluded that there was some justification in developing country views that current rules and conventions on *commercial policy* were relatively unfavourable to them. A committee was then established to look at the matter further, and to this can be traced in part the inclusion of specific developing-country issues in the Kennedy Round. In the meantime, decolonization led to the accession to the GATT of more developing countries. Some of them, and others outside it, began to view to *United Nations* system as a better potential mechanism for improvements in issues of interest to them. This eventually led to the convening of *UNCTAD* (United Nations Conference on Trade and Development) in 1964 and its establishment in the same year as a permanent body. Later, this was followed by calls for a *New International Economic Order* and a *Charter of Economic Rights and Duties of States*, both to be negotiated under United Nations auspices. In the GATT, the big breakthrough for developing countries came with the launch of the Kennedy Round in 1963. For the first time, the negotiating mandate for a round referred specifically to developing countries. According to the Ministerial Declaration launching the Round, one objective was the adoption of measures for the expansion of trade of developing countries as a means of furthering their economic development. Results of the Round for developing countries were mixed. They benefited from tariff cuts particularly in non-agricultural items of interest to them. They also obtained *Part IV of the GATT* which freed them from the requirement to accord reciprocity to developed countries in trade negotiations. This, however, could be no more than a symbolic gesture, and its value to developing countries has been debated ever since. On the other hand, the *Long-Term Arrangement Regarding International Trade in Cotton Textiles*, which put severe restrictions on their ability to expand their exports of cotton textiles, was extended for another three years and was well on its way to becoming a feature of the *multilateral trading system* in the form of the *Multi-Fibre Arrangement* until its replacement by the WTO *Agreement on Textiles and Clothing* more than thirty years later. In 1968, UNCTAD II adopted a resolution calling for the establishment of a *GSP* (Generalized System of Preferences) which would give developing countries preferential access to developed-country markets. The idea had been around for some years. In 1963, the *European Economic Community* had signed the *Yaoundé Convention* which gave special benefits to some African countries. The GATT faced up to the new reality in 1971 when it adopted a ten-year waiver for such schemes. The developing countries had therefore achieved formally both of their main aims of non-reciprocity and preferential market access. They succeeded in buttressing their gains in the *Tokyo Round* through the adoption of the *Enabling Clause* which put *special and differential treatment* on a firmer footing. It also was seen as providing a permanent waiver for the GSP. However, neither of these achievements seemed to take the developing countries much further in the direction of achieving fuller participation in the multilateral trading system. Some of them certainly did very well as exporters of manufactures and as destinations for investment, but they had effectively given away their influence over the rules of the game. As far as many developed countries were concerned, there was little point in agreeing on rules with players who were not obliged to play by them. The years following the conclusion of the Tokyo Round therefore led to many calls for new GATT rules for developed countries, the so-called *GATT plus* proposals. Their adoption would have formalized the outsider role of developing countries further. The opposite was true of the *Leutwiler Report* of 1985 which called for greater emphasis on encouraging developing countries to take advantage of their competitive strength and to integrate them more fully into the trading system. In other words, they should look towards adopting more of the GATT's obligations in order to benefit more from its rights. This view gained some support from the more outward-looking developing countries. The *Uruguay Round* outcome reversed the trend. Developing countries then appeared to be accepting the fact that they would only have bargaining power if they were bound by all the results of negotiations. Some indications of this can be gained from the negotiations under the *General Agreement on Trade in Service* (GATS) where the obligations of developing countries are nearly equal to those of developed countries, the main difference being the relative number of listings to be made in the *schedules of commitments*. Now the pendulum may have swung the other way again. The multilateral trade negotiations launched in November 2001 are formally known as the *Doha Development Agenda*, but it is too early to say how this issue will play itself out. See also *graduation* and *infant-industry argument*. [Gallagher 2000]

Development agenda: see *Doha Development Agenda*.

Development assistance: aid given to developing countries in the form of loans, grants, credits or in kind, regardless of whether this is done by non-governmental organizations or as *official development assistance*. See also *trade-related technical assistance*.

Development Assistance Committee: DAC. A body established within the *OECD* as a forum for the consideration of bilateral and multilateral *development assistance* activities of member countries. See also *capacity-building* and *official development assistance*.

Development box: a proposal for an amendment to the WTO *Agreement on Agriculture* made by the *Like-minded Group of Developing Countries* in 2000. The main aims of the development box would be (a) to protect and enhance domestic food production, (b) to sustain and enhance employment, (c) to allow flexible support for small farmers, (d) to protect poor farmers from subsidized imports and harmful fluctuations in import prices and quantities, and (e) to promote improved internal distribution and exports of surplus production. Proponents of the development box argue that it would give developing countries more effective means to promote rural development, *food security* and alleviation of poverty. See also *amber box*, *blue box*, *green box* and *food security box*.

Development Round: a name for the multilateral trade negotiations launched at Doha, Qatar, on 14 November 2001. The work program for this round reflects the concerns of developing countries more than any previous round. See also *developing countries and the multilateral trading system* and *Doha Development Agenda*.

Diagonal cumulation: permissible under the system of *preferential rules of origin* administered by the *European Community*. The production of eligible goods must involve at least three partners. It is available to partner countries belonging to a network of *free-trade agreements* which have the same rules of origin and which allow this type of accumulation. See also *Pan-European Cumulation Area*. [Commission of the European Communities 2003]

Dialogue partners: these are countries that are not members of any given *intergovernmental organization*, but that have more than *observer status* in its work. Dialogue partners often can attend the formal sessions of a meeting, and they receive the official documents. They also have the opportunity, usually towards the end of the session, to have a separate meeting with the member states of the organization.

Dictum: see *obiter dictum*.

Differential and More Favourable Treatment, Reciprocity and Fuller Participation of Developing Countries: see *Enabling Clause*.

Differential export tax: the reverse of *tariff escalation* in the case of imports. Raw materials for export are taxed heavily, but processed materials made from the same raw material are taxed lightly. The purpose of this practice is to ensure that raw materials are processed before export.

Differential pricing: putting a price on a good or service that differs according to the market. In some cases this may contravene a country's *competition laws*.

Diffuse reciprocity: see *reciprocity at the margin*.

Digital divide: the gap between developed and developing countries in the use of, and access to, information and communications technology products and services.

Digital product: a term frequently used in *free-trade agreements* concluded by the United States. The agreements define digital products as "computer programs, text, video, images, sound recordings and other products that are digitally encoded, regardless of whether they are fixed on a carrier medium or transmitted electronically". An example of a digital product would be a recorded piece of music which could be made available through a compact disc, a tape or through downloading from the Internet.

Dillon Round: the fifth round of *multilateral trade negotiations*, held in Geneva from 1960–61. It was named after Douglas C Dillon, the then United States Under-Secretary of State. Much of the Dillon Round was concerned with tariff renegotiations resulting from the establishment of the *European Economic Community* and its *common external tariff*, but more general tariff negotiations were conducted also. Despite the use of the term "round", it really was the last of the old-style tariff negotiating conferences. Its results were modest. About 4,400 tariff *concessions* were exchanged, compared to about 45,000 during the *Geneva Tariff Conference, 1947*.

Dilution doctrine: an aspect of the law concerning *trademarks*. It gives owners of *famous marks* protection against the use of the mark in a way that makes it unlikely that confusion occurs. For example, if someone were to use the name of an expensive car to describe cheap running shoes, few consumers would be misled to think that by buying the shoes they were buying something produced by or associated with the car factory. The owner of the car brand might, however, consider that using the mark in this way would be taking away something the reputation the brand has in the market. In other words, he might feel that the use of the brand in this way would dilute the reputation of the mark. Nevertheless, allowing the use of a famous mark for apparently unrelated purposes may be part of a sales strategy by the owners of the mark. Dilution is different to *passing off*, where there is a clear intention to deceive the buyers that they are buying the genuine product.

Diminished giant syndrome: a term coined by Jagdish Bhagwati to describe what then appeared to be an erosion of the prominent status of the United States in the world economy. He saw the diminished giant syndrome as one of the indirect causes "encouraging the notion that other countries are trading unfairly and that this calls for aggressive trade legislation, tougher and more restrictive interpretation of unfair trade practices, 'hardball' international negotiations, and confrontational tactics". See also *aggressive unilateralism* and *Section 301*. [Bhagwati 1988]

Diplomatic protection: protection of an investment in a foreign country through the diplomatic mission of the investor's home country located in that country. [Sornarajah 1994]

Direction of trade: a term describing the set of a country's trading partners, and how important its trade with single or groups of countries is. The principal statistical work containing this information is the *IMF Direction of Trade Statistics Yearbook*, published annually.

Directive: an official *European Community* act which is binding on the member states to which it is addressed. Member states are then free to implement the directive in their preferred manner, provided that they give complete effect to its content. See also *European Community legislation*.

Directly competitive or substitutable product: a phrase used in Article III (National Treatment) of the GATT where, however, it is not further defined. In *Korea – Taxes on Alcoholic Beverages* the *Appellate Body* held that "products are competitive or substitutable when they are interchangeable, or if they offer, as the *Panel* [on the same case] noted 'alternative ways of satisfying a particular need or taste'". See also *like product*. [WT/DS75/AB/R, WT/DS84/AB/R]

Directly competitive products: a term used in Article XIX of the GATT (Emergency Action on Imports of Particular Products) and the *Agreement on Safeguards*. See *like or directly competitive products*.

Direct payments: subsidies to people engaged in agricultural production that are independent, or nearly independent, of the amount produced by them. See also *decoupling*.

Dirty Dozen: a group of developed countries first established during the *Uruguay Round* when it had twelve members. It is apparently named after an American motion picture popular at the time. Its core participants included Australia, Canada, European Community, Iceland, Japan, Norway, New Zealand, Switzerland and the United States.

Dirty dozen substances: a list of substances named in the *Convention on Persistent Organic Pollutants*, the use of which either has to be eliminated or restricted. They are aldrin, chlordane, DDT, dieldrin, endrin, heptachlor, hexachlorobenzene, mirex, toxaphene, polychlorinated biphenyls (PCB) and the by-products plychlorinated dibenzo-p-dioxins and dibenzofurans (PCCD/PCDF), hexachlorobenzene (HCB) and polychlorinated biphenyls.

Dirty quotification: excessive discretion used in setting and administering *tariff rate quotas* for trade in agricultural products.

Dirty tariffication: see *water in the tariff*.

Discretionary/mandatory distinction: see *GATT-consistency of national legislation*.

Discrimination: making a distinction between trading partners and treating some of them differently. Examples of allowable discrimination are according tariff-free entry to a *free-trade agreement* partner and giving *preferential tariff treatment* to a developing country under a *GSP scheme. See also arbitrary and unjustifiable discrimination and non-discrimination.*

Disguised restriction on international trade: several of the agreements administered by the WTO require members to ensure that certain measures taken under them are not in fact "disguised restrictions on international trade". Among these are Article XX of the GATT (General Exceptions), Article VII (Recognition) and Article XIV of the *General Agreement on Trade in Services*, Article 3 (National Treatment) of the *Agreement on Trade-Related Aspects of Intellectual Property Rights* and Article 3 (Assessment of Risk and Determination of the Appropriate Level of Sanitary and Phytosanitary Protection) of the *Agreement on the Application of Sanitary and Phytosanitary Measures*. The phrase has no clear definition. In *European Communities – Measures Affecting Asbestos and Asbestos-Containing Products* the *panel* noted that the key to understanding this phrase lay not so much in the word "restriction" as in the word "disguised". One can therefore assume that a "disguised restriction on international trade" is a measure that has been framed, sometimes inadvertently and sometimes intentionally, to serve one purpose (e.g. promotion of public health), but which in fact has a protectionist aim or effect. Whether the measure has been announced publicly or whether it is, on the surface at any rate, not related to trade, is in the opinion of the panel of no great moment. What matters is whether the measure has a trade effect. [WT/DS135/R]

Disguised trade barriers: measures taken by governments ostensibly to achieve a goal unrelated to trade, but which can have a direct impact on imports. Among the measures sometimes so used are consumer protection laws, product standards and quarantine rules. See also *sanitary and phytosanitary measures, shelf-life restrictions* and *technical barriers to trade*.

Dispersed tariff rates: a *tariff schedule* in which there is a wide discrepancy between low rates and high rates. Also, relatively few concentrations of similar tariff rates appear in such a schedule. See also *flat-tariff structures* and *peak tariffs*.

Dispute settlement: resolution of conflict arising between governments over the interpretation of trade or other rules, often through a compromise between opposing claims, sometimes through an intermediary. Dispute settlement can acquire a strongly adversarial or rules-based. Dispute settlement in the WTO usually starts after *consultation* has failed. The basic rules for consultation and dispute resolution are set out in Articles XXII and XXIII of the *GATT* for goods, Articles XXII and XXIII of the *General Agreement on Trade in Services* for services and Article 64 of the *Agreement on Trade-Related Aspects of Intellectual Property Rights* for intellectual property. The detailed rules to be followed in all cases are those contained in the *Dispute Settlement Understanding*. See also *Appellate Body* and *Dispute Settlement Body*. [Sacerdoti, Yanovich and Bohanes, 2006]

Dispute Settlement Body: DSB. The WTO *General Council*, when it convenes to settle disputes arising between members. The DSB has the sole authority to establish *panels*, adopt panel and appellate reports, maintain surveillance of implementation of rulings and recommendations, and authorize *retaliation* in cases where its recommendations are ignored. The WTO secretariat says that a case should normally take about one year to complete, and fifteen months if it goes to the *Appellate Body*. See also *dispute settlement* and *Dispute Settlement Understanding*.

Dispute Settlement Mechanism: see *dispute settlement*, *Dispute Settlement Body* and *Dispute Settlement Understanding*.

Dispute Settlement Panel: see *panel* and *Dispute Settlement Understanding*.

Dispute Settlement Understanding: DSU. Formally the WTO *Understanding on Rules and Procedures Governing the Settlement of Disputes*. This is one of the *Uruguay Round* outcomes. Its underlying theme is that prompt settlement of disputes is essential for the proper functioning of the WTO. The understanding therefore sets out in some detail the procedures and timetable to be followed in resolving disputes. There is little scope for delaying tactics. The first stage in the resolution of a dispute consists of *consultation* between the parties who may call on the WTO Director-General to mediate. If consultation is unsuccessful, the formation of a *panel* is almost automatic. If the parties disagree with the panel's findings, they may appeal to the *Appellate Body*, but the grounds for such appeals must be confined to legal issues.

Distortion: a measure, policy or practice that shifts the market price of a product above or below what it would be if the product were traded in a competitive market. Measures causing distortions include *subsidies*, *import restrictions* and *restrictive business practices*.

Distribution foreign direct investment: this refers to *foreign direct investment* by a firm with the aim of finding outlets for its products. This happens, for example, when an oil company invests in a chain of service stations.

Diversionary dumping: the export of a product at dumped prices to an intermediate country from where it is exported to its true destination. The purpose of diversionary dumping may be to take advantage of the pricing structure of the intermediate country to avert *anti-dumping measures*. See also *circumvention* and *dumping*.

Docking: sometimes used to describe the joining of two *preferential trade arrangements*.

Doctrine of Dilution: see *dilution doctrine*.

Doctrine of reasonable expectations: the assumptions that once countries have made commitments or pursued practices under their international trade regimes, these commitments will be honoured for the foreseeable future. An example frequently quoted to illustrate this doctrine is *Australian subsidy on ammonium sulphate* where a *GATT* working party found that Australia had not acted illegally in removing a subsidy on sodium nitrate imported from Chile while maintaining it on ammonium sulphate. However, in the view of the working party, Chile could have reasonably assumed that the subsidy would be maintained on both products as long as there was a domestic shortage of them in Australia. See also *non-violation*.

Doha Development Agenda: the sum of the issues arising from the *Doha Ministerial Conference* which launched a new round of *multilateral trade negotiations* on 13 November 2001. Development objectives are prominent in the Doha Ministerial Declaration. Developed countries have also committed themselves to assist developing countries with *capacity-building* initiatives.

Doha Development Agenda Global Trust Fund: a fund established in March 2002 by WTO members to provide technical assistance to developing countries and to assist them with capacity-building efforts. See also *Integrated Framework for Trade-Related Assistance to Least Developed Countries*.

Doha Ministerial Conference: the *WTO Ministerial Conference* held in Doha, Qatar, from 9 to 13 November 2001. It resulted in the Doha Ministerial Declaration which launched the first round of multilateral trade negotiations under the auspices of the WTO. This is now known as the *Doha Development Agenda*. The negotiations were to have been completed by 1 January 2005. They were suspended in July 2006. Main areas for negotiations are *implementation* issues, agriculture, services, market access for non-agricultural products, WTO rules on anti-dumping and subsidies, and the creation of a multilateral system of *geographical indications*. The mandate also entailed exploratory work on *trade and investment*, *trade and competition policy*, *transparency in government procurement*, *trade facilitation* and *trade and environment*, especially the relationship between existing WTO rules and specific trade obligations set out in *multilateral environment agreements*. Trade facilitation became part of the negotiations in 2004 through the *July package*. The fifth WTO Ministerial Conference, held in 2003 in Cancún, was meant to decide on negotiations in these areas, but it ended without agreement on them. Separately, the WTO *Committee on Trade and Environment* will examine the effect of environmental measures on market access for goods and services, provisions in the *Agreement on Trade-Related Aspects of Intellectual Property Rights* relevant to trade and environment, and labelling requirements for environmental purposes. The Cancún Conference also was meant to decide whether negotiations on these three issues were desirable, but this again ended in disagreement. Other subjects listed for examination or review and possible future negotiations are electronic commerce, small economies, trade, debt and finance, trade and transfer of technology, technical cooperation and *capacity building*, *least developed countries* and *special and differential treatment*. The Doha conference also issued a *Decision on Implementation-related Issues and Concerns* and a *Declaration on the TRIPS Agreement and Public Health*.

Doha Ministerial Declaration: see *Doha Ministerial Conference*.

Doha Round: an unofficial name for the multilateral trade negotiations launched at Doha, Qatar, on 14 November 2001. See *Doha Development Agenda* and *Doha Ministerial Conference*.

Domestically prohibited goods: see *export of domestically prohibited goods*.

Domestic content requirements: see *local content requirements*.

Domestic exports: goods for export that are wholly or mainly of domestic origin, either because they have been grown or manufactured there, or because that is where they have undergone *substantial transformation*. See also *re-exports*.

Domestic International Sales Corporation: a corporate structure used in the United States until 1984, generally known as DISC. The principal benefit conferred by it was permission to defer payment of federal taxes on income from export profits until these had been distributed to their shareholders. DISCs covered mainly goods trade. In services, they were more or less confined to activities related to construction. In 1973, the *European Economic Community* notified the GATT of a dispute over the alleged subsidies DISCs enjoyed in steel exports. The *panel* found against the United States which then launched a retaliatory action on certain types of tax treatment available in the European Economic Community. The dispute was finally settled in 1982. In 1984, the DISC legislation was replaced by the *Foreign Sales Corporation* (FSC) program, thought to be more in keeping with the GATT rules. A WTO panel then found that some aspects of it too were against the WTO rules.

Domestic support: another term for *assistance*, *internal support* or *subsidy*. In agriculture, any domestic subsidy or other measure which acts to maintain producer prices at levels above those prevailing in international trade. It also refers to *direct payments* to producers, including *deficiency payments*, and input and marketing cost reduction measures available only for agricultural production. See also *Agreement on Agriculture* and *Agreement on Subsidies and Countervailing Measures*.

Dominant supplier provision: a provision in the United States *Trade Expansion Act* of 1962 which permitted a reduction to zero in the tariff of any category of products in which the United States and the *European Economic Community* together had 80% or more of the global market. See also *zero-for-zero tariff reductions*.

Domino theory of regionalism: proposed by Richard Baldwin. He said that the growing interest in the early 1990s in a United States-Mexico *free-trade agreement* and the *European Community*'s *Single Market* was not due to dissatisfaction with the slow progress in the *Uruguay Round* as some claimed. Rather, in his view, it was due to fears by countries outside these arrangements that they would be disadvantaged once the arrangements were in force. These fears would then prompt them to seek membership also. Baldwin says that in any country the political equilibrium determines the country's stance on regional liberalization. If enough exporters feel they are threatened by an emerging free-trade arrangement, they can bring about a change in the country's policy towards that arrangement. The expanding membership of the arrangement so prompted would then induce yet others to seek membership also because they in turn might now be harmed or at least feel disadvantaged as non-members. [Baldwin 1993]

Donor countries: a term used to describe the countries maintaining a *GSP* scheme. See also *beneficiary countries*.

Double écart **formula:** a formula for linear tariff negotiations proposed by the *European Economic Community* (EEC) during the *Kennedy Round*. It was based on the identification of significant disparities in the tariff rates of the major participants, particularly the EEC, Japan, the United Kingdom and the United States. Under this formula, tariff rates would have been considered disparate if there was a ratio greater than 2 : 1 between the rates compared. It would only have applied if the difference was at least 10 percentage points *ad valorem*. See also *ad valorem tariffs*, *écrêtement*, *tariff negotiations* and *thirty-ten formula*.

Double pricing: the practice of ensuring that domestic processors and manufacturers can purchase raw materials at a lower price than they are sold in export markets. This aim may be achieved through *export quotas*, *export tariffs* and other measures with a similar aim.

Double transformation: occurs when a good undergoes two *substantial transformations* in succession. Examples would be the transformation of bauxite into alumina, followed by the transformation of alumina into aluminium, or the spinning of raw fibres into yarn, followed by weaving yarn into a fabric. See also *triple transformation*.

Double-zero reductions: the same as *zero-for-zero tariff reductions*.

Downpayment: an initial conditional offer of tariff reductions, an undertaking to follow an agreed negotiating plan or another stratagem demonstrating a serious interest in the outcome of proposed negotiations. In *APEC*, an initial instalment on the longer-term commitment to free and open trade and investment as shown in an *APEC individual action plan*. This was agreed as part of the November 1995 *Osaka Action Agenda*.

Downstream dumping: a name given to the practice of selling a component of a product at less than full cost to a home country producer. This producer then transforms the component or incorporates it in another product, thereby gaining a price advantage on export markets. See also *anti-dumping measures* and *dumping*.

Downstream flexibility: a provision in the WTO *Agreement on Agriculture* which permitted WTO members to exceed their commitments on *export subsidies* in any of the second to fifth year the *implementation period* provided, *inter alia*, that the excess in any year was no greater than 3% of the annual outlay and that the cumulative outlay over the implementation period was no greater than under conditions with full compliance.

Dracula effect: explained by Jagdish Bhagwati as "exposing evil to sunlight helps to destroy it". See also *notification*, *surveillance* and *transparency*. [Bhagwati 1988]

Draft Act on the Protection of Geographical Indications: prepared by the *WIPO* Secretariat to assist countries intending to introduce a law to register and protect *geographical indications* and to provide remedies for infringement. It uses the definition given in Article 22.1 of the WTO *Agreement on Trade-Related*

Aspects of Intellectual Property Rights, i.e. that "a geographical indication means an indication which identifies a good as originating in the territory of a country, or a region or locality in that territory, where a given quality, reputation or other characteristic of the good is essentially attributable to its geographical origin". [www.wipo.org]

Draft International Agreement on Illicit Payments: an instrument produced under *ECOSOC* auspices in 1979, but not adopted by the *United Nations General Assembly*. It would have made punishable by criminal penalties under national laws (a) the bribing of any public official to influence his actions in connection with an international commercial transaction, and (b) asking for a bribe by any public official for the same purpose. The Agreement would have required each party to it to establish a system of appropriate criminal penalties. See also *Convention on Combating Bribery of Foreign Public Officials in International Business Transactions*, *trade and illicit payments* and *United Nations Convention Against Corruption*.

Draft International Antitrust Code: produced in 1993 by the International Antitrust Code Working Group, also called the Munich Group, consisting of twelve scholars. Four principles governed the approach of the Working Group: (a) national laws should be used to deal with international competition issues, (b) national treatment should be accorded to any party, (c) there should be recognized minimum standards for national antitrust rules, and (d) an International Antitrust Authority should be established. The Working Group also proposed that the Draft Code should be developed into a *plurilateral agreement* under the WTO. The Draft Code has not attracted sufficient international support for any kind of intergovernmental consideration. See also *antitrust laws*, *competition policy* and *trade and competition*. [Fikentscher and Immenga 1995]

Draft International Code of Conduct on the Transfer of Technology: an instrument under negotiation in *UNCTAD* between 1976 and 1985. The aim of the Draft Code is to establish general and equitable standards for the conduct of parties engaged in the *transfer of technology*. Substantial differences remained when negotiations were suspended. There are no current plans to resume discussions. See also *trade and transfer of technology*.

Draft United Nations Code of Conduct on Transnational Corporations: a proposed multilateral instrument aimed at guiding the behaviour of *transnational corporations* in countries other than their home country. Work on it began in the late 1970s. The latest version of the Draft Code is that of 1990. Much detailed drafting has been done, but substantial differences remain among negotiators, including the extent to which the Draft Code should be mandatory.

Drawback: the practice of refunding customs, sales and excise duties on goods imported and then re-exported either in processed form or after having been incorporated in other products. See also *border tax adjustments*, *duty deferral program* and *maquiladora*.

Droit de suite: an inalienable right, expressed in Article 14ter of the *Berne Convention*, of the author of a work of fine art to a royalty on the resale of the work after its first sale by the author. It is an aspect of the rules governing *copyright*. In the *European Community*, for example, the resale right applies to sales involving market professionals such as art dealers, art galleries and show-rooms. It covers works of graphic or plastic art, but not original manuscripts of writers or composers. The royalty is paid by the seller according to a fixed scale. Other jurisdictions also have laws concerning *droit de suite*. See also *moral rights*. [Berne Convention on the Protection of Literary and Artistic Works; European Community Directive 2001/84/EC]

DSB: the *Dispute Settlement Body*, i.e. the WTO *General Council* meeting to settle trade disputes.

DSU: Dispute Settlement Understanding. The Uruguay Round *Understanding on Rules and Procedures Governing the Settlement of Disputes*.

Dual pricing: the practice by countries of maintaining different prices for a product, depending on whether it is sold on domestic or export markets. It is also called *double pricing*.

Dual purpose exports: trade in goods, services and technologies suitable for civil-ian and military use. There can be disagreements over the extent to which prod-ucts clearly made for civilian mass markets, such as advanced personal comput-ers, can be applied to military purposes. Much depends on one's perception of the strategic balance at the time of the proposed sale. See also *COCOM*, *strate-gic exports* and *Wassenaar Arrangement on Export Controls for Conventional Arms and Dual-Use Goods and Technologies*.

Dual-use products: goods or services which may be applied to more than one purpose. An example from the negotiations towards the *Information Technology Agreement* may illustrate the point. Some said that a certain type of glue was only used in the production of motherboards, etc., and should be considered a relevant product, but others said glue was a chemical substance and therefore not an information technology product. The question of dual-use products often arises in *sectoral trade negotiations*.

Due restraint provision: see *peace clause*.

Dumped imports: in its strict meaning this refers to imported goods meeting the conditions for a finding of *dumping* as set out in Article VI of the *GATT* and the *Anti-Dumping Agreement*. The expression is often used loosely, however, to describe imported goods exerting downward pressure on the prices of similar goods produced locally, even if there is no indication of dumping.

Dumping: occurs when goods are exported at a price less than their normal value, generally meaning they are exported for less than they are sold in the domestic market or third-country markets, or at less than production cost. GATT Article VI, which deals with anti-dumping and countervailing duties, does not prohibit dumping. It merely says that GATT *contracting parties* recognize that dumping is to be condemned if it causes or threatens *material injury* to an established industry or retards the establishment of a domestic industry in the territory of another member. If enquiries in the importing country show that dumping is taking place and causing material injury to an industry, governments may take *anti-dumping measures*. The basis of comparison is usually the ex-factory price in the exporting country and the transaction price of the goods at the border of the importing country, less transport and other costs incurred after the good has left the factory. It appears, however, that some equate sales below the domestic price with sales below cost. This interpretation is strictly speaking incorrect. Dumping has on occasion been confused with the import of products benefiting from the payment of *subsidies*. In *trade policy*, dumping refers to the conduct of individual firms that see some advantage in discriminatory pricing arrangements and that finance these from their own resources. Subsidies, on the other hand, are paid, directly or indirectly, to industries by governments. The effect of subsidized and dumped products on the importing market can of course be the same. Commentators are wont to point out that the apparently simple concept of dumping has led to innumerable disputes over its occurrence and the appropriate remedy. A demonstration that dumping has occurred often depends on very detailed cost calculations. It may be difficult to allocate costs accurately even in cases where the accounting is exceedingly precise. Often, assumptions have to be made on how a cost is to be treated. A simple comparison between the two prices may be impossible when the pricing and accounting mechanism of a firm is so opaque as to prevent any meaningful insight into its cost structure. At other times, comparisons may be inappropriate because the exported product is not sold on the home market at all or only in small quantities. Dumping as a perceived trade problem has been around for a long time, but it only turned into a major trade policy issue after World War I and particularly during the Great Depression of the 1930s. In the United States anti-dumping laws and *antitrust* laws appear to have originated in a perception that certain commercial practices were directly opposed to the public interest. Antitrust laws were enacted to deal with anti-competitive practices of domestic firms. Anti-dumping laws, on the other hand, were aimed at perceived anti-competitive practices of foreign firms which manifested themselves through sales that undercut domestic firms. In time perceptions of the causes of dumping and its effect on domestic markets, as well as the correct remedies, diverged markedly from the antitrust policies. Much effort has gone into investigations of the reasons for dumping. Three examples of motivational classifications will suffice. In 1923 Jacob Viner devised a classification according to motive and to continuity in his *Dumping: A Problem in International Trade*. First, *sporadic dumping* disposes of surplus stocks and is unintentional. At any rate, most businesses would use it at some time. Second, *short-run or intermittent dumping* arises when a firm is meeting temporary low prices in existing markets, is attempting to develop new markets, forestalls competition and retaliates against dumping in the reverse direction. Third, *long-run or continuous dumping* occurs when firms maintain full production without cutting domestic prices, when they wish to obtain economies of larger-scale production without cutting domestic prices, and when they do it for purely mercantilist reasons. Greg Mastel divides motivations for dumping into *overcapacity dumping* (prevalent in industries that face longer-term reduced demand), *government-supported dumping* (firms are able to take advantage of below-cost inputs supported by governments), *tactical dumping and discriminatory pricing* (selling the same product in different markets at different prices, partly in order to meet the competition) and *predatory dumping* (undercutting the competition in order to drive it out of business). Robert Willig has devised one of the most useful approaches to the analysis of dumping, particularly because it provides some useful insights into the motivations for dumping, though his approach does not enjoy wholehearted support from the trade policy community. He divides the activity into non-monopolizing and monopolizing dumping. Non-monopolizing dumping includes *market-expansion dumping* (higher net prices in the home market support lower prices in the export market), *cyclical dumping* (aimed at eliminating substantial excess production to a down-turn in demand) and *state-trading dumping* (practiced particularly by economies in which exchange rates may be fixed at levels unrelated to the market, the dominant aim is to obtain hard currency, or price signals do not matter). Monopolizing dumping includes *strategic dumping* (injury caused in the importing market through an overall strategy or general anti-competitive circumstances prevailing in the exporting country) and *predatory-pricing dumping* (exporting at low prices aimed driving rivals out of business to achieve monopoly power in the importing country). At the time of the negotiations leading to the **Havana Charter**, participants identified four categories of dumping: (a) **price dumping** for which the rules ultimately appearing in GATT Article VI were made; (b) **service dumping**, where a price advantage for a product comes about because dumping occurs in the provision of shipping services; (c) **exchange dumping**, based on manipulation of the exchange rate to achieve a competitive edge; and (d) **social dumping**, caused by the import at low prices of goods made by prison or sweated labour. No rules were made for latter three categories. For the trade policy community today, the main sub-categories of dumping are (a) **hidden dumping**, defined in an **ad note** to GATT Article VI as the sale by an importer at a price below that corresponding to the price invoiced by an exporter with whom the importer is associated, and also below the price in the exporting country, i.e. dumping is achieved through transfer pricing; (b) **indirect dumping,** where a product is imported via a third country where it would not be considered as having been dumped; and (c) **secondary dumping** which is the export of a product containing components imported at what would normally be considered dumped prices. Sometimes, a firm may be able to sell at a higher price abroad, a condition called *reverse dumping*. Few other trade policy topics are surrounded as much by emotion as they are by rational analysis. The literature on this subject is accordingly voluminous. A few examples of thoughtful analysis must suffice. K W Dam has drawn attention to an apparent contradiction in the dumping concept. He says that according to the rules, local firms suffer injury whenever the import price is the same or lower than the price they charge. Yet, he says, the injury is no greater when dumping is present than when the import price merely reflects the comparative advantage of the exporter. Professor Deardorff has pointed to the close connection between dumping and the degree of competition in the home market. He notes that if both the market and the firm are protected, they will almost certainly have to resort to selling at less than the domestic price if they are to make any export sales at all. Gabrielle Marceau sums it up well when she says that the origin of dumping remains the existence of different national economic and legal policies between two national markets. She adds that national differences are normal and reasonable unless internationally agreed standards exist. See also *anti-circumvention*, *Anti-Dumping Agreement*, *circumvention*, *competition policy and anti-dumping measures*, *de minimis dumping margins* and *persistent dumping clause*. [Dam 1970, Deardorff 1990, Marceau 1994, Mastel 1996, Russell 1999, Viner 1923, Willig 1998]

Dunkel Draft: the Draft Final Act embodying the results of the *Uruguay Round* negotiations which was issued by Arthur Dunkel, then Director-General of the *GATT*, in December 1991. As it happened, negotiations continued for another two years, especially over agriculture, but much of the Dunkel Draft was eventually adopted with minor revisions only.

Dutiable goods: goods subject to *customs duties* on entering or leaving a *customs territory*.

Duties and other regulations of commerce: an expression occurring in Article XXIV of the *GATT* which governs the formation of *free-trade areas* and *customs unions*. The expression is not defined further. Article XXIV requires in both cases that duties and other regulations of commerce applicable to third parties must not be higher after the formation of the arrangement than they were before.

Duties and other restrictive regulations of commerce: an expression occurring in Article XXIV of the *GATT* which governs the formation of *free-trade areas* and *customs unions*. Parties to such arrangements must eliminate duties and restrictive regulations of commerce on substantially all the trade between them. The expression is not defined further, except that, where necessary, measures permitted under Article XI (General Elimination of Quantitative Restrictions), Article XII (Restrictions to Safeguard the Balance of Payments), Article XIII (Non-discriminatory Administration of Quantitative Restrictions), Article XIV (Exceptions to the Rule of Non-discrimination), Article XV (Exchange Arrangements) and Article XX (General Exceptions) may still be maintained. See also *substantially-all-trade criterion*.

Duty: a levy, tax or impost charged by governments within their entire jurisdiction on production, transactions and, less frequently, the ownership of an asset. The amount of duty levied is usually related to the value of the transaction. *Customs duties*, consisting of import and export tariffs, are such charges. They are levied at the border. A WTO requirement is that duties must not be used to discriminate against imported products once they have passed legally through the border. Whatever clear distinction there may have been once between a duty and a tax has now become blurred in day-to-day use. To the economist, their impact is the same, but for the lawyer and the tax administrator the distinction may be important. See also *Lerner's symmetry theory*.

Duty absorption: occurs when a producer or exporter who is faced with *anti-dumping duties*, decides to adjust the price of the good so as to make sure that its cost in the importing market changes little. See also *absorption* and *anti-absorption*.

Duty deferral program: a mechanism which exempts an importer from paying customs duties on products that are re-exported or used in the production of an article to be re-exported as was the case, for example, under the *maquiladora* system. See also *drawback*.

Duty drawback: see *border tax adjustment*.

Duty evasion: the attempt to paying the due duty to the customs authorities. Common means for this are *under-invoicing* and *smuggling* as well as seeking to import a good under a tariff classification mandating a lower tariff.

Dynamic comparative advantage: see *comparative advantage*.

E

EAEC: East Asia Economic Caucus. A consultative group proposed in the early 1990s by Malaysia which, if implemented, would consist of East Asian countries. See also *ASEAN+3*.

EALAF: East Asia-Latin America Forum. Now replaced by the *Forum for East Asia-Latin America Cooperation*.

E-APEC strategy: a framework aimed at creating a digital society adopted in 2001 at the Shanghai *Economic Leaders' Meeting*. Its three pillars are: (a) to create an environment for strengthening market structures and institutions, (b) to facilitate an environment for infrastructure investment, and (c) to enhance human capacity building and promote entrepreneurship.

Early harvest: agreement among negotiating partners that some of their targets could or should be reached and implemented without waiting for the formal end to the negotiations. The *Doha Ministerial Declaration*, for example, states that ". . . agreements reached at an early stage [of the negotiations launched by the Declaration] may be implemented on a provisional or a definitive basis". An example of an early harvest in the *Uruguay Round* was the creation of the *Trade Policy Review Mechanism*. See also *single undertaking*.

Early Voluntary Sectoral Liberalization: EVSL. A program for tariff liberalization initiated at the November 1996 *APEC Economic Leaders' Meeting*. Nine sectors were selected for implementation in 1999: environmental goods and services, energy sector, fish and fish products, toys, forest products, gems and jewellery, medical equipment and instruments, chemicals and a telecommunications mutual recognition arrangement. More preparatory work was to be done on the remaining six sectors: environmental goods and services, natural and synthetic rubber, fertilizers, automotive, oilseeds and oilseed products, and civil aircraft. The program covered tariff and non-tariff measures as well as elements of trade facilitation and economic and technical cooperation. In November 1998 the initiative was converted into **accelerated tariff liberalization** and forwarded to the WTO for further work. See also *individual action plans*. [Okamoto 2004]

Earth Summit: the United Nations Conference on Environment and Development. See *UNCED*.

East African Community: EAC. Established on 15 January 2001 as the successor to the East African Cooperation. It consists of Kenya, Tanzania and Uganda. EAC's objectives are to widen and deepen cooperation among its member states in political, economic, social and cultural fields, research and technology, defence, security, and legal and judicial affairs. Members established a *customs* *union* on 16 February 2004. This is to be followed a *common market*, to be followed by a monetary union and ultimately a Political Federation of the East African States. Its secretariat is in Arusha, Tanzania.

East African Cooperation: see *East African Community*.

East African Development Bank: a regional development bank located in Kampala. It was established in 1967. Its members are Kenya, Tanzania and Uganda.

East ASEAN Growth Area: see *BIMP-EAGA*.

East Asia Free-Trade Agreement: EAFTA. Several versions exist of a possible EAFTA. The two main proposals are the *ASEAN+3 free-trade agreement* and the *ASEAN+6 free-trade agreement*. Preparatory work for both of them was initiated in 2006. See also *ASEAN+3* and *North East Asia Free-Trade Area*.

East Asia Economic Caucus: see *EAEC*.

East Asian Community: also East Asia Community. This refers to various proposals, such as that of the *East Asia Vision Group* in 2001, for the creation of a regional grouping with political, economic, social and cultural aims. Both the coverage and the membership of the proposed Community remain to be defined. One suggestion is that it should consist of *ASEAN+3*, but others have proposed adding at least Australia and New Zealand. See also *East Asia Summit*.

East Asia Summit: EAS. An annual meeting of heads of government first held in Kuala Lumpur on 14 December 2005. Participants are the *ASEAN* countries, China, Japan, Republic of Korea, India, Australia and New Zealand. Some refer to the EAS as ASEAN+6.

East Asia Vision Group: a group established in 1999 which consists of two academics nominated by each of the members of the *ASEAN+3* countries. Its mandate is to examine ways to promote regional cooperation.

East Caribbean Common Market: see *Organization of Eastern Caribbean States*.

East-South trade: described trade between the *Comecon* members and developing countries. The term is now obsolete in that meaning.

East-West trade: described trade between the *OECD* countries and the *Comecon* countries. Such trading posed special problems arising largely from the non-convertibility of the currencies of Comecon countries and the *transfer of technology*. The term is now obsolete in its original meaning, but some continue to use it for trade between Eastern and Western Europe. See also *dual purpose exports*.

EBA: *Everything But Arms*. The *European Union* initiative giving tariff-free access to all products from *least developed countries* except arms.

EC: European Communities. The official name of the *European Union* in the WTO. See also *common commercial policy* and *European Community*.

ECAFE: Economic Commission for Asia and the Far East. One of the original *United Nations regional economic commissions*. It was succeeded in 1974 by *ESCAP* (Economic and Social Commission for the Asia-Pacific).

ECDC: Economic Cooperation between Developing Countries. A mechanism operating mainly within the United Nations system designed to promote the economic advancement of developing countries through cooperative activities. See also *Committee on Trade and Development* and *GSTP*.

ECLA: Economic Commission for Latin America, superseded in 1985 by the *Economic Commission for Latin America and the Caribbean*.

ECLAC: see *Economic Commission for Latin America and the Caribbean*.

Eclectic theory of international investment: a theory of *foreign direct investment* that assumes that investment decisions are driven by the identification of ownership, location and internalization advantages, and these three components are viewed as interacting. First, direct investment gives the investor control over the asset. Second, it allows the investor to choose the location of a production facility that fits in best with the company's aims. Third, foreign direct investment allows the investor company to utilize its existing intellectual capital in the best way.

Eco-dumping: used in common parlance for the production of goods for export under lax environmental conditions. The term does not have proper standing in trade policy formulation. The practice is assumed to give producers a cost advantage in export markets where more stringent conditions apply. It appears, however, that production costs that can be ascribed to environmental regulations are a much smaller factor in total costs than other production costs. Generally, it is likely that they account for no more than 2% of total production cost. See also *eco-duties* and *trade and environment*.

Eco-duties: proposed levies on imported products to compensate for a perceived unfair competitive advantage arising to producers operating under less stringent, and therefore less expensive, environmental standards for industry. This is a contentious concept which, if implemented, could be misused as a protectionist device. See also *eco-dumping* and *trade and environment*.

Eco-labelling: a voluntary market mechanism designed to encourage industry to produce goods which have a reduced environmental impact and to encourage consumers to buy them in preference to others. A trade concern about eco-labelling schemes is that they can include production-related criteria discriminating against imports which only reflect the environmental preferences of the importing country. See also *eco-duties*, *genetic labelling*, *social labelling* and *trade and environment*.

Economic and Social Commission for the Asia-Pacific: see *ESCAP*.

Economic and Social Commission for Western Asia: ESCWA. Originally established in 1973 as the Economic Commission for Western Asia (ECWA) and given its present name in 1985. It is one of the *United Nations regional economic commissions*. It seeks to improve the economic well-being of its member states and their economic relations with each other. Its secretariat is located in Amman.

Economic and Social Council: a body established under the Charter of the *United Nations*. It is widely known as *ECOSOC*. It oversees broadly the trade and economic work of the various United Nations bodies, but it has no rule-making function.

Economic Commission for Africa: ECA. One of the *United Nations regional economic commissions*. Established in 1958. It seeks to promote economic advances in African countries. Its secretariat is located in Addis Ababa.

Economic Commission for Europe: UN-ECE. One of the *United Nations regional economic commissions*. Established in 1947. It has done much useful work particularly in the area of standards affecting international trade and in *trade facilitation* more generally. Its secretariat is located in Geneva. See also *EDIFACT*.

Economic Commission for Latin America and the Caribbean: ECLAC. One of the *United Nations regional economic commissions*. It was established in 1948 as the Economic Commission for Latin America (ECLA) and given its current name in 1985. It aims to promote economic progress in Latin American countries. Its secretariat is located in Rio de Janeiro.

Economic Commission for Western Asia: see *Economic and Social Commission for Western Asia*.

Economic Community of Central African States: see *African regional integration arrangements*.

Economic Community of the Great Lakes: see *Communauté Economique des Pays des Grands Lacs*.

Economic-complementarity agreements: another name for *partial-scope trade agreements* and *sectoral free-trade areas* sometimes negotiated by developing countries under the *Enabling Clause*.

Economic cooperation agreement: a bilateral or plurilateral agreement to promote deeper economic cooperation between the partners. Such agreements do not follow a set pattern, but usually they do not contain *market access* provisions. Other names used for this type of instrument include *economic framework agreement*, *trade and economic agreement* and *trade and investment framework* (or *facilitation*) *agreement*.

Economic Cooperation Area of Black Sea Countries: see *Black Sea Economic Cooperation Organization*.

Economic Cooperation between Developing Countries: see *ECDC*.

Economic Cooperation Organization: ECO. Established in 1985 to promote the economic development of its members, at that time Iran, Pakistan and Turkey. Since 1992 the members of ECO have been Afghanistan, Azerbaijan, Iran, Kazakhstan, Kyrgyz Republic, Pakistan, Tajikistan, Turkey, Turkmenistan and Uzbekistan. ECO's broad objectives were redefined in the Treaty of Izmir of 14 September 1996. Trade and customs, transport and communications and money and finance form major parts of its work program. The ECO secretariat is located in Teheran. [www.ecosecretariat.org]

Economic framework agreement: a treaty between two or more parties setting out basic rules for the conduct of economic relations between them. Provisions included in such agreements do not follow set patterns. At a minimum, they usually contain elements of *trade facilitation*. They also provide for *non-discrimination* between the parties. Depending on the level of obligations, there may also be

143

a mechanism for consultation and dispute settlement. Among other names for this type of agreement are *economic partnership agreement*, *trade and economic agreement*, *trade and investment framework agreement* and *trade and investment facilitation agreement*.

Economic impact criterion: a test sometimes suggested for use in the *GATT* to assess whether a domestic measure is impairing *national treatment*. Under this criterion, the proof for a finding that the national treatment obligation had been breached would have to be found in changing trade flows. Finding the proof might pose many practical difficulties because there may be other reasons why a country's imports of a product might have changed. GATT dispute settlement panels have rejected the use of this criterion in favour of a test assessing whether there is *equality of competitive opportunity*.

Economic integration: all economies, even those given to practising *autarky*, are to some extent integrated with others, but the term is usually reserved for groups of economies that are manifestly combining their activities more quickly among themselves than with others. It is usual to distinguish between *market-led integration* (spontaneous integration without the formal involvement of governments) and *policy-led integration* (integration through intergovernmental frameworks). Another distinction is that between *shallow integration* and *deep integration*. The former is confined, for example, to the formation of a *free-trade area* in which each member retains autonomy in economic policies. The latter implies cooperation or harmonization of matters such as *competition laws*, monetary and financial policies, standards and other regulations, etc., as would be the case in a *common market*. See also *globalization* and *internationalization*.

Economic integration agreements: used in Article V of the *General Agreement on Trade in Services* to cover free-trade arrangements in services. This term was chosen because free trade in services requires the possibility of *commercial presence* in the importing country as well as the free movement of consumers and producers of services. This is seen as involving a greater degree of economic integration than might occur under conditions of free trade in goods. Economic integration agreements must have *substantial sectoral coverage* and provide for the absence or elimination of substantially all discrimination between its members to conform to WTO rules. See also *free-trade areas* and *trade in services*.

Economic international commodity agreements: these are *international commodity agreements* that seek to influence the price of the commodity through *buffer stocks*, *export quotas* and other measures manipulating the amounts reaching the market. See also *administrative international commodity agreements*.

Economic nationalism: the view that economic advances can only be achieved at the expense of other participants in the international economy. See also *autarky*, *beggar-thy-neighbour policies*, *mercantilism* and *zero-sum nationalism*.

Economic needs test: a mechanism controlled by government, industry or professional associations to decide whether the entry into the market of new foreign, and sometimes domestic, firms is warranted on economic grounds. Such mechanisms are often opaque. They may be discretionary and protectionist. Sometimes economic needs tests purport to protect the interests of consumers, but these are not always asked for their views on additional competition in the market. Article XVI of the *General Agreement on Trade in Services* setting out *market access* rules proscribes the use of economic needs tests.

Economic partnership agreement: EPA. A bilateral or plurilateral agreement. The content of such agreements varies greatly. Some merely promote voluntary economic cooperation between the partners. Others are proper *free-trade agreements*. Japan, for example, tends to refer to its free-trade agreements as EPAs. The *ACP-EC Partnership Agreement*, an *asymmetrical trade agreement*, provides for the negotiation of economic partnership agreements with *ACP* regions compatible with the WTO rules. These are expected to enter into force by 1 January 2008 at the latest. See also *economic cooperation agreement* and *trade and economic agreement* for other instruments of this type.

Economic regulation: see *regulation*.

Economic sanctions: economic and commercial measures sometimes taken by governments to achieve their foreign policy objectives. These measures include *trade embargoes*, investment restrictions or prohibitions, travel restrictions, etc. Most commonly such measures are taken in the pursuit of *United Nations economic sanctions*. In their analysis of economic sanctions imposed over a long period, Hufbauer and his colleagues have concluded that is not true to say that sanctions "never work" *(Economic Sanctions Reconsidered: History and Current Policy)*. Rather, they consider that sanctions are of limited utility in achieving foreign policy goals that depend on compelling the target country to take actions it is determined to resist. Nevertheless, they consider that in the case of small target countries and comparatively modest policy goals, sanctions have brought about changes in behaviour. See also *security exceptions* and *retaliation*.
[Hufbauer, Schott and Elliott 1990]

Economic summits: see *G8*.

Economic union: any group of countries with a *common market* for goods and services, free movement capital and labour amongst themselves and operating a mechanism for harmonizing financial and monetary policies.

Economic unity theory: an element of the *competition policy* of the *European Community*. It holds that for the purposes of an *antitrust* action under Community law against a subsidiary of a company located within the Community, the two are considered a single economic unity. In other words, the parent company is deemed itself to be involved.

Economies in transition: economies making the transformation from *centrally-planned economies* to *market economies*. Sometimes, the expression is used also for developing countries that have embarked upon substantial economic *deregulation*. The *Transition Report*, published annually by the European Bank for Reconstruction and Development (EBRD), contains detailed information on the economic performance of transition economies.

Economy: the formal name of the members of *APEC*.

Eco-packaging: the use of packaging materials that have the smallest impact on the environment, either because their production is environmentally friendly or because they can easily be re-used or recycled. Insistence on certain types of non-standard eco-packaging could result in protectionist effects if the supplying country cannot meet the required standards. See also *trade and environment*.

Eco-protectionism: measures aimed protecting local industries under the guise of protecting the environment. See also *trade and environment* and *trade and labour standards*.

ECOSOC: United Nations Economic and Social Council. It has 54 members of the United Nations who are elected by the United Nations General Assembly for a three-year term. Representation on ECOSOC is based on an agreed geographical distribution. Its annual high-level sessions of WTO, *World Bank* and *IMF* heads are considered to be helpful in promoting coherence of economic policy between countries. See also *ECOSOC and the GATT* and *Draft International Agreement on Illicit Payments*.

ECOSOC and the GATT: the Charter of the *United Nations* gave *ECOSOC* a range of responsibilities in international economic and social cooperation, including the ability to call international conferences on matters falling within its competence. The United States, the main power in the immediate post-war years promoting multilateral trade agreements, accordingly proposed that ECOSOC should convene what became the *United Nations Conference on Trade and Employment*. The United States distinguished, however, between the aims of establishing an international trade organization and the negotiation of a multilateral tariff agreement. This was because it derived its mandate for negotiating the tariff agreement from the *Reciprocal Trade Agreements Act* of 1934 which did not envisage the establishment of any permanent institution to oversee international trade. Once ECOSOC had passed the resolution calling for a conference, it effectively was given no further role in the negotiations. From its inception, the GATT therefore was virtually independent of the United Nations system. This principle has been carried forward into the WTO. Of course, the WTO has a close working relationship with many United Nations bodies. See also *United States Reciprocal Trade Agreements Program*.

Eco-standards: product, production or consumption standards imposed to reduce or eliminate damage to the environment. See also *technical barriers to trade* and *trade and environment*.

ECOTECH: economic and technical cooperation among *APEC* members. The ECOTECH goals, as agreed in 1996, are (a) attain sustainable growth and equitable development in the Asia-Pacific region, (b) reduce economic disparities among APEC economies, (c) improve the economic and social well-being of the people, and (d) deepen the spirit of community in the Asia-Pacific.

ECOWAS: Economic Community of West African States. Established in 1975. It consists of the members of the then West African Economic Community (Benin, Burkina Faso, Côte d'Ivoire, Mali, Mauritania, Niger and Senegal), the members of the *Mano River Union* (Guinea, Liberia and Sierra Leone), and Cape Verde, The Gambia, Ghana, Guinea-Bissau, Nigeria and Togo. Mauritania withdrew on 31 December 2000. The original ECOWAS was only partly successful in achieving its trade liberalization aims. It was relaunched in 1993 with a program for free trade in all unprocessed products and progressive liberalization of trade in industrial products. Members are also working towards the creation of a *customs union* and ultimately a common market and an economic union. A program is also under way for the free movement of persons throughout ECOWAS. Its secretariat is located in Lagos. See also *African regional integration arrangements*. [www.sec.ecowas.int]

Ecrêtement: *Fr.* removing the peaks. A proposal for tariff harmonization through targeted reductions made early in the *Kennedy Round* (1963–67) by the *European Economic Community* (EEC). The proposal stemmed from an EEC view that its own tariffs were mostly in the 10% to 20% range, whereas the United States tariffs in many cases ranged from 30% to 50%, with some going up to 100%. The EEC therefore proposed lowering tariffs by half to target levels of 10% for manufactures, 5% for semi-manufactures and zero for raw materials. The proposal was not acceptable to the United States because it would have forced it to accept much larger tariff cuts in the face of an EEC unwillingness to do something on agriculture. See also *double écart formula* and *thirty-ten formula*.

EC wine labelling regulation: this regulation aims to give consumers more comprehensive information about the product they are buying and at harmonizing different approaches to labelling across the *European Union*. For example, labels have to show information such as the sales designation, volume, alcoholic strength of the wine, the lot number and the name of the bottler or importer. Certain bottle shapes identified with a particular wine or wine region are protected. Some optional terms, such as production methods, *traditional expressions* (described as having three characteristics: a legislative, simple and precise definition, a traditional use on the European Union market, i.e. at least ten years, and a *notoriety* in the mind of the consumer resulting from that definition and traditional use), names of vineyards and the meaning of "vintage year" are also defined. The regulation also sets out labelling requirements for wines originating outside the European Union. It entered into force on 1 August 2003 and was amended on 23 February 2004. [Regulation (EC) No 753/2002]

EC-92 program: see *European Community Single Market*.

EDI: Electronic Data Interchange. The transfer of data in a standardized electronic form between companies through the use of networks such as the internet.

EDIFACT: Electronic Data Interchange for Administration, Commerce and Transport. Developed under the auspices of the United Nations *Economic Commission for Europe* (UN-ECE). It is defined officially as a "set of internationally agreed standards, directories and guidelines for the electronic interchange of structured data, and in particular that related to trade in goods and services between independent, computerized information systems".

EEP: the United States *Export Enhancement Program*. It gives American farmers export subsidies mainly to enable them to compete with subsidized agricultural exports from the *European Community* on certain export markets.

Effective market access: defined by some as the absence of domestic regulatory policies and other *structural impediments* that unintentionally limit competition or transparency. *Tariff* and *non-tariff measures* such as *subsidies* and *voluntary restraint arrangements* would be assessed separately.

Effective market presence: defined by some as the ability of foreign firms to compete in the market through investing, i.e. through enjoyment of the *right of establishment*. See also *trade and investment*.

Effective rate of assistance: ERA. Sometimes also called effective rate of protection. It is a framework for making clear the difference between the hypothetical situation of no domestic assistance to industry and the situation actually obtaining. The ERA concept is useful because it can measure government interventions such as subsidies or purchasing preferences that may influence trade flows without actually restricting flows at the border, including *tariffs* and *non-tariff measures*. It also shows the additional costs borne by consumers because of domestic assistance. The ERA does not distinguish between measures that may be considered legal or illegal under the WTO agreements. See also *nominal rate of protection* and *tariff escalation*.

Effective rate of protection: see *effective rate of assistance*.

Effects doctrine: the principle that a state may have *antitrust laws* covering *conduct* outside of its territory if such conduct has an actual or potential effect on commerce within its territory. For example, the 1986 *Third Restatement of the Foreign Relations Law of the United States* says that "any agreement in restraint of United States trade that is made outside of the United States, and any conduct or agreement in restraint of such trade that is carried out predominantly outside of the United States, are subject to the jurisdiction to prescribe of the United States, if a principal purpose of the conduct is to interfere with the commerce of the United States, and the agreement or conduct has some effect on that commerce". The effects doctrine is subject to a test of reasonableness. Other jurisdictions, including the *European Community*, apply a version of the effects doctrine. See also *competition policy*, *extraterritoriality* and *implementation doctrine*.
[American Law Institute 1986]

Efficiency-seeking investment: a term for *foreign direct investment* undertaken to supply other markets in the most competitive manner. See also *market-seeking investment*.

EFTA: European Free Trade Association. Entered into force on 3 May 1960 through the Convention of Stockholm. Founding members were Austria, Denmark, Norway, Portugal, Sweden, Switzerland and the United Kingdom. Iceland joined in 1970. Finland became a full member in 1986 after having been an associate member. Denmark and the United Kingdom left on 31 December 1972 to join the *European Economic Community*. They were followed by Portugal in 1985 and Austria, Finland and Sweden on 1 January 1995. EFTA now comprises

Iceland, Liechtenstein, Norway and Switzerland. EFTA has always had much more modest aspirations for economic integration than the European Economic Community. Nevertheless, it has provisions on *restrictive business practices* and the *right of establishment* of enterprises of member countries. Agricultural products are for the most part exempt from the provisions of the Convention. The *EFTA Convention 2001* revised the Stockholm Convention in major ways. See also *European Economic Area*.

EFTA Convention 2001: the revised *Convention Establishing the European Free Trade Association*, or *EFTA*, concluded on 21 June 2001 at Vaduz, Liechtenstein. Members are Iceland, Liechtenstein, Norway and Switzerland. It reflects progress in European economic integration since the formation of EFTA in 1960 and removes the anomalies arising from the fact that, alone of the EFTA members, Switzerland is not a member of the *European Economic Area*. Among the main changes in the EFTA framework are expanded mutual recognition of conformity assessments and broader rules on *intellectual property rights*. The Convention now contains comprehensive provisions liberalizing investment, *trade in services* and the movement of persons. Transport services remain restricted. EFTA members have opened their *government procurement* further to each other. Some slight improvements have been made to trade in agricultural goods, but this remains by far the least liberal part of the Convention.

Egregious: defined in the *Concise Oxford Dictionary* as "shocking". An adjective which, but for the efforts of United States legislators, might well be unknown among *trade policy* makers. See *Special 301* and *Super 301*.

E-IAP: the electronic version of the *individual action plans* prepared periodically by *APEC* members.

Electronic commerce: often abbreviated to e-commerce. The production, advertising, sale and distribution of products via telecommunications networks ranging from ordinary telephones to use of the internet or other large-scale electronic networks. Many definitions for this term exist. None enjoys universal support. *UNCTAD* publishes annually the *E-Commerce and Development Report* which analyzes trends in e-commerce from a development perspective. See also *EDIFACT*, *Global Trade Point Network* and *UNCITRAL model law on electronic commerce*.

Electronic Data Interchange: see *EDI*.

Embedded liberalism: a term coined by John Ruggie to describe the post-war economic liberalism which resulted in the GATT and the *Bretton Woods agreements*. The essence of economic liberalism is a multilateral economic framework subject to domestic interventionism. This would safeguard domestic stability and at the same time end discriminatory trade and exchange practices. [Ruggie 1982]

Embodied services: services embodied in a physical product, such as the intellectual component of computer software sold in the form of floppy disks or CD-ROMs. Some say that the estimated share of services in global trade statistics would double if embodied services were included in service trade statistics. This proposition may well be true, but a demonstration of it could only be achieved with great additional reporting burdens. Reporting embodied services separately would mean, for example, that iron ore exports would consist at least of a commodity component and services components involving at least prospecting, transport, marketing and management. It of course makes sense for a manufacturing firm to know what the services components of its products are worth, but it cannot sell its products separately from these. The customer therefore is charged a single unit price. See also *trade in services statistics*.

Emergency protection: see *escape clause*.

Emergency safeguard mechanism: ESM. Article X of the *General Agreement on Trade in Services* requires negotiations on the question of emergency safeguard measures based on the principle of non-discrimination. The results of these negotiations were to enter into effect by 1 January 1998, but so far it has not been possible to find much common ground either on (a) the necessity or desirability of an ESM or (b) its feasibility. Both proponents and opponents of an ESM appear to have as their starting point taken Article XIX of the *GATT* which permits the use of *safeguards* in the goods trade. Issues raised have accordingly included (a) how an import surge in a service sector would manifest itself, (b) how, in the absence of detailed *trade in services statistics*, an investigation could produce a reliable picture, and (c) what the remedy would be, bearing in mind the different *modes of services delivery* and in particular how *commercial presence* (mode 3) would be dealt with. The permitted duration of a safeguard, compensation for the affected party and possible *structural adjustment* in the relevant sector would also need to be considered. Developing countries have argued a need for an ESM for services as a political requirement for making liberalisation of services more acceptable in their economies. This of course was precisely the reason for the inclusion of the *escape clause* in agreements negotiated under the *United States reciprocal trade agreements program* and later the GATT. Developed countries have tended to view the proposed ESM as a mechanism inviting *protectionism* because its use would necessarily depend to an even greater extent on perception than is the case for trade in goods.

Emerging market economies: a term used by *UNCTAD*. It includes Argentina, Brazil, Chile, Mexico, Peru, Korea, Malaysia, Singapore, Taiwan, Thailand, Czech Republic, Hungary, Poland and the Russian Federation. [Trade and Development Report 2003]

Empire preferences: see *imperial preferences arrangement*.

Enabling Clause: the *Decision on Differential and More Favourable Treatment, Reciprocity and Fuller Participation of Developing Countries*, one of the outcomes of the *Tokyo Round*. It allows developed WTO members to take action favouring developing countries without according the same treatment to other members. Main measures covered by it include the *GSP*, *non-tariff measures* covered by the GATT, regional and global trading arrangements between developing countries and special treatment for the *least developed countries*. The Enabling Clause was intended to promote greater participation of developing countries in the world trading system, but there is doubt that it achieved its purpose. See also *developing countries and the multilateral trading system, GSTP, Part IV of the GATT, regional trade arrangement* and *special and differential treatment*.

Energy Charter Treaty: concluded in December 1994 with the signature of the Final Act of the European Energy Charter Conference. More than 50 countries have signed it. Membership includes most *OECD* countries, Central and East European countries and members of the *Commonwealth of Independent States*. The purpose of the treaty is to establish "a legal framework in order to promote long-term co-operation in the energy field, based on complementarities and mutual benefit". It covers broadly trade, investment and other matters relevant to energy. In Article 3 members agree to promote access to international markets on commercial terms, and generally to develop an open and competitive market for energy materials and products. The Treaty does not cover national energy policies, and it is not a framework for *development assistance*. In 1998 the Treaty was amended to bring into line with the *WTO Agreement*. At the same time its rules were extended to cover energy-related equipment.

Enforcement: actions taken by governments through regulatory agencies and the courts to ensure that laws, regulations, rulings, etc., are observed by those to whom they are addressed. See also *compliance, compliance panel, consultations, cross-retaliation, dispute settlement* and *retaliation*.

Enlargement: used especially for the *accession* of new member states to the *European Union*. In 1958 the original six members of the *European Economic Community* were Belgium, Federal Republic of Germany, France, Italy, Luxembourg and the Netherlands. The first enlargement came on 1 January 1973 when Denmark, Ireland and the United Kingdom brought its membership to nine. Greece joined in 1981. The enlargement to twelve came in 1986 when Portugal and Spain acceded. The accession of Austria, Finland and Sweden on 1 January 1995 brought its membership to fifteen. On 1 May 2004 Cyprus, Czech Republic, Estonia, Hungary, Latvia, Lithuania, Malta, Poland, Slovak Republic and Slovenia joined. Bulgaria and Romania joined on 1 January 2007. Membership criteria used to be informal, but in June 1993 the European Council adopted the Copenhagen criteria to judge the readiness for membership of new applicants. These are (a) stability of institutions guaranteeing democracy, the rule of law, human rights and respect for and, protection of minorities, (b) existence of a functioning market economy, as well as the capacity to cope with competitive pressure and market forces within the Union; and (c) an ability to take on the obligations of membership, including adherence to the aims of political, economic and monetary union. See also *Agenda 2000* and *Treaty of Nice*. [Gillingham 2003]

Enlightened mercantilism: see *GATT-Think*.

Enquiry points: some WTO agreements as well as some *free-trade agreements* require members to establish points in their trade administrations where other members can obtain information on the sector covered by the agreement. Sometimes they are called contact points. The exchange of information is at the governmental level. Examples of such agreements are the ***General Agreement on Trade in Services*** (GATS), the ***Agreement on Trade-Related Aspects of Intellectual Property Rights*** and the ***Agreement on Technical Barriers to Trade***. The GATS also requires developed-country members to establish contact points where private firms from developing countries can find out about trade opportunities.

Enterprise-based definition of investment: see *investment*.

Enterprise for ASEAN Initiative: EAI. An initiative announced by President Bush on 26 October 2002. It offers individual *ASEAN* countries ready to do so the opportunity to enter into *free-trade agreement* negotiations with the United States. Countries taking up this offer ought to be members of the WTO. They also ought to have concluded a ***Trade and Investment Framework Agreement*** with the United States as a preparatory step.

Enterprise for the Americas Initiative: EAI. A United States program launched in June 1990 by President Bush to strengthen Latin American and Caribbean economies. The main components of the initiative are trade, investment and debt reduction programs. The *FTAA*, now under negotiation, had its origin under this initiative. See also ***Alliance for Progress***, ***Andean Trade Preference Act***, ***Andean Trade Promotion and Drug Eradication Act*** and ***Caribbean Basin Initiative***. [Green 1993]

Entities: a term used in the WTO ***Agreement on Government Procurement*** to describe any organization or body covered by the Agreement. Typical listings include central and provincial government ministries and offices and enterprises and service providers under their control. These can include water and electricity utilities, port and airport authorities, research organizations, medical services providers, transport enterprises, and so on.

Entrepôt trade: shipping goods through a port in one economy for re-export to another economy as, for example, is the case for the export of some Indonesian or Malaysian products through Singapore, or goods from China through Hong Kong. Goods entering and leaving as entrepôt trade are not subject to tariffs. Apparent discrepancies in bilateral trade statistics may arise because goods may be recorded first as entering the intermediate country and then as re-exports to the final destination without any indication of the true country of origin. See also *rules of origin*.

Environmental dumping: see *eco-dumping* and *eco-duties*.

Environmental goods and services: many definitions of this sector are available. A representative one is that produced jointly by the *OECD* and Eurostat in 1999. It divides the environmental industry into three sectors: products, systems and services for pollution management, cleaner technologies and products, and resources management. Each of these is divided further as follows: (a) pollution management includes air pollution control, wastewater treatment, waste management, remediation and clean-up of contaminated land and water, noise and vibration control, environmental analysis and assessment, environmental research and development, general administration (public sector) and environmental management (private sector), (b) cleaner technologies and products which includes cleaner/resource-efficient technologies and processes and cleaner/resource-efficient products, and (c) resources management which includes portable water treatment and distribution, recycled materials, renewable energy plant and nature protection.

Environmentally preferable products: products or services that affect the environment less than other products having the same purpose. Such products typically contain recycled materials, save energy and water in their production, reduce waste and minimize toxic by-products. See also *life cycle assessment*.

Environmentally preferable purchasing: policies that result in the purchase of products and services affecting the environment less than other products having the same purpose. Some governments have programs to promote such policies. The United States Environmental Protection Agency, for example, has developed a framework of five principles for this purpose: (a) include environmental considerations as part of the normal purchasing process, (b) emphasize pollution prevention early in the purchasing process, (c) examine multiple environmental attributes throughout a product's or service's life cycle, (d) compare relevant environmental impacts when selecting products and services, and (e) collect and base purchasing decisions on accurate and meaningful information about environmental performance. See also *life cycle assessment*. [www.epa.gov.]

Environmental rules under the WTO: The WTO does not have a system of rules specifically dealing with environmental matters, but that does not mean that it is indifferent to environmental concerns. The basic WTO tenet is that governments are free to set and enforce their own environmental standards in their territories if they do it without discriminating against other members, such as contravening the *most-favoured-nation rule* or the *national treatment* principle. *GATT* Article XX (General Exceptions), which permits the suspension of obligations under the Agreement to the extent necessary in narrowly defined circumstances, can be used to enforce some environmental objectives. Article XX(b) can be invoked to adopt or enforce measures necessary to protect human, animal or plant life or health. Article XX(d) can be used to ensure compliance with laws and regulations otherwise consistent with the GATT. Article XX(g) enables adoption or enforcement of measures relating to the conservation of exhaustible natural resources if such measures are made effective in conjunction with restrictions on domestic production or consumption. Some have argued that Article XX should be supplemented by a provision permitting the suspension of GATT obligations to promote environmental protection, but this proposition remains contentious. Article XIV of the *General Agreement on Trade in Services* permits in some cases suspension of the Agreement's provisions to protect human, animal or plant life or health. The WTO forum for the consideration of environmental matters is the *Committee on Trade and Environment*. The *Doha Ministerial Conference* launched negotiations on the relationship between existing WTO rules and specific trade obligations set out in *multilateral environment agreements*. It also extended the WTO work program on *trade and environment* by establishing a work program to examine (a) the effect of environmental measures on market access, (b) the environmental provisions of the *Agreement on Trade-Related Aspects of Intellectual Property Rights* and (c) labelling requirements for environmental purposes. Some prominent GATT and WTO disputes with an environmental component were *superfund*, *tuna I* and *tuna II*. See also *Agreement on Sanitary and Phytosanitary Measures*, *eco-labelling*, *general exceptions*, *race-to-the-bottom argument* and *sanitary and phytosanitary measures*.

Environment and trade: see *trade and environment*.

Equality of competitive opportunity: the principle underlying the *national treatment* obligation contained in Article III of the *GATT*. It means that national laws and regulations have to be drafted so that imported products to compete effectively with domestic products. Normally, this means that regulations for imported and domestic products are identical, but there may be formally different rules for imports if this is the only way to achieve equal opportunity. See also *competitive neutrality*, *economic impact criterion* and *implicit discrimination*.

Equitable competition: a concept based on the assumption that there ought to be some degree of international harmonization of labour, environmental and other standards seen to affect the cost of production to achieve a framework in which firms compete on more equal terms. The wisdom underlying this concept is that countries permitting inadequate standards give their firms a cost advantage which translates into enhanced international competitiveness for them. See also *fair competition*, *level playing field*, *social clause*, *trade and labour standards* and *trade and the environment*.

Equitable share of the market: an elusive concept enshrined in GATT Article XVI:3 (Subsidies) concerning allowable subsidies for *primary products*. GATT members have held the view at least since 1955 that it was desirable to satisfy world requirements of primary commodities in the most effective and economic manner, and that account should be taken of any special factors regarding the exporting country's share of world trade in the product concerned during a representative period. The *panel* in *French wheat and wheat flour* in 1958 made useful observations on the concept of "equitable share", but these have not been developed and refined by later panels. Article 9 of the *Tokyo Round Agreement on Interpretation and Application of Articles VI, XVI and XXIII of the General Agreement on Tariffs and Trade* (the Subsidies Code) notes that with regard to new markets, traditional patterns of supply of the product to the region in which the new market is located must be taken into account in determining "equitable share of world export trade". GATT Article XIII (Non-discriminatory Administration of Quantitative Restrictions) also seeks to ensure the principle of fair market share. It requires the distribution of trade in a product subject to *quantitative restrictions* to approach as closely as possible the shares exporting countries might obtain in the absence of restrictions, and it sets out ways of how this might be done.

Equivalence: a principle set out in the WTO *Agreement on the Application of Sanitary and Phytosanitary Measures*. It says that if an exporting country demonstrates objectively to an importing country that its sanitary and phytosanitary measures achieve the levels set by the importing country, the levels should be considered equivalent. The measures taken by the two countries need not be identical.

Equivalence of advantages: achieved through the granting of a benefit to another party in return for a benefit of about the same size. See also *reciprocity*.

Equivalent measure of support: EMS. A term used in the WTO *Agreement on Agriculture*. It describes an annual level of support to agricultural producers, expressed in monetary terms, which cannot be calculated in accordance with the methods used for determining the *aggregate measure of support*.

Erga omnes: *Lat.* "against all" or "in relation to all". It is a term sometimes used in trade agreements, as in "If a party lowers its tariffs *erga omnes*. . ."

Erga omnes **obligations:** obligations to the international community as a whole, regardless of consent. Crawford says that "one can infer that the core cases of obligations *erga omnes* are the non-derogable obligations of a general character which arise either directly under general international law or under under generally accepted multilateral treaties (e.g. in the field of human rights)". He continues that such obligations are "virtually coextensive with peremptory obligations (arising under norms of *jus cogens*)". Where the parties to an international regime have a common legal interest, i.e. where it is necessary to join a multilateral treaty for the legal interest to arise, the obligation is known as *erga omnes partes*. [Crawford 2000, Pauwelyn 2002]

ESCAP: the Economic and Social Commission for the Asia-Pacific. One of the *United Nations regional economic commissions*. It was established in 1947 as the Economic Commission for Asia and the Far East (ECAFE) and given its present name in 1974. It has major work programs on regional economic cooperation, environment and sustainable development, poverty alleviation, transport and communications, statistics and issues concerning least developed, landlocked and island developing countries. ESCAP's secretariat is located in Bangkok. See also *Bangkok Agreement*.

Escape clause: a provision in trade agreements which permits a party to suspend its obligations when imports cause or threaten to cause *serious injury* to the domestic producers of similar goods. GATT Article XIX contains the escape clause for trade in goods used by WTO members. It allows a member to suspend its obligations or to modify liberalizing commitments if there are *unforeseen developments* and if any product is imported in such increased quantities likely to cause or causing harm to domestic producers. The Article is supplemented by the detailed rules of the *Agreement on Safeguards*. One clarification it makes is that *customs unions* may choose between imposing a safeguard measure on behalf of the entire union or on behalf of one member only. The decision has to be made at the time of the investigation. The *General Agreement on Trade in Services* does not yet have an escape clause, though Article X establishes the mandate for this.

Two main reasons are usually given for the inclusion of safeguard provisions in agreements. First, they encourage greater liberalization since countries making liberalizing commitments will have the opportunity to step back from them if they have unwittingly provoked a surge in imports clearly harming domestic industry. Second, they increase the flexibility of the *multilateral trading system* by promoting its longer-term stability. The immediate reason for including an escape clause in the GATT was United States Executive Order 9832 of February 1947 which made it mandatory for American trade negotiators to include in all future trade agreements an escape clause similar to that contained in the United States-Mexico Trade Agreement of December 1942. See also *parallelism in safeguards*, *safeguards* and *Section 201*. [Mueller 2003]

ESM: see *emergency safeguard mechanism*.

Essential facilities doctrine: an *antitrust* term meaning broadly that the owner of an "essential", "bottleneck" or "gate-keeper" facility, such as a public electricity or water utility, a telecommunications network or a railway, must give access to competitors at a reasonable price so that they in turn can conduct their own businesses. The interpretation of this doctrine varies from country to country.

Essential products: WTO members may in defined circumstances impose restrictions on imports under GATT Article XII to safeguard their balance of payments. Developing-country members may also use Article XVIII. In doing so, they may give priority to the import of products deemed more essential than others. The *Understanding on the Balance-of-Payments Provisions of the GATT*, concluded during the *Uruguay Round*, defines "essential products" as those which meet basic consumption needs or those which contribute to an improvement of the balance-of-payments situation, such as capital goods or other inputs into production.

EST: environmentally–sound technology.

EST&P: environmentally–sound technology and products.

Establishment: see *post-establishment*, *pre-establishment*, *right of establishment* and *right of non-establishment*.

Estoppel: a rule in the law of evidence that a party in legal proceedings cannot deny or assert something when that would be inconsistent with its own statements or conduct. M. N. Shaw puts it this way: "states deemed to have consented to a state of affairs cannot afterwards alter their position". [Shaw 1997]

Eurasian Economic Community: EURASEC. It was first established in 1995 and given its present name on 30 May 2001. It consists of Belarus, Kazakhstan, Kyrghyz Republic, Russia and Tajikistan. Moldova and Ukraine are observers. EURASEC aims to form a *customs union* and a *single economic space*.

Euro: €. The single European currency introduced in January 1999. Those using it are Austria, Belgium, Finland, France, Germany, Ireland, Italy, Luxembourg, Netherlands, Portugal, Spain and Greece.

Euro-Mediterranean Association Agreements: the *preferential trade arrangements*, often known informally as *Mediterranean Agreements*, between the *European Community* and some countries located on the rim of the Mediterranean

Sea. They are divided into first-generation cooperation agreements concluded in the 1960s and 1970s (now superseded by other agreements) and those concluded in the late 1990s. The modern association agreements include provisions concerning many trade and economic matters, including the establishment of a WTO-consistent *free-trade area* over twelve years. Other provisions deal with cooperation in social affairs and migration. They also include a *democracy clause* and a *human rights clause*. See also *Barcelona Process*.

Euro-Mediterranean Economic Area: EMEA. A *free-trade area* proposed in November 1995 at a meeting in Barcelona which would cover the fifteen members of the *European Union* and twelve Mediterranean Rim countries: Algeria, Cyprus, Egypt, Israel, Jordan, Lebanon, Malta, Morocco, the Palestinian Authority, Syria (Mashrek), Tunisia (Maghreb) and Turkey. Libya is an observer at some meetings. The EMEA is expected to become effective by 2010. See also *Mediterranean Agreements*.

Europe Agreements: a type of *Association Agreement* used by the *European Community* for its political and economic relations under preferential conditions with the countries of Central and Eastern Europe. They were concluded in the first half of the 1990s. The agreements covered trade-related issues, political dialogue and legal aspects. Under these agreements, Central and East European countries undertook to align their laws to those of the European Community in areas such as capital movement, *competition laws*, *intellectual property rights* and *government procurement*. Europe Agreements allowed for the possibility of eventual full membership of the Community, but they did not guarantee it. Most have now been superseded because the parties joined the European Community. See also *enlargement* and *Mediterranean Agreements*.

European Agricultural Guidance and Guarantee Fund: the mechanism through which the *European Community* finances the *Common Agricultural Policy*. The Fund is in two parts: (a) the Guidance part which funds structural policy, and (b) the Guarantee part which supports markets and prices.

European Coal and Steel Community: ECSC. Established in 1951 by the Treaty of Paris. It created a single market for coal and steel among member countries. Members delegated their powers in this regard to a newly created High Authority, a supra-national authority. The successful working of the ECSC was one of the factors leading to the negotiation of the *Treaty of Rome* which created the *European Economic Community*. In 1965, the *Treaty Establishing a Single Council of the European Communities* (the Merger Treaty) unified the High Authority with the Commission of the European Economic Community. The Treaty establishing the ECSC expired on 23 July 2002. See also *European Communities*.

European Commission: one of the *European Union* institutions in which political authority resides. The Commission is responsible for ensuring that the provisions of the various treaties making up the legal framework of the European Union are observed. It is the formal initiator of policy and legislative proposals, the implementer of European Union policy and the enforcer of *European Community* law. The *Treaty of Nice* established on 1 November 2004 a Commission of 25 members, including the president. Each member state is entitled to one commissioner. The Commission is divided into more than 20 Directorates-General (DGs). The DGs used to be numbered. For example, DG-I was concerned with external economic relations, including negotiations in the WTO, DG-IV with competition and DG-VI with agriculture. Now all the Directorates-General are known by a name which indicates their responsibilities, such as Trade, Agriculture, Competition, and Economic and Financial Affairs. Under Article 228 of the *Treaty of Rome* and some other articles, external agreements are to be negotiated by the Commission and concluded by the *Council of the European Union* (the Council of Ministers). In broad terms, the Council of Ministers lays down general negotiating guidelines which the Commission then follows in the negotiations.

European Communities: a term created with the adoption of the Merger Treaty *(Treaty Establishing a Single Council of the European Communities)* in 1965 which created, among other institutional changes, a single Commission of the European Communities. The Commission unified the bodies administering the European Atomic Energy Community, the *European Coal and Steel Community* (ECSC) and the *European Economic Community*. Article XI of the *WTO Agreement* refers to the European Communities as a member of the WTO. This is because there were doubts at that time whether the *European Community* had *competence* over matters falling within the ambit of the ECSC and the Atomic Energy Community. These doubts proved unjustified. See also *European Commission*. [Schroeder 2003, Wessel 2003]

European Community: created as a legal entity by the *Treaty of Maastricht* as the successor of the *European Economic Community* (EEC or the *Common Market*). Often shortened to EC. The term "European Community" was often used before the entry into force of the Treaty of Maastricht to mean the EEC. The exact meaning is usually clear from the context. See also *enlargement*, *European Union* and *Treaty of Maastricht*.

European Community and European Union treaties: this entry outlines the main treaties underlying the European Union. The *European Economic Community* was established on 1 January 1958 through the *Treaty of Rome*. The *Merger Treaty* of 1965 unified the separate bodies heading the European Atomic Energy Community, the *European Coal and Steel Community* and the European Economic Community into the *European Commission*. The *Single European Act* of 1987 eliminated remaining barriers between the member states. The *Treaty of Maastricht* established the *European Union* on 1 November 1993. The *Treaty of Amsterdam* which entered into force on 1 May 1999 simplified and consolidated the treaties constituting the law of the European Union. The *Treaty of Nice*, which entered into force on 1 February 2003, prepared the ground for the *enlargement* likely to occur over the next few years.

European Community legislation: the *European Community* has five legislative avenues to carry out its mandate. *Regulations* are official European Community acts which are binding in their entirety and which apply directly in all member states. Regulations therefore promote legislative harmonization, since community law prevails over national law where there is a conflict. *Directives* are official European Community acts which are binding on the member states to which they are addressed as far as their objectives are concerned, but member states are free to decide how to give effect to directives. This approach can make the implementation of controversial measures more acceptable. *Decisions* are binding in their entirety on those to whom they are addressed. *Recommendations* and *opinions* have no binding force, but they can be as effective as other measures.

European Community Single Market: launched in 1987 through the *Single European Act*, an amendment to the *Treaty of Rome*, and achieved in 1992. It entailed the elimination of the remaining physical (customs), technical (standards and licensing) and fiscal barriers between the then twelve members of the *European Community*. This not only meant that goods and services produced in one member state had unhindered access to the other member states if they were wanted there, but also that foreign goods and services, once they were lawfully imported by one member state, could then be transferred to any other member state. Even then, there was a view at the time of its creation that it would not lead to a single market, and that without further reforms the European Community market would remain a collection of twelve national markets. See also *European Community legislation* and *four freedoms*.

European Court of Justice: the judicial organ charged with ensuring that the law is observed in the interpretation and application of the treaties establishing the *European Communities* as well as the provisions laid down by the various Community institutions. The Court of Justice is the pre-eminent legal body in the Community, but the courts of the member states retain a role in the application of Community laws, especially where the member states are charged with carrying out certain functions and where Community instruments confer directly individual rights on nationals of member states. The European Court of Justice is located in Strasbourg.

European Economic Area: EEA. Entered into force on 1 January 1994. It comprises the 27 members of the *European Community* (EC) and three of the four members of *EFTA* (Iceland, Liechtenstein and Norway) in a single market. Switzerland decided in December 1992 not to join the EEA. For the EFTA countries membership of the EEA represents an intermediate step between a separate EFTA and its full EC membership. Applying to join the EC would be a separate step. The agreement establishing the EEA covers the *four freedoms* (free movement of goods, persons, services and capital), but agriculture and fisheries are mostly excluded. The *Common Comercial Policy* does not apply. Members of the EEA must adopt the *acquis communautaire* dealing with competition. EFTA states are also bound by the European Community rules on social policy, consumer protection, environment, company law and statistics.

European Economic Community: EEC. Established by the *Treaty of Rome* which was signed on 25 March 1957. It entered into force on 1 January 1958. The Treaty was intended to "lay the foundations of an ever closer union among the peoples of Europe". Among its principal aims were the elimination of *tariff* and *non-tariff barriers* among member states and the formation of a *common market* entailing also the free movement of persons, services and capital. Among the elements making up the EEC were the *Common Agricultural Policy*, the *Common Commercial Policy* and a common transport policy. The EEC has been replaced by the *European Community* through the *Treaty of Maastricht*. See also *enlargement*, *European Union* and *four freedoms*. [Gillingham 2003]

European Free Trade Association: see *EFTA*.

European Patent Convention: the *Convention on the Grant of European Patents* concluded on 5 October 1973. It establishes a common system of law for the grant of patents in member states. These European patents have the effect of national patents granted by member states.

European Recovery Program: see *Marshall Plan*.

European Union: EU. Created by the *Treaty of Maastricht*, signed in February 1992. It entered into force on 1 November 1993. The European Union consists of three parts: (i) the *European Community* (which remains the principal pillar), (ii) a common foreign and security policy and (iii) cooperation in the fields of justice and home affairs. Only the European Community has a legal personality and can sign international agreements, but scholars have pointed out, for example, that in their accession treaties Austria, Sweden and Finland became "members of the European Union and contractual parties of the treaties, on which the Union is founded". The 27 members of the European Union are Austria, Belgium, Bulgaria, Cyprus, Czech Republic, Denmark, Estonia, Finland, France, Germany, Greece, Hungary, Ireland, Italy, Latvia, Lithuania, Luxembourg, Malta, Netherlands, Poland, Portugal, Romania, Slovak Republic, Slovenia, Spain, Sweden and the United Kingdom. In the WTO the European Union is known officially as the *European Communities*. See also *Treaty of Amsterdam* and *Treaty of Nice*. [Gillingham 2003, Schroeder 2003, Wessel 2003]

European Union–Mercosur Cooperation Agreement: adopted on 15 December 1995 in Madrid. It sets out the process for future cooperation between the two groups of partners. The areas to be covered include economic, commercial, industrial, customs, statistics, *intellectual property*, investment, energy, transport, science and technology, telecommunications and information technology, environment, education, culture and drug trafficking. The work is done through a ministerial Council of Cooperation. Negotiations are under way for an *association agreement*. See also *Mercosur*.

EU-US aircraft agreement: formally the *Agreement Between the European Community and the Government of the United States Concerning the Application of the GATT Agreement on Trade in Civil Aircraft on Trade in Large Aircraft* which took effect on 17 July 1992. The Agreement (a) prohibits government funding for the production of large civil aircraft [i.e. aircraft with more than 100 seats], (b) limits the level of government funding for the development of new aircraft, (c) limits the amount of "indirect" government support for developing new aircraft, (d) restricts government intervention in competition for sales, and (e) provides for the exchange of information concerning government support. See also *Agreement on Trade in Civil Aircraft* and *Large Aircraft Sector Understanding*.

Evasion of customs duties: see *smuggling*, *trafficking* and *under-invoicing*.

Everything But Arms: EBA. A *European Union* initiative for duty-free and quota-free access to all products except arms originating in *least developed countries*. It took effect on 5 March 2001 for most products. Sugar, rice and bananas will receive free access in stages by 2009.

EVSL: *Early Voluntary Sectoral Liberalization*. An *APEC* initiative for *sectoral trade negotiations*.

Ex aequo et bono: *Lat.* according to what is just and good.

Ex ante: *Lat.* before a measure is applied.

Exchange controls: conditions or limits imposed by governments on the extent to which residents may have access to foreign exchange reserves. WTO members may use exchange controls imposed in accordance with the Articles of Association of the *IMF*, but they may not use them to frustrate the intent of the GATT. For *trade in services*, they may not apply restrictions on international transfers and payments for current transactions where they have made *specific commitments*. In both cases, exchange controls may be possible to safeguard the balance of payments under strictly defined conditions. See also *balance-of-payments consultations, currency board* and *trade and foreign exchange*.

Exchange dumping: suggested in the past by some as a category of *dumping*. This was assumed to occur through manipulation of the *exchange rate* to give exporters an advantage in the importing market. So-called exchange dumping was discussed at the time of the *Havana Charter* negotiations, but no rules were established to deal with this practice. Some of the calls for negotiations on *trade and foreign exchange* appear to be based on the view that some forms of exchange dumping still persist.

Exchange of concessions: agreed bilateral outcomes arrived at as the result of *requests and offers* in *multilateral trade negotiations*. A *concession* is in its narrow sense a *binding*, but it is also used for tariff reductions more generally.

Exchange rate: the cost of a currency in terms of another currency. Some exchange rates are fixed. This is done through a government decision, usually against a currency showing moderate fluctuations in value. Floating exchange rates are determined by free markets in response to supply and demand. See also *currency board*.

Excise duty: a *duty* sometimes levied by governments on the production, purchase, sale or use of a commodity. A typical example is the duty levied on the distilling and sale of alcohol. Foreign and domestic products have to be given the same level of excise duty under the WTO rules on *national treatment*.

Exclusive Economic Zone: see *United Nations Convention on the Law of the Sea*.

Exclusive export rights: the right given to governmental and non-governmental enterprises to be the sole exporter of, usually, an agricultural commodity. See also *single-desk selling*.

Exclusive import rights: the practice of giving holders of *patents*, *copyright* and other *intellectual property rights* the ability to stop *parallel imports* of products embodying the same intellectual property rights. Some countries assign exclusive importing rights in particular products to *state trading* operations. See also *trading rights*.

Exclusive marketing rights: EMRS. A concept used in the *Agreement on Trade-Related Aspects of Intellectual Property Rights* relating to *patent* protection for pharmaceuticals and agricultural chemical products. EMRS may be available for five years in cases where defined transitional arrangements are used to bring the provisions of the Agreement into effect.

Exclusive service suppliers: a small number of service suppliers established or authorized by the government. They usually operate in an environment of little or no competition.

Exemption: a dispensation from conforming with a certain measure, such as having the right to apply an *MFN exemption* under the *General Agreement on Trade in Services*.

Exhaustion doctrine: also called first-sale doctrine. This is the proposition that once a product embodying *intellectual property rights* (IPRs) has been placed on the market lawfully (i.e. with the consent of the owner of the rights), the owner of the rights cannot prevent or prohibit the resale or transfer of the product in that market. In other words, the owner's rights over the product are held to have been "exhausted". In reality, the situation is not quite as simple as this. Some intellectual property laws and conventions do set some limits on the resale or transfer of a product, depending on the IPR in question. Works of art, for example, may be subject to a *droit de suite*. *Moral rights* may apply in matters of *copyright*. Aside from these and other limitations, nobody disputes that the doctrine applies to products sold and resold on the same market. Its application to products traded internationally is, however, contentious. Some jurisdictions recognize the concept of "international exhaustion". This is the proposition that once a product has been placed on the market anywhere, it can be resold or transferred to any other market without the consent of the owner of any IPRs it may embody. The application of this proposition then permits *parallel imports*. The *Agreement on Trade-Related Aspects of Intellectual Property Rights* does not establish any rule on exhaustion. See also *Community exhaustion*, *international exhaustion*, *national exhaustion* and *regional exhaustion*.

Ex officio: a responsibility or entitlement one obtains through holding another office or another position.

Exon-Florio amendment: Section 5021 of the *Omnibus Trade and Competitiveness Act* of 1988 which authorizes the President to block on national security grounds mergers, acquisitions and joint ventures involving foreign investment. It offers considerable flexibility in its application. See also *foreign investment screening*, *national interest* and *security exceptions*.

Ex parte communications: the WTO *Dispute Settlement Understanding* expressly prohibits *ex parte* communications (communications with one party only to a dispute) with a *panel* or the *Appellate Body* concerning a matter they may be considering. Written submissions to a panel or the Appellate Body are treated as confidential, but they must be available to the parties to the dispute.

Explicit consensus: see *consensus* and *decision-making in the WTO*.

Explicit harmonization: a form of cooperation between governments to achieve defined and legally binding uniform bilateral, regional or global standards. It entails some movement away from complete national autonomy for the making of standards towards decision making in an international framework or within international institutions. See also *harmonization* and *zero-margin harmonization*.

Export: a good or a service sold by residents of one country to residents of another in return, usually, for foreign exchange. See also *barter* and *countertrade*.

Exportation: the same as *export*.

Export ban: a prohibition on the export of a good.

Export cartel: see *cartel*.

Export competition: the practice of competing internationally in markets for agricultural commodities through, for example, *export subsidies*, subsidized *export credits*, *state-trading enterprises*, *differential pricing*, abuse of food aid and non-transparent market support systems.

Export controls: measures instituted by exporting countries to supervise export flows. Reasons for them include compliance with *United Nations economic sanctions*, adherence to *voluntary restraint arrangements*, observance of *export quotas* under *international commodity arrangements*, management of *strategic exports* and administration of rules concerning *dual purpose exports*, as well as a policy of preserving some raw materials and other articles for domestic production or consumption. See also *grey-area measures* and *Wassenaar Arrangement on Export Controls for Conventional Arms and Dual-Use Goods and Technologies*.

Export credits: the granting to the importer (purchaser) of goods and services an extended term to pay for them. *OECD* members handle their government-supported export credits according to the *Arrangement on Guidelines for Officially Supported Export Credits*. The accepted practice today is to consider repayment terms of less than two years as short-term, between two and five years as medium-term and above five years as long-term. Many exporting countries have mechanisms to manage, support or guarantee export credits since, especially in the case of large contracts like power stations or port facilities, favourable terms of credit can influence considerably the competitiveness of a bid. The WTO *Agreement on Subsidies and Countervailing Duties* declares export credits prohibited if they are made at less than commercial rates. Export credits extended by OECD members in accordance with the OECD Arrangement are exempt from this prohibition.

Export culture: a recognition among individuals, firms and governments that competitive exports contribute significantly to national economic welfare, and that participation in international markets must be a high priority. Promoting and sustaining an export culture requires a consistent effort to abolish domestic structural impediments to exporting and to ensure the availability of non-discriminatory *market access* in other countries.

Export duties: a tariff levied at the time a good is exported. See *export tariffs*.

Export Enhancement Program: EEP. A United States subsidy program introduced in 1985. Its objective is to help American exporters compete against subsidized prices in specific markets. Commodities able to benefit from this program are wheat, wheat flour, rice, frozen poultry, barley, barley malt, table eggs and vegetable oil. EEP enables exporters to sell these products abroad for less than the price they paid for them. The subsidies, called bonuses under the program, are paid in cash by the *Commodity Credit Corporation* (CCC). See also *Dairy Export Incentive Program* and *Farm Security and Rural Investment Act* of 2002 which extended the program until 2007.

Export earnings guarantee schemes: mechanisms usually aimed at ensuring that individual commodity producers or countries mainly dependent on export earnings from commodities are not exposed fully to sharp drops in their incomes. They are also known as *compensatory financing arrangements*. Examples of such mechanisms were *STABEX* and *SYSMIN*, both operated by the *European Community* under the *Lomé Convention*. They have been replaced in the *ACP-EC Economic Partnership Agreement* by a scheme to support national budgets in defined cases. The *IMF Compensatory and Contingency Financing Facility* has a broader scope.

Export Expansion and Reciprocal Trade Agreements Act: the *fast-track* proposal tabled by President Clinton in September 1997. It was not adopted. See also *Trade Promotion Authority* and *United States trade agreements legislation*.

Export incentives: Measures adopted by governments to promote the expansion of exports by domestic companies. Such measures can include direct subsidies, bounties, reduced import tariffs for components where they are incorporated into products to be re-exported, taxation concessions, etc. The *Agreement on Subsidies and Countervailing Duties* makes some types of export incentives illegal, including subsidies related to the export of products. See also *bounty* and *export subsidies*.

Export inflation insurance schemes: schemes operated by governments particularly in the high-inflation environment of the 1970s. They were designed to minimize or eliminate the effects of monetary inflation on the cost of export contracts. Countries not maintaining such schemes held that they conferred a competitive advantage to exporters benefiting from them. These exporters could bid more aggressively in international markets, since they were secure in the knowledge that they would not have to bear the cost of inflation alone. A *panel* established by the GATT in 1978 to examine whether such schemes amounted to a *subsidy* concluded that this would be true if the premium rates were "manifestly inadequate to cover long-term operating costs and losses". It also noted that the meaning of "long-term" still would have to be defined. In the current environment of low inflation any schemes of this nature which might still exist appear to be unused.

Exporting unemployment: The woolly idea that domestic economic activity can be raised, and employment thereby increased, if the flow of imports is stemmed in some way. In other words, proponents of this idea hold that it is possible to transfer the unemployment burden to some other country and protect and increase employment at home through keeping imports at bay. Generally, the more acceptable term of *import substitution* is used for this practice. Such policies may work in the short term, but only at the expense of lower *competitiveness* of the domestic industry. Factors to consider in the imposition of import substitution policies are that many imported products are inputs into the production process. Raising their prices raises the costs of domestic producers. Increased costs are a disincentive to purchasers, and this may lead to a dampening of economic activity. The aim of exporting unemployment can therefore lead to increased unemployment at home. See also *beggar-thy-neighbour policies*, *local content rules* and *optimal-tariff argument*.

Export of domestically prohibited goods: allowing the manufacture of goods for export, but not for domestic consumption. Said to be done for reasons of health, safety, etc. Practical examples are hard to find. Views differ on the extent to which importing countries should agree to open their markets to these exporters. Some say that if a country does not allow such products in its domestic market, it should ban their export also. Others say that importing countries have no obligation to accept such products. At its worst, the arguments therefore amount to blatant *protectionism* on the part of those who dispute the right of countries to engage in such exports, but in many cases the reality is not so simple. This difficult issue has been on the GATT work program since 1982. A solution is not readily apparent.

Export of jobs: the erroneous view sometimes expressed sometimes by trade unions and manufacturers in *sensitive sectors* that the import of products means the export of jobs because any order placed abroad means that someone in a foreign country now has a job. The remedy usually suggested is higher tariffs to promote *import substitution*. However, such policies lead to higher costs for the economy overall, and they therefore make it less competitive with resulting higher unemployment. See also *exporting unemployment* and *outsourcing*.

Export participation rate: a measurement indicating how many firms in a given industry in an economy are engaged in exporting or attempting to export goods and services. The export participation rate is a useful device for assessing the extent to which a country has acquired an *export culture*.

Export performance measure: A requirement that a certain quantity of production must be exported. See *export performance requirements*.

Export performance requirements: conditions imposed by the country authorizing foreign investment within its territory that are aimed at expanding that country's exports. At its simplest, the enterprise established with foreign investment has to export a certain percentage of its output, expressed either in value or quantity. Wholesale and retail traders may have to balance their imports with exports. The *Agreement on Trade-Related Investment Measures* bans most of these requirements. See also *performance requirements*.

Export pessimism: a view prevalent particularly in the 1950s in the heyday of *import substitution* policies by developing countries in the Latin-American region. It was based on the assumption that the smallness of their exports would not be able to promote economic development, and that international integration would undermine whatever competitiveness an economy might have achieved. The conclusion was that import substitution was the only realistic policy. See also *dependence theory*.

Export price: the price at which a good is exported from a country. It has a special significance if *anti-dumping measures* are considered against the good. If the export price is lower than *normal value* (the comparable price for the *like product* when it is intended for consumption in the exporting country), *dumping* may have occurred.

Export propensity: the share of domestic production of goods and services that is exported. See also *export participation rate*.

Export processing zones: see *free-trade zones*.

Export quotas: restrictions or ceilings imposed on the total value or volume of certain exports. They are designed to protect domestic producers and consumers from temporary shortages of these products or to improve the prices of specific products on world markets by shortening their supply. The latter is only possible where a country, or a group of countries, is the dominant exporter of a product. *International commodity agreements* with economic provisions can underpin their aim of price stabilization through export quotas, sometimes together with a *buffer stock*. Article XX(h) (General Exceptions) of the GATT allows members to adopt measures in support of obligations they have accepted under any intergovernmental commodity agreements conforming to the 1947 *ECOSOC* principles. This is also reflected Chapter VI of the *Havana Charter*. GATT Article XX(i) permits WTO members to maintain "restrictions on exports of domestic materials necessary to ensure essential quantities of such materials to a domestic processing industry during periods when the domestic price of such materials is held below the world price as part of a governmental stabilization plan", but such restrictions must not be used to increase exports of the commodity concerned or to give it greater protection. Reasons adduced at one time or another against export quotas include (a) their tendency to discriminate against low-cost producers and new entrants into the market, (b) their inability to alleviate shortages, (c) they may lead to unreasonable expectations of defensible price levels among producers, (d) they may work against the aim of putting less on the market by guaranteeing less efficient producers a minimum price,

(e) artificially high prices encourage consumers to use substitutes, synthetics or new technologies reducing the need for that commodity, (f) the general difficulty of negotiating and policing quotas, especially when there are structural changes in the market brought about, for example, by a shift in consumer preferences or the entry of new producer-based technologies, (g) ensuring that all significant producers are members of an agreement with export quotas is always difficult, and (h) in times of even minor oversupply a small additional exporter can have a disproportionate effect. Some argue that the *Integrated Programme for Commodities* would offer a defence against most of these perceived difficulties because of the universality of its membership. Others believe that the history of commodity negotiations since 1976, when the integrated programme was negotiated, does not support this claim adequately. See also *commodity policy*.

Export restitution: an export subsidy under the *Common Agricultural Policy* which bridges the gap between domestic and world prices.

Export restraint arrangement: see *voluntary restraint agreement*.

Export subsidies: government payments or other financial contributions by governments provided to domestic producers or exporters if they export their goods or services. They are illegal for manufactured products under the *Agreement on Subsidies and Countervailing Measures*. See also *export incentives*.

Export support: any form of governmental action that (a) reduces the cost of the exported product to the importer to less than its true market price or (b) reduces the cost of exporting or marketing for export to less than the cost actually incurred. Either of these actions is held, at any rate by those benefiting from them, as making the exporting country more competitive. However, the difference between the true cost and the actual return must be met somehow, and the taxpayer usually fills that role. See also *export competition* and *export subsidies*.

Export targeting: the practice by an exporting country of selecting some countries as particularly promising markets for its products. The practice becomes reprehensible in the eyes of producers in importing countries when *unfair trading practices* are used. As such, they may give grounds for action under *Section 301*. See also *import targets* and *voluntary import expansion programs*.

Export tariffs: a levy on goods or commodities at the time they leave a *customs territory*. Reasons for imposing export tariffs include raising revenue, the desire to promote further processing of commodities within the country and a policy of ensuring that commodities perceived as scarce and necessary for domestic production are reserved as much as possible for local industry. See also *differential export tax*, *double pricing*, *export quotas*, *Lerner's symmetry theorem* and *short-supply products*.

Ex post: after a measure is applied.

Expressions of folklore: see *folklore* and *traditional cultural expressions*.

Expropriation: confiscation by the host country of property owned by foreign nationals or taking action to nullify the value of property, usually under the guise of some public policy goal. Article III of the United States model bilateral investment treaty, for example, says that parties may only expropriate an investment for a public purpose, in a non-discriminatory manner, upon payment of prompt, adequate and effective compensation, and in accordance with due process of law. *Bilateral investment treaties* and *investment promotion and protection agreements* seek to establish procedures for just compensation of former owners See also *Hull formula*. [Shaw 1997, Brownlie 1990]

Extended Balance of Payments Services Classification: EBOPS. A product-based classification of traded services developed in response to the new statistical information needs arising from the *General Agreement on Trade in Services*. It supplements the fifth edition of the *IMF* Balance of payments Manual. See also *trade in services statistics*.

Extended Moratorium on Customs Duties on Electronic Transmissions: see **Moratorium on Customs Duties on Electronic Transmissions**.

Extension of protection for geographical indications: the WTO *Doha Ministerial Conference* agreed to examine the question of extending protection of *geographical indications* to products other than wines and spirit and that this examination would be handled by the *Council for TRIPS*. Few dispute that an extension of protection of geographical indications to other products is feasible in principle. The *Paris Convention*, the observance of which is a requirement under the *Agreement on Trade-Related Aspects of Intellectual Property Rights*, requires its members in Article 1 to protect indications of source or appellations of origin as a form of *industrial property*. It defines "industrial property" as not only including industry and commerce proper, but also "agricultural and extractive industries and all manufactured or natural products, for example, wines, grain, tobacco leaf, fruit, cattle, minerals, mineral waters, beer, flowers and flour". Most countries already protect these forms of industrial property, not only as geographical indications but also as *trademarks*, *certification marks*, etc. Some say that the proposal for extending protection is impracticable, and they doubt that the cost of doing extending protection to other products would balance the likely benefits. This group also argues that, as far as extension is feasible, the same ends can be achieved through simpler means, such as protection of trademarks. Proponents of extension say that there are no economic or systemic reasons for protecting geographical indications for certain products differently from others, and that the administrative costs of doing so would negligible. See also *multilateral system of notification and registration of geographical indications*.

External trade: this can mean the same as foreign trade generally. It can also refer to the foreign trade conducted by members of a *preferential trade arrangement* with non-members. The trade between the partners to such an arrangement is then called internal trade.

Extraordinary challenge: a procedure available under *NAFTA* Article 1904.13 concerning the settlement of disputes about anti-dumping or countervailing duty matters. The provision allows parties to challenge a panel decision on the claim that (a) a panel member was guilty of gross misconduct, bias, a serious conflict of interest or violating the rules of conduct in other ways, (b) the panel seriously departed from a fundamental rule of procedure, or (c) the panel manifestly exceeded its powers, and that any of these conditions materially affected the panel's decision and threatened the integrity of the panel review process.

Extraterritoriality: the enforcement of the laws of a country outside its territory. This is much disliked except by those economically powerful enough to benefit from it. See also *antitrust laws*, *effects doctrine*, *Iran-Libya Sanctions Act* and *Helms-Burton legislation*.

Ex-works price: a concept used in the administration of some *preferential rules of origin*. It is the value of a good when it leaves the factory. One major component is the value of all materials used in its manufacture. The other major component is all costs incurred in the manufacture of the good, such as wages, electricity, licences for *intellectual property*, etc. In most cases, highly complex and probably irritating calculation methods have been developed under *free-trade agreements* using this method.

F

Fabric formation rule: see *fabric forward rule*.

Fabric forward rule: a *rule of origin* much favoured by the United States. The rule says that some specified fabrics and made-up non-apparel articles (e.g. *flat goods*) are deemed to originate in the country where the fabric is woven, knitted or otherwise formed, regardless of any further finishing which may have been performed on the fabrics afterwards. The reasoning behind this rule is the assumption that fabric formation is the most important step in the production of such goods. See also *yarn forward rule*.

Facilitation payments: another name for bribes. See also *trade and illicit payments*.

Factor proportion theory: see *Heckscher-Ohlin theorem*.

Failing-firm doctrine: a doctrine established under United States and some other *antitrust-laws*. It permits mergers that might otherwise be illegal, if some conditions are met. These usually are (a) a grave possibility of a business failure, (b) a lack of any other prospective buyer and (c) a small chance for a successful reorganization of the firm. See also *crisis cartel*.

FAIR Act: see **Federal Agriculture Improvement and Reform (FAIR) Act**.

Fair and equitable treatment: an obligation found in Article XVII (State Trading Enterprises) of the GATT concerning the conduct of *state trading* in relation to government import purchases. This obligation does not have the same force as *most-favoured-nation treatment*, but it was originally meant to give non-discriminatory treatment to the maximum extent possible. The expression is common in *bilateral investment treaties* and other treaties concerned with investment, though it is not usually defined exactly. Some say that the phrase should be understood in its plain meaning, i.e. treatment has to be "fair" and "equitable". Others say that it is the same as the *minimum standard of treatment*. [UNCTAD 1999]

Fair competition: in *trade policy* the proposition that international trade should be conducted within the non-discriminatory rules of the *multilateral trading system*. Sometimes this is also known as the *level playing field*. One element of fair competition in trade is that competition is kept within certain bounds. Otherwise, *anti-dumping measures*, *countervailing duties*, etc., may apply. See also *equitable competition* and *fair trade*.

Fair labour standards: a term with much the same meaning as *core labour standards*. See also *international labour standards* and *social clause*.

Fair trade: this has several meanings. It can be a trading system in which rights and obligations are balanced and observed by participants in the system. To others it means trade without reliance on *dumping* or *subsidies*. In the 1980s, fair trade came to be defined by some as meaning something more akin to *managed trade*, such as the effort to achieve forced bilateral *balance of trade*. In *competition policy*, fair trade refers to the conduct of commercial activities without resort to anti-competitive practices as described by a country's *competition laws*. The context usually makes clear the intended meaning.

Fair-use doctrine: the proposition that works under *copyright* may be drawn on to a limited extent through quotation of excerpts, particularly for scholarly purposes, without leading to claims of *piracy*. Whether use would be considered fair in a particular instance would depend on the circumstances of the case. See also *intellectual property rights* and *intellectual property right infringements*.

Fallacy of composition: the dilemma, as explained for example in the 2002 UNCTAD *Trade and Development Report*, that "on its own a small developing country can substantially expand its exports without flooding the market and seriously reducing the prices of the products concerned, but this may not be true for developing countries as a whole". Proponents of this view often use the analogy of spectators in a football stadium. If the people in the front rows stand up to see better, those in the seats behind also have to stand up. The result is that hardly anybody is better off. The fallacy lies in assuming that if something works for one economy, it could or should work for lots of others also. See also *prisoner's dilemma*. [Mayer 2002]

False indications of source: see *indications of source*.

Famous mark: a *trademark* which is obviously known to many, but the meaning of the term does not appear to be defined further. Courts of law, in deciding whether a mark is famous, make use of criteria such as the geographical extent of the area where the mark is used or known, what distribution channels are used for the goods bearing the mark, the degree of recognition of the mark among those that buy and sell the good, and so forth. See also *dilution doctrine* and *well-known mark*.

FAO: see *Food and Agricultural Organization*.

FAO Consultative Sub-Committee on Surplus Disposal: see *Consultative Sub-Committee on Surplus Disposal*.

Farmer's privilege: the right of farmers to make use of seeds produced from stock protected under the United States *Plant Variety Protection Act* of 1970 without infringing the *intellectual property rights* of the owner of the protected stock. [Abbott *et al.* 1999]

Farmers' rights: a concept developed by the *Food and Agricultural Organization* (FAO) through the *International Undertaking on Plant Genetic Resources*, adopted in 1983. An interpretative resolution to the Undertaking passed in 1989 defines farmers' rights as "rights arising from the past, present and future contribution of farmers in conserving, improving and making available plant genetic resources, particularly those in the centres of origin/diversity". The FAO says that farmers' rights are not assigned to specific varieties, types of plants, or to specific farmers as, for example, *intellectual property rights* are. The purpose of farmers' rights is to encourage farmers and farming communities to nurture, conserve, utilize and improve plant genetic resources. Farmers' rights are therefore seen as a way to compensate farmers for improvements they have made over a long time, and for which they may not be able to benefit from protection through intellectual property rights. See also *traditional knowledge*.

Farm Security and Rural Investment Act: the United States agricultural law, signed by President Bush on 13 May 2002, which replaces the *Federal Agriculture Improvement and Reform Act* of 1996. Among many other provisions, it extends the *Export Enhancement Program*, the *Food for Progress* program and the *Food for Peace* program until 2007. Critics claim that this Act authorizes substantial handouts to anyone engaged in farming and related activities without apparently promoting structural adjustment. Its provisions can be seen both as a cause of and a reaction to the problems caused by distorted agricultural production and trade policies elsewhere in the world.

Fast-track: a mechanism, now renamed *Trade Promotion Authority*, available since the passage of the 1974 United States Trade Act under which Congress can only approve or disapprove in its entirety a regional or multilateral trade package negotiated by *USTR*. The main conditions are (a) that Congress is informed of the likely outcome of negotiations well before they are concluded to allow for consultations with the Administration, (b) that committees would report on the bill within a short time, and (c) that debate over the bill in both houses would be limited. Some WTO members think that the United States cannot negotiate seriously in *multilateral trade negotiations* until it has received fast-track authorization. There is much truth in this view, but Congress tends to take in any case a strong interest in all phases of the negotiations and make its views known to the Administration. Others see the main benefit of fast-track authority as giving other countries the signal that the United States is ready to negotiate. See also *reverse fast-track*. [Hornbeck and Cooper 2006]

Favourable-balance-of-trade objective: see *mercantilism*.

FCN treaties: see *Treaties of Friendship, Commerce and Navigation*.

Federal Agriculture Improvement and Reform (FAIR) Act: the formal name of the comprehensive farm bill covering both production and trade aspects passed by the United States Congress on 28 March 1996 and signed into law by President Clinton on 4 April. The Act largely retained the existing export subsidy programs, such as the *Dairy Export and Incentive Program* and the *Export Enhancement Program*, but it put a ceiling on expenditure on them. The Act also envisaged a seven-year program to remove the link between production and payments to some farmers, particularly those growing rice, cotton, feedgrains, wheat and oilseeds. It has now been succeeded by the *Farm Security and Rural Investment Act*. See also *Commodity Credit Corporation*.

FEOGA: Fonds européen d'orientation et de garantie agricole. See *European Agricultural Guidance and Guarantee Fund*.

Fetish of industrialization: an expression used by Clair Wilcox in *A Charter for World Trade* (written in 1949) to describe what he calls an insistent demand in undeveloped countries that standards of living be improved, and an irrational belief that this improvement is to be obtained only through a rapid industrialization of their economies. He noted that this was almost always accompanied by severe restrictions on foreign trade. See also *developing countries and the multilateral trading system*, *import substitution* and *infant-industry argument*.

Fibre-forward rule: a *rule of origin* favoured especially by the United States. It requires that fibres must be made in the territories of the partners to these trade agreements and subsequent processing must also occur there if the product is to receive preferential treatment. See also *fabric-forward rule* and *yarn-forward rule*.

Fifth Protocol to the General Agreement on Trade in Services: gives effect to the commitments on trade in *financial services* following negotiations in 1996 and 1997. It entered into force on 1 March 1999.

Final determination of dumping: once all aspects of a petition for *anti-dumping measures* have been examined, the investigating authority will give the reasons for its decision in a final determination. This may have been preceded by a *preliminary determination of dumping*. The final determination can either be negative (i.e. the requirements for imposing anti-dumping measures have not been met) or positive (i.e. the requirements have been met). Investigations leading to a final determination normally will be concluded within twelve months of the initiation, but in exceptional cases it may last up to eighteen months. All determinations have to be published. See also *dumping*.

Final goods and services: goods and services bought by end-users. They are not used in any further production process. This distinguishes them from intermediate goods and services. The distinction depends entirely on who buys them. A teapot bought for use at home is a final product, but teapots bought by hotels for the provision of breakfast tea are clearly an intermediate good for the provision of a final service.

Final rate: in a program of phased or staged tariff reductions the rate reached when the last reduction has been made.

Financial services: banking, general insurance, life insurance, funds management, securities trading and advisory services related to these activities. See *Understanding on Financial Services*.

First Account: the program under the *Common Fund for Commodities* which finances international *buffer stocks* and internationally coordinated national stocks, but only if they are operated in the framework of *Integrated Programme for Commodities*. This program is inactive. See also *Second Account*.

First Agreement on Trade Negotiation Among Developing Countries of ESCAP: see *Asia-Pacific Trade Agreement*.

First-difference negotiations: another name for the technique of bilateral *requests and offers* followed in the WTO system for trade in goods and services.

First-difference reciprocity: a term used by Bhagwati to describe bargaining for tariff cuts based on perceived advantages at the margin. He contrasts this with negotiations that would lead to perceived equality of market access and reverse market access. See also *first-difference negotiations*. [Bhagwati 1988]

First-in, first-out: a method of inventory management which uses the cost of the oldest goods in stock as the valuation basis. Its main relevance to trade policy stems from the need to calculate a *regional value content* under the *rules of origin* adopted in some *free-trade agreements*. See also *last-in, first-out* and *averaging*.

First in time, first in right: the principle that the first person acquiring an *intellectual property right*, such as a *trademark* or a *geographical indication*, is the person who has the right to use it.

First-mover advantage: the benefits said to be available to a firm because it is the first in the market with a new technology or a new process.

First-order protectionism: the trade-restrictive measures falling broadly into the category of *voluntary restraint arrangements*. This term is based on the incontrovertible intention that any such measures should be protectionist. See also *protectionism*.

First regionalism: used by Jagdish Bhagwati to describe the wave of *preferential trade arrangements* concluded during the 1950s and 1960s. The two main surviving arrangements from that time are the *European Community* and *EFTA*. [Bhagwati 1993]

First-sale doctrine: see *exhaustion doctrine*.

First-to-file: a procedure to determine priority of *patent* rights. Most countries, the United States and the Philippines being the main exceptions, accord priority of invention to the person registering first regardless of when the invention took place. The United States and the Philippines use the "first-to-invent" principle to accord priority. The main advantage of the first-to-file method is that, if a dispute arises about the precedence of claims, it establishes a clear starting point for any determination of which inventor may have priority rights. Under the first-to-invent method, the applicable date may have to be established laboriously through the use of notebooks and other records. See also *intellectual property rights*.

First-to-invent: see *first-to-file*.

Five Interested Parties: FIPs. A group formed during the negotiations on agriculture under the *Doha Development Agenda*. It consists of Australia, Brazil, European Community, India and the United States. It is known also as the P-5 and the NG-5.

Fixed exchange rate: see *exchange rate*.

Fixed quota: a quota set for the volume of import of goods that may not be exceeded in set period. See also *tariff rate quota*.

Flag of convenience: a nationality of a ship, indicated by the flag it flies, different to the nationality of the ship's owner. Flag-of-convenience registries offer the shipowner a choice of the least onerous conditions in terms of registration costs, mandatory manning requirements, wages and, possibly, safety requirements.

Flat goods: in the textiles trade items such as bed linen, quilts, blankets, table linen, wall hangings, curtains, interior blinds, towels, etc.

Flat-tariff structure: a *tariff schedule* in which all tariff rates are equal or nearly equal. The famous example is that of Chile which in 2003 had an *applied MFN tariff rate* of 6% for nearly all imports. The *bound rate* for most of these tariffs was 25%. See also *dispersed tariff*.

Flexibility provisions: these relate to the reductions to be made in agricultural export subsidies as a result of the *Uruguay Round* negotiations. If a country's export subsidies increased since the 1986–90 *base period* on which the negotiations were based, it had the option of using 1991–92 as the base period. However, the end-points for achieving the reductions remained the same. Flexibility provisions were also part of the *Agreement on Textiles and Clothing*. They permitted swing (transfer of part of an export quota for one product to another product), carryover (the use in the current year of an unused export quota from the previous year) and carry forward (the use of part of next year's quota during the current year). The flexibility provisions listed in the Agreement on Textiles and Clothing had their origin in the *Multi-Fibre Arrangement*. See also *Agreement on Agriculture*.

Floating exchange rate: see *exchange rate*.

Floating initial negotiating rights: see *initial negotiating rights*.

Floor price: a guaranteed price level for commodity producers. It may be higher or lower than the world market price for that commodity. In *international commodity agreements* the floor price may be the level at which the *buffer stock* manager must buy in an effort to reduce supply to the market and in this way support the price. See also *Common Agricultural Policy*, *loan rate* and *trigger price mechanism*.

Florence Agreement: *Agreement on the Importation of Educational, Scientific and Cultural Materials*. Adopted under *United Nations Educational, Scientific and Cultural Organization* (UNESCO) auspices in 1950. Parties to the Agreement undertake not to levy import duties on books, publications, documents and educational, scientific and cultural materials listed in the annexes. A protocol to the Agreement adopted in 1977 modernized the lists of materials covered.

Flying-geese paradigm: the proposition that economic development in a given region can be led by a major economy, with other following behind, similar to the V-pattern adopted by flying geese. It apparently was originally proposed by the Japanese economist Kaname Akamatsu in the 1930s. [Kasahara 2004]

FOB: free on board. The producer, seller or exporter of a good meets all costs and charges for the handling of a good until it has been loaded on a ship in the agreed port. For example, an exporter might quote the price of a good as "FOB Antwerp". The buyer would then be responsible for the cost of freight and insurance from the point it has been put aboard the ship in Antwerp. See also *CIF*.

FOB value method: one of the methods used to establish whether a good imported from another party to a *free-trade agreement* qualifies for the *preferential tariff*. In the free-trade agreement between Japan and Singapore the formula is:

$$QVC = \frac{FOB - NQM}{FOB} \times 100$$

where QVC is the qualifying value content (in other agreements often described as the *regional value content*) of a good, expressed as a percentage, FOB is the free-on-board value of a good payable by the buyer to the seller regardless of the mode of shipment, and NQM is the non-qualifying value of the materials used in the production of the good. This method is the same as the *build-down method* and the *transaction value method*.

Folklore: an aspect of *traditional knowledge*. The protection of folkloric expressions against illicit exploitation has been discussed in the *United Nations Educational, Scientific and Cultural Organization* and *WIPO* for many years. Some have suggested that it should also become part of the WTO agenda. See also *traditional cultural expressions*.

Food Aid Convention: see *International Grains Agreement*.

Food and Agricultural Organization: FAO. Established in 1945 as one of the *United Nations specialized agencies*. Its aims, as set out in the preamble to its constitution, are (a) raising levels of nutrition and standards of living of the peoples of member states, (b) securing improvements in the efficiency of the production of all food and agricultural products, (c) bettering the condition of rural populations, and (d) in this way contributing toward an expanding world economy and ensuring humanity's freedom from hunger. The FAO has, among others, committees on commodity problems, agriculture, and world *food security*. One of these is the *Consultative Sub-Committee on Surplus Disposal*. The FAO is active in land and water development, plant and animal production, forestry and fisheries. Together with the World Health Organization, the FAO administers the *Codex Alimentarius* Commission, intended to promote the harmonization of requirements for food and thereby facilitate international trade. The FAO is located in Rome. See also *International Treaty on Plant Genetic Resources for Food and Agriculture*, *International Undertaking on Plant Genetic Resources* and *World Food Programme*.

Food for Peace program: see *PL 480*.

Food for progress program: a United States program established under the *Food Security Act* of 1985. It encourages agricultural policy reform in developing countries through food donations and sales at concessional prices. Commodities are provided under this program to developing countries and emerging democracies that have committed themselves to some elements of free enterprise in their agricultural economies. All edible commodities managed by the *Commodity Credit Corporation* are eligible for exports under this program. The *Farm Security and Rural Investment Act* of 2002 renewed the program until 2007.

Food-importing Group: this was established early in the *Uruguay Round* to represent the interests of developing countries dependent on imports of food.

Food security: a concept aimed at ensuring that the nutritional needs of a country are met. It is sometimes used to discourage opening the domestic market to foreign agricultural products on the principle that a country must be as self-sufficient as possible for its basic dietary needs. See also *Food and Agricultural Organization*, *food security box* and *World Food Programme*.

Food security box: a proposal made in 2001 by India to amend the WTO *Agreement on Agriculture*. Key elements of the box would be: (a) government service programs, food security stocks, domestic food aid, natural disaster relief, structural adjustment programs, environmental support measures, poverty alleviation, rural development and rural employment programs to be exempt from subsidy reduction programs, (b) developing countries to have flexibility in providing agricultural subsidies, (c) flexibility for developing countries in the administration of tariff bindings and (d) developing countries to be exempt from making minimum market access commitments. See also *development box*.

Foot dragger: a party to *multilateral trade negotiations* which uses the *consensus* rule to prevent a decision or to water down the force of a provision to suit its own purposes. See also *convoy problem*.

Footloose industries: a term used for industries for which the location is relatively unimportant for production and sales because they do not depend on an elaborate physical infrastructure or large fixed investment. They can easily move elsewhere in search of a cheaper and better operating environment. Sometimes they have to do this in order to satisfy new *rules of origin*. Some service activities, such as information processing, are thought to fall into the category of footloose industries. *Globalization*, which can spread the production process over many countries, is thought to give some impetus to the emergence of such industries. Remember, though, that in the long run all industries are footloose. See also *delocalization*.

Forced technology transfer: the practice of requiring firms to transfer some of their technology to the host country as part of receiving approval to invest when there is no existing law or regulation concerning the *transfer of technology*. See also *compulsory licensing*.

Foreign Corrupt Practices Act: FCPA. A United States law adopted in 1977 which imposes criminal liability on its corporations and individuals who are involved in offering inducements to officers of foreign governments to obtain or retain business. The FCPA is therefore directly relevant to rules and practices governing *government procurement*. See also *trade and illicit payments*.

Foreign direct investment: defined by the *IMF* as "direct *investment* that is made to acquire a lasting interest in an enterprise operating in an economy other than that of the investor, the investor's purpose being to have an effective voice in the management of the enterprise". Much thought has been given to the meaning of "lasting interest". The *OECD* has recommended that 10% or greater ownership should satisfy this requirement. The OECD also defines direct investment flows as (i) the direct investor's net purchases of the company's share capital and net loans, trade and other credits advanced, and (ii) the direct investor's share of reinvested earnings. See also *APEC Non-Binding Investment Principles*, *Foreign Investment Advisory Service*, *non-equity-based investment*, *portfolio investment* and *World Bank Guidelines on the Treatment of Foreign Direct Investment*.

Foreign exports: see *re-exports* and, for comparison, *domestic exports*.

Foreign Investment Advisory Service: FIAS. An advisory service originally established by the *International Finance Corporation* and now operated jointly by it with the *World Bank*. It assists developing countries in attracting increasing amounts of *foreign direct investment*. Its main activities include giving advice to governments on foreign investment laws, the institutions needed to administer foreign investment and to develop investment promotion strategies. See also *Multilateral Investment Guarantee Agency*.

Foreign investment screening: a mechanism operated by many countries to ensure that projects financed with foreign investment meet national development objectives and *economic needs tests*, and that foreign equity in specific sectors or companies does not exceed legal limits. Screening also aims to promote *bona-fide* investment proposals. The importance of foreign investment screening for *trade policy* stems from the fact that some see it as capable of being a trade impediment in cases where foreign investment is essential for effective *market access*. The screening process may result in the refusal of an application to invest and therefore to a denial of market access. See also *Exon-Florio amendment* and *pre-establishment*.

Foreign investment protection agreements: see *bilateral investment treaties* and *investment promotion and protection agreements*.

Foreign parity: see *most-favoured-nation treatment*.

Foreign sales corporation: FSC. A corporation established and maintained in a foreign country responsible for the export, sale and lease of goods and services produced in the United States. In this way, it may benefit from some tax exemptions and special administrative pricing rules. An FSC need not be affiliated with or controlled by a United States corporation to qualify for the benefits, but the benefits are greatest if such a relationship exists. Accordingly, most FSCs are subsidiaries of United States corporations. The FSC scheme was introduced in the early 1980s as the successor to the *domestic international sales corporation* (DISC) after a GATT panel ruled in 1976 that DISC was inconsistent with GATT rules. In 1998 the *European Communities* requested the establishment of a WTO *panel* because in its view the United States provisions for FSCs constituted a subsidy and that, therefore, the United States had violated its obligations under the *Agreement on Subsidies and Countervailing Measures*. The panel found against the United States. Following an appeal by the United States, the *Appellate Body* ruled that the FSC constituted a prohibited subsidy under this Agreement on Subsidies and Countervailing Duties and under the *Agreement on Agriculture*.

Formula cuts: tariff reductions across whole sectors done through the use of a formula, such as the *Swiss Formula*.

Formula-plus tariff reductions: the use of *linear tariff cuts*, accompanied by other methods to achieve tariff reductions.

Formula tariff reductions: see *linear tariff cuts*.

Fortress effect: this refers to the possibility that *regional integration agreements* may lead to more protectionist attitudes by member countries towards non-members. Much careful analysis of this problem has not led to conclusive evidence either way.

Fortress Europe: a term expressing the fear by some that the formation of the *European Community Single Market* would turn the Community into an inward-looking market more difficult to penetrate. Such fears have not been justified.

Forum-shopping: the practice of introducing a proposal or pursuing a dispute in one forum after another until a favourable outcome has been achieved. Sometimes also called forum-hopping.

Four freedoms: the free movement of goods, capital, labour and *services*. The expression is often used in the context of the *Treaty of Rome* where they are mandated in Titles I and III. See also *deep integration* and *European Economic Area*.

Four pillars of trade liberalization: described by Gerard Curzon in *Multilateral Commercial Diplomacy* as *most-favoured-nation treatment*, reliance on the *customs tariff* rather than *non-tariff measures*, *tariff negotiations* leading to reduction of tariffs and tariff stabilization through rules enabling the binding of tariffs. [Curzon 1965]

Fourth Protocol to the General Agreement on Trade in Services: gives effect to the commitments on *basic telecommunications services* negotiated after the conclusion of the *Uruguay Round*. It entered into force on 5 February 1998. See also *Agreement on Basic Telecommunications Services*.

Framework Agreement on the ASEAN Investment Area: entered into force on 21 June 1999. See *ASEAN Investment Area*.

Framework Agreements: the name given to four outcomes of the *Tokyo Round* negotiations dealing particularly with developing-country issues. The four instruments are (i) the *Enabling Clause*, (ii) the Declaration on Trade Measures Taken for Balance-of-Payments Purposes, (iii) the Decision on Safeguard Action for Development Purposes and (iv) the Understanding Regarding Notification, Consultation, Dispute Settlement and Surveillance. The term "framework agreements" was taken from paragraph 2 of the *Tokyo Declaration* which sought, among other matters, an "improvement of the international framework for the conduct of world trade" in response to developing-country concerns that the trading system did not meet fully their needs. See also *developing countries and the multilateral trading system* and *Tokyo Round agreements*.

Framework Convention on Climate Change: see *United Nations Framework Convention on Climate Change*.

Framework for Comprehensive Partnership between Japan and the Association of South East Asian Nations: see *ASEAN-Japan Comprehensive Economic Partnership*.

Francophone countries: a grouping of countries where French is spoken or wher French culture is influential. They are members of the Organisation Internationale de la Francophonie (OIF). French is the national language or one of the national languages in the following countries: Belgium, Benin, Burkina-Faso, Burundi, Cameroon, Canada, Central African Republic, Chad, Comoros, Democratic Republic of Congo, Djibouti, France, Gabon, Guinea, Haiti, Côte d'Ivoire, Luxembourg, Madagascar, Mali, Monaco, Niger, Republic of Congo, Rwanda, Senegal, Seychelles, Switzerland, Togo and Vanuatu. Some twenty other countries are member states of the OIF because of the role French plays in their cultures.

Free and fair trade: the idea, enunciated particularly well in United States tariff and trade policy, that from the perspective of economic development and global welfare *free trade* is a highly desirable objective, but only if one's trading partners also play fairly under the rules they have accepted. If they adhere to unfair practices, they should not be entitled to the benefits of open market access. There is a well-documented view, for example, that the thinking underpinning the emergence of *Section 301* is aimed not at protecting the United States market, but to ensure that other economies similarly open their markets. See also *level playing field*.

Freedom-of-emigration provision: see *Jackson-Vanik amendment*.

Freedom of transit: the right, available to members of the WTO under Article V of the GATT, to transport goods unhindered across the territory of another member for them to be able to reach their final destination. The right includes the use of vessels and other means of transport for the purpose. Members may not discriminate between goods and means of transport from other members, and they may not levy *customs duties* on goods in transit. They are, however, entitled to recover administrative expenses based on the actual cost of any services provided in connection with the transit.

Freedoms of the air: aviation experts divide the right of airlines to fly through or over their domestic territories into eight categories called freedoms of the air, though only the first six are in common use. The eight are (i) the right to fly over a country, (ii) the right to land in a country to refuel or similar purposes, but not to pick up or set down passengers or cargo, (iii) the right to set down passengers or cargo in another country, (iv) the right to pick up passengers or cargo in another country and set them down in the airline's home country, (v) the right to carry passengers or cargo between third countries using one's own country as a hub, (vi) the ability to combine rights acquired under the third and fourth freedoms, (vii) the right to operate air services between third countries entirely outside one's home country, and (viii) the right to provide air services within a country, often called *cabotage*. These freedoms are usually negotiated between governments on behalf of domestic airlines. See also *bilateral air services agreement*, *Chicago Convention*, *Multilateral Agreement on the Liberalization of International Air Transportation* and *open-skies arrangements*.

Free imports: goods that can be imported without the payment of any *customs duties*. See also *free list* and *zero rating*.

Free list: a listing of products that can be imported free of customs duties or that are not subject to *import licensing* requirements.

Free riders: casual term used to imply that a country which does not make any trade concessions, profits, nonetheless, from tariff cuts and concessions made by other countries under the most-favoured-nation principle. From an economic perspective, free riders do themselves harm because they deny themselves the benefits of trade liberalization. See also *most-favoured-nation treatment*.

Free trade: in principle, the free movement across borders of goods, services, capital and people. In practice, national policy and regulatory objectives put greater or lesser constraints on the movement of each. The meaning of "free trade" itself has changed over the years. Observers have noted that in the case of American policy free trade meant a tariff under 20% in the early nineteenth century. By the late nineteenth century freetraders advocated tariff levels below 40%. By the middle of the twentieth century free trade meant a tariff of less than 5%. In the case of *AFTA*, free trade is understood to be a tariff ranging from 0% to 5%. Under Article XXIV of the GATT, *customs unions* and *free-trade areas* have to eliminate duties and other restrictive regulations of commerce on substantially all the trade between the parties to meet the free-trade criterion. The norm there is the abolition of all tariffs between the partners either immediately or over several years. See also *Bogor Declaration, economic integration arrangements, four freedoms* and *free and fair trade*.

Free-trade agreement: a contractual arrangement between two or more countries under which they give each other *preferential market access*, usually called *free trade*. In practice, free-trade agreements tend to allow for all sorts of exceptions, many of them temporary, to cover *sensitive products*. In some cases, free trade is no more than a longer-term aim. In other cases the agreement creates a form of managed trade liberalization. Observers have noted that many recent free-trade agreements have run to several hundred pages, whereas a true free-trade agreement would require only a few lines. *Preferential rules of origin*, an essential part of any free-trade agreement, can be too strict for the Agreement to be of much benefit to exporters. Indeed, some recent analytical evidence strongly suggests that many free-trade agreements do not make a worthwhile contribution to trade expansion between the parties. See also *best practice for RTAs/FTAs in APEC, customs union, free-trade area, FTA syndrome, regional integration arrangement* and *regional trade arrangement*. [Adams, Dee, Gali and McGuire 2003, Bartels and Ortino 2006, Crawford and Fiorentino 2005, Dent 2006, Desker 2004, World Trade Organization 2003]

Free-trade area: a group of two or more countries or economies, *customs territories* in technical language, that have eliminated *tariff* and all or most *non-tariff measures* affecting trade among themselves. Participating countries usually continue to apply their existing tariffs on external goods. Free-trade areas are called reciprocal when all partners eliminate their tariffs and other barriers towards each other. There are cases where developing country partners are exempt from making equivalent reductions, as is the case with *SPARTECA* and the *ACP-EC Partnership Agreement*, even though they get free access to developed-country markets. These are called non-reciprocal free-trade areas. See also *customs union*, *trade creation*, *trade deviation* and *trade diversion*.

Free Trade Area of the Americas: see *FTAA*.

Free Trade Area of the Asia-Pacific: FTAAP. A proposal for a *free-trade area* consisting of the *APEC* members, but other configurations may also be possible. It is not yet on the negotiating table.

Free-trade zones: these are defined areas, also called export processing zones, normally located near transport nodal points and designated by governments for the duty-free import of raw materials or manufacturing components intended for further processing or final assembly and their re-export afterwards. Such products are exported to markets in other countries. Successful free-trade zones tend to have a plentiful supply of relatively cheap and adequately skilled labour. Countries establishing free-trade zones usually are characterized by non-competitive domestic industries and regulatory frameworks, and this is one way in which they gain access to foreign investment and markets. Such zones sometimes lead to technology transfers to host countries, but often that is not an objective of companies establishing operations in them.

French plan: see *Pflimlin plan*.

***French wheat and wheat flour* case:** in 1958 Australia lodged a complaint in the *GATT* that because of subsidies granted by the French Government on exports of wheat and wheat flour, French exports of these products had displaced Australian exports to its traditional wheat flour markets in Ceylon (now Sri Lanka), Indonesia and Malaya (now Malaysia). Australia maintained that France was acting inconsistently with its obligations under GATT Article XVI:3. This Article states that members should seek to avoid the use of export subsidies on the export of *primary products*, and that if they were using them, it should not be done in such a manner as to result in them obtaining a more than *equitable share of world trade* in that primary product. The case therefore centred on the meaning of "equitable share". French exports of wheat and wheat flour in the previous 25 years had fluctuated widely, but there was a sudden increase in wheat, and especially wheat flour, exports beginning in 1954. Prices charged for French wheat flour exports had on the whole been lower than those of other exporters. The *panel* found that the French practices resulted in the payment of subsidies on the export of wheat and wheat flour and therefore fell within the ambit of Article XVI:3. The panel then turned to the question of whether France had in this way obtained more than an equitable share of the world market for wheat and wheat flour. It noted that GATT Article XVI did not offer a definition of "equitable share". There was, however, implicit agreement among GATT members in the light of their negotiations of the negotiations of the *Havana Charter* and the *GATT review session* of 1955 that "equitable share" applied to the global market and not to exports to an individual market. It was understood also, the panel said, that the need for the efficient and economic supply of world markets should not be ignored. The panel recalled that French exports of wheat and wheat flour had risen substantially from 1954 above the levels achieved in the previous twenty years, and that they also represented an increase in France's share of world exports in these products. It concluded on the basis of the evidence on tonnages and price levels that France's subsidy arrangements had contributed to a large extent to a share of world exports that had to be considered more than equitable. The panel recommended that France consider measures to avoid creating adverse effects on Australian exports of flour to Southeast Asian markets. This might be done through changing its payments system or entering into consultations with Australia before new contracts were concluded by French exporters of flour to these markets.

Friends of Multifunctionality: an informal group active at one time formed to promote acceptance of the concept of *multifunctionality* of agriculture in the WTO and elsewhere. Core members are the European Community, Japan, Mauritius, Norway, Republic of Korea and Switzerland.

Frontier traffic: usually refers to trade across a frontier by local inhabitants in a clearly defined geographical area who have well-developed kinship ties or a long-standing economic association. Under Article XXIV of the GATT countries may decide not to apply all of the usual customs formalities to border trade. Goods traded in this way are not expected to find their way into the broader economy on either side of the border. The GATT does not specify what distance each side of the frontier is to be considered to lie within the frontier zone, but many pre-war trade agreements settled on a limit of fifteen kilometres on either side of the border. The *General Agreement on Trade in Services* states that *most-favoured-nation treatment* need not apply in the case of exchanges of services in contiguous frontier zones if they are produced and consumed locally.

Frontloading: refers to the practice of ensuring that liberalization commitments under an agreement or arrangement are proportionately heavier at the beginning of the implementing period. See also *Agreement on Textiles and Clothing* and *backloading*.

FTAA: Free Trade Area of the Americas. Also called Western Hemisphere Free Trade Agreement. Agreed as an objective at the Miami Summit of the Americas in December 1994 to cover all the Americas, except Cuba. Negotiations were launched at the Summit of the Americas held in March 1998 in Santiago de Chile with 2005 is the target date for its entry into force. Eleven working groups covering market access, customs procedures and rules of origin, investment, standards and technical barriers to trade, sanitary and phytosanitary measures, subsidies, anti-dumping and countervailing duties, smaller economies, government procurement, intellectual property rights, services, and competition policy have been established. See also *Enterprise for the Americas Initiative*.

FTAAP: see *Free Trade Area of the Asia-Pacific*.

FTA syndrome: entering into negotiations for *free-trade agreements* for the sole or main reasons that other countries are also negotiating them. This is sometimes also called "competitive proliferation of FTAs". [Nagai 2003]

Full balance-of-payments consultations: consultations in the WTO following the invocation by a member of the WTO provisions permitting measures to safeguard its external financial position. Full consultations are distinguished from the simplified consultations used mainly for *least developed countries*. Consultations are done using documentation prepared by the member itself, a factual background paper drafted by the WTO Secretariat and an analysis prepared by the *IMF* on recent economic developments. The consultations cover the member's *balance of payments* and prospects, alternative methods to restore equilibrium, system and methods of restrictions and the effects of restrictions. See also *balance-of-payments consultations*.

Full cumulation: used in the administration of *preferential rules of origin*. Any processing of a good within the area covered by a *preferential trade agreement* is counted as *qualifying value content* regardless of whether the process is sufficient to turn it into an *originating good*. In this case, the whole preferential area is considered a single territory, and any processing within it is counted towards the determination of origin. [Commission of the European Communities 2003, Productivity Commission 2003]

Full parallelism: see *parallelism in export support*.

Full preferential trade agreement: describes a *preferential trade agreement* under which all of the parties accord each other free trade in all or nearly all products. See also *partial preferential trade agreement*.

Functional trade agreement: a form of trade agreement now seldom used. It seeks to deal with a particular type of form of trade, measure or occurrence. Examples are *government procurement*, measures to restrict or manage trade and the imposition of *countervailing duties*.

Functioning of the GATT System: FOGS. One of the negotiating groups established at the start of the *Uruguay Round*. Its negotiating mandate was defined as enhancing the surveillance in the GATT of national trade policies, improving the overall effectiveness and decision-making of the GATT as an institution and increasing the contribution of the GATT to greater coherence in global economic policy-making. One of its achievements was the establishment of the *Trade Policy Review Mechanism*.

Fundamental principles and rights at work: see *Declaration on Fundamental Principles and Rights at Work*.

Fungible goods: also called fungibles or fungible materials. It is a term used in the administration of *rules of origin*. In *NAFTA.* for example, fungible goods are described as goods or materials that are virtually the same and that can be used interchangeably. See also *identical goods* and *similar goods*.

G

Gaiatsu: a Japanese expression meaning pressure from outside. It is used to describe, both in Japanese and in foreign-language texts, the pressure sometimes brought to bear on Japan by other countries to reform this or that policy.

Gains-from-trade theory: that part of the theory of *international economic relations* which demonstrates that two countries with different price structures are maximizing their economic returns if they trade with each other rather than pursuing *autarky*. The gain lies in the ability of either country to buy more at a lower cost from the other than it would be if it attempted to be self-sufficient. The consequence is specialization in production. See also *absolute advantage, comparative advantage, Heckscher-Ohlin theorem, globalization, international division of labour, internationalization, self-reliance* and *self-sufficiency*.

Gate-keeper effect: control by a company of an infrastructure facility that is essential for others to develop their businesses. See also *essential facilities doctrine*.

GATS: see *General Agreement on Trade in Services*.

GATS 2000: refers to the new round of negotiations on *trade in services* mandated by Article XIX of the *General Agreement on Trade in Services* which began in 2000 and which has been subsumed in the *Doha Development Agenda*.

GATT: *General Agreement on Tariffs and Trade*. This has two meanings. The first is the international organization and the secretariat that administered the Agreement. This has been superseded by the WTO. The second meaning is the text of the Agreement itself. The GATT entered into force on 1 January 1948 as a provisional agreement and remained so until it was superseded by the WTO framework on 1 January 1995. It consists of four parts. Parts I to III are, with minor changes, the original GATT adopted in 1947. Part IV was added in 1966. Part I, in Article I, contains the obligation to extent *most-favoured-nation treatment* to all other members of the Agreement. Article II requires each member (called *contracting party* in the Agreement) to maintain a schedule which sets out the terms and conditions under which a good may be imported. This is usually known as the tariff schedule. Part II contains most of the provisions applicable to trade in goods. Article III requires members to apply internal taxes and other charges to imported goods only to the extent that the same charges are applied to goods made locally. This is the *national treatment* obligation. Article IV contains some special provisions relating to films. Screen quotas must conform to certain conditions. Article V guarantees *freedom of transit* through the territory of each member. Goods in transit are exempt from customs duties. Article VI sets out the conditions under which *anti-dumping measures* and *countervailing duties* may be imposed. The *Anti-Dumping Agreement* (formally *Agreement on Implementation of Article VI of the General Agreement on Tariffs and Trade 1994*) now contains much more detailed provisions for the use of anti-dumping measures. Similarly, the *Agreement on Subsidies and Countervailing Measures* sets out the procedures to be followed when countervailing duties are considered. Article VII states that the value of imported goods for customs purposes should be based on the actual value of the goods. Assessments must not be based on national origin or on fictitious values. The *Agreement on Implementation of Article VII of the General Agreement on Tariffs and Trade 1994*, usually known as the *Customs Valuation Agreement*, now contains much more detailed provisions on *customs valuation* procedures. Article VIII says that all fees connected with the import or export of goods must be limited to the approximate cost of the services rendered. Under Article IX *marks of origin* must not be used to disadvantage the products of other members or to discriminate between them. Article X requires each member to publish promptly all laws, regulations, judicial decisions and *administrative rulings of general application* concerning its import and export trade to enable other governments to become familiar with them. Measures must be published officially before they can be applied. This is the *transparency* obligation. Article XI requires the general elimination of *quantitative restrictions*. Quotas, import or export licences are banned except for some closely defined circumstances. The *Agreement on Import Licensing Procedures* now contains rules for the non-discriminatory administration of import licensing. Under Article XII members may resort to import restrictions to safeguard their external financial position, but no more than is necessary to prevent the imminent threat of a serious decline in monetary reserves or to achieve a reasonable increase in monetary reserves if these are low. The *Understanding on Balance-of-Payments Provisions of the General Agreement on Tariffs and Trade 1994* is also relevant for the use of this Article. Members may not, under Article XIII, discriminate between other members when they apply quantitative restrictions. The *Agreement on Import Licensing Procedures* contains rules for the administration of such restrictions. Article XIV states that discrimination in the use of restrictions may be permitted under defined conditions if the benefits to the parties concerned outweigh substantially any injuries to the trade of other members. Article XV sets out the basis of the relationship between the GATT and the *IMF* (International Monetary Fund). This is aimed to coordinate the relationship between *exchange rate* policy and quantitative restrictions. Article XVI requires members to notify all *subsidies* and to seek to avoid the use of subsidies in the export of *primary products*. The *Agreement on Subsidies and Countervailing Measures* sets out more detailed rules concerning the use of subsidies in non-agricultural trade. Under Article XVII *state trading enterprises* must act in a manner consistent with the principle of *non-discrimination* prescribed for private traders. The *Understanding on the Interpretation of Article XVII of the General Agreement on Tariffs and Trade 1994* is also relevant. Article XVIII sets out the conditions under which developing countries may deviate from other provisions of the GATT if they have to support lower standards of living or are in the early stages of development. Action open to them may include balance-of-payments measures or measures for the promotion of *infant industries*. The *Understanding on Balance-of-Payments Provisions of the General Agreement on Tariffs and Trade 1994* is also relevant for the use of this Article. Article XIX allows members to impose temporary import restrictions if, as a result of *tariff concessions*, an import surge threatens to cause or causes *serious injury* to domestic producers. This is the *safeguards* article. All safeguard measures must be applied in a non-discriminatory manner. The *Agreement on Safeguards* now contains detailed procedures concerning the impositions of such measures. Article XX contains the *general exceptions* and Article XXI the *security exceptions*. Article XXII requires each member to respond sympathetically to requests for *consultations* on matters covered by the GATT. Article XXIII forms the legal basis for initiation of *dispute settlement* and sets out the basic procedures to be followed. The *Dispute Settlement Understanding* now contains far more detailed procedures to be followed in the case of consultations and dispute settlement. Part III of the GATT begins with Article XXIV which governs conditions concerning the formation of *free-trade areas* and *customs unions*. It exempts *frontier traffic* from the GATT provisions, and it obliges members to take reasonable measures to ensure observance of the Agreement by regional and local government authorities. Article XXV authorises members to take *joint action*, now overtaken by the provisions of the *WTO Agreement*, and to adopt *waivers*. The *Understanding in Respect of Waivers of Obligations under the General Agreement on Tariffs and Trade 1994* terminated all waivers in existence at the time of the establishment of the WTO unless they had been reauthorized under WTO rules. Article XXVI, now also superseded by the WTO Agreement, describes the conditions under which governments could have become GATT members, and when the Agreement would enter into force. Article XXVII has also been superseded by the WTO Agreement. It states that members do not have to observe the results of tariff negotiations with countries that did not in the end join the GATT or that terminated their membership. Article XXVIII sets out the conditions under which members may modify or withdraw tariff concessions. These used to be valid for three years and were then open to negotiated changes. Rights to *compensation* are also defined. The *Understanding on the Interpretation of Article XXVIII of the General Agreement on Tariffs and Trade 1994* now sets out the conditions applying to *principal supplying rights* which may be used to initiate *tariff negotiations*. Under Article XXVIIIbis members may launch multilateral tariff negotiations from time to time. Article XXIX describes how the GATT was to be treated if the *Havana Charter* had entered into force. Article XXX deals with amendments to the GATT. Any amendments would now have to be done under the WTO Agreement. Article XXXI authorized members to withdraw by giving six months' notice. Withdrawals from the GATT are now only possible as part of withdrawal from the WTO Agreement. Article XXXII deals with membership matters and Article XXXIII with accessions. Both of these articles have been superseded by the WTO Agreement. The only way to adopt the GATT obligations is by joining the WTO. Article XXXIV states that the annexes are an integral part of the Agreement. Eight of these annexes are mainly of historical interest. The ninth, Annex I, contains notes and supplementary provisions important for the interpretation of many of the articles. These are the *ad notes*. Article XXXV describes the conditions under which a member does not have to apply its obligations towards another member. This provision has been superseded by the *non-application* article of the WTO Agreement. *Part IV of the GATT* is concerned trade and development. In Article XXXVI members agree that measures are needed to ensure more favourable market access for products of interest to developing countries. Developed countries agree that that they do not expect *reciprocity* when they act in favour of developing countries. In Article XXXVII developed members undertake to give high priority to reducing and eliminating trade barriers to products of interest to developing countries. Developing countries undertake to open their markets to other developing countries to the extent that their circumstances permit. In Article XXXVIII GATT members agree to collaborate to further these objectives. Some of the articles have *ad notes*. These are later additions to the articles. See also *GATT 1947* and *GATT 1994*. [Jackson 1969, Jackson 1997, Hoekman and Kostecki 1995]

GATT à la carte: a derisory term used by some commentators to describe the situation prevailing up to the end of the *Uruguay Round* whereby GATT members could to a large extent decide themselves which of the *Tokyo Round agreements* they should join. See also *single undertaking*.

GATT Analytical Index: a two-volume guide to the interpretation and application of the *GATT (General Agreement on Tariffs and Trade)* prepared by the Legal Division of the WTO. The *Analytical Index* contains at a highly detailed level the interpretations of the GATT articles made by its membership, dispute settlement panels, etc. up to 1994. It is now superseded by the *WTO Analytical Index*. See also *GATT Basic Instruments and Selected Documents*.

GATT Basic Instruments and Selected Documents: BISD. Reports published annually by the GATT Secretariat between 1952 and 1994 which contain decisions, conclusions and reports adopted in the reporting period. The BISD is indispensable for the administration and study of the GATT and related agreements and codes. It has now been succeeded by the *WTO Basic Instruments and Selected Documents.*

GATT-consistency of national legislation: under the *Protocol of Provisional Accession* national legislation in effect before 1 January 1948 was allowed to remain in force even if it was inconsistent with the provisions of the GATT through the *grandfather clause*. Laws passed after that date had to be in conformity with the GATT, though certain exceptions, for example in the form of strictly circumscribed *waivers*, are still possible. In the *Manufacturing Clause* case, the panel found that amendments to grandfathered legislation may be possible if they do not make it more inconsistent with the GATT, or if they do not cancel rightful expectations of other members. Another panel ruling, this time in the *Superfund* case, held that the mere existence of national legislation permitting discretionary action inconsistent with the GATT did not constitute a violation of obligations under the GATT. The current approach to this question is that outlined in *United States – Measures Affecting the Importation, Internal Use and Use of Tobacco* that [p]anels had consistently ruled that legislation which mandated action inconsistent with the General Agreement could be challenged as such, whereas legislation which merely gave the discretion to the executive authority of a contracting party to act inconsistently with the General Agreement could not be challenged as such; only the actual application of such legislation inconsistent with the General Agreement could be subject to challenge". [GATT BISD 31S, GATT BISD 34S, Naiki 2004, Sim 2003]

GATT Council of Representatives: established on 4 June 1960 to administer the GATT more effectively in view of its expanding work program. Until then, an intersessional committee composed of seventeen members had provided continuity between the annual sessions of the *contracting parties*. The Council's main functions were to consider matters requiring urgent attention between the annual sessions of the contracting parties and to supervise the work of committees, working parties and other subsidiary bodies. All GATT members automatically became members of the Council which met about once a month. In the WTO, the body most nearly performing the functions of the GATT Council is the *General Council*.

GATT plus: an expression implying imposition or acceptance of international trade disciplines more stringent than those prescribed by the GATT or extending the GATT rules to areas beyond trade in goods. One of the most ambitious examples of "GATT plus" was the proposal in 1976 by the Atlantic Council of the United States that there should be a code of *trade liberalization* within the GATT framework with stronger rules for the conduct of trade relations between industrialized countries willing to accept them. According to its proponents, the benefits would have been extended to all GATT members according to the most-favoured-nation clause. The code would also have been open to new members willing to accept its obligations, but only code members would have been able to initiate *tariff negotiations* with another code member. The proposal did not find favour with GATT members as a whole. See also *most-favoured-nation treatment* and *WTO plus*. [Atlantic Council of the United States 1976]

GATT review session: the ninth session of the contracting parties (members) of the GATT, held from October 1954 to March 1955. It reviewed all aspects of the operations of the GATT. Several articles were amended as a consequence, most notably Article XVIII dealing with economic development issues and the rights and obligations of developing countries. Most other changes were minor. See also *developing countries and the multilateral trading system*.

GATT-Think: characterized by Paul Krugman as three simple rules about the objectives of negotiating countries in the GATT: 1. Exports are good. 2. Imports are bad. 3. Other things equal, an equal increase in imports and exports is good.

He says that GATT-Think is enlightened *mercantilism* and economic nonsense. Despite all this, Krugman concedes that the GATT has after all played a useful role in liberalizing the world trading system. [Krugman 1991]

GATT 1947: *General Agreement on Tariffs and Trade 1947*. The old (pre-1994) version of the GATT, adopted at the conclusion in 1947 of the Second Session of the Preparatory Committee of the *United Nations Conference on Trade and Employment*, and as subsequently rectified, amended or modified. It was in force from 1 January 1948 until the conclusion of the *Uruguay Round* when it was replaced by the *GATT 1994*. The two basic texts are virtually identical, but legally distinct, in that the GATT 1947 was an international treaty, whereas the GATT 1994 is only one of the components of the *WTO Agreement*.

GATT 1994: *General Agreement on Tariffs and Trade 1994*. The new version of the *GATT*, which governs trade in goods. It is the formal name for the *GATT 1947* and the collected amendments, interpretations, additions, etc. to it made since its entry into force. It is a part of the agreement establishing the WTO, and it has no independent legal status. It consists, in addition to the provisions contained in the GATT 1947 (not the GATT 1947 agreement itself), of protocols and certifications relating to tariff concessions, protocols of accession, decisions on waivers still in force and other decisions taken by the GATT contracting parties, but not the *grandfather clause*. It also includes six understandings interpreting several GATT articles and the Marrakesh Protocol to GATT 1994 which covers tariff concessions made by members. Countries joining the WTO accept all the rights and obligations contained in the GATT 1994, but they cannot accede separately to it. See also *WTO Agreement* and *single undertaking*.

General Affairs Council: see *Council of the European Union*.

General Agreement on Trade in Services: frequently known as GATS. One of the *Uruguay Round* outcomes. Parts I, II, IV, V and VI apply to all services. Part III applies to the extent that a member has made *specific commitments* on services activities. Part I deals with scope and definitions. Article I states that the GATS covers all trade in services except bilateral air traffic rights. It also describes the four modes of delivery for services: (1) cross-border supply (seller and customer do not meet); (2) consumption abroad (customer goes abroad to buy the services); (3) commercial presence (seller establishes an office in the export market); and (4) through the presence of natural persons. Part II covers general obligations and disciplines. Article II prescribes *most-favoured-nation treatment* for services and services suppliers. It is possible to obtain exemptions from this obligation for individual traded services under defined conditions. These are the *MFN exemptions*. Article III deals with *transparency*. This is the obligation to publish domestic regulations on trade in services as well as major changes to them, and to notify international agreements on trade in services to the WTO. Members also must establish enquiry points where information on regulations may be obtained. Article IV seeks to promote greater participation by developing countries in international services trade. Articles V and V*bis* describe, respectively, the conditions under which members may conclude *economic integration arrangements* and *labour markets integration agreements*. *Free-trade agreements* for services fall under these two articles. Article VI requires members to ensure that all general domestic regulations affecting trade in services are administered reasonably and impartially. Adequate procedures must be in place for verifying professional qualifications. Under Article VII members may not use recognition of qualifications and experience as a disguised barrier to trade. Members may recognize the qualifications of another country and enter into *mutual recognition arrangements* without the need to extend the same conditions to third countries. Article VIII requires members to ensure that monopolies and exclusive service suppliers behave in accordance with the most-favoured-nation principle and the specific commitments they have made. Article IX recognizes that some business practices may restrain competition and restrict trade in services. Members therefore have the right to ask for consultations with a view to eliminating such practices. Article X authorizes negotiations on an article covering emergency *safeguard* measures. Under Article XI members may not impose restrictions on payments and transfers for current transaction in sectors where they have made a specific commitment other than as set out in Article XII (restrictions to safeguard the balance the payments). Any restrictions so imposed must be non-discriminatory. Article XIII exempts *government procurement* from the most-favoured-nation, market access and national treatment provisions. Artciles XIV and XIV*bis* contain the *general exceptions* and *security exceptions*. Article XV recognizes that subsidies may distort trade in services. It also requires members to enter into negotiations on rules concerning subsidies. Part III of the Agreement contains the rules applying to specific commitments. Article XVI covers *market access for services* and Article XVII guarantees *national treatment*. Formally different treatment of foreign firms is possible if formally identical treatment were found to be disadvantaging them. Article XVIII permits members to make *additional commitments* going beyond market access and national treatment. These may include matters concerning qualifications, standards or licensing. Part IV establishes the framework for progressive liberalization of trade in services. Article XIX mandates new round of negotiations and outlines the conditions under which these negotiations will be conducted. Article XX describes the contents of the *schedules of specific commitments*. Entries on market access and national treatment arc obligatory. Article XXI requires that, as a rule, a commitment cannot be reduced or withdrawn inside three years. If such a change is made, *compensation* may be necessary. Unilateral improvements may be made at any time. Part V deals with institutional matters. Article XXII contains the right to *consultations*. Article XXIII states that if a member considers that the outcome of consultations has not been satisfactory, it may seek a solution through *dispute settlement*. In this case, the unified WTO procedures will apply. These are set out in the *Dispute Settlement Understanding*. Article XXIV establishes the *Council for Trade in Services* which in turn may establish subsidiary bodies. Article XXV makes technical cooperation available to developing countries through the Council for

Trade in Services. Article XXVI authorizes the WTO *General Council* to make arrangements for cooperation with United Nations bodies and other *intergovernmental organizations* concerned with services. Part VI contains the final provisions. Under Article XXVII it is possible to deny the benefits of the Agreement to a service supplier under closely defined conditions. Article XXVIII contains more definitions. Article XXIX contains eight annexes. *Annex on Article II exemptions*: Article II of the GATS contains the obligation to extend MFN treatment to the other members of the agreement. Exceptions to this rule are possible under the conditions prescribed in the annex. MFN exemptions must have a specific aim, and they should not last longer than ten years. *Annex on movement of natural persons supplying services under the Agreement*: this annex states that the GATS does not apply to measures regarding citizenship, residence or employment on a permanent basis. GATS members may regulate entry to their territories, but they must not use this right to negate their specific commitments. The *Third Protocol to the General Agreement on Trade in Services* contains new commitments in this area. *Annex on air transport services*: the GATS does not apply to bilateral air traffic rights or services directly related to them. This exception is to be reviewed after five years. *Annex on financial services*: this annex describes in greater detail how the GATS rules apply to trade in financial services. *Second annex on financial services*: this annex is the basis for the negotiations on trade in financial services which concluded on 28 July 1995. The results of these negotiations are contained in the *Second Protocol to the General Agreement on Trade in Services*. The outcome of further negotiations on financial services is contained in the *Fifth Protocol to the General Agreement on Trade in Services*. *Annex on negotiations in maritime transport services*: MFN treatment and MFN exemptions in maritime services will only enter into force once the negotiations on maritime transport services have concluded. *Annex on telecommunications*: members must ensure that foreign service suppliers have access to public telecommunications networks on reasonable and non-discriminatory terms. The annex specifies how this should be done. *Annex on negotiations on basic telecommunications*: MFN treatment and MFN exemptions in basic telecommunications will only enter into force once the negotiations have concluded. The *Fourth Protocol to the General Agreement on Trade in Services* contains the outcome of the negotiations. The negotiations mandated in Article XIX began in 2000. They are now part of the *Doha Development Agenda*. [Sauvé 1995, Sauvé and Stern 2000]

General Agreement on Tariffs and Trade: see *GATT*.

General Considerations and Practical Approaches Concerning Conflicting Requirements Imposed on Multinational Enterprises: see *Decision on Conflicting Requirements*.

General Council: this is a body composed of all WTO members. It has general authority to supervise the various agreements under the jurisdiction of the WTO. It exercises authority between the biennial *WTO Ministerial Conferences* and on behalf of them. It meets about once a month. See also *Dispute Settlement Body* and *Trade Policy Review Mechanism*.

General Exception List: in *AFTA* a list of goods not subject to liberalizing commitments for reasons of national security, protection of human, animal or plant life or health, and the protection of articles of artistic, historic and archaeological value. Similarly, the *ASEAN Investment Area* permits members to include in a General exceptions List industries and investment measures that cannot be opened up for investment or granted *national treatment* for reasons of national security, public morals, public health or environmental protection. See also *Sensitive List*.

General exceptions: the *General Agreement on Trade in Services* (GATS) in Article XIV and the *GATT* in Article XX give WTO members the right not to apply the provisions of these agreements in specified circumstances. But these articles may not be invoked to discriminate between countries or as a *disguised restriction on international trade*. Under the GATT this right may be used, to the extent that it is necessary to do so, (a) to protect public morals, (b) to protect human, animal or plant life or health, (c) to cover trade in gold and silver, (d) to ensure compliance with laws and regulations otherwise consistent with the GATT, customs enforcement, enforcement of monopolies, the protection of intellectual property rights and prevention of deceptive practices, (e) to deal with products made by *prison labour*, (f) to protect national treasures of artistic, historic or archaeological value, (g) to conserve exhaustible natural resources, but only in combination with domestic restrictions on production and consumption, (h) to pursue obligations under international commodity agreements, (i) to restrict exports of domestic materials under strictly defined conditions, and (j) to adopt measures essential for the acquisition or distribution of products in general or local short supply. The GATS, apart from identical provisions on public morals and human, animal and plant life, also mentions public order in cases of genuine and sufficiently serious threat to one of the fundamental interests of society. Its other exceptions cover compliance with laws and regulations not inconsistent with GATS rules, collection of direct taxes and double taxation agreements. See also *security exceptions*. [Klabbers 1992]

Generalized System of Preferences: see *GSP*.

Generally Accepted Accounting Principles: GAAP. These are accounting rules that have achieved the status of widely-used principles to measure and report financial data. They vary between industries and between countries. Their purpose is to present credible financial data to investors, creditors and regulatory authorities. The calculation of the *regional value content* under *preferential rules of origin* sometimes depends on these rules. In the *free-trade agreement* between Canada and Chile GAAP is described as "recognized consensus or substantial authoritative support in the territory of a party with respect to the recording of revenues, expenses, costs, assets and liabilities, disclosure of information and preparation of financial statements. These standards may be broad guidelines of general application as well as detailed standards, practices and procedures". See also *international accounting standards*.

General most-favoured-nation treatment: see *most-favoured-nation treatment*.

General obligations: obligations which should be applied to all services sectors at the entry into force of the *General Agreement on Trade in Services*.

General tariff: this term nowadays is often used instead of *most-favoured-nation tariff* in that it applies to the bulk of one's trading partners. Before the emergence of general *most-favoured-nation treatment* with the entry into force of the GATT in 1948, the general tariff often referred to the tariff applied to countries not receiving *preferences* of one kind or another. In some cases, countries still distinguish between a general tariff and a most-favoured-nation tariff, and the rates contained in the former are usually higher. See also *normal trade relations*.

General trade: goods traded under the rates contained in the *general tariff*. In modern usage it often means goods receiving *most-favoured-nation treatment*.

Generic geographical indications: refers to *geographical indications* which once had meaning in describing a product as having special characteristics because it came from a defined area, but which now has become a common name for a product of that kind. *Moutarde de Dijon* or *Dijon Mustard* and *Swiss Cheese* are the standard examples of generic indications. Once a geographical indication has become generic, it no longer enjoys protection under the relevant laws or treaties. Difficulties can arise when a name is considered a geographical indication in its home country, but a generic name in others. See also *semi-generic geographical indications*. [Audier 2000; Council Regulation (EEC) 2081/92; WIPO SCT/8/4]

Generic springboarding: this is the contentious process by which a firm starts to prepare for the commercial production and sale as a generic product of an item which is still under *patent* protection. The aim of springboarding is to ensure that producers of generic products can enter the market as early as possible once the patent term expires. In the case of pharmaceuticals, where several years may be required to develop a generic drug, springboarding enables firms to manufacture an item still under patent protection for the purpose of meeting pre-regulatory requirements. But commercial activity is not permitted at this stage, and doing so would involve an *intellectual property right infringement*. See also *Bolar exception*, *decompilation*, *intellectual property* and *reverse engineering*.

Genetically modified organism: GMO. An organism in which the genetic material has been altered in a way that would not occur in the natural world.

Genetically modified micro-organism: GMM. A micro-organism in which the genetic material has been altered in a way that would not occur in the natural world.

Genetic labelling: a system of product labelling advocated by some to indicate whether the product or its components have been modified genetically. Proponents argue that doing so is in the interest of consumers and users. Opponents say that this yet another unnecessary *technical barrier to trade* because, for reasons of cost, many producers would prefer not to keep genetically modified crops separate from others. All *European Community* members were required to enact genetic-labelling legislation by 31 July 1997 to ensure that firms located in member states use the labels when necessary. See also *eco-labelling* and *social labelling*.

Geneva Convention: *Convention for the Protection of Producers of Phonograms Against Unauthorized Duplication of their Phonograms*. It protects a producer of phonograms of another member state against the making of duplicates without consent. "Phonogram" means an exclusively aural fixation, i.e. a recording (record, compact disc, tape, etc.). The term does not include sound films or videocassettes.

Geneva Tariff Conference, 1947: consisted of tariff negotiations between the participants in the Preparatory Committee of the *United Nations Conference on Trade and Employment*. About 45,000 *concessions* were exchanged. This was the first occasion when tariff negotiations were conducted multilaterally. Negotiations were conducted under the *principal supplier rule*. In other words, the granting of a concession only had to be considered if the country supplying the largest part of the product made a request for a tariff reduction. The Geneva Tariff Conference is deemed to have been the first round of *multilateral trade negotiations*. See also *principal supplier right*.

Geneva Tariff Conference, 1955–56: a minor round of multilateral tariff negotiations, largely because the United States Congress had limited the negotiating authority of its delegation. It was the last of the formal *tariff conferences*, and it is deemed the fourth round of *multilateral trade negotiations*. See also *Dillon Round*.

Geographical indications: GIs. A category of *indications of source* enjoying protection under *intellectual property* laws or treaties. A geographical indication on a product denotes a close connection between it and the place where it was harvested, processed or produced which gives it a special quality, reputation or characteristic. Some use the term interchangeably with *appellation of origin*. A *WIPO* committee of experts considered in 1990 whether to replace the concepts of "appellations of origin" and "indication of source" with the single term "geographical indication", but it was not able to reach agreement. There seems to be agreement, however, that "appellation of origin" is a narrower term than "geographical indication". Geographical indications are protected by laws or treaties against imitation or misuse. In this way, the good name of a region (e.g. a wine-growing region) built up over a long time cannot be exploited by a company or producers located in another part of the country or abroad. Depending on a country's legal system and the product in question, this can be done through laws concerning *geographical indications*, *trademarks* or under laws governing *unfair competition* or *passing off*. Broadly speaking, the systems of geographical indications for wines and spirits are most developed, partly because it is in this sector that the protection of geographical indications was first implemented in many countries. The protection of geographical indications is sometimes linked with verification of production processes. One cannot assume that all of the wine taken from a bottle bearing a certain geographical indication is necessarily from that area. Mixing regulations often permit the addition of wines brought in from elsewhere. However, the *European Community* rules on wine permit member states to make use of a geographical indication conditional on the wine being produced exclusively in the territory whose name it bears. Efforts to protect geographical indications for cheeses through, for example, the *Stresa Convention*, have been less successful. There is little dispute that geographical indications should be protected unless they have become generic, but opinions on how best to do this vary considerably. Here we can only give an outline of the issues. Intellectual property experts broadly divide the rules for protecting geographical indications into the Lisbon model and the TRIPS model. The Lisbon model is named after the *Lisbon Agreement* which does not, however, use the term "geographical indication". Instead it refers to "appellation of origin". In Article 2(1) the Agreement defines appellation of origin as "the geographical name of a country, region, or locality, which serves to designate a product originating therein, the quality and characteristics of which are due exclusively or essentially to the geographical environment, including natural and human factors". Article 2(2) continues that the "country of origin is the country whose name, or the country in which is situated the region or locality whose name constitutes the appellation of origin which has given the product its reputation". The TRIPS model is named after the WTO *Agreement on Trade-Related Aspects of Intellectual Property Rights* (TRIPS) which contains two levels of protections. First, Article 22.1 defines geographical indications as "indications which identify a good as originating in the territory of a Member, or a region or locality in that territory, where a given quality or other characteristic is essentially attributable to its geographical origin". Second, a higher level of protection obligations applies for geographical indications for wines and spirits. In Article 23.1 it requires WTO members to afford the legal means to interested parties to prevent the use of geographical indications for wines and spirits not originating in the place indicated by the geographical indication, even where the true origin of the goods is indicated or the geographical indication is translated or accompanied by expressions such as "kind, "type, "style", "imitation", etc. This is close to the language on appellations of origin in the Lisbon Agreement. For geographical indications identifying products other than wines and spirits, the TRIPS Agreement requires its members to have in place the legal means for interested parties to prevent the use of a designation that indicates or suggests that the good in question originates in an area other than the true place of origin or any use constituting an act of *unfair competition*. Making provision for interested parties to protect their geographical indications does not necessarily mean that WTO members have to pass new laws, but sometimes legislative action may be necessary. *WIPO* has prepared a *Draft Act on the Protection of Geographical Indications* for this purpose. One difference between the two models is that under the Lisbon Agreement the quality and characteristics of a product must be due exclusively or essentially to the geographical environment, including natural and human factors. In the TRIPS model the quality, reputation or other characteristic of a product must be attributable essentially to its geographical origin. The Lisbon model therefore would appear to be more strict or more narrow than the TRIPS model in that the latter's definition of geographical indications would seem to capture a greater number of them. Some see the relationship between the Lisbon provisions and the TRIPS provisions as contentious. They say that the TRIPS provisions should supersede the Lisbon disciplines to the extent that there is an inconsistency between them. The TRIPS Agreement provides some exceptions to the protection of geographical indications, such as the possibility in Article 24 to continue to use a geographical indication of another country identifying wines or spirits if this use had lasted for at least the ten years preceding the conclusion of the TRIPS Agreement. Members of this Agreement are not obliged to afford protection to a geographical indication of another country if it is not protected in its country of origin. The administration of systems for the protection of geographical indications has always required a degree of flexibility. One reason for this is the occurrence of *homonymous geographical indications* (the same name occurring in more than one country). In some cases geographical indications can turn into *semi-generic geographical indications* or *generic geographical indications*. Once this happens, only a most determined effort can turn the situation around, but in most cases it will be a lost cause. A complicated situation arises when a name of a product is deemed to be the equivalent of a geographical indication even though it is not a placename. This is the case, for example, with *Liebfraumilch* or *Liebfrauenmilch* (Milk of Our Lady), a German white wine of varying quality. Originally the name was used for wines coming from the vineyards of the Liebfrauenkirche (Church of Our Lady) in Worms. German law now requires that wine carrying this name must come from the Rheinhessen, Rheinpfalz, Rheingau or Nahe regions. At issue here is not whether the owners of the name *Liebfraumilch* should enjoy protection against its unlawful use, but whether a name that is clearly no longer a geographical indication should be treated as one because the product bearing it must always come from a defined area. In other words, it is a proxy for a geographical indication. One may contrast this with, for example, the name *Château Giscours*, a French wine. In this case it is possible, through reliance on title registers, maps and local knowledge, to define exactly the locations that are entitled to use this name. At the *Doha Ministerial Conference* WTO members agreed to negotiate "the establishment of a multilateral system of notification and registration of geographical indications for wines and spirits" by the time of the fifth ministerial conference. They also agreed that issues related to the *extension of protection for geographical indications* provided for in Article 23 to products other than wines and spirits will be addressed as an implementation issue. Negotiations are now under way. See also *Organisation for an International Geographical Indications Network*. [Lisbon Agreement for the Protection of Appellations of Origin and their International Registration; WIPO SCT/5/3, SCT/8/4, SCT/9/4; Council Regulation (EC) No 1493/1999; Abbott *et al.* 1999; Addor and Grazioli 2002, Audier 2000, Rangnekar 2003]

Geographical names: many goods traded internationally have displayed on them or their packaging their geographical origin. Audier notes that "a geographical name applied to a product can mean three different things: an *indication of source*, with no special implications in terms of the product's characteristics, and a *geographical indication* or *appellation of origin*, which implies that the product will have a quality or characteristic attributable to its place of origin". The broadest of these names, according to *WIPO* usage, are indications of source. More narrow are geographical indications. Narrower still are appellations of origin. The use of "denomination" in the *Stresa Convention* seems to be roughly equal to geographical indication. In the *European Community* the term *protected designation of origin* is evidently more narrow than a *protected geographical indication*. The definition of geographical names can overlap in laws and treaties. Geographical names themselves are used in different ways. Consider an example given by the International Trademark Association: Swiss cheese, Napa Valley chardonnay and Philadelphia cream cheese. The word "Swiss" is used as a generic expression, "Napa Valley" is a geographical indication and "Philadelphia" is used as a *trademark*. The commercial implications flowing from the three categories are considerable. Any dairy factory can choose to make a cheese loosely resembling the original *Emmental* cheese, though the characteristic large holes are often missing, and sell it as "Swiss cheese". The "Philadelphia cheese" trademark may only be used by its rightful owner who can use it to produce the cheese wherever this is commercially attractive. The owner can also insist that licensed producers make the product in accordance with his standards. "Napa Valley wine", however, may only originate in the territory described as Napa Valley, and this results in a theoretical production ceiling. Many wineries are able to use this geographical indication, and this means that the quality and characteristics of the wines produced in the area show marked variations. See also *extension of protection for geographical indications*, *generic geographical indications*, *homonymous geographical indications*, *multilateral system of notification and registration of geographical indications* and *semi-generic geographical indications*. [Audier 2000; WIPO SCT/8/4; International Trademark Association 2000]

Georgetown Agreement: adopted on 6 June 1975 in Georgetown, Guyana. It established the group of *ACP states*. It was revised on 26 November 1992 with the objective of promoting the aims of the *Lomé Convention*. Membership is open to all states that are members of the Convention, now the *ACP-EC Partnership Agreement*. Cuba is a member of the Georgetown Agreement, but not the ACP-EC Partnership Agreement. The Convention's secretariat is in Brussels.

German imports of sardines: in 1952 Norway brought a complaint to the GATT concerning the alleged discrimination by Germany on imports of *clupea pilchardus* (sardines), *clupea sprattus* (sprats) and *clupea harengus* (herring). In the course of its economic liberalization program, Germany had decided to place sardines on a list allowing unrestricted imports, but sprats and herring remained subject to *quantitative restrictions*. This led to a substantial decrease of Norwegian exports of sprats and herring to Germany. The *panel* was asked by Norway to find that the German measures were in conflict with GATT Articles I:1 (General Most-Favoured-Nation Treatment) and XIII:1 (Non-discriminatory Administration of Quantitative Restrictions) which require imports of *like products* from different countries to receive similar treatment. It considered whether sardines, sprats and herrings should be considered like products, and it noted that Germany in its accession negotiations had always thought the three to be separate products. The panel decided that insufficient evidence had been presented to permit a judgement of discriminatory treatment. See also *Brazilian unroasted coffee*. [GATT BISD 1S]

Glass-Steagall Act: the United States Bank Act of 1933, largely repealed in 1999. It separated commercial and investment banking. Banks, including foreign bank branches and subsidiaries, could not underwrite or deal in securities of non-governmental issuers. See also *financial services*.

Global Alliance for Sugar Trade Reform and Liberalization: see *Global Sugar Alliance*.

Global Classification and Labelling System for Chemicals: also called Globally Harmonised System or GHS. Adopted by the *United Nations Economic Commission for Europe* in December 2002. It is a labelling system for chemicals based on pictograms. GHS aims to provide all countries with a structure to classify and label hazardous chemicals and to ensure that coherent information is provided on all imported and exported chemicals worldwide.

Global commons: defined by the *World Commission on Environment and Development* as the oceans, outer space and Antarctica, i.e. those parts of the planet that fall outside national jurisdictions. See also *trade and environment*.

Global Compact: proposed by the Secretary-General of the United Nations to business leaders at the *World Economic Forum* on 31 January 1999. It consists of nine principles: (1) support and respect the protection of international human rights within the sphere of influence of business, (2) make sure corporations are not complicit in human rights abuses, (3) freedom of association and effective recognition of the right to collective bargaining, (4) elimination of all forms of forced and compulsory labour, (5) effective abolition of *child labour*, (6) elimination of discrimination in respect of employment and occupation, (7) support a precautionary approach to environmental challenges, (8) undertake initiatives to promote greater environmental responsibility, and (9) encourage the development and diffusion of environmentally-friendly technologies. See also *trade and human rights*, *trade and labour standards* and *trade and environment*.

Global Environment Facility: GEF. A mechanism for the provision of grants and concessional funding for programs protecting the global environment and promoting sustainable economic growth. It concentrates on climate change, biological diversity, international waters and stratospheric ozone. GEF projects and programs and funds for them are awarded and supervised by the *World Bank*, the *United Nations Development Programme* (UNDP) and the *United Nations Environment Programme* (UNEP). See also *trade and environment*.

Global Information Infrastructure: GII. A proposal formulated by the United States in 1994 for international cooperation in the development of a more efficient and more versatile global telecommunications and information network. Five basic principles would have governed the establishment of the GII: encouraging private sector investment, promoting competition, providing open access, creating a flexible regulatory environment, and ensuring universal service. See also *Okinawa Charter on Global Information Society*.

Globality: sometimes used to refer to one of the general negotiating principles that form part of the *Punta del Este Declaration*. The principle held that the launching, conduct and implementation of the negotiations were to be treated as parts of a *single undertaking*. This principle was often expressed in the phrase "nothing is agreed until everything is agreed".

Globalization: from an economist's point of view, at its simplest, a decline in costs of doing business across space. The term describes the increasing integration of national economic systems through growth in international trade, investment and capital flows. Definitions of globalization, both benevolent and malevolent, are too numerous to list here. The *World Commission on the Social Dimension of Globalization* says in its report that "the term 'globalization' has acquired many emotive connotations . . . At one extreme, [it] is seen as an irresistible and benign force for delivering economic prosperity to people throughout the world. At the other, it is blamed as a source of all contemporary ills". Many analysts distinguish globalization from *internationalization* which they tend to see as more benign. In reality, globalization and internationalization exist side by side. Globalization is promoted by rapid improvements in international transport and communications and the lowering of barriers to trade and investment. But many do not see globalization simply as an economic matter. This is because one of its effects is the relocation and integration of production processes among countries, reflecting the most appropriate technology and the best production cost. Globalization implies therefore a degree of reciprocal action and interdependence and a greater exposure to global economic developments, described by some as a loss of independence by national governments. Greater participation in the international economy has social and political implications. Inflows of foreign investment into developing countries cause changes in employment and national income. Opponents of globalization claim that it increases the gap not only between rich and poor countries, but also among the peoples especially of developing countries. Some claim that globalization simply means corporations chasing ever cheaper labour and raw materials, and governments willing to ignore consumer, labour and environmental laws. To holders of this view, globalization is an insidious result of market forces, the economic power of *multinational corporations* and the growth of world trade. This is the *race-to-the-bottom argument*. Holders of this view sometimes also tend to look to restricted trade and investment flows as the preferred remedy. Defenders of globalization say poverty has many causes, including weak and corrupt governmental. They claim that developing countries that have opened their economies have seen the greatest reductions in poverty, and they cast doubt on the notion of rising global inequality. David Dollar points out that since 1980 the growth rates of developing countries have accelerated, that the number of poor people in the world has declined significantly, that global inequality among citizens of the world has seen a modest decline, that there is no general trend towards higher inequality within countries, and that wage inequality is rising worldwide. He says that solutions may depend partly on improved economic development strategies of developing countries and better access by them to the markets of developed countries. In other words, the solution to the problems caused by globalism, assuming that one accepts this proposition, lies in fact in greater global integration and more globalization. See also *anti-globalization*, *autarky*, *borderless world*, *delocalization*, *deindustrialization*, *trade and poverty* and *Washington Consensus*. [Dollar 2002, Kohl 2003, Stiglitz 2202, Wolf 2004, World Commission on the Social Dimension of Globalization 2004]

Global negotiations: full name *Global Negotiations Relating to International Cooperation for Development*. The plan for global negotiations grew out of the proposals for a *New International Economic Order*. The negotiations were expected to be launched by the *United Nations General Assembly* in 1980 after more than three years of consultations on a possible agenda, procedures and timeframes, but in the end this did not happen. See also *Charter of Economic Rights and Duties of States* and *North-South dialogue*.

Global Plan of Action for the Conservation and Sustainable Utilization of Plant Genetic Resources for Food and Agriculture: adopted in Leipzig on 23 June 1996 under the auspices of the *Food and Agriculture Organization*. The Global Plan is based on the view that countries are interdependent in respect of plant genetic resources for food and agriculture. Its main aims are (a) to ensure the conservation of plant genetic resources for food and agriculture as a basis for *food security*, (b) to promote sustainable utilization of plant genetic resources for food and agriculture, (c) to promote a fair and equitable sharing of the benefits arising from the use of plant genetic resources, (d) to assist countries and institutions responsible for conserving and using plant genetic resources to identify priorities for action, and (e) to strengthen national, regional and international programs for the conservation and utilization of plant genetic resources for food and agriculture. See also *International Undertaking on Plant Genetic Resources for Food and Agriculture* and *International Treaty on Plant Genetic Resources for Food and Agriculture*.

Global quota: a limit set by a country on the total quantity of a product that may be imported or exported within a specified period, usually one year. See also *tariff quota*.

Global reciprocity: a term used by Paemen (and possibly others) to describe *multilateralism*. [Paemen, no date]

Global safeguards: the safeguard measures available through GATT Article XIX.

Global Sugar Alliance: formally Global Alliance for Sugar Trade Reform and Liberalization. A group of sugar producers which aims to reform international trade in sugar. It was formed in 1999. Its members include producers in Australia, Brazil, Canada, Chile, Colombia, El Salvador, Guatemala, Honduras, India, Nicaragua, Panama, South Africa and Thailand.

Global System of Trade Preferences: see *GSTP.*

Global Trade Point Network: established by *UNCTAD* to enhance the participation of developing countries and *economies in transition* in international trade, to reduce transaction costs and to allow them better access to trade-related information and global networks. Some 100 national Trade Points now exist. They are connected electronically. They act as *trade facilitation* centres where all necessary formalities can be transacted under one roof, and they provide information to traders on export opportunities. In November 2002 the program was transferred from UNCTAD to the World Trade Point Federation, located in Geneva. See also *Trade Efficiency Programme* and *electronic commerce*.

Good faith: also referred to as *bona fides*. Malcolm N. Shaw calls it "perhaps the most important general principle underpinning many international legal rules". He adds that "[i]n the absence of a certain minimum belief that states will perform their treaty obligations in good faith, there is no reason for countries to enter into such obligations with each other". The principle is defined in the *Vienna Convention on the Law of Treaties* to the effect that a state is "obliged to refrain from acts which would defeat the object and purpose of a treaty". The WTO *Dispute Settlement Understanding* exhorts members to enter and engage in *consultation*, *dispute settlement* and *arbitration* procedures in good faith. The Understanding does not describe the meaning of "good faith". One panel report *(United States – Section 310)* thought is was "notoriously difficult, or at least delicate, to construe the requirement that a treaty shall be interpreted in good faith . . . , not least because of the possible imputation of bad faith to one of the parties". The *Appellate Body* observed in *United States – Continued Dumping and Subsidy Act Offset Act of 2000* that "[n]othing, however, in the covered agreements supports the conclusion that simply because a WTO member is found to have violated a substantive treaty provision, it has therefore not acted in good faith. In our view, it would be necessary to prove more than mere violation to support such a conclusion." The *Dispute Settlement Understanding* gives some helpful pointers on the meaning of "good faith". Article 3.7 asks members to exercise their judgement whether an action would be fruitful. It stresses that the aim of the dispute settlement mechanism is to secure a positive solution to a dispute, and that a solution acceptable to both parties and consistent with the WTO rules is clearly preferable. Article 3.10 says that requests for conciliation and the use of the dispute settlement procedures should not be intended or considered as contentious acts, and hence that all members would engage in the procedures in good faith to resolve the dispute. It continues that complaints and counter-complaints in regard to distinct matters should not be linked. At the very least we can therefore say that the WTO setting for the settlement of disputes should not be considered a suitable venue for vexatious behaviour, and that members should do nothing to undermine the intent of the rules. But *panel* proceedings always are adversarial. Industries asking for the initiation of consultations and their political backers expect results. The heat is therefore easily turned up. Against this background it is surprising how few disputes brought before the WTO have led to bad blood. Equally impressive is the extent to which parties so far have participated in dispute settlement and implemented panel decisions in good faith. See also *legitimate expectation*. [Shaw 1997, Jung and Lee 2003]

Good governance: highly desirable attributes of decision-making and decision-implementing processes. The main attributes are participation by all who may be affected, respect for the rule of law, transparency, responsiveness to the views of participants, consensus, equity and inclusiveness, and effectiveness and efficiency. Most importantly, those making and implementing decisions must be accountable to those affected by them.

Good offices: a form of *mediation* between parties to a dispute. It describes an offer by a disinterested third party, often a person of distinction in the field, to examine what can be done to settle a difficult dispute. The offer to assist may be made spontaneously, or it may be part of a framework for settling disputes. Good offices and mediation always consist of giving advice. The never have the binding force of *arbitration*. Article 5 of the WTO *Dispute Settlement Understanding* says that the parties may use the good-offices procedure, assuming they agree among themselves to do so. Either party may call for its introduction. It may begin or be terminated at any time. The procedure may run parallel to a panel process. Also, the Director-General of the WTO may offer his good offices in an *ex officio* capacity. See also *arbitration*.

Government procurement: also called public procurement. It covers purchases of goods and services by governments and governmental authorities for their own use. An OECD study in 2002 estimated that government procurement accounts for about 20% of GDP in OECD countries, and for about 15% in non-OECD countries. The *GATT* and the *General Agreement on Trade in Services* exempt government procurement from the application of their rules. See also *Agreement on Government Procurement*, *APEC Non-binding Principles on Government Procurement* and *Working Group on Transparency in Government Procurement*. [OECD 2002]

Government trading monopolies: the exclusive allocation by a country to one firm, often state-owned, of the right to trade internationally in certain products. See also *single-desk selling* and *state trading*.

Government use: arises in the case of *patents* when the government itself uses or authorises other persons to use the rights over a patented product or process, for government purposes, without the permission of the patent owner. See also *compulsory licensing*.

Graduation: the removal of tariff preferences accorded to developing countries under *GSP* (Generalized System of Preferences) programs because a country has exceeded a certain level of per capita GDP. Many countries also have graduating mechanisms allowing the removal of GSP concessions for particular products once a supplier country captures more than a defined share of the import market for that product. See also *a priori limitation* and *competitive-need limitation*.

Graduation clause: paragraph 7 of the *Enabling Clause* notes that less-developed GATT members expect that their capacity to make contributions under the GATT provisions would improve with the progressive development of their economies and trade. Accordingly, they would expect to participate more fully in the framework of rights and obligations under the GATT. See also *developing countries and the multilateral trading system* and *graduation*.

Grains Trade Convention: see *International Grains Agreement*.

Grandfather clause: refers to a provision in the *Protocol of Provisional Application* adopted by the original members of the GATT in 1947 which states that Part II of the GATT would be applied "to the fullest extent not inconsistent with existing legislation". This was a device which permitted the continuing existence of national legislation in violation of the GATT articles. It was based on the view that the entry into force of the GATT would be delayed indefinitely if members first had to bring their legislation into conformity with it. This provision became known as the "grandfather clause" because it accepted as a *fait accompli* legislation predating the agreement. The grandfather clause has not been carried forward into the *GATT 1994*. See also *GATT-consistency of national legislation*.

Greater Arab Free Trade Area: GAFTA. Agreed in 1997 by the member states of the Arab League for implementation by 31 December 2007. The fifteen member states deciding to join GAFTA were Algeria, Bahrein, Egypt, Iraq, Jordan, Kuwait, Lebanon, Libya, Morocco, Oman, Qatar, Saudi Arabia, Syria, Tunisia and the United Arab Emirates. In 2002 the participating countries agreed to eliminate all tariffs by 2005. A *customs union* would supersede this within ten years and prepare the way for the formation a Common Arab Market.

Greater China: used mainly by economic analysts to refer to the economies of China, Hong Kong, Macao and Taiwan as a group. The term has no other significance.

Greater Horn of Africa: consists of Burundi, Djibouti, Eritrea, Ethiopia, Kenya, Rwanda, Somalia, Sudan, Tanzania and Uganda. See also *Horn of Africa*.

Green box: domestic support policies for agricultural products exempt from the *Uruguay Round* reduction commitments and permitted without limits. Green box policies include genuine relief to farmers through a wide range of assistance measures which have a minimal impact on trade, such as disaster relief, research, disease control, infrastructure, environmental protection and *food security*. See also *Agreement on Agriculture*, *amber box* and *blue box*.

Greenhouse gases: an omnibus term for atmospheric gases that absorb and emit infra-red radiation. Scientific evidence suggests that there is a long-term build-up of such gases. This has led to predictions of an adverse *climate change*. The main greenhouse gases are water vapour (H_2O), carbon dioxide (CO_2), methane (CH_4), nitrous oxide (N_2O), surface ozone (O_3), perfluorocarbons

(PFCs), hydrofluorocarbons (HFCs) and sulphur hexafluoride (SF$_6$). See also *Kyoto Protocol* and *United Nations Framework Convention on Climate Change*.

Greening the GATT: a term popularized by Daniel Esty in a book of the same title. It expresses the hopes of those who would like the WTO to be more responsive to their particular environmental concerns and who see it as necessary for the GATT to reflect clearly the aims of environmental protection. See also *trade and environment*. [Esty 1994]

Green labelling: see *eco-labelling*.

Green Paper: a report originally bearing a green cover issued by a government as part of a consultation process to stimulate public discussion of policy issues. Although governments do not usually consider themselves bound to adopt any particular proposal examined in a Green Paper, the ideas explored by them often turn into policy proposals. See also *White Paper*. [www.europa.eu.int]

Green procurement: purchasing policies and practices that favour environ-mentally-friendly parts and materials.

Green protectionism: see *eco-protectionism* and *trade and environment*.

Green Room: a meeting room in the WTO building in Geneva sometimes used for working out compromises in trade negotiations, often under the leadership of the WTO Director-General. As the room is quite small, only a small part of the WTO membership can take part in such meetings. For this reason, opponents of the WTO sometimes use the Green Room as an example of alleged non-transparent decision-making. Against this, it can be argued that in multilateral negotiations difficult decisions cannot be made in plenary meetings, especially if some parties have to back down.

Grey-area measures: discriminatory export and import restraints agreed between governments which are usually contrary to the principles governing the *multi-lateral trading system*, but which were not clearly illegal under the multilateral rules until the end of the *Uruguay Round*. Examples of grey-area measures are *orderly marketing arrangements* and *voluntary export arrangements*. These are now illegal under the WTO *Agreement on Safeguards*. Existing grey-area measures had to be eliminated by 1999. Emerging grey-area measures may be *cartel* arrangements between private firms implicitly sanctioned by governments and *voluntary import expansion* agreements between governments.

Grey marketing: a North American expression denoting the practice of *parallel imports*. Goods so imported are known as "grey market goods" or as "grey market imports".

Group of Latin American and Caribbean Countries: see *GRULAC*.

Group of Negotiations on Goods: GNG. A group established to manage all nego-tiating issues relating to the GATT and trade in goods in the *Uruguay Round*, including trade-related aspects of intellectual property rights and trade-related investment measures.

Group of Negotiations on Services: GNS. A group established to handle all issues relating to *trade in services* in the *Uruguay Round*.

Group of Three: a free-trade arrangement between Colombia, Mexico and Venezuela. It entered into force on 1 January 1995. See also *free-trade area*.

Group of Twenty: refers either to the *G-20* promoting dialogue on financial and monetary matters or the *G-20*, a group of developing countries active in WTO negotiations.

Group of 15: see *G-15*.

Group of 24: see *G-24*.

Group of 77: G77. A loosely organized group of developing countries, originally numbering 77, which was formed at the first meeting of *UNCTAD* in 1964. The G77 quickly became the main force in setting the agenda for the UNCTAD work program. It now has over 130 members. The group's aim is to help developing countries to articulate and promote their collective interests, and to enhance their joint negotiating capacity in all major economic areas of the United Nations system. Existing members use broad economic and political criteria to decide whether a country should be admitted to membership. The G77 chairmanship rotates at fixed intervals among the groups representing the African, Latin-American and Asian countries. The G77 also functions in other parts of the United Nations system, but it does not operate in the WTO. China is not a formal member of the G77, but it cooperates with it through the arrangement known as *Group of 77 and China*. See also *group system*.

Group of 77 and China: an informal association between the *Group of 77* and China, begun in 1991. China contributes to the funding of the Group of 77 and can participate in all of its proceedings.

Group system: the system on which negotiations in *UNCTAD* in particular were based for a long time. The UNCTAD membership is divided formally into four groups: Asian and African countries (Group A), OECD countries (Group B), Latin-American and Caribbean countries (Group C) and the socialist countries of Eastern Europe and Russia (Group D). Positions of responsibility in the various UNCTAD committees rotated among the groups according to agreed guidelines. At UNCTAD I in 1964, Groups A and C decided to meet jointly, creating the *Group of 77*. In legal terms, Groups A and C continue to exist, but they only meet sporadically. Negotiations were carried out through group coordinators upon whom it fell to arrive at a common group position. Often, this left them little leeway for flexibility because they always had to negotiate with other groups on the basis of delicately balanced compromises within their own groups. The group system was one of the factors preventing UNCTAD from reaching its full potential because it forestalled the emergence of subject-oriented coalitions where some developed and developing countries had shared interests.

Growth triangles: sub-regional economic zones identified by governments as holding particular promise for rapid economic development by virtue of their location or factor endowment. On a map, they sometimes look like triangles, but other Euclidian shapes may be found. They are often conceived in the form of *free-trade zones*. Growth triangles in most cases include territory of two or three states who cooperate in their development, but they may be contained within a single country. See also *BIMP-EAGA*.

GRULAC: the Group of Latin American and Caribbean Countries which operates informally within the WTO.

GSP: Generalized System of Preferences. First proposed at UNCTAD II in 1968. Entered into force in 1971. It gives developing countries a *margin of preference* in the tariff rates their goods face in the markets of developed countries and in this way increases their competitiveness. Countries maintaining GSP schemes are usually called *donor countries*. Those using them are called *beneficiary countries*. The massive tariff reductions since 1971 as a result of *multilateral trade negotiations* and unilateral actions, as well as changes in productivity, have reduced the importance of the GSP to many developing country exporters, but it remains an important plank in the trade policies of many developing countries. *UNCTAD* is the main forum for a discussion of GSP issues.

GSTP: Global System of Trade Preferences Among Developing Countries. It entered into force in 1989. It aims to promote the development of economic cooperation among developing countries through the exchange of *tariff preferences*. *Non-tariff preferences* may also be exchanged. *Least developed countries* do not have to offer reciprocal concessions. Membership of the GSTP is open to members of the *Group of 77*. Negotiations are conducted under *UNCTAD* auspices. 44 countries participate in the GSTP. See also *ECDC* and *trade negotiations between developing countries*.

Guarantee mark: see *certification mark*.

Guidelines for Mutual Recognition Agreements or Arrangements in the Accountancy Sector: a set of non-binding principles adopted by the WTO on 29 May 1997 aimed at making it easier for governments to negotiate the mutual recognition of professional qualifications. Part A of the Guidelines deals with the conduct of negotiations and the relevant obligations governments have under the *General Agreement on Trade in Services*. Part B sets out various issues that may have to be addressed in negotiations, such as the intended participants, the purpose and scope of the arrangement, the conditions under which mutual recognition will be accorded, the mechanism for implementation, and other related matters. See also *mutual recognition arrangements* and *Working Party on Professional Services*.

Guiding Principles Concerning Environmental Policies: an *OECD* recommendation adopted on 26 May 1972. The five principles it contains deal mainly with the international economic and trade implications of environmental policies. First, costs of public measures to reduce pollution and to allocate resources better should be met through the *polluter-pays principle*. Second, it encourages harmonization of environmental standards, though it allows that this may be difficult to achieve. In any case, it deems striving towards more stringent standards as desirable. Measures to protect the environment should avoid the creation of *non-tariff* barriers to trade. Third, measures to protect the environment should be applied in accordance with the principles of *national treatment* and ***non-discrimination***, described as identical treatment for imported products regardless of their national origin. Fourth, procedures should be established for checking conformity to product standards. The fifth principle is that differences in environmental policies should not lead to the introduction of compensating import levies or export rebates. See also ***trade and environment***.

Gulf Cooperation Council: GCC. Formal name *Cooperation Council of the Arab States of the Gulf*. Established in 1981. It consists of Saudi Arabia, Kuwait, Bahrain, Qatar, the United Arab Emirates and Oman. Among its major political and economic aims is that of drawing up similar regulations in the economic and financial fields, trade, customs and transport, information and tourism. In 1981 the GCC members also established a ***free-trade area*** covering industrial and agricultural products, but not petroleum products. A ***customs union*** is to be established no later than 2007, to be followed by the Gulf Common Market. Its secretariat is located at Riyadh.

G7: the group of seven leading industrial countries. They are Canada, France, Germany, Italy, Japan, United Kingdom and the United States.

G8: comprises Canada, France, Germany, Italy, Japan, Russia, the United Kingdom and the United States. The European Commission also participates. The group originated at a meeting of France, Germany, Italy, Japan, the United Kingdom and the United States in 1975 at Rambouillet. Canada joined in 1976 and the European Commission in 1977. The group then was known as the G7. Russia became a full member in 1998. The G8 attempts to set broad directions for international economic and monetary activity. Its members participate annually in an economic summit which often deals with trade policy matters. See also ***Okinawa Charter on Global Information Society***.

G8 African Action Plan: adopted by the *G8* summit at Kananaskis, Canada, on 27 June 2002. It seeks to support the implementation of the ***New Partnership for Africa's Development***. Chapter III on fostering trade, investment, economic growth and sustainable development is aimed at (a) helping Africa to attract investment from African and other countries and implementing policies conducive to economic growth, (b) facilitating capacity-building and the transfer of expertise for the development of infrastructure projects, (c) providing greater market access for Africa, (d) increasing the funding and improving the quality of support for trade-related technical assistance and capacity-building in Africa, (e) supporting African efforts to advance regional economic integration and intra-African trade, and (f) improving the effectiveness of ***official development assistance***. Other chapters with a mainly economic focus deal with implementing debt relief, expanding knowledge and digital opportunities, and increasing agricultural productivity.

G-10: a group of WTO members that are net food importers, formed during the negotiations on agriculture under the ***Doha Development Agenda***. It consists of Bulgaria, Chinese Taipei (Taiwan), Iceland, Israel, Japan, Korea, Liechtenstein, Mauritius, Norway and Switzerland.

G-15: a group originally of fifteen developing countries acting as the main political organ for the Non-Aligned Movement. It was established in 1990. Its members now are: Algeria, Argentina, Brazil, Chile, Colombia, Egypt, India, Indonesia, Iran, Jamaica, Kenya, Malaysia, Mexico, Nigeria, Peru, Senegal, Sri Lanka, Venezuela and Zimbabwe. It gives primary attention to issues of investment, trade and technology. The G-15's main objectives are to harness the potential for greater cooperation among developing countries, to review the impact of the world economic situation and the state of international relations on developing countries, to serve as forum for consultations among developing countries with a view to coordinating policies and actions, to identify and implement new schemes for *South-South* cooperation and to pursue a more productive *North-South dialogue*.

G-20: a group of developing countries established on 20 August 2003 so named because it had twenty members at the time. It exerted considerable influence on the outcome of the WTO *Cancún Ministerial Conference*. Its membership has fluctuated. As of October 2006 it consisted of Argentina, Bolivia, Brazil, Chile, China, Cuba, Egypt, Guatemala, India, Indonesia, Mexico, Nigeria, Pakistan, Paraguay, Philippines, South Africa, Tanzania, Thailand, Uruguay, Venezuela and Zimbabwe.

G-20: an informal forum established in 1999 which seeks to promote dialogue between industrial economies and emerging-market economies on issues related to the international monetary and financial system. It also seeks to strengthen the international financial architecture. Its members are the finance ministries and central banks of Argentina, Australia, Brazil, Canada, China, France, Germany, India, Indonesia, Italy, Japan, Korea, Mexico, Russia, Saudi Arabia, South Africa, Turkey, United Kingdom and United States. The European Union is represented by the presidency and the European Central Bank. The G-20 has no permanent secretariat. The country chairing it for the year performs that task. [www.g20.org]

G-24: Intergovernmental Group of Twenty-Four on International Monetary Affairs, established in 1971. Its objective is to coordinate positions of developing countries on monetary and development finance issues. Members are divided into three regions. Region I (Africa) is represented by Algeria, Côte d'Ivoire, Democratic Republic of Congo, Egypt, Ethiopia, Gabon, Ghana, Nigeria and South Africa. Region II (Latin America and the Caribbean) is represented by Argentina, Brazil, Colombia, Guatemala, Mexico, Peru, Trinidad and Tobago and Venezuela. Region III (Asia and developing countries of Europe) is represented by India, Iran, Lebanon, Pakistan, Philippines, Sri Lanka and Syrian Arab Republic. China is an observer.

G-33: see *Alliance for Strategic Products and Special Safeguard Mechanism*.

G-77: see *Group of 77*.

G-90: in the WTO the *ACP states* and the *least developed countries* when they meet jointly.

Haberler Report: in late 1957 GATT members decided to commission an examination of past and current international trade trends and their implications. It was to enquire particularly (a) into the failure of the trade of less developed countries to develop as rapidly as that of industrialized countries, (b) excessive short-term fluctuations in the prices of primary products and (c) widespread resort to agricultural protection. This was the first such examination in the GATT looking particularly at issues facing developing countries. A panel of distinguished economists was assembled, led by Gottfried Haberler of Harvard University. The panel report, titled *Trends in International Trade*, was issued in October 1958. It became known immediately as the Haberler Report. The report contained 60 conclusions. The first fifteen are factual accounts of short-term fluctuations and long-term trends in commodities and manufactures trade prevailing at the time. The next eight conclusions deal with the interpretation of past trends, future import requirements and prospects for exports. The report was unable to conclude whether there had been an increase in agricultural protection in industrial countries in recent years, but it also cautioned against counting on any improvement in the *terms of trade* of the non-industrialized countries to raise their ability to purchase imports. The next 33 conclusions were the most important ones. The called for the stabilization of particular commodity markets, but not in a too ambitious way. They also argued for a moderation of agricultural *protectionism* in North America and Western Europe. One prediction was concerned with the diversion of trade in raw materials and foodstuffs away from outside sources to European sources as real incomes in Europe rose. In the final four conclusions, the experts agreed that although the issues covered in the report would affect primarily the policies of the highly industrialized countries, they too would gain from the proposed changes. The experts concluded in any case that there was some justification in developing country views that current rules and conventions on commercial policies were relatively unfavourable to them. The Haberler Report had quite a small immediate impact on rule-making in the GATT, although it furnished some ideas for the Programme for the Expansion of Trade, adopted in November 1958, which ultimately led to the *Dillon Round*. See also *commodity policy* and *developing countries and the multilateral trading system*.

Hague System for the International Deposit of Industrial Designs: a system for the protection of *industrial designs* in more than one country through its registration with the International Bureau of *WIPO*. A design must be new or original to be eligible for registration. The normal term of protection is five years, and it can be renewed for up to fifteen years. The instrument under which this is done is *The Hague Agreement Concerning the International Deposit of Industrial Designs*, done on 6 November 1925 and revised several times since, most recently through the *Geneva Act* of July 1999.

Hard core cartel: a type of *cartel* defined in the OECD *hard core cartel recommendation* as an "anti-competitive agreement, anti-competitive concerted practice, or anti-competitive arrangement by competitors to fix prices, make rigged bids (collusive tenders), establish output restrictions or quotas, or share or divide markets by allocating customers, suppliers, territories, or lines of commerce". It does not include agreements aimed at lawful cost-reduction, agreements excluded by a member country's competition law, or those authorised in accordance with those laws. [OECD C(98)35/FINAL)]

Hard core cartel recommendation: an OECD recommendation adopted in 1998 which asks member countries to "provide for (a) effective sanctions, of a kind and at a level adequate to deter firms and individuals from participating in such cartels; and (b) enforcement procedures and institutions with powers adequate to detect and remedy hard core cartels, including powers to obtain documents and information and to impose penalties for non-compliance". OECD members are asked to cooperate with each other in enforcing their laws against such cartels. [OECD C(98)35/FINAL)]

Hard-core waiver: a decision taken in the GATT in 1955 to allow members in certain cases to retain *quantitative restrictions* that had been maintained over several years because of persistent balance-of-payments difficulties. The *waiver* was subject to some conditions. For example, members had to demonstrate that a sudden removal of a quantitative restriction would result in serious *injury* to a domestic industry, and they had to carry out a policy of progressive liberalization. See also *residual quantitative restrictions*.

Hard law: in *trade policy* usage, international arrangements that entail legally enforceable *rights and obligations* on their members. Examples of hard law are the WTO obligations as embodied in the *GATT (General Agreement on Tariffs and Trade)* and the *General Agreement on Trade in Services* (GATS). Such arrangements are usually in the form of treaties, or they have the status of a treaty. See also *soft law*.

Harmonization of standards and qualifications: the adoption of a single standard or qualification requirement by two or more countries where previously each might have had its own set of requirements. Harmonization may involve the creation of an entirely new standard, the adoption of the standard of the most influential participant in the arrangement, the adoption of the most reasonable standard or a mixture of them. Achieving harmonization often entails laborious negotiations. See also *Agreement on Technical Barriers to Trade*, *explicit harmonization*, *International Electrotechnical Commission*, *International Organization for Standardization*, *managed mutual recognition* and *mutual recognition arrangements*.

Harmonized Commodity Description and Coding System: see *Harmonized System*.

Harmonized rules of origin: see *rules of origin*.

Harmonized System: formally the *Harmonized Commodity Description and Coding System*. An international nomenclature developed by the **World Customs Organization**. The Harmonized System's aims are (a) to achieve international uniformity in the classification of goods for customs purposes; (b) to facilitate the collection, analysis and comparison of world trade statistics; (c) to provide a common international system for coding, describing and classifying goods for commercial purposes; and (d) to provide an updated nomenclature to take account of technological developments and changes in international trade patterns. It is arranged in six-digit codes under 97 chapters. Chapter 77 has not yet been allocated to any product group, hence the reference to 96 chapters in some descriptions. In addition, chapters 98 and 99 are reserved for special use by individual countries. Beyond the six-digit level countries are free to break product groups down further.

Harmonized tariff reductions: one of the ways to reduce tariff levels explored in the *Tokyo Round* negotiations. It was aimed at bringing tariffs of the participants for the same products to roughly similar levels. Harmonization is as difficult now as it was 25 years ago because of its impact on *sensitive products*. See also *linear tariff cuts* and *tariff negotiations*.

Harmonizing formula: used in tariff negotiations for much steeper reductions in higher tariffs than in lower tariffs to bring them closer together, i.e. to harmonize them.

Harries Report: a report commissioned by the Australian Government in 1978 to examine the nature of Australia's relationship with the *Third World* and to make proposals for the development of that relationship. The report was published in 1979 under the title *Australia and the third world*. It contributed to a better understanding of the issues subsumed in the *North-South dialogue* and the *New International Economic Order*.

Hatters' fur: a dispute in 1950 between the United States and Czechoslovakia about the interpretation of *"unforeseen developments"*. This is one of the conditions set out in GATT Article XIX (Emergency Action on Imports of Particular Products) which have to be satisfied before emergency action to cut imports can be taken. The United States argued that a change in hat fashions was an unforeseen development and therefore justification for action against the import of hatters' fur from Czechoslovakia. Czechoslovakia argued that changes in fashions were normal and should be expected. The United States won. John Jackson said of this case in *World Trade and the Law of the GATT* that one could almost conclude that an increase in imports could itself be an unforeseen development. The WTO *Agreement on Safeguards* now permits the use of safeguards action only if it has been properly determined that a product is being imported in such increased quantities to cause or threaten to cause serious *injury* to domestic industry that produces like or directly competitive products. [GATT/CP/106, Jackson 1969, Mueller 2003]

Havana Charter: the final draft of the *Charter for an International Trade Organization* (*ITO*), adopted at Havana in 1948. The breadth of its provisions can be gauged from its chapter headings: employment and economic activity, economic development and reconstruction, investment, restrictive business practices, inter-governmental commodity agreements, and commercial policy. The Charter never became part of international trade law for quite complex reasons. It was meant to be a binding set of articles, but successive rounds of negotiations on its contents gradually turned more and more of them into best-endeavours obligations. Developing countries opposed an open investment regime. Ultimately, the aims of the Charter became entangled in United States domestic politics and concerns that it would constrain domestic sovereignty. The Executive therefore delayed bringing the Charter before Congress, but in 1950 it decided that it would no longer seek to have the Charter adopted by Congress. This served as a signal to other countries not to pursue further any ratification proceedings. Much of the contents of the chapter on commercial policy survived as the *GATT* (*General Agreement on Tariffs and Trade*). This had been negotiated separately in 1947, and it entered provisionally into force on 1 January 1948. See also *Protocol of Provisional Application*. [Brown 1950]

Hawley-Smoot tariff: see *Smoot-Hawley tariff*.

Hazard Analysis and Critical Control Points: HACCP. A system for assuring the safe manufacture of food products. It consists of seven steps: (1) analysis of hazards, (2) identification of critical control points, (3) establishing critical limits for each control point, (4) monitoring of the control points. (5) establishing a system of corrective action, (6) effective record-keeping, and (7) establishing procedures to verify that the system is working properly. HACCP had its origin in the food safety requirements developed by NASA for the United States space program.

Hazardous wastes: see *Basel Convention*.

Heading: a four-digit entry in the *Harmonized System*. Examples are 1701 (cane or beet sugar and chemically pure sucrose, in solid form), 5001 (silk-worm cocoons suitable for reeling) and 9108 (watch movements, complete and assembled). See also *chapter* and *sub-heading*.

Heckscher-Ohlin theorem: states that countries will export those goods whose production is relatively intensive in the factors with which they are well endowed. The basic assumption underlying the theorem is that demand patterns do not differ much between countries. The theorem was first formulated by Eli Filip Heckscher in 1919 and publicized by Bertil Gotthard Ohlin in 1933, both eminent Swedish economists. It has been refined considerably over the years as a result of a patient statistical analysis. Essentially, the theorem is a restatement of the *theory of comparative advantage*. See also *new trade theory* and *Stolper-Samuelson theorem*.

Helms-Burton legislation: The United States *Cuban Liberty and Democratic Solidarity (Libertad) Act* of 1996. Its stated aims are "to seek international sanctions against the Government of Cuba headed by Fidel Castro" and "to plan for support of a transition government leading to a democratically elected government in Cuba". The Act contains several economic provisions. Section 108 requires the President to submit to Congress an annual report detailing (1) a description of all bilateral assistance given to Cuba by all other foreign countries, (2) a description of Cuba's commerce with other countries, (3) a description of all joint ventures entered into by foreign nationals with Cuba, (4) a determination of whether the facilities described under (3) are subject of a claim by a United States national against Cuba, (5) a determination of Cuba's foreign debt, (6) a description of the steps taken to ensure that no Cuban goods enter the United States and (7) an identification of countries purchasing arms from Cuba. Section 110 prohibits the import into the United States of any merchandise wholly or partly made in Cuba or transported from or through Cuba. Title III contains the most contentious economic provisions. It deals with the protection of property rights of United States nationals and sets out in some detail the proposed remedies. The precepts of this Title are that (a) the Government of Cuba has confiscated the property of many United States nationals, (b) it is now making some of this property available to foreign investors, (c) this "trafficking" in property undermines the foreign policy of the United States, (d) the international judicial system lacks fully effective remedies for this type of problem, (e) international law recognizes that a law may be applied extraterritorially if it is intended to have effect substantially within its home territory, and (f) that United States nationals whose property was confiscated should be able to have recourse through the United States courts. Section 306 states that damages may be sought against anyone engaged in trafficking after 1 November 1996. See also *effects doctrine* and *extraterritoriality*.

***Herring and salmon*:** a case brought before the GATT by the United States against Canada in 1987 concerning Canadian regulations prohibiting the export or sale for export of unprocessed herring and pink and sockeye salmon. The facts were that Canada had proclaimed a regulation under the authority of the *Fisheries Act* of 1970 that "no person shall export from Canada any sockeye or pink salmon unless it is canned, salted, smoked, dried or frozen and has been inspected in accordance with the *Fish Inspection Act*". A similar provision applied to the export from the Province of British Columbia of food herring, roe herring, herring roe or herring spawn. Canada had also maintained since the early decades of the twentieth century governmental measures for the conservation, management and development of salmon and herring stocks in the waters off British Columbia. These measures included intergovernmental agreements and conventions. At the time of this dispute, sockeye and pink and herring fisheries dominated commercial fishing of the Canadian West Coast. They gave employment to almost five-sixths of the workers in the British Columbia fish processing industry.

Canada stated that the measures concerned were an integral and long-standing component of its West Coast fisheries conservation and management regime. They were therefore completely justified under GATT Article XX(g) which gives members the right not to apply the provisions of the Agreement if this necessary to conserve exhaustible natural resources, but only in conjunction with domestic restrictions on production and consumption. Canada also said that its strict quality and marketing regulations for the three species were necessary to maintain its reputation for safe, high-quality fish products. In making its findings, the *panel* noted that Canada prohibited the export of fish not meeting its standards, but that it banned the export of certain unprocessed herring and salmon even if they met Canadian export standards. The panel therefore found that the export prohibitions were not necessary to maintain standards. The panel agreed that salmon and herring stocks were "exhaustible natural resources" and that harvest limitations were "restrictions on domestic production" as intended by Article XX(g). It considered, however, that while a trade measure did not have to be essential to the conservation of an exhaustible natural resource, it had to be aimed primarily at conservation. The panel concluded finally that Canada's export prohibitions could not be considered as aimed primarily at the conservation of salmon and herring stock because they only related to the export of these species in their unprocessed form. Canada only limited the purchases of unprocessed herring and salmon stocks by foreign processors and consumers, but not those by domestic processors and consumers. The panel therefore decided that the export prohibitions were not justified by Article XX(g) also. See also *general exceptions* and *trade and environment*. [GATT BISD 35S]

Hidden dumping: a form of *dumping* said to occur when a firm exports goods at ostensibly market prices to a related firm, but in reality at a lower cost. The second firm then sells the goods in the importing country at about that price, but the transaction has all the time been below market price. See also *anti-dumping measures*.

High-income economies: a group of 56 economies so classified by the *World Bank* and listed in the 2007 *World Development Report* as having had in 2005 a per-capita GNI (gross national income) of more than $10,726. See also *low-income economies*, *lower-middle-income economies* and *upper-middle-income economies*.

Highly sensitive products: under *AFTA* various types of rice on which Malaysia, Indonesia and the Philippines can maintain tariffs of 20% or more as the *final rate*.

Historical preferences: in the WTO framework this refers to benefits under *preferential trade arrangements* in existence before the GATT entered into force on 1 January 1948. Such arrangements were allowed to continue even though they contravene *most-favoured-nation treatment*, but under Article I of the GATT (General Most-Favoured-Nation Treatment) the maximum *margin of preference* cannot be increased. The *imperial preferences arrangement* is one example of historical preferences. The value of historical preferences decreased steadily as *most-favoured-nation tariffs* came down. Most have now disappeared.

Hit-and-run dumping: see *sporadic dumping*.

Hollowing-out: see *deindustrialization* and *delocalization*.

Home market visibility test: finding out how prominent a product is in its home market. This is important in investigations of whether *anti-dumping measures* can be imposed. Part of the investigation will establish the *normal value* of the product. The *Anti-Dumping Agreement* requires that at least 5% of the sales of the product in question should occur in its home market (called "exporting market" in the Agreement) to give a reliable indication of its normal value in that market. If the home market is smaller, it may be necessary to determine normal value through the use, for example, of an *analogue country* or a *constructed* value.

***Homestyle* exemption:** refers to Section 110(5) of the United States Copyright Act, as amended by the *Fairness in Music Licensing Act* of 1998. It permits some shops and food service or drinking establishments of a defined size to broadcast radio and television programs using a limited number of loudspeakers or television sets without leading to an infringement of *copyright*. Main assumptions are that this would be the kind of equipment normally used at home, and that the establishment using it would be too small to subscribe to a commercial background music service. Section 110(5) does not apply to the playing of recorded music, such as compact discs or cassettes. In 1999 the *European Communities* sought the establishment of a *panel* on the grounds that this Section violated the obligations of the United States under the *Agreement on Trade-Related Aspects of Intellectual Property Rights*, especially those relating to the *Berne Convention*. The panel found in favour of the European Communities. [WT/DS160/R]

Homonymous geographical indications: identical *geographical indications* in use in more than one country. These can occur whenever countries share a language, but especially when emigrants take the placenames of their home country with them.

Hong Kong, China: the formal name of Hong Kong in the WTO, *APEC* and some other international organizations.

Hong Kong Ministerial Conference: the sixth *WTO Ministerial Conference*, held from 13 to 18 December 2005.

Horizontal arrangements: see *competition policy*.

Horizontal commitments: a component of the *schedules of commitments* attached by WTO member countries to the *General Agreement on Trade in Services*. Horizontal commitments apply to all services trade covered in a schedule of commitments. Generally, they relate to investment, formation of corporate structures, land acquisition, the movement of personnel, etc. See also *commitment*.

Horizontal foreign direct investment: this refers to *foreign direct investment* by a firm in the area of activities it already pursues at home. For example, a car manufacturer in country A invests in a car plant in country B. See also *tariff-jumping investment*.

Horizontal keiretsu: see *keiretsu relationships*.

Hormone growth promotants: chemical substances which accelerate the growth of animals through increasing the efficiency of feed conversion. Proponents of their use say that they permit the animal to produce more muscle and less fat without adverse effects if they are administered properly. The use of hormone growth promotants is legal in the United States and other major beef-producing countries. In 1989 the *European Community* banned the import of beef and beef products produced with the addition of hormone growth promotants on the grounds that their use led to dangerous levels of residues. United States producers claim that their beef products are safe, and that the European Community action was motivated above all by the need to deal with a mounting beef surplus. Accusations and counter-accusations led nowhere, and in 1996 the United States brought the dispute before the WTO. Australia, Canada and New Zealand supported the United States action. The *panel* handed down its decision in mid-1997, and it found against the European Community. See also *sanitary and phytosanitary measures*.

Horn of Africa: consists of Djibouti, Eritrea, Ethiopia, Somalia and Sudan. See also *Greater Horn of Africa*.

Host country operational measures: HCOMs. An *UNCTAD* contribution to the analysis of *international investment agreements*. It describes "the vast array of [investment] measures implemented by host countries concerning the operation of foreign affiliates once inside their jurisdictions". UNCTAD divides HCOMs into three groups. The first, so-called "red light" HCOMs, contains measures explicitly prohibited by multilateral agreements, such as the *Agreement on Trade-Related Investment Measures*. The second group, the "yellow light" HCOMs, is made up of measures additionally prohibited, conditioned or discouraged by inter-regional, regional or bilateral agreements. The third group, the "green light" HCOMs, are not generally prohibited through international investment rules. See also *traffic light approach*.

Hub and spokes: a concept used in the analysis of *free-trade areas*. It postulates that a large country could be a member of several free-trade arrangements, but that smaller countries might only belong to one of these arrangements each. The large country would then be the hub, and the others would form the spokes in a series of discriminatory bilateral trade arrangements. Unlike in the case of a free-trade area, where all parties negotiate as equals, under a hub-and-spokes arrangement the larger country generally sets the terms and conditions for membership. Some, however, argue that hub-and-spoke arrangements may be stepping stones to larger free-trade areas. Others maintain that the country forming the hub would have no incentive to extend such arrangements and trade preferences to others. This argument remains unresolved. However, as the 1995 WTO study on *Regionalism and the World Trading System* notes, in the case of a hub-and-spoke system, the essence is always the same: goods and services (and perhaps capital and labour) flow more freely between the hub and each spoke than they do between the spokes.

Hull formula: sometimes Hull rule. The view expressed in 1938 by Cordell Hull, then United States Secretary of State, in response to Mexican agrarian nationalisation measures that there should be "prompt, adequate and effective" compensation in cases of *expropriation*. [Seid 2002]

Human Development Report: a report published annually by the *United Nations Development Programme* (UNDP). Its theme changes from year to year, but its focus usually is on progress made by UNDP towards achieving one or more of its main goals.

Human rights: many definitions are available for this term. All share the idea that human rights belong to all humans and cannot be taken away from them, i.e. that they are "inalienable". The starting point for post-war human rights actions is the *Universal Declaration of Human Rights*, adopted by the *United Nations General Assembly* on 10 December 1948. Entries in this dictionary concerned with human rights include *core labour standards*, *Declaration on Fundamental Principles and Rights at Work*, *International Covenant on Economic, Social and Cultural Rights*, *Millennium Declaration*, *Millennium Development Goals*, *Right to Development*, *trade and gender*, *trade and human rights* and *trade and poverty*.

Human rights clause: a provision in national trade laws or international treaties which promotes the observance of human rights. The *ACP-EC Partnership Agreement*, for example, requires from its members respect for all human rights and fundamental freedoms as an essential element of the Agreement. The *Mediterranean Agreements* concluded by the *European Community* also require respect for human rights and democracy. Some have suggested that Article XX (General Exceptions) of the *GATT* should be supplemented by a reference to human rights, but this has not yet attracted widespread support. See also *trade and human rights*, *democracy clause* and *social clause*. [Bal 2001, Petersmann 2001]

I

IBRD: International Bank for Reconstruction and Development. See *World Bank*.

ICC Guidelines for International Investment: adopted in 1972 by the *International Chamber of Commerce* (ICC) to serve as a model for international agreements. They have been used in this way by the *OECD* and some other international organizations. A feature of the guidelines is that they combine the rights and obligations of states and firms in a single instrument.

ICITO: Interim Commission for the International Trade Organization. Established in 1948 to prepare the administrative arrangements for entry into force of the *ITO*. At the same time, it was agreed that ICITO would supply the secretariat services for GATT. As the ITO did not enter into force, ICITO's only reason for existence was the latter arrangement.

ICSID: International Centre for Settlement of Investment Disputes, located in Washington DC, chaired *ex officio* by the president of the *World Bank*. It was established by the *Convention on the Settlement of Investment Disputes between States and Nationals of Other States* which entered into force on 14 October 1966. ICSID provides facilities for conciliation and arbitration of disputes. It describes its main objective as the promotion of a climate of mutual confidence between states and foreign investors conducive to an increasing flow of resources to developing countries. It publishes the *ICSID Review: Foreign Investment Law Journal* which is a source of commentary and analysis of the legal treatment of foreign investment, including investment treaties. See also *foreign direct investment*.

ICT: Information and Communication(s) Technology. See also *Digital Divide* and *Okinawa Charter on Global Information Society*.

Identical goods: defined in the *Customs Valuation Agreement* as "goods that are the same in all respects, including physical characteristics, quality and reputation. Minor differences in appearance would not preclude goods otherwise conforming to the definition from being regarded as identical". Among other conditions, goods are not regarded as "identical goods" unless they were produced in the same country as the goods being valued. See also *accordion of likeness*, *fungible goods*, *like products* and *similar goods*.

ILO: see *International Labour Organization*.

ILO Convention No. 138: see *child labour*.

ILO Convention No. 182: the *Convention Concerning the Prohibition and Immediate Action for the Elimination of the Worst Forms of Child Labour*.

ILO Declaration on Fundamental Principles and Rights at Work: see *Declaration on Fundamental Principles and Rights at Work*.

ILO Tripartite Declaration of Principles Concerning Multinational Enterprises and Social Policy: a non-binding set of principles which became effective in 1978, adopted by the *International Labour Organization*. It is aimed at encouraging the positive contribution multinational enterprises can make to economic and social progress. It is also aimed at minimizing and resolving difficulties that may arise through the operation of such enterprises. The Declaration exhorts multinational enterprises to take fully into account the established policy objectives of host countries. It sets out principles governing employment, training, conditions of work and life, and industrial relations. The Declaration is therefore relevant to the consideration of *trade and labour standards*.

IMF: International Monetary Fund. One of the organizations established at the 1944 United Nations Monetary and Financial Conference held at Bretton Woods. It oversees the international monetary system through (a) encouraging international monetary cooperation, (b) facilitating the expansion of balanced growth of international trade, (c) assisting member countries in correcting balance of payments deficits through short- to medium-term credits and (d) promoting foreign exchange stability and orderly exchange relations among its members. *GATT* Article XV provides for consultation and coordination between the two organizations on matters concerning monetary reserves, balances of payment or foreign exchange arrangements. GATT members either had to join the IMF or enter into a special exchange arrangement with the other GATT members to ensure that the provisions of the Agreement were not frustrated by foreign exchange measures. The relationship of the WTO with the IMF is based on the provisions that have governed the GATT's relationship with it. The IMF participates in *balance-of-payments consultations* conducted under Articles XII and XVIII:B of the GATT. See also *Bretton Woods Agreements* and **Trade Integration Mechanism**.

IMF Buffer Stock Financing Facility: see *buffer stocks*.

IMF Compensatory and Contingency Financing Facility: a facility available to *IMF* members who experience balance-of-payments difficulties because of temporary shortfalls in export earnings. Commodity exporters are the main users of this facility. It can also be used by members in cases of unforeseen adverse external shocks beyond their control, such as a sharp drop in export earnings, sharp rises in import prices or international interest rates. Availability of funds is usually conditional on a commitment by the recipient to address the causes of the payments imbalance. See also *structural adjustment*.

Impairment: a negative effect on a WTO member's rights under one or more of the agreements administered by the WTO. See *nullification and impairment*.

Impediments to trade: see *barriers to trade*.

Imperial preferences arrangement: established formally at the 1932 Ottawa Imperial Conference. The basic feature of the arrangement was that pairs of countries making up the British Empire at the time exchanged reciprocal trade preferences. The United Kingdom was a party to the agreements in most cases. The arrangement became a target of United States *commercial policy* at the time of the drafting of the *Atlantic Charter* in 1941, and again in Article 7 of the *mutual aid agreement* between the United Kingdom and the United States of 1942. The Article sought "the elimination of all forms of discriminatory treatment in international commerce". When the GATT entered into force in 1948, it prohibited an increase in all *margins of preference*. This ceiling, combined with negotiated tariff reductions under the GATT, ensured that preference margins were soon eroded. Most have disappeared. The increasing use of the term "British Commonwealth of Nations" in the inter-war years also led to the more widespread use of Commonwealth preferences instead of Imperial preferences. The modern *Commonwealth* has not had any role in the arrangement. See also *historical preferences* and *preferential trade arrangements*.

Implementation: putting into effect the undertakings made in trade negotiations. This is usually considered much less exciting by trade policy people than negotiating new things. In the WTO, implementation often refers to a set of issues argued for by *developing countries*. The first is that some of their *Uruguay Round* obligations are too heavy for them. The second is that there should be negotiations to redress the unfair balance carried by developing countries. Third, that they can only meet some of their other obligations through extended deadlines and increased technical assistance. The *Doha Ministerial Conference* adopted a *Declaration on Implementation-related Issues and Concerns* which seeks to find solutions to some of these problems. See also *capacity-building*.

Implementation doctrine: the principle in *competition law* that *conduct* by firms may be actionable in the country or group of countries where it occurs, even though it may have been decided on elsewhere. See also *antitrust laws, competition policy* and *effects doctrine*.

Implementation periods: see *staging*.

Implicit discrimination: a legislative, tax or other measure applicable to domestic and imported goods and services that may indirectly or unintentionally discriminate against the imported product or service. Having to conform with certain domestic measures maintained by the importing country may cause them to lose their competitive advantage. See *wine gallon assessment* for a practical example of this concept.

Implicit tariff equivalent: an *import quota* on a good normally restricts its availability on the market. Such an induced scarcity may push the good's price up, much in the same way as a *tariff* increases the price of a good on the import market. The *implicit tariff equivalent*, denoted as a percentage, expresses the difference between the cost of the good under quotas and what it would have been without quotas. [Kreinin 1998]

Import: a good or a service bought by residents of one country from residents in another in return, normally, for foreign exchange. See also *barter* and *countertrade*.

Importation: the same as *import*.

Import cartel: see *cartel*.

Import deposit schemes: mechanisms administered by governments or on behalf of governments which require the lodging of a monetary deposit at the time an import order is placed. Such schemes are often part of *import licensing* systems. Their purpose is to ensure that import orders are actually executed or that a minimum import price is met.

Import discipline hypothesis: the proposition that a liberal trading regime has a beneficial effect on the efficiency of domestic firms and the welfare of the consumer through preventing the formation of economic rents.

Import licensing: the need to obtain a permit for importing a product. It is defined in the WTO *Agreement on Import Licensing Procedures* as "administrative procedures used for the operation of import licensing regimes requiring the submission of an application or other documentation to the relevant administrative body as a condition for importing". Import licensing is considered automatic when applications are approved in all cases. See also *import deposit schemes*.

Import licensing agreement: see *Agreement on Import Licensing Procedures*.

Import market value: a system for the valuation of goods to be imported for the purpose of levying *customs duties* which is based on the value of the same goods currently sold in the internal markets of the importing country. This system never was common. It has been superseded by the *transaction value* method described in the WTO *Customs Valuation Agreement*. See also *customs valuation*.

Import quotas: restrictions or ceilings imposed by an importing country on the value or volume of certain products that may be bought from abroad. They are designed to protect domestic producers from the effects of lower-priced imported products. Import quotas are a form of *quantitative restrictions*.

Import relief: protection of domestic producers against competition from imports, mainly through the use of *safeguards*. See also *anti-dumping measures*.

Import restriction: any governmental *measure* that makes import flows smaller than they would be in the absence of the measure. Examples are foreign exchange restrictions, *import licensing* and *import quotas*. Import *cartels* may have the same effect.

Import risk assessment: see *risk assessment*.

Import substitution: a policy for the development of a domestic productive capacity in goods and services to reduce or displace imports, often with the expectation of increases in employment and reductions in the *current account* deficit. Import substitution also seems to be a natural policy to follow when countries seek to deal with the phenomenon described by the *Singer-Prebisch thesis*. This thesis postulates that the *terms of trade* of commodity-producing developing countries in their trade with developed countries will deteriorate over time. The suggested remedy for this was often seen in policies promoting industrialization. Countries practising import substitution often find that their foreign exchange reserves do not show any improvement at all, partly because they still have to import capital goods. To the extent that this policy involves restrictions on imports or domestic subsidies, it raises domestic costs and limits a country's exports.

Import substitution subsidy: a *subsidy* payable only if local materials or components are used in the production of a good, regardless of whether this is the sole condition for its availability. All such subsidies are prohibited under the WTO *Agreement on Subsidies and Countervailing Measures*.

Import surcharge: a levy added to the normal *customs duties*. Countries sometimes apply a surcharge to improve a *current account* deficit, usually with limited success because persistent *trade deficits* tend to reflect a particular type of economic structure or, sometimes, more deep-seated economic problems. Import surcharges also raise the cost of domestic producers and cause them to become less competitive against international standards. The imposition of a surcharge may be legal under the WTO rules if it does not exceed the margin between the *applied tariff rates* and the *bound rates*. See also *primage*.

Import target: see *voluntary import expansion*.

Import tariffs: these are *customs duties* levied at the border on products imported from other economies. See also *customs territory*, *export tariffs*, *multi-column tariff* and *single-column tariff*.

In a manner contrary to honest commercial practices: the *Agreement on Trade-Related Aspects of Intellectual Property Rights* gives natural and legal persons the right to have *undisclosed information* protected by governments and governmental agencies against disclosure, acquisition or use by others in a manner contrary to honest commercial practices. Such practices are defined as at least a breach of contract, breach of confidence and inducement to breach. They include the acquisition of undisclosed information by third parties who knew, or were grossly negligent in failing to know, that such practices were involved in the acquisition. An identical provision can be found in Article 1721 of *NAFTA*. See also *trade secrets*.

In-bond manufacturing: the production of goods within a *free-trade zone*, or a facility recognized for the purpose by the customs authorities, where no duties have to be paid on the import of components or raw materials as long as they are exported to another customs territory.

Inclusion list: part of the *CEPT* mechanism under *AFTA*. Products on this list enjoy the full preferential tariff rates for intra-ASEAN trade. See also *General Exception List*, *Sensitive List* and *Temporary Exclusion List*.

Income equalization: see *agricultural subsidies*.

Incoterms: standard definitions of trade terms used in international sales contracts. Examples are FAS (free alongside ship), FOB (free on board) and CIF (cost, insurance and freight). The Incoterms are administered by the *International Chamber of Commerce*.

Incremental progress: when little or no progress has been made, more likely the latter, but something positive has to be said anyway about the event.

Independence of protection: an *intellectual property* concept enshrined in the *Paris Convention*. It means, for example, that any Australian patent granted under the Paris Convention enjoys protection in Australia quite independently of any protection it may enjoy in respect of the same invention under patents granted in other countries, whether or not these are signatories of the Paris Convention.

Independent Commission on International Development Issues: see *Brandt Report*.

Indian Ocean Rim Association for Regional Cooperation: IOR-ARC. An organization for promoting regional economic cooperation, sustained growth and balanced development launched in 1997 at meeting in Mauritius. It aims to promote the expansion of trade and investment among its members. The IOR-ARC has eighteen members (Australia, Bangladesh, India, Indonesia, Iran, Kenya, Madagascar, Malaysia, Mauritius, Mozambique, Oman, Singapore, South Africa, Sri Lanka, Tanzania, Thailand, United Arab Emirates and Yemen). China, Egypt, France, Japan and the United Kingdom are *dialogue partners*.

Indications of geographical origin: see *geographical indications*.

Indications of source: names on a good itself or on its packaging material of the country, and sometimes also the region, where it has been produced or made. The *Paris Convention* requires its members to seize goods with a false indication of source both in the country where the unlawful use occurred or the country into which the good was imported. The *Madrid Agreement for the Repression of False or Deceptive Indications of Source on Goods* requires its members additionally, as the name of the agreement implies, to seize all goods bearing a false or deceptive indication of source on import or in the country where the unlawful use occurred. Article 4 leaves it to national courts to decide what generic products should not be protected by the Agreement, except for "regional appellations concerning the source of products of the vine". In other words, the Agreement discriminates in favour of such products. Neither the Paris Convention nor the Madrid Agreement defines the meaning of "indication of source". Addor and Grazioli offer this definition: "any expression or sign used to indicate that a product or a service originates in a country, region or a specific place, without any element of quality or reputation". The *Lisbon Agreement* offers additional protection for *appellations of origin*, a sub-category of indications of source, which are protected "as such" in the country of origin and registered with the *International Bureau of Intellectual Property* within *WIPO*. See also *geographical indications*, *geographical names*, *marks of origin* and *rules of origin*. [Addor and Grazioli 2002]

Indicators of market openness: conceptual frameworks for the measurement of the extent to which markets can be contested by new entrants, particularly those located in other countries. There are three basic approaches to constructing such indicators. The first assesses levels of *tariff* barriers, *non-tariff barriers* and *tariff equivalents*. The second looks at the results of liberalization through examining its effect on trade flows, extent and growth of *intra-industry trade*, etc. This is done through modelling work. The third approach is aimed at the interaction between barriers and the competitive process in a given market. In other words, it looks at the structural openness of markets to competition. There is considerable agreement on the most appropriate methods for the first two approaches, but they can differ rather more for the third class of indicators. See also *international contestability of markets* and *trade and competition*.

Indigenous knowledge: distinctive knowledge held by indigenous peoples and transmitted to future generations. It is a sub-category of *traditional knowledge*. [WIPO/IPTK/MCT/02/INF.4]

Indirect dumping: the usual definition of *dumping* is the sale of a product abroad for less than it is sold on the home market. This definition assumes that only two countries are involved, i.e. the product is exported from country A to country B. An allegation of indirect dumping would claim that the article causing injury was first exported from country A to country B where it would not be considered as having been dumped, then from country B to country C. See also *dumping*, *hidden dumping* and *anti-dumping measures*.

Indirect material: this is either a good used in the production, testing or inspection of a good, but not physically incorporated into the good, or it is a good used in the maintenance of buildings or the operation of equipment associated with the production of a good. Examples of indirect materials are fuel and energy, tools, spare parts, safety equipment, lubricants and greases. See also *rules of origin*.

Individual action plan: see *APEC individual action plan*.

Industrial designs: the shape, configuration, pattern or ornamentation of a useful article, but not a method or principle of construction. See also *Hague System for the International Deposit of Industrial Designs*, *intellectual property* and *Locarno Agreement Establishing an International Classification for Industrial Designs*.

Industrial property: mainly deals with *inventions*, *trademarks* and *industrial designs*, but also the repression of *unfair competition*. See also *intellectual property*.

Industrial research: defined in the WTO *Agreement on Subsidies and Countervailing Measures* as planned search or critical investigation aimed at discovery of new knowledge, with the objective that such knowledge may be useful in developing new products, processes or services, or in bringing about a significant improvement to existing products, processes or services. *Assistance* qualifying as *non-actionable subsidies* for up to 75% of the cost of such industrial research may be allowable under the Agreement if it is limited to costs of personnel, instruments, equipment, land and buildings, consultancy, additional overhead costs directly related to research and other running costs incurred directly as result of the research activity. See also *pre-competitive development activity*.

Industrial tariffs: in strict terms, *tariffs* levied on manufactures and semi-manufactures to distinguish them from tariffs on primary agricultural and mineral commodities. Sometimes used, however, to refer to tariffs on non-agricultural products generally. See also *non-agricultural market access*.

Industry policy: in its wide meaning, this term refers to policies adopted by governments towards all industries or industrial development generally. In its narrow meaning, it covers governmental policy towards selected industrial sectors to ensure their development or restructuring. This can be done in many ways, and one of them is **protection**. Sometimes, calls for an active industry policy reflect no more than a desire to pursue **mercantilism**, freer availability of **subsidies**, preference for domestic manufacturers in **government procurement** and **local content requirements**. See also **infant-industry argument**, **learning-by-doing argument**, **national champions**, **picking winners**, **strategic trade theory** and **structural adjustment**.

Industry-to-industry understandings: a euphemistic name given to **voluntary restraint arrangements**. They are understandings between industries only because governments insist on them, though in some cases industries are quite happy to accept them because of the opportunity for windfall profits they offer to importers and exporters alike.

Inertial policy determinism: adherence to policies long after they have outlived their ostensible utility. See also **conventional wisdom**, **QWERTYprinciple** and **vestigial thought**.

Infant-industry argument: this argument holds that if a given industry with a potential **comparative advantage** was accorded **protection**, usually in the form of **tariffs**, **subsidies**, **local content requirements**, **bounties**, **import quotas**, etc., to allow it to establish itself, it would be able in the long run to succeed in the market without the need for special protection. One of the flaws in the argument is that if the cost of current protection is to be repaid in the future, above-average returns will be needed after the industry is established, and that is at best problematical. In practice, few infant industries grow up of their own volition. Instead, they tend to seek to perpetuate their protection. See also **learning-by-doing argument**, **picking winners** and **strategic trade theory**.

Infant-industry provision: Article XVIII of the GATT (Governmental Assistance to Economic Development) allows developing countries under certain conditions to impose measures aimed at fostering the development of infant industries. See also **developing countries and the multilateral trading system** and **infant-industry argument**.

Informal trade: describes trade in goods, usually between neighbouring countries, which does not pass formally through customs controls. Informal trade seems to range from **border trade** to **smuggling**. See also **unrecorded trade**.

Information Technology Agreement: an outcome in the WTO of the December 1996 **Singapore Ministerial Conference**. Parties agreed to eliminate **customs duties** and any other duties on a wide range of information technology products through equal rate reductions beginning in 1997 and ending in 2000. They also bound the zero tariffs. Because of its wide membership, the Agreement covers more than 90% of world trade in information technology products, including computers, telecommunications equipment, semiconductors, semiconductor manufacturing equipment, software and scientific instruments. It does not cover consumer electronic goods.

Information Technology Agreement II: a proposal made in 1997 for expanding the **Information Technology Agreement** through the addition of provisions on **non-tariff measures**, expansion of product coverage and the **transfer of**

technology. These negotiations now have been overtaken by the *Doha Development Agenda*.

Initial commitments: trade-liberalizing commitments in services which WTO members are prepared to make early in negotiations.

Initial negotiating right: INR. The right of a WTO member to ask for tariff *concessions* by another member in a WTO negotiating round even though it is not the principal supplier. INRs remain negotiating tools for countries with important trade interests in a product or commodity, though these rights no longer hold the importance they once had in trade negotiations. The question of who has initial negotiating rights does not arise in the case of *linear tariff cuts* because all participants agree to cut tariffs on specified product categories by the same percentage rate, regardless of their importance to any given trading partner. It may, however, come up in subsequent bilateral negotiations. WTO members have therefore agreed to create so-called floating initial negotiating rights. These are initial negotiating rights that would be enjoyed by members having *principal supplier rights* at the time of the renegotiation of a tariff item that had earlier been subject to *linear cuts*. Such initial negotiating rights are called "floating" because they remain hypothetical until a concrete case arises. See also *principal supplying interest* and *principal supplier rule*.

Initiative for ASEAN Integration: a program launched in November 2000 by the *ASEAN* countries with the twin aims of integrating ASEAN as a whole better into the world economy and to integrate the four newer ASEAN members (Cambodia, Laos, Myanmar and Vietnam) better into the ASEAN framework.

Injury: an adverse effect on domestic industry assumed to be caused by the actions of exporters from other countries, for example, through *dumping*, *subsidies* or import surges. In the case of dumping, action can be taken if there is *material injury*. In *safeguards*, *serious injury* must be threatening or have occurred. Both terms allow for a subjective assessment, but serious injury is deemed to be more grave than material injury. The WTO has a highly developed framework for the assessment of injury and any remedial action in the case of injury or threat of injury. The *Agreement on Textiles and Clothing* permits members to impose *transitional safeguards* under certain conditions in cases of *serious damage*, or the threat of serious damage, to domestic industry as a result of increased imports. See also *Agreement on Safeguards* and *anti-dumping measures*.

Inland parity: see *national treatment*.

Inorganic integration: described by some as the process resulting from formal and politically oriented trade agreements forged among countries to reduce or eliminate tariff and non-tariff barriers and harmonize trade-relevant domestic economic policies. See also *economic integration*.

Input dumping: said to be done of products that are not in themselves dumped, but which are claimed to contain components acquired at dumped prices. See also *secondary dumping*.

In-quota rate: the *tariff* applicable to a product imported within the limits of a *tariff quota*.

In-quota trade: the trade that occurs within a given *tariff rate quota*.

Insufficient operations: also called insufficient processing or non-qualifying operations. This is a term used in the administration of *preferential rules of origin* to signify that a product imported from one party to a *free-trade agreement* does not qualify for the *preferential tariff rate* because it has not undergone *substantial transformation* in that party. The free-trade agreement between Japan and Singapore, a typical example, describes as insufficient operations: (a) preservation of products in good condition during transport and storage, (b) changes of packaging, (c) affixing marks or labels on the products or their packaging, (d) disassembly, (e) placing in bottles, cases or boxes, and other simple packaging operations, (f) simple cutting, (g) simple mixing, (h) simple assembly of parts to form a complete product, (i) simple making up of sets of articles, and (j) any combination of these operations. See also *minimum operations*.

Insufficient processing: see *insufficient operations*.

Integrated Data Base: IDB. Maintained by the WTO Secretariat. It contains information supplied by members concerning *applied MFN tariff rates*, import statistics, etc. Tariff and trade data are matched at the tariff line level. See also *Consolidated Tariff Schedules*. [WTO TN/MA/S/2]

Integrated Framework for Trade-Related Technical Assistance to Least Developed Countries: adopted in 1998 to improve the trade-related benefits available to *least developed countries* from the WTO and five other multilateral agencies (*IMF*, *International Trade Centre WTO-UNCTAD*, *UNCTAD* and the *United Nations Development Programme*). See also *Doha Development Agenda Global Trust Fund*.

Integrated Programme for Commodities: IPC. A program adopted at UNCTAD IV in 1976 which envisaged the negotiation of international agreements or arrangements for eighteen specified commodities. These were bananas, bauxite, cocoa, coffee, copper, cotton and cotton yarns, hard fibres and products, iron ore, jute and products, manganese, meat, phosphates, rubber, sugar, tea, tropical timber, tin, vegetable oils, including olive oils and oilseeds. Other products may at any time be added to this list. The IPC has several objectives, including avoiding excessive price fluctuations, the achievement of price levels which would be remunerative to producers and equitable to customers, increased export earnings for developing countries, improvements in market access and reliability of supply. The *Common Fund for Commodities*, a financing facility for the IPC, was created at the same time. See also *buffer stocks*, *international commodity arrangements*, *international commodity bodies* and *UNCTAD*.

Integrated Tariff of the European Community: TARIC. An annual publication by the *European Community* (EC) listing tariffs and other trade measures applied to EC imports and exports. The tariff information is also available electronically in a continually updated version.

Integration: see *deep integration*, *economic integration*, *inorganic integration*, *market-led integration*, *organic integration* and *policy-led integration*.

Integration program: the phasing out of *Multi-Fibre Agreement* (MFA) restrictions in four stages starting on 1 January 1995 and ending on 1 January 2005.

Integrity in customs: see *Arusha Declaration*.

Intellectual property: generally includes *patents*, *trademarks*, *industrial designs*, *lay-out designs of integrated circuits*, *copyright*, *geographical indications* and *trade secrets* (confidential business information). See also *Agreement on Trade-Related Aspects of Intellectual Property Rights*, *WIPO*, *traditional knowledge* and *United Nations Educational, Scientific and Cultural Organization*.

Intellectual property protection: the safeguarding of an owner's *intellectual property rights* through national legislation and international agreements especially concerning *copyright*, *patents* and *trademarks*. Many commentators insist that the strength or weakness of a country's system of intellectual property protection seems to have a substantial effect on the kinds of technology firms transfer to another country. See also *intellectual property right infringements*, *sui generis right* and *transfer of technology*.

Intellectual property rights: ownership of expressions of ideas, including literary and artistic works protected by *copyright*, *inventions* protected by *patents*, signs for distinguishing goods of an enterprise protected by *trademarks* and other elements of *industrial property*. Intellectual property rights give the innovator an exclusive legal right, i.e. a monopoly, to exploit the innovation for a certain time. This serves as a reward and encourages others to innovate. Thus intellectual property rights can be in conflict with *competition policy* which seeks to remove impediments to the efficient functioning of the markets through, for example, minimizing the power of monopolies. The challenge in the drafting of intellectual property laws therefore is to ensure that innovators receive sufficient encouragement to be creative and, at the same time, that owners of intellectual property rights are not in a position to abuse these rights. See also *Agreement on Trade-Related Aspects of Intellectual Property Rights* and *competition laws*. [Gervais 2003]

Intellectual property right infringements: such infringements on a commercial scale are classified as *piracy* if they involve the unauthorized reproduction of copyright materials, or as *counterfeiting* where there is copying of *trademarks* with the intention of passing the goods off as those of the authentic producer. Trademarks can be infringed through the unauthorized use of a mark that is identical or so similar to an existing mark that it may lead to confusion among consumers. *Patents* can be infringed through unauthorized manufacture, use or sale in the country of registration of the invention claimed in the patent. See also *Agreement on Trade-Related Aspects of Intellectual Property Rights* and *dilution doctrine*.

Inter-Agency Task Force on Statistics of International Trade in Services: see *trade in services statistics*.

Inter-American Convention Against Corruption: see *corruption*.

Inter-American Convention on International Commercial Arbitration: adopted by the member states of the *Organization of American States* on 30 January

1975. The parties agree in Article I that "an agreement in which the parties undertake to submit to arbitral decision any differences that may arise between them with respect to a commercial transaction is valid". Article 4 states that any arbitral decision or award that cannot be appealed against under the applicable law has the force of a final judicial judgement. See also *arbitration*.

Interconnection: see *telecommunications termination services*.

Interconnection charge: a charge levied by telecommunications network operators to cover the cost of connecting calls originating from or destined for another network.

Interested parties: persons who may have rights when an enquiry or investigation leading to possible *anti-dumping measures*, *safeguards* or *countervailing measures* is undertaken. They must be notified of the information required by the authorities, they must be given ample time to make their case, and they must have a full opportunity for a defence of their interest. The WTO *Anti-Dumping Agreement*, which sets out the rules applicable for the handling of anti-dumping cases, defines interested parties as (a) an exporter or foreign producer or the importer of a product subject to investigation, or a trade or business association which has a majority of producers, exporters or importers of such products as members, (b) the government of the exporting member and (c) a producer of the *like product* in the importing member or a trade and business association with a majority of members who produce the like product in the territory of the importing member. The WTO *Agreement on Subsidies and Countervailing Measures* has the same definition, but it does not mention the government of the exporting member. The WTO *Agreement on Safeguards* also requires members about to impose a *safeguards* action to give an opportunity for consultations to those members with a substantial interest in the product concerned, but it does not define how the term "substantial interest" is to be understood.

Interested third parties: the WTO *Dispute Settlement Understanding* allows for the consideration of the interests of member countries in a dispute in which they are not directly involved. Such members have the right to be heard by a *panel* and to make submissions to it, but to do so they must be able to show through trade figures that they have a substantial interest in the matter. This, as the panel in *Korea – Definitive Safeguard Measures on Imports of Certain Dairy Products*, held, this does not necessarily mean an economic interest. In *European Communities – Regime for the Importation, Sale and Distribution of Bananas* the *Appellate Body* ruled "substantial interest" could not be interpreted either as meaning a "legal interest" only. [WT/DS27/AB/R, WT/DS98/R]

Intergovernmental conference: a mechanism available to the *European Union* to consider revisions of and amendments to the framework of treaties constituting it. Intergovernmental conferences can stretch over months and even years, but they usually lead to substantial steps forward.

Intergovernmental control agreements: see *commodity policy*.

Intergovernmental Group of Twenty-Four on International Monetary Affairs: see *G-24*.

Intergovernmental organizations: IGs. These are organizations usually established through a *treaty* bringing together governments regionally or multilaterally for the pursuit of a common purpose. IGs usually are administered by a secretariat which supports the organization's governing body, consisting of representatives of member states, as well as subsidiary bodies established by the governing body. IGs and their staffs often enjoy full or partial diplomatic privileges in the country hosting them.

Interim agreement necessary for the formation of a customs union or a free-trade area: an instrument mentioned in GATT *Article XXIV* which deals with *customs unions* and *free-trade areas*. Such agreements have to be notified to the WTO, together with a timetable for their implementation. Few interim agreements appear to have been notified to the GATT or the WTO. Nor have working parties, in examining notified agreements, always been able to agree whether they were dealing with an interim agreement or a final agreement. However, in a sense nearly all notified free-trade agreements have been interim agreements even though the parties may have regarded them as final agreements. This is because many free-trade agreements intended to conform immediately to Article XXIV contain phase-in provisions for the elimination of trade restrictions in *sensitive products*.

Interim Commission on Phytosanitary Measures: see *Commission on Phytosanitary Measures*.

Interim Co-ordinating Committee for International Commodity Arrangements: see *commodity policy*.

Interlaken Declaration on the Kimberley Process Certification Scheme for Rough Diamonds: see *Kimberley Process Certification Scheme*.

Intermediate agricultural products: these are agricultural products that have been processed to some extent, but not generally enough to be sold to consumers. Examples are hides and skins, animal fats and raw sugar.

Intermediate goods and services: see *final goods and services*.

Intermediate material: a term used in the *rules of origin* of *free-trade agreements*. It means a material produced by the producer of a good and used in the production of that good. Such goods may be included in the calculation of the value of a product to make it qualify for preferential customs treatment under the Agreement.

Internal market: used both for a market lying within a single jurisdiction and the market made up through the formation of a *customs union*, a *free-trade area* or a *common market*, such as the *European Community*.

Internal support: encompasses any measure which acts to maintain producer prices at levels above those prevailing in international markets. This is done through direct payments to producers, such as *subsidies* and *deficiency payments*, and input and marketing cost reduction measures available only for agricultural production.

Internal taxes: government charges applied to sale of goods and services inside a *customs territory*. Article III (National Treatment on Internal Taxation and

Regulation) of the GATT requires that such charges are levied at the same rate for domestic products as for imported products. In other words, *national treatment* is a fundamental obligation in this regard. See also *behind-the-border issues*.

Internal trade: usually the trade between the partners to a *preferential trade arrangement*. Their trade with third countries is known as external trade. Sometimes internal trade is used to describe commercial activity within a single economy, but the use of *commerce* for this is often preferred.

International accounting standards: accounting standards being developed by the International Accounting Standards Committee (IASC) with the aim of enhancing the comparability of financial information, improving disclosure, reducing compliance cost and encouraging uniform financial reporting by multinational companies. These standards are therefore seen as a means for a better and more efficient allocation of financial resources. See also *Generally Accepted Accounting Principles*, *Guidelines for Mutual Recognition Agreements or Arrangements in the Accountancy Sector* and *harmonization of standards and qualifications*.

International Agreement on Jute and Jute Products: entered into force in 1984 under the *Integrated Programme for Commodities*. It was renegotiated in 1989 with entry into force in 1991. It expired on 11 April 2000 and was replaced by the *International Jute Study Group*. This Agreement was confined to the aims of achieving better markets for jute and jute products, transparency in international trade and improved production and processing techniques. It was administered by the International Jute Organization, located in Dhaka.

International Agreement on Olive Oil and Table Olives: first concluded in 1956 and renegotiated in 1963, 1979 and 1986. The current agreement, adopted in 2005, is valid until 31 December 2014. Until 1986 it was known formally as the *International Olive Oil Agreement*. The Agreement aims to develop long-term markets, to promote research and development, to expand consumption, to forestall unfair competition practices and ensure reliability of supplies. It does not have a *buffer stock*. Membership consists mainly of the *European Community* and about a dozen other countries, mostly Mediterranean. The Agreement is administered through the International Olive Oil Council, located in Madrid.

International Bovine Meat Agreement: one of the *WTO plurilateral agreements*, originally negotiated in the *Tokyo Round* as the *Arrangement Regarding Bovine Meat*. Its objectives were (a) expanding, liberalizing and stabilizing trade in meat and livestock, (b) encouraging greater international cooperation in all aspects of trade in bovine meat and livestock, (c) to secure additional benefits for developing countries and (d) to expand trade further on a competitive basis, taking into account the traditional position of efficient producers. Until it was terminated at the end of 1997, it was administered by the International Meat Council.

International Bureau of Intellectual Property: this is the secretariat administering the governing bodies of *WIPO* and its Unions. A Union consists of the states that have acceded to one of the *intellectual property* conventions. The

International Bureau also maintains international registration services in the fields of *patents*, *trademarks*, *industrial designs* and *appellations of origin*. It is located in Geneva.

International Centre for Settlement of Investment disputes: see *ICSID*

International Centre for Trade and Sustainable Development: a *non-governmental organization* established in 1996 to promote a better understanding of the relationship between international trade, *sustainable development* and environmental issues more generally. It is located in Geneva.

International Chamber of Commerce: ICC. A business organization represented in more than 130 countries. The ICC promotes an open international trade and investment system and the market economy. Among the services it provides to its members is the *International Court of Arbitration*. Its headquarters are in Paris. See also *Incoterms*.

International Civil Aviation Organization: see *Chicago Convention*.

International Cocoa Agreement: first concluded in 1972 and renegotiated in 1975, 1980, 1986, 1993 and 2001. The current agreement entered into force on 1 October 2003 for five years. The Agreement no longer operates a *buffer stock*. The objectives of the current Agreement include, among others, (a) the development and strengthening of cooperation in the international cocoa economy, (b) contributing to a balance between supply of and demand for cocoa in the world market, and (c) promotion of transparency in the world cocoa economy through the collection and dissemination of statistics and other data on cocoa. The Agreement's administrative body, the International Cocoa Organization, is in London.

International Code of Conduct on the Transfer of Technology: see *Draft International Code of Conduct on the Transfer of Technology*.

International Coffee Agreement: first concluded in 1962 and renegotiated in 1968, 1976, 1983, 1994 and 2001. The current Agreement will be in force until 30 December 2007. It no longer seeks to stabilize prices through the imposition of *export quotas*, and it does not operate a *buffer stock*. The objectives of the current Agreement are: (1) to promote international cooperation on coffee matters, (2) to provide a forum for intergovernmental consultations and negotiations on coffee, (3) to provide a forum on consultations with the private sector, (4) to facilitate the expansion and transparency of international trade in coffee, (5) to collect, disseminate and publish economic and technical information, statistics and studies, (6) to encourage the development of a sustainable coffee economy, (7) to encourage the consumption of coffee, (8) to advise on projects for the benefit of the world coffee economy, (9) to promote quality and (10) to promote the transfer of technology relevant to coffee. The Agreement is administered by the International Coffee Organization, located in London.

International commercial dispute resolution: resolution of disputes between private parties in different countries outside the framework of courts. This can be done through negotiation, mediation and conciliation, expert determination and expert appraisal, *arbitration* and a combination of such processes. The method selected depends on the views of the parties. See also *ICSID* and *International Court of Arbitration*.

International commodity agreements: ICAs. These are intergovernmental agreements intended to improve the functioning of global commodity markets by balancing the interests of producers and consumers. They are of two types: (a) administrative agreements aimed at increasing consumption of the commodity, promoting transparency in production and market conditions through, for example, statistical work, and (b) economic agreements which seek to influence the market price of the commodity. The agreement establishing the *Common Fund for Commodities*, negotiated under *UNCTAD* auspices, which aims at the conclusion of economic agreements, sets out four elements it deems necessary for an ICA: (a) agreements and arrangements must be concluded between governments, (b) agreements should promote international cooperation in that commodity, (c) producers and consumers must be included and (d) the agreement should cover the bulk of world trade in the commodity concerned. Some of them are made up of producers only. Most ICAs are negotiated for periods normally ranging from three to six years, when their operations are reviewed. ICAs with economic provisions typically contain obligations aimed at stabilizing prices, financing a *buffer stock*, disposal of non-commercial stockpiles, commitments to improve market access and to promote consumption. Some agreements also seek to encourage further processing in producing countries, and they contain provisions for the exchange of information on production, trade and consumption. Most also include consultation and dispute settlement provisions. The 1954 sugar and tin agreements carried a "fair labour standards" clause which stipulated that labour engaged in the production of the relevant commodity should receive fair remuneration, adequate social security protection and other satisfactory employment conditions. The 2001 *International Coffee Agreement* contains a clause promoting improvement of standards of living for populations engaged in the coffee sector. At the same time, members agreed that they would not use this provision for protectionist purposes. Most ICAs are administered by a body established for the purpose. Members are divided into producers and consumers, with the two categories having an equal number of total votes. Producer countries often also import the same commodity, and consumer countries also export. The definition of producer and consumer therefore can hinge on whether a country is a net exporter or importer. Voting is usually based on the share of international trade a member has in that commodity. ICAs commonly operate autonomously, but their negotiation or renegotiation usually takes place under UNCTAD auspices which, upon its establishment in 1964, acquired responsibility for commodity matters within the *United Nations* system. Two agreements have, however, been negotiated in the *GATT*, and they were part of the *WTO plurilateral agreements* until the end of 1997. The two are the *International Dairy Agreement* and the *International Bovine Meat Agreement*. Both were ostensibly aimed at expanding, liberalizing and stabilizing trade in the commodities under their purview. See also *commodity policy*, *Integrated Programme for Commodities* and *international commodity bodies*.

International commodity bodies: ICBs. These are organizations that either administer *international commodity agreements* or are constituted as commodity study groups. The *Common Fund for Commodities* established through *UNCTAD* has designated 24 organizations which represent more than 30 commodities as ICBs. The first group consists of the International Cocoa Organization, International Coffee Organization, International Copper Study Group, International Cotton Advisory Committee, International Grains Council, International Jute Study Group, International Lead and Zinc Study Group, International Network for Bamboo and Rattan, International Nickel Study Group, International Olive Oil Council, International Rubber Study Group, International Sugar Organization and the International Tropical Timber Organization. The second group consists of bodies located within the *Food and Agricultural Organization* Intergovernmental Sub-Group on Bananas, Intergovernmental Group on Citrus Fruit, Intergovernmental Sub-Committee on Fish Trade, Intergovernmental Group on Grains, Intergovernmental Group on Hard Fibres, Intergovernmental Sub-Group on Hides and Skins, Intergovernmental Group on Meat, Intergovernmental Group on Oils, Oilseeds and Fats, Intergovernmental Group on Rice, Intergovernmental Group on Tea and Intergovernmental Sub-Group on Tropical Fruits. The third group is the UNCTAD Committee on Tungsten. All these bodies are eligible to sponsor projects for financial support by the Common Fund. See also separate entries for some of the agreements administered by these bodies.

International commodity-related environment agreement: ICREA. A type of voluntary intergovernmental instrument suggested by *UNCTAD* as conducive to the promotion of environmental objectives in commodity production and to facilitate cooperation among producers and consumers in this regard. ICREAs could either be concerned with the setting of standards, or they could be aimed at funding the transition to more sustainable production methods. See also *commodity policy* and *trade and environment*.

International Competition Network: ICN. This is an international body concerned with issues in the enforcement of competition law. It does not make rules. Membership is open to any national or multinational competition authority. [www.internationalcompetitionnetwork.org]

International Conference on Financing and Development: see *Monterrey Consensus*.

International contestability of markets: used for assessing from the perspective of exporters in other countries the extent to which markets are free of distortion caused by regulation and anti-competitive governmental or private action. International contestability is determined by such factors as *tariff* and *non-tariff measures*, regulatory conditions affecting the import of services, *structural impediments* in the form of, for example, distribution systems, internal regulation of investment and competition, and private anti-competitive practices. A fully contestable market would be one in which firms can compete purely on the basis of price and ability to deliver the product or service wanted by the market. See also *indicators of market openness* and *trade and competition*.

International Convention for the Protection of New Varieties of Plants: concluded in 1961 in Paris and revised in 1978 in Geneva. It provides for the grant of *patents* or special titles of protection to breeders of new plant varieties. It is administered by the International Union for the Protection of New Varieties of Plants (UPOV), rather than by *WIPO*. See also *intellectual property rights*.

International Convention for the Protection of Performers, Producers of Phonograms and Broadcasting Organizations: see *Rome Convention*.

International Convention for the Use of Appellations of Origin and Denomination of Cheeses: see *Stresa Convention*.

International Convention on Mutual Administrative Assistance for the Prevention, Investigation and Repression of Customs Offences: adopted in Nairobi on 9 June 1977 under the auspices of the *World Customs Organization*. Parties to this Convention undertake to give each other assistance aimed at preventing, investigating and repressing customs offences. Its provisions do not cover requests for the arrest of persons or the recovery of duties.

International Convention on the Harmonized Commodity Description and Coding System: see *Harmonized System*.

International Convention on the Simplification and Harmonization of Customs Procedures: see *Kyoto Convention*.

International Copper Study Group: ICSG. An intergovernmental organization established under *UNCTAD* auspices in 1992. Its members consist of 24 national governments and the European Community. They represent more than 80% of world trade in copper. The ICSG's main functions are the exchange of information on the international copper economy, to collect and disseminate improved statistics and to consider any special issues that might arise. Its secretariat is located in Lisbon. See also *CIPEC* and *international commodity bodies*.

International Cotton Advisory Committee: ICAC. Established in 1939 as an association of cotton producers and restructured in 1945 to admit consumers also. It collects and disseminates statistics on cotton production and trade and promotes measures for the development of the global cotton economy. Its secretariat is located in Washington, DC. See also *international commodity bodies*.

International Court of Arbitration: established in 1923 as the *arbitration* body of the *International Chamber of Commerce*. It offers resolution of commercial disputes without litigation in national court systems. See also *alternative dispute resolution*.

International Court of Justice: the principal judicial organ of the *United Nations*. Its two functions are to settle legal disputes between states and to give advisory opinions on legal questions submitted by authorized international organizations and agencies, all of them being United Nations agencies. The sources of law used by the Court include international treaties and conventions, international custom, general principles of law, judicial decisions and academic work. The Court was established in 1946 as the successor to the Permanent Court of International Justice. It is located at The Hague.

International Covenant on Economic, Social and Cultural Rights: entered into force on 3 January 1976. This Covenant, especially aspects of Part III, is relevant to the discussion of *trade and labour standards* and *trade and human rights*. In Article 6 the parties recognize the right to work, including access to technical and vocational guidance and training programs. Article 7 recognizes the right to fair wages and equal remuneration for work of equal value, safe and healthy working conditions, equal opportunity to be promoted and rest, leisure and reasonable limitation of working hours. In Article 8 the Parties undertake to ensure the right of everyone to form and join trade unions, the right of trade unions to establish national federations and to form or join international trade-union organizations, the right of trade unions to function freely, and the right to strike in accordance with the law. Article 9 recognizes the right of everyone to social security, including social insurance. See also *Universal Declaration of Human Rights*. [Centre for Human Rights 1988]

International Dairy Agreement: one of the *WTO plurilateral agreements*, negotiated during the *Tokyo Round* as the *International Dairy Arrangement*, but terminated in 1997. Its objectives were (a) to achieve the expansion and ever greater liberalization of world trade in dairy products under market conditions as stable as possible on the basis of mutual benefit to exporting and importing countries, and (b) to further the economic and social development of developing countries. The Agreement covered trade in fresh and preserved milk and cream, butter, cheese and curd, and casein. It was administered by the International Dairy Council.

International Dairy Arrangement: see *International Dairy Agreement*.

International Dairy Council: see *International Dairy Agreement*.

International Development Association: IDA. This is an agency of the *World Bank* which makes concessional loans to the poorest of developing countries. Its aim is to reduce disparities between and within countries, and it concentrates on primary education, basic health, water supply and sanitation. IDA mainly lends to countries that do not have the financial ability to borrow from the World Bank on commercial terms. In 2004 most of the countries eligible for IDA funds had an annual per capita income of less than $865. In some cases, countries are eligible for combined IDA/World Bank loans. The IDA is funded mainly through contributions from the wealthier member countries, rather than by borrowing on financial markets as is the case for the World Bank itself. See also *International Finance Corporation* and *Multilateral Investment Guarantee Agency*.

International division of labour: the arranging of production processes to promote ever greater specialization of labour, economies of scale and standardized products. Its aim is to enable firms to compete through the price mechanism. The international division of labour was originally based on the analogy of dividing the manufacture of a product in such a way that the greatest possible part of it could be produced by cheaper unskilled and semi-skilled labour, but the complexity of many products now produced and traded internationally has greatly undermined this rationale. See also *delocalization*, *globalization*, *new international division of labour* and *product cycle theory*.

International economic relations: includes directly, in addition to international trade, international monetary and financial cooperation and activities, such as capital movements and foreign investment. More indirectly, almost any international activity can have an economic aspect or effect.

International Electrotechnical Commission: IEC. The main international body for cooperation on *standards* and *conformity assessment* in the fields of electricity, electronics and related technologies. It provides a forum for the preparation and implementation of consensus-based voluntary international standards. The IEC is associated with the WTO through the *Agreement on Technical Barriers to Trade*. Its secretariat is located in Geneva. See also *International Organization for Standardization*.

International Energy Agency: IEA. An intergovernmental organization established in 1974 after the first oil shock. It consists of *OECD* member countries. Its main concerns are increased energy efficiency, energy conservation and the development of new sources of energy. The IEA's secretariat is in Paris.

International exhaustion: the proposition that once a product embodying *intellectual property rights* (IPRs) has been lawfully placed on the market anywhere (i.e. with the consent of the owner of the IPRs), it can be resold or transferred to any other market without the further consent of the owner of these IPRs. See also *exhaustion doctrine*, *regional exhaustion* and *parallel imports*. [Maskus 2000]

International Finance Corporation: IFC. The part of the *World Bank* charged with providing finance for private enterprise in developing countries to promote their economic development. The IFC coordinates its activities closely with the World Bank, but it operates essentially as an independent agency. See also *International Development Association* and *Multilateral Investment Guarantee Agency*.

International financial institutions: IFIs. A term used for intergovernmental organizations, such as the *IMF*, the *World Bank* or the Asian Development Bank. They are concerned mainly with the promotion of sound economic management by member states or the provision of financial support to member states for defined purposes. Developing countries often can obtain financial assistance for the development of their economies under concessional conditions, such as extended repayment periods and interest below market rates. See also *multilateral development banks* and *structural adjustment*.

International Fund for Agricultural Development: IFAD. One of the *United Nations specialized agencies*. It began operations in 1977 with a mandate to finance agricultural development projects leading to improved food supplies and *food security* in developing countries. The bulk of its loans are made available to *low-income countries*, usually on highly concessional terms. See also *Food and Agricultural Organization* and *World Food Programme*.

International Grains Agreement: IGA. The successor to the *International Wheat Agreement*. It entered into force on 1 July 1995 for three years, with provision for renewal every two years. The IGA consists of two instruments: the *Grains Trade Convention* and the *Food Aid Convention*. The former aims to promote international cooperation in the wheat and coarse grains trade, mainly through improving *market transparency*. The latter provides annually specified minimum amounts of food aid to developing countries in the form of grains suitable for human consumption, much of it through the *World Food Programme*. The IGA is administered by the International Grains Council located in London. See also *Food and Agricultural Organization* and *food security*.

International investment agreement: IIA. This is an agreement between two or more parties for the treatment of investment flows between them. Most of these agreements aim to protect and promote investment, but more recent ones also liberalise conditions for investment. *Treaties of friendship, commerce and navigation* are among the oldest such instruments. Current forms are *investment promotion and protection agreements* and *bilateral investment treaties*. The *Energy Charter Treaty* is an example of a regional investment agreement. An ambitious attempt to establish common rules for international investment was the OECD *Multilateral Agreement on Investment*, but negotiations towards it were abandoned in 1999. IIAs typically have provisions concerning the *standard of treatment* to be accorded to foreign investors and their investments. These standards include *most-favoured-nation treatment, national treatment, minimum standard of treatment* and *fair and equitable treatment*. The former two are found in virtually every agreement, the latter only in some. Other main provisions include rules on *establishment* (i.e. act of investing), entry of personnel to manage the investment, *expropriation* and compensation, dispute settlement between the parties and *investor-state disputes*. Beginning with the entry into force of *NAFTA* in 1994 many *free-trade agreements* have included comprehensive investment chapters, such as *NAFTA Chapter 11*. Some of these investment chapters perform the concurrent functions of promoting, protecting, liberalizing and facilitating investment, a development already anticipated by some bilateral investment treaties. Such agreements proscribe, for example, *performance requirements*. Others emphasize liberalization and leave promotion and protection to separate instruments. *International Investment Instruments: A Compendium*, which is published by *UNCTAD* and has now reached fourteen volumes, is an essential tool for a detailed study of IIAs. See also *non-conforming measures*.

Internationalization: the extension of economic activity across national borders to harness the benefits of lower costs in other economies, with countries specializing in a particular stage of production. It is one of the results of decreasing costs of transport and communications which promotes the integration of markets for goods, services, technology, ideas, capital and human resources. Analysts tend to distinguish internationalization from *globalization*. Some see the former as allowing countries to retain their economic independence and the latter as weakening national sovereignty.

International Jute Study Group: established on 13 March 2001 as the successor to the *International Agreement on Jute and Jute Products*. The objective of the study group is to provide an effective framework for international cooperation, consultation and policy development in all aspects of the world jute economy. Its secretariat is in Dhaka.

International Labour Organization: ILO. Established in 1919 as part of the Treaty of Versailles. It became a *United Nations specialized agency* in 1946. Its objectives are to improve working and living conditions through the adoption of international conventions and recommendations setting minimum standards for wages, hours of work, conditions of employment, social security, etc. It is located in Geneva. See also *child labour*, *core labour standards* and *trade and labour standards*.

International labour standards: expressions of international agreement in the form of conventions and recommendations arrived at in the *International Labour Organization*. They cover labour conditions, social policy, human rights and civil rights matters. Among them are freedom of association, the right to organize, collective bargaining, abolition of forced labour, and equality of opportunity and treatment. See also *core labour standards* and *trade and labour standards*.

International Lead and Zinc Study Group: ILZSG. Established in 1959 as the successor to the Lead and Zinc Study Committee. It is a forum for consultation between producers and consumers on issues related to the production of and trade in lead and zinc, including the compilation of statistics. The ILZSG is located in London, but its meetings are conducted under the auspices of *UNCTAD*. See also *international commodity bodies*.

International Maritime Organization: IMO. One of the *United Nations specialized agencies*. It was established in 1959 as the Inter-Governmental Maritime Consultative Organization and given its present name in 1982. The IMO provides a forum for intergovernmental cooperation on matters such as facilitation of international maritime traffic, maritime safety standards, liability and compensation issues and measures to prevent pollution from ships. It is located in London. See also *maritime transport services*.

International Meat Council: the body which administered the *International Bovine Meat Agreement*, one of the *WTO plurilateral agreements*, until its termination at the end of 1997.

International Monetary Fund: see *IMF*.

Internationally recognized labour standards: see *core labour standards* and *international labour standards*.

International Natural Rubber Agreement: first concluded in 1979, renewed in 1987 and terminated in 1999. It was administered by the International Natural Rubber Organization, located in Kuala Lumpur. See also *International Rubber Study Group*.

International Nickel Study Group: INSG. It was established in 1986 under *UNCTAD* auspices and entered into force on 23 May 1990. It promotes international cooperation on issues concerning nickel, especially by improving statistics and other information on the nickel market, and it provides a forum for discussing nickel issues of common interest and concern. INSG members account for about 80% of world nickel mine production. Its secretariat is located at The Hague.

International non-governmental organizations: see *non-governmental organizations.*

International Observatory on Creative Industries for Development: proposed for establishment by *UNCTAD* to analyse policies in developing countries on *creative industries* and to collect statistics on them. [UNCTAD TD(XI)BP13]

International Office of Epizootics: an intergovernmental organization established in 1924 with the following main objectives: (a) to inform governments of the occurrence and course of animal diseases throughout the world and of ways to control these diseases, (b) to coordinate studies devoted to the surveillance and control of animal diseases, and (c) to harmonize regulations for trade in animals and animal products among member countries. It cooperates closely with the members of the WTO in the administration of the *Agreement on the Application of Sanitary and Phytosanitary Measures*. The Office is better known by its French name Office International des Epizooties (OIE). In 2003 it adopted the name World Organisation for Animal Health to describe its activities better, but its statutory name remains unchanged. [www.oie.int]

International Olive Oil Agreement: see *International Agreement on Olive Oil and Table Olives*.

International Organization for Standardization: ISO. A world-wide federation of national standards bodies established in 1947 to promote the development of standardization and related activities with a view to facilitating the international exchange of goods and services. Each country is represented by one organization only. The ISO also promotes the development of cooperation in intellectual, scientific, technological and economic activities. It is associated with the WTO especially through work concerning the *Agreement on Technical Barriers to Trade* which seeks to ensure that standards are not used as disguised barriers to trade. See also *International Electrotechnical Commission*, *ISO 9000* and *ISO 14000*.

International Organisation of Vine and Wine: OIV. Established as the successor to the International Vine and Wine Office through the *Agreement Establishing the International Organisation of Vine and Wine*, done at Paris on 3 April 2001, which became effective on 1 January 2004. It is located in Paris. Article 1 of Agreement the states that it "is an *intergovernmental organisation* of a scientific and technical nature of recognised competence for its work concerning vines, wine, wine-based beverages, grapes, raisins and other vine products". Its main activities are (a) to promote and guide scientific and technical research and experimentation, (b) to draw up and implement recommendations concerning conditions for grape production, oenological practices, definition and/or description of products, labelling and marketing conditions, methods for analysing and assessing vine products, and (c) to examine proposals relating to guaranteeing the authenticity of vine products, protecting *geographical indications*, especially vine- and wine-growing areas and the related *appellations of origin* and improving scientific and technical criteria for recognizing and protecting new grape plant varieties.

International Patent Classification: IPC. See *Strasbourg Agreement Concerning the International Patent Classification*.

International Plant Protection Convention: entered into force on 3 April 1952 and revised in 1979. It is administered by the *Food and Agricultural Organization*. Its objective is securing common and effective international action to prevent the introduction and the spread of pests of plants and plant products and to promote measures for their control. The Convention was amended in 1997 partly to meet the standard-setting requirements of the WTO *Agreement on the Application of Sanitary and Phytosanitary Measures*. The revised convention entered into force on 2 October 2005.

International political economy: broadly defined as the academic discipline concerned with the relationship between the political and economic domains in contemporary international society. *Trade policy* is one aspect of this relationship.

International Programme on the Elimination of Child Labour: IPEC. A programme initiated in 1992 by the *International Labour Organization* to assist member countries in their efforts to eliminate child labour. Activities under IPEC include the development of national action programmes, establishing demonstration projects and awareness programmes for government, non-government organizations, workers and employers. Some twenty countries are now participating in IPEC. See also *child labour*, *core labour standards*, *social clause*, *trade and labour standards* and *worst forms of child labour*.

International Rubber Study Group: IRSG. A body consisting of producer and consumer countries established in 1944. Its purpose is to act as a forum for the discussion of matters related to the production, consumption and trade in natural and synthetic rubber. It also publishes an extensive range of statistical material. Its secretariat is located in London. See also *International Natural Rubber Agreement* and *International Trpartite Rubber Organization*.

International Standard Industrial Classification of All Economic Activities: ISIC. This is a classification of the entire range of economic activities regardless of ownership. It allows entities to be classified according to the activity they carry out. ISIC is maintained by the United Nations Statistical Office. [www.unstats.un.org]

International Standards for Phytosanitary Measures: ISPM. These are plant quarantine standards established under the *International Plant Protection Convention* which have been endorsed by the *Food and Agricultural Organization*, the Interim Commission on Phytosanitary Measures or the *Commission on Phytosanitary Measures*. These standards are part of the international standards, guidelines and recommendations recognized under the WTO *Agreement on the Application of Sanitary and Phytosanitary Measures*.

International standards for sanitary and phytosanitary measures: the *Agreement on the Application of Sanitary and Phytosanitary Measures* requires WTO members to base their sanitary and phytosanitary measures on international standards, guidelines or recommendations where these exist. Among these are (a) the standards for food safety established by the *Codex Alimentarius Commission* relating to food additives, veterinary drug and pesticide residues, contaminants, methods of analysis and sampling, and codes and guidelines of hygienic practice, (b) for animal health the standards developed by the *International Office of Epizootics*, (c) for plant health the standards established under the *International Plant Protection Convention*, and (d) any other international standards set by international organizations open for membership to all.

International steel cartel: a *cartel* allegedly dividing the world steel market into two hemispheres, with the dividing line running through Burma. According to the those claiming knowledge of the existence of this cartel, steel mills on either side of the line did or do not export to markets on the other side. See also *Multilateral Steel Agreement*.

International Sugar Agreement: the first sugar agreements were negotiated in the 1860s. A new agreement was concluded in 1931 between producer associations whose governments then had to give effect to its provisions. At the same time, a permanent secretariat was established at The Hague. The agreement aimed to liquidate surplus stocks through *export quotas*, but it failed in this because non-members raised their production. A second agreement was negotiated in 1937. It provided for representation of consumers and producers. The first post-war sugar agreement was concluded in 1954 and renegotiated in 1958, 1968, 1973, 1977 and 1984. The agreement ran a *buffer stock* until 1977. The 1984 agreement did not contain economic provisions, but set itself the task of negotiating a new agreement of this type. A successor administrative agreement entered into force in 1993 for five years, with no limit on the number of possible extensions. The administering body, the International Sugar Organization, is located in London.

International Tea Agreement: first entered into force in 1933 as a producer-only arrangement and expired long ago. Tea is one of the commodities included in the *Integrated Programme for Commodities*, but efforts to negotiate a new tea agreement have not been successful.

International Telecommunication Union: ITU. Established in 1865 and restructured in 1947 as one of the *United Nations specialized agencies*. Its responsibilities are (a) to maintain and extend international cooperation for the improvement and rational use of telecommunications of all kinds, (b) to promote the development of technical facilities and their most efficient operation with a view to improving the efficiency of telecommunications services, increasing their usefulness and making them, so far as possible, generally available to the public, and (c) to harmonize the actions of members in the attainment of those ends. The ITU secretariat is in Geneva. See also *Agreement on Basic Telecommunications*.

International Textiles and Clothing Bureau: a body located in Geneva whose objective are (a) to achieve the elimination of discrimination and protectionism directed against members' exports of textiles and clothing and (b) to promote the full application of GATT principles to trade in these products. Members are Argentina, Bangladesh, Brazil, China, Colombia, Costa Rica, Democratic People's Republic of Korea, Egypt, El Salvador, Guatemala, Honduras, Hong Kong-China, India, Indonesia, Macau-China, Maldives, Pakistan, Paraguay, Peru, Republic of Korea, Sri Lanka, Thailand, Uruguay and Vietnam. Cuba, Mauritius and Singapore are observers.

International Tin Agreement: first concluded in 1931 and renewed in 1934. These early agreements did not allow for consumer representation. The third agreement, concluded in 1937, invited the two largest consumer countries to attend its meetings. The agreement was renegotiated to include producers and consumers in 1954, then 1961, 1966, 1971, 1975 and in 1980 for a duration of five years. All versions of the agreement established a *buffer stock* and ran a system of *export quotas*. This, in the end, became one of the reasons for the undoing of the Agreement in 1985. It appears that the buffer stock manager's forward dealings on the London Metals Exchange resulted in a funds shortage. Another reason was that some major producers and consumers were not members, and they therefore were not bound by the Agreement's provisions. Views differ on the causes of the Agreement's demise. See also *International Tin Study Group*.

International Tin Study Group: established in 1989 as a result of the United Nations Tin Conference, but not yet operational because too few participants have notified their acceptance. The aims of the group are to ensure enhanced international cooperation on tin, improve statistical information and exchange information on production and trade. See also *International Tin Agreement*.

International Trade Centre UNCTAD/WTO: ITC. Established in 1964 as the focal point in the United Nations system for technical cooperation with developing countries in *trade promotion*. Its work program now covers product and market development, development of trade support services, trade information, human resource development, international purchasing and supply management and trade promotion needs. The centre is located in Geneva. See also *trade facilitation*.

International Trade Commission: ITC. A United States governmental agency charged with reporting on the effects of *tariffs* and *non-tariff measures* maintained by other countries on United States exports. Originally established in 1916 as the United States Tariff Commission. Its mandate also covers the determination of *dumping*, action concerning the effects of *export subsidies* by other countries and *safeguard* action. It also advises the President whether agricultural imports interfere with agricultural price support programs. The ITC does not make *trade policy*, but its findings are among the basic determinants of United States trade policy.

International trade law: the body of multilateral, regional and bilateral trade agreements and other international agreements having a bearing on the way international trade is conducted. For many countries, the WTO agreements are the most important of these instruments for trade relations with countries that are also WTO members. In the remaining cases, bilateral agreements and other instruments form the body of applicable international trade law. Another stream of international trade law is concerned with the activities of private firms. See also *private international law*, *public international law* and *UNCITRAL*.

International Trade Organization: see *ITO*.

International trade writ large: a term used by Ernest Preeg to describe the international exchange of goods, services and the factors of production. Many now see this overall approach as more relevant than simply looking at import and export trade. See also *four freedoms*.

International Treaty on Plant Genetic Resources for Food and Agriculture: adopted by the *Food and Agricultural Organization* on 3 November 2001. The objectives of the Treaty are the conservation and sustainable use of plant genetic resources for food and agriculture and the fair and equitable sharing of the benefits arising out of their use, in harmony with the *Convention on Biological Diversity*, for sustainable agriculture and *food security*. The Treaty recognizes *farmers' rights*, establishes a multilateral system of access and benefit-sharing for plant genetic resources listed in Annex I to the Treaty, and it enjoins the parties to implement the rolling *Global Plan for the Conservation and Sustainable Use of Plant Genetic Resources for Food and Agriculture*. See also *International Undertaking on Plant Genetic Resources*.

International Tripartite Rubber Organization: established in 2001 after the collapse of the *International Natural Rubber Organization*. It consists of Indonesia, Malaysia and Thailand. Its main aim is to bolster prices for natural rubber. Members have established the International Tripartite Rubber Corporation to achieve this.

International Tropical Timber Agreement: ITTA. Concluded in 1983 under the auspices of the *Integrated Programme for Commodities* and succeeded in 1994 by a new agreement lasting for four years with the option of two three-year extensions. A successor agreement was concluded on 27 January 2006. It is expected to enter into force in 2008. The ITTA does not contain economic provisions. Its main objective is to provide an effective framework for consultation, international cooperation and policy development among all members with regard to all relevant aspects of the world timber economy. Other trade-related aims include (a) to provide a forum for consultation to promote non-discriminatory timber trade practices, (b) to enhance the capacity of members to form sustainable export strategies, (c) to promote the expansion and diversification of international trade in tropical timber from sustainable sources, (d) to improve market intelligence, (e) to promote increased and further processing in producer member countries, (f) to improve marketing and distribution, and (g) to encourage information-sharing on the international timber market. The administering body, the International Tropical Timber Organization, is in Yokohama. See also *trade and environment*.

International Undertaking on Plant Genetic Resources: adopted by the *Food and Agricultural Organization* (FAO) in 1983. The objective of the Undertaking is to ensure that plant genetic resources of economic and/or social interest, particularly for agriculture, will be explored, preserved, evaluated and made available for plant breeding and scientific purposes. In the view of the FAO, the Undertaking is at the cross-roads where agriculture, environment and trade meet. A revised and expanded Undertaking was adopted on 3 November 2001 in the form of the *International Treaty on Plant Genetic Resources for Food and Agriculture*. See also *farmers' rights*.

International Union for the Conservation of Nature and Natural Resources: see *CITES*.

International Union for the Protection of New Varieties of Plants: UPOV. See *International Convention for the Protection of New Varieties of Plants*.

International Vine and Wine Office: see *International Organisation of Vine and Wine*.

International Wheat Agreement: in its final version this consisted of two instruments: (a) the *Wheat Trade Convention* of 1986 which was a consultative forum with a program for the collection and dissemination of statistics and (b) the *Food Aid Convention* concluded at the same time. On 1 July 1995 the Agreement was succeeded by the *Grains Trade Convention* under the *International Grains Agreement*. All parties to the Agreement were members of the International Wheat Council, now the International Grains Council, located in London.

Intervention price: a mechanism under the *Common Agricultural Policy* whereby the *European Community* buys an agricultural commodity at a certain price. The intervention price expresses the intention to support the current income levels of farmers even when output is above requirements. See also *floor price*.

Intra-firm trade: international trade conducted between units of the same company. The bulk of this type of trade is conducted between units of multinational enterprises. Estimates of the size of intra-firm trade differ, but studies suggest that it may account for about one-third of total trade. Some commentators see intra-firm trade as a form of *managed trade* on the assumption that a multinational enterprise would rather purchase from its own units, even if a cost difference is involved, than using the open market. Opinion on this proposition remains divided. See also *globalization*.

Intra-industry trade: the concurrent export and import by an industry of essentially the same product. For example, an automotive industry in one economy may both import and export automotive parts. Intra-industry trade has been debated intensively by economists since the 1970s, with some holding that it is a special case of international trade. There is no disagreement, however, on the importance of intra-industry trade in terms of international trade flows. See also *globalization*.

Invention: the creation of something new which may turn into *industrial property*. To benefit from *intellectual property protection* in the form of a *patent*, an invention has to be new (i.e. not already described or used somewhere), it must be non-obvious (in *WIPO* terms, it would not have occurred to a specialist asked to provide a solution to the particular problem) and it must be capable of industrial use.

Investigation: an examination to ascertain whether, for example, a case has been made for the imposition of *anti-dumping measures*, *countervailing measures* or *safeguards*. If a petition has been received for the imposition of any of these *trade remedies*, the authority making the investigation must follow the rules set out in the *Anti-Dumping Agreement*, the *Agreement on Safeguards* or the *Agreement on Subsidies and Countervailing Measures*, as the case may be.

Investigation effect: refers to the possibility that an investigation into alleged *dumping* or an examination of the desirability of *safeguards* may itself have the effect of lowering imports of the products being examined. See also *trade harassment*. [Lee and Jun, 2004]

Investment: a stake in a business, a company or an enterprise. Many definitions exist. The *World Investment Report 2003* divides the definitions used in *international investment agreements* into asset-based, transaction-based and enterprise-based. An example of an asset-based definition is that used in the *Energy Charter Treaty*, concluded in December 1994, which defines investment as every kind of asset, owned or controlled directly or indirectly by an investor. It includes: (a) tangible and intangible, and movable and immovable, property, and any property rights such as leases, mortgages, liens and pledges, (b) a company or business enterprise, or shares, stock, or other forms of equity participation in a company or business enterprise, (c) claims to money and claims to performance pursuant to contract having an economic value and associated with an investment, (d) intellectual property, (e) returns, and (f) any right conferred by law or contract or by virtue of any licences and permits granted pursuant to law to undertake an economic activity in the energy sector. The working definition used by the participants in the negotiations for the *Multilateral Agreement on Investment*, which were abandoned in early 1999, was also asset-based. It states that investment means every kind of asset owned or controlled directly by an investor, including: (a) an enterprise (a legal person, whether or not for profit, private or government-owned or -controlled, including a corporation, trust, partnership, sole proprietorship, branch, joint venture, association or organization), (b) shares, stocks or other forms of equity participation in an enterprise, and rights reserved therefrom, (c) bonds, debentures, loans and other forms of debt, and rights derived therefrom, (d) rights under contracts, including turnkey, construction, management, production or revenue-sharing contracts, (e) claims to money and claims to performance, (f) intellectual property rights, (g) rights conferred pursuant to law or contract or concessions, licences, authorizations and permits, and (h) any other tangible and intangible, movable and immovable property, and any related property rights, such as leases, mortgages, liens and pledges. The transaction-based method is used in the 1961 *OECD Code of Liberalisation of Capital Movements*. It defines direct investment as "investment for the purpose of establishing lasting economic relations with an undertaking such as, in particular, investments which give the possibility of exercising an effective influence on the management thereof by means of (1) creation or extension of a wholly owned enterprise, subsidiary or branch, acquisition of full ownership of an existing enterprise, (2) participation in a new or existing enterprise, and (3) a loan of five years or longer". *NAFTA*, which entered into force on 1 January 1994, uses the enterprise-based approach. It defines investment as (a) an enterprise, (b) an equity security of an enterprise, (c) a debt security of an enterprise where the enterprise is an affiliate of the investor and the original maturity of the debt security is at least three years, (d) a loan to an enterprise which is an affiliate of the investor and where the original maturity of the loan is at least three years, (e) an interest in an enterprise that entitles the owner to share in income or profits, (f) an interest in an enterprise that entitles the owner to share in the assets of that enterprise on dissolution, (g) real estate or other property, tangible or intangible, acquired in the expectation or used for the purpose of economic benefit or other business purposes, and (h) interests arising from the commitment of capital or other resources in the territory of a party to NAFTA. **See** also *foreign direct investment*.

Investment Policy Review: IPR. An *UNCTAD* program to assist *least developed countries* in improving their potential to attract *foreign direct investment* (FDI) and to identify their competitive strengths. IPRs analyse a country's competitive position in attracting FDI, its policy framework and procedures and its policy options.

Investment promotion and protection agreements: agreements concluded bilaterally by many countries aimed at promoting the flow of capital for economic activity and development. Such agreements typically contain provisions entailing the application of *most-favoured-nation treatment*, and setting out conditions concerning entry of personnel, *expropriation* and nationalization, transfers of funds, *dispute settlement* between the parties, etc. See also *bilateral investment treaties* and *World Association of Investment Promotion Agencies*.

Investment-related trade measures: governmental measures aimed at promoting investment by foreign firms in one's economy. Sometimes these measures include high tariff barriers aimed at giving these firms a captive market. See also *Agreement on Trade-Related Investment Measures* and *tariff-jumping investment*.

Investment services directive: ISD. A *European Community* directive aimed at improving the *right of establishment* and freedom to provide services in the securities sector. It entered into force on 1 January 1996. Under the terms of this *directive*, investment firms are allowed to operate anywhere within the European Community once they have obtained authorization in their home member state. The activities authorized by the home country may be carried out through establishment in another member country or through *cross-border trade*. No additional authorization, endowment capital or any other measure having an equivalent effect may be requested. See also *financial services*.

Investment substitution: a term used by some to describe the replacement of GATT-restricted measures with other, sometimes more distorting practices, including domestic policy instruments. See also *Agreement on Trade-Related Investment Measures*.

Investor-state disputes: treaties, whether bilateral, regional or multilateral, are between states, and they convey rights and obligations on the states (parties) to them. If a natural or judicial person residing in one of the member states wishes to have its concerns over another party's operation of the treaty addressed under the consultation or dispute settlement provisions of the treaty, it must first convince its own government to take up the case. There are exceptions. *NAFTA*, for example, allows investors in some circumstances to submit to *arbitration* claims that another party has breached an obligation in relation to investment obligations in the agreement and in matters concerning monopolies and/or state enterprises. A claim may only be made if an investor has incurred loss or damage because of the alleged breach, and it must be made no more than three years after the investor first acquired, or should have first acquired, knowledge of the alleged breach and loss of damage. The *free-trade agreement* between Australia and Thailand also has a provision on investor-state disputes. It states that an investor cannot pursue a claim against matters concerning conditions placed on the establishment, acquisition or expansion of an investment, or the enforcement of such conditions. See also *NAFTA Chapter 11*. [UNCTAD 2005]

Invisible barriers to trade: see *non-tariff measures*.

Invisible earnings: income derived from the sales of services in other countries, as well as profits, dividends, royalties, etc., resulting from investments abroad.

Invisible hand: an expression used by Adam Smith in *An Inquiry into the Nature and Causes of the Wealth of Nations* when he deals with the motivation of those investing capital in industry. He rejects the view that a trader or investor intends to promote the public interest, or that he even knows how much he might be promoting it. Smith claims that the trader or investor "by directing [domestic] industry in such a manner as its produce may be of the greatest value, he intends only his own gain, and he is in this, as in many other cases, led by an invisible hand to promote an end which was not of his intention".

Invisibles Group: an informal group of capital-based senior officials from WTO member countries, both developed and developing, which meets irregularly, usually in Geneva. It concerns itself with an exploration of major issues of common concern on the WTO work program. It has no decision-making powers. See also *Consultative Group of Eighteen*.

Invisible tariffs: an older expression for what is now broadly subsumed under the category of *non-tariff barriers*, *non-tariff measures*, trade-restrictive use of *customs valuation* procedures and *trade remedies*.

Invisibles trade: see *trade in services*.

IOR-ARC: see *Indian Ocean Rim Association for Regional Cooperation*.

IOSCO: International Organization of Securities Commissions, located in Montreal. Its objectives are to (a) cooperate to promote high standards of regulation in order to maintain just, efficient and sound markets, (b) exchange information on respective experiences in order to promote the development of domestic markets,

(c) establish standards and an effective surveillance of international securities transactions, and (d) provide mutual assistance to promote the integrity of the markets by a rigorous application of the standards and by effective enforcement against offences. IOSCO has more than 130 members.

IPRs: see *intellectual property rights*.

Iran and Libya Sanctions Act: ILSA. A United States law adopted on 5 August 1996 for five years and extended in 2001 for another five years. The Act is intended to (a) help deny Iran and Libya revenues that could be used to finance international terrorism, (b) limit the flow of resources necessary to obtain weapons of mass destruction and (c) to put pressure on Libya to comply with a range of *United Nations* resolutions. It does this by allowing the President to impose sanctions on foreign companies that provide new investments over $US40 million for the development of petroleum resources in Iran or Libya. Possible sanctions include denial of export licences, prohibitions on loans or credits from United States financial institutions, prohibition on designation as a *primary dealer* for United States government debt instruments, denial of United States *government procurement* opportunities, and a ban on imports of the violating company. On 23 April 2004 the President terminated the application of ILSA to Libya. See also *extraterritoriality*.

Iron law of subsidies: the proposition that *subsidies* delay reforms and depress productivity by keeping inefficient producers in business, unless the granting of the subsidy is accompanied by strict and enforced rules for reform. See also *law of constant protection*.

ISIC: see *International Standard Industrial Classification of All Economic Activities*.

ISO 9000: a series of quality systems standards developed by the *International Organization for Standardization* (ISO). These are standards for evaluating the way a firm does its work. They should not be confused with product standards. Quality systems standards enable firms to identify the means of meeting consistently the requirements of its customers.

ISO 14000: a series of environmental management standards prepared by the *International Organization for Standardization* (ISO) covering six areas: environmental managing systems; environmental auditing; environmental labelling; environmental performance evaluation; life cycle assessment; terms and definitions. Most of the standards are intended as guidance documents on environmental tools and systems to help companies and other organizations integrate environmental considerations into their normal business processes. Only one of the standards, ISO 14001 on environmental management systems, contains specifications for certification or registration purposes. ISO 14000 does not create production or pollution control requirements. See also *trade and environment*.

Istanbul Convention: the *Customs Convention on Temporary Admission* which entered into force on 27 November 1993. This Convention updates the *Customs Convention on the ATA Carnet for the Temporary Admission of Goods*. It created a single instrument to simplify and harmonize temporary admission formalities. Goods admitted temporarily must be re-exported to the country of origin. They must not undergo any transformation while they are under temporary admission. The Convention is administered by the *World Customs Organization*.

ITA: the *Information Technology Agreement*, or formally the *Ministerial Declaration on Trade in Information Technology Products*, under which participants removed tariffs on IT products by 2000.

ITA II: Negotiations aimed at expanding the *ITA*'s product coverage. See also *Information Technology Agreement II*.

ITC: the International Trade Centre UNCTAD/GATT, originally established by the old GATT. It is now operated jointly by the WTO and the *United Nations*, the latter acting through *UNCTAD*. The ITC is a focal point for technical cooperation on trade promotion of developing countries.

ITCB: see *International Textiles and Clothing Bureau*.

Item: in the administration of *rules of origin* this sometimes refers to a *tariff line* of seven or more digits.

Item-by-item tariff negotiations: tariff negotiations in which each item is looked at separately. The method is more laborious than *formula cuts*, *linear tariff reductions* or *sectoral trade negotiations*, but it may be the only possible method for achieving results, especially if *sensitive products* are involved.

ITO: International Trade Organization. The proposal for the establishment of an ITO was one of the outcomes of the 1944 Bretton Woods conference. The ITO was meant to cover a wide range of economic issues, including *investment*, *restrictive business practices*, *commodity arrangements*, rules for international trade and trade issues related to economic development. All these topics were subject to intensive negotiations at Havana in 1947 and 1948. A compromise of sorts was reached in the end, but at the expense of an agreement with fewer teeth than its early main proponents would have liked. The only surviving part was the set of trade rules and tariff commitments now known as the GATT which was based on the chapter on *commercial policy*, but which had been negotiated on a parallel track. The ITO accordingly was never established. See also *Bretton Woods agreements*, *Havana Charter*, *Organization for Trade Cooperation* and *WTO*. [Toye 2003]

Jackson-Vanik amendment: an amendment to the 1974 United States *Trade Act* proposed by Senator Henry Jackson (D) and Representative Charles Vanik (D) and enacted as Section 402. It denies the granting of *most-favoured-nation treatment* (MFN) to *non-market economies* if they (a) deny their citizens the right to emigrate, (b) impose more than a nominal tax on emigration and (c) impose more than a nominal charge on citizens if they wish to emigrate. The President may waive the requirement for full compliance with Section 402 if he determines that this will substantially promote the freedom-of-emigration provisions, and if he has received assurances that the emigration practices of the country will lead substantially to the achievement of this objective. The Jackson-Vanik amendment was aimed originally at the USSR, but it was also used against other countries. Withdrawal of MFN means that the high tariff rates contained in the *Smoot-Hawley Tariff Act* (the *Tariff Act* of 1930) apply. These would make an exporter quite uncompetitive in the United States market. See also *conditional most-favoured-nation treatment* and *normal trade relations*.

Japanese measures on leather: a case launched under the GATT in 1983 by the United States. It concerned *import restrictions* maintained by Japan on bovine, equine, sheep, lamb, goat and kid leather. Japan explained that its restrictions reflected the historical, cultural and socio-economic background of the "Dowa problem". The Dowa are a national minority traditionally performing jobs considered less desirable, such as tanning. Japan noted that they were a product of its feudal society before the Meiji Reformation (1868). The people of Dowa districts had been, as an established social institution, classified as being outside and below the hierarchy of samurais, peasants, artisans and merchants. They had been subjected to severe institutional discrimination in all aspects of social life. Since 1871, the Japanese Government had initiated various measures to emancipate them, although the elimination of poverty still had a long way to go. Likewise, Japan submitted, psychological discrimination in Japanese society at large still existed, though this was now reduced to a large extent. The Japanese tanning industry, traditionally an occupation of Dowa people, employed about 12,000 people in small, backward enterprises. Its low technological level made it uncompetitive. Japan claimed that if the import restrictions on leather were eliminated immediately, the industry would collapse with "unmeasurable social, regional-economic and political problems". The *panel* noted that Japan's case rested almost entirely on considerations resulting from the particular problems connected with the population group known as the Dowa people. It continued that it could not take into account the special circumstances mentioned by Japan since its terms of reference were to examine the matter "in the light of the relevant GATT provisions". These provisions did not allow such a justification for import restrictions. Accordingly, it found that the Japanese import restrictions on leather contravened GATT Article XI (General Elimination of Quantitative Restrictions). The fact that the restrictions had existed for a long time could not alter this finding. See also *Belgian family allowances* for another case dealing with social issues. [GATT BISD 27S]

JI: Joint Implementation. See *Kyoto Protocol*.

Johannesburg Declaration on Sustainable Development: see *World Summit on Sustainable Development*.

Johannesburg Plan of Implementation: see *World Summit on Sustainable Development*

Joint action: action taken by all the *contracting parties* (members) of the GATT concerning administration of the provisions of the Agreement or with a view to furthering its objectives. Joint action was necessary, for example, for granting a *waiver*. Whenever you see CONTRACTING PARTIES written in this way, you know that joint action had been taken by the contracting parties (members).

Joint Implementation: see *Kyoto Protocol*.

Joint Integrated Technical Assistance Program: JITAP. This is a program managed jointly by the WTO, *UNCTAD* and the *International Trade Centre UNCTAD/WTO* to assist African developing countries, some of them *least developed countries*, in participating in the *multilateral trading system*. The program is supported through a trust fund supported by thirteen donor countries.

Joint Recommendation Concerning Provisions on the Production of Well-Known Marks: adopted by *WIPO* on 29 September 1999. It establishes criteria for determining whether a mark is well known. These are (a) the degree of knowledge or recognition the mark enjoys, (b) duration, extent and geographical area of use of the mark, (c) duration, extent and geographical area of any promotion of the mark, (d) duration and geographical area of any registration or application for registration of the mark, (e) the record of successful enforcement of rights in the mark and (f) the value associated with the mark. The Recommendation also contains detailed provisions for dealing with conflicting marks (reproduction, imitation, translation or transliteration of a mark liable to create confusion with the well-known mark).

Joint Trade Committee: a mechanism normally instituted under *bilateral trade agreements* for periodic meetings reviewing bilateral trade flows and issues arising from them. Meetings may be held at ministerial or officials level, and their location normally alternates between the two countries involved. See also *mixed commission*.

Joint venture: a cooperative association between two or more firms or individuals to carry out a specific activity. Joint ventures may be dissolved when a task, such as the construction of a bridge or a research and development project, has been completed. In the case of a production facility, there may be agreement to dissolve the joint venture after a fixed number of years, usually along previously agreed guidelines. The main reasons for the formation of joint ventures include the pooling of financial, technical or intellectual resources, sharing risks or developing new markets. Sometimes, forming a joint venture with a local company is the only realistic way to enter a new market. See also *ASEAN Industrial Cooperation Scheme*, *intellectual property protection* and *transfer of technology*.

Jones Act: the United States *Merchant Marine Act* of 1920. Section 27 of the Act requires that all goods transported by water between United States ports must be carried in vessels built and registered in the United States, owned by United States citizens and fully crewed by United States citizens. See also *cabotage*.

Judicial economy: a term apparently embodying several principles. Among these are that the time of courts should not be wasted, that legitimate cases should be dealt with speedily, that frivolous cases should be dismissed, and that judges should hear and decide all related parts of a case at the same time.

Judicial review: the review by a tribunal of a decision made by a government authority or agency, usually following an appeal by a person affected by the decision. Such tribunals are normally independent of the body that made the decision. Grounds for review vary, but a common thread tends to be at a minimum the launch of an enquiry whether the process leading to the decision followed the prescribed administrative steps. See also *administrative ruling of general application*.

July package: the WTO *General Council* decision of 1 August 2004 which sets out a work program leading to the conclusion of negotiations under the *Doha Development Agenda*. It takes its name from the intensive negotiations during July 2004 leading up to the decision. [WT/L/579]

Juridical person: a term used in the *General Agreement on Trade in Services*. A legal entity, such as a corporation, trust, partnership, joint venture, sole proprietorship, association, etc., formed for the purpose of supplying *services*.

JUSCANZ: refers to Japan, United States, Canada, Australia, New Zealand Switzerland, Norway and Turkey especially in *climate change* negotiations. The loosely-organized group sometimes coordinates positions, but mainly it compares them. [Bayne and Woolcock 2003]

Jus cogens: peremptory forms of international law from which it is not possible to depart. Article 53 of the *Vienna Convention of the Law of Treaties* states that "A treaty is void if, at the time of its conclusion, it conflicts with a peremptory norm of general international law. For the purposes of the present Convention, a peremptory norm of general international law is a norm accepted and recognized by the international community of States as a whole as a norm from which no derogation is permitted and which can be modified only by a subsequent norm of general international law having the same character." Article 64 of the same Convention states that "If a new peremptory norm of international law emerges, any existing treaty which is in conflict with that norm becomes void and terminates". [Brownlie 1990, Starke 1989]

K

Kaleidoscopic comparative advantage: a term suggested by Jagdish Bhagwati to describe situations of industries in which many countries concurrently have a fragile *comparative advantage*. In other words, the comparative advantage may change very quickly like the image seen through a kaleidoscope. Slight changes in the domestic environment might in these circumstances bring about a shift of industries across countries as they seek to maintain their competitive edge. This then may result in *footloose industries* or *screwdriver operations*. See also *globalization* and *delocalization*. [Bhagwati 1995]

Keiretsu **relationships:** a term denoting complex traditional Japanese distribution systems and industrial conglomerate arrangements seen to make it difficult for newcomers to compete on price. Historically, *keiretsu* relationships appear to have been based on a desire by firms for continuity of supplies and orders. Today *keiretsu* relationships are sometimes seen by United States exporters in particular as major *non-tariff barriers* or *restrictive business practices*. Japanese commentators tend to argue that the power of *keiretsus* is overrated, and that the relationships generally are not strong enough to negate price signals. Some distinguish between horizontal *keiretsus* (arrangements between firms in several sectors) and vertical *keiretsus* (arrangements between firms at different production and distribution stages in the same sector). See also *Market-Oriented Specific Sector talks* and *Structural Impediments Initiative*.

Kennedy Round: the sixth round of GATT *multilateral trade negotiations*, held from 1963 to 1967. It was named after President John F Kennedy in recognition of his support for the reformulation of the United States trade agenda which resulted in the *Trade Expansion Act* of 1962. This Act gave the President the widest-ever negotiating authority. (See *United States trade agreements legislation* for a brief description of how this is done). As the *Dillon Round* went through the laborious process of *item-by-item tariff negotiations*, it became clear, long before the Round ended, that a more comprehensive approach was needed to deal with the emerging challenges resulting from the formation of the *European Economic Community* (EEC) and *EFTA*, as well as Europe's re-emergence as a significant international trader more generally. Japan's high economic growth rate portended the major role it would play later as an exporter, but the focal point of the Kennedy Round always was the United States-EEC relationship. Indeed, there was an influential American view that saw what became the Kennedy Round as the start of a transatlantic partnership that might ultimately lead to a transatlantic economic community. To an extent, this view was shared in Europe, but the process of European unification created its own stresses under which the Kennedy Round at times became a secondary focus for the EEC. An example of this was the French veto in January 1963, before the round had even started, on membership by the United Kingdom. Another was the internal crisis of 1965 which ended in the *Luxembourg Compromise*. Preparations for the new round were immediately overshadowed by the *Chicken War*, an early sign of the impact *variable levies* under the *Common Agricultural Policy* would eventually have. Some participants in the Round had been concerned that the convening of *UNCTAD*, scheduled for 1964, would result in further complications, but its impact on the actual negotiations was minimal. In May 1963 Ministers reached agreement on three negotiating objectives for the round: (a) measures for the expansion of trade of developing countries as a means of furthering their economic development, (b) reduction or elimination of tariffs and other barriers to trade, and (c) measures for access to markets for agricultural and other primary products. The working hypothesis for the tariff negotiations was a linear tariff cut of 50% with the smallest number of exceptions. A drawn-out argument developed about the trade effects a uniform linear cut would have on the dispersed rates (low and high tariffs quite far apart) of the United States as compared to the much more concentrated rates of the EEC which also tended to be in the lower half of United States tariff rates. The EEC accordingly argued for an evening-out or harmonization of peaks and troughs through its *écrêtement*, *double écart* and *thirty : ten proposals*. Once negotiations had been joined, this lofty working hypothesis was soon undermined. The *special-structure countries* (Australia, Canada, New Zealand and South Africa), so called because their exports were dominated by raw materials and other primary commodities, negotiated their tariff reductions entirely through the item-by-item method. In the end, the result was an average 35% reduction in tariffs, except for textiles, chemicals, steel and other sensitive products; plus a 15% to 18% reduction in tariffs for agricultural and food products. In addition, the negotiations on chemicals led to a provisional agreement on the abolition of the *American Selling Price* (ASP). This was a method of valuing some chemicals used by the United States for the imposition of import duties which gave domestic manufacturers a much higher level of protection than the tariff schedule indicated. However, this part of the outcome was disallowed by Congress, and the American Selling Price was not abolished until Congress adopted the results of the *Tokyo Round*. The results of the Kennedy Round in agriculture overall were poor. The most notable achievement was agreement on a *Memorandum of Agreement on Basic Elements for the Negotiation of a World Grains Arrangement* which eventually was rolled into a new International Grains Arrangement. The EEC claimed that for it the main result of the negotiations on agriculture was that they "greatly helped to define its own common policy". The developing countries, who played a minor role throughout the negotiations in this Round, benefited nonetheless from substantial tariff cuts particularly in non-agricultural items of interest to them. Their main achievement at the time, however, was seen to be the adoption of *Part IV of the GATT* which absolved them from according *reciprocity* to developed countries in trade negotiations. In the view of many developing countries, this was a direct result of the call at UNCTAD I for a better trade deal for them. There has been argument ever since whether this symbolic gesture was a victory for them, or whether it ensured their exclusion in the future from meaningful participation in the *multilateral trading system*. On the other hand, there was no doubt that the extension of the *Long-Term Arrangement Regarding International Trade in Cotton Textiles*, which later became the *Multi-Fibre Arrangement*, for three years until 1970 led to the longer-term impairment of export opportunities for developing countries. Another outcome of the Kennedy Round was the adoption of an Anti-dumping Code which gave more precise guidance on the implementation of Article VI of the GATT. In particular, it sought to ensure speedy and fair investigations, and it imposed limits on the retrospective application of anti-dumping duties. The Code, however, also ran into difficulties with the United States Congress which precluded it from operating as had been intended. The United States nevertheless claimed that it was complying fully with the new code. See also *anti-dumping measures* and *developing countries and the multilateral trading system*. [Preeg 1970]

Kimberley Process Certification Scheme: KPCS. Entered into force on 1 January 2003. It aims to eliminate trade in conflict diamonds, defined as "rough diamonds used by rebel movements or their allies to finance conflict aimed at undermining legitimate governments . . .". Sometimes they are also called "blood diamonds". The KPCS requires its member countries to ensure that a Kimberley Process Certificate accompanies each shipment of rough diamonds exported from it. It bans trade in rough diamonds with countries not participating in the scheme. Participants also are exhorted to establish a system of internal controls and to share information on the functioning of the scheme and to encourage closer cooperation between law enforcement and customs agencies of member countries. More than fifty countries and customs territories now participate in the KPCS.

Knowledge-based economy: defined in APEC as "an economy in which the production, distribution and use of knowledge is the main driver of growth, wealth creation and employment across all industries". Features of a knowledge-based economy are held to be an openness to trade, new ideas and new enterprises; sound macroeconomic policy; the importance attached to education and life-long learning; and the enabling role of information and telecommunications infrastructure. See also *creative industries*. [APEC 2000]

Knowledge-based industry: an industry thought to rely more than others on the creation of new ideas and new expressions of ideas. Accordingly, knowledge-based industries rely heavily on *intellectual property protection*.

Kodak-Fuji case: proceedings in the WTO launched in 1997 by the United States against Japan. The case takes its name from the principal companies thought to have been at the bottom of it. The United States alleged that Japanese governmental measures denied fair and equitable market opportunities to its suppliers of consumer photographic film and paper. The United States also claimed that the Japanese measures of particular concern were (a) vertical distribution channels handling Japanese products only, (b) a law restricting the growth of large department stores and (c) measures restricting the use of sales promotions. The United States case consisted of three elements: (a) a *non-violation* claim, (b) an infringement of GATT Article III (national treatment) and (c) an infringement of GATT Article X (transparency). The *panel* held that the United States had not been able to show under any of the three elements that Japan had contravened its WTO obligations. [WT/DS44/R, Komuro 1998]

Korean beef: three separate cases launched against the Republic of Korea by Australia, New Zealand and the United States in 1988 concerning its beef *import restrictions*. Korea claimed that the restrictions had been imposed for *balance-of-payments* reasons. The *panel* found that the restrictions contravened GATT Article XI (General Elimination of Quantitative Restrictions). Nor were they needed to shore up Korea's rapidly improving balance of payments. See also *balance-of-payments consultations*. [GATT BISD 36S]

Kyoto Convention: *International Convention on the Simplification and Harmonization of Customs Procedures*. Entered into force in 1974. It contains many annexes, each setting out procedures related to a particular area of customs administration. Each member decides which of these it will adhere to. Not all of the annexes have entered into force. The Convention also contains rules for the determination of origin for a product. It is administered by the *World Customs Organization*. In 1999 the Convention was revised to take account of developments in trade, transport and administrative techniques. See also *Harmonized System*, *Istanbul Convention* and *rules of origin*.

Kyoto Protocol: a protocol to the *United Nations Framework Convention on Climate Change* (UNFCC), adopted on 11 December 1997 in Kyoto and entered into force on 16 February 2005. It aims to reduce greenhouse gas emissions by the *Annex I countries* to agreed targets in the commitment period (2008 to 2012). Several paths are available to countries to meet their obligations. First, they can reduce their actual emissions through domestic measures. Second, they can buy emission credits from countries that are below their targets through emissions trading. Third, a country can earn emission reduction credits through Joint Implementation (JI). It would do this through funding a project in another country which would result in lower emissions there. Fourth, the Clean Development Mechanism (CDM) allows developed countries to earn credits by financing projects resulting in reduced emissions in developing countries. Countries are not allowed to rely solely on either emissions trading, Joint Implementation or the Clean Development Mechanism to achieve their emission targets. See also *climate change* and *greenhouse gases*.

L

Labelling: see *eco-labelling*, *genetic labelling*, *marks of origin* and *social labelling*.

Labour markets integration agreements: listed in the *General Agreement on Trade in Services* as a subset of *economic integration agreements*. WTO members may join an agreement establishing full integration of the labour market between the parties if (a) citizens of the parties to the agreement do not have to obtain residency and work permits and (b) if the agreement is notified to the *Council for Trade in Services*. Full integration of labour markets is described as citizens of the parties concerned having the right of free entry to the employment markets of the other parties. Integration should also cover measures such as conditions of pay, other conditions of employment and social benefits.

Labour market testing: the practice of ascertaining whether qualified local people might be available when assessing whether to support an application for the employment of foreign nationals. Article XVI of the *General Agreement on Trade in Services* states, among other things, that in sectors where market access *commitments* have been made, limitations or numerical quotas may not be maintained or adopted on the total number of persons employed.

Labour standards in international trade: see *core labour standards*, *human rights*, *international labour standards*, *social clause*, *trade and human rights* and *trade and labour standards*.

LAFTA: Latin American Free Trade Association. An intergovernmental organization created by the Treaty of Montevideo in February 1960, designed to establish gradually a *free-trade area* which would provide the basis for a Latin American Common Market. By 1980, only 14% of the trade of member countries was covered by the LAFTA rules. Following LAFTA's perceived inability to produce concrete results, *ALADI* (Latin-American Integration Association) was formed in that year.

Lagos Plan of Action: see *African regional integration arrangements*.

LAIA: Latin American Integration Association. See *ALADI* (Asociación Latinoamericana de Integración).

Laissez-faire policies: economic policies based on minimum governmental intervention to allow the market to produce the best outcomes. See also *invisible hand*.

Large Aircraft Sector Understanding: LASU. Refers to Annex III to the *Arrangement on Guidelines for Officially Supported Credits* maintained under *OECD* auspices. It sets out the permissible export credit arrangements for the sale or lease of new large civil aircraft (defined as aircraft with more than 70 seats) and engines fitted to such aircraft as part of an original order. The Understanding defines a new aircraft as one "owned by the manufacturer, i.e. an aircraft which has not been delivered nor previously used for its intended purpose of carrying fare-paying passengers and/or freight". See also *Agreement on Trade in Civil Aircraft*.

Last-in, first-out: a method of inventory management which uses the cost of the newest goods in stock as the valuation basis. Its main relevance to trade policy stems from the need to calculate a *regional value content* under the *rules of origin* adopted in some *free-trade agreements*. See also *first-in, first-out* and *averaging*.

Lasting interest: see *foreign direct investment*.

Last substantial transformation: a concept used in the administration of *rules of origin* to decide whether a good will be eligible for the *preferential tariff*. It means that the good has to have undergone sufficient processing or re-working to meet, for example, the *change-in tariff-classification* criterion or a *value-added criterion*. The last substantial transformation has to occur in one of the parties to the *preferential trade agreement* in question, and it has to be done immediately before the good is exported. See also *substantial transformation*.

Latin American and Caribbean regional integration arrangements: this entry summarizes the main *regional integration arrangements* concluded by Latin American and Caribbean countries since the 1960s. It only lists arrangements with at least three members. *LAFTA* (Latin American Free Trade Area) was formed in 1960 by Argentina, Brazil, Chile, Mexico, Paraguay, Peru and Uruguay. In 1980 it was replaced by *ALADI* (Latin American Integration Association) with Bolivia, Colombia, Ecuador and Venezuela as additional members. The Andean Pact was established in 1969 as a sub-group of LAFTA. In 1997 it became the *Andean Community*. Its members are Bolivia, Colombia, Ecuador, Peru and Venezuela. The *Central American Common Market* entered into force in 1961. The original members were Costa Rica, El Salvador, Guatemala, Honduras and Nicaragua. It was revitalized in 1993 through *SIECA* (Central American Integration System) and now also includes Panama. The Caribbean Free Trade Association (CARIFTA) was established in 1969. It became the *Caribbean Community and Common Market* (CARICOM) in 1973. The *CARICOM Single Market and Community* will supersede it in about 2005. *Mercosur*, which consists of Argentina, Brazil, Paraguay and Uruguay, was formed in 1991. In December 2003 the members of Mercosur, plus Bolivia, Chile, Colombia, Ecuador, Peru and Venezuela, signed the *South American Free Trade Agreement* (SAFTA). Latin American and Caribbean countries, apart from Cuba, are among the negotiators for the *FTAA* (Free Trade Area of the Americas) which was to be concluded by early 2005, but which is running late. The *Rio Group* discusses, among other matters, macro-economic issues, but it is not a regional integration arrangement *per se*. [Bhalla and Bhalla 1997, Crawford and Fiorentino 2005]

Latin American Economic System: see *SELA*.

Latin American Integration Association: see *ALADI*.

Lattice regionalism: describes the view that an interlacing framework of bilateral *free-trade agreements* among regional economies could be the forerunner of broader regional economic integration. See also *docking*. [Dent 2006]

Law of constant protection: a term proposed by Jagdish Bhagwati to mean that if *protectionism* is stopped in some form or other, it will arise in some other guise elsewhere. See also *iron law of subsidies*. [Bhagwati 1988]

Law of Similars: a Brazilian law, now rarely used, which permits the authorities to impose a high tariff on an imported product if a similar domestic product is available. The law was meant to support an *import substitution policy*.

Lay-out designs of integrated circuits: one of the forms of *intellectual property* enjoying protection under the *Agreement on Trade-Related Aspects of Intellectual Property Rights*. Protection is often afforded through a *sui generis right*, a method applying in this case specifically to lay-out designs (or topography) of integrated circuits. It prohibits the unauthorized reproduction or distribution of such designs. *Reverse engineering* is allowed under the laws of many countries.

LCA: see *life cycle assessment*, also called life cycle analysis. A method to assess whether a good or service is environmentally friendly by taking into account, among other factors, how it will be disposed of.

LDCs: see *least developed countries*.

Lead economy: in *APEC* and some other international groupings the member economy which has been given the task of coordinating or managing a project or activity.

Leaders' Statement to Implement APEC Transparency Standards: see **APEC principles on transparency standards**.

League of Nations: the forerunner of the United Nations, established in 1919 as part of the Treaty of Versailles. The League's main aims were collective security, arbitration of international disputes, reductions in armaments and open diplomacy. By the 1930s there were serious doubts about its efficacy, though it continued to have a legal existence until 1946 when it was formally abolished. The League had a work program on international trade, but the onset of the Great Depression in the late 1920s and the deteriorating international political situation eliminated any great enthusiasm to engage in joint action for the revival of international trade. The League dissolved itself on 18 April 1946.

Learning-by-doing argument: a variation of the *infant-industry argument*. It proposes that government protection of an industry is warranted if the industry can in this way learn to be competitive. See also *import substitution*.

Least developed countries: abbreviated either to LDC or, especially in older material, to LLDC. A group of 49 developing countries so designated by *ECOSOC* on the basis of the following indicators: per capita GNP, life expectancy at birth, per capita calorie supplies, combined primary and secondary enrolment ratio, adult literacy rate, share of manufacturing in GDP, share of employment in industry, per-capita electricity consumption, and their export concentration ratio. These indicators and the list of countries designated as LDCs are reviewed by ECOSOC every three years. The list currently includes Afghanistan, Angola, Bangladesh, Benin, Bhutan, Burkina Faso, Burma (Myanmar), Burundi, Cambodia, Cape Verde, Central African Republic, Chad, Comoros, Democratic Republic of the Congo, Djibouti, Equatorial Guinea, Eritrea, Ethiopia, Gambia, Guinea, Guinea-Bissau, Haiti, Kiribati, Lao People's Democratic Republic, Lesotho, Liberia, Madagascar, Malawi, Maldives, Mali, Mauritania, Mozambique, Nepal, Niger, Rwanda, Samoa, Sao Tome and Principe, Senegal, Sierra Leone, Solomon Islands, Somalia, Sudan, Timor-Leste, Togo, Tuvalu, Uganda, United Republic of Tanzania, Vanuatu, Yemen and Zambia. Some of the WTO provisions recognize the special difficulties and needs of LDCs in several ways. First, LDCs can avail themselves of *Part IV of the GATT* and the *Enabling Clause* which allow developed countries to take measures in their favour without expecting reciprocal treatment. In addition, the ministerial *Decision in Favour of Least Developed Countries* taken at Marrakesh in April 1994 allows them to undertake *commitments* and *concessions* to the extent consistent with their individual development, financial and trade needs. The decision also seeks a quick implementation of tariff and *non-tariff measures* of interest to LDCs and improvements to the *GSP*. LDCs also receive increased technical assistance to enable them to expand their trade. Several of the agreements administered by the WTO contain provisions concerning LDCs. For example, the *Agreement on Trade-Related Aspects of Intellectual Property Rights* allows LDCs ten years before they have to apply its provisions. The *General Agreement on Trade in Services* requires its members to take measures enabling LDCs to participate more actively in global *services* trade. *UNCTAD* publishes annually the *Least Developed Countries Report* which deals with key developmental issues facing LDCs, their short-term outlook and prospects for growth. See also *Everything But Arms*, *food security*, *Integrated Framework for Trade-Related Technical Assistance to Least Developed Countries*, *Joint Integrated Technical Assistance Program* and *SNPA*.

Least Developed Countries Report: published annually by *UNCTAD*. See *least developed countries*.

Least-trade-restrictive-alternative test: when a *panel* is set up to adjudicate in a dispute over the legality of a *trade measure*, its finding may be that the aim of the measure was legitimate. The panel may then have to consider whether the measure used was appropriate in the circumstances. A yardstick it can use is an examination of what kind of measure achieving the same aim would have the least impact on trade flows. If it finds that such a measure would have been reasonably available, it may rule against the defendant. This test differs from the *necessity test* which asks whether the measure was needed in the first place.

Leather: see *Japanese measures on imports of leather*.

Left-over tariffs: see *residual tariffs*.

Legal persons: incorporated companies, as opposed to *natural persons*, i.e. people.

Legitimate expectation: a doctrine used in the WTO, not defined precisely, which holds that a country should have reasonable grounds to expect that a *market access* commitment, once made, would not be undermined or negated through a later action. The doctrine is therefore an aspect of *good faith*. It refers to changes in conditions which could not have been reasonably foreseen. For example, an exporting country might have a legitimate expectation that there would be no sudden change in a product standard in the importing country, but such a change was for some reason made anyway. This may result in a disruption of trade. The doctrine does not apply to changes caused by the use of *trade remedies*. The assumption in these cases is, for example, that if *dumping* has been identified, the importing country may be entitled to impose *anti-dumping measures*, and the exporting country should be aware of this. See also *non-violation*. [Jung and Lee 2003]

Leontief Paradox: see *new trade theory*.

Lerner's symmetry theorem: named after the economist Abba Lerner who demonstrated in 1936 that a tax on exports has the same effect on the economy as a tax on imports. [Lerner 1936]

Less-advantaged countries: a term used by *AITIC* and others for a group of countries that traditionally have not been active in international trade negotiations. It includes the *least developed countries*, some other developing countries and some *economies in transition*.

Less-developed countries: a term in common use until the 1970s for what we now call *developing countries*.

Lesser-duty principle: the principle in the administration of *anti-dumping measures* that additional duties imposed on products found dumped should be less than the *margin of dumping* if a duty less than that is enough to eliminate the *injury*.

Less than fair value: under United States anti-dumping laws, broadly a lower export price of a product than its value on the exporter's home market. If the export price is less than the domestic price, less than fair value is deemed to exist. The difference, the *margin of dumping*, together with material *injury*, if that has been established, then forms part of the assessment for possible *anti-dumping measures*.

Leutwiler Report: in late 1983, about one year after the inconclusive 1982 GATT Ministerial Meeting which was seen by many as the low point in the GATT history, the Director-General of the GATT assembled a group of seven eminent people from business, government and academia, led by Dr Fritz Leutwiler, then chairman of the Swiss National Bank. The Group's task was to look at the state of the international trading system, the fundamental reasons for the difficulties it faced and to make proposals for action. The resulting report, *Trade Policies for a Better Future*, appeared in March 1985. Its fifteen recommendations influenced considerably the impetus for a new round of trade negotiations and the mandate for it. Most of them can be seen reflected in the *Uruguay Round* outcome, though not necessarily with the same degree of ambition. In summary, the recommendations were that (i) the making of *trade policy* should be brought into the open in each country, (ii) agricultural trade should be based on clearer and fairer rules, (iii) a timetable should be established to bring ***grey-area measures*** within GATT rules, (iv) trade in textiles and clothing should be fully subject to GATT rules, (v) rules on subsidies should be made more effective, (vi) the GATT codes on ***non-tariff distortions*** should be improved, (vii) the rules permitting ***free-trade areas*** and ***customs unions*** needed to be clarified and tightened up, (viii) there should be more international ***surveillance*** of trade policies and actions, (ix) emergency ***safeguard*** protection should be provided only in accordance with the rules, (x) greater emphasis should be placed on encouraging developing countries to take advantage of their competitive strength and to integrate them more fully into the trading system, (xi) the possibility of multilateral rules for ***trade in services*** should be explored, (xii) ***dispute settlement*** procedures and implementation of ***panel*** recommendations should be improved, (xiii) a new round of GATT negotiations should be launched, (xiv) a permanent Ministerial-level body should be established to encourage prompt negotiations on problems, and (xv) efforts towards satisfactory resolution of the world debt problem, adequate flows of development finance, better international coordination of macroeconomic policies and greater consistency between trade and financial policies.

Level playing field: a term used to describe *fair trade*, with all adherents playing by the rules. There are differing views on what is meant by a level playing field. Some concede that the available trade rules do not favour one party over another in a strictly legal sense, but they are of the view that there is a tilted playing field, often said to consist of otherwise unidentified ***non-tariff measures*** and ***subsidies***. Hence, in their view, some of the players will always face an inherent up-hill struggle if they agree to play by the rules. The level playing field has therefore been used increasingly by those who favour various forms of ***protection*** to suggest that for trade to be "fair", all distortions must be removed. If that cannot be done, as is obviously the case, at least in the near future, then government intervention against imports is justified. Failing that, no further domestic ***trade liberalization*** should be undertaken until the others have mended their way. As many commentators have pointed out, it is possible to have a level playing field within an economy because everyone plays by the same rules. It is rather more difficult to achieve it when the rules of many players are involved. Apart from this, the level-playing-field concept is so loaded with individual assumptions that it is of no use as an analytical concept.

Lex posterior (derogat priori): (*Lat.* later law prevails over an earlier law). A rule used in the interpretation of international treaties which holds that if a country becomes a party to two treaties which have conflicting provisions, the obligations it assumes in the later accession are the ones applicable.

Lex specialis (derogat legi generali): (*Lat.* specific law prevails over general law). This principle applies to situations that could be dealt with under two different laws. In such cases, the courts will apply the specific law because the situation is one of many that might fall under the general law.

Life cycle assessment: LCA. A way of ascertaining the environmental effects of a product, process or service over its entire life. This includes the ultimate disposal of the product. A life cycle assessment covers the entirety of the resources consumed in the production of a good or a service, as well as the impact on the environment caused by the existence of these products. Sometimes, a life cycle assessment is also called a cradle-to-grave assessment. See also *trade and environment*.

Like domestic product: see *like product*.

Like-Minded Group of Developing Countries: a group active in WTO negotiations. Its core members are Cuba, Dominican Republic, Egypt, Honduras, India, Indonesia, Jamaica, Kenya, Malaysia, Mauritius, Pakistan, Sri Lanka, Tanzania, Uganda and Zimbabwe.

Like or directly competitive products: a term used in Article XIX of the GATT (Emergency Action on Imports of Particular Products) and the *Agreement on Safeguards*. Both of them permit the imposition of *safeguards* under defined conditions. One of these is that a product is imported in such increased quantities as to cause or threaten *serious injury* to domestic producers of like or directly competitive products. In WTO usage "like" is deemed to equate to "same", but "directly competitive" is much harder to define. A luxury car and basic car are broadly speaking like products, but they are hardly directly competitive. This is one of the reasons why the *Appellate Body* has referred to an *accordion of likeness*. See also *directly competitive or substitutable products*.

Like product: this expression occurs in several of the agreements administered by the WTO. It is one of the standards that can be used to examine whether discrimination against the imported product has occurred. In disputes concerning the meaning of "like products", *panels* have been inclined to look at criteria such as international usage and accepted customs classifications. The tendency has been, however, to equate "like" with "same". This approach has been formalized in the case of *anti-dumping measures* where action may only be taken if the industry producing the like product has suffered material *injury*. Under the relevant WTO rules, the term "like product" means a product which is identical, i.e. alike in all respects to the product under consideration. If such a product is not available, another product may be used which, although not alike in all respects, has characteristics closely resembling those of the product under consideration. *Brazilian unroasted coffee* and *German imports of sardines* are disputes based on the meaning of "like product". See also *accordion of likeness*.

Linear country: a term used particularly during the *Kennedy Round* for countries disposed to make *linear tariff cuts*.

Linear tariff cuts: also known as formula approach. These are tariff cuts of equal magnitude, usually expressed in percentage points, across whole classes of products. They were first introduced formally into *multilateral trade negotiations* during the *Kennedy Round* (1963–67), but the EEC's initial offer in the *Dillon*

Round (1960) had already envisaged them. The main reason this method was not adopted before the Kennedy Round was the lack of United States negotiating authority for doing so. The United States rejected linear tariff cuts for the *Uruguay Round*. See also *Swiss formula* which was used in the *Tokyo Round* tariff negotiations.

Lisbon Agreement: *Agreement for the Protection of Appellations of Origin and their International Registration.* Concluded in Lisbon in 1958 and revised in 1967. It provides for the protection of *appellations of origin*. Such names are registered by *WIPO* upon request of the interested state. All members must protect the internationally registered name as long as it continues to be protected in the country of origin, except in the case where a member declares within one year that it cannot ensure the protection of a registered name. See also *intellectual property*.

Living modified organism: LMO. Defined in the *Cartagena Protocol* as any living organism that possesses a novel combination of genetic material obtained through the use of modern biotechnology.

LLDC: see *least developed countries*.

Loan rate: part of the agricultural support framework administered by the United States *Commodity Credit Corporation*. The loan rate is the price at which the Corporation is prepared to purchase crops against which it has issued loans. It therefore acts a *floor price*.

Local content requirements: sometimes also called mixing requirements. Governmental measures setting out certain minimum levels of locally made components to be incorporated in goods or services produced domestically. Minimum levels of local content may be set in the form of weight, volume, value, etc. The aims of such programs include, among others, encouraging the development of local industry, finding an assured market for an uncompetitive industry and the promotion of regional development. All local content schemes entail a degree of *protection* for the suppliers of the component in question and therefore a higher cost for consumers. This is self-evident, since competitive industries have no need to search for captive markets. However, governments sometimes consider that these costs are outweighed by the prospective benefits of the program. GATT Article III:5 (National Treatment on Internal Taxation and Regulation) prohibits internal quantitative regulations relating to the mixture, processing or use of products in specified amounts or the mandatory use of domestic products. See also *Agreement on Trade-Related Investment Measures*.

Local content rules in broadcasting: such rules generally require radio and television broadcasters to use at least defined minimum amounts of locally produced materials during certain time slots. The definition of a local product may be based on any combination of the nature of the content of the material, the nationality of the production house, the producer, director and the main actors, funding sources, etc. See also *audiovisual services*, *broadcasting directive*, *cultural identity* and *trade and culture*.

Local presence: the requirement to maintain a branch office, representative office or to station people in the territory of the importing country for the purpose of selling goods and services. See also *commercial presence* and *right of establishment*.

Locarno Agreement Establishing an International Classification for Industrial Designs: concluded in Locarno on 8 October 1968 and amended on 28 September 1979. It establishes a single classification for *industrial designs* which consists of a list of 32 classes and 223 sub-classes It also contains an alphabetical list of goods in which industrial designs are incorporated, with an indication of the classes and sub-classes into which theses goods fall. More than 6,600 indications are so listed. The Agreement is administered by *WIPO*. See also *Hague System for the International Deposit of Industrial Designs*.

Locomotive effect: the impetus given by economic growth in large economies to economic development in smaller economies.

Log-rolling: an American expression for helping each other out in the political arena, with the implication that this may be done at the expense of someone else. Also known as trading of votes. [Dam 2001 and many others]

Lomé Convention: the umbrella agreement, first signed in 1975 as the successor to the *Yaoundé Convention* and last renegotiated in 1990 for ten years (Lomé-IV), for a type of association by 71 African, Caribbean and Pacific (ACP) states with the *European Economic Community* (EEC), now the *European Community*. Associated countries receive tariff-free access to the EEC for nearly all products, and significant aid flows. They also had access to two *export earnings guarantee schemes* offering concessional loans if their export earnings suffered a serious and sudden decline. These were *STABEX* and *SYSMIN*. The EEC did not have tariff-free access to the *ACP states*. The Lomé Convention has been superseded by the *ACP-EC Partnership Agreement*.

London Guidelines for the Exchange of Information on Chemicals in International Trade: adopted on 25 May 1989 under the *United Nations Environment Programme* (UNEP). The guidelines aim to enhance the sound management of chemicals through the exchange of scientific, technical, economic and legal information, including the use of the *prior-informed-consent* principle. There are special provisions for banned or severely restricted chemicals in international trade. See also *trade and environment*.

Long-Term Arrangement Regarding International Trade in Cotton Textiles: LTA. An arrangement in the GATT for *managed trade* in cotton textiles and clothing which entered into force in 1962 for five years as the successor to the *Short-Term Arrangement Regarding International Trade in Textiles*. It was extended for another three years as part of the *Kennedy Round* outcome. After a further extension in 1970, the arrangement was replaced in 1973 by the *Multi-Fibre Arrangement*. See also *Agreement on Textiles and Clothing* which brought trade in textiles and clothing again under the normal multilateral trade rules on 1 January 2005.

Low-income economies: a group of 54 economies so classified by the *World Bank* and listed in the 2007 *World Development Report* as having had in 2005 a per-capita GNI (gross national income) of $875 or less. The group includes many of the *least developed countries*. See also *high-income economies*, *lower-middle-income economies* and *upper-middle-income economies*.

Lower-middle-income economies: a group of 58 economies classified as such by the *World Bank* and listed in the 2007 *World Development Report* as having had in 2005 a per-capita GNI (gross national income) ranging from $876 to $3,465. See also *high-income economies*, *low-income economies* and *upper-middle-income economies*.

Lusophone countries: the countries that have Portuguese as their official language. They are Angola, Brazil, Cape Verde, Timor Leste (East Timor), Guinea-Bissau, Mozambique, Portugal, and Sao Tome and Principe.

Luxembourg Compromise: the resolution in January 1966 of a crisis within the *European Economic Community* which had held up negotiations in the *Kennedy Round* for about six months. It had as its immediate cause the failure of France and Germany to agree on how the *Common Agricultural Policy* should be financed. The larger issue, however, appears to have been France's intention to seek a change in the envisaged transition from unanimous decisions to majority voting which would have undermined its ability to use its veto power. The compromise consisted of agreement to disagree on the voting question and to agree that agricultural pricing would be looked at again in the context of the Kennedy Round agricultural negotiations. [Gillingham 2003]

M

Made-to-measure tariffs: describes *tariffs* that are just high enough to allow domestic producers to cover their costs plus normal profits. Because industries have differing cost structures, this results in a complicated tariff structure as each industry receives tariff support apparently made to measure. Some call them tailor-made tariffs.

Madrid Agreement Concerning the International Registration of Marks: concluded on 14 April 1891 and last revised in Stockholm on 14 July 1967. The Agreement was supplemented in 1989 by the *Protocol Relating the Madrid Agreement* which entered into force on 1 April 1996. Together they constitute the Madrid Union. The Agreement and the Protocol are separate treaties, and membership of one is possible independent of the other. The Agreement enables nationals of member countries to secure international protection for their marks applicable to goods and services registered in the country of origin by filing them with the *International Bureau of Intellectual Property* of *WIPO*. This saves them the expense and the effort of registering in each market separately. The Protocol aims to make this system acceptable to more countries.

Madrid Agreement for the Repression of False or Deceptive Indications of Source on Goods: concluded in Madrid on 14 April 1891 and revised several times, lastly in 1967. It is administered by *WIPO*. The Agreement provides for the cases and the manner in which seizure may be requested and effected for goods bearing a false or deceptive indication of source. It prohibits the use of all publicity indications capable of deceiving the public as to the source of the goods. Each member state may decide what appellations, because of their generic character, are not covered by the Agreement, except for "regional appellations concerning the source of products of the vine". See also *appellations of origin*, *geographical indications*, *indications of source* and *Lisbon Agreement*.

Madrid Protocol: see *Madrid Agreement Concerning the International Registration of Marks*.

Madrid Union: see *Madrid Agreement Concerning the International Registration of Marks*.

Maghreb states: this often refers to Algeria, Morocco and Tunisia which in 1976 concluded cooperation agreements with the *European Economic Community* (EEC) under which they enjoy preferential non-reciprocal market access to the EEC. See also *Arab Maghreb Union*.

Mailbox: refers to a requirement of the *Agreement on Trade-Related Aspects of Intellectual Property Rights* applying to WTO members which do not yet provide product patent production for pharmaceuticals and for agricultural chemicals. Since 1 January 1995, when the WTO agreements entered into force, these countries have had to establish a means by which applications of patents for these products can be filed. They must also put in place a system for granting *exclusive marketing rights* for the products whose patent applications have been filed.

Mala fides: *Lat.* bad faith, often met as *mala fide* (in bad faith). Taking on an obligation without meaning to keep it. More or less the opposite of *good faith*.

Malevolent mercantilism: see *mercantilism*.

Managed liberalism: used by some to describe the practice by existing members of *free-trade agreements* of exempting particular sectors from the operations of the agreement, particularly when new members accede to it. See also *block exemptions*.

Managed mutual recognition: postulated by Kalypso Nicolaïdis as the process adopted by the *European Community* to achieve *mutual recognition* of qualification, licensing and certification requirements. The proposition is that managed mutual recognition does not require extensive prior harmonization of qualifications across borders. Rather, it accepts that there are differences in the way professions are regulated, and it deals with these differences flexibly. See also *harmonization of standards and qualifications*. [Nicolaïdis 1997]

Managed trade: international trade in which some sectors or products are not traded according to the demands of market forces. Means for this include *voluntary restraint arrangements*, *orderly marketing arrangements*, *quantitative restrictions* and other *non-tariff measures*. The aim of managed trade in these cases always is to protect domestic industry. More modern versions of managed trade seek not to restrict access, but to increase exports through numerical targets, usually at the expense of third-country exporters. See also *fair trade*, *grey-area measures*, *Multi-Fibre Arrangement* and *voluntary import expansion*.

Managed trade liberalization: see *managed liberalism*.

Mandatory but not compulsory: a description of the status of *retaliatory action* under *Super 301*, used during congressional hearings in 1988 on the *Omnibus Trade and Competitiveness Act*. It made sense to those involved.

Mandatory/discretionary distinction: see *GATT-consistency of national legislation*.

Manila Action Plan for APEC: the work program adopted at the November 1996 *APEC* leaders meeting in Manila. It integrates the *APEC individual action plans*, *collective action plans* and the work programs prepared by the various bodies established within APEC.

Mano River Union: a preferential trade area established in 1973. It consists of Guinea, Liberia and Sierra Leone. Its secretariat is in Freetown, Sierra Leone. See also *ECOWAS*.

Mansholt proposals: two proposals named after Sicco Mansholt, *European Economic Community* Commissioner for Agriculture during the *Kennedy Round*. The first was concerned with establishing a common EEC pricing regime for cereals. Member states whose prices were lowered through the proposed harmonization were to be compensated by direct EEC payments. The second proposal formed the outline of the EEC offer on agriculture for the Round. In essence, it offered to bind the *montant de soutien* (level of internal support) for three years on the basis of reciprocity. The EEC was able to reach internal agreement on the first proposal, but its negotiating partners in the Round remained unconvinced of the merits of the second. See also *agriculture and the multilateral trading system*.

Manual on Statistics of International Trade in Services: see *trade in services statistics*.

Manufacturing Clause: a dispute brought before the GATT in 1983 by the *European Communities*. The facts were that Section 601 (the *Manufacturing Clause*) of United States Public Law 97–215 of 1982 prohibited, with certain exceptions, the import into the United States or public distribution there of a work under *copyright* consisting mainly of non-dramatic material unless the material had been manufactured in the United States or Canada. The definition of "manufacture" included typesetting, printing and binding. The *Manufacturing Clause* had originally been enacted in 1891 and amended several times. The 1976 amendment included a *sunset clause* applicable before 1 July 1982. The Act expired and was re-enacted on 13 July 1982 with 1986 as the new expiry date. The main interest in this case was in whether the amended Act was covered by the *Protocol of Provisional Accession*. This protocol allowed GATT members to retain legislation not fully consistent with GATT rules if it was in force on 30 October 1947. The *panel* held that legislative changes to the *Manufacturing Clause* did not necessarily disqualify it as "existing legislation". It considered, however, that the insertion of the sunset clause in the 1976 Act constituted a policy change representing a move towards greater GATT conformity. The re-enactment in 1982 postponing the expiry date was a reversal of the move towards greater conformity and therefore an increase in the degree of inconsistency with the GATT. The panel accordingly found in favour of the European Communities on this point. [GATT BISD 31S]

Maputo Declaration: see *Arusha Declaration*.

Maquiladora **industries:** Mexican production facilities engaged in processing or secondary assembly of imported components for re-export, primarily to the United States. The *maquiladora* program was created in the late 1960s by Mexico to alleviate economic and social problems. Materials could be imported free of tariffs if they were re-exported. Article 303 of *NAFTA* has changed the *maquiladora* program substantially. This article prohibits the refunding, waiving or reducing the amount of customs duties on goods imported into the territory of a party, if a condition is that the product is exported to another party or used in the production of a good to be exported to another party. Of course, all tariffs between the United States and Mexico will be eliminated by 2008 in any case.

Marginalization: putting people on the sidelines where they don't matter or can't influence things. It is an expression favoured by *UNCTAD*, among others, to describe what it considers a complex phenomenon existing on two levels. First, it can be seen as a social condition referring to disadvantaged groups within individual societies. Second, it can be an economic phenomenon affecting entire countries and jeopardizing their economic and development prospects. Countries affected in this way may find it difficult to reap the benefits of increasing *integration*. Marginalization is often regarded as a process occurring alongside *globalization*.

Margin of dumping: a key concept in *dumping* enquiries which determines the extent to which *anti-dumping measures* may be imposed. The margin of dumping is the difference between the assessment by the relevant authority of what should be considered *normal value* and the export price of the product exported from one country to another. Procedures to be followed in ascertaining the margin of dumping are set out in the WTO *Anti-Dumping Agreement*. The authorities may only impose anti-dumping measures to the extent necessary to cover the margin of dumping. See also *de minimis dumping margins* and *lesser-duty principle*.

Margin of preference: the difference between the duty that would be paid under some kind of *preferential trade arrangement* and the duty payable on a *most-favoured-nation* (MFN) basis.

Maritime transport services: in 1995 the *Council for Trade in Services* established a Negotiating Group on Maritime Transport Services (NGMTS) with the aim of increasing commitments under the *General Agreement on Trade in Services* (GATS) in international shipping, auxiliary services and access to, and use of, ports. The NGMTS was intended to conclude its negotiations by 30 June 1996, but it proved impossible to arrive at an agreed result. Negotiations on maritime transport services resumed in 2000 as part of the new round of services negotiations mandated by Article XIX of the GATS. See also *cabotage*, *Jones Act* and *progressive liberalization*.

Market access: one of the basic concepts in international trade. It describes the extent to which an imported good or service can compete in another market with goods or services made there. In the WTO framework it is a legalistic term outlining the government-imposed conditions under which a product may enter a country under non-discriminatory conditions. Market access in the WTO sense is expressed through border measures, i.e. *tariffs* and *non-tariff measures*, in the case of goods, and regulations inside the market in the case of *services*. Traditionally, multilateral *trade policy* has sought to make market access predictable and, preferably, more liberal. This is done through the reduction of tariffs and "binding" them at the lower level. A *binding* is a contractual obligation not to raise the tariff above the levels specified in the *schedules of concessions*. The removal of market access impediments in the form of non-tariff measures is more complex since some of them may escape precise legal definition. The rapid growth of *trade in services* and the process of *globalization* have drawn attention to market access impediments inside the border. Of the WTO agreements, the *General Agreement on Trade in Services* has gone furthest in seeking to deal with trade-restrictive regulatory measures, but other instruments, such as the *Agreement on Subsidies and Countervailing Measures* have also extended the reach of trade rules into the domestic domain. The coverage of these rules is, however, patchy, and there have been calls for the insertion of *competition policy* into the WTO system. In competition frameworks, market access is described as the ability to compete effectively in a market. Its aim is the regulation or removal of anti-competitive private *conduct* and *regulation*. A merging of these two market access concepts, if it turned out to be feasible, could make a powerful contribution to the furthering of the *international contestability of markets*. Access for *foreign direct investment* can also influence market access. One school of thought holds that market access is too limiting a concept, and that it should be replaced by the more embracing concept of *market presence*. See also *equality of competitive opportunity*, *market access for agriculture*, *market access for services*, *national treatment* and *most-favoured-nation treatment*.

Market access for agriculture: an omnibus term covering the *tariffs* and *tariff quotas* negotiated during the *Uruguay Round* negotiations on agriculture. These negotiations comprised the three key elements of market access, *domestic support* and *export subsidies*, all of which had to be accepted as a package. The Uruguay Round outcome restricted the expansion of trade-distorting measures and maintained or opened new access to markets for agricultural products. See also *agriculture and the multilateral trading system*.

Market access for services: the *General Agreement on Trade in Services* promotes the goal of open and non-discriminatory market access for services and their suppliers. It does not define market access, but in Article XVI it lists six types of measures which must not be maintained or adopted for sectors listed in a country's *schedule of specific commitments on services*. Broadly, they are (i) limitations on the number of service suppliers, (ii) limitations on the total value of service transactions, (iii) limitations on the total number of service operations, (iv) limitations on the number of persons that may be employed, (v) entity restrictions or joint-venture requirements and (vi) limitations on the level of foreign equity. *Economics needs tests* governing market access are to be eliminated.

Market disruption: one of the justifications used for the imposition of *safeguards* measures. Such situations are said to occur when an increasing flow of imports puts serious strain on the ability of domestic producers to stay in business. In the textile trade, market disruption emerged as a key concept in the *Long-Term Arrangement Regarding International Trade in Cotton Textiles* where it referred to any sudden large flow of very low-priced imports from one or more trading partners. This concept was carried forward into the *Multi-Fibre Arrangement*. See also *Transitional Product-Specific Safeguard Mechanism*.

Market dominance: the rationale in many countries for creating the need for *competition policy*. Market dominance is the ability of a firm to influence the behaviour of other firms, either upstream or downstream. In most cases, competition policy accepts the existence of market dominance, but is concerned with eliminating its abuse. See also *antitrust laws* and *market power*.

Market economy: an economy in which the price mechanism determines what is produced and traded, though too often price signals are distorted by *subsidies*, *industry policy* and other types of government intervention. See also *centrally-planned economies* and *non-market economies*.

Market-expansion dumping: see *dumping*.

Market failure: an economist's term for imperfectly functioning markets. It does not mean that the market has collapsed. Market failure can occur when participants in the market are insufficiently informed, when there are few buyers or few sellers (*monopoly* or *monopsony* conditions) or when the costs and benefits of producing a product are of relevance to some market participants only.

Marketing boards: private or public bodies sometimes established by producer countries to promote, market and export agricultural commodities. Their functions may include the funding of research for more efficient production and storage, processing and identifying new uses. Marketing boards sometimes have a statutory monopoly on exports. Their administration is often funded through levies on producers. See also *single-desk selling* and *state trading*.

Market-led integration: regional economic integration occurring through or promoted by business activities. This may happen without an intergovernmental framework for integration. See also *policy-led integration*.

Market-opening initiatives: a term used especially by the United States to describe its activities aimed at eliminating alleged persistent trade barriers against its exports. Typical examples are the *Market-Oriented Sector-Specific talks* of 1985 and the *Structural Impediments Initiative* of 1989, both directed against Japan. Market-opening initiatives are often managed under *Section 301*.

Market-Oriented Sector-Specific talks: the MOSS talks. A 1985 United States initiative to open up the Japanese market for forest products, pharmaceuticals and medical equipment, electronics, telecommunications equipment, auto parts and transportation machinery. See also *Structural Impediments Initiative* and *United States-Japan Framework for a New Economic Partnership*.

Market power: the fundamental assumption underlying *antitrust laws*. It is based on the view that firms may have the ability to increase their prices without suffering a decrease in their sales. Antitrust laws are aimed at ensuring the existence of price competition in the market. See also *competition policy* and *market dominance*.

Market presence: a term thought to reflect better than *market access* the fact that firms may need to establish some kind of operation in the importing country if they are to succeed. Market presence includes the notion that firms may wish to invest, and that they need adequate opportunities to compete. See also *commercial presence* and *right of establishment*.

Market-seeking investment: a term used for *foreign direct investment* undertaken with the dominant aim of supplying one or more markets. See also *tariff-jumping*.

Market-sharing arrangements: schemes supported or instituted by governments to ensure that the share of local industry in a given activity does not fall below a certain level. They can apply to goods and services. In services, two important examples are the *bilateral air services agreements* and the *United Nations Convention on a Code of Conduct for Liner Conferences*. There may be strong competition within each of the defined shares. *Voluntary restraint arrangements* are also a form of market-sharing.

Market transparency: the extent to which participants in a market are able to assess, on the basis of the information available to them, how the market is likely to behave. The information necessary to enable a good assessment is to a large extent statistical, including data on production, sales and pricing. Advance notice of major investment proposals may also be desirable. Many *international commodity agreements* have market transparency as their main aim. See also *administrative international commodity agreements* and *APEC principles on transparency standards*.

Marks of origin: a mark on a product which signifies the country of its origin, usually beginning with "Made in . . ." or "Product of . . .". See also *certificate of origin*, *indications of source* and *rules of origin*.

Marrakesh Agreement Establishing the World Trade Organization: see *WTO Agreement*.

Marshall Plan: a plan for the post-war economic rehabilitation of Europe first proposed by George C. Marshall, then United States Secretary of State, in a speech at Harvard University on 5 June 1947. It was put into effect on 3 April 1948 when President Truman signed the *Foreign Assistance Act*. The United States made available an estimated $13,000 million between 1948 and 1952 for this purpose. The Marshall Plan was administered through the *Organisation for European Economic Cooperation* (OEEC), the predecessor of the *OECD*. Apart from its direct contribution to the reconstruction of the participating economies, the Plan also gave impetus to the later European economic integration through the *European Economic Community* and *EFTA*.

Mashreq countries: Egypt, Jordan, Lebanon, Syria, West Bank and Gaza Strip.

Massachusetts Burma Law: adopted by the Massachusetts state legislature in 1996 to promote improvements in human rights in Burma. The law gave companies avoiding doing business with Burma a 10% preference margin in purchases by the Massachusetts state government. Following a challenge by the National Foreign Trade Council the Supreme Court held in 1998 that the law was an infringement of the exclusively federal constitutional right to regulate foreign trade.

Material injury: a condition that has to be satisfied before *anti-dumping measures* can be taken. The WTO *Anti-Dumping Agreement* does not define the term. It requires, however, that a determination of injury must be based on positive evidence and involve an objective examination of (a) the volume of the dumped imports and their effect on prices in the domestic market for *like products* and (b) the impact of such imports on domestic producers. See also *injury*.

Material retardation of the establishment of an industry: a phrase occurring in both the *Anti-Dumping Agreement* and the *Agreement on Subsidies and*

Countervailing Measures. Neither agreement defines it. However, it seems that material retardation should be considered a less severe event than *injury*, *material injury*, *threat of injury* or *threat of material injury*.

Material transfer agreement: the legal instrument used to protect the transfer of genetic material from a provider/user to another user. Such an agreement is normally considered subject to *trade secrets* law.

Maximum-minimum tariff: a *tariff schedule* that gives for some tariff items the maximum and the minimum rate the customs authorities may apply to imported products. Such tariffs usually were developed autonomously by national legislatures. The intention was to reward those countries perceived as having relatively open markets with the lower rates and to impose the higher rates on countries considered relatively closed. *General most-favoured-nation treatment* rules out the use of a maximum-minimum tariff among WTO members in this way, though it would still be legal in the conduct of their trade relations with non-members. See also *conventional tariff* and *negative reciprocity*.

MEA: see *multilateral environment agreement*.

Means-and-ends test: an examination to ascertain (a) whether the objectives of a *trade measure* are in themselves defensible, and (b) whether the methods proposed for attaining the objectives are going to do that. See also *least-trade-restrictive-alternative test* and *necessity test*.

Measure: normally any law, rule, regulation, policy, practice or action carried out by government or on behalf of a government.

Measurement of commercial policy: assigning a numerical value to the impact of a *trade measure*. This is relatively straightforward in the case of *ad valorem tariffs* since they are normally expressed as a percentage of the *transaction value* of a good. *Specific tariffs* (e.g. a duty of $5 per 100 litres regardless of the value), are more complex to assess since their impact varies with the price of the good. Most difficult to assess is the impact of *non-tariff measures*. Some of these are intended to control the flow of imports or even to stop them, but others ensure no more than that the imported good is of the same standard as the domestically produced good. See *quantification of non-tariff measures* for a brief discussion of the technical issues.

Mediation: now in most cases indistinguishable from *good offices*. It used to have the meaning of direct negotiations between the parties under the guidance of a mediator. The WTO *Dispute Settlement Understanding* allows the parties to accept mediation, either by a third party or the WTO Director-General.

Mediterranean Agreements: the *preferential trade arrangements*, formally known as *Euro-Mediterranean Association Agreements*, between the *European Community* and some Mediterranean countries other than Turkey, Cyprus and Malta. See also *Association Agreements*, *Euro-Mediterranean Economic Area* and *Europe Agreements*.

Mega-tariff: a journalistic term for an extremely high tariff. See also *prohibitive tariff*.

Melanesian Spearhead Group Trade Agreement: a *preferential trade arrangement* concluded in 1999 between Papua New Guinea, Solomon Islands and Vanuatu. The agreement does not establish a timetable for the elimination of *tariffs* or the removal of trade restrictions.

Members: WTO governments (first letter capitalized, in WTO style).

Mercado Comum do Sul: see *Mercosur*.

Mercado Común del Sur: see *Mercosur*.

Mercantilism: a enduring 17th-century set of views which holds that the aim of international trade should be the accumulation of an increased share of global wealth in the form of bullion. In the modern world the aim is to accumulate as much foreign exchange as possible. Mercantilism always seeks to maximize exports and minimize imports. Lars Magnusson points out in *Mercantilism: the shaping of an economic language* that mercantilism in its traditional form was not a well-structured doctrine containing principles to describe economic behaviour or to prescribe policy measures. Rather, it was characterized by a strong emphasis on the means to achieve national wealth and power. Douglas Irwin notes in *Against the Tide : an intellectual history of free trade* that virtually all mercantilists would have agreed with the following proposition: exports of manufactures were beneficial and exports of raw materials (for use by foreign manufacturers abroad) were harmful; imports of raw materials were advantageous and imports of manufactured goods were damaging. This proposition sounds quite familiar to the contemporary policy maker. A shorter way of expressing it is that trade is good, but imports are bad. Most mercantilists also were in favour of expanding trade to promote economic development. A. W. Coats distinguishes in *Mercantilism: Economic Ideas, History, Policy* between three levels of mercantilist ideas: (a) the ultimate ends or objectives of economic policy, e.g. the promotion of the wealth, power and security of the state, (b) the intermediate ends, e.g. adequate supply of precious metals, stable exchange rate, favourable balance of trade, protection of home industry, etc., and (c) the means to achieve the intermediate ends, e.g. bounties on exports, duties and prohibitions on imports of finished goods, prohibitions on the export of precious metals, etc. Robert Gilpin distinguishes in his *Political Economy of International Relations* between benign mercantilism (aimed at protecting the national economic interest as the minimum required for the security of the state) and malevolent mercantilism (aimed at imperialist expansion and national aggrandisement). Adherents of mercantilism implicitly assume that global wealth is fixed. They portray trade as a zero-sum activity in which one country can only prosper at the expense of another. Mercantilism is therefore a form of economic nationalism. The massive growth of world trade and wealth over the past two hundred years or more demonstrates that trade is, in fact, a positive-sum activity. It also shows that all can prosper through efficient specialization. See also *balance of trade* and *neo-mercantilism*. [Coats 1987, Gilpin 1987, Irwin 1996, Magnusson 1994]

Merchandise trade: the import and export of physical goods, i.e. raw materials, semi-manufactures and manufactures. See also *balance on merchandise trade* and *trade in services*.

Mercosul: Mercado Comum do Sul. Southern Common Market. The name in Portuguese of *Mercosur*.

Mercosur: Mercado Común del Sur (Southern Common Market). Currently a *customs union* covering trade in goods except sugar and automobiles. Mercosur objectives include the free transit of all goods, services and the factors of production, and the lifting of non-tariff restrictions. It was established on 29 November 1991 through the Treaty of Asunción and amended on 17 December 1994 through the Protocol of Ouro Preto which covers mainly institutional issues. It includes Argentina, Brazil, Paraguay and Uruguay. Chile signed an association agreement on 1 October 1996. Bolivia did so on 1 March 1997. Membership is open to *ALADI* members. The Mercosur secretariat is located in Montevideo.

Merger Treaty: a treaty concluded in 1965 which created a single Commission of the *European Communities* to replace the bodies administering the European Atomic Energy Community, the *European Coal and Steel Community* and the *European Economic Community*. See also *European Commission*, *European Community and European Union treaties*.

METI: the Japanese Ministry of Economy, Trade and Industry. Until 6 January 2001 it was known as MITI (Ministry of International Trade and Industry). Many see the *dirigiste* industrial and trade policies administered by MITI as a major reason for Japan's post-war economic success. Others have tried to emulate MITI, but without much success. METI itself has now become a market-oriented ministry.

MFA: the *Multi-Fibre Arrangement* under which countries whose markets are disrupted by increased imports of textiles and clothing were able to negotiate quota restrictions.

MFN applied tariff: see *applied MFN tariff rate*.

MFN: *most-favoured-nation treatment*, i.e. the principle of not discriminating between one's trading partners. It is required by Article I of the GATT, Article II of the *General Agreement on Trade in Services* and Article IV of the *Agreement on Trade-Related Aspects of Intellectual Property Rights*.

MFN exemption: under the *General Agreement on Trade in Services* (GATS), permission granted to a member country not to apply *most-favoured-nation treatment* in a given sector. In most cases, these are necessary because of earlier treaty obligations, such as membership of a *market-sharing agreement*, a preferential arrangement or a cooperation agreement. MFN exemptions are for a maximum of ten years, and they have to be reviewed after five years. Many WTO members took out MFN exemptions when the GATS entered into force. Others have since been granted exemptions upon accession. It is possible for existing members to take out new MFN exemptions, but this can only be done with the agreement of 75% of the WTO membership at a *WTO Ministerial Conference*. See also *waiver*.

MFN rules of origin: the *rules of origin* applied by a country to goods imported under its *MFN tariff*. See *non-preferential rules of origin*.

MFN tariff: the tariff rates applied to goods imported from countries enjoying *most-favoured-nation treatment* under one's trade laws.

Miami Summit: see *FTAA*.

Middle East Free Trade Area Initiative: a proposal offering "a vision of openness, trade integration and economic development for the Middle east" launched by President Bush in 2003. It has six elements: (1) United States support for countries seeking WTO membership, (2) an expanded *GSP* scheme, (3) an offer to negotiate *Trade and Investment Framework Agreements*, (4) an offer to negotiate *bilateral investment treaties*, (5) comprehensive *free-trade agreements* and (6) aid for *capacity-building*.

Midrand Declaration: a non-binding statement adopted at *UNCTAD* IX (May 1996) which sets out broadly UNCTAD's task for the next for the next four years. Its main themes are the impact of *globalization* and liberalization, partnerships for development through cooperation between developed and developing countries, the focal points for UNCTAD's future work, partnerships involving the private sector and institutional reform of UNCTAD.

Millennium Declaration: adopted by the United Nations on 8 September 2001, mainly concerned with political and security matters, but it has a bearing also on *trade policy*. The Declaration stresses *good governance* at home and internationally as well as *transparency* in the financial, monetary and trading system. It contains a commitment to an open, equitable, rule-based, predictable and non-discriminatory multilateral trading and financial system. The Declaration calls on developed countries to give duty-free and quota-free access for essentially all exports from the *least developed countries*, and it encourages the pharmaceutical industry to make essential drugs more widely available and affordable by all who need them in developing countries. It also forms the basis of the *Millennium Development Goals*.

Millennium Development Goals: the eight goals for human development adopted in 2000 and given a realization target of 2015 as part of the *Millennium Declaration*. They are (1) eradicate extreme poverty and hunger, (2) achieve universal primary education, (3) promote gender equality and empower women, (4) reduce child mortality, (5) improve mental health, (6) combat HIV/AIDS, malaria and other diseases, (7) ensure environmental sustainability and (8) develop a global partnership for development. See also *United Nations Development Programme*. [Human Development Report 2003]

Millennium Round: a name suggested in 1997 by Sir Leon Brittan, then Vice-President of the *European Commission*, for the new round of *multilateral trade negotiations* that he and others expected would get under way in about 2000 or 2001. The name did not take on. See also *Seattle Ministerial Conference* and *Doha Ministerial Conference*.

Minilateralism: a preference for conducting *trade policy* in the company of a few countries. No exact definition exists for "minilateral". It definitely describes a relationship that is more than bilateral, but less than plurilateral which, of course, is equally inexact. The *Quadrilaterals*, however, would fit the bill well. See also *creative minilateralism* and *plurilateralism*.

Minimal operations or processes: if goods are to qualify for *preferential market access*, i.e. if they meet the *preferential rules of origin*, the exporting country has to add value equalling or exceeding an agreed threshold. Minimal operations or processes are those that do not meet this threshold. Among these are preservation of goods in storage, packaging, cleaning, simple assembly of parts, etc. See also *insufficient operations*.

Mini-ministerial meeting: an informal meeting to which a limited, but representative, number of ministers is invited. These meetings are normally used to seek ways to maintain impetus in negotiations or to discuss key issues in negotiations. Accordingly, the selection of ministers to be invited depends to some extent on the topics to be discussed.

Minimum access tariff quotas: a mechanism giving a minimum level of access opportunities for agricultural products where *non-tariff measures* have been converted into tariffs. The *Uruguay Round* negotiations led to a formula whereby the level of access to be opened for a certain product was based on the import/consumption ratio during the 1986–88 *base period*. In countries where imports were less than 3% of consumption during the base period, access was to be increased immediately to 3% and expanded to 5% by the end of the Uruguay Round implementation period for agriculture commitments. See also *Agreement on Agriculture*, *current access tariff quotas* and *tariffication*.

Minimum customs values: the arbitrary allocation by customs authorities of a value to an imported good, usually above its market value. See *customs valuation*.

Minimum labour standards: see *core labour standards* and *international labour standards*.

Minimum operations: in the administration of *preferential rules of origin* this generally refers to work on a product deemed insufficient to make it qualify as a product of the exporting country. Hence the product would not benefit from any *preferential tariff*. Such operations can include simple assembly, final quality testing or packaging. See also *insufficient operations* and *substantial transformation*.

Minimum standard of treatment: some *international investment agreements* investment chapters in *free-trade agreements*, such as Article 1105 of *NAFTA*, require the parties to accord to investments of investors of another party a minimum standard of treatment. This is generally held to be treatment in accordance with international law, including fair and equitable treatment and full protection and security. This provision has caused considerable comment and analysis, though, as many have pointed out, such provisions have been around for some time. One difference is that NAFTA has the judicial environment where this provision can be enforced. Views on the meaning and impact of this provision are still evolving. A recent judgment in a NAFTA dispute illustrates the issue.

The judge in *The United Mexican States v. Metalclad Corporation* held that Article 1105 was framed in absolute terms, "intended to establish a minimum standard so that a party may not treat investments of another investor worse than this standard irrespective of the manner in which the Party treats other investors and their investments". He quoted with approval the tribunal's view on 13 January 2000 in *S. D. Myers, Inc. v. Government of Canada* (another NAFTA case) that the "minimum standard" was a floor below which treatment of foreign investors must not fall, even if a government were not acting in a discriminatory manner. He noted that the introductory phrase to Article 1105 referred to "treatment in accordance with international law". Hence, in order to qualify as a breach of Article 1105, the treatment in question must fail to accord with international law. So the judge. The significance therefore of the "minimum standard" is that it establishes an absolute standard for treatment of investors, in contrast to the relative standards implied by *most-favoured-nation treatment* (non-discrimination between foreign investors) and *national treatment* (non-discrimination between foreign and domestic investors). Neither of these two standards prescribes how well a party must treat foreign investors, except in terms of its own practices.

Ministerial Conference: see *WTO Ministerial Conference*.

Ministerial Declaration on Trade in Information Technology Products: see *Information Technology Agreement*.

Mini-trading area: used by some to describe a *free-trade area*, but for others it is a *growth triangle*. The context will make clear what is meant.

Minor exceptions doctrine: Article 13 of the *Agreement on Trade-Related Aspects of Intellectual Property Rights* requires WTO members to confine limitations or exceptions to exclusive rights in the area of *copyright* to "certain special cases which do not conflict with a normal exploitation of the work and do not unreasonably prejudice the legitimate interests of the right holder". These conditions make clear that exceptions meeting these criteria would always have to be of a minor nature, especially since they have to be read in the context of Articles 11 and 11[bis] of the *Berne Convention* which give authors exclusive rights to authorize public performances, recordings and broadcasts of their works.

Mirror-image reciprocity: the expectation that trade benefits offered to another country will be matched exactly. See also *reciprocity* and *reciprocity at the margin*.

Mirror retaliation: the suspension of the same obligations as have been breached by the country against which the *retaliation* is aimed. It is also known as reciprocal retaliation.

MITI: Ministry of International Trade and Industry. See *METI*.

Mixed Commission: usually a body established under a *bilateral trade agreement* which consists of representatives of both parties. The task of a mixed commission is to review periodically the operation of the agreement. See also *Joint Trade Committee*.

Mixed credits: the provision by developed donor countries to developing countries of credits partly on commercial terms and partly at subsidized interest rates. The aim of such credits usually is to fund projects capable of making an important contribution to the economic development of the recipient country. The assumption is that these projects would not proceed if they had to rely entirely on commercial funding. See also *official development assistance* and *trade and aid*.

Mixed export cartel: see *cartel*.

Mixed tariff: see *compound tariff*.

Mixed trade policies: the concurrent application of the mix deemed most appropriate of trade policies having different immediate aims, though they all are meant to expand a given country's exports. These might be (a) unilateral policies to improve the competitiveness of domestic industries through market-opening measures, (b) stronger emphasis on *reciprocity* in market access to other countries, accompanied by market-opening initiatives, and (c) the use of *contingent protection* (anti-dumping, countervailing and safeguard measures) and, sometimes, other, less transparent measures to protect domestic producers. See also *competitive liberalization*.

Mixing requirements: see *local content requirements* and *performance requirements*.

Mobility of business people: see *business mobility*.

Modalities: ways or forms of organizing work in the WTO, including trade negotiations. They set broad outlines, such as formulas or approaches for tariff reductions, for final commitments.

Model Arbitration Clause: also called Separate Arbitration Agreement. It is contained in the *UNCITRAL Arbitration Rules*. It reads as follows: "Any dispute, controversy or claim arising out of or relating to this contract, or the breach, termination or invalidity thereof, shall be settled by arbitration in accordance with the UNCITRAL Arbitration Rules as present in force. Parties may wish to consider adding: (a) The appointing authority shall be ___ (name of institution or person); (b) The number of arbitrators shall be ___ (one or three); (c) The place of arbitration shall be ___ (town or country); The language(s) to be used in the arbitral proceedings shall be ___." See also *arbitration*.

Model measures for RTAs/FTAs: a set of indicative examples of provisions being developed in *APEC* that might be included in a *free-trade agreement*. The model measures are not in legal language, and they are not binding. The chapters concluded so far are trade in goods, trade facilitation, technical barriers to trade, government procurement, transparency, dispute settlement and cooperation. See also *Best Practices for RTAs/FTAs in APEC*.

Modes of services delivery: in the *Uruguay Round* negotiations on the *General Agreement on Trade in Services* participants agreed to divide services trade into four modes: 1. *cross-border supply*, where the producer remains in one territory and the consumer in another; 2. *consumption abroad*, where the consumer travels from one country to the country of the service producer to obtain the service;

3. *commercial presence*, where services are provided through *establishment* of an operation in the other country; and 4. *presence of natural persons*, where the producer travels from one country to another to produce or deliver a service. This approach is useful for analytical purposes, but it does not necessarily reflect the way services are traded, and it has made the listing of *commitments* more complex than need be the case. See also *cross-border trade in services*, *services* and *trade in services*.

Monetary assessments: refers to proposals arising from time to time for the use of fines instead of trade sanctions to secure compliance with dispute settlement panel decisions made under *free-trade agreements*. Assessing the damage suffered by the winning party because of the losing party's failure to remedy its failings is of course possible. It is less certain that an adequate mechanism could be found to enforce a reasonably prompt payment of these assessments.

Monetary Compensation Amounts: MCAs. A system of border levies and subsidies in force in the *European Economic Community* until 31 December 1992. MCAs were abolished as part of achieving the *European Community Single Market* which did away with internal borders for economic activities.

Monetary union: the use by two or more economies of the same currency and the pursuit of a common monetary policy. See also *EURO*.

Monitoring and Enforcement Unit: a unit established on 5 January 1996 and located within *USTR* with the task of monitoring all trade agreements to which the United States is party and of pursuing actions to enforce rights under these agreements. Priorities of the unit include barriers affecting high-volume and high-value exports, barriers affecting job creation, ensuring that United States industries are competitive, ensuring that widespread barriers in the fastest-growing and largest markets are addressed, and that small and medium-sized businesses are competitive and can expand in the global market place. See also *Section-306 monitoring*.

Monopoly: a single provider or seller of goods and services who is often maintained through legislation permitting no others to perform the same activities. Monopolies can also occur through natural market development in the private sector, but they tend to be under constant threat from prospective new entrants. See also *deregulation*, *essential facilities doctrine*, *re-regulation* and *single-desk selling*.

Monopsony: the existence of a single buyer of certain goods or services, usually maintained through legislation.

Montant de soutien: *Fr.* margin of support. An element in the proposal by the *European Economic Community* for negotiations on agriculture during the *Kennedy Round*. According to the definition offered by the EEC, "the margin of support for a given agricultural product is equal to the difference between the price of the product on the international market and the remuneration actually obtained by the national producer". Critics at the time noted that this definition had the advantage, from the EEC's perspective, of directing attention to the support mechanisms of others, but that it had serious flaws. The most important one was the absence of a competitive world price for major agricultural products since these prices were themselves influenced by domestic price support systems and subsidies.

Monterrey Consensus: adopted on 22 March 2002 in Monterrey, Mexico, as the outcome of the International Conference on Financing and Development, organized under the auspices of the *United Nations*. It seeks to achieve the goal of eradicating poverty, achieving sustained economic growth and promoting sustainable development through calls for (a) mobilizing domestic financial resources for development, (b) harnessing international trade as an engine for development and reaffirming the commitment of participants to trade liberalization, (c) increasing international financial and technical cooperation for development, and (d) appropriate strategies for dealing with external debt. Conference participants also committed themselves to keeping fully engaged to ensuring proper follow-up to implementation of conference commitments.

Montreal mid-term review: see *Uruguay Round*.

Montreal Protocol: *Montreal Protocol on Substances that Deplete the Ozone Layer*. Adopted in 1987. The Protocol addresses concerns about the impact that uncontrolled production or consumption by non-parties would have on the effectiveness of controls agreed by the parties. It contains provisions designed to restrict the relocation of industries using or producing CFCs (chloroflurocarbons) from signatory countries to countries that are not signatories. These provisions may be in conflict with the WTO *most-favoured-nation* principle. Developing countries may apply for funding from the Multilateral Fund for the Implementation of the Montreal Protocol to support the implementation of their commitments under the Protocol. See also *multilateral environment agreements*.

Moral hazard: the risk that a policy or mechanism aimed at preventing a certain event makes it more likely that the event will occur. This term is mainly used in discussions of finance and insurance matters. For example, a borrower may become more profligate if he or she knows that emergency funds are available if a default seems possible. [Lane and Phillips 2000]

Moral rights: the idea expressed in Article 6bis of the *Berne Convention* that "independently of the author's economic rights, and even after the transfer of the said rights, the author shall have the right to claim authorship of the work and to object to any distortion, mutilation or other modification of, or derogatory action to, the said work, which would be prejudicial to his honour or reputation". Moral rights therefore pertain to the author's person, whereas *copyright* pertains to the work itself. Not all members of the Berne Convention recognize moral rights in their national copyright legislation. See also *intellectual property* and *WIPO*.

Moratorium: in *trade policy* negotiations this is the same as a *standstill*. It is usually is imposed before the start of negotiations to ensure the participants do not raise their *tariffs* or change their regulations with the sole aim of using them as *negotiating coin*.

Moratorium on Customs Duties on Electronic Transmissions: adopted as part of the WTO *Ministerial Declaration on Global Electronic Commerce* in 1998. This was a non-binding undertaking not to impose customs duties on products ordered and delivered (transmitted) electronically. The *Doha Ministerial Conference* extended the moratorium until the *Cancún Ministerial Conference*. *APEC* adopted a similar moratorium in 2000 and converted it into a long-term action in 2002.

More than an equitable share of the market: see *equitable share of the market* and *wheat flour case*.

Most-favoured-nation tariff: MFN tariff. The *tariff* applied by WTO members to goods from other WTO members with which they have not concluded a *preferential trade arrangement*. Strictly speaking, the MFN tariff also applies to *non-originating goods* imported from free-trade partners. In the case of WTO non-members, the application of these rates may be a requirement of a *bilateral trade agreement*. See also *general tariff* and *most-favoured nation treatment*.

Most-favoured-nation treatment: MFN. This is the rule, usually established through a trade agreement, that a country gives each of the trading partners with which it has concluded relevant agreements the best treatment it gives to any of them in a given product. MFN is not in itself an obligation to extend any favourable treatment to another party, nor is it an obligation to negotiate for better treatment. The fundamental point of MFN therefore is equality of treatment of other countries, and in some older treatises it is indeed called "foreign parity". Despite the apparently static nature of MFN, it has acted as a powerful motor for *trade liberalization*. Together with *national treatment*, MFN makes up the principle of *non-discrimination*. The MFN rule, in one form or another, can be traced back at least to the sixteenth century. Typical of these older provisions is the formulation contained in the *Treaty of Peace and Friendship between Great Britain and Spain* of 1713, part of the instruments making up the *Treaty of Utrecht*. This says that "the subjects of each kingdom ... shall have the like favour in all things as the subjects of France, or any other foreign nation, the most favour'd, have, possess and enjoy, or at any time hereafter may have, possess or enjoy". An MFN clause was included in the *Cobden-Chevalier Treaty* between England and France of 1860. This is thought to be the ancestor of its modern application. At any rate, the MFN rule was then copied into many other European trade agreements. In the years before the First World War, the MFN rule suffered a decline. The war years led to its virtual demise. In the third of his fourteen points, President Wilson called in January 1918 for the removal, as far as possible, of all economic barriers and the establishment of an equality of trade conditions among all the nations consenting to the peace and associating themselves for its maintenance. This is deemed by some to have been the equivalent of a call for MFN. The Versailles peace conference did not discuss trade barriers, but in the peace treaty Germany and the other central powers were required to extend unconditional MFN for three years to the trade of the allied powers. The

Covenant of the *League of Nations* only referred to "equitable treatment" of commerce of other League members. This fell well short of an MFN clause. The Geneva World Economic Conference of May 1927 pronounced strongly in favour of the widest possible interpretation of the MFN clause, and it stressed that its use in commercial treaties ought to be normal. In 1933, the League of Nations published a 300-word model text of an MFN clause. By that time, economic conditions had been very difficult for several years, and the MFN principle was not able to attract broad support. The *Atlantic Charter* of 1941 revived the MFN principle and made it the cornerstone of the post-war *multilateral trading system* as exemplified by the *GATT*. In the WTO, MFN is the binding general obligation that any *concession* made to another country must immediately be extended to all other members. All WTO members grant each other treatment for trade in goods as favourable as they give to any other country in the application and administration of customs regulations, tariffs and related charges. A similar provision applies to *trade in services*. There are, however, exceptions to the MFN obligation. Here, we mention only some of the important ones. MFN members satisfying the conditions of GATT *Article XXIV* and *Article V* of the *General Agreement for Trade in Services* (GATS) for membership of preferential *free-trade areas* or *customs unions* are not obliged to give countries that are not members of the same *preferential trading arrangement* the same kind of access. *Part IV of the GATT* and the *Enabling Clause* allow discriminatory treatment in favour of developing countries. Developed countries may maintain *GSP* schemes which give preferential treatment to developing country imports. It is possible to ask for a *waiver* which provides the legal basis for treating some members more favourably. There is also the possibility of *non-application* under which an existing WTO member can deny the benefits of the agreement to a newly acceding member. The GATS also permits the taking out of a time-bound *MFN exemption*. A concern sometimes voiced about the MFN principle is that it allows *free riders* to take advantage of trade-liberalizing actions of others without making an equivalent effort. See also *conditional most-favoured-nation treatment*, *Jackson-Vanik amendment*, *minimum standard of treatment* and *normal trade relations*.

Moutarde de Dijion: see *generic geographical indications*.

Movement of goods: another way to describe what happens when goods are trade internationally.

Movement of natural persons: a term used in the *General Agreement on Trade in Services* to signify the temporary entry by service suppliers, i.e. people, into another jurisdiction for the purpose of selling or supplying a service. See also *business mobility* and *modes of services delivery*.

Multi-column tariff: a *tariff schedule* that discriminates between the various trading partners. Tariff rates in the first column might be reserved for countries not receiving *most-favoured-nation treatment* (MFN) and the second column for countries accorded MFN. The third and additional columns would contain the rates applicable to various *preferential trade arrangements*, such as *free-trade area* partners or those given to developing countries under the *GSP* (Generalized System of Preferences). See also *single-column tariff*.

Multidomestic corporation: a form of *transnational corporation* which adopts a strategy for its units centred in each case on individual countries. Typically, it sets up an operation in another country mainly to supply the market of that country.

Multi-Fibre Arrangement: MFA, formally *Agreement Regarding International Trade in Textiles*. This was an agreement between textile-producing and consuming countries concluded in 1973 and renegotiated periodically afterwards to manage trade in textile products through the concept of *market disruption*. The MFA was replaced by the WTO *Agreement on Textiles and Clothing* under which restrictions had to be phased out over ten years starting on 1 January 1995. See also *Short-Term Arrangement Regarding International Trade in Cotton Textiles* and *Long-Term Arrangement Regarding International Trade in Cotton Textiles*.

Multifunctionality: the idea that agriculture has many functions in addition to producing food and fibre. These functions may be environmental protection, landscape preservation, rural employment, etc. The term appears to have originated in a communiqué issued in March 1998 by agricultural ministers from *OECD* countries. The recognition of the various roles agriculture can play is hardly new, but multifunctionality has quickly become one of the dividing lines of agricultural *trade policy*. Those who stress its importance are seen as leaning towards *protectionism*. Those who oppose its use like to think of themselves as promoters of agricultural trade liberalization. Some simply think it is an ugly word that states the obvious. See also *co-existence and diversity*, *Friends of Multifunctionality* and *non-trade concerns*. [OECD 2003]

Multilateral agreement on competition: a proposal for future inter-governmental negotiations, but not yet on any negotiating agenda. Some see its prospective purpose as enabling cooperation between national competition authorities on enforcement matters. Others would prefer an agreement for the international administration of *antitrust laws* which would entail common rights and obligations. See also *Draft International Antitrust Code* and *trade and competition*.

Multilateral Agreement on Investment: MAI. The *OECD* Ministerial Council Meeting of June 1995 decided to launch negotiations for an agreement on investment liberalization which would also be open to OECD non-members. Ministers hoped that the agreement would contain high standards for liberalizing national investment regimes and that it would have effective dispute settlement provisions. After a promising start the negotiations quickly got bogged down in nearly all areas as the complexities of the matter became clearer. Negotiators also were increasingly attacked by *non-governmental organizations* for their alleged secrecy and their purported aim to create an unhindered investment flow between member countries. Neither assessment was accurate, though negotiators were slow to make the negotiating text available publicly. More probably, the negotiations collapsed because of irreconcilable differences between members on key provisions and, to outsiders at any rate, the increasingly incomprehensible language of the draft MAI as negotiators tried to reach compromises. Moreover, it appeared that very few non-member countries would seek to accede to the agreement. By 1998, when the negotiating deadline had been extended by one year, one sensed that some governments had decided that the political cost of the proposed agreement had become very high. Negotiations were abandoned in early 1999.

Multilateral Agreement on the Liberalization of International Air Transportation: MALIAT. This Agreement seeks to promote *open-skies arrangements*. Members agree to open route schedules, open traffic rights (including *seventh-freedom cargo services*), open capacity, multiple airline designation, third-country code-sharing and a minimal tariff-filing regime. Members also agree to maintain airline investment provisions based on effective control and principal place of business which at the same time protect against *flag-of-convenience* carriers. The Agreement entered into force on 21 December 2001. Its members are Brunei Darussalam, Chile, New Zealand, Peru, Samoa, Singapore, Tonga and the United States. See also *freedoms of the air*. [www.maliat.gov.nz]

Multilateral Agricultural Framework: an idea emerging in the later stages of the *Tokyo Round* for a mechanism which would oversee the negotiating results in agriculture, and which also would provide a forum for the exchange of information aimed at preventing problems in agricultural trade. In particular, it was thought that the framework would eliminate continuing political and commercial confrontations in this sector. The proposal also aimed to establish an International Agriculture Consultative Council under GATT auspices. When the Tokyo Round ended on 12 April 1979, participants were still far from an agreement on this proposal, and post-Round negotiations did not lead to a result. See also *agriculture and the WTO*.

Multilateral development banks: institutions established to provide financial support and advice to support the economic and social development of developing countries through long-term loans on commercial terms, credits on concessional terms and grants. Membership of these banks consists of developed and developing countries. The main ones are the African Development Bank (based in Abidjan, Côte d'Ivoire), the Asian Development Bank (Manila), the European Bank for Reconstruction and Development (London), the *World Bank* and the Inter-American Bank Group (both in Washington DC). See also *international financial institutions*.

Multilateral environment agreements: agreements, conventions and protocols agreed multilaterally and aimed at eliminating or reducing damage to the environment. Some 200 have reportedly been concluded. At least eighteen of them contain specific trade provisions. Among these are the *Basel Convention*, *Cartagena Protocol on Biosafety*, *CITES*, *Convention on Biological Diversity*,

Convention on Persistent Organic Pollutants, Convention on the Prior Informed Consent Procedure for Certain Hazardous Chemicals and Pesticides in International Trade, Montreal Protocol, United Nations Framework Convention on Climate Change and the *Kyoto Protocol*. Some other agreements contain provisions which could have an effect on the formulation of trade policy, including *Agenda 21* and the *Rio Declaration on Environment and Development*. [Brack 1999]

Multilateral Fund for the Implementation of the Montreal Protocol: see *Montreal Protocol*.

Multilateral Investment Fund: established in 1993 by the Inter-American Development Bank to encourage growth in the private sector in Latin America and the Caribbean. It is located in Washington, DC.

Multilateral Investment Guarantee Agency: MIGA. Established on 12 April 1988 under the auspices of the *World Bank*. Its purpose is to encourage increased levels of private direct investment in developing countries. It acts as an insurer of investment against certain political risks in the host country. It also offers technical assistance to help developing countries to improve their investment climates and to attract new investment. MIGA is located in Washington, DC. See also *foreign direct investment* and *World Association of Investment Promotion Agencies*.

Multilateralism: an approach to the conduct of international trade based on cooperation, equal *rights and obligations, non-discrimination* and the participation as equals of many countries regardless of their size or share of international trade. This is the basis of the rules and principles embodied in treaties such as the *WTO Agreement* and its components.

Multilateral procurement: the purchase of goods and services by multilateral bodies (e.g. *United Nations, IMF,* WTO, etc.) for their own use or for use on projects funded and managed by them.

Multilateral Specialty Steel Agreement: MSSA. A proposal for a sectoral agreement made in early 1996 by industry associations in Europe and the United States for an agreement that would (a) ban subsidies, (b) remove tariff and non-tariff barriers and (c) eliminate trade-distorting anti-competitive practices in global specialty steel trade. It would also address the problem of surplus production capacity. The Specialty Steel Industry of North America, a private-sector organization, would in addition like such an agreement "to ensure the effectiveness of United States trade law and to make the *Section 201* injury standard compatible with the WTO *injury* standard". The proposed agreement is not yet on any negotiating agenda. See also *Multilateral Steel Agreement*.

Multilateral Steel Agreement: MSA. In the second half of the *Uruguay Round* negotiations the United States proposed the conclusion of an MSA with coverage of subjects such as tariff reductions, the elimination of *quantitative restrictions*, subsidies, the imposition of *anti-dumping measures, countervailing duties*, etc., related specifically to trade in steel. Negotiations were conducted on a track separate to the Uruguay Round negotiations, and 36 countries took part in them. However, negotiations broke down in March 1992. There have been periodic suggestions since, especially by the American Iron and Steel Institute, that the MSA should remain a trade policy objective for the United States. Its proponents argue that it should contain a mechanism for *alternative dispute resolution* because it would be faster and cheaper than trade litigation, partly because it would not require proof of injury in cases where the MSA had been violated. See also *Multilateral Specialty Steel Agreement* and *sectoral trade negotiations*.

Multilateral system of notification and registration of geographical indications: negotiations for such a system were mandated by Article 23.4 of the WTO *Agreement on Trade-Related Aspects of Intellectual Property Rights* and set in train by the *Doha Ministerial Conference*. Negotiations were meant to conclude by the *Cancún Ministerial Conference*, but agreement was not possible. See also *geographical indications*.

Multilateral trade agreements: intergovernmental agreements aimed at expanding and liberalizing international trade under non-discriminatory, predictable and transparent conditions set out in an array of *rights and obligations*. The motivation for taking on these obligations is that all members will increase their welfare by adhering to a common standard of conduct in the management of their trade relations. Typically, such agreements have numerous members representing small, medium-sized and large trading nations. Membership of this kind of agreement is open-ended, but countries wishing to accede usually have to demonstrate that their trade regimes are in keeping with the aims of the agreement, and that the access conditions to their markets roughly match those of existing members. If necessary, they must make adjustments. Before the *GATT*, entered into force in 1948, trade agreements were mostly bilateral, or they were preferential, such as the *imperial preferences arrangement*. In the WTO, the term "Multilateral Trade Agreement" refers to the arrangements and associated legal instruments contained in Annexes 1, 2 and 3 to the *WTO Agreement*. See also *accession*, *bilateral trade agreements*, *plurilateral trade agreements* and *prisoner's dilemma*.

Multilateral trade negotiations: MTN. Also known as *rounds*. They aim to strengthen the rules that ensure orderly and fair conduct of international trade and to reach mutually beneficial agreements reducing barriers to world trade. Eight rounds have been held under GATT auspices since 1947. Each round has consisted of long bargaining sessions. The eight completed rounds and the names by which they are commonly known were: Geneva (1947), Annecy (1949), Torquay (1950), Geneva (1955–56), Dillon (1960–61), Kennedy (1963–67), Tokyo (1973–79) and Uruguay (1986–94). The ninth round, the *Doha Development Agenda*, was launched by the *Doha Ministerial Conference* in November 2001 The content of the rounds up to the *Kennedy Round* was tariff reductions only. The early rounds essentially were made up of a series of bilateral negotiations, the results of which were then made available to other members on a ***most-favoured-nation*** (MFN) basis. From the Kennedy Round onwards, ***non-tariff measures*** and ***systemic issues*** were also on the agenda. The abbreviation "MTN" was in common use during the ***Tokyo Round***, and it is often used to refer specifically to that Round. See also ***Annecy Tariff Conference***, ***Dillon Round***, ***Geneva Tariff Conference, 1947***, ***Geneva Tariff Conference, 1955–56***, ***Millennium Round***, ***Torquay Tariff Conference*** and ***Uruguay Round***.

Multilateral trading system: the non-discriminatory arrangement for international trade which came into existence with the ***GATT*** in 1947 and which is now represented by the WTO system.

Multi-modal: transport using more than one mode. In negotiations under the ***General Agreement on Trade in Services*** the term relates essentially to door-to-door services that include international shipping.

Multinational enterprises: see ***transnational corporations***.

Multiple transformations: see ***double transformation*** and ***triple transformation***.

Munich Group: see ***Draft International Antitrust Code***.

Mutatis mutandis: *Lat.* with the appropriate and/or necessary changes.

Mutual aid agreement: an agreement concluded on 23 February 1942 between the United Kingdom and the United States concerning the principles applying to mutual aid in the prosecution of the war against aggression. It builds on the ***Atlantic Charter*** and is one of the important steps which ultimately led to the convening of the ***United Nations Conference on Trade and Employment*** in 1947, the negotiation of the ***GATT*** in 1947 and the emergence of the ***Havana Charter*** in 1948. Article 7 of the Agreement dealt with international economic relations. It looked forward to agreed action between the two countries, which would be "open to participation by all other countries of like mind, directed to the expansion, by appropriate international and domestic measures, of production, employment, and the exchange and consumption of goods, which are the material foundations of the liberty and welfare of all peoples; to the elimination of all forms of discriminatory treatment in international commerce, and to the reduction of tariffs and other trade barriers".

Mutual recognition arrangements: agreements between two or more countries to recognize each other's standards, qualifications, licensing requirements or testing procedures and results. They can cover goods, services, education and professional qualifications. Mutual recognition can contribute to the expansion of trade through removing some technical obstacles. Achieving mutual recognition may require the parties to meet agreed minimum standards, and it can lead to laborious negotiations. Members of the ***General Agreement on Trade in Services*** who recognize each other's standards and qualifications do not have to extend recognition to others on a ***most-favoured-nation*** basis. If a third country wishes to demonstrate that it, too, can meet the requirements for recognition of qualifications, it must be given an opportunity to do so. A 1979 ruling by the European Court of Justice in the *Cassis de Dijon* case established the principle of ***European Community*** mutual recognition of similar product standards, rather than identical standards. This made mutual recognition within the Community simpler, and it also removed standards from the category of very difficult issues. See also *Guidelines for Mutual Recognition Agreements or Arrangements in the Accountancy Sector*, *harmonization of standards and qualifications*, *managed mutual recognition*, *technical barriers to trade* and *zero-margin harmonization*.

N

NAFTA: North American Free Trade Agreement. Entered into force on 1 January 1994. Its members are Canada, United States and Mexico. This agreement, though long and complex, has exerted a strong influence on the architecture of later *free-trade agreements* negotiated by countries other than the United States. Only a basic introduction to its structure can be given here. NAFTA's objectives, as set out in Chapter 1, are to eliminate barriers to trade in goods and services, promote fair competition, adequate and effective protection of *intellectual property rights*, effective procedures for settlement of disputes and to provide a framework for further trilateral, regional and multilateral cooperation. Chapter 2 contains definitions. Chapter 3 provides for *national treatment* of goods. Most tariffs were eliminated over ten years. All will have gone by 2008. *Anti-dumping rules* are also part of this chapter. Chapter 4 sets out the *rules of origin*. These use the *change-in-tariff classification* method. Common customs procedures are listed in Chapter 5. Energy and trade in basic petrochemicals, dealt with in Chapter 6, are to be liberalized. Chapter 7 contains the rules for agriculture and *sanitary and phytosanitary measures*. Chapters 8, 9 and 10, respectively, set out the *safeguards*, *technical barriers to trade* and *government procurement* provisions. *NAFTA Chapter 11* is the investment chapter. *National treatment* and *most-favoured-nation treatment* apply to investment. This chapter also outlines the concept of a *minimum standard of treatment*. Chapter 12 concerns *cross-border trade in services*. The agreement covers all *modes of services delivery*, but mode 3 (commercial presence) is covered by the investment rules. This followed by more specific rules for telecommunications and financial services in Chapters 13 and 14, respectively. Chapter 15 covers *competition policy*, monopolies and state enterprises. Chapter 16 deals with the temporary entry of business persons. *Intellectual property* provisions are contained in Chapter 17. Chapter 18 deals with the publication, notification and administration of laws, i.e. *transparency*. Chapters 19 and 20 deal, respectively, with review and dispute settlement in antidumping and countervailing duty matters, and institutional arrangements and dispute settlement procedures. Chapter 21 covers exceptions. It has provisions on *general exceptions*, national security, taxation, balance of payments, disclosure of information and *cultural industries*. Chapter 22 covers matters such as entry into force, amendments and withdrawals. Side agreements were concluded in the form of the *North American Agreement on Labor Cooperation* and the North American Agreement on Environmental Cooperation. Some agricultural matters have also been dealt with in separate agreements. A Cabinet-level Free Trade Commission supervises the implementation and operation of NAFTA. It is assisted by a secretariat consisting of national sections. Each party funds its own secretariat staff. The secretariat is responsible, among other things, for administering panels and committees established for the settlement of disputes. See also *investor-state disputes*.

NAFTA Chapter 11: contains the *NAFTA* rules on investment. It provides for *national treatment* (Article 1102) and *most-favoured-nation treatment* (Article 1103). The better of the two treatments is to be applied to NAFTA member investors and their investments (Article 1104). Article 1105 provides for a *minimum standard of treatment*. It requires each party "to accord to investments of investors in another party treatment in accordance with international law, including fair and equitable treatment and full protection and security". Article 1106 prohibits a broad range of *performance requirements*. No party may impose export requirements, domestic content rules, domestic purchase rules, a relationship between import and export flows, measures relating the sale of goods and services to foreign exchange earnings, requirements to transfer technology or exclusive supplier provisions to specific markets. Article 1110 permits *expropriation* under certain conditions. Under Article 1116 an investor of one party may file a claim of *arbitration* against another party on the grounds that it has breached an obligation under the investment chapter or against the behaviour of state enterprises, but only within three years of the alleged breach. That is, this chapter permits *investor-state disputes*.

Nagging rights: used by some to describe provisions in trade agreements which allow a party to exhort another party to adopt new measures or commitments. The party so addressed is not contractually obliged to respond, but it may decide to take some action anyway if the request is made often enough.

Nairobi Convention: see *Convention on the Means of Prohibiting and Preventing the Illicit Import, Export and Transfer of Cultural Property* or *International Convention on Mutual Administrative Assistance for the Prevention, Investigation and Repression of Customs Offences*.

NAM: see *Non-Aligned Movement*.

NAMA: non-agricultural market access. This refers to the tariff negotiations under the *Doha Development Agenda* for goods other than agricultural ones.

Narrow competition policy: this deals with the range of practices usually covered by *antitrust laws* or by laws aimed at controlling *restrictive business practices*. The main targets of narrow competition policy are horizontal and vertical arrangements, misuse of *market power* and the control of anti-competitive conditions resulting from mergers and acquisitions. See also *competition policy* and *wider competition policy*.

National champions: companies designated in some countries to act as promoters of new technologies, new processes or new management methods from whom other companies will be able to learn. Often, they already enjoy a pre-eminent position in their sector when they are nominated. National champions usually benefit from preferential tax treatment and other support measures. They may also be exempt from some *competition laws*. The impact of such firms on the domestic markets can be considerable, but their role in international markets may be quite minor. There is no way of telling whether a national champion will fulfil the expectations of its proponents, or whether it will simply turn into a protected and uncompetitive entity. See also *infant-industry argument*, *learning-by-doing argument* and *picking winners*.

National exhaustion: the doctrine that once a product embodying *intellectual property rights* has been sold in a national market with the consent of the owner of these rights, the product can be resold or transferred within that market without the further consent of the owner of these rights. See also *exhaustion doctrine*, *international exhaustion* and *parallel imports*. [Maskus 2000]

National interest: a term describing a range of criteria, seldom described exactly or even listed in writing, whose fulfilment is considered basic to the welfare of the state. Interest or lobby groups often equate the national interest with their own aims. In a strict sense, only national governments have the competence to judge and invoke the national interest by virtue of the responsibilities assigned to them by the constitution and the laws flowing from it. There are cases when the use of this discretionary power leads to vigorous debate about their appropriateness, especially when the specific criteria triggering the national-interest clause are not spelt out. Nevertheless, there is widespread agreement that the administration of some sectors of government requires the flexibility offered by national-interest provisions. See also *Exon-Florio amendment*, *foreign investment screening*, *general exceptions*, *rule of reason* and *security exceptions*.

National policy space: another way to say that governments need flexibility in their observance of their rights and obligations under international trade or investment agreements. Many treaty provisions are in fact drafted to allow this. See also *national interest*. [World Investment Report 2003]

National schedules: the equivalent of *tariff schedules* in *GATT*, laying down commitments accepted unilaterally or through negotiation by WTO members.

National Trade Estimate Report on Foreign Trade Barriers: an annual report to the President and Congress by *USTR* as required under Section 181 of the *Trade and Tariff Act* of 1984, as amended by the *Omnibus Trade and Competitiveness Act* of 1988. The report covers (a) significant barriers to United States exports of goods, services, intellectual property and foreign direct investment, (b) the trade-distorting effects of these barriers and the value of lost trade and investment opportunities, (c) a listing of *Section 301* and other actions taken to remove these barriers, or an explanation why no action was taken, and (d) United States priorities to expand exports. See also *National Treatment Study*.

National treatment: the principle of giving other states and/or their products the same treatment as one's accords to one's own nationals and/or products. In the older literature, this principle is sometimes called "inland parity". It is a simple proposition, but it has been the cause of many disputes, partly because a strict interpretation of national treatment may in fact disadvantage foreign suppliers. The classic example of this possibility is the *wine gallon assessment*. For this reason, the national treatment principle has been refined over the years to allow for different or formally better treatment of foreign products if that is the only way to guarantee that foreign products are not disadvantaged. Sometimes countries deliberately give foreign investors better than national treatment to attract suitable firms. The basic principle underlying Article III of the *GATT*, which deals with national treatment for goods, is that of *equality of competitive opportunity*. The Article starts with the general statement that GATT members recognize that internal taxes and other charges, laws and regulations affecting the internal sale, transport and distribution, and internal quantitative regulations should not be applied to imported or domestic products to give protection to domestic production. It then says that imported products must not be subject to internal taxes or other internal charges above those applied to domestic products. The Article also requires that all laws, regulations, etc., must apply equally to imported and domestic products. Additionally, internal quantitative restrictions must be applied in a non-discriminatory way. In *intellectual property*, under the *Agreement on Trade-Related Aspects of Intellectual Property Rights* a WTO member must, in terms of Article 3, accord to the nationals of other members treatment no less favourable that it accords to its own nationals. There may be some exceptions to this because of pre-existing rights under the *Paris Convention*, the *Berne Convention* or the *Rome Convention* and the *Treaty on Intellectual Property in Respect of Integrated Circuits*. For *services*, national treatment, as described in Article XVII of the *General Agreement on Trade in Services*, is the obligation to guarantee foreign service providers and their services equivalent treatment to that given to domestic service providers and the services they supply, but only for activities inscribed in the *schedules of specific commitments on services*. Treatment for foreign suppliers may be formally different if that is required to achieve equality of opportunity. See also *economic impact criterion*, *implicit discrimination*, *minimum standard of treatment*, *most-favoured-nation treatment* and *non-discrimination*.

National treatment instrument: an *OECD* instrument. It consists of the *national treatment* section of the 1976 *Declaration on International Investment and Multinational Enterprises* and the *Third Revised Decision on National Treatment*, adopted in 1991. It requires OECD members to notify all their investment measures that are exceptions to national treatment. These notifications are examined at least every three years with a view to eliminating the measures. Members may notify measures of any other member if they consider that it is acting contrary to its undertakings. The national treatment instrument is therefore a strong promoter of non-discriminatory foreign investment in OECD countries.

National Treatment Study: published every four years under the *Omnibus Trade and Competitiveness Act* of 1988 by the United States Department of the Treasury. It contains detailed information on regulatory frameworks and market conditions in banking and securities services for a large number of countries. The *National Treatment Study* has established itself as a basic reference work for the study of global rules applying to trade in *financial services*. See also *National Trade Estimate Report on Foreign Trade Barriers*.

Natural monopoly: the supply, usually of a service, rarely a good, deemed to be most efficiently provided when there is only one supplier. Until quite recently gas, water, electricity, telecommunications and mail delivery services were thought to be natural monopolies. Few would argue so now. It is now not too difficult to supply these services under competitive conditions with considerable benefits to the consumer. See also *competition* and *competition law*.

Natural persons: people, as distinct from *juridical persons* or *legal persons*, such as companies. If they are service suppliers to other members of the *General Agreement on Trade in Services*, they have rights under the Agreement.

Natural resource-based products: NRBPs. In the GATT environment these include minerals, ores, fish and fisheries products, forest products, timber and paper. They were the subject of a separate negotiating group in the *Uruguay Round*.

Natural trading blocs: a term used by some economists for modelling purposes to describe countries which are close together, have low transport costs and that therefore trade with each other.

Natural trading partners fallacy: the view that the concept of *natural trading partners*, regardless of whether it is based on geographic proximity, complementary economies or whether the prospective participants already are major trading partners, has limited value in analysing whether a proposed *free-trade area* will lead to increasing trade between the prospective partners. The statistical evidence certainly appears to indicate that geographical proximity is no guide to the intensity of trade within the free-trade area. [Schiff and Winters 2003]

Natural-trading-partners hypothesis: the proposition that *free-trade areas* between countries already conducting the bulk of their trade with each other yield the greatest gain. See also *natural trading partners fallacy*.

Necessity test: sometimes used to refer to the steps necessary to justify invoking the *general exceptions* of the *GATT*. WTO members may adopt or enforce measures necessary to protect public morals (Article XX(a)), necessary to protect human, animal or plant life or health (XX(b)), necessary to secure compliance with laws or regulations not inconsistent with the provisions of the GATT (XX(d)), and restricting exports of domestic materials necessary to ensure the supply of essential quantities to domestic industry (XX(e)), provided that this does not constitute arbitrary or unjustifiable discrimination between countries or a disguised restriction on international trade. The GATT *security exceptions* (Article XXI) allow WTO members to take any action they consider necessary for the protection of their essential security interests. The *General Agreement on Trade in Services* contains similar necessity tests in Article XIV (General Exceptions) and Article XIVbis (Security Exceptions). See also *least-trade-restrictive-alternative test* and *means-and-ends test*.

Negative comity: also called traditional comity. It is a term used, for example, in the administration of *competition policy*. It means that, under the terms of relevant bilateral arrangements, a country has to take account of the interests of the other country when it initiates an action under its *competition laws*. See also *positive comity*.

Negative deindustrialization: occurs when labour no longer needed in industry cannot find productive employment in the services sector. This results in persistent unemployment. See also *positive deindustrialization*. [Trade and Development Report 2003]

Negative integration: the removal of barriers to *cross-border trade* without the creation of new regulatory frameworks. See also *positive integration*.

Negative listings: a method used in *free-trade agreements* to list commitments in services and investment. The starting point for this method is that an investment or a service supply is permitted unless it is restricted through an inscription in the *schedules of commitments*. The inscription specifies the reason for the restriction, usually a limitation on *market access* or *national treatment*. Investment chapters often use a more elaborate form of negative listing called the *two-annexe method*. In this case, the first annexe, the list of *non-conforming measures*, lists all sectors and activities that are not in full conformity with the agreement. Again, it describes the reason for this. Non-conforming measures are expected to be brought into conformity with the agreement over time. The second annexe, the *reserved list*, lists sectors and activities for which the government wishes to retain flexibility of regulation. It reserves the right to alter the rules at any time and to make them more restrictive. Inclusion of a sector in the reserved list does not necessarily mean that foreign investment is prohibited in that area. Developed countries have used negative listing for their commitments on financial services under the *General Agreement on Trade in Services*. See also *positive listings*.

Negative margin of dumping: in *dumping* investigations, a finding that the *export price* is greater than the *normal value*. In other words, no dumping has occurred. See also *positive margin of dumping*.

Negative reciprocity: this term is now of historical interest only. It describes the practice followed by the United States and some others in the nineteenth- and early twentieth-centuries of raising tariffs against those countries that were seen as maintaining unreasonably high tariffs themselves. Negative reciprocity was, however, regarded mainly as a market-opening mechanism. Proponents of this practice took scant regard of the generally high level of their own tariff, and the basis of their thinking was always *mercantilism*.

Negligible imports: defined in Article 5.8 of the *Anti-Dumping Agreement* as a volume of dumped imports from a particular country accounting for less than 3% of imports of the *like product* in the importing country. If this situation applies, an anti-dumping investigation will have to cease immediately in respect of such a country. The situation is different if the dumped imports of the like product from several countries combined exceed 7% of imports. In this case, imports will no longer be considered negligible even though each country looked at separately accounts for less than 3% of dumped imports of the like product. See also *anti-dumping measures*, *de minimis dumping* and *dumping*.

Negotiated protectionism: a term sometimes used to describe the growing acceptance in the early 1980s of negotiated instruments for restricting trade, such as *orderly marketing arrangements* and *voluntary restraint arrangements*.

Negotiating coin: what one is willing to give away in negotiations in order to secure something one would like. Sometimes one's negotiating coin is imaginary, but it becomes important in questions such as the payment for *autonomous liberalization*. See also *bargaining tariff*.

Negotiating credits: the informal practice in WTO negotiations whereby countries take into account unilateral tariff reductions made by other participants before a fixed date, usually a date associated with the start of the negotiations. The practice is meant to ensure that participants do not have to lower their barriers without receiving adequate *compensation* in the form of lower barriers by others. In this way the practice encourages countries to liberalize their trade whenever the time is appropriate. The entire concept is based on the erroneous idea that trade liberalization is a cost to the liberalizing country.

Negotiating Group on Basic Telecommunications: (NGBT). Established by the *Council for Trade in Services* to achieve the progressive liberalization of trade in telecommunication transport networks. Its work resulted in the *Agreement on Basic Telecommunications Services*. See also *Fourth Protocol to the General Agreement on Trade in Services*.

Negotiating Group on Maritime Transport Services: see *maritime transport services*.

Negotiating rights: one of the purposes of the WTO is to act as a forum for the reduction and elimination of trade barriers. This is done through negotiations, but the right to engage in them is subject to certain rules. The bulk of barrier reductions is now done through *multilateral trade negotiations*, the so-called rounds, and sometimes *sectoral trade negotiations*. All WTO members have the right to participate in them. In other circumstances, they may not have automatic negotiating rights. Whether they do may depend on the fulfilment of some conditions, including the *principal supplier rule* and the *substantial supplier rule*. The entry on *renegotiation of tariffs* contains instances where negotiating rights may arise. See also *initial negotiating rights*.

Neighbouring rights: exclusive rights, also called related rights, of performers, producers of phonograms and broadcasters. Such rights have historically been considered to "neighbour" on the traditional areas of copyright protection. Neighbouring rights are said to relate to derivative subject matter (e.g. a recording company recording a musical composition) where it may be relatively more difficult to identify the creative person deserving of reward. See also *Berne Convention* and *copyright*.

Neo-mercantilism: a *trade policy* founded on the belief that governments need to control trade and industry to secure national prosperity. Specifically, neo-mercantilism seeks to promote enhanced domestic production accompanied by rising employment, to increase exports and to decrease imports. See also *infant-industry argument*, *mercantilism* and *pop mercantilism*.

NEPAD: see *New Partnership for Africa's Development*.

Net cost value method: one of the methods used to establish whether a good imported from another party to a *free-trade agreement* has undergone *substantial transformation* and qualifies for the *preferential tariff*. In the free-trade agreement between Canada and Chile the formula is:

$$RVC = \frac{NC - VNM}{NC} \times 100$$

where RVC is the *regional value content* expressed as a percentage, NC is the net cost of the good and VNM is the value of *non-originating materials* used by the producer in the production of the good. The net cost is the total cost incurred in respect of all goods produced by a producer minus any costs related to sales promotion, marketing, after-sales service, royalties, shipping, packaging and non-allowable interest payments. The resulting net cost incurred in producing all goods is then "reasonably" allocated to the good in question.

New-age agreement: sometimes used by Japanese negotiators to refer to *free-trade agreements* supplemented by extensive provisions for cooperation in related economic fields, such as those contained in the *Japan-Singapore Economic Partnership Agreement for a New Age*, concluded in 2001.

Newcomer provision: systems for the allocation of *quotas* under *import licensing* regimes sometimes are based on the ability of a quota holder to fill previous allocations. An arrangement purely based on historical performance would prevent prospective new entrants from obtaining a quota since they have no performance to point to. This problem can be remedied through a newcomer provision which ensures that part of the global quota is open to competition from new entrants. The *Anti-Dumping Agreement* also contains a newcomer provision. Here it means that an anti-dumping order against products from a certain country cannot be applied automatically against new exporters (i.e. exporters not in the market during the anti-dumping investigation) of the same product from that country. However, a review may be conducted to ascertain whether they should also be subject to anti-dumping duties. New exporters will then have to show that they are not related to any of the exporters from that already subject to anti-dumping duties.

New commercial policy instrument: NCPI. A *regulation* first adopted by the *European Community* in 1984. It was substantially revised in 1994 and issued as the *Trade Barriers Regulation*, partly to bring it into line with the European Community's obligations under the WTO instruments. The objective of the regulation was to give European companies and European Community member states the means to request the European Commission to seek the elimination of trade barriers, described as obstacles to trade, maintained by third countries. The NCPI appears to have been modelled to some extent on *Section 301* under United States law. It differs from Section 301, however, in that it emphasized the protection of the European Community against foreign practices rather than the opening up of other markets. [Regulation (EC) No 3286/94]

New economy: the economic boom caused in the late 1990s by the perception that massive investment in information technology and extensive use of the internet would give firms doing so a decisive commercial advantage. Its premise seems to have been that those engaged in the *old economy* would not be able to adapt to a rapidly changing environment where business would be conducted over the Internet. The boom's symbol was the *dot.com* company. Many who invested in this boom later wished they had never heard of it. See also *first-mover advantage*. [Gadrey 2003]

Newer ASEAN members: Cambodia, Laos, Myanmar and Vietnam. They are also known as the CLMV countries. See *ASEAN*.

New industrial policies: NIPs. This is a term sometimes used for targeted industrial development policies that differ both from *laissez-faire* policies which allow the market to determine the broad lines of industrial development and simple protectionism which seeks to give industries a shield against competition from imports. NIPs include governmental measures to increase savings and capital investment, compulsory or guided sharing of technology among enterprises, forced mergers to promote efficiency, shared research and development facilities, possibly subsidized, etc. See also *national champions*.

New international division of labour: an evolution of the concept of the *international division of labour* in which price competition is no longer the sole or dominant determinant of how a firm manufactures its products. The system in part reflects a recognition of the power of the consumers, but it also gives them many pseudo-choices. Analysts say that this system requires, among others, product flexibility, rapid innovation, a multiskilled workforce and closer integration of production schedules and product development of related production units. Corporations distribute their production units internationally in the way that best satisfies their competing requirements. See also *globalization*, *product cycle theory* and *transnational corporations*.

New International Economic Order: NIEO. A campaign launched in the early 1970s by developing countries to bring about radical changes in the international economic order. It was based on a perception that the economic and technological progress since the end of World War II had not enriched the lives of people in developing countries in any meaningful way. Developing countries dependent on commodity exports in particular felt that they were caught by the early 1970s between the so-called revolution of rising expectations and falling commodity prices. A perception was also building up that development through concessional, but conditional, loans only increased the debt burden of developing countries and thus put them increasingly at the mercy of developed country policies and actions. Demands for the NIEO gained considerable impetus through the decision by the 1973 *OPEC* ministerial conference to raise oil prices fourfold. The evident success of this policy in increasing the revenues of OPEC member countries encouraged the view that other commodities would lend themselves to the furthering of developing country aspirations. The NIEO consisted of a *Declaration on the Establishment of a New International Economic Order* and a *Programme of Action on the Establishment of a New International Economic Order* in the form of General Assembly resolutions 3201 (S-VI) and 3202 (S-VI), respectively. The *Declaration* was concerned particularly with the problems of raw materials and development, noting that since 1970 the world economy had experienced a series of grave crises with severe repercussions on developing countries. It stressed the reality of interdependence of all countries and proposed a new international economic order based on the following principles, given here in abbreviated form: (a) sovereign equality of states and self-determination of all peoples, (b) broadest cooperation of all states to banish prevailing disparities and to secure prosperity, (c) full and effective participation on the basis of equality in the solving of world economic problems in the common interest of all countries, (d) the right of every country to adopt the economic and social system it deems the most appropriate for its own development, (e) full and permanent sovereignty of states over their natural resources and all economic activities, including the right to nationalization or transfer of ownership to its nationals, (f) the right of all states under foreign occupation to restitution and full compensation for the exploitation of natural resources, (g) regulation and supervision of the activities of transnational corporations by taking measures in the interest of the national economy, (h) the right of developing countries under colonial domination to achieve their liberation and regain effective control over their natural resources and economic activities, (i) extension of assistance to developing countries under foreign domination or subjected to other coercive measures, (j) just and equitable relationship between the prices of raw materials, primary commodities and manufactures exported by developing countries and their capital goods and other imports with the aim of improving their unsatisfactory **terms of trade**, (k) active and unconditional assistance to developing countries by the whole international community, (l) a reformed international monetary system assisting the developing countries and ensuring an adequate flow of resources to them, (m) improved competitiveness of natural materials facing competition from synthetic materials, (n) preferential and non-reciprocal treatment for developing countries in all fields of international economic cooperation, (o) securing favourable conditions for the transfer of financial resources to developing countries, (p) access for them to science and technology achievements, promotion of the **transfer of technology** and the creation of indigenous technology, (q) an end to the waste of natural resources, including food products, (r) developing countries to concentrate all their technical resources for development, (s) strengthened technical cooperation among developing countries as well as through economic, trade and financial activities, and (t) facilitating the role of producer associations in promoting sustained growth in the world economy and accelerated development. The *Programme of Action* was equally ambitious. It sought solutions to the fundamental problems of raw materials and primary commodities as related to trade and development, and the food crisis. It also proposed a long list of trade actions, including *compensatory financing arrangements*, an improved *GSP* and the setting up of commodity *buffer stocks*. Improvements were sought also in transport and insurance and the international monetary system. Many of these items were pursued in *UNCTAD*, leading, for example, in 1976 to the proposal for the establishment of a *Common Fund for Commodities* and the *Integrated Programme for Commodities*. Aspects of the NIEO ran into fierce opposition from developed countries, but some of the major developed-country commodity producers were seduced by the prospect of higher export returns if the commodity measures could be made to work. Other international organizations, including the GATT in the concurrent *Tokyo Round*, also paid greater attention to developing country views, but the NIEO as a program had run its course by the early 1980s. See also *Charter of Economic Rights and Duties of States* and *North-South dialogue*. [Bhagwati 1977, Sauvant and Hasenpflug 1977, Singh 1977]

Newly Independent States: this group of countries comprises Armenia, Azerbaijan, Belarus, Georgia, Kazakhstan, Kyrgyz Republic, Moldovia, Tajikistan, Turkmenistan, Ukraine and Uzbekistan which were part of the USSR. See also *Commonwealth of Independent States* which in addition includes Russia.

Newly industrializing economies: also called newly industrializing countries. A term used particularly in the 1980s for developing economies which were transforming significant parts of their economies to a stage where they had many of the characteristics of industrialized economies. Examples of such economies include Hong Kong, Mexico, Malaysia, Republic of Korea, Taiwan and Singapore.

Newly liberalizing countries: a term for the countries of Central and Eastern Europe, those making up the *Commonwealth of Independent States*, and China which are transforming their previously *centrally-planned economies* into *market economies*. At the same time, their centralized foreign trade regimes are being liberalized.

New Miyazawa Initiative: the finance package made available by Japan to countries affected by the 1997 Asian economic crisis. Main elements of the initiative were $30 billion in short-term and long-term and funds, purchase of bonds issued by Asian governments and provision of concessional yen loans. See also *Chiang Mai Initiative*.

New Partnership for Africa's Development: NEPAD. Adopted by African leaders at Abuja on 23 October 2001. It contains, among other chapters, a program of action for achieving sustainable development in the twenty-first century with the long-term objectives of (a) eradicating poverty in Africa and to place African countries on a path of sustainable growth and development to halt the marginalization of Africa in the globalization process and (b) to promote the role of women in all activities. One of the means identified by the program of action to reach these goals is the market access initiative. This envisages diversification of production in African economies, improving the performance of the mining sector, increasing the competitiveness of the manufacturing sector, developing tourism, promotion of a sound environment for private-sector activities, promotion of African exports, enhanced participation in the world trading system and efforts to improve access to the markets of industrialized countries through the removal of their non-tariff barriers. See also *G8 Africa Action Plan*.

New protectionism: a term common in the 1980s. It was used to refer to measures such as *quantitative restrictions*, *voluntary restraint arrangements*, *orderly marketing arrangements*, etc., in contrast to protective action expressed through high tariffs. See *grey-area measures*. [Salvatore 1987]

New trade agenda: a term used by some to describe the *market access* issues still needing resolution. From this perspective, the traditional trade agenda is represented by efforts to reduce border measures consisting of *tariffs* and *non-tariff measures*. The new trade agenda, on the other hand, is aimed more at impediments inside the market, such as standards, excessive reliance on *sanitary and phytosanitary measures*, and private and public anti-competitive practices. To some extent, the new trade agenda overlaps with the *new trade issues*, but in other respects it seeks to promote optimal results from existing multilateral trade agreements. See also *technical barriers to trade*.

New trade issues: issues arising because of the emergence of new trading patterns, new products, new technologies or the confluence of *trade policy* and social policies. The term "new trade issues" often simply means that there is not yet a formal multilateral trade framework in existence for dealing with relevant matters or that they have only recently been taken up within the WTO. New trade issues include *trade and competition*, *trade and illicit payments*, *trade and investment* and *trade and labour standards*. Some add *trade and environment* to this list, but the decision to establish a *Committee on Trade and Environment* in the WTO has persuaded many that this is now an established, if unresolved, issue. Intermittently there are suggestions that *trade and culture*, *trade and foreign exchange* and *trade and taxation* should also be looked at. Since the *Doha Ministerial Conference* the WTO has had a work program on *trade and the transfer of technology*. See also *Singapore issues*.

New trade order: in contemporary literature this term refers commonly to the global trading system that began with the establishment of the WTO, but it does not have a precise meaning. Some use it to describe what in their view would be a desirable trading system, if only certain instruments or rules could be negotiated.

New trade theory: an approach to the analysis of international trade that had its origin in the "Leontief Paradox". In 1953 the American economist Wassily Leontief found in his analysis of input-output statistics that the United States, a capital-rich country, exported labour-intensive products more successfully than capital-intensive products. This was contrary to what he had expected under the *Heckscher-Ohlin theorem* which is a restatement of the theory of *comparative advantage*. Attempts by economists to explain this eventually led to the new trade theory which also takes into account the influence of factors such as technology and research and development. These factors can allow a country to acquire a comparative advantage where before it had none. An important medium-term result was the *product cycle theory* which appeared in 1967. The final stage was the *strategic trade theory* of which there are differing interpretations. The theory certainly has been used to defend *targeting* and *picking winners*. That does not appear generally to be the aim of economists supporting it. See also *competitive advantage*.

New Transatlantic Agenda: endorsed on 3 December 1995 at a *European Union*-United States summit in Madrid. It enables the two sides to join forces on a wide range of international economic, social and political issues. Objective III of its four objectives deals with strengthening the world trading system and achieving closer economic cooperation. It aims at (a) moves to ensure that the WTO works as well as intended and cooperation on the *new trade issues*, (b) efforts to achieve further bilateral reduction, or elimination, of tariffs in industrial products and to accelerate reductions due under the *Uruguay Round*, and (c) concrete steps to remove regulatory and other obstacles to transatlantic trade through the creation of the *New Transatlantic Marketplace*. The other three objectives are promoting peace, development and democracy around the world, responding to global challenges, and building bridges across the Atlantic. See also *Transatlantic Business Dialogue*.

New Transatlantic Marketplace: one of the objectives of the *New Transatlantic Agenda* with a work program covering a joint study to facilitate trade in goods and services and eliminating *tariff* and *non-tariff barriers*; confidence building through resolving bilateral trade issues; standards, certification and regulatory issues; veterinary and plant health issues; *government procurement*; *intellectual property rights*; expansion of the bilateral dialogue on *financial services*; conclusion of a customs cooperation and mutual assistance agreement; expanding the bilateral Information Society Dialogue and cooperation on information technology and telecommunications; deepening cooperation in competition matters; discussion of data protection issues; expanded cooperation on air and maritime transport matters; intensified cooperation on energy-related issues; biotechnology; and safety and health. See also *Transatlantic Business Dialogue*.

New York Convention: the *United Nations Convention on the Recognition and Enforcement of Foreign Arbitral Awards*, adopted on 10 June 1958. Article II requires the contracting states to recognize an agreement in writing under which parties undertake to submit to *arbitration* differences which have arisen between them. Article III requires each contracting state to recognize arbitral awards as binding and enforce them under the conditions set out in subsequent articles of the Convention.

New Zealand Australia Free Trade Agreement: NAFTA. The trade agreement governing trade relations between Australia and New Zealand from 1966 to 1982. It achieved significantly liberalized trade between the two countries, but well short of free trade. It was replaced on 1 January 1983 by *ANZCERTA (Australia New Zealand Closer Economic Relations Trade Agreement)*.

NGBT: see *Negotiating Group on Basic Telecommunications*.

NGMTS: see *maritime transport services*.

NGO: see *non-governmental organization* and *civil society*.

NG-5: Negotiating Group of 5. This is the same as the P5 and the Five Interested Parties (FIPS). It was formed during the negotiations on agriculture under the *Doha Development Agenda*. Its members are Australia, Brazil, *European Community*, India and the United States.

Nice Agreement Concerning the International Classification of Goods and Services for the Purposes of the Registration of Marks: concluded in 1957 and last revised in 1979. It created a system of 42 classes of goods and services which is used for the assessment and registration of trademarks. The Agreement is administered by *WIPO*.

Noerr-Pennington doctrine: the principle in United States law that attempts to lobby a governmental or administrative body with the aim of influencing legislation or law enforcement cannot be prosecuted under the *Sherman Act* even if the lobbying has anti-competitive aims. See also *antitrust laws*.

Nominal rate of assistance: defined by the Australian Productivity Commission as "the percentage change in gross returns per unit of output relative to the (hypothetical) situation of no assistance". [Productivity Commission 2000]

Nominal rate of protection: indicates the extent by which the domestic price of a product exceeds the price at the border (i.e. before the application of any customs duties). It as usually expressed as a percentage. See also *effective rate of protection* and *price wedges*.

Nominal tariff: the tariff rate appearing in a country's *tariff schedule* for a given product. It may differ from the *applied tariff rates* (the tariff rate actually levied by the customs administration when the product is imported). See also *binding*.

Non-actionable subsidies: a class of subsidies identified in the WTO *Agreement on Subsidies and Countervailing Measures*. It includes assistance to research and development, assistance to disadvantaged regions and assistance to promote the adaptation of existing facilities to new, more burdensome, environmental requirements. The Agreement describes in some detail how the subsidies are to be interpreted. If another WTO member believes that a subsidy which otherwise would be non-actionable is causing serious adverse effects, it may seek a determination and recommendation on the matter. The Agreement does not apply to agricultural subsidies. These are covered by the *Agreement on Agriculture*. See also *actionable subsidies*, *prohibited subsidies* and *subsidies*.

Non-agricultural market access: NAMA. Tariff negotiations on products other than those covered by the *Agreement on Agriculture*. This term was created in the preparatory phase for the *Seattle WTO Ministerial*.

Non-agricultural products: in the *non-agricultural market access* negotiations, products not covered by Annex 1 of the *Agreement on Agriculture*. Fish and forestry products are therefore non-agricultural, along with industrial products in general.

Non-Aligned Movement: NAM. A group of about 115 members, mainly developing countries, which has its origin in the 1955 Asia-Africa Conference, held in

Bandung, Indonesia. The first NAM summit was convened in Belgrade in 1961. Membership criteria include the requirement that the joining country should have adopted an independent policy based on the coexistence of states with different political and social systems and on non-alignment or should be showing a trend in favour of such a policy. NAM's early years were dominated by political issues, but since the early 1990s it has increasingly paid attention to global economic problems. See also *Group of 77*.

Non-application: Article XIII of the *WTO Agreement* lays down that this Agreement and the other agreements administered by the WTO do not apply between two members if either of them does not consent to their application at the time either of them becomes a member. Non-application is therefore available only at the time a *customs territory* accedes to the WTO. See also *denial of benefits*.

Non-automatic import licensing: an *import licensing* system under which it is necessary to obtain a permit each time a designated good is imported. See also *automatic import licensing*.

Non-conforming measures: in a *free-trade agreement* using *negative listings* for scheduling commitments concerning services and investment laws, regulations, policies, etc., these are measures that do not comply fully with the provisions of the agreement when it enters into force. In the case of investment, the provisions usually cover *national treatment*, *most-favoured-nation treatment*, *performance requirements* and senior management and boards of directors. In the case of services, the applicable provisions usually are national treatment, most-favoured-nation treatment, *market access* and *local presence*. Some agreements limit themselves to national treatment, market access and local presence. The listings explain why the measure is non-conforming. The parties usually agree that such measures will be brought into conformance with the agreement over time. See also *positive list*, *ratchet effect*, *reserved list* and *two-annex method*.

Non-discrimination: treating all of one's trading partners in the same way. This is a fundamental concept in the multilateral trade framework. A country may not discriminate among foreign supplier countries, and it may not apply adverse discriminatory treatment to products once they have entered its territory legally. The WTO rules permit some exceptions to this concept under strictly defined conditions. For example, members of a *free-trade area* or a *customs union* may discriminate against non-members in the application of tariff rates. WTO members may also maintain preferential tariff schemes for developing countries. See also *GSP*, *most-favoured-nation treatment* and *national treatment*.

Non-dutiable goods: goods that are not subject to customs duties on entering or leaving a *customs territory*. See also *free list*.

Non-economic objectives: see *non-trade concerns*.

Non-equity-based investment: investments in the form of licensing agreements, management contracts, production-sharing arrangements, risk-sharing contracts, international sub-contracting, licensing agreements, etc. See also *foreign direct investment*, *investment* and *portfolio investment*.

Non-establishment: see *right of non-establishment*.

Non-governmental organizations: NGOs. A category of national or international organizations that are independent of governments. NGOs have a specific mandate (e.g. promotion of human rights, protection of the environment, advancement of women, the professional development of members, etc.). These are sometimes called "advocacy" NGOs because they seek to influence the behaviour of governments and *intergovernmental organizations*. Others deliver services. These are classified as "operational" NGOs. Most NGOs do not seek to make a profit, but they usually charge a membership fee. Sometimes they ask for, and receive, business or government funding. In many cases, NGO membership is available to anyone who agrees to support its aims. Professional bodies usually require a minimum standard of qualifications. See also *civil society* and *inter-governmental organizations*.

Non-market economies: similar to *centrally planned economies*, but sometimes with the difference that some sectors of these economies may show all or most characteristics of a similar sector in a *market economy*.

Non-originating goods: in the administration of *rules of origin* for *preferential trade agreements* these are goods not receiving preferential treatment because they are deemed not to be the product of the country normally receiving preferential access. See also *originating goods*.

Non-originating materials: components of a good traded under a *preferential trade arrangement* which do not originate in the territory of a partner to the arrangement.

Non-paper: an informal proposal, usually on plain paper, issued by a country acting alone or in a group, aimed to test whether a new approach to a problem is worth pursuing. A on-paper is a useful way to deal with deadlock since its rejection is not seen as reflecting adversely on its sponsor.

Non-preferential rules of origin: refers to *rules of origin* applied by an importing country to all goods traded under *most-favoured-nation* conditions. These are also called *MFN rules of origin*. A joint work program is under way in the WTO and the *World Customs Organization* to harmonize non-preferential rules of origin.

Non-price predation: the action of seeking to drive efficient competitors out of business through abusive litigation and other means of imposing major costs on them. Abusive litigation would, for example, be aimed at ensuring that competitors could not use some crucial *intellectual property rights*, rather than ensuring that these rights are protected. See also *predatory pricing*.

Non-product-related process and production: a way of looking at the production process which concentrates on the finished product and which, in a hypothetical extreme case, would pay no attention to how the product is made. What matters is the result of the production process. An example would be the production of a steel bar. Examined from this perspective, it would not matter whether the bar was made from recycled iron and steel, or whether it was made in a process beginning with iron ore and coking coal. Of course, the steelmaker would still have to meet, for example, health and safety standards, and the steel would have to meet the applicable technical specifications. See also *product-related process and production*.

Non-qualifying operations: see *insufficient operations*.

Non-reciprocal free-trade area: see *free-trade area*.

Non-reciprocity: in trade negotiations, acceptance of the principle that an offer or undertaking by a party to do something need not be matched, either wholly or partly, by the party standing to benefit from the offer. This principle is contained, for example, in *Part IV of the GATT* (Article XXXVI:8) which states that the "developed *contracting parties* do not expect *reciprocity* for commitments made by them in trade negotiations to reduce or remove tariffs and other barriers to the trade of the less-developed contracting parties". See also *Enabling Clause*.

Non-tariff barriers: see *non-tariff measures*.

Non-tariff distortions: adverse influences on trade flows caused by the existence of *non-tariff measures*.

Non-tariff measures: NTMs. Measures other than *tariffs* applied by governments at the border that determine the extent to which a good has access to the import market. This term is used by many in preference to *non-tariff barriers* (NTBs) because it conveys more clearly the fact that many of these measures are not meant to be import barriers, and that they do not place the imported good at a disadvantage. An example of this reasoning is the case where an NTM would merely consist of applying the rules governing domestically-produced goods to imported goods also. This would be the case with product standards agreed internationally. Assuming these standards were met, the good could be imported to whatever extent would make commercial sense. From this perspective, calling the measure an NTM would be appropriate. If, however, there was an element of putting the foreign good at a disadvantage, it would be better to refer to the measure as an NTB. Many commentators prefer to use NTM instead of NTB because the former is less likely to prejudge whether a given measure has a protectionist effect. In practice, though, the two terms are often used interchangeably. Laird and Vossenar have suggested the following classification of NTMs: (a) *measures to control the volume of imports*, including both quantitative restrictions and export restraint arrangements, (b) *measures to control the price of imported goods*, such as *trigger price* mechanisms, *variable levies*, *anti-dumping measures*, *countervailing duties*, etc., (c) *monitoring measures including price and volume investigations and surveillance*, (d) *production and export measures*, mainly *subsidies* or taxation measures, and (e) *technical barriers*, such as various standards imposed for health and safety reasons. Deardorff and Stern have proposed a different classification. They suggest (a) *quantitative restrictions and similar specific limitations* such as *import quotas*, export limitations, licensing, prohibition, etc., (b) *non-tariff charges and related policies affecting imports*, including variable levies, *advance deposits*, anti-dumping duties, countervailing duties and *border tax adjustments*, (c) *government participation in trade, restrictive practices, and more general government policies*, such as subsidies and other aids, government procurement policies, *state trading*, *competition poli-cies*, etc., (d) *customs procedures and administrative practices*, and (e) *technical barriers to trade*, including safety and industrial standards, health and sanitary regulations, packaging and labelling regulations, and advertising and media reg-ulations. Strictly speaking, anti-dumping duties and countervailing measures are non-tariff measures to the extent that investigations and related procedures may cause a *trade chill effect*. In a quantitative assessment of non-tariff measures, any duties imposed after an investigation would count as a *tariff*. See also *Agree-ment on Safeguards* and *Tariffication*. [Deardorff and Stern 1997, Laird and Vossenar 1991, Laird 1997]

Non-tariff preferences: discrimination in favour of some trading partners in the use of *non-tariff measures*. This sometimes happens under *free-trade agreements*.

Non-tradeables: goods and services that are not, or only rarely, traded interna-tionally because they are abundant and cheap everywhere or because the cost of support services needed for trading them would exceed the value of the product in the importing market. A list of non-tradeables would change considerably over the years and probably become shorter. Two examples will suffice. Sand and gravel, at one time quarried locally and considered non-tradeable, have be-come tradeable for a range of reasons, including more stringent environmental measures governing their extraction. Haircuts remain among the non-tradeable services even though a person living very close to a border may find it con-venient to hop across the border for a haircut. See also *semi-tradeables* and *tradeables*.

Non-trade concerns: used in the agricultural trade negotiations as a more neu-tral expression than, for example, *multifunctionality*. The preamble of the *Agreement on Agriculture* specifies *food security* and environmental protec-tion as examples. Also cited by WTO members are rural development and employment, and poverty alleviation. See also *non-trade objectives in trade policy*.

Non-trade objectives in trade policy: this refers to the formulation of trade rules to achieve aims other than the traditional goals of freer, predictable and non-discriminatory trade. Such aims can include the protection of the environment, the promotion of *core labour standards* or *human rights*, support for democratic values and social and political ideas more generally. Some also include rules concerning competition and investment in this category, but others dispute this because of the frequently complementary relationship between *trade policy* and investment or competition. Arguments about the validity of non-trade objectives are often fierce. A basic principle seems to be that my concerns are legitimate, but yours are suspect and probably protectionist. See also *animal rights*, *democracy clause*, *human rights clause*, *multifunctionality*, *trade and competition*, *trade and environment*, *trade and human rights*, *trade and investment* and *trade and labour standards*.

Non-violation: action taken under the WTO dispute settlement rules falls into one of two categories. The first is violation cases. The plaintiff believes that the defendant has violated one or more of his obligations under the WTO rules. Most disputes are of this kind. The second category covers non-violation cases. Here the plaintiff does not argue that the defendant has acted contrary to the rules and, indeed, may agree that they were observed to the letter. The plaintiff will seek to show, however, that the defendant has altered some other conditions with the result that he was denied a benefit available him before the action was taken. In other words, the defendant may have had "nullified or impaired" what he considers his reasonable expectations by a measure either consistent with the rules or not subject to them. An example of this would be to cancel out the lowering of a tariff with some other measure either consistent with the rules or not covered by them. *Australian subsidy on ammonium sulphate*, *Kodak-Fuji case* and *oilseeds* are examples of non-violation cases. See also *nullification or impairment*. [Cho 1998, Mavroidis 2000]

Nordic countries: refers to Denmark, Finland, Iceland, Norway and Sweden and their autonomous territories associated with them. The latter are Åland (Finland), Faroe Islands and Greenland (both Denmark). They cooperate officially through the Nordic Council, a parliamentary cooperation body, and the Nordic Council of Ministers, a governmental cooperation body. The two bodies maintain separate secretariats in Copenhagen.

Normal trade relations: the term now often used by the United States instead of **most-favoured nation treatment**. See also *permanent normal trade relations* and *temporary normal trade relations*.

Normal value: a key concept used in determining whether *dumping* has taken place. GATT Article VI condemns the introduction of products into the commerce of another member at less than normal value. Article 2 of the *Anti-Dumping Agreement* sets out the meaning of "normal value" and the procedures for its determination. A product is considered dumped, or introduced at less than normal value, if its price, when being exported in the *ordinary course of trade*, is less than the comparable price for the like product when destined for consumption in the exporting country. If there are no sales in the domestic market of the exporting country or if these sales do not permit a proper comparison, the export price to an appropriate and representative third country may be used. A third method is using the cost of production in the country of origin plus a reasonable amount for administrative, selling and general costs and for profits. Precise rules are available if the product is found not to have been exported in the ordinary course of trade, or for trade that may have been short term only. If no export price is available, or if it appears that the export price is unreliable because of an association between the exporter and the importer or a third party, the export price may be constructed on the basis of the price at which the imported products are sold to an independent buyer. The comparison between export price and normal value must be made under similar conditions, with allowance for unavoidable differences. See also *anti-dumping measures*.

North: see *developed country* and *North-South dialogue*.

North American Agreement on Environmental Cooperation: see *NAFTA*.

North American Agreement on Labor Cooperation: an agreement containing binding obligations signed by the Canada, Mexico and United States in September 1993 as part of their obligations under *NAFTA* with the main objective of improving working conditions and living standards in the territory of each party. The parties to the Agreement undertake to promote eleven labour principles which include, in addition to the *core labour standards*, the right to strike, minimum employment standards, equal pay for women and men, prevention of occupational injuries and illnesses, compensation in cases of occupational injuries and illnesses and protection of migrant workers. The Agreement permits trade measures to enforce the observance of standards relating to occupational safety and health, *child labour* or minimum wage technical standards, but not the core labour standards such as freedom of association or the right to bargain collectively. The administration of the Agreement is supervised by a Commission for Labour Cooperation consisting of a ministerial council and a secretariat.

North American Free Trade Agreement: see *NAFTA*.

North Atlantic Free Trade Area: a proposal for a *free-trade area* between the United States and the European Economic Community which appeared sporadically in the 1960s. Irreconcilable differences concerning agricultural trade, the friction it was meant to resolve above all else, meant that it did not reach the negotiating table. See also *TAFTA*.

North East Asia Free-Trade Area: NEAFTA. Proposed in 1999 by Prime Minister Obuchi of Japan as a long-term project for closer regional economic integration. Prospective members could include Japan, Republic of Korea, China, Hong Kong and others. No timetable for negotiations exists. See also *East Asia Free-Trade Agreement*.

North-South: A Programme for Survival: see *Brandt Report*.

North-South dialogue: a process of discussions and negotiations, frequently acrimonious and fruitless, between the developed or industrialized countries (the North) and the developing countries (the South). Some see it as having begun in the early 1960s with, for example, the *Alliance for Progress* and the moves leading to the establishment of *UNCTAD* (United Nations Conference on Trade and Development) in 1964 and the concurrent formation of the *Group of 77*. Others date the beginning of the North-South dialogue to the *Conference on International Economic Cooperation* (CIEC), convened by France in 1975, which itself concluded in 1977 without any concrete results. The more or less formal end of the dialogue came with the 1980 Special Session of the *United Nations General Assembly*. There is little disagreement on this point. Whatever exact starting point one accepts for the North-South dialogue, it followed the arrival in the United Nations and its specialized agencies of a large number of newly-independent developing countries. Their numbers allowed them increasingly to define or influence the work program of these bodies. This, coupled with the view advocated strongly by many developing countries that their legitimate concerns about development, economic growth and participation in the global trading system were not being taken seriously by the developed countries, led by the early 1970s to a realization by the North that something had to be done. The *OPEC* decision in 1973 to quadruple the price of oil provided an additional incentive for this. What followed was a range of political and economic initiatives, many of which did not endure. In outline, in 1974 the United Nations General Assembly passed a resolution on the *New International Economic Order*, in effect a vast claim for the transfer of resources from the North to the South. The adoption of the *Charter of Economic Rights and Duties of States*, an attempt to redefine aspects of international law, occurred in the same year. Early in 1975 followed the first *Lomé Convention* which, though producing advantages for developing countries, also showed that probably they did not have the power to force a rapid change. This became clearer at CIEC, mentioned above, held in the same year. There had been moves in the United Nations system since 1977 to start a program of *Global Negotiations* in 1980. The launch of the *Brandt Report* in 1980 appeared to give promise of a new start. However, by that time the gap between the two sides had become unbridgeable, their positions largely incapable of movement, and the dialogue petered out. There have been periodic calls for the revival of the North-South dialogue, but discussions on how to do it always got bogged down in the preliminaries. See also *Harries Report*.

Nothing is agreed until everything is agreed: a frequent understanding between participants in trade negotiations at the start of proceedings. This principle preserves each party's bargaining power, and it ensures that the result is considered balanced by all. See also *ad referendum agreement*, *globality* and *single undertaking*.

Notification: an obligation to report to the relevant body of the WTO the adoption of trade measures that might have an effect on the members of the agreement it administers. Notifying promotes *transparency* and assists *surveillance*. Notifying has no bearing on whether the measure itself will be judged to be in conformity with the rules. The *Decision on Notification Procedures* taken at Marrakesh in April 1994 contains an illustrative list of twenty types of notifiable measures as follows: tariffs, tariff quotas and surcharges, quantitative restrictions (including voluntary export restraints and orderly marketing arrangements), other non-tariff measures such as licensing and mixing requirements and variable levies, customs valuation, rules of origin, government procurement, technical barriers, safeguard actions, anti-dumping actions, countervailing actions, export taxes, export subsidies, export tax exemptions, concessionary export financing, free-trade zones (including in-bond manufacturing), export restrictions, any other government assistance, role of state-trading enterprises, foreign exchange controls related to imports and exports, government-mandated countertrade, etc. In drawing up the list, negotiators have cast a wide net, and few measures could in principle escape it. The WTO Secretariat maintains a list of all notified measures and reminds members when they have to put in a standard notification. See also *reverse notification*, *surveillance* and *transparency*.

Not inconsistent with: an expression frequently used by *panels* in WTO *dispute settlement* reports. It means that, as far as the panel can establish, the measure being examined does not contravene any WTO rules. Accordingly, the party maintaining the measure is not required to change it. The use of this expression appears to stem partly from the fact that the *GATT 1947* was in force provisionally only, and partly from a desire by panels to shield themselves against the possibility of undiscovered facts. See also *Protocol of Provisional Application*.

Not indispensable, but necessary: in *Korea – Various Measures Affecting Imports of Fresh, Chilled and Frozen Beef* the *Appellate Body* considered whether a measure might not be indispensable, but nevertheless necessary, to attain a certain objective. It noted that sometimes "indispensable" and "necessary" would have the same meaning, but on other occasions the meaning of "necessary" might be limited to "making a contribution to". The Appellate Body found that sometimes one would not get around considering "the relative importance of the common interests or values that the law or regulation to be enforced is intended to protect". Accordingly, "the more vital or important those common interests or values are, the easier it would be to accept as 'necessary' a measure designed as an enforcement instrument". The Appellate Body noted that this issue could be looked at from other angles. For example, the more important a measure was to realize an end, the more easily it might be deemed "necessary". Yet another angle would be that of the restrictive effect of the measure on imports. The less the impact was, the easier it might be considered "necessary". In other words, a measure might not be "indispensable", but it could still be "necessary". [WT/DS161/AB/R, WT/DS169/AB/R]

Not-made-here syndrome: see *techno-nationalism*.

Not-on-the-whole-higher-or-more-restrictive criterion: one of the criteria used in the assessment of whether a *customs union* is in conformity with the rules of the *GATT*. Article XXIV requires that the *common external tariff* of a new customs union must not on the whole be higher or more restrictive than the national tariffs of the members were before they joined the union. Much argument has arisen over the method to be used in ascertaining whether the criterion has been met, especially over the question of the use of the *average tariff* or a *trade-weighted average tariff*. Outcomes clearly can be quite different depending on which calculation is used. The *Understanding on the Interpretation of Article XXIV* concluded as part of the *Uruguay Round* clarified the matter. It says that an evaluation of tariff levels must be based on an overall assessment of weighted average tariff rates and of *customs duties* collected.

Notoriety: a word used by *intellectual property* specialists to indicate whether something, e.g. a *trademark*, is well known.

NTBs: *non-tariff barriers*. See also *non-tariff measures* or *NTMs*.

NTMs: *non-tariff measures*, such as quotas, import licensing systems, sanitary regulations, prohibitions, etc.

Nuisance tariff: a *tariff* so low that it costs the government more to collect it than the revenue it generates. Sometimes also used to refer to any tariff without a protective effect. Some countries defend this as necessary to raise revenues. See also *revenue tariff*.

Nullification or impairment: damage to a country's benefits and expectations from its WTO membership through another country's change in its trade regime or failure to carry out its WTO obligations. If the matter cannot be solved through *consultation*, it is then open to members to resort to formal *dispute settlement* procedures. Nullification and impairment can occur through a violation of the rules, but the same is possible through *non-violation*.

O

Obiter dictum: a remark or observation by a court that is not essential for deciding a case. It is not binding on the lower courts nor later on the court that made it. See also *stare decisis*.

Observer status: participation in a meeting to observe the formal proceedings, but without the right to intervene in the debate or take part in making decisions. Observers are not usually admitted to informal sessions or negotiating meetings. They have, however, the right in most cases to address formal meetings, usually after all of the ordinary participants have had their say. They also normally receive all of the formal documents. See also *dialogue partner*.

OECD: Organisation for Economic Cooperation and Development. Established in 1961 as the successor to the *Organisation for European Economic Cooperation* (OEEC). Sometimes called a "rich-country club" because its members account for more than 70% of global output. Its objectives are (a) to achieve the highest sustainable economic growth and employment and a rising standard of living in member countries, while maintaining financial stability, and thus to contribute to the development of the world economy, (b) to contribute to sound economic expansion in member as well as in non-member countries in the process of economic development, and (c) to contribute to the expansion of world trade on a multilateral, non-discriminatory basis in accordance with international obligations. The OECD can point to considerable achievements in the trade and economic fields over the last thirty years, assisted to some extent by the homogeneous nature of its membership. Membership consists of Australia, Austria, Belgium, Canada, Czech Republic, Denmark, European Communities, Finland, France, Germany, Greece, Hungary, Iceland, Ireland, Italy, Japan, Korea, Luxembourg, Mexico, Netherlands, New Zealand, Norway, Poland, Portugal, Slovak Republic, Spain, Sweden, Switzerland, Turkey, United Kingdom and the United States. The highest OECD body is the annual Ministerial Council Meeting, usually held in May or June. The OECD secretariat is located in Paris. See also *Arrangement on Guidelines for Officially Supported Credits*, *Convention on Combating Bribery of Foreign Public Officials in International Business Transactions*, *Guiding Principles Concerning Environmental Policies*, *Joint Group on Trade and Competition*, *Large Aircraft Sector Understanding*, *Multilateral Agreement on Investment*, *OECD Guidelines for Multinational Enterprises*, *OECD Recommendation on Trade and Competition*, *OECD shipbuilding agreement* and *trade and illicit payments* and other entries beginning with OECD.

OECD Action Plan for Electronic Commerce: adopted on 9 October 1998. It contains four themes: (a) building trust for users and consumers through protection of privacy and personal data, secure infrastructure and technologies, authentication and certification, and consumer protection, (b) establishing transparent and predictable ground rules for the digital market place, (c) enhancing the information infrastructure for electronic commerce, including access to and use of the information infrastructure, and (d) maximising the benefits of electronic commerce, paying attention to its economic and social impact. See also *electronic commerce*. [OECD SG/EC(98)9/REV5]

OECD Guidelines for Multinational Enterprises: a set of voluntary guidelines in the form of recommendations for the behaviour of multinational enterprises (MNEs) first adopted by *OECD* member countries in 1976 and last revised in 2000. The guidelines are not intended to distinguish between MNEs and domestic enterprises. Rather, they are meant to reflect good practice for all. Chapter II contains a range of general policies (contribute to economic, social and environmental progress in host countries, respect for human rights, encouragement of local capacity-building, encourage human capital formation, support and uphold good corporate principles, etc.). Chapter III recommends that enterprises should ensure disclosure of timely, regular, reliable and relevant information regarding their activities, structure, financial situation and performance. Chapter IV on employment and industrial relations asks enterprises, among other things, to respect the right of employees to be represented by trade unions, to contribute to the effective abolition of *child labour* and the elimination of all forms of forced or compulsory labour, not to discriminate among employees on grounds of race, colour, sex, religion, etc., and to provide employee representatives with assistance in developing effective collective agreements. Chapter V asks enterprises to take due account of the need to protect the environment, public health and safety and to contribute to the wider goal of *sustainable development*. Chapter VI asks companies neither to offer nor to accept bribes. Chapter VII on consumer interests recommends taking all reasonable steps to ensure the safety and quality of goods and services. Chapter VIII aims to promote the transfer and rapid diffusion of technologies and know-how and to perform science and technology development work in host countries. Chapter IX asks enterprises to conduct their activities in a competitive manner. Chapter X stresses the important contribution of enterprises to public finances of host countries by paying their taxes on time. See also *Draft United Nations Code of Conduct on Transnational Corporations* and *ILO Tripartite Declaration of Principles Concerning Multinational Enterprises and Social Policy*.

OECD Recommendation on Trade and Competition: formal name *Revised Recommendation of the Council for Cooperation Between Member Countries on Anticompetitive Practices Affecting International Trade*. It was first adopted in 1986 and revised several times since, the last time in 1995. It is a non-binding instrument. It sets out a range of measures, including procedural arrangements aimed at transparency, consultation and conciliation, members could take to minimize friction between trade and competition policies of different jurisdictions.

OECD shipbuilding agreement: formal name *Agreement Respecting Normal Competitive Conditions in the Commercial Shipbuilding and Repair Industry*. It was concluded on 21 December 1994, but it is not yet in force. The Agreement seeks to eliminate the use of subsidies in the construction and repair of self-propelled seagoing vessels of more than 100 gross tons. It does not cover military vessels and fishing boats destined for own use by a party. Annex I contains a list of support measures that are inconsistent with the Agreement, including *export credits* or subsidies and, domestic support and some support measures for research and development. Parties to the agreement also will have access to a mechanism to deal with injurious pricing which is based on the *anti-dumping measures* available under the WTO agreements. There is also a dispute settlement mechanism. The Agreement is open for signature to countries outside the OECD.

Offer: in a negotiation, a country's proposal for its own further liberalization, usually an offer to improve access to its markets.

Office international de la vigne et du vin: OIV. Established in 1924 to collect and disseminate scientific, technical, economic and legal information on matters related to wine. Its work is of relevance to international trade in wine because many important wine-growing countries adopt its standards for their wine industries. Its secretariat is located in Paris. On 1 January 2004 it became the Organisation internationale de la vigne et du vin (*International Organisation of Vine and Wine*). See also *appellation contrôlée* and *geographical indications*.

Office International des Epizooties: see *International Office of Epizootics*. This body is now also known as World Organization for Animal Health.

Official development assistance: defined by the *Development Assistance Committee* of the *OECD* as grants or loans by its members to a defined list of developing countries. To qualify as official development assistance, activities must be (a) undertaken by the official sector of the donor country, (b) aimed mainly at the promotion of economic development and welfare, and (c) at concessional financial terms. Technical cooperation activities are included, but grants, loans and credits for military purposes do not qualify.

Official support: assistance by governments to exporters through export credit insurance and guarantees, interest-rate support, credits, etc.

Official tariff rate: the tariff rate listed in the government's tariff schedule. It is often higher than the *applied tariff rate*.

Offsets: measures used to encourage the development of local industry or to improve the *balance of trade* by means of *local content requirements*, licensing of technology, investment requirements, *countertrade* or similar requirements. Some of these measures are illegal under the *Agreement on Trade-Related Investment Measures*. The *Agreement on Government Procurement* prohibits all such offset requirements for its members. Governments are normally attracted to offsets as a form of infant industry development. As with all forms of *protection*, offsets may raise domestic costs and therefore harm a country's export efforts. See also *infant-industry argument*.

Oilseeds: this was a long drawn-out dispute originally brought by the United States against the European Economic Community (EEC) in 1989. It is an example of the application of the GATT rule on *non-violation*. The first *panel* report on this case, adopted in 1990, found that the EEC regulations authorizing payments to seed processors, on condition that the oilseeds originated in the EEC, were inconsistent with the *GATT national treatment* obligation. The panel also found that the *subsidy* scheme for oilseeds operated by the EEC isolated EEC producers completely from the movement of prices on international markets. Therefore, *tariff concessions* in the form of *zero bindings* made by the EEC could not have any impact on the competitiveness of imported oilseeds. In December 1991 the panel was reconvened at the request of the United States to determine whether the changes made by the EEC as a result of the earlier panel would eliminate the difficulties. The panel found that the revised support scheme still rendered the level of EEC production substantially insensitive to the movement of world market prices. It therefore continued to impair the benefits the United States could expect to accrue to it under the relevant tariff concessions. The panel then recalled that over two years had passed since the original report had been adopted, and it recommended that the EEC should act expeditiously to eliminate the impairment of tariff concessions. In other words, the EEC's right to institute subsidies on certain products and the level of these subsidies was not at issue and not inconsistent with GATT rules. However, the use of subsidies as they affected oilseed producers impaired and nullified the rights of other GATT members. This is the basis of the non-violation argument in this case. The panel decision was not the end of the matter. It remained an irritant in European Community–United States trade relations for the remainder of the *Uruguay Round*. It was resolved as part of the *Blair House Accord* in November 1992 when the European Community agreed to set acreage limits for oilseeds production. [GATT BISD 37S]

Okinawa Charter on Global Information Society: adopted at the *G8* summit in Okinawa in July 2000. Participants agreed on several key principles, including (a) promoting competition and opening markets for information technology and telecommunications products and services, (b) protection of *intellectual property rights*, (c) commitment to using software in full compliance with intellectual property rights, (d) importance of efficient telecommunications, transport, trade and customs procedures, (e) promoting cross-border *electronic commerce*, (f) adopting consistent approaches to taxation, (g) desisting from imposing customs duties on electronic transmissions, (h) promoting market-driven standards, (i) promoting consumer trust in the electronic market place, (j) developing effective and meaningful privacy protection for consumers, and (k) developing electronic authentication, electronic signature, cryptography and other means to ensure the security of transactions. The G8 members also pledged themselves to making efforts to bridge the *digital divide*.

Old economy: the economy as we knew it until talk in the late 1990s about the superiority of the *new economy* and the accompanying investment boom made it briefly unfashionable. It turned out that managers of the old economy were much more adaptable than the proponents of the new economy thought possible.

OMA: see *Orderly Marketing Arrangement*.

OMC: Organisation Mondiale du Commerce. See *WTO*.

Omnibus Trade and Competitiveness Act: passed by the United States Congress in 1988. Its name reflected the many different legislative acts that had been rolled into it. This Act gave the President *fast-track* negotiating authority until 1 June 1991 to participate in the *Uruguay Round*. Fast-track was renewed twice, the second time until 15 December 1993 which became the definitive deadline for the negotiations. New trade provisions in the Act were *Super 301* authorising *market-opening actions* on behalf of many industries and *Special 301* dealing particularly with the protection by other countries of United States-owned *intellectual property rights*. See also *mandatory but not compulsory*, *priority foreign country* and *Trade Promotion Authority*.

OMPI: Organisation Mondiale de la Propriété Intellectuelle. The World Intellectual Property Organization. See *WIPO*.

One village, one product: a Japanese proposal made at the WTO *Hong Kong Ministerial Conference*. It is intended to help developing countries to identify products capable of being exported and to find markets for them.

One-way free-trade area: see *asymmetrical trade agreement*.

OPEC: Organization of Petroleum Exporting Countries. Established in 1960. Its members are Algeria, Angola, Indonesia, Iran, Iraq, Kuwait, Libya, Nigeria, Qatar, Saudi Arabia, United Arab Emirates and Venezuela. It aims to coordinate and unify production and export policies. Membership is open to countries with a substantial net export of crude petroleum. Its secretariat is located in Vienna.

Open-accession clauses: provisions, for example, in *free-trade agreements*, which invite or enable additional countries to join the agreement. See also *accession* and *enlargement*.

Openness: the extent to which a country is open to competition from goods and services from other countries. See also *contestability of markets*.

Open regionalism: a term which implies that any regional arrangement should be outward-looking and lowering barriers to economies outside the arrangement as well as those within it. For some, open regionalism means that full *most-favoured-nation treatment* will apply to tariff reductions by members of an arrangement. For others it allows the possibility of a *preferential trade arrangement*, coupled with easy access to membership.

Open-season negotiations: an opportunity available every three years to GATT members under Article XXVIII to conduct technical tariff negotiations when *bindings* expired. Bindings originally were made for three years. Such negotiations often led to modifications or withdrawals of *concessions*. Resort to such negotiations is less common now that bindings are deemed to be permanent. See also *renegotiation of tariffs*.

Open-skies arrangements: these are arrangements between governments to give each other unrestricted access to their airports for scheduled passenger and cargo flights. Most international air routes and service frequencies are still allocated on the basis of *bilateral air services agreements*. These agreements usually specify the maximum number of passenger seats that may be offered and the airports that may be used. See also *freedoms of the air* and *Multilateral Agreement for the Liberalization of International Air Transportation*.

Opinio juris (sive necessitatis): the expectation by nations that in a given situation they will be obliged to follow a certain course of action. See also *customary international law*. [Starke 1989, Shaw 1997]

Opinion: one of the ways in which the *European Community* institutions are able to influence the actions of member states. An opinion is not binding, but it expresses a preference for a certain type of action. See also *European Community legislation*.

OPTAD: Organization of Pacific Trade and Development. This was proposed in 1979 as an organization linking the countries of the Pacific Rim, but it never reached the negotiating stage. Its proponents thought that it would act as forum for the resolution of economic problems, to provide a stimulus for investment and trade flows into the region, to provide a forum for the longer-term economic transformation of the region and to form the foundation for a more constructive approach to the expansion of relations with the Soviet Union, China and Vietnam. Its prospective membership would have included most of the economies that are now the *APEC* members.

Optimal-intervention principle: the use of the instrument that attains the policy goal with the least amount of undesired side-effect, usually the one that attacks the identified policy problem directly at its source.

Optimal-tariff argument: also called optimum-tariff argument. Its starting point is that the imposition of a tariff leads to a reduction in the volume of trade that would have occurred if there had been no tariff. The result is a change in the *terms of trade* of the importing and exporting country, but these effects cancel each other out. Both countries are now worse off. The optimal-tariff argument postulates that if a country is large enough, and if the tariff is not high, the effect of the tariff will lead to an improvement in that country's terms of trade which will exceed the loss of real income caused by the reduction in the volume of trade. The improvement in the terms of trade will only be beneficial for a reduced import volume. Small countries, however, would invariably maximize their welfare by not having the tariff. Harry G Johnson noted that only the optimum-tariff argument provides an economic justification for tariffs, and that all other arguments for protection are arguments for subsidies. [Johnson 1968, Kjeldsen-Kragh 2001, Kreinin 1995]

Orderly Marketing Arrangement: OMA. A bilateral arrangement whereby an exporting country (government or industry) agrees to reduce or restrict exports so as to shield the importing country from having to make use of quotas, tariffs or other import controls. OMAs fall in the same category of trade distortions as *voluntary restraint arrangements* and *voluntary import expansion* schemes. See also *Agreement on Safeguards*.

Ordinary course of trade: the WTO *Anti-Dumping Agreement* requires that the price comparison between the *normal value* of a product and its *export price* be based on the comparable price, in the ordinary course of trade, for the *like product* when it is intended to be sold in the exporting country. The Agreement does not say how the "ordinary course of trade" should be interpreted. The phrase does, however, point in the direction of established or customary behaviour by the importer and exporter in the trade of a particular product. The United States Department of Commerce, among others, has developed a definition of this phrase which says that "generally, sales are in the ordinary of course of trade if made under conditions and practices that, for a reasonable period of time prior to the date of sale of the subject merchandise, have been normal for the sales of the foreign like product". See also *anti-dumping measures*. [Durling and Nicely 2002]

Organic integration: private cross-border flows of capital, goods and services, technology and information, driven in large part by multinational enterprises. See also *economic integration*.

Organisation for an International Geographical Indications Network: ORIGIN. An organization of producers from more than twenty countries seeking better international protection for *geographical indications* which was established in June 2003. It seeks the extension of the additional protection for wines and spirits available under the WTO *Agreement on Trade-Related Aspects of Intellectual Property Rights* to other products and the establishment of a legally binding *multilateral system of notification and registration of geographical indications* for all products. See also *World Wine Trade Group*. [www.orign-gi.com]

Organisation for European Economic Cooperation: OEEC. Established in 1948 as the body administering the *Marshall Plan* and superseded in 1961 by the *OECD*.

Organization for International Economic Cooperation: the successor organization to the *Council for Mutual Economic Assistance*. Its mandate is to advise member states on trade and economic matters. It now is inactive.

Organization for Trade Cooperation: OTC. Proposed in 1955 through a GATT working party report as a permanent mechanism for administering the GATT. Its mandate would have been a limited version of what had been expected of the *ITO*. All GATT members would automatically have become members of the organization. One interesting point raised in the report of the working party is that countries appointed to the Intersessional Committee, which at that time was the only means of conducting business between the annual sessions, might consider appointing representatives of suitable calibre and the necessary authority to live in Geneva or nearby capitals so that they could contribute to its deliberations. Another of its recommendations was that the organization should be brought into a specialized agency relationship within the *United Nations*. The proposal for an OTC failed to get United States congressional approval, and it lapsed. See also *GATT Council of Representatives*, *United Nations specialized agencies* and *WTO*.

Organisation Internationale de la Francophonie: see *francophone countries*.

Organisation internationale de la vigne et du vin: OIV. See *International Organisation of Vine and Wine*.

Organization of African Unity: OAU. Established on 25 May 1963. Many of its aims are political, but one of them is economic cooperation, including transport and communications. All independent sovereign nations of Africa may become members, and 53 have taken that step. Its secretariat is located in Addis Ababa. Superseded in July 2001 by the *African Union*. See also *African Economic Community*.

Organization of American States: OAS. Established through the Bogotá Charter of 1948 which entered into force in 1951. 35 sovereign states of the Americas participate in it. Cuba was excluded from membership in 1962. OAS seeks, among mainly political objectives, to solve economic problems that may arise among member states and to promote, by cooperative action, their economic, social and cultural development. The OAS secretariat is located in Washington.

Organization of Eastern Caribbean States: OECS. Established in 1981 to promote, among other objectives, economic cooperation among its members. At the same time, it superseded the East Caribbean Common Market. OECS members are Anguilla, Antigua and Barbuda, British Virgin Islands, Commonwealth of Dominica, Grenada, Montserrat, St Kitts and Nevis, St Lucia, and St Vincent and the Grenadines. OECS decided in July 2001 to establish an economic union to enable the free movement of people, goods, services and capital. Its economic affairs secretariat is located at St John's, Antigua and Barbuda, but the OECS central secretariat is at Castries, St Lucia.

Organization of the Islamic Conference: OIC An intergovernmental organization of 57 states established in 1969. Among its objectives are cooperation in political, economic and other fields and strengthening Islamic solidarity among member states. It is located in Jeddah.

Origin: see *rules of origin*.

Original membership of the WTO: deemed to have been attained by the members of the *GATT 1947* who had on 1 January 1995 (a) accepted the *WTO Agreement*, (b) the multilateral trade agreements annexed to it, and (c) annexed schedules of *concessions* to the *GATT 1994* and schedules of specific commitments to the *General Agreement on Trade in Services*. Countries meeting these requirements did not have to undergo the *accession* formalities, but original membership did not confer any other rights.

Originating goods: in the administration of *rules of origin* for *preferential trade agreements* these are goods deemed to be a product of the party enjoying preferential access. See also *non-originating goods*.

Originating materials: components of a good traded under a *preferential trade arrangement* which have been produced in the territory of a partner to the arrangement. See also *non-originating materials*.

Osaka Action Agenda: the agenda for trade and investment liberalization and economic cooperation agreed by *APEC* leaders on 19 November 1995 at their meeting in Osaka. It is a step towards realizing the aims of the 1994 *Bogor Declaration*. The action agenda consists of three pillars: (a) trade and investment liberalization, (b) trade and investment facilitation and (c) economic and technical cooperation. The aims of the action agenda are to be achieved through encouraging and converting the evolving efforts of voluntary liberalization in the region, taking collective actions to advance liberalization and facilitation objectives, and stimulating and contributing to further momentum for global liberalization. The Agenda's guiding principles are *comprehensiveness*; *transparency*; *standstill*; *non-discrimination*; simultaneous start, continuous process, differentiated timetables; flexibility and cooperation. Individual action plans had to be submitted to the 1996 APEC Ministerial Meeting. Their overall implementation began in January 1997, followed by annual reviews. See also *comparability*, *APEC individual action plan* and other entries beginning with *APEC*.

Other regulations of commerce: see *duties and other regulations of commerce* and *duties and other restrictive regulations of commerce*.

Other restrictive regulations of commerce: see *duties and other restrictive regulations of commerce*.

Ottawa Imperial Conference: the conference held in 1932 which established the *imperial preferences arrangement* for the countries then making up the British *Commonwealth*. The arrangement entered into force in October 1932.

Our Common Future: see *World Commission on Environment and Development*.

Out-of-cycle reviews: this is a mechanism created by *USTR* to administer *Special 301*. Under the provisions of the *Omnibus Trade and Competitiveness Act*, USTR must make an annual report on its monitoring and enforcement activities and the compliance of other countries with trade agreements of which the United States is a member. Where the matter is considered serious enough, USTR will start a review without waiting for the cycle of annual reports. That then is an "out-of-cycle review". See also *Monitoring and Enforcement Unit*.

Out-of-quota rate: the *tariff* rate applicable to products imported in excess of a *tariff quota*. This rate is meant to discourage imports above the quota limit. It is usually much higher than the one applied to imports within the quota. See also *in-quota tariff*.

Outsourcing: also known as business process outsourcing or BPO. This refers to the purchasing of goods and services, more often the latter, necessary for the running of an organization from outside that organization rather than relying on one's staff to provide them. Sometimes this is done because of cost advantages, but another reason is that specialist providers are much more likely to be familiar with changing technology and practices. In the environment of a corporation or a government department outsourcing could mean, for example, purchasing all information technology services from a suitable provider and having provider staff located permanently within the organization. More recently, the term has also been used for obtaining services from another country, mainly because the foreign country can supply the service at a lower cost. In some countries the practice has provoked strong adverse reactions. However, purchasing services from abroad because they can be made more cheaply elsewhere is really no different to importing manufactures. See also *comparative advantage*.

Outward-oriented development: a strategy of economic development based on an expansion of exports and reliance on financing from global capital markets. [Moon 2000]

Outward processing: exporting a part-finished good for further processing and re-importing it for final manufacture. Outward processing may affect the status of the good under *preferential rules of origin*. Many such systems have strict limits on the value that may be added to a good in this way.

Over-invoicing: preparing or presenting an invoice giving a price for goods or services that is higher than the pprice actually paid. One reason for this practice is to transfer funds abroad in contravention of foreign exchange regulations. See also *under-invoicing*.

Over-quota tariff rate: see *out-of-quota rate*.

Over-quota trade: trade in a given product subject to a *tariff rate quota* which occurs outside that quota. Where over-quota trade is permitted, it always attracts a higher than that set for *in-quota trade*.

P

Pacific Agreement on Closer Economic Relations: PACER. An agreement adopted in August 2001 by the *Pacific Islands Forum* which sets out the framework for the development of trade relations between the Forum members. It is not a *free-trade agreement*, but it allows for the establishment of *free-trade areas*. One of these is the *Pacific Island Countries Trade Agreement*. PACER entered into force on 3 October 2002. See also *SPARTECA*.

Pacific Community: an organization to promote economic and social cooperation in the Pacific area. Its members are American Samoa, Australia, Cook Islands, Federated States of Micronesia, Fiji, France, French Polynesia, Guam, Kiribati, Marshall Islands, Nauru, New Caledonia, New Zealand, Niue, Northern Mariana Islands, Palau, Papua New Guinea, Pitcairn Islands, Samoa, Solomon Islands, Tokelau, Tonga, Tuvalu, United States, Vanuatu and Wallis and Futuna. It is administered by the *Secretariat of the Pacific Community*, located at Noumea.

Pacific Free Trade Area: PAFTA. An idea for a regional preferential trade arrangement that has been around since the 1960s. Most of the various proposals brought forward over the years have included either the United States or Japan, often both, as the centre of any prospective arrangement. None of them have reached the negotiating stage. Some say that the formation of *APEC* has made PAFTA redundant. See also *Free Trade Area of the Asia-Pacific*, *OPTAD*, *PBEC* and *PECC*.

Pacific Island Countries Free Trade Agreement: PICTA. A *free-trade agreement* adopted in August 2001 by the *Pacific Islands Forum*. It entered into force on 13 April 2003. The Agreement calls for the establishment of a *free-trade area* over the next ten years. Australia and New Zealand are eligible to join if they wish. See also *SPARTECA*.

Pacific Islands Forum: PIF. Founded in 1971 as the South Pacific Forum. Renamed in 2000. This is an annual meeting of the heads of government of South Pacific states. Its membership is Australia, Cook Islands, Federated States of Micronesia, Fiji, Kiribati, Nauru, New Zealand, Niue, Palau, Papua New Guinea, Republic of the Marshall Islands, Samoa, Solomon Islands, Tonga, Tuvalu and Vanuatu. The PFI also has about ten dialogue members. It concerns itself with regional political and economic questions, including the aim of closer regional economic cooperation. It has no written charter. Its secretariat is located in Suva.

Pacific Rim: an imprecise term for the countries bordering the Pacific Ocean. Also known as Pacific Basin. See *APEC*, *PBEC* and *PECC*.

Packaging directive: a *directive* issued by the *European Community* in 1994 and updated several times since. It seeks to prevent the formation of packaging waste, and it encourages the recovery and recycling of used packaging. The recovery target is 50% to 60%. The recycling target is 25% to 45% of materials, with a minimum of 15% by weight for each packaging material. Both of these targets had to be met by 30 June 1996. See also *eco-packaging*. [Directive 94/62/EC]

*Pacta sunt servanda***:** the principle in international treaties law, as expressed in Article 26 of the *Vienna Convention on the Law of Treaties*, that "every treaty is binding upon the parties to it and must be performed by them in *good faith*".

Panel: an independent group of three experts established by the *Dispute Settlement Body* to examine and issue recommendations on particular dispute in the light of WTO provisions. Sometimes used figuratively for the actual finding or decision made by a panel. Panels are not guided by extraneous factors or rules established outside the WTO framework. See also *dispute settlement* and *Dispute Settlement Understanding*.

Pan-European Cumulation System: a name commonly used for a scheme established on 1 January 1997 under which goods consisting of components made in more than one participating country are treated in the same way as domestically produced goods. The system consists of the *European Community* and most of its European trading partners. See also *preferential rules of origin*.

Pan-Pacific Free Trade Area: one of several names for a proposed *free-trade agreement* for Asia and perhaps the Pacific also. See also *East Asia Free Trade Area* and *Free Trade Area of the Asia-Pacific*.

Paperless trading: eliminating the requirement for paper documents, such as customs declarations and freight manifestos, to be used in the conduct of international trade and using electronic documents instead. The successful introduction of paperless trading requires overcoming legal and authentication barriers (ensuring that the document transmitted electronically is genuine and has not been tampered with), harmonization of documentation requirements between participants and agreement on the technical standards to be used. See also *APEC paperless trading initiative*.

Parallel imports: also called "grey-market imports. The term denotes the import outside the manufacturer's or distributor's authorized channel of a product with an *intellectual property* content from another country where the product has been lawfully placed on the market by the owner of the *intellectual property right* or with the owner's consent. Such imports compete with the same product produced or distributed, also with the authorization of the holder of the rights, in the domestic market. They are therefore said to be imported in parallel with the authorized channels. The motivation for doing so arises when the parallel import can be put on the market more cheaply. Some say that strictly speaking the same person should hold the intellectual property rights in both countries, but the term more generally now describes situations where ownership has been split by contract. Parallel importing remains a contentious practice, and its legality varies according to jurisdiction. Competition authorities tend to be in favour of this practice because the consumer clearly benefits from it. Others, however, hold that the practice undermines the system of *intellectual property rights* which is designed to foster innovation and creativity. Neither the WTO *Agreement on Trade-Related Aspects of Intellectual Property Rights* nor the *WIPO Copyright Treaty* concluded in December 1996 preclude governments from permitting parallel imports. See also *exhaustion doctrine*. [Maskus 2000]

Parallelism in export support: an expression used by the *European Union* (EU) in the *Doha Development Agenda* negotiations on agriculture. When the EU offered to enter into negotiations leading to the elimination of *export subsidies* for agricultural products, it did so on condition that all other forms of *export support* would also be put on the negotiating table. Sometimes this was also referred to as full parallelism.

Parallelism in safeguards: a concept that made its first appearance in the *Appellate Body* report concerning *Argentina – Safeguard Measures on Footwear*. The first of its two parts is that (a) a country may make a determination of *serious injury* under the conditions set out in Article 2.1 of the *Agreement on Safeguards* and (b) in its investigation whether serious injury has occurred, it has to take into account the factors listed in Article 4.2 of the Agreement. The second part is Article 2.2 which states that "safeguard measures shall be applied to a product being imported irrespective of its source". The Appellate Body held that "the imports included in the [injury] determination made under Articles 2.1 and 4.2 should correspond to the imports included in the application of the measure, under Article 2.2". The Appellate Body gave as its reason that the words "product ... being imported" occurred in both Articles 2.1 and 2.2, and that they ought to have the same meaning. [WT/DS121/AB/R, Pauwelyn 2004]

Parallel trade: see *parallel imports*.

Para-tariffs: a name sometimes used for charges levied on imports instead of, or in addition to, *tariffs*. These can consist of service fees, additional import surcharges or other fees levied on imported products inside the market. Para-tariffs are illegal if they are levied on imports inside the market, but not at the same time on domestic products. Their imposition in such cases would be a denial of *national treatment*.

Pareto optimum (or efficiency): the principle defined by Vilfredo Pareto that resources are allocated efficiently when no person can be made better off without some other person being made worse off. Intermediate situations between the current stage and the optimum are called Pareto-superior.

Paris Club: a forum consisting mainly of *OECD* member countries which was established to bring together creditor and debtor countries in cases where there are difficulties in meeting loan repayments. It seeks to avoid defaults on loans through debt rescheduling and other mechanisms. The French Treasury provides a secretariat for the Paris Club.

Paris Convention: full name *Paris Convention for the Protection of Industrial Property* which established the Paris Union. It came into force in 1884, and it has been revised several times. The latest version is the 1967 Stockholm

Revision. The Convention is administered by *WIPO*. It provides protection for *patents*, *trademarks*, *industrial designs* and applies broadly to *industrial property*, including *geographical indications* and *appellations of origin*. The main features of the Convention are *national treatment*, *right of priority* (a person filing for a patent in one member country has a right of priority to file in another country within one year), and *independence of protection* (patents applied for in member countries by nationals of member countries are independent of patents obtained for the same invention in other countries). See also *Agreement on Trade-Related Aspects of Intellectual Property Rights*.

Paris Union: see *Paris Convention*.

Partial-scope trade agreements: another name for *sectoral free-trade areas* sometimes negotiated by developing countries under the *Enabling Clause*.

Partial preferential trade agreement: a term used to describe either *preferential trade agreements* confined to trade in some sectors or an *asymmetrical trade agreement* under which only some of the participants grant free access to products from the other members. See also *full preferential trade agreement*.

Part IV of the GATT: a protocol to the GATT which had its origin in the *Kennedy Round* and entered into force on 27 June 1966. It added Articles XXXVI to XXXVIII to the GATT. In these three articles developed countries agreed broadly that they would not expect *reciprocity* for tariff reductions and removal of trade barriers where the trade of developing countries is affected. Developed countries would also take measures to ensure that the trade of developing countries would not be disadvantaged by actions taken by developed countries and to work together with them to promote and expand their trade. Although these three articles impose few legal conditions on developed countries, they have shaped to a considerable extent the form of the trading system since 1965 through lessening expectations of what developing countries could or should be required to do. See also *Enabling Clause*, *developing countries and the multilateral trading system* and *special and differential treatment*.

Partners for Progress: an *APEC* mechanism based on mutual assistance and voluntarism to promote economic and technical cooperation more efficiently within APEC. It was established by the November 1995 *APEC* Ministerial Meeting. The mechanism is aimed at activities that support directly the liberalization and facilitation of trade and investment. See also *Bogor Declaration* and *Osaka Action Agenda*.

Partnership and Cooperation Agreements: PCAs. The name for the agreements between the *European Community* and the *Newly Independent States*. The parties offer each other *most-favoured-nation treatment* (MFN) for trade in goods. There are provisions also on *trade in services*, *right of establishment*, *intellectual property protection* and other areas. PCAs are seen by the Community in terms of rights and obligations as half-way between its standard framework agreements which do not offer preferences and the *Europe Agreements*, though there is no presumption of an automatic progression to a *preferential trade arrangement*.

Passing off: the use of someone else's reputation, *trademark*, design or other distinctive characteristic in the manufacture or sale of a product and implying, overtly or implicitly, that the product is, or could be, the work of the rightful owner of these properties. Passing off always involves a degree of deception. See also *piracy*. [McKeough 1992]

Passive reciprocity: a concept introduced by William R Cline which means that two countries may agree cooperatively that reciprocal trade liberalization offers benefits to both of them. Under WTO rules, such liberalization would have to be extended to all WTO members on a *most-favoured-nation treatment* basis. See also *aggressive reciprocity* and *reciprocity*. [Cline 1983]

Pass-through operations: the process of first shipping goods into a *free-trade area* through the member country that has the lowest general tariff or which is known for a relatively lax administration of customs rules and then forwarding the goods to their intended market, another member of the free-trade area, in the expectation that no further duties will be payable. This practice is also known as *trans-shipment*. Strictly enforced *rules of origin* are aimed at preventing this practice. See also *preferential rules of origin*, *preferential trade arrangements* and *substantial transformation*.

Pass-through subsidy: a *subsidy* given to producers of a good at a given stage, the benefits of which are deemed to flow on automatically to producers at a later stage of the production process. For example, a subsidy given to loggers might be assumed to benefit sawmills also. [WT/DS257/R]

Pasta: launched by the United States against the *European Economic Community* (EEC) in 1982 on the grounds that EEC export subsidies on pasta products (macaroni, spaghetti and similar products) manufactured from durum wheat were inconsistent with Article 9 of the *Tokyo Round* Subsidies Code. This article states that signatories shall not grant export subsidies on products other than certain primary products. The EEC argued that pasta products were a type of *primary product*. The facts were that the EEC operated a common system for the internal market in cereals and cereal-based products. It provided for a single system of internal prices for the whole Community and a common trading system with third countries which prevented price fluctuations of the world market from affecting internal cereal prices. The system also provided for export licensing and for application of export refunds in a prescribed manner. Export refunds could be granted to cover the difference between the internal prices and those on third markets for cereals exported in natural state or in the form of specified goods. Pasta products were included in this list of specified goods. The funding of the export refund on durum wheat in the form of pasta was made by a public contribution from the EEC budget which also paid the export refunds on cereals. In its findings, the *panel* was of the opinion that pasta was not a primary product, but a processed agricultural product. It also concluded that the EEC system of granting refunds had to be considered a form of subsidy in the sense of GATT Article XVI (Subsidies). The panel held that the terms of Article XVI, as interpreted in Articles 9 and 10 of the Subsidies Code, excluded the possibility of considering the export of a processed product on the same terms as the export of its constituent components. Accordingly, it concluded that the EEC export refunds were granted on the exports of pasta products and operated to increase these exports and that the EEC subsidies on exports of pasta products were granted in a manner inconsistent with Article 9 of the Subsidies Code. [GATT SCM/43]

Patent: the exclusive right given to an inventor through a certificate to prevent others for a specified period from making, using, selling or importing an *invention*. To qualify for a patent an invention must be useful (capable of industrial application, novel (it must not already be in the public domain), and it must be non-obvious (it must involve some inventive step from the point of view of someone skilled in that area). Patents are available for products and processes. They can be bought, sold or licensed to others. Some countries issue *petty patents*. These require a less strict test for inventiveness and the period of protection is shorter. See also *intellectual property*, *Agreement on Trade-Related Aspects of Intellectual Property Rights* and *Strasbourg Agreement Concerning the International Patent Classification*.

Patent Cooperation Treaty: provides for the filing of an international *patent* application in member states. Filing has to be done through the patent office of which the applicant is a national or resident, and it has the same effect in member states as filing an application with a national patent office of that state. The Treaty has more than 100 members. It is administered by *WIPO*. See also *intellectual property* and *intellectual property right infringements*.

Pathfinder approach: agreement at the 2001 *APEC Economic Leaders' Meeting* that groups of member economies able to proceed more quickly towards the realization of the aims of the *Bogor Declaration* may do so through developing "pathfinder initiatives".

Pauper-labour argument: the argument that industry in countries paying high wages cannot withstand the competition from low-wage countries, and that some form of *protection* is therefore needed. See also *core labour standards*, *race-to-the-bottom argument*, *social clause*, *trade and labour standards* and *wage-differential argument*.

PBEC: Pacific Basin Economic Council. A non-governmental organization established in 1967 and consisting of more than 1,100 companies located in 19 economies around the Pacific Rim. It seeks to promote a business environment conducive to open trade and investment and encouraging competitiveness. It also contributes to the development of policies in *APEC*. PBEC has a secretariat based in Hong Kong.

Peace clause: a provision in Article 13 of the WTO *Agreement on Agriculture* which prevented challenges to agricultural subsidies until 31 December 2003 under other WTO agreements under this and other WTO agreements, especially the *Agreement on Subsidies and Countervailing Measures* and the *GATT*.

Peak tariffs: if the *tariff* rates contained in a typical national tariff schedule were represented chapter by chapter as a continuous line in a graph, the result probably would be something like a series of plateaus interspersed with sudden peaks. Each peak would mean that that product, or group of products, is benefiting from higher *protection* than the products expressed by plateaus. Peak tariff rates are to a large extent a relative concept, though during the *Uruguay Round* they were defined for negotiating purposes as above 15%. That figure is also used in the *OECD*. A rate of 10% in a schedule averaging 4%, as many of the developed-country rates for industrial products are as a result of the Uruguay Round, would represent a peak just as a rate of 40% would in the environment of rates around 20%. The presence of pronounced peak tariff rates may show only one aspect of the protection available to domestic producers. There are cases where their absence is masked by a range of *non-tariff measures* with the same or a greater impact. See also *sensitive products*.

PECC: Pacific Economic Cooperation Conference. Established in 1980. It consists of business, academic and governmental representatives. PECC has 23 members (Australia, Brunei Darussalam, Canada, Chile, China, Colombia, Ecuador, Hong Kong, Indonesia, Japan, Korea, Malaysia, Mexico, New Zealand, Peru, the Philippines, Russia, Singapore, Pacific Islands Forum, Chinese Taipei, Thailand, United States and Vietnam) and two associate members (France and Mongolia) who share their perspectives and expertise on of economic cooperation issues in the Asia-Pacific region. Its secretariat is in Singapore.

PECC competition principles: a non-binding set of fifteen principles and key requirements adopted by *PECC* in May 1999. Their aim is to promote competition throughout *APEC*. The core first-level principles are (a) comprehensiveness (competition policy to apply to all goods and services), (b) transparency (principles, policies and processes to be clear to all), (c) accountability (those responsible for applying competition principles to be accountable for departures from them), and (d) non-discrimination (ensuring competitive neutrality in respect of different modes of domestic and international supply). See also *APEC Principles to Enhance Competition and Regulatory Reform*.

Pelly Amendment: see *Tuna I*.

Percentage criterion method: some *free-trade agreements* have *rules of origin* which require that qualifying for *tariff preferences* must have at least a minimum amount of value added to them by the exporting country. This is usually expressed as a percentage. The rule may apply either across the board, as in *AFTA*, or to some goods only, sometimes together with a mandatory *change in tariff heading*. See also *value-added criterion*.

Performance requirements: see *export performance requirements*.

Peril points: a provision first included in the United States *Trade Agreements Extension Act* of 1948, but deleted in 1949. It was reintroduced in the *Trade Agreements Extension Act* of 1955. The provision required the United States Tariff Commission to set, through a process involving public hearings, a floor tariff rate for each product which indicated that a reduction below that rate would cause or threaten to cause *injury* to domestic industry. The President could go below the peril point, but he had to explain his decision to Congress.

This provision was not incorporated in the *Trade Expansion Act* of 1962. See also *United States trade agreements legislation*.

Permanent Group of Experts: a body established under the WTO *Agreement on Subsidies and Countervailing Measures*. It consists of five independent persons who are qualified in the fields of subsidies and trade relations. The function of the Group is to assist *panels* that may have been convened to adjudicate on the alleged existence of *prohibited subsidies* and to give advisory opinions on proposed or existing subsidies.

Permanent normal trade relations: PNTR. An American expression for according permanent *most-favoured-nation treatment* to countries that have been subject to annual renewals. See also *normal trade relations* and *temporary normal trade relations*.

***Per se* conduct:** used in the administration of *antitrust* laws for *behaviour* by a firm that is always against the rules. *Per se* rules have the advantage of setting a definite legal standard, and they are relatively cheap to enforce since it is only necessary to show that the *conduct* has occurred. See also *competition policy* and *rule of reason*.

Persistent Dumping Clause: a provision in United States Tariff Act of 1930 which allows the Department of Commerce to initiate an anti-dumping investigation in the absence of a petition. This can be done if (a) more than one anti-dumping order is in effect with respect to imports of a class or kind of merchandise, (b) there is reason to believe that there is an extraordinary pattern of persistent dumping from one or more additional supplier countries, and (c) this extraordinary pattern is causing a serious commercial problem for the domestic industry. This clause therefore deals with an aspect of *circumvention* of *anti-dumping measures*. See also *recidivist dumping*.

Persistent Organic Pollutants: see *Convention on Persistent Organic Pollutants*.

Petty patent: see *patent*.

Pflimlin plan: this was a proposal by France in 1951 for a 30% average tariff reduction by all GATT members. The plan would have allowed for extensive waivers for developing countries which would have exempted them from similarly large cuts. It was discussed extensively, but in the end the limited United States negotiating authority, which did not permit anything but item-by-item tariff reductions, put paid to this plan. M Pierre Pflimlin was the French Minister for Foreign Economic Relations at the time. See also *waiver*.

Phase-in for rules of origin: sometimes part of a system of *preferential rules of origin* under which the qualifying threshold for *preferential market access* is raised or lowered over some years. For example, the *regional value content* may move up or down, depending on what has been agreed.

Phase-in periods: the staged introduction of a new agreement or new *commitments*, sometimes according to an agreed timetable. The end-point is fixed. For example, the tariff reductions agreed during the *Uruguay Round* could be phased in through five annual equal reductions, though faster action was of course possible. Most *free-trade agreements* have a phase-in mechanism for some of the tariffs to be eliminated. Other examples of phase-in periods are those applicable under the *Agreement on Textiles and Clothing* or the *Information Technology Agreement*. See also *implementation* and *staging*.

Phonogram: a recording of the sound of a performance on, for example, a tape or a compact disk. See *Geneva Convention*, *Rome Convention* and *WIPO Performances and Phonograms Treaty*.

Picking winners: the occasional inclination of governments to identify some industrial activities as having particular promise for the future, and to institute support frameworks to promote the development of these industries. High-technology industries are especially favoured. Successes globally have been at least balanced by failures, and in most cases industries so picked have performed no better than the average of industries or firms not favoured by special attention. It is worth recalling, too, Adam Smith's admonition that "[i]t is thus that every system which endeavours, either by extraordinary encouragements to draw towards a particular species of industry a greater share of the capital of the society than what would naturally go to it, or, by extraordinary restraints, force from a particular species of industry some share of the capital which would otherwise be employed in it, is really subversive of the great purpose which it means to promote. It retards, instead of accelerating, the progress of the society towards real wealth and greatness; and diminishes, instead of increasing, the real value of the annual produce of its land and labour." See also *national champions* and *strategic trade theory*.

Piecemeal tariff reform: tariff reductions for certain groups of goods only. See also *concertina approach* and *concertina theorem*.

Pipeline protection: the practice of according protection of *intellectual property rights* to inventions before a *patent* has been granted formally. Products benefiting from this practice include particularly agricultural chemicals and pharmaceuticals.

Pipeline sanctions: a international problem in 1982 involving the application of United States *extraterritoriality*. It was aimed at ensuring that American suppliers, their affiliates and foreign firms using American technology would be prevented from participating in the construction of Russian pipelines. European firms were affected heavily, and the United States action led to considerable tension in its relations with the *European Community*. The matter was in due course settled amicably. See also *Westinghouse case*.

Piracy: unauthorized copying of materials protected by *intellectual property rights* (such as *copyright*, *trademarks*, *patents*, *geographical indications*, *neighbouring rights*, etc.) for commercial purposes and unauthorized commercial dealing in copied materials. See also *bootlegging* and *fair-use doctrine*.

Plant breeders' rights: a *sui generis right* of *intellectual property protection* available under the *International Convention for the Protection of New Varieties of Plants*. To be eligible for protection, a plant variety must be (a) distinct (i.e. distinguishable from other commonly known varieties), (b) stable (i.e. repeated reproduction must not change its characteristics), (c) homogeneous as far as reproduction or propagation is concerned, and (d) novel in that it has not previously been offered for sale or marketed in the source country with the agreement of the holder of the right. Protection is normally accorded for fifteen to twenty years. See also *International Plant Protection Convention*.

Ploughshares War: an expression used by Nicholas Butler to describe the trade friction in the agricultural area between the United States and the European Community since the establishment of the *Common Agricultural Policy*. See also *Chicken War*. [Butler 1983]

Plurilateral trade agreements: refers to the agreements under the WTO accession to which is not a pre-condition for WTO membership. See *WTO plurilateral trade agreements*.

Plurilateralism: doing things in small groups involving more than *bilateralism* (two participants), but less than *multilateralism* (many participants). See also *minilateralism* and *WTO plurilateral agreements*.

Plus-three countries: also plus-3 and +3. Usually China, Japan and the Republic of Korea in the context of *ASEAN +3*.

PL 480: Public Law 480. The United States *Agricultural Trade and Development Assistance Act* of 1954 which established the *Food for Peace* program. It consists of three titles. Title I permits government to government sales of agricultural commodities to developing countries under long-term credits. Title II enables the United States to donate agricultural commodities as humanitarian food aid to foreign governments. Title III permits government to government grants to support long-term economic development in *least developed countries*. The main exports under this Act have been wheat, feedgrains, rice, cotton oilseeds and dairy products. The *Farm Security and Rural Investment Act* of 2002 extended this program until 2007. See also *Commodity Credit Corporation* and *Food for Progress*.

PNTR: see *permanent normal trade relations*.

Policy competitiveness: the aim of governments to ensure that major firms establish new production facilities within their jurisdictions through offering better terms and conditions than other prospective sites. It is a consequence of the view that it is possible to benefit at the expense of others. Often the taxpayer is the unwitting underwriter of attempts to achieve policy competitiveness.

Policy-led integration: regional economic integration promoted through a formal arrangement, usually through a preferential *regional trade arrangement*. See also *market-led integration*.

Politically optimal tariff: the proposition that a tariff would be optimal from a government's perspective if the tariff could be set without taking into account the views of other governments or any effect on the *terms of trade*. [Godek 1986]

Political will: from the point of view of a trade negotiator, the trait missing among opponents who are unwilling to change their positions. Calls for a demonstration of political will usually are tantamount to a request for more flexibility by the other side. Thus it is by no means uncommon that all negotiators join in a call for a show of political will, no matter how stubbornly they defend their own positions.

Polluter-Pays Principle: a principle embodied in the OECD *Guiding Principles Concerning Environmental Policies*. It states that the polluter should bear the expenses of carrying out measures decided by public authorities to reduce pollution and to reach a better allocation of resources. The cost of these measures should be reflected in the cost of goods and services which cause pollution in production and/or consumption. Such measures should not be accompanied by subsidies that would create significant distortions in international trade and investment. See also *trade and environment*.

Pollution haven: a country intent, at least perceived by some to be so, on attracting trade and investment regardless of the consequences for the environment. The assumption that pollution havens exist, and the perceived need to contain their spread, is one of the motivations for the discussion of *trade and environment*.

Pollution-haven hypothesis: the proposition that (a) countries with lax environmental standards will use their trade and investment regimes to attract all manner of industries with the intention of exporting goods made regardless of adverse environmental consequences, and (b) that countries with strict environmental production standards will import these goods and ignore the conditions under which they were made. The pollution-haven hypothesis differs from the *race-to-the-bottom* hypothesis. The latter predicts an equilibrium among all countries at low, possibly unsatisfactory, standards. [Frankel and Rose 2002]

Pop mercantilism: not a serious *trade policy* term, but of interest all the same. According to Mark Harrison of the University of Warwick, it describes the popular view that (a) industries or activities can be classed as essential or inessential, or ranked in order of national priority, and (b) when competition occurs in international markets, some countries gain and others lose. See also *mercantilism* and *neo-mercantilism*. [Harrison 2001]

Portfolio investment: minority holdings of shares, bonds and other securities as part of a diversified portfolio. The main difference between portfolio investment and *foreign direct investment* is generally seen in the amount of investment involved. Equity holdings of less than 10% would normally be considered portfolio investment. See also *investment* and *non-equity-based investment*.

Positive adjustment programs: see *structural adjustment*.

Positive comity: a term used in the administration of *competition policy*. It means that a country may, under the rules of a relevant bilateral arrangement, request the other country to initiate an action under the *competition laws* of that country. This can result in action that may otherwise not have been taken by the authorities of the other country. Article IX (Business Practices) of the *General Agreement on Trade in Services* incorporates the principle of positive comity. See also *negative comity*.

Positive deindustrialization: occurs when labour no longer needed in industrial production finds new employment opportunities in the services sector. See also *negative industrialization*. [Trade and Development Report 2003]

Positive integration: economic integration achieved through the creation of new institutions and regulatory frameworks established for the purpose. See also *negative integration*.

Positive intervention: often another way of referring to a *subsidy*, especially by those who would like to get one.

Positive listings: then countries inscribe their commitments under the *General Agreement on Trade in Services* in the form of positive listings, they list the activities they wish to be covered. Only these activities are then covered by all GATS articles, importantly the *market access* and *national treatment* obligations. The disadvantage of this method is that all services have to be listed even if there are no market access or national treatment limitations in the sense of the Agreement. Most countries have made all of their listings in this form. Some *free-trade agreements* have positive lists for services and investment commitments. See also *negative listings* and *market access for services*.

Positive margin of dumping: in *dumping* investigations, a finding that the *export price* is less than the *normal value*. In other words, dumping has occurred. See also *negative margin of dumping*.

Post-establishment: after an investment has been made. See also *pre-establishment* and *right of establishment*.

Poverty: this has many meanings. Usually it is concerned with "extreme poverty" or "destitution" on a large scale in developing countries and less with pockets of poverty in developed countries. The *World Development Report* 2000/2001 describes several ways in which poverty can be measured. First, one can calculate actual household income and compare it with a benchmark assumed to be the upper line of poverty in a given place. This is known as the "poverty line". Extreme poverty is often defined as having an income of less than one or two dollars a day. Another way is to look at health, especially mortality rates, and education, especially enrolments in primary schools. More difficult to use is the concept of *vulnerability*. This can mean either the risk that a household will experience income or health poverty over time or that it is exposed to other risks, such as violence, crime or natural disasters which will lead to poverty. A fourth way described in the Report is that of measuring voicelessness and powerlessness. All of these ways pose analytical problems. Measuring income is easiest, but it is in some ways less good at portraying the impact of poverty on people than the other methods are. *ECOSOC* uses a range of indicators when it determines its list of *least developed countries*. Views differ sharply on the causes of poverty in developing countries. Some poverty is doubtless due to inappropriate domestic policies made worse in some cases by a range of external causes. In other cases, awful government, persistent civil strife or endemic corruption should be included in the list of main causes. See also *Millennium Development Goals* and *trade and poverty*.

Poverty reduction: see *trade and poverty*.

Poverty Reduction and Growth Facility: PRGF. A program established by the *IMF* in 1999 to integrate better into its operations in *low-income countries* the

Fund's objectives of poverty reduction. Strategies to reduce poverty are formed by the countries themselves, with the assistance of the IMF. Individual programs are aimed mainly at prudent macro-economic policies, structural reforms and better fiscal management. Eligible countries can borrow at concessional interest rates from a trust fund established for this purpose.

PPM: see *process and production method*.

PPM labelling: a label on a good which gives information on how it was produced. In other words, it indicates what processes and production methods were applied. See *process and production method*.

Prebisch thesis: the proposition that the *terms of trade* of commodity-exporting developing countries will deteriorate in the long term. It is named after Raúl Prebisch, an Argentinean economist who was the first Secretary-General both of *ECLA* and of *UNCTAD*. See *Singer-Prebisch thesis*.

Precaution: see *precautionary principle*.

Precautionary approach: see *precautionary principle*.

Precautionary principle: this refers to Principle 15 of the *Rio Declaration on Environment and Development*. In the *Cartagena Protocol on Biosafety* it is called the precautionary approach. Trade negotiators sometimes simply refer to "precaution". The principle states that where there are threats of serious or irreparable damage [to the environment], lack of full scientific certainty shall not be used as a reason for postponing cost-effective measures to prevent environmental degradation. The precautionary principle has been incorporated in Article 5.7 of the *Agreement on the Application of Sanitary and Phytosanitary Measures*. This principle is one of the contentious issues in trade negotiations. Those who seek to enshrine it in trade rules are often accused by opponents of protectionism. In fact, most countries use the precautionary principle when it suits them, though it may be more or less informal. The *European Community* has established formal conditions for the application of the precautionary principle. These are: (a) where the scientific data are insufficient, inconclusive or uncertain and (b) where a preliminary scientific evaluation shows that potentially dangerous effects for the environment and human, animal or plant health can reasonably be feared. Additionally, three rules must be obeyed: (1) a complete scientific evaluation carried out by an independent authority to determine the degree of scientific uncertainty, (2) an assessment of the potential risks and the consequences of inaction, and (3) the participation, under conditions of maximum transparency, of all the interested parties in the study of possible measures. See also *rebuttable presumption* and *trade and environment*. [Cameron 1999]

Pre-competitive development activity: a concept used in the WTO *Agreement on Subsidies and Countervailing Measures*. Assistance, i.e. subsidies, for research activities conducted by firms or on their behalf is permitted if it does not cover more than 50% of pre-competitive development activities. These are defined as the translation of industrial research findings into a plan, blueprint, or design for new, modified or improved products, processes or services whether intended for sale or use, including the creation of a first prototype which would not be capable of commercial use. It may also include the conceptual formulation and design of products, processes or services.

Predatory pricing: the setting of prices at aggressively low levels, also known as ruinous competition, below-cost pricing, etc. This is the concept thought to underlie the treatment in the GATT of *dumping*, but it is not actually mentioned in its provisions. No single definition of predatory behaviour enjoys unanimous support, but there is agreement that to qualify as predatory pricing, an action should be aimed at driving efficient competitors out of the market. It has always been difficult to determine what the dividing line between competitive pricing and predatory pricing might be. Predation is a costly activity, and it would only be worth it to the predator if in the end all the costs incurred and the revenues foregone could be recovered. This is a doubtful proposition. See also *Areeda-Turner test* and *non-price predation*.

Predatory-pricing dumping: see *dumping*.

Pre-establishment: the phase in a foreign direct investment proposal between a decision by a company to invest and the receipt of approval from relevant authorities to proceed. In many cases, pre-establishment is simply a necessary planning stage, but it can be contentious if *foreign investment screening* is involved.

Pre-expiration testing: the analysis of patented products, often pharmaceutical products, shortly before the *patent* on them expires with a view to bringing a product with the same characteristics on the market shortly after the patent has expired. See also *Bolar exception*, *generic springboarding* and *reverse engineering*.

Preference erosion: disappearing *margins of preference* as countries reduce their *MFN tariffs* to levels at or below the margin of preference. See also *historical preferences*.

Preferences: favours extended to some trading partners, usually in the form of lower tariffs or non-application of some *non-tariff measures*. See also *historical preferences*, *GSP*, *GSTP*, *most-favoured-nation treatment* and *preferential trade arrangements*.

Preferential investment arrangements: formal or informal arrangements which give better access terms to investment capital and investors from selected countries or groups of countries. This may include expedited consideration of investment proposals, permission to invest in activities closed to others, higher ceilings for foreign equity, etc. Investment chapters in *free-trade agreements* fall in this category.

Preferential market access: any *market access* conditions afforded to a trading partner that are more favourable than the non-discriminatory *most-favoured-nation treatment*. Preferential access may be reciprocal or symmetrical as in *customs unions*, *free-trade areas*, or through the now residual imperial preferences. It can also be non-reciprocal or asymmetrical, as is the case with the

ACP-EC Partnership Agreement, the *Caribbean Basin Initiative*, *SPARTECA* and other such agreements.

Preferential rules of origin: a system of *rules of origin* (ROOs) to determine whether a good exported under a preferential trading arrangement, such as a *free-trade area*, will be admitted by another member of the arrangement under the applicable preferential rules. In most cases this would be free of *customs duties*. Preferential rules of origin are therefore meant to ensure that preferences given to the other members of the arrangement do not leak to third countries. *Wholly obtained goods* always qualify. In the case of other goods these rules seek to determine whether a *substantial transformation* has occurred, i.e. whether the imported good has been given its present form in the exporting country. One yardstick commonly applied to determine whether a good originates in the other member is the *regional value content* (RVC), expressed as a percentage of the total value of the good. The RVC is the share of the value of the good that can be ascribed to the exporting member or, in the case of several countries, the other members combined. It is the ratio between *originating materials*, which receive preferences, and *non-originating materials*, which do not. Two main methods have been devised to determine the RVC. All can entail complicated cost calculations. First, the *ex-factory cost method*, also known as the *net cost method*, takes into account all costs incurred by the producer up to the point where the good leaves the factory. Related to this is the *build-up method* which is based on a calculation of the value of originating materials. Second, the *FOB value method*, also known as *transaction value method* or *build-down method*, takes into account all costs, including a profit component, up to the point where the good has been loaded on the ship in the port of export. The calculation is based on ascertaining the value of non-originating material. A second yardstick used in the determination of the origin of a good is the *change in tariff heading*, also known as *change in chapter heading*. The basis of this method is that if a good has entered the country under one chapter heading, usually specified as a *chapter*, a *heading* or a *sub-heading* in the *Harmonized System*, it will necessarily be classified as a different product when it is exported. A calculation of the value added in the producing country is not necessary. The third yardstick used is a system of specific processing operations that must be met. Many free-trade agreements use more than one of these yardsticks. Sometimes the exporter can choose the method best suited to his products, but in other cases the product exported determines what rule will be used. A country that is a member of several free-trade agreements will have a different system of ROOs for each. [Estevadeordal and Suominen 2003, LaNasa 1995, Vermulst, Waer and Bourgeois 1994, WTO WT/REG/W/45]

Preferential tariff: a *tariff schedule* which shows the tariff rates applicable under *preferential trade arrangements*. The applicable tariff is usually lower than *general tariff* or the *most-favoured-nation tariff*. Preferential tariffs can be contractual as in a *free-trade agreement* or autonomous as under a *GSP* scheme.

Preferential Trade Area for Eastern and Southern African States: see *Common Market for Eastern and Southern Africa*.

Preferential trade arrangements: these are trade arrangements under which a party agrees, either unilaterally or as a result of negotiations, to accord one or more other parties preferential treatment in trade in goods or services. The scope for establishing such arrangements is subject to reasonably precise WTO rules, though developing countries have more flexibility. They may give each other preferences in the form of reduced tariffs, their complete elimination or, in the case of services, partial or complete liberalization. Developed countries must establish either a *free-trade area*, a *customs union* under *Article XXIV* of the *GATT* or, in the case of services, an *economic integration agreement* under *Article V* of the *General Agreement on Trade in Services*. That is, they must remove substantially all barriers to trade among those receiving preferences. If, for example, they wanted to give each other a preference in some product lines only, they would have to offer the same access conditions to all of their trading partners under the rule of *most-favoured-nation treatment*. Under the WTO rules, preferential trade arrangements are legal also in the form of *GSP* schemes set up by developed countries, and participation in the *GSTP* scheme by developing countries. For preferential arrangements other than these, it would be necessary to obtain a *waiver*. Some classify *treaties of friendship, commerce and navigation* as preferential agreements because the parties to them might be guaranteeing certain standards of behaviour towards the other party without giving trade preferences. See also *Caribbean Basin Initiative, imperial preferences arrangement, ACP-EC Partnership Agreement, preferential market access* and *SPARTECA*.

Preliminary affirmative determination of subsidization: no earlier than 60 days after the start of an investigation whether *countervailing duties* can be imposed, an investigating authority may determine that enough evidence exists to do so. It may then decide to impose *provisional countervailing duties*, but for a period not exceeding four months. It is at this stage that a *price undertaking* may be sought or accepted.

Preliminary determination of dumping: when an investigating authority examines a petition for the imposition of *anti-dumping measures*, it may conclude that there is enough evidence of *dumping* before all aspects of the case have been examined. It can then issue a preliminary determination of dumping and impose *provisional anti-dumping duties*. These may be imposed no earlier than 60 days after the start of the investigation. Their duration limited to between four to six months. After that, a *final determination of dumping* is needed to maintain the additional duties. All determinations have to published with the reasons for them.

Preparatory work: see *travaux préparatoires*.

Presence of natural persons: one of the *modes of services delivery*. The producer travels to another country to sell or deliver the service.

Preshipment inspection: PSI. Inspection of goods by specially appointed firms before they are shipped to other countries. PSI is defined in the WTO *Agreement on Preshipment Inspection* as "all activities imposed by a WTO member

341

relating to the verification of the quality, quantity, price, including currency, exchange rates and financial terms, and/or the customs classification of goods to be exported to its territory".

Pressure valve actions: refers mainly to *anti-dumping measures* and *safeguards*, but sometimes also to tariff renegotiations possible under GATT Article XXVIII. [Finger, Ng and Wangchuk 2001]

Price bands systems: mechanisms for the management of commodity prices. Two main varieties occur. The first is a mechanism maintained by some countries to ensure that the price on internal markets of mainly agricultural commodities is kept in a certain relationship to the international market price through a moving floor price to afford domestic producers a measure of protection. The way this is done is that when the price of the imported product is high compared to the domestic price, the *tariff* is lowered. If the imported price is low compared to the domestic price, the tariff is raised. Some have therefore described this kind of price band system as a *variable tariff*. The second variety of price band systems underpins the operations of *buffer stocks*. The simplest system consists of three bands, related to the market price of the commodity. When the price is low, the manager may buy. When it is at a medium level, the manager may buy or sell. When the price is high, the manager usually sells. [Valdés and Foster 2003]

Price collusion: a tacit or explicit agreement between firms to fix prices of certain goods in a market, usually with the aim of not undercutting each other. See also *antitrust laws* and *competition policy*.

Price-contingent subsidy: a subsidy that is only payable if the price for the good or the service in question moves outside a certain range. This is the case when the return to the producer is very low, or when the consumer would otherwise have to pay a very high price.

Price depression: a term used in the WTO *Agreement on Subsidies and Counter-vailing Measures*, but not defined there. It is, however, generally taken to mean a price forced lower than would have been the case without state intervention, i.e. the payment of a *subsidy*. It seems to have virtually the same meaning as *price suppression*. [WT/DS273/R]

Price dumping: a category of *dumping* identified at the time of the *Havana Charter* negotiations which is now subject to Article VI of the GATT. It is based on the concept that the exporter sells goods abroad at a lower price than in the domestic market, and that this may have an injurious effect on industry in the importing country producing similar goods. See also *anti-dumping measures* and *predatory pricing*.

Price equalization mechanism: a mechanism designed to ensure that market prices for commercially produced and traded commodities, and therefore returns to their producers, do not fluctuate excessively. This aim is seen as promoting the orderly development of the industry by assuring producers of more predictable remunerative returns. At the same time, it is thought to benefit consumers who can look forward to modest price changes at any one time. Such mechanisms operate in many different ways. The main challenge for all of them is to ensure that it does not turn into a more or less permanent *subsidy*. This can be done if the producers are responsible for the funding of the mechanism. In this way, price signals will not be ignored. See also *buffer stocks*, *common agricultural policy*, *floor price*, *international commodity agreements*, *price band system* and *variable tariff*.

Price suppression: a term used in the WTO *Agreement on Subsidies and Countervailing Measures*, but not defined there. It seems to have virtually the same meaning as *price depression*. [WT/DS273/R]

Price taker: a firm or a country that is too small on its own to influence the price of a good.

Price undertaking: an undertaking by an exporter to raise the export price of the product to avoid the possibility of an anti-dumping or countervailing duty. In the case of the former, a price undertaking is not supposed to exceed the alleged *margin of dumping*, and preferably it should be at the lowest possible level that would be adequate to remove the threat of *injury* from domestic industry. In the case of the latter, the price increases must not be higher than necessary to eliminate the amount of the subsidy. Authorities are not compelled in either case to agree to offers of price undertakings. See also *anti-dumping measures*, *countervailing duties*, *lesser-duty principle* and *trade harassment*.

Price wedge: the difference between the price of a product in a protected market and its price under fully competitive conditions.

***Prima facie*:** *Lat.* variously rendered as on the face of it, at first sight, on first impression, etc.

***Prima facie* case:** enough evidence to allow the plaintiff to win the case unless the defence presents additional evidence or legal argument to rebut it. The *Appellate Body* described such a situation in *Canada – Measures Affecting the Export of Civil Aircraft* as "a case which, in the absence of effective refutation by the defending party . . . , requires a panel, as matter of law, to rule in favour of the complaining party presenting a *prima facie* case".

Primage: a term denoting the temporary imposition of an *import surcharge* or a similar measure having the effect of increasing the normal *customs duties*.

Primary dealers: in the United States banking system, these are firms that have established a trading relationship with the Federal Reserve Bank of New York. To qualify as a primary dealer, a firm must be willing to make markets in the full range of Treasury issues for a reasonably diverse group of customers, and it must satisfy minimum capital requirements. Some United States acts, such as the *Iran and Libya Sanctions Act*, may lead to the cancellation of a primary dealer licence if the firm engages in activities declared illegal under the acts.

Primary products: defined in GATT Article XVI:4 for the purposes of the applicable subsidies regime as "any product of farm, forest or fishery, or any mineral, in its natural form or which has undergone such processing as is customarily required to prepare it for marketing in substantial volume in international trade".

The reference to "minerals" was omitted when the *Agreement on Interpretation and Application of Articles VI, XVI and XXIII of the General Agreement on Tariff and Trade* (the Subsidies Code) was adopted in 1979 as part of the **Tokyo Round** outcome. In 1957, GATT members rejected a United States suggestion that subsidies should be permitted for the export of cotton textiles if the subsidy was essentially the payment that would have been made on raw cotton if the raw material had been exported in its natural form. In the *pasta* case the panel found that pasta was not a primary product, but a processed agricultural product. The European Economic Community had argued that the disputed exported refund in that case was granted in respect of the durum wheat that had been used, that the refund did not include any component by way of processing aid, and that durum wheat was undeniably a primary product. See also *Agreement on Agriculture* and *basic agricultural products*.

Principal supplier right: the right, obtained by virtue of one's status as the largest supplier of a particular tariff line to another trading partner, to ask for tariff negotiations under the *principal supplier rule*.

Principal supplier rule: a major feature of the system governing tariff negotiations in the GATT, particularly in the earlier negotiating rounds. Under this rule, requests for tariff concessions to a particular GATT member could only be made by the principal supplier of the product in question. The rule is based on the assumption that the country making the *concession* will only be able to get compensated for it once, and that the country invited to make the concession will be able to maximize its returns by dealing with the largest supplier. It is also meant to reduce the unintended benefits *free riders* may otherwise obtain. In practice, reliance on this system alone led to the effective exclusion of smaller and developing countries from the negotiating process. The method of *linear tariff reductions* in the **Kennedy Round** and the **Tokyo Round**, as well as the practice of negotiations across broader product categories, such as the *Information Technology Agreement*, have reduced the importance of the principal supplier rule. See also *initial negotiating rights*, *principal supplying interest* and *sectoral trade negotiations*.

Principal supplying interest: a right to participate in WTO tariff negotiations for specified product items based on a ranking of export interest in a given product. It is held by the WTO member having the highest ratio of exports affected by the item. It is therefore a right based on the relative magnitude of trade flows. A principal supplying interest differs from *principal supplier rights* which are based on absolute magnitude of trade flows. It also is unlike *initial negotiating rights* which are accorded by one member to another through negotiations. In determining whether a country has a principal supplying interest, the WTO secretariat may only take into account products traded on a most-favoured-nation basis. One of the purposes of the concept of principal supplying interest is to allow smaller and medium-sized traders an opportunity to initiate tariff negotiations in products of major importance to them. See also *substantial supplying interest*.

Prior art: a term used in *patent* examinations to describe all publicly available information relevant to the *invention* for which the patent has been sought.

Prior informed consent: PIC. A voluntary procedure governing trade in chemicals or pesticides banned or severely restricted by national governments because of the health and environmental risks they pose. It is being implemented jointly by the *Food and Agricultural Organization* and the *United Nations Environment Programme* (UNEP). The procedure entails notifying a central agency of the ban or restriction. The notification is then circulated, and other governments advise the agency whether they consent to the import of chemicals or pesticides listed in this way. Exporting countries in turn undertake only to export these substances to countries that permit their import. The procedure in itself is not a recommendation to ban or restrict the use of chemicals. See also *Convention on the Prior Informed Consent Procedure for Certain Hazardous Chemicals and Pesticides in International Trade*, *multilateral environment agreements* and *trade and environment*.

Priority foreign country: this is a term used in sections 1302 and 1303 of the *Omnibus Trade and Competitiveness Act* of 1988. These two sections are usually known as *Super 301* and *Special 301*, respectively. Super 301 requires *USTR* to inform Congress of priority foreign countries maintaining practices which, if eliminated, would have the greatest potential for increasing United States exports. Special 301 requires a similar list of countries, known as the priority watch list, that deny adequate and effective protection of *intellectual property rights* to United States firms. In this case, priority foreign countries are countries that have (a) the most onerous or *egregious* acts, policies or practices that deny adequate and effective intellectual property rights or deny fair and equitable *market access* to United States persons that rely upon *intellectual property* protection, and (b) that are not prepared to enter into bilateral or multilateral negotiations to find remedies. Once a country has been identified as a priority foreign country, USTR must start a *Section 301* investigation. Countries may be deleted from the list, but USTR must give reasons for doing so.

Priority foreign country practices: see *Super 301*.

Priority watch list: see *priority foreign country* and *Special 301*.

Prisoner's Dilemma: a device used to demonstrate that apparently rational micro-level decisions do not necessarily lead to rational macro-level outcomes. It is often used in game theory to explain the virtue of collective action as practiced under the *multilateral trading system*. The dilemma, which occurs in many variations, has in outline the following features. Several prisoners face separate interrogation. Each knows that if none of the others confess, it will result in freedom for all. Each also knows that if one of them confesses, but none of the others do, the one making the confession will get freedom. All of the others will receive severe sentences. If all confess, they will all be punished, but less severely than if only one confessed. The apparently rational decision by each individual prisoner therefore is to confess without bothering too much about the others. The moral is that they all are worse off by confessing than if they had been able to agree among themselves not to confess at all. This proposal was apparently first presented formally by A. W. Tucker in 1950, but it seems to have existed in some form or other before that.

Prison labour: GATT Article XX(e) allows WTO members to adopt restrictions on the import of goods made by prison labour. Many countries have adopted laws enabling them to ban the import of such products, but the extent to which they enforce them varies. See also *core labour standards* and *social dumping*.

Private cartel: see *cartel*.

Private international cartel: a *cartel* with member firms in more than one economy or affecting markets in more than one jurisdiction.

Private international law: the field of law dealing with relations between individuals domiciled in different jurisdictions. As no two countries have the same legal system, the question arises as to which law should prevail. This area of the law is therefore also known as conflict of laws. See also *public international law*.

Privatization: the process by which public assets, previously owned and managed by the state, are restructured as public entities with share capital being offered to the public. Governments sometimes retain a substantial share of the privatized enterprise. The expression is also sometimes used to describe the conversion of a publicly listed company into a private one. See also *deregulation*.

Procedural protectionism: the abuse especially of *anti-dumping measures*, *countervailing duties* or *safeguards* in a way that turns them into protectionist mechanisms.

Process and production method: PPM. A term used in discussions concerning *trade and environment*. It deals with the environmental effects of processes by which goods and services are produced. A negative effect may occur in two main ways: (a) through the transformation of the product itself and (b) through a production process that does not affect the characteristics of the finished good. What is important is that the process and production resulting in the good is in itself deemed to determine how the finished good should be dealt with. Some have argued that a labelling system should be established to let the consumer know what processes have been used in the production of a good. This is the so-called PPM-labelling. See also *non-product-related process and production*.

Process protectionism: a term used by I. M. Destler to describe a domestic system under which *trade remedies* can be invoked more easily than under the standard WTO rules. [Destler 1993]

Procès-verbal: the preparation of minutes, recording of agreed conclusions and other written descriptions of transactions occurring in a meeting.

Producer subsidy equivalent: PSE. A term used in agricultural negotiations. PSE is defined as the subsidy that would be necessary to compensate agricultural producers for removing government support. Expressed as a percentage, it is the ratio of the total value of transfers to producers as a result of government policies to total producer income. When this ratio is positive, the PSE indicates that the producer is receiving *assistance*. When it is negative, the producer is taxed. See also *consumer subsidy equivalent*.

Product-by-product negotiations: see *item-by-item tariff negotiations*.

Product cycle theory: proposed by Raymond Vernon in 1966. It states that highly industrialized countries enjoy a *comparative advantage* in the research and development of new products because they have better access to capital and specialized human resources. The product cycle is assumed to consist of several stages, beginning with production in a small custom-oriented market, later becoming the domain of the multi-national firm and reaching its apex with the manufacture of the product in lower-cost countries from where the product is re-exported to the market in which it had been developed originally. See also *Heckscher-Ohlin theorem*. [Vernon 1966]

Product-mandating: a governmental requirement that a new investor export to certain countries or regions. See also *export performance requirements*.

Product-specific non-preferential rules of origin: refers to *rules of origin* applied by an importing country to goods traded under *most-favoured-nation* conditions. Such a system of rules prescribes product by product the conditions that have to be met for a product to be considered originating from a given country. An example of such rules is the requirement that chemical products may have to be the result of a chemical reaction in the exporting country. Mere mixing of components would not be enough.

Produit similaire: see *like product*.

Professional services: a class of *services* usually provided by persons having specialist educational qualifications or training. Sometimes permission to offer such services also depends on membership of a professional body. Examples of professional services are those offered by accountants, architects, auditors, chemists, engineers, doctors, lawyers, librarians, pharmacists, physiotherapists, psychologists, surveyors and veterinarians. In *NAFTA* professional services are defined as services where the delivery requires specialized post-secondary education or equivalent training or experience, subject to a right to practice being granted by a party to the Agreement. Services provided by tradespersons or ship and aircrew members do not qualify as professional services.

Profit-shifting tariff: a concept in economic theory founded in *mercantilism* which proposes that it is possible to shift monopoly rents from a foreign country to one's own territory through the imposition of a tariff. The tariff would cream off the excess profit the foreign firm would otherwise be making. Economists have noted that the profit-shifting tariff is yet another mercantilist argument for restricting imports and promoting exports. See also *balance of trade*.

Programme of Action on the Establishment of a New International Economic Order: see *New International Economic Order*.

Progressive liberalization: a principle enshrined in the *General Agreement on Trade in Services*. It had its origin in the Punta del Este Declaration which launched the *Uruguay Round*. There it was identified with *transparency* and economic growth as one of the aims for the forthcoming services negotiations.

This principle was carried forward into Article XIX of the GATS which requires members to enter into successive rounds of negotiations at least every five years and no later than 1 January 2000. See also *WTO built-in agenda*.

Progressivity and flexibility: virtually the same as *special and differential treatment*. Its underlying principle is that developing countries should be able to take on new obligations selectively and in stages.

Prohibited subsidies: a concept used in the WTO *Agreement on Subsidies and Countervailing Measures* to denote subsidies contingent on export performance or subsidies contingent on the use of domestic rather than imported goods. WTO members are not allowed to maintain this type of subsidies. See also *actionable subsidies*, *local-content rules*, *non-actionable subsidies*, *subsidies* and *Agreement on Trade-Related Investment Measures*.

Prohibitive tariff: a tariff rate set so high that it acts as a strong barrier to imports. See also *protective tariff*.

Proportionality: a concept used to compare the trade costs of a measure with the benefits that the measure might have for other areas of governmental policy. The idea is that there should be some rational relationship between the cost impact of a measure and the benefits it is likely to produce. It is one measure that can be used for determining the necessity of a trade measure.

Proprietary information: see *trade secrets*.

Proprio motu: *Lat.* on one's own initiative. For example, Article 144.4 of the Japan-Singapore free-trade agreement states that the "arbitral tribunal may, at the request of a Party or *proprio motu*, select, in consultation with the parties, no fewer than two scientific or technical experts who shall assist the arbitral tribunal ... "

Prospect theory: the proposition, developed by D. Kahnemann and A. Tversky in 1979, that in making decisions, people overemphasize small probabilities of success and underemphasize large probabilities of success. Or, as Kenneth Dam puts it, "groups work harder to avoid a loss than to gain a benefit". See also *conservative social welfare function*. [Kahnemann and Tversky 1979, Dam 2001]

Protected appellation of origin: an *appellation of origin* protected under the *Lisbon Agreement*. This Agreement defines "appellation of origin" as "the geographical name of a country, region, or locality, which serves to designate a product originating therein, the quality and characteristics of which are due exclusively or essentially to the geographical environment, including natural and human factors". The Agreement gives protection against any usurpation or imitation, even if the true origin of the product is indicated, or if the appellation is in translated form, accompanied by terms such as "kind", "type", "imitation", or the like. Recognition of a protected appellation is usually done through a law, decree or other administrative act following an investigation of the claim for recognition. See also *geographical indications*. [Lisbon Agreement for the Protection of Appellations of Origin and their International Registration; Audier, 2000; WIPO SCT/8/4]

Protected designation of origin: PDO. In the *European Community* the registered name of a region, a specific place or, in exceptional cases, a country used to describe an agricultural product or a foodstuff which (a) is originating in that region, specific place or country, and (b) the quality or characteristics of which are essentially or exclusively due to a particular geographical environment with its inherent natural and human factors, and the production, processing and preparation of which take place in the defined geographical area. This definition in some cases also covers traditional geographical or non-geographical names for an agricultural product or a foodstuff originating in a region or specific place. Foodstuffs include beer, natural mineral waters and spring waters, beverages made from plant extracts, bread, pastry, cakes, confectionery, biscuits and other baker's wares, and natural gums and resins. Generic names may not be registered. The *regulation* establishing PDOs does not apply to wines and spirits. See also *appellations of origin*, *geographical indications*, *certificate of specific character* and *protected geographical indication*. [Council Regulation (EEC) No 2081/92; Audier, 2000]

Protected geographical indication: PGI. In the *European Community* the registered name of a region, a specific place or, in exceptional cases, a country, used (a) to describe an agricultural product or a foodstuff originating in that region, place or country, and (b) which possesses a specific quality, reputation or other characteristics attributable to that geographical origin and the production and/or processing and/or preparation which take place in that geographical area. Foodstuffs include beer, natural mineral waters and spring waters, beverages made from plant extracts, bread, pastry, cakes, confectionery, biscuits and other baker's wares, and natural gums and resins. Generic names may not be registered. The *regulation* establishing PGIs does not apply to wines and spirits. See also *appellations of origin*, *certificate of specific character*, *geographical indications* and *protected designations of origin*. [Council Regulation (EEC) No 2081/92; Audier 2000]

Protection: the extent to which domestic producers and their products are shielded from the competition of the international market. The incidence or cost of protection can be measured or estimated with a high degree of accuracy. *Tariffs* are the starting point in the case of goods, but the matter becomes more complicated where tariffs are accompanied by *non-tariff measures*, or if protection consists entirely of non-tariff measures, or government regulation in the case of services. Methods are available also for estimating the cost of protection of service industries, but these are rather less accurate than the ones for goods. Protection differs considerably from *protectionism*. See also *assistance*, *bounty*, *effective rate of protection*, *international contestability of markets*, *optimal tariff* and *subsidy*.

Protectionism: economic policies which prevent the exposure of domestic producers to the rigours of the international market, often under the guise of some other policy objective. The basic means for achieving this are *tariffs*, *subsidies*, *voluntary restraint arrangements* and other *non-tariff measures*, with an emphasis on the less transparent measures. More complex cases can involve alleged cultural, *sanitary and phytosanitary measures*, environmental and other considerations. Protectionism can also be promoted through the vigorous use of *contingent protection*. In most cases, protectionism merely delays the inevitable adjustment of inefficient industries to the market. See also *cultural identity*, *structural adjustment* and *trade and environment*.

Protectionist statements and claims: this entry lists claims often made by protectionist who would have us believe that although they are fully persuaded of the merits of freer trade, and sometimes even of free trade, some unmet conditions prevent them from accepting any anything but a good measure of protection. The list of claims and statements is by no means complete, but their drift will be clear anyway. *I am a free-trader, but ...* This always means that the speaker is not a free-trader at all, as the concluding part of the sentence always makes clear. *We should reduce our tariffs, but only when the others have reduced theirs.* The implication seems to be that but for the high tariffs of others, the industry would be able to export. This statement is usually made by representatives of industries operating behind high protective walls and that have no chance of exporting. *Let us not eliminate tariffs purely to meet some academic ideal.* The meaning is that elimination of tariffs is not wanted regardless of what academic theory may be at stake. *Now is not the time to reduce tariffs.* Nor probably, in the view of the claimants, would any other time be right. *Comparative advantage doesn't apply to agriculture.* One can only assume that holders of this view know that the claim is nonsense, and that they have run out of anything else to say.

Protection of geographical names: see *Agreement on Trade-Related Aspects of Intellectual Property Rights*, *appellation d'origine contrôlée*, *appellations of origin*, *certification mark*, *collective mark*, *designations of origin*, *Draft Act on the Protection of Geographical Indications*, *extension of protection for geographical indications*, *geographical indications*, *indications of source*, *Lisbon Agreement*, *Madrid Agreement for the Repression of False or Deceptive Indications of Source on Goods*, *Paris Convention*, *protected appellation of origin*, *protected designation of origin*, *registered geographical indications* and *Stresa Convention*.

Protective tariff: a *tariff* designed to shelter part of the national productive capacity from the full impact of foreign competition. See also *protection*, *protectionism* and *revenue tariff*.

Protocol: a protocol is a *treaty* drafted to supplement another treaty or convention. It contains all the elements found in other types of treaties (preamble, definitions, signature, ratification, entry into force, etc.), and it shares the same legally binding quality. A protocol must be consistent with its parent treaty. If a conflict arises, the parent treaty prevails over the protocol. A protocol is needed each time the results of multilateral negotiations have to be added to the WTO instruments. Note, however, that some instruments designated as protocols are treaties in their own right.

Protocol of accession: the instrument which sets out the terms and conditions under which a country becomes a member of the WTO, or for that matter, other international organizations. In the WTO, these protocols are largely standardized, but they sometimes reflect particular circumstances of the acceding country. See also *accession*.

Protocol of Ouro Preto: see *Mercosur*.

Protocol of Provisional Application: PPA. This was adopted by the original members of the *GATT* in 1947 to apply the Agreement provisionally pending a decision to do so permanently. That decision never was taken. The PPA is not part of the *GATT 1994*.

Protocol of Tegucigalpa: see *SICA*.

Provisional anti-dumping duties: duties or charges imposed once it becomes evident that there is a *prima facie* case of *dumping*. The WTO rules on *anti-dumping measures* permit governments to impose provisional anti-dumping duties under three conditions. These are that (a) a proper investigation has been initiated, (b) a preliminary affirmative determination has been made of dumping and consequent *injury* to domestic industry, and (c) the authorities deem provisional duties necessary to prevent injury being caused during the investigation period. Provisional anti-dumping duties may not exceed the provisionally estimated *margin of dumping*. The WTO rules stress, however, that asking for a cash or bond security would be preferable. In principle, provisional anti-dumping duties should be imposed for no longer than four months, though this may be extended to up to nine months in some circumstances.

Provisional countervailing duties: once a government has initiated an investigation concerning alleged subsidies applied by another WTO member, it may impose provisional countervailing measures. The three main conditions to be fulfilled are (a) that the investigation has been initiated according to the rules, (b) that a preliminary finding has been made that a *subsidy* exists and that it is causing *injury* to domestic industry, and (c) that there is a view that further injuries would occur if subsidization was maintained during the remainder of the investigation. Provisional countervailing measures may be in the form of cash deposits or bonds equal to the amount of subsidization. Provisional measures cannot be applied earlier than 60 days after the start of an investigation, and they must not remain in force for more than four months.

Provisional safeguard measures: may be applied under the WTO *Agreement on Safeguards* if a preliminary determination shows that increased imports have caused or are threatening to cause serious *injury*. Provisional safeguard measures may be applied for no longer than 200 days. WTO members have to go through the full safeguards procedures if they want to continue the measures beyond that limit. Many *free-trade agreements* have a similar provision in the articles governing *bilateral safeguards*.

Prudence: see *prudential regulation*.

Prudential regulation: in *financial services*, terms used to describe an objective of market regulation by authorities to protect investors and depositors or to avoid instability or crises. Prudential measures require banks and insurance companies to maintain certain capital reserves and mandatory asset ratios. They have to meet strict reporting requirements. There is no agreement on what an optimal level of prudential control might be. Opinion is in favour of clear and enforceable prudential measures, but they have not prevented some spectacular exploits by financial services firms or company crashes. Prudential measures are not normally considered impediments to trade in financial services, and they do not have to be listed under the GATS as measures capable of affecting *market access* and *national treatment*.

PSI: *preshipment inspection*. The practice of employing specialized private companies to check shipment details of goods ordered overseas, i.e. price, quantity, quality, etc. See also *Agreement on Preshipment Inspection*.

Public cartel: see *cartel*.

Public interest test: the WTO *Agreement on Safeguards* requires countries starting an investigation whether *safeguards* are justified to consider, among other matters, whether the application of a safeguard measure would be in the public interest. The term is not defined further, but the agreement refers to importers, exporters and other interested parties. The public interest therefore goes beyond the interests of the industry petititoning for an investigation. Some have advocated that the public interest should be one of the factors to be considered before *anti-dumping measures* can be taken. This might include the impact of the measures on users of the product, the impact on consumers, effect on competition in the market place, efficient allocation of resources, etc. The public interest is not identical to the *national interest*, but one assumes that an effective public-interest provision would similarly permit the relevant authority to suspend all or part of a proposed anti-dumping measure. Some anti-dumping laws already allow for or require a public interest test. Such tests are also administered in other areas of public administration, such as *competition policy*. See also *Community interest clause*. [Leclerc 1999; Marceau 1994; Steele 1996]

Public international law: the law concerning relations between states or between states and international organizations. See also *International Court of Justice* and *private international law*.

Public procurement: see *government procurement*.

Public telecommunications transport services: defined in the *Annex on Telecommunications* to the *General Agreement on Trade in Services* as "any telecommunications transport service required, explicitly or in effect, by a Member to be offered to the public generally. Such services may include, *inter alia*, telegraph, telephone, telex, and data transmission typically involving the real-time transmission of customer-supplied information between two or more points without any end-to-end change in the form or content of the customer's information".

Public telecommunications transport network: defined in the *Annex on Telecommunications* to the *General Agreement on Trade in Services* as "the public telecommunications infrastructure which permits telecommunications between and among defined termination points".

Punitive tariff: a tariff set so high, often as a form of *retaliation*, that in most cases trade no longer occurs under it. It has the same effect as a *prohibitive tariff*.

Punta del Este Declaration: the Ministerial Declaration formally launching the *Uruguay Round* on 25 September 1986.

Purchase abroad: the same as *consumption abroad*, one of the *modes of services delivery*.

Pure export cartel: see *cartel*.

P-4 Agreement: see *Trans-Pacific Strategic Economic Partnership Agreement*.

P5: an informal grouping concerned with issues of agricultural trade. It consists of Australia, Brazil, the European Community, India and the United States. The group is known also as the Five Interested Parties (FIPs) and the NG-5.

P-5: short for Pacific-5. It includes Australia, Chile, New Zealand, Singapore and the United States. At the time of the Auckland *APEC* meetings (1999) Fred Bergsten suggested that the P-5 should consider forming a *free-trade agreement* among themselves.

Q

QRs: see *quantitative restrictions*.

Quadrilaterals: established in 1981 as periodic *trade policy* talks between the United States, the *European Community*, Japan and Canada. Now also applied to the four acting together. Often shortened to Quad. See also *minilateralism*.

Qualifying area: one of the criteria used in the administration of *rules of origin*. It is the territory within which a product must have been produced or from which it must have been exported to enjoy *preferential treatment* in the importing country. For *free-trade areas* this is usually the territory of the parties to the agreement. Under other schemes, such as the *GSP*, the qualifying area may include other developing countries. This criterion may have to be met together with others, such as the *regional value content* or *substantial transformation*. See also *Pan-European Cumulation Area*.

Qualifying value content: in the administration of *rules of origin* the same as *regional value content*. It denotes the point at which a product is considered to be the product of another party because enough value has been added to it. The product is accordingly eligible for preferential customs treatment.

Quantitative export restrictions: see *export quotas* and *voluntary restraint arrangement*.

Quantitative restrictions: specific limits on the quantity or value of goods that can be imported (or exported) during a given period. Article XI of the GATT proscribes the use of quantitative restrictions, subject to specified exceptions, including those listed in Article XX which covers *general exceptions*. See also *export quotas*, *import quotas* and *tariff quotas*.

Quarantine measures: see *sanitary and phytosanitary measures*.

Quint: consists of the agriculture ministers of Australia, Canada and Japan, the United States Secretary of Agriculture and the European Commissioner for Agriculture. The group was established during the *Uruguay Round*. It now meets at irregular and infrequent intervals.

Quota: a restriction on the amount of a good that may be imported by a country or exported from it. See also *import licensing*.

Quota-hopping: the transfer of production of products subject to an export quota from a country with a limited quota availability to one where a quota may be obtained more easily. See also *rules of origin*.

Quota modulation: when a WTO member applies a *safeguard* on a product subject to *import quotas*, the normal expectation would be that any restrictions on imports would more or less preserve the allocated shares. The *Agreement on Safeguards* makes it possible, however, to depart from this principle (i.e. to modulate a quota), but only in cases of *serious injury*. Conditions are (a) that imports from certain members have increased disproportionately, (b) the departure can be justified, and (c) the change is equitable to all suppliers of the product concerned.

Quota right: the right granted to an importer or exporter to make use of the more favourable trading conditions available under a defined *quota*.

QWERTY principle: not an accepted trade policy concept, but illustrative of the dangers of accepting uncritically established ideas. It was first proposed by the economic historian Paul Davis in 1982 and popularized greatly in the 1990s by Paul Krugman. The principle takes its starting point from the QWERTY layout of computer keyboards which dates back to the earliest manual typewriters. The latter apparently were likely to jam when the typing was too quick, and the QWERTY layout forced the typist to slow down (note that there is argument whether this is really true). Later mechanical improvements made the QWERTY layout unnecessary, but inertial thinking ensured its survival into the computer age, because it had become "locked in". More recently, the validity of the assertion that the QWERTY layout is an inferior solution has been questioned, and it may indeed be no more than a myth. Be that as it may, Krugman notes that the emergence of the QWERTY layout leads one to reject the idea that markets invariably lead the economy to a unique best solution, and that in fact the outcome of market competition often depends crucially on historical accident. The principle also stands for the idea that investigating the validity of long-held beliefs and practices is intrinsically worthwhile. See also *conventional wisdom* and *vestigial thought*.

R

Race-to-the-bottom argument: expresses the fear that the need to compete with imports from countries with low labour costs and lower labour standards will reduce wages and labour conditions in the developed countries. This argument forms part of the rationale for discussions on a *social clause* and *trade and labour standards*. A similar argument has been made in relation to environmental standards where it is thought that lower environmental requirements in some countries could give them a competitive advantage. See also *core labour standards*, *globalization*, *social dumping*, *trade and environment*, *wage-differential argument* and *workers rights*.

Ratchet mechanism: refers to provisions on trade in services in some *free-trade agreements* whereby autonomous liberalization measures by a member between negotiating sessions are automatically included in that member's *schedule of commitments* under the agreement in question. See also *non-conforming measures*. [OECD TD/TC(2002)8/FINAL]

Rational ignorance: a decision by voters not to spend time or money on getting to understand electoral matters not concerning them since the marginal cost of getting the information would be greater than the marginal benefit derived from it. [Dam 2001]

REACH: Registration, Evaluation and Authorization of Chemicals. This is a *European Union* (EU) proposal launched in 2003 to improve protection in the EU of human health and the environment from the hazards of *chemicals* and to enhance the competitiveness the EU chemicals industry. REACH requires the registration of all chemical substances produced or imported in volumes greater then one tonne per year. The extent of required evaluation and the granting of authorization will depend on the nature of the substance. See also *Global Classification and Labelling System for Chemicals* and *Convention on Persistent Organic Pollutants*.

Reasonable period of time: a term used in the WTO *Dispute Settlement Understanding*. It denotes the time, generally a maximum of 15 months, that may elapse between the adoption of a *panel* or *Appellate Body* report and the point when a trade regime found inconsistent with the WTO rules has to be brought into conformity with them. Where a WTO member refuses to take the necessary actions, the member notifying the dispute may impose the *suspension of concessions or other obligations* after the same reasonable period of time has passed. Three options are available for defining what may be a reasonable period of time. The first is the time proposed by the member itself, subject to the agreement of the *Dispute Settlement Body*. If this does not work, the second option is for the parties to agree on a period of time within 45 days of the adoption of the ruling. If there is still no agreement, an arbitrator will be appointed to settle on a period of no more than fifteen months from the adoption of a *panel* or *Appellate Body* report. The significance of this approach is that a WTO member has little opportunity or incentive to waste time over taking action in an adverse ruling since the clock starts when the Dispute Settlement Body adopts the panel or Appellate Body Report.

Rebuttable presumption: a legal term in common use in the United States meaning that an action is deemed to conform to the law until shown otherwise. Some say that the word "rebuttable" is redundant since any presumption can be challenged and, indeed, rebutted. The term is sometimes used in discussions of the *precautionary principle*.

Recidivist dumping: sometimes used, especially by American negotiators, for companies that persist in *dumping* their products, and that allegedly see dumping as a way of doing business. See also *anti-dumping measures* and *Persistent Dumping Clause*.

Reciprocal dumping: occurs when firms from two countries engage in *dumping* in each other's markets. Krugman and Brander have demonstrated that this can occur if monopoly profits exceed transport costs. [Krugman and Brander 1983]

Reciprocal free trade: the proposition that one should liberalize *market access* only to those who are prepared to open their markets in turn. There is no implication that this would necessarily lead to the condition usually defined as *free trade*. See also *reciprocity*.

Reciprocal free-trade area: see *free-trade areas*.

Reciprocal trade agreement: a trade agreement which gives members equal rights and obligations. This form of agreement does not imply any particular content, but sometimes it may mean an agreement for reciprocal tariff reductions negotiated under the *United States Reciprocal Trade Agreements Program*.

Reciprocal retaliation: see *Mirror retaliation*.

Reciprocal Trade Agreements Program: see *United States Reciprocal Trade Agreements Program*.

Reciprocity: the practice in the WTO, but not a contractual requirement, by which governments extend similar *concessions* to each other, as when one government lowers tariffs or other barriers impeding imports in exchange for equivalent concessions from a trading partner. This is also known as achieving a *balance of concessions*. Concessions made as a result of reciprocal bargaining must be extended through the *most-favoured-nation rule* to all WTO members. See also *mirror-image reciprocity* and *reciprocity at the margin*.

Reciprocity at the margin: a term meaning that the overall value of *concessions* offered to trading partners should roughly match the value of concessions received in turn. See also *mirror-image reciprocity*.

Recognition: the act of recognizing by one country of the qualifications, standards, licence requirements or testing methods of another country. Such recognition can have a considerable impact on the conduct of trade. Under the *General Agreement on Trade in Services*, recognition may be done unilaterally, mutually or through harmonization. If a country accords recognition to another country, it does not have to extend it to others, as *most-favoured-nation treatment* would require. It must, however, give others an opportunity to demonstrate that they, too, can meet the required standards. See also *Agreement on Technical Barriers to Trade*, *harmonization of standards and qualifications* and *mutual recognition arrangements*.

Recommendation: one of the means available to the *European Community* to influence the actions of member states, even though recommendations are not binding. Recommendations are also commonly used in the *OECD*. See also *European Community legislation*.

Rectifications: adjustments to a country's *tariff schedule*, usually to remove errors made in its preparation. See also *renegotiation of tariffs*.

Re-exports: goods brought into a country temporarily and destined ultimately for other markets, sometimes after some value has been added. See also *entrepôt trade*, *free-trade zones* and *remanufactured goods*.

Reference paper on telecommunications services: a set of definitions and principles concerning the regulatory framework for *basic telecommunications services*, adopted by the WTO on 24 April 1996. The reference paper seeks to prevent anti-competitive practices, ensure interconnection under non-discriminatory terms, and to promote a transparent, non-discriminatory and competitively neutral universal service obligation. It makes the public availability of licensing criteria mandatory. It also postulates the existence of independent regulatory authorities. Allocation of scarce resources, including frequencies, numbers and rights of way, is to be done in an objective, timely, transparent and non-discriminatory manner. See also *Agreement on Basic Telecommunications Services* and *competitive neutrality*.

Reference price: a benchmark for valuing goods adopted by some customs authorities to arrive at the amount of customs duties payable. Its main aim is to prevent *under-invoicing* as this would lead to a lower revenue collection. The reference is usually meant to reflect the market price for the goods, but it can be higher. See also *customs valuation*.

Reform process/program: The Uruguay Round *Agreement on Agriculture* starts a reform process for global agricultural trade. It sets out a first step in the process, i.e. a program for reducing subsidies and production and other reforms. The negotiations launched under Article 20, now subsumed in the *Doha Development Agenda*, are aimed at continuing the reform process. See also *continuation clause*.

Refusal to deal: see *boycott*.

Regatta approach: a term sometimes used in the context of *enlargement* of the *European Community*. Under this approach, some applicant countries would start accession negotiations more or less at the same time, and those with the fewest adjustment difficulties to overcome would reach the finishing line first.

They would then be admitted without awaiting equal progress by the others. See also *Agenda 2000* and *Treaty of Nice*.

Regional economic communities: African regional arrangements established under the Lagos Plan of Action. See *African regional integration arrangements*.

Regional economic integration organization: REIO. This is an omnibus term covering *free-trade agreements*, *common markets*, *customs unions* and other economic partnerships of various kinds.

Regional exhaustion: the doctrine that once a product embodying *intellectual property rights* has been sold in a regional market with the consent of the owner of these rights, the product can be resold or transferred within any of the countries or economies making up that regional market without the further consent of the owner of these rights. See also *Community exhaustion, exhaustion doctrine, international exhaustion* and *parallel import*. [Maskus 2000]

Regional integration arrangement: RIA. A bilateral or regional economic agreement that may go beyond the reach of a *regional trade arrangement*. RIAs typically seek to achieve a degree of economic integration based on, for example, *harmonization* of various national policies or the adoption of policies aimed at similar outcomes.

Regionalism: actions by governments to liberalize or facilitate trade on a regional basis, sometimes through *free-trade areas* or *customs unions*. Many see regionalism, which apparently is often no more than *bilateralism*, as complementary to *multilateralism* because it appears to offer a quicker way to achieve results for the participating economies than the full multilateral process. This is not necessarily the case. Often, the perceived faster pace of regional liberalization, where this actually occurs, is due only to the fact that multilateral outcomes may take a long time to negotiate. Moreover, the apparently faster pace of regional negotiations is often balanced by extended phase-in arrangements or *carve-outs* for *sensitive products*. The time difference in reaching the end-points may therefore be less than seems to be the case. See also *APEC*, *hubs and spokes*, *spaghetti-bowl effect* and *open regionalism*.

Regional Trade and Investment Framework Agreement: a type of agreement negotiated by the United States with groups of countries, aimed at addressing trade and investment issues and eliminating or reducing barriers to trade. See also *Trade and Investment Framework Agreement*.

Regional trade arrangement: RTA. A *free-trade agreement*, *customs union* or *common market* consisting of two or more countries (e.g. *ANZCERTA*, *NAFTA* or the *European Community*). Some analysts see RTAs as building blocks for a freer non-discriminatory multilateral trading system, others as agents for its undermining. John Whalley has listed six reasons why countries negotiate regional trade arrangements. First, they can obtain the traditional *gains of trade*. Second, countries use legally binding agreements to strengthen domestic policy reform. Third, countries hope to increase their multilateral bargaining power in this way. Fourth, free-trade arrangements can offer guaranteed access to markets. Fifth, for some countries the possibility of strategic linkages is important. The sixth reason is that countries may be able to benefit from the multilateral and regional interplay by emphasizing their interest in bilateral negotiations at critical points in the multilateral negotiations. Many commentators have noted that the current WTO rules on regional trade arrangements suffer from three main defects. First, they allow significant sectoral exemptions. Second, they skirt around problems caused by *grey-area measures*, *contingent protection* and *rules of origin*. Third, they fail to track regional agreements after they have been signed and if later rule changes are made. In early 1996 the WTO established a Committee on Regional Trade Agreements to examine further their effect on the global trading system. See also *best practice for RTAs/FTAs in APEC*, *first regionalism*, *hub and spokes*, *second regionalism* and *substantially-all-trade criterion*. [Crawford and Fiorentino 2003, Pomfret 1997, Whalley 1996, www.wto.org]

Regional value content: RVC. Also known as qualifying value content. This is a concept used in the administration of *rules of origin* under *preferential trade arrangements*, especially *free-trade agreements*. The RVC is the share of the good exported from one partner to another that determines whether *preferential market access* will be given. It represents the value added to the good by one or more partners to the arrangement. The RVC is usually expressed as a percentage. If the RVC is below the prescribed threshold, the good will have to enter under a higher tariff, usually the *most-favoured-nation tariff*. Various calculations have been devised to arrive at the RVC, such as the *net cost value method* and the *FOB value method*. See also *non-originating products*, *originating products*, *preferential rules of origin* and *substantial transformation*.

Registered geographical indication: a title of protection similar to *protected appellation of origin*. The main difference is that protected appellations of origin are created by law or decree, whereas a registered geographical indication is usually created through registration of a *geographical indication* through a body established for this purpose. [WIPO SCT/8/4]

Registration, Evaluation and Authorization of Chemicals: see *REACH*.

Regulated exports: goods that may be exported under certain conditions, such as *export quotas* or licensing requirements.

Regulation: an omnibus term covering all overt and covert actions or procedures instituted by governments with a view to influencing industry or customers of an industry in a particular manner. Government regulation may be imposed to correct perceived *market failure* or to redistribute income for the public good. Regulation may also refer to a system of rewards and penalties designed to influence the behaviour of firms and consumers. Other types of regulation include measures such as safety and environmental standards, market entry restrictions and price controls. Analysts of regulatory activities sometimes divide them into three categories: *economic regulation* (aimed at improving the efficiency of markets), *social regulation* (aimed at influencing the way companies approach social values and rights), and *administrative regulation* (aimed at improving the administrative efficiency of government agencies and to support governmental activities). In *European Community legislation* a regulation is an act binding all member states directly. See also *deregulation*, *privatization*, *prudential regulation* and *re-regulation*.

Related rights: see *neighbouring rights*.

Relative reciprocity: the expectation in a reciprocal arrangement that the partners would not have the same level of obligations towards each other. See also *reciprocity at the margin*.

Relevant market: a concept used in the administration of *competition policy*. When a competition authority investigates, for example, what the effect of a proposed merger between companies might be on competition in that industry, it has to consider what market might be affected by the merger. That determination is called the relevant market. It is not necessarily the same as the geographical area of the market of the companies concerned.

Remanufactured goods: these are goods made up from a combination of new parts and parts taken from used goods. They usually last as long as a new good of the same type, and they meet the same performance standards.

Remedy: a legal term used to describe the action imposed or recommended by a court or tribunal in cases where a person has contravened a law.

Remissions: see *border tax adjustments*.

Renegotiation of tariffs: most *tariff* negotiations are now conducted as part of *multilateral trade negotiations* or as sectoral negotiations like those resulting in the *Information Technology Agreement*, but the GATT sets out several ways of renegotiating tariffs during other periods. The listing provided by John Jackson and William Davey in *Legal Problems of International Economic Relations* is particularly useful. First, GATT Article XXVIII:1 permits parties with a *principal supplying interest* or parties who have had earlier bilateral tariff negotiations to reopen these negotiations every three years. The period of three years originally reflected the United States practice of renewing the President's negotiating authority for three years at a time, and this was adopted as the period during which bindings could not be changed. Second, Article XXVIII:4 allows parties to request another party for special circumstance renegotiations. These would be small-scale negotiations confined to a few items resulting in a speedy conclusion, and they are meant to help countries relying on a relatively small number of primary commodities to diversify their economies. Third, Article XXVIII:5 envisages reserved renegotiations. This means that parties can reserve the right to modify their *tariff schedules* during the next three-year period in accordance with normal procedures, including the obligation to offer compensation to affected parties. Fourth, whenever two or more countries agree to form a *customs union* resulting in a *common external tariff*, part of the tariff schedules of participating members must necessarily be changed. Tariff renegotiations are therefore required under Article XXIV:6 to ensure that the overall level of tariffs of the members of the customs area does not exceed the levels in force when there were separate tariffs. Fifth, developing countries have the right under Article XVIII:7 to change, under defined conditions, a tariff schedule as part of promoting an *infant industry*. Sixth, Article XXVII gives parties the right to change a tariff concession negotiated with a country that either did not become a member of GATT or ceased to be one. Seventh, renegotiations of tariffs are possible also in the form of minor technical rectifications where clearly a mistake was made. WTO members tend to very careful to ensure that such technical changes do not amount to disguised substantive tariff increases which might entitle others to *compensation*. See also *tariff negotiations*. [Jackson and Davey 1986]

Repeat dumping: see *recidivist dumping*.

Repression of unfair competition: see *unfair competition*.

Requests and offers: market access negotiations in the WTO for goods and services usually proceed on the basis of bilateral requests and offers, except in the case of *accession* negotiations which are confined to requests by existing members. Requests are normally made by countries which have a significant interest in the traded product. Offers can be made in response to requests or concurrently. When two parties have reached agreement on the extent of new *market access* they are willing to give and accept, the result must be extended to all other WTO members on a most-favoured-nation basis. See also *first-difference negotiations*, *initial negotiating rights*, *most-favoured-nation treatment*, *principal supplier rights* and *principal supplying interests*.

Re-regulation: the institution of a new regulatory framework as part of the *deregulation* of an industry. This may seem contradictory at first glance, but it aims to ensure that competition feature in the deregulated market is genuine. Deregulation often takes away the *monopoly* function of service providers, but it tends to leave them as important players in the market which is now open to others. Because the former monopoly provider is well established, it may have sufficient dominance to retain a *de facto* monopoly. It may therefore be necessary to enact new *competition laws* to ensure that the former monopoly does not abuse its *market power*, and that new entrants get a proper chance to establish their viability in the market.

Resale right: see *droit de suite*.

Resentment, inefficiency, bureaucracy, and stupid signals: identified by Michael Aho as ingredients for the emergence of a series of regional trade blocs. [Aho 1990]

Reservation: an exemption from the obligations of an international agreement, such as a *free-trade agreement* or *international investment agreement*, which applies to specified goods, services or investment activities. Reservations made under bilateral or regional trade and investment agreements are usually the result of negotiations between the parties. They may be permanent or time-bound. In the latter case they may be subject to a *ratchet mechanism*. See also *MFN exemption*, *non-conforming measures* and *two-annex method*. [UNCTAD 2006b]

Reserved list: in *free-trade agreements* using *negative lists* for investment laws, regulations, policies, etc., this is a list of sectors and activities for which the government retains complete flexibility of regulation. In other words, the government retains the right to make unilateral changes to its laws. Inscription of a sector in a reserved list does not necessarily mean that foreign investment in that sector is discouraged or even prohibited. See also *national interest* and *non-conforming measures*.

Reserved negotiations: see *renegotiations of tariffs*.

Residual quantitative restrictions: this normally refers to *quantitative restrictions* imposed to safeguard foreign exchange reserves, but which are still maintained after these difficulties have disappeared.

Residual rules of origin: an aspect of the administration of *non-preferential rules of origin*. These rules must always result in a determination of the origin of a good so that, for example, it may be captured in import statistics. In a given case, a country may have chosen to use a *change in tariff classification* as its normal criterion. If that criterion is not met, possibly because the good went through some minor processing only in the country from which it was exported, the customs authorities then use additional criteria, known as residual rules. One of these might be determining the last country where the good underwent a *substantial transformation*. Another residual rule in this case may be a value-added criterion. These rules are applied until the origin of the goods has been settled satisfactorily. An element of arbitrariness may be inevitable. [Inama 2000]

Residual tariffs: used by some to describe the low tariffs on industrial products that are now the rule in developed economies. Some see them as "left-overs" from the *Uruguay Round* that now should be eliminated completely.

Res judicata: the principle that once a matter has been dealt with by a court, it should not be reopened. [Brownlie 1990]

Resources diplomacy: national and intergovernmental actions and policies aimed at ensuring non-discriminatory and reliable access to supplies and remunerative markets for raw materials. For examples of issues and mechanisms see *agriculture and the multilateral trading system*, *Charter of Economic Rights and Duties of States*, *commodity*, *commodity cartels*, *commodity policy*, *commodity terms of trade*, *Common Fund for Commodities*, *Global Negotiations*, *Integrated Programme for Commodities*, *international commodity agreements*, *international commodity bodies*, *New International Economic Order*, *Singer-Prebisch thesis* and *UNCTAD*.

Restrictive business practices: RBPs. Anti-competitive behaviour by private firms of the type dealt with by national *competition laws* and policies. These can include collusion, abuse of dominant position, refusals to deal, price discrimination, resale price maintenance, exclusive dealing, vertical and horizontal arrangements, etc. There is no accepted international standard on what constitutes RBPs or how they are to be dealt with. The *Havana Charter* included a chapter on them, but the Charter did not enter into force. In 1980, *UNCTAD* adopted the *Set of Multilaterally Agreed Equitable Principles and Rules for the Control of Restrictive Business Practices*, but it does not contain binding obligations. Much work has also been in the *OECD* on this subject. See also *antitrust laws*, *Arrangements for Consultations on Restrictive Business Practices*, *competition* policy, *Revised Recommendation Concerning Cooperation Between Member Countries on Restrictive Business Practices Affecting International Trade* and *trade and competition*.

Results-based trade policy: an idea steeped in *mercantilism* based on the notion that certain benefits can be obtained through attacking carefully chosen targets. Advocates of such a policy usually expect the other side to make the *concessions*. At the same time they defend their own trade regimes as being as perfect as might reasonably be expected in an imperfect world. The results, as always, tend to be mixed.

Retaliation: action taken by a country to restrain imports from a country that has increased a tariff or imposed other measures adversely affecting its exports. There are strict rules and procedures requiring exhaustion of *dispute settlement* under the WTO for retaliatory action, but countries sometimes are tempted to act outside these. In any case, the level of the retaliatory measures must not exceed the level of the measures they seek to deal with. Retaliation is also available to the United States under *Section 301*. See also *cross-retaliation* and *suspension of concessions or other obligations*.

Retaliatory tariff: a tariff aimed mainly at countering tariff increases by others, usually at a punitive level. Governments may feel satisfied that by imposing a retaliatory tariff they have defended the *national interest*, but in reality they have also managed to raise costs for domestic producers and consumers alike. See also *beggar-thy-neighbour policies*.

Retroactive anti-dumping duties: in most circumstances *anti-dumping duties* may be levied at the earliest from the time a *preliminary determination of dumping* was made and *provisional anti-dumping duties* were imposed. In some cases, however, it is possible to levy anti-dumping on goods imported up to 90 days before that determination. This can happen (a) when there is a history of dumping causing *injury*, or (b) that the importer was aware, or should have been, that the exporter practises dumping causing injury, and (c) the injury is caused by massive dumped imports in a relatively short time which is likely to undermine the remedial effect of prospective *definitive anti-dumping duties*. The importers must, however, be given a chance to comment on the proposed action.

Retroactive countervailing duties: normally *countervailing duties* cannot be imposed before a decision has been made, after an investigation, to impose *preliminary countervailing duties*. It is possible, however, to levy countervailing duties on imports which were entered for consumption no more than 90 days before the application of provisional measures. This is the case when the investigating authority finds that the *injury* is difficult to repair because it is caused by massive imports in a relatively short time, and it concludes that retroactive duties are necessary to preclude the recurrence of injury.

Revealed comparative advantage: see *comparative advantage*.

Revenue tariff: a *tariff* with a minimal protective function aimed mainly at producing a steady revenue stream for government. For some developing countries the tariff is one of the principal sources of income. They may therefore be reluctant to cut tariffs, unless another revenue source can be identified. See also *nuisance tariff*.

Reverse consensus: the principle that a report or decision is deemed adopted unless there is a *consensus* not to do so.

Reverse engineering: the controversial concept of acquiring a technological capacity through imitation of a product, generally by taking it apart to work out how it operates. The resulting product must not result in *intellectual property right infringements*. See also *decompilation*.

Reverse fast-track: a proposal by Senator Max Baucus in July 2000 that the United States Congress should be able to legislate not only for *fast-track*, but that it also should be able to withdraw fast-track entirely or in respect to a particular negotiation. See also *Trade Promotion Authority*.

Reverse notification: the normal way to achieve transparency in the GATT, and now the WTO, is for governments to notify other members of trade measures they have taken or are about to take. A different approach was adopted at the end of the *Tokyo Round* when a database was established within the GATT Secretariat based on notifications made by governments of measures contained by others, i.e. through reverse notification. See also *notification*.

Reverse preferences: preferences accorded by developing countries to developed countries.

Reverse special and differential treatment: a term devised by Jagdish Bhagwati to describe the proposition that developing countries should introduce measures to ensure minimum labour and environmental standards. The idea is that this would bring their costs into a more realistic relationship to those borne by developed countries already adhering to these standards. See also *core labour standards* and *trade and environment*. [Bhagwati 1995]

Reverse transfer of technology: a term used particularly in the *United Nations* system to describe the flow of scientists and highly trained specialists from developing countries to developed countries. This is the so-called brain drain. Numerous meetings on this subject have led neither to agreement on its causes nor on possible remedies. Suggestions by developing countries that recipient developed countries should pay some form of compensation have fallen on barren ground.

Revised Recommendation Concerning Cooperation Between Member Countries on Restrictive Business Practices Affecting International Trade: a 1995 *OECD* instrument, based on a recommendation first adopted in 1967 which promotes cooperation between members through (a) notification and request for restraint in cases where companies of other member states are involved, (b) coordination in cases where action is taken by more than one member state against the same company, (c) notification by a member state and request for action in some cases, and (d) conciliation procedures. This recommendation is not binding. See also *negative comity*, *positive comity* and *restrictive business practices*.

Revised Treaty of Chaguaramas Establishing the Caribbean Community Including the CARICOM Single Market and Economy: see *CARICOM Single Market and Economy*.

Right of establishment: the right to establish a commercial entity in another country for the purpose of producing for the local market or importing products from another economy and distributing them. Establishment normally entails some form of investment, including acquisitions, mergers and takeovers. See also *commercial presence*, *foreign direct investment*, *joint venture*, *post-establishment* and *pre-establishment*.

Right of non-establishment: the right to do business in another country without the need to establish a permanent operation there. This principle is often incorporated in the chapter on *Cross-border trade in services* in *free-trade agreements*. See also *commercial presence*.

Right of priority: a right available to signatories of the *Paris Convention*. It means that a person filing for a *patent* in one country has a priority right to file for the same invention in another country within one year. In practical terms this means that once a company has filed for a patent in its home country and it then files for the same patent in another country, the patent will be protected from the date of the earlier application at home rather than the later one abroad. See also *intellectual property*.

Right to Development: refers to a declaration adopted by the United Nations General Assembly in Resolution 41/128 on 4 December 1986. In ten articles it sets out rights and duties of states to promote economic, social, cultural and political development. This declaration is relevant for a discussion of *trade and human rights* and *trade and labour standards*. [Chowdhury, Denters and de Wart 1992]

Rio Declaration on Environment and Development: a set of principles aimed at protecting the integrity of the global environmental and developmental systems adopted on 14 June 1992 at a meeting of *UNCED* (United Nations Conference on Environment and Development) in Rio de Janeiro. Principle 12 holds that "States should cooperate to promote a supportive and open international economic system that would lead to economic growth and sustainable development in all countries, to address better the problems of environmental degradation. *Trade policy* measures for environmental purposes should not constitute a means of *arbitrary or unjustifiable discrimination* or a *disguised restriction on international trade*. Unilateral actions to deal with environmental challenges outside the jurisdiction of the importing country should be avoided. Environmental measures addressing transboundary or global environmental problems should, as far as possible, be based on an international consensus." This Principle is mentioned as a relevant text in the terms of reference for the WTO *Committee on Trade and Environment*. See also *Agenda 21*.

Rio Group: an intergovernmental grouping consisting of Argentina, Bolivia, Brazil, Chile, Colombia, Costa Rica, Dominican Republic, Ecuador, El Salvador, Guatemala, Honduras, Mexico, Nicaragua, Panama, Paraguay, Peru, Uruguay and Venezuela and one country representing the entire Caribbean region. It was founded in Rio de Janeiro in 1983 to consider security issues in the region, but it expanded its role in 1986 to include the promotion of democracy and human rights. As part of this new mandate, the group now also discusses macro-economic issues.

Risk assessment: members of the WTO may apply food safety, animal health and plant health regulations to their international trade, but they must not use them to discriminate arbitrarily or unjustifiably between members in similar conditions. The WTO *Agreement on the Application of Sanitary and Phytosanitary Measures* sets out rules for achieving this. It encourages members to harmonize measures and to base them on international standards, guidelines and recommendations where these are available. If members wish to maintain higher standards, they must carry out risk assessments. A risk assessment can be an evaluation of the likelihood of the introduction or spread of a pest or disease in the light of the sanitary and phytosanitary measures applied. It can also be an evaluation of the potential for adverse effects on human or animal health arising from the presence of additives, contaminants, toxins or disease-causing organisms in food, beverages or feedstuffs. Risk assessment must take into account available scientific evidence, relevant *processes and production methods*, relevant inspection, sampling and testing methods, prevalence of specific diseases or pests, existence of pest- or disease-free areas, relevant ecological and environmental conditions, and quarantine or other treatment. An assessment of the economic factors involved is also required with the objective of minimizing negative trade effects if measures are taken. This is balanced by a consideration of the damage to production if a disease enters the country, the cost of control and eradication and the cost-effectiveness of possible alternative measures. See also *acceptable level of risk* and *sanitary and phytosanitary measures*. [Peel 2004]

Robinson-Patman Act: an amendment to paragraph 2 of the *Clayton Act*. It prohibits price discrimination between different purchasers of goods of the same grade or quality. The Act essentially applies to commerce within the United States only. See also *antitrust laws* and *competition policy*.

Rollback: multilateral or unilateral action taken to remove barriers to trade through the dismantling of existing measures. Often combined with a *standstill*. See also *trade liberalization*.

Rolling specificity: a term used in *APEC* to describe the process of developing action plans leading to free trade by 2010/2020. The idea is that countries will be able to be quite specific about their near-term plans, but less so about their medium- to long-term actions. Action plans will therefore be updated periodically and become more specific on a rolling basis. See also *Bogor Declaration* and *APEC individual action plans*.

"Roll-up" principle: see *absorption principle*.

Rome Convention: the *International Convention for the Protection of Performers, Producers of Phonograms and Broadcasting Organizations*. This Convention protects the rights of performers in performances. Phonogram producers have the right to authorize the reproduction of their phonograms, and broadcasting organizations have the rights concerning their broadcasts. The Convention is administered jointly by *WIPO*, *UNESCO*, and the *International Labour Organization*. See also *Agreement on Trade-Related Aspects of Intellectual Property Rights* and *neighbouring rights*.

Rotterdam Convention on the Prior Informed Consent Procedure for Certain Hazardous Chemicals and Pesticides in International Trade: see *Convention on the Prior Informed Consent Procedure for Certain Hazardous Chemicals and Pesticides in International Trade*.

Round: see *multilateral trade negotiations*.

Ruinous competition: see *predatory pricing*.

Rule of reason: a method used in the administration of *competition policy* to ascertain whether an ostensibly anti-competitive business practice may have a balancing pro-competitive impact. If this is the case, competition authorities may decide not to take action if the law gives them that flexibility. See also *antitrust laws* and *per se rules*.

Rules of origin: ROOs. These are any laws, regulations, administrative rulings, etc., applied by governments to determine the country of origin of goods, services or investments. The origin of goods, services or investment is important because it may influence how they are treated in the receiving country. For example, some countries only permit investment in some activities if the investor is a national of a defined country. Similarly, permission to sell a service may depend on the origin of the seller. The origin of a good will determine the *tariff* applied to it. Another reason is that statistical authorities need to be able to ascribe an import to a supplying country. If a country maintains any administrative restrictions or *tariff quotas*, it may need to know what country has filled its quota. If a country is a member of the *Agreement on Government Procurement*, it may have obligations towards some supplying countries, but not to others. ROOs enable it to determine whether any goods it intends to buy are indeed the product of the country having the right to bid for contracts and to supply. The origin of a product thus can have a significant bearing on its cost in the import market or its access to it, and therefore on its *competitiveness*. ROOs accordingly can be one of the considerations leading to an investment decision. ROOs for goods fall into two main categories. The first applies to goods traded under non-discriminatory conditions, i.e. *non-preferential rules of origin* or MFN rules of origin, where the main purpose is to establish the country of origin. This is easy in the case of basic commodities, such as wheat, sugar and iron ore, or products wholly manufactured in one country, such as paving bricks, carded wool, etc. More complex manufactures traded internationally may consist of components imported from several countries. A country may produce a car containing a Japanese gearbox, an Indonesian engine, a German ignition system, seats made with Australian leather and a Korean sound system. In this case the customs authorities would probably decide that the car is the product of the country where all of the components were assembled to make a product ready for the showroom. The situation would be more complicated if the car was assembled in one country and exported to another for cleaning and polishing and then re-exported it to its final destination. The country doing the polishing may deem the car as its product, but the customs authorities may decide that that the bulk of production occurred in the country of assembly. It is easy to see that, as *globalization* of production increases, the role of non-preferential ROOs in the administration of international trade rules will also increase. Work is now under way in the WTO and the *World Customs Organization* to harmonize ROOS for non-preferential trade. The second main category of ROOs applies to goods traded within *free-trade areas* under a *preferential tariff*. Free-trade area partners usually will seek to ensure that only products produced in one of the other partners will qualify for preferential treatment. The criteria for determining this consist of a set of *preferential rules of origin*. Goods qualifying for preferential treatment are usually called *originating goods*. Goods not receiving a preference are called *non-originating goods*. Preferential ROOs differ from agreement to agreement. They can be complex though, in all fairness, in many cases this is no more than a perception. All the same, examples of unashamed protectionist intent can easily be found. Three main systems are used for deciding where a product originates regardless of whether trade is preferential or not. They all seek to establish whether *substantial transformation* has occurred in the exporting country. First, there is the *change in tariff heading*, based on whether a product has been sufficiently transformed in the exporting country to be classified now under a different *chapter*, *heading* or *sub-heading* in the national *tariff schedule*. For example, a country may import dressed timber and export it as furniture ready for self-assembly. Second, an assessment can be made in terms of the value that may have been added to the product in the exporting country. Labour costs could be one factor. Third, the origin may be determined in terms of specific processing operations necessary to give the product its characteristics. Such rules often apply to dairy and textile products. In the case of services and investment, the most important criteria for determining the origin of the activity are the place of incorporation, the nationality of the owners, the location of the company head office and the place where business is actually conducted. See also *Kyoto Convention*. [Estevadeordal and Suominen 2003, Inama 2000, LaNasa 1995, Vermulst, Waer and Bourgeois 1994, UNCTAD/ITCD/TSB/2, WTO WT/REG/W/45]

Rules of origin phase-in: see *phase-in for rules of origin*.

S

S&D: also S+D or SDT. "Special and differential treatment" provisions for developing countries contained in several agreements administered by the WTO. See *special and differential treatment*.

S&D box: refers to Article 6.2 of the WTO *Agreement on Agriculture* which exempts from reduction commitments some government measures maintained by developing countries in support of agriculture. This includes (a) measures of assistance, whether direct or indirect, to encourage agricultural and rural development which are an integral part of development programs, (b) investment subsidies generally available to agriculture, (c) agricultural subsidies generally available to low-income or resource-poor producers, and (e) support to producers to encourage diversification from growing illicit narcotic crops. See also *amber box*, *blue box* and *green box*.

SAARC: see *South Asian Association for Regional Cooperation*.

SACU: the *Southern African Customs Union* which comprises Botswana, Lesotho, Namibia, South Africa and Swaziland.

Safeguards: action taken to protect a specific industry from an unexpected build-up of imports causing, or threatening to cause, *serious injury*. Safeguards measures usually refer to action taken under Article XIX (Emergency Action on Imports of Particular Products) of the GATT, the so-called *escape clause*. However, safeguards action is possible also under Article XII (Restrictions to Safeguard the Balance of Payments) and Article XVIII (Governmental Assistance to Economic Development). A useful outline of the ways safeguards action may be instituted under the WTO rules has been devised by trade policy analysts within the *World Bank*, but this approach is not necessarily accepted by all WTO members. According to this view, safeguards action may be taken in six different ways, all of which are subject to conditions ensuring that action is taken only if valid reasons exist. There are also certain procedural steps which have to be followed in each case. First, Article VI of the *GATT* permits governments to take action if *dumping* occurs. The provisions of this article are refined further in the *Agreement on Implementation of Article VI of the GATT 1994* (the Anti-dumping Agreement). Second, under Articles XII and, in the case of developing countries, XVIII:B, they may restrict imports in order to protect their external financial position and their *balance of payments*. Third, Article XVIII:A and XVIII:C allow developing countries to provide governmental assistance to promote economic development. Fourth, Article XIX allows a country to suspend its obligations or to modify liberalizing commitments if there are *unforeseen developments* and if any product is being imported in such increased quantities or under such conditions as to cause or threaten serious *injury* to domestic producers of like or directly competitive products. Except in defined circumstances, safeguards action taken under Article XIX must be aimed at a particular product, regardless of its source. Discriminatory action aimed against the countries perceived to be the main problem is against the rules. If action is taken, there is an obligation to provide compensation to affected parties in the form of lower tariffs and/or better access conditions in other product lines. The *Agreement on Safeguards* establishes the detailed rules for the application of safeguard measures as provided for in Article XIX of the GATT. Fifth, it is possible to renegotiate commitments under GATT Article XXVIII with the aim of gaining relief from imports. Sixth, the *general exceptions* and the *security exceptions* under the *General Agreement on Trade in Services* and the GATT can also be viewed as a form of safeguards action. See also *anti-dumping measures*, *bilateral safeguards*, *hatters' fur*, *selectivity*, *Transitional Product-Specific Safeguard Mechanism* and *transitional safeguards mechanism*. [Finger 1998, Lee 2003]

Safe-haven agreement: used by some commentators to describe a *regional trade arrangement* to which a smaller country accedes in the expectation of obtaining secure access for its exports.

SAFTA: see *South American Free Area.*

SAFTA: South Asian Free Trade Area. A framework agreement now under negotiation between Bangladesh, Bhutan, India, Maldives, Nepal, Pakistan and Sri Lanka. The target date for regional free trade is 2005. See also *South Asian Association for Regional Cooperation*.

Same-condition substitution duty drawback: a practice relating to trade in agricultural products prohibited under *NAFTA*. It concerns the refund, waiving or reduction in the amount of customs duties owed on any agricultural good imported into the territory and substituted for an identical or similar good subsequently exported to the territory of another party. A similar prohibition applies to customs duties on manufactured products. See also *maquiladora industries*.

Sanitary and phytosanitary measures: measures necessary to protect human health, animal or plant life or health. They are often called quarantine measures. The WTO *Agreement on the Application of Sanitary and Phytosanitary Measures* (the SPS agreement) defines them as any measure applied (a) to protect animal or plant life or health from risks arising from the entry, establishment or spread of pests, diseases, disease-carrying organisms or disease-causing organisms, (b) to protect human or animal life or health from risks arising from additives, contaminants, toxins or disease-causing organisms in foods, beverages or foodstuffs, (c) to protect human life or health from risks arising from diseases carried by animals, plants or products thereof, or from the entry, establishment or spread of pests, or (d) to prevent or limit other damage form the entry, establishment or spread of pests. The Agreement sets out broadly the rights and obligations of WTO members in enforcing such measures. Among other things, they must be based on scientific principles, sufficient scientific evidence and on *risk assessments*. Measures must not be applied in a manner which would constitute a means of *arbitrary or unjustifiable discrimination* between members where the same conditions prevail. Where international standards exist, these are to be used as the basis for national standards, but national standards may be higher if there is scientific justification for doing so. Sanitary and phytosanitary measures must not be used as a *disguised restriction on international trade*. See also *acceptable level of risk*, *appropriate level of sanitary or phytosanitary protection*, *International Office of Epizootics*, *International Plant Protection Convention* and *Standards and Trade Development Facility*. [Anderson, McRae and Wilson 2001, Peel 2004, Schoenbaum 2002]

Santiago Initiative for Expanded Trade in APEC: a multi-year program to promote further trade and investment liberalization among *APEC* economies and to intensify work on trade facilitation. It was adopted in November 2004 by the *APEC Economic Leaders' Meeting*. [www.apecsec.org.sg]

São Paulo Consensus: a statement adopted on 18 June 2004 at *UNCTAD* XI at São Paulo. It offers policy analysis and UNCTAD's reponse in four main areas: (development strategies in a globalizing world economy, (b) building productive capacities and international competitiveness, (c) assuring development gains from the international trading system and trade negotiations, and (d) partnership for development. The statement is essentially a broad outline of UNCTAD's work program until UNCTAD XII. [UNCTAD TD/410]

SAPTA: *SAARC Preferential Trading Arrangement*, launched as a first step towards a regional free-trade area in April 1993 with a program of tariff reductions on specified goods and commodities. *Para-tariffs*, *non-tariff measures* and direct trade measures may also be dealt with. The target date for regional free trade is 2005. SAPTA consists of Bangladesh, Bhutan, India, Maldives, Nepal, Pakistan and Sri Lanka which make up the South Asian Association for Regional Cooperation (SAARC). It is administered by the SAARC Secretariat in Dhaka. See also *SAFTA* and *South Asian Association for Regional Cooperation.*

Schedules of specific commitments on services: a requirement under the *General Agreement on Trade in Services*. They show what level of *market access for services* each WTO member is willing to accord other members. Similarly, they indicate whether *national treatment* is offered. These schedules perform a function similar to the *tariff schedules* for goods under the GATT.

Schedule of concessions: a list of *bound tariff rates* negotiated under WTO auspices. It sets out the terms, conditions and qualifications under which goods may be imported. No additional duties or charges may be imposed at the border other than internal taxes also levied on similar domestic products, *anti-dumping measures* or *countervailing duties* or a fee-for-service charge. See also *tariff*.

Scientific tariff: the ideal set of *tariff* rates sought over the years by many governments. Its aim would be to ensure that one's products can compete internationally on an equal basis with those of others, to promote employment at home and to offset perceived *unfair trading practices* by others. No country has yet succeeded in formulating a scientific tariff, though not for want of effort. In any case, even if it could be devised, it would be in direct conflict with the ideas of the *international division of labour* and *comparative advantage*, and in this way negate the advantages of efficiencies available elsewhere. See also *optimal-tariff argument*.

SCM Agreement: see *Agreement on Subsidies and Countervailing Measures*.

Screwdriver **case:** dispute settlement proceedings initiated by Japan against the *European Economic Community* (EEC) in 1988 concerning *anti-dumping measures* taken by the EEC against Japanese products assembled or produced there from imported parts. The background was that the EEC had in the mid-1980s imposed anti-dumping duties on, among other things, hydraulic excavators, electronic weighing scales and electronic typewriters imported from Japan. EEC producers subsequently submitted that that although these duties were now applied, the prices of the relevant Japanese products had not increased, and in some cases they had even gone down. The producers alleged that this was possible because the Japanese companies, said to be multi-nationals with large financial resources at their disposal, were able to import the parts of the offending equipment at normal duty rates. They were then assembled within the EEC or third countries. EEC producers alleged that the cost of assembling these products by a "screwdriver" process was relatively low. In response to these complaints the EEC then proceeded to impose also anti-dumping duties on products made or assembled in the EEC of imported parts. It further sought undertakings from the enterprises concerned that they would limit the use of parts or materials originating in Japan. One of the arguments in the case by the EEC was that the anti-dumping duties on imported parts were justified as an *anti-circumvention* measure. The *panel* did not see it that way. It held that both of EEC's actions contravened the *national treatment* requirement of the GATT. [GATT BISD 37/S]

Screwdriver operations: a pejorative term for manufacturing operations concerned mainly with the assembly of components. This often involves little or no *transfer of technology*. Screwdriver operations are more likely to be found where there is an adequate supply of comparatively inexpensive labour. They are partly a cause and a result of *globalization* driven by the need to find the most efficient production arrangement. They can also be due to *preferential rules of origin* which encourage firms to establish operations inside *free-trade areas* to get around *market access* impediments. See also *delocalization*, *export processing zones*, *footloose industries*, *maquiladora industries* and *rules of origin*.

Seasonal tariff: a tariff rate related to the seasonal supply of domestic agricultural products. Tariffs are low when domestic offerings are out of season and high when domestic production starts to reach the market. The imported product need not be exactly the same as the domestic product.

Seattle Ministerial Conference: the *WTO Ministerial Conference* held in Seattle from 30 November to 3 December 1999. See also *Doha Ministerial Conference*. [Schott 2003]

Second Account: the finance program established under the *Common Fund for Commodities* to fund commodity development measures aimed at improving the structural conditions in markets and enhancing the long-term competitiveness and prospects of particular commodities. See also *First Account*.

Secondary dumping: the export of a product which incorporates components that have been landed at dumped prices. For example, the frame of a bicycle may have been imported by a firm in the exporting country at less than market price. Because of this, the firm enjoys a price advantage even if it is selling its completed bicycles at the market price prevailing in its own economy. The *injury* impact of secondary dumping is difficult to substantiate. See also *anti-dumping measures*, *dumping*, *hidden dumping* and *indirect dumping*.

Second banking coordination directive: SBCD. A *directive* issued by the *European Community* in 1989 which permits a bank authorized to operate in any member state, including subsidiaries of foreign banks, to operate in any other member state in fourteen defined activities, but only if it is allowed to do so by its own licensing authority. This includes traditional banking as well as underwriting of, dealing in and distribution of securities. The authorities in the host countries may not limit the activities of banks allowed to operate in this way even if their domestic banks cannot participate in them. See also *European Community legislation*.

Second beer panel: a dispute in 1991 in the GATT between the United States and Canada. It concerned the import, distribution and sale of certain alcoholic drinks by Canadian provincial marketing agencies. There had been a case on the same issue in 1988, hence the name of this case. The Canadian marketing agencies ("liquor boards"), created by provincial laws, had a monopoly on the supply and distribution of alcoholic beverages within provincial boundaries. They also had a monopoly on the import of alcoholic beverages from other provinces or foreign countries. A provincial licence was needed for the brewing and selling of beer in a province, and most domestic beer had to be brewed in the province in which it was sold. All provinces operated government liquor stores, but they also allowed beer sales at privately-owned retail outlets and brewery stores. The 1988 *panel* had concluded that mark-ups on imported products that were higher than those on domestic products could only be justified in precisely defined circumstances, that the *burden of proof* in this regard lay with Canada, and that the listing requirements and the availability of points of sale discriminating against imported alcoholic beverages were restrictions made effective through state-trading operations contrary to Article XI (General Elimination of Quantitative Restrictions). In 1988, following the first panel, Canada concluded an agreement with the *European Community* aimed at resolving some of the points at issue. This agreement was to be implemented by the provinces on a *most-favoured-nation* basis. The panel concluded that, with the exception of one province, the United States had not substantiated its claim concerning Canadian listing and delisting practices. As to restrictions on access to points of sale, the panel considered that imported beer had access to fewer of them. It found that these restrictions were contrary to the provisions of the GATT. It concluded that the mere fact that imported and domestic beer were subject to different delivery systems was not in itself enough to establish inconsistency with the GATT since formally identical *national treatment* might leave the imported product worse off. The panel then considered the methods for assessing mark-ups and taxes on imported beer and found that they were inconsistent with Article III:4 (National Treatment). The panel next turned to the question of minimum prices and concluded that the maintenance by an import monopoly of any minimum price for an imported product at a level at which a directly-competing, higher-priced domestic product was supplied was inconsistent with Article III:4. The panel considered that the taxes on beer containers had been dealt with as part of its consideration of restrictions on private delivery. It concluded that provincial notification procedures did not violate Article X (Publication and Administration of Trade Regulations). Finally, the panel concluded that Canada had failed to comply in several aspects of this case with its obligations under GATT Article XXIV:12 which enjoins GATT members to take reasonable measure to ensure compliance with the provisions of the Agreement by regional and local governments and authorities within its territories. See also *implicit discrimination* and *second-level obligations*. [GATT BISD 39S]

Second-level obligations: the obligations under the WTO agreements of central governments of federated states in respect of states or provinces constituting their jurisdictions. Two examples will suffice. The provisions of the *GATT* require WTO members to take such reasonable measures as may be available to them to ensure observance of GATT rules by regional and local governments and authorities within their territories. The *General Agreement on Trade in Services* applies to measures taken by central, regional or local governments and authorities.

Second Protocol to the General Agreement on Trade in Services: the *protocol* giving effect to the commitments on trade in *financial services* made in the 1995 negotiations. It entered into force on 1 September 1996.

Second regionalism: used by Jagdish Bhagwati to describe the trend towards *preferential trade arrangements* that began in 1985 with the conclusion of the United States-Israel Free Trade Agreement. See also *first regionalism*. [Bhagwati 1993]

Second United Nations Conference on the Least Developed Countries: see *SNPA*.

Secretariat of the Pacific Community: an *intergovernmental organization* established in 1947 as the South Pacific Commission to give training and assistance in social, economic and cultural areas to the Pacific island countries. Its members are American Samoa, Australia, Cook Islands, Federated States of Micronesia, Fiji, France, French Polynesia, Guam, Kiribati, Marshall Islands, Nauru, New Caledonia, New Zealand, Niue, Northern Mariana Islands, Palau, Papua New Guinea, Pitcairn Islands, Samoa, Solomon Islands, Tokelau, Tonga, Tuvalu, United States, Vanuatu and Wallis and Futuna. Its secretariat is located at Noumea.

Section 22 waiver: refers to Section 22 of the United States *Agricultural Adjustment Act* which required the Administration to impose *quantitative restrictions* or surcharges (above normal tariffs) whenever agricultural imports interfered with a United States farm program. In 1955, the United States was granted a *waiver* without a time limit to exempt this section of the Act from the GATT disciplines. Quotas imposed under Section 22 have been converted to tariff protection as a result of the *Uruguay Round* negotiations. See also *agriculture and the multilateral trading system* and *tariffication*.

Section 201: a section, usually called the *escape clause*, of the United States *Trade Act* of 1974 and subsequent versions of the Act. It gives American firms relief from imports that are considered causing, or threatening to cause, serious injury to an industry. It applies to products that are traded fairly. In other words, products are not considered subsidized or dumped. Relief may be brought about through temporary tariff increases, *import quotas*, negotiated restraint arrangements or direct assistance to the industry concerned. See also *safeguards* and *voluntary restraint agreement*.

Section 232 investigation: an investigation under Section 232 of the United States *Trade Expansion Act* of 1962, as amended, to determine the effects of imports on national security. Tariff reductions may not be made if this would affect national security.

Section 301: the section so numbered of the United States *Trade Act* of 1974. Section 301 is designed to enforce United States rights under trade agreements and to provide for responses to foreign unfair trading practices following petition and investigation. Unfair trading practices may take place in the United States, in the offending country itself or in third countries. Section 301 may also be used to obtain increased market access for United States goods and services, to secure fairer conditions for its investors abroad and to promote more effective protection in other countries for United States intellectual property rights. It also allows *USTR* to limit imports from countries that unfairly restrict United States trade in particular products. It is generally used for single product sectors. The threat of a Section 301 action is most unwelcome to trade policy makers, not only because it may mean rethinking the rules in the targeted areas, but also because the defence requires much effort that is otherwise unproductive. Taking action is equally resource-intensive for the Americans, and USTR tends to pick cases it perceives as winnable to the extent that it has the choice. That flexibility has been eroded over the years. Some say that the history of Section 301 actions against the European Economic Community, Japan and Korea has shown that its imposition can be quite ineffectual if there is not already an inclination in the target country to reform access to the sector anyway. This is definitely an underestimate of its impact. Others say that the WTO *Understanding on Rules and Procedures Governing Settlement of Disputes* has taken the teeth out of Section 301. This is not the case. Section 301 is still available for retaliation if a WTO member does not act in accordance with the outcome of the dispute settlement process. Section 301 may also still be used as originally intended in all cases where there are no WTO rules covering an action perceived as unfair. See also *Special 301* and *Super 301*.

Section-306 monitoring: a mechanism specified in the *Omnibus Trade and Competitiveness Act*. It requires *USTR* to monitor the implementation of measures taken under *Section 301*. If USTR considers that a foreign country is not implementing a measure or an agreement satisfactorily, it must determine what further action to take. Such a determination is considered to satisfy the requirements for further action under Section 301. In other words, no further investigation is necessary to justify additional action. See also *Monitoring and Enforcement Unit*.

Section 337: a provision of the 1930 United States*Tariff Act*, also known as *Smoot-Hawley Act*, which allows the granting of fast-track relief from present or potential *injury* caused by unfair imports. Section 337 is quite broad in its application, but it has been used particularly for cases involving infringements of *intellectual property rights*.

Sectoral commitments: these are entries covering specific service sectors or subsectors in the *schedules of commitments* under the *General Agreement on Trade in Services* (GATS). Examples are accountancy, freight-forwarding or life insurance. A sectoral commitment attracts a higher level of GATS rights and obligations in relation to *market access* and *national treatment*. Once a commitment has been made, the market access conditions applying to it may not be made more restrictive for at least three years. See also *market access for services*.

Sectoral customs union: see *sectoral free-trade area*.

Sectoral free-trade area: a *free-trade area* or a *customs union* covering some traded sectors only. This option is only available to developing countries under the *Enabling Clause*. Developed countries may conduct *sectoral trade negotiations*, but they must extend the benefits of sectoral trade liberalization on a *most-favoured-nation* basis.

Sectoral Initiative in Favour of Cotton: proposed by Benin, Burkina Faso, Chad and Mali in July 2003. It envisages (a) the complete elimination of of support for cotton production and export over three years, and (b) financial compensation for cotton-producing *least developed countries* until support for cotton production has been phased out. In July 2004 this proposal became part of the WTO negotiations on agriculture.

Sectoral rules of origin: refers to *rules of origin*, especially *preferential rules of origin*, that apply to defined groups of goods only. Common examples of such goods are agricultural products, textiles, clothing, footwear, chemicals and cars.

Sectoral trade negotiations: the idea of achieving efficiencies in trade negotiations through tackling clusters of tariff items rather than through the *item-by-item negotiations* pursued in the early rounds of *multilateral trade negotiations*. It was first attempted on a large scale during the *Kennedy Round*. The main sectors so treated were aluminium, chemicals, cotton textiles, iron and steel, and pulp and paper. Though the results varied greatly, one thoughtful assessment of the Round considered that enough progress had been made for free trade between selected industry sectors to become a possible future means of tariff reductions. Canada then advocated during the *Tokyo Round* the sectoral reduction or elimination of tariff and non-tariff barriers. Canada argued that in some sectors it would be possible in this way to go beyond the trade liberalization resulting from the accepted negotiating techniques. In this way it would be feasible for all trade barriers from the raw-material stage to the finished product to be removed. Developing countries found this proposal attractive because it could have been adapted to the export products of main interest to them, and it might also have provided a solution to the problem of *tariff escalation*. However, resistance by others ensured that this proposal was not adopted. During the *Uruguay Round* sectoral trade negotiations took place at two levels. First, at a broad level, the negotiations on agriculture, textiles and services resulted, respectively, in the conclusion of the *Agreement on Agriculture*, the *Agreement on Textiles and Clothing* and the *General Agreement on Trade in Services*. All of these agreements achieved some trade liberalization, though not all that much in the case of services. Second, there were tariff negotiations in smaller sectoral groups. These eliminated among the main trading countries tariffs on pharmaceuticals, construction equipment, medical equipment, beer, farm machinery, wood and paper products, some fish products and toys. The United States and the *European Community* agreed in addition to reduce their tariffs on chemicals to about 3%. An attempt to negotiate a *Multilateral Steel Agreement* was unsuccessful. Sectoral trade negotiations continued after the Uruguay Round in the financial services, telecommunications and maritime services. An outstanding example of what can be achieved through sectoral trade negotiations is the *Information Technology Agreement*. A main reason why this Agreement succeeded so well is that it was supported by industry and government alike in all major producing and trading countries. The most recent example of trade negotiations in the WTO is the *Doha Ministerial Conference* mandate for negotiations on *environmental goods and services*. *APEC* trade ministers decided in May 1997 to explore sectoral trade liberalization through the *Early Voluntary Sectoral Liberalization* initiative. Their intention was to identify sectors where all APEC economies could agree to reduce or eliminate tariffs and non-tariff barriers. This attempt was unsuccessful. Some see sector-by-sector negotiations as the best way to achieve trade liberalization. When they work, they achieve results efficiently. Their main drawback is that they put the burden of adjustment on a single industry which then sees itself as bearing all the costs. If the degree of resistance is too great, governments may decide not to push ahead. This is despite the fact that all trade liberalization results in gains for the economy. It is therefore likely that multilateral liberalization in agriculture, a *sensitive sector* in many countries, will for a long time only be possible in the setting of a round of *multilateral trade negotiations*. These rounds allow governments to strike a balance between sectors in that they see "gains" here and "losses" there. Industries, too, can see that they have not been singled out for what they consider "sacrifices". See also *zero-for-zero tariff reductions*.

Secure Trade in APEC Region: STAR. An initiative launched at the 2002 *APEC Leaders Meeting* "to accelerate action on screening people and cargo for security before transit; increasing security on ships and airplanes while on route; and enhancing security in airports and seaports". The action plan to implement STAR has the following main elements: (a) identifying and examining high-risk containers, (b) implementing by 2005 common standards for electronic customs reporting, (c) cooperation to fight piracy in the region, (d) introducing new baggage screening procedures and equipment in all major APEC airports by 2005, (e) implementing a common global standard on advance passenger information, (f) adopting biometrics standards and (g) reforming immigration service procedures. See also *Container Security Initiative*. [www.apecsec.org]

Security exceptions: the right of WTO members under the *General Agreement on Trade in Services* (Article XIVbis), the GATT (Article XXI) and Article 73 of the *Agreement on Trade-Related Aspects of Intellectual Property Rights* to suspend their obligations under these agreements if important national security issues are at stake. The circumstances when this might arise are (a) the right to refuse disclosure of information if this would be contrary to essential security interests, (b) the need to take action necessary for the protection of essential security interests relating to fissionable materials, traffic in arms, ammunition and implements of war, and in times of war or other international emergencies, and (c) the pursuit of action taken by the United Nations to preserve peace and security. These provisions are rarely used. See also *general exceptions*.

SELA: Sistema Económico Latinoamericano, or Latin American Economic System. A regional organization, based in Venezuela, which includes 27 Latin American and Caribbean countries. It aims to promote intra-regional cooperation to accelerate the economic and social development of its members, and to provide a permanent institutional structure for the adoption of unified strategies in international forums.

Selective safeguards: see *selectivity*.

Selectivity: the imposition of *import restrictions* against one or more countries seen as the main threats to domestic producers rather than the use of non-discriminatory *safeguard* measures as required in most instances under WTO rules. Some selectivity is permitted in case of *serious injury* under Article 5.2(b) of the *Agreement on Safeguards* if (i) it is clear that imports from certain countries have increased disproportionately in the period under consideration, (ii) all the other conditions for taking safeguard action have been satisfied, and (iii) if this would be equitable to other suppliers. See also *escape clause* and *quota modulation*.

Self-certification: a method under some systems of *rules of origin* which allows, producers, exporters and/or importers to certify that the goods in question qualify for *preferential treatment*. Self-certification is easier and cheaper than obtaining a *certificate of origin* from a chamber of commerce or a governmental agency.

Self-produced material: used to describe in the *rules of origin* of *NAFTA* a material that is produced by the producer of a good and used in the production of that good. See also *intermediate material*.

Self-reliance: an economic development policy based on relying mainly on locally available natural resources, capital and skills. One of its characteristics is a profound disinclination to spend foreign exchange on factors of production that do not immediately and directly result in greater inflows of foreign exchange. A consequence is that domestic enterprises and research institutes spend much of their time and funds on re-inventing products and processes already available elsewhere, but they never seem to catch up. Outward-looking economies avoid this trap and seek instead to find their place in the system of international specialization through international trade and foreign investment. See also *autarky*, *comparative advantage*, *self-sufficiency* and *techno-nationalism*.

Self-sufficiency: an economic policy under which a country aims to produce to the greatest extent what it consumes itself. Foreign trade does occur in countries practising such policies, but it tends to be confined to importing essential raw materials not available locally and the export of raw materials and other products not needed on the local market. Such a policy disregards the gains to be made from international specialization, and it acts therefore as a brake on the expansion of trade and the economy more broadly. See also *autarky*, *comparative advantage*, *international division of labour*, *self-reliance* and *techno-nationalism*.

Semi-conductor: a dispute with the United States and Japan brought before the GATT Council by the *European Economic Community* (EEC) in 1986. The case made by the EEC stemmed from an arrangement made between the United States and Japan in 1986 concerning trade in semi-conductors. This provided for better market access for imported semi-conductors in Japan and the monitoring of export prices by the Government of Japan to prevent *dumping* in the United States. The provisions on monitoring and dumping were applicable to third-country markets. Japan used its *COCOM* enforcement mechanism to monitor export prices which caused delays in the granting of export approvals. The EEC claimed that (a) the Japanese monitoring measures, especially those applied to third-country markets, contravened Articles VI (Anti-dumping) and XI (General Elimination of Quantitative Restrictions), (b) the provisions for access to the Japanese market contravened Article I (General Most-favoured-nation Treatment), and (c) the lack of transparency surrounding the whole issue contravened Article X (Publication and Administration of Trade Regulations). It argued that third-country monitoring was aimed at ensuring, now that the arrangement had increased prices in the United States, that United States companies would not be disadvantaged in these markets. The *panel* first considered the claims concerning Article XI and found that the request to Japanese companies not to export semi-conductors at prices below company-specific costs to GATT members other than the United States, combined with the complex system of monitoring price, was inconsistent with Article XI, as was the system of administering export licences. It also found that the evidence submitted did not demonstrate preferential market access to Japan by United States firms in contravention of the most-favoured-nation clause. The panel held that Article VI was silent on actions by exporting countries to prevent dumping, and that it was therefore not a justification for export restrictions or export price measures. It also noted that Article VI was silent on the right of exporting countries to impose *anti-dumping measures* on their exports. [GATT BISD 35S]

Semi-generic geographical indications: names widely used to describe some wines and other products not necessarily produced in the place where the name originated. Examples for wine are *Burgundy* and *Chablis*. The use of such names is permitted in some jurisdictions if the correct place of origin is also indicated on the product. A hypothetical example of permitted use would be "Chablis, product of Iceland". In other jurisdictions this kind of labelling may be illegal. See also *geographical indications* and *generic geographical indications*.

Semi-tradeables: goods and services that exhibit features putting them in the category of *tradeables* and others that may make them *non-tradeables*. The distinction between these categories can be difficult to make in practice.

Sensitive List: a list maintained by *AFTA* members which covers unprocessed agricultural products, the so-called sensitive products. Internal liberalization in listed products does not have to be achieved until 2010. Similarly, the *ASEAN Investment Area* allows for sensitive lists of industries and investment measures that do not have to be liberalized, but which are to be reviewed periodically. See also *General Exception List* and *highly sensitive products*.

Sensitive products: these are products more likely than others to encounter *import restrictions*. Typical examples are many agricultural products, textiles, clothing and footwear, passenger motor vehicles, chemicals and, sometimes, steel. The reasons for the sensitivity surrounding these products are complex. It may be the perceived need to protect the traditional occupation of a national minority, as is the case with Japanese tanneries. In other cases, technological changes and new investment may lead to lower-cost foreign competitors and an inability by domestic producers to adjust quickly. Agriculture, as shown by the European and American examples, is particularly complicated. Traditional political power combined with a vague community perception that the rural population expresses the national spirit and must therefore be preserved, may render any reform of the rural sector a delicate matter. See also *Japanese leather* and *sensitive sectors*.

Sensitive sectors: parts of the domestic economy posing special challenges to trade policy makers for various reasons, including relative technological backwardness, cultural factors, over-production or political clout. Among them are agriculture, audiovisual services and cultural activities more generally, defence-related industries, financial services, shipbuilding, textiles and footwear. In fact, almost any industry can turn itself into a sensitive sector if it feels the pressure of imports, and if it is willing to organise itself. The long-term solutions for dealing with the problems caused by sensitive sectors are usually found through *structural adjustment* or, if nothing else is done, through accidental obsolescence and the disappearance of some of the sector as players. See also *cultural identity*, *sensitive products* and *sectoral trade negotiations*.

Separate Arbitration Agreement: see *Model Arbitration Clause*.

Seoul Declaration: the declaration on *APEC* objectives made at the November 1991 APEC Ministerial Meeting in Seoul. The four objectives are: (i) to sustain the growth and development of the region for the common good of its peoples and, in this way, to contribute to the growth and development of the world economy; (ii) to enhance the positive gains, both for the region and the world economy, resulting from increasing economic inter-dependence, including by encouraging the flow of goods, services, capital and technology, (iii) to develop and strengthen the open multilateral trading system in the interest of Asia-Pacific and all other economies, and (iv) to reduce barriers to trade in goods and services and investment among participants in a manner consistent with GATT principles, where applicable, and without detriment to other economies. See also *Bogor Declaration* and *Osaka Action Agenda*.

Sequential foreign direct investment: defined by *UNCTAD* as *foreign direct investment* by firms that are already established in the market. In most cases, such investment consists of reinvested earnings. See also *associated foreign direct investment*.

Serious damage: the condition that has be satisfied, for example, to justify action under the *specific transitional safeguard mechanism* to restrain the import of textiles and clothing. The *Agreement on Textiles and Clothing* does not define "serious damage", but it explains that the claim of serious damage can be assessed by the effect of the imports of the product in question on the particular industry, as reflected, for example, in changes of output, productivity, utilization of capacity, inventories, market share, exports, wages, employment, domestic prices, profits and investment. See also *injury*.

Serious injury: defined in the WTO *Agreement on Safeguards* as "a significant overall impairment in the position of a domestic industry". The term is not further defined, but authorities investigating whether serious injury exists are required to "evaluate all relevant factors of an objective and quantifiable nature". These include the rate and amount of the increase in imports of the product concerned in absolute and relative terms, the share of the domestic market taken by increased imports, changes in the level of sales, production, productivity, capacity utilization, profits and losses, and employment. See also *injury*.

Serious prejudice: this exists under the WTO *Agreement on Subsidies and Countervailing Measures* when subsidies have certain effects on the interests of other members. Broadly, this arises in cases (a) when the total subsidy on a product exceeds 5%, (b) when subsidies are awarded to cover the operating losses of an industry, (c) of subsidies covering operating losses to allow the development of long-term solutions and to avoid acute social problems, and (d) direct forgiveness of debt owed to government. The member country must take appropriate action in these cases. The Agreement also describes a range of situations in which serious prejudice may, rather than will, arise. Different rules apply to agricultural subsidies under the WTO *Agreement on Agriculture*. See also *actionable subsidies*, *prohibited subsidies* and *subsidies*.

Service dumping: said to result from the use of subsidized or discriminatory pricing arrangements in the provision of shipping services. The resulting freight at less than cost is thought to give the exporter an advantage that may be reflected in the landed price of the product. The product itself may have been landed at *normal value*, but the freight reduction could still lead to a charge of dumping. This concept was discussed during the drafting of the *Havana Charter*, but it is not reflected in the current anti-dumping rules. See also *anti-dumping measures*.

Service mark: a *trademark* uniquely associated with the provision of a service. It can be a mark, word, name or symbol, or a combination of them.

Services: these include key economic activities such as telecommunications, banking, insurance, land and water transport, aviation, accountancy, law, engineering, entertainment, etc., which can be produced in their own right or as a component of some product or another service. Services account for about 60% to 75% of GDP in most countries. The variations can be explained partly by structural factors and partly because of the use of different statistical methods. The importance of services was not always recognized. Adam Smith's view was that "the labour of some of the most respectable orders in the society is, like that of menial servants, unproductive of any value, and does not fix or realize itself in any permanent subject, or vendible commodity, which endures after that labour is past, and for which an equal quantity of labour could afterwards be procured . . . In the same class must be ranked, some both of the gravest and most important, and some of the most frivolous professions: churchmen, lawyers, physicians, men of letters of all kinds; players, buffoons, musicians, opera-singers, opera-dancers, etc.". If this view of services was not consciously held by later generations, there was nevertheless frequently a tendency to underplay their role in the economy. There is no universally accepted definition of services. Several approaches have been tried, but none has received full approval. First, services are often characterized as intangible, invisible, incapable of storage and therefore requiring simultaneous production and consumption. These characteristics are already implicit in Adam Smith's remarks. Technological advances have, however, made this an obsolescent definition. Second, the institutional approach assumes that anything not classified as primary or secondary industry must be a service or a service occupation. Third, there is the functional approach, pioneered by T P Hill in 1977 when he defined services as "a change in the condition of a person or of a good belonging to some economic unit, which is brought about as the result of the activity of some other economic unit with the prior agreement of the former person or economic unit". Some have argued that this definition is deficient because it does not cover, for example, security services or preventive medicine. The United States Office of Technology Assessment has proposed classification into two types: (a) knowledge-based services (insurance, professional and technical services, certain banking services, information technology services, etc.), and (b) tertiary services (leasing, shipping, distribution, franchising, retail trade, travel, etc.). In the *Work of Nations*, Robert Reich offers three different categories of services according to occupations. The first is routine production services entailing repetitive tasks guided by standard procedures and codified rules, much in the way assembly work is done by blue-collar occupations. These services can be traded globally. The second category he calls in-person services, also entailing simple and repetitive tasks, but they must be provided person-to-person. He notes that these providers often must have a pleasant demeanour, and they must smile and exude confidence and good cheer even when they feel morose. His third category is symbolic-analytic services. This covers problem-solving, problem-identifying and strategic-brokering activities. These services can be traded internationally, but they are not standardized. They include many business, professional, financial and engineering services. This list of classification systems is by no means exhaustive. Draft version 2 of the *United Nations Central Product Classification* has a quite comprehensive listing of services. See also *trade in services statistics*. [Hill 1977, Reich 1991, Smith 1776]

Set-aside programs: instituted particularly by the United States and the European Community, but also Japan, to take agricultural land out of production as one way to reduce agricultural over-production. Farmers receive financial compensation for participating in these programs.

Set of Multilaterally Agreed Equitable Principles and Rules for the Conduct of Restrictive Business Practices: see *restrictive business practices*.

Seventh-freedom cargo services: the right of an airline to operate cargo services between countries entirely outside its home country. See also *freedoms of the air* and *Multilateral Agreement on the Liberalization of International Air Transportation*.

Shallow integration: a situation in which economies pursueeconomic policies sharing some characteristics, but each economy is free to pursue its own ends. An example of this occurs under *free-trade arrangements* or when economies adopt the results of *multilateral trade negotiations*. See also *deep integration*.

Sham litigation: see *non-price predation* and *trade harassment*.

Shanghai Accord: an appendix to the statement issued after the 2001 Shanghai *APEC Economic Leaders' Meeting*. The Shanghai Accord consists of five elements. The first is a commitment to broadening and updating the *Osaka Action Agenda*. It will cover in particular the *e-APEC strategy* and APEC's work on strengthening the functioning of markets. Second, member economies agreed to the *pathfinder approach* to promote progress towards the goals listed in the *Bogor Declaration*. Third, they will promote the adoption of appropriate trade policies for the *New Economy*. Fourth, members will aim to reduce trade transaction costs by 5% through implementing the *APEC Trade Facilitation Principles*. Fifth, members will pursue the implementation of the *APEC transparency principles*.

Shanghai Cooperation Organization: known until June 2001 as the "Shanghai Five". It consists of China, Kazakhstan, Kyrgyz Republic, Russia, Tajikistan and

Uzbekistan. It is mainly concerned with cooperation in security and strategic matters. Its secretariat is Beijing.

Shelf-life restrictions: usually public health regulations covering especially food items, chemicals, pharmaceuticals, etc., to ensure that a product only remains on sale in the shops as long as its quality and safety can be maintained and assured. If the shelf-life of a product is declared artificially short, *market access* by foreign suppliers may be impeded since the time needed for transport and customs clearance has to be allowed for. This reduces the time the product can be left on the shelf, and it increases the importer's costs because there might be greater wastage. It may even deter shops from stocking the product. Shelf-life restrictions then become *technical barriers to trade*. Motivations for shelf-life restrictions vary. They can be based on a desire to protect local manufacturers, a genuine belief that shelf-life should not exceed a certain period for health and safety reasons, a reluctance to accept the efficiency of certain types of packaging and hesitation to accept the validity of new testing methods.

Sheltered industries: industries benefiting from a *protective tariff* which ensures that they are not exposed to full international competition.

Schengen agreement: an instrument permitting the free movement of people between most of the members of the *European Union*. It removed checks at borders between members and replaced them with external border controls. The original agreement entered into force in 1995. It became part of European Union law through the *Treaty of Amsterdam*.

Sherman Act: a United States law passed in 1890 with the aim of prohibiting monopolies and restraints in interstate commerce as well as foreign trade. It remains the basis of the American system of *antitrust laws* and policies. The United States Supreme Court said of it in 1958: "The *Sherman Act* was designed to be a comprehensive charter of economic liberty aimed at preserving free and unfettered competition as the rule of trade". Section 1 of the Act states that "Every contract, combination in the form of trust or otherwise, or conspiracy, in restraint of trade or commerce among the several States, or with foreign nations, is hereby declared to be illegal." In the early days this was interpreted literally, but a 1911 Supreme Court judgment held that only unreasonable or undue restraints of trade were to be covered. Section 2 of the Act states that "Every person who shall monopolize, or attempt to monopolize, or combine and conspire with any other person or persons, to monopolize any part of the trade or commerce among the several States, or with foreign nations, shall be deemed guilty of a felony . . ." See also *Webb-Pomerene Act*.

Sherpa: in the *G-8* the personal representative of a head of government who is responsible, together with the sherpas from the other member countries, for preparing the *Economic Summit*. Each sherpa is normally assisted by two sous-sherpas drawn from the foreign and finance ministries. The term is apparently drawn from the Nepali word for a person who guides climbers to Himalayan summits. [Bayne and Woolcock 2003]

Shortage clause: a provision sometimes included in *free-trade agreements* to enable a party to impose export restrictions because of a shortage of a commodity on the internal market. The free-trade agreement between the *European Community* and Mexico, for example, states that a party may adopt export restrictions or export customs duties if major difficulties arise, or are likely to arise, for the exporting party because of (a) a critical shortage, or threat thereof, of foodstuffs or other products essential to the exporting party, or (b) a shortage of essential quantities of domestic materials to a domestic processing industry when prices are held below the world market price as part of a governmental stabilization plan, or re-export to a third country against which the exporting party maintains export customs duties or export prohibitions or restrictions. If such measures are taken, they must not be arbitrarily or unjustifiably discriminatory, and they must not be used to protect the domestic industry.

Short-supply products: Article XI of the GATT prohibits, with some defined exceptions, import and export quotas. One of these exceptions is that it permits *export quotas* if they are needed temporarily to prevent or relieve critical shortages of foodstuffs or other products essential to the exporting country.

Short-supply regulations: a framework of regulations under discussion in 1997 in the context of amended United States legislation on *anti-dumping measures*. The argument for such regulations was that some manufacturing operations are dependent on a competitive supply of components to maintain sales of their products. Sometimes these components are temporarily in short supply from domestic sources, but they may at the same time be subject to anti-dumping procedures. In such a situation, the anti-dumping action should in the view of importers be disregarded. This would allow firms to continue to benefit from lower prices charged for imported components and this way maintain their competitiveness. This argument was in the end rejected by the legislators.

Short-Term Arrangement Regarding International Trade in Cotton Textiles: an arrangement under the GATT between large textile exporters and importers to manage trade in these products through selective quantitative restrictions. It entered into force in 1961 for one year and was replaced in 1962 by the *Long-Term Arrangement Regarding International Trade in Cotton Textiles* which in turn was superseded in 1973 by the *Multi-Fibre Arrangement*. See also *Agreement on Textiles and Clothing* which brought the textiles trade again under the normal rules of the WTO.

SICA: Sistema de la Integración Centroamericana. The Central American Integration System, created through the Protocol of Tegucigalpa adopted by Belize, Costa Rica, El Salvador, Guatemala, Honduras, Nicaragua and Panama on 13 December 1991. It entered into force on 1 February 1993. SICA's objective is to bring about the integration of Central America so that it will constitute a region of peace, freedom, democracy and development. Among its aims are strengthening the region as an economic bloc and improving the Central American financial system. See also *SIECA*.

Sideswipe problem: an expression used particularly by Canadian trade analysts to describe any negative effects on Canada by United States actions aimed primarily at third countries.

SIECA: Secretaría de Integración Económica Centroamericana. The Permanent Secretariat of the General Treaty on Central American Integration, located in Guatemala City. The General Treaty entered into force on 12 October 1961. Its members are Costa Rica, El Salvador, Guatemala, Honduras, Nicaragua and Panama. The aims of SIECA were redefined in the Protocol of Guatemala to the General Treaty of 29 October 1993. They include, among others, the gradual establishment first of a *free-trade area*, then of a common *commercial policy* and a *customs union* and the free movement of factors of production. See also *SICA*.

Similar goods: defined in the *Customs Valuation Agreement* as "goods which, although not alike in all respects, have like characteristics and like component materials which enable them to perform the same functions and to be commercially interchangeable". The quality of the goods, their reputation and the existence of a trademark are among the factors to be considered in determining whether products are similar. Among other conditions, goods are not regarded as "similar goods" unless they were produced in the same country as the goods being valued. See also *accordion of likeness*, *fungible goods*, *identical goods* and *like products*.

Simplified balance-of-payments consultations: consultations in the WTO after the invocation by a *least developed country* member of the WTO provisions permitting measures to safeguard its external financial position. They are distinguished from the *full balance-of-payments consultations* normally used in the case of other WTO members. See also *balance-of-payments consultations*.

Singapore issues: so named because they entered the WTO work program through the declaration issued by the *Singapore Ministerial Conference*. The issues are *trade and investment*, *trade and competition*, *transparency in government procurement* and *trade facilitation*.

Singapore Ministerial Conference: the first of the biennial WTO meetings at ministerial level, held in December 1996. See also *Cancún Ministerial Conference*, *Doha Ministerial Conference*, *Seattle Ministerial Conference* and *WTO Ministerial Conference*.

Singapore Treaty on the Law of Trademarks: a revision adopted in 2006 of the *Trademark Law Treaty*, but not yet in force. It allows the registration of two-dimensional and three-dimensional *trademarks*, including hologram marks, colour marks and marks consisting of non-visible signs, such as sound and taste marks. It also establishes an assembly of contracting parties to deal with matters arising from the treaty. [www.wipo.int]

Singer-Prebisch thesis: refers to the proposition advanced in 1950 by the economists Hans Singer and Raúl Prebisch that the *terms of trade* of commodity-producing developing countries in their trade with developed countries will deteriorate over time. Singer and Prebisch arrived at the proposition independently of each other and from different assumptions. The proposition is known also as Prebisch-Singer thesis. The reason that Singer is often mentioned first is that apparently Prebisch was able to make good use of analytical work performed by Singer. On the other hand, the eventual popularity of the thesis owed much to its advocacy by Prebisch first as Secretary-General of *ECLA* and later as the first Secretary-General of *UNCTAD*. The starting point for Prebisch appears to have been the role of the labour market in developed and developing countries. He argued that because trade unions in developed countries, i.e. the countries producing manufactures, were strong, wages there tended to rise quickly in good times, but wage reductions in bad times were much slower. He saw this as an important factor in maintaining the price of manufactures. In developing countries, the weakness of trade unions meant that wages rose less quickly in good times and fell more quickly in bad times. This situation, according to Prebisch, meant that the gap between the cost of commodities and that of manufactures was increasing. Singer, on the other hand, was concerned more with price and income elasticities. He said that the demand for primary commodities had a relatively low income elasticity, and this meant that a rise in income tended to lower demand, and therefore the price, of commodities more than was the case for manufactures. He also held that technological improvements tended to reduce the demand for raw materials through, for example, the production of man-made substitutes and more efficient use of existing raw materials. This meant over time a lower growth in demand for primary commodities than for manufactures. Both Singer and Prebisch agreed that the solution for commodity-producing developing countries was to encourage industrialization. The Singer-Prebisch thesis became an important aspect of development economics, but it has always been controversial, partly because it appeared to encourage *protectionism* by developing countries. Certainly, one of its effects in Latin America especially was the widespread resort to *import substitution policies*. Additionally, the statistical evidence for a long-term deterioration of commodity terms of trade does not appear conclusive. It is always possible to find periods during which the terms of trade for commodity-producing developing countries decline, but equally other periods can be found to show the opposite. The heyday of the thesis spanned two decades beginning with the early 1960s. Today few economics textbooks discuss it in any depth. Its influence, however, is continuing in the *GSP* (Generalized System of Preferences), the *Integrated Programme for Commodities*, the concept of *special and differential treatment*, the *Enabling Clause*, the *GSTP* (Global System of Trade Preferences Among Developing Countries), etc. All of these are aimed at promoting increased participation by developing countries in world trade. See also *core-periphery thesis* and *export pessimism*. [Prebisch 1950, Prebisch 1963, Singer 1950, Cuddington, Ludema and Jayasuria 2002, Ghatak 2003, Toye and Toye 2003]

Single-column tariff: a *tariff schedule* under which all trading partners are treated in the same way. The schedule does not allow preferences, and it permits importers to seek the best possible suppliers. A single-column tariff represents the ideal state of the *multilateral trading system*. See also *multi-column tariff*.

Single commodity producers: refers mainly to developing countries that rely on one or two commodities for a large part of their exports. Such economies can experience large fluctuations in export income as demand and supply rise and fall.

Single-desk selling: the practice in some countries of marketing abroad and exporting agricultural commodities through *marketing boards*. Often, these have a monopoly on exporting and, sometimes, for imports also. In *market economies* at least, they usually operate on commercial principles in response to market signals. See also *state trading*.

Single economic space: an imprecise term which can mean anything from a *free-trade area* to a *common market*. See also *common economic space* and *Eurasian Economic Community*.

Single European Act: an amendment in 1987 to the *Treaty of Rome* with the aim of transforming relations among European Community member states into a European Union, and to contribute to making concrete progress towards European unity. The content of the Act is, however, mainly economic. It extended the Community's competence to include the internal market, monetary policy, social policy, economic and social cohesion, research and technology, and the environment. It made possible the *European Community Single Market*. The *Single European Act* also contains important institutional changes, such as making a formal linkage between the *European Communities* and European Political Cooperation. See also *European Community and European Union treaties*.

Single-firm behaviour: an aspect of company behaviour usually regulated under *antitrust laws* or *competition laws*. Its main manifestations are *predatory pricing*, price discrimination and fidelity rebates.

Single Market: see *European Community Single Market*.

Single Payment Scheme: the single payment, independent of production, which is available to *European Union* agricultural producers since 1 January 2005 under the revised *Common Agricultural Policy*.

Single undertaking: a guiding principle in the framework of multilateral trade negotiations. The *Doha Ministerial Declaration* states that ". . . the conduct, conclusion and entry into force of the outcome of the negotiations shall be treated as part of a single undertaking." The Punta del Este Declaration which launched the *Uruguay Round*, also said that the conduct of the negotiations, their conclusion and entry into force were to be treated as a single process. "Single undertaking" has also been used to refer to the requirement that WTO members must join all the agreements administered by it, except for the two *plurilateral agreements*. Membership of these remains optional. Before the WTO was established, GATT members could elect to a large extent which of the agreements under the purview of the GATT, other than the GATT itself, they wanted to join. See also *early harvest*.

SITC: Standard International Trade Classification. A *United Nations* classification which covers transportable goods. Services and non-traded sectors are not included. SITC is the most commonly used statistical classification for measuring trade in goods. See also *Harmonized System, International Standard Industrial Classification of All Economic Activities* and *UNCPC*.

Sliding-scale tariff: a *tariff schedule* which sets tariff rates according to the value of the imported products. In most cases, the rates rise as the value of the goods increases.

Slippery slope: has roughly the same meaning as the *thin edge of the wedge*. It refers to the beginning of a process that will almost inevitably lead to undesirable results from the point of view of those who do not wish to be anywhere near it.

Small and vulnerable economies: an imprecise term sometimes used to cover economies sharing several or all of the following characteristics: (a) domestic markets of a limited size, (b) limited diversification in export structure, both in terms of products and markets, (c) vulnerability to internal and external shocks, such as natural disasters or rapid increases in prices for imported energies, (d) long distance from markets and high transport costs, (e) shortage of suitably qualifies human resources, and (f) shortfalls in institutional and administrative capacities. See also *weak and vulnerable economies*. [www.wto.org]

Small economies: a WTO work program established at the *Doha Ministerial Conference* which aims at the fuller integration of small, vulnerable economies into the *multilateral trading system*.

Small island developing states: SIDS. A group of 41 countries and territories recognized by the United Nations as having unique problems and special vulnerabilities in achieving *sustainable development*. The Alliance of Small Island States (AOSIS) operates within the group as a lobby and negotiating voice, but not all AOSIS members are part of SIDS. AOSIS pays attention especially to the vulnerability of SIDS to the effects of *climate change*.

Smoot-Hawley Tariff Act: the 1930 United States *Tariff Act*. It was passed at the onset of the Great Depression and is chiefly remembered for having raised tariffs to the highest level in United States history. The tariff rates specified by this Act, like those of its predecessor, the *Tariff Act* of 1909, were fixed and could not be reduced through negotiation. It was amended in 1934 by the *Reciprocal Trade Agreements Act*. This launched the Reciprocal Trade Agreements Program which permitted negotiated tariff reductions. The effect on international trade of the Smoot-Hawley tariff is still being debated. There is a widespread belief, expressed in many economic histories, that it was one of the major causes of the deepening recession. As far as the United States economy is concerned, this may be a misreading of the influence of the higher tariff. At that time, United States imported only amounted to about 6% of gross national product. In any case, the full domestic impact of the tariff was not felt until the Depression had become chronic. Countries for whom the United States was a major market were of course very much affected by the higher rates. Regardless of the effect of the Act on trade, it was symptomatic of the *beggar-thy-neighbour policies* pursued by many countries in the inter-war years. The Smoot-Hawley tariff rates are still in force, and they apply to products from countries not receiving *most-favoured-nation treatment* by the United States, i.e. countries with which the United States does not have *normal trade relations*. This act also bans the import into the United States of goods produced by *prison labour*, forced or indentured labour. See also *autonomous tariff*, *Section 337* and *United States Reciprocal Trade Agreements Program*.

Smuggling: taking goods illegally across borders. If the goods could be imported legally into the country after the payment of applicable *customs duties*, the main motivation may simply be the avoidance of these duties. If the import of the good is illegal in the first place, other motivations of course come into play. See also *trafficking*.

Snapback provision: a mechanism sometimes built into *preferential trade agreements* or other trade agreements which allows an importing country to increase temporarily the *tariff* on a specified good or limit the quantities of that good that may be imported at the preferential tariff if its value at the border drops below a certain point. See also *safeguards*.

SNPA: the *Substantial New Programme of Action for the 1980s for the Least Developed Countries*. Adopted in Paris on 14 September 1981 by the United Nations Conference for the Least Developed Countries to promote the advancement of *least developed countries*. Progress on the implementation of the SNPA was reviewed and new targets set for it at the Second United Nations Conference for the Least Developed Countries held in September 1990, also in Paris. For the Third United Nations Conference on the Least Developed Countries (Brussels, 14 to 20 May 2001) see *Brussels Declaration*.

Social Chapter: see *Social Charter*.

Social Charter: formal name *Community Charter of Fundamental Social Rights for Workers*. It was adopted by the *European Community* members, apart from the United Kingdom, in December 1989. It was appended in a slightly altered form to the *Treaty of Maastricht* and became then known also as the *Social Chapter*. The *Intergovernmental Conference* held in June 1997 in Amsterdam agreed that the appendix should become a formal part of the Treaty. The Charter seeks to ensure that all citizens of the European Community should benefit from the *European Single Market*, and not business alone. The Charter contains provisions on freedom of movement, employment and remuneration, improvement of living and working conditions, social protection, freedom of association and collective bargaining, vocational training, equal treatment for men and women, information, consultation and participation of workers, health protection and safety at the workplace, protection of children and adolescents, elderly persons, and disabled persons. Some see the Charter as a possible model for a discussion of *trade and labour standards* in international organizations.

Social clause: short for the question of whether trade penalties in the form of WTO measures should be able to be applied to member countries found in breach of internationally agreed labour practices. The aim of a social clause would be to improve labour conditions in exporting countries by permitting sanctions against exporters who fail to observe certain minimum labour standards formulated by the *International Labour Organization* (ILO). There is no agreement yet on its feasibility or desirability, though similar measures have been discussed for well over a century in other forums. It was discussed in December 1996 at the WTO *Singapore Ministerial Conference* where ministers agreed that labour standards were a matter for the ILO. It is worth recalling, though, that the 1954 international sugar and tin agreements contained, for example, a "fair labour standards" clause which sought to ensure that labour engaged in the production of the commodity concerned would enjoy fair remuneration, social security benefits and other satisfactory conditions. The 1976 World Employment Conference held that the competitiveness of imports from developing countries should not be achieved at the expense of fair labour standards. Four years later, the first *Brandt Report* also recommended that fair labour standards should be internationally agreed to facilitate trade liberalization. The *International Coffee Agreement* of 2001 contains a clause promoting improved standards of living for populations engaged in the coffee sector. See also *child labour*, *Convention Concerning the Prohibition and Immediate Action for the Elimination of the Worst Forms of Child Labour*, *democracy clause*, *human rights clause*, *international commodity agreements*, *trade and labour standards* and *workers rights*.

Social conditionality: the attachment of social objectives to trade rules and making adherence to these rules conditional on the observance of certain social practices. See also *social clause*, *trade and human rights* and *trade and labour standards*.

Social dimension of the liberalization of international trade: this is a concept concerned with the effects on people of the structural changes brought about by the liberalization of international trade. Underlying this issue are the thoughts that not everyone benefits from these changes, and that workers in certain occupations are under threat from imports made by workers in countries allowing inadequate labour standards. The *International Labour Organization* established a working party to examine this subject. This has now been superseded by the *Working Party on the Social Dimension of Globalization*. See also *core labour standards*, *social clause*, *trade and labour standards* and *World Commission on the Social Dimension of Globalization*.

Social dumping: an imprecise term for actions assumed to occur when goods produced by prison or sweated labour are exported at very low prices. It was one of the putative categories of dumping identified by some participants in the *Havana Charter* negotiations. No rules were drafted for this type of alleged dumping, and it is not an accepted *trade policy* concept. The GATT contains a *general exception* in Article XX(e) covering goods made by *prison labour*. More recently, the term "social dumping" has also been used for products allegedly produced and exported under conditions that do not reflect standards, other than technical ones, prevailing in developed economies. See also *dumping*, *pauper-labour argument*, *social clause*, *trade and labour standards* and *workers rights*.

Social labelling: the practice of attaching a label or a mark to a product to indicate that it has been made under conditions of *fair labour standards*. There are no international rules on this, and many fear that compulsory social labelling would be the first step towards discriminatory treatment of *sensitive products* to protect some domestic industries. Proponents of the idea say that such is not their intent. *Rugmark* is an example of voluntary labelling. Products bearing this label are made without *child labour*. See also *eco-labelling*, *genetic labelling* and *social clause*.

Social regulation: see *regulation*.

Socially-responsible investing: the practice of taking into account ethical and economic criteria when making a decision to invest.

Social subsidies: some claim that these occur when governments permit the existence particularly in export industries of labour standards lower than those applied internationally, or if they do not enforce their own standards. The perceived resulting lower operating costs of enterprises benefiting from these practices are seen as an indirect export subsidy. Analysis tends to indicate, however, that lower labour standards have little effect on export competitiveness and, indeed, that they may impede it. Nor is the concept of social subsidies an accepted part of the *trade policy* vocabulary. See also *core labour standards*, *pauper-labour argument* and *social clause*.

Social tariff: a *tariff* intended to take into account social conditions in the importing country. For example, an industry may be given higher tariffs if it can show that it satisfies certain employment conditions, etc. The social tariff is best seen as an argument for *protectionism*. See also *Australian argument for protection*.

Soft law: in *trade policy* parlance, international arrangements that do not require parties to them to enforce the *measures* contained in them. In other words, they are hortatory arrangements. Examples of instruments entailing soft law are the *Set of Multilaterally Agreed Equitable Principles and Rules for the Control of Restrictive Business Practices* negotiated under *UNCTAD* auspices, the *OECD Guidelines for Multinational Enterprises* and the *APEC Non-Binding Principles on Government Procurement*. See also *hard law*.

Soft loan: a loan made by a government or a *multilateral development bank* at interest rates that are lower than commercial rates and possibly extended repayment periods.

SOLVIT: a *European Community* mechanism for *alternative dispute resolution*. It can be used by natural or legal persons that have run into problems resulting from the possible misapplication of internal market rules by another member state. The target deadline for finding a solution is ten weeks.

Sous-sherpa: see *sherpa*.

South: see *developing country*.

South American Free Trade Agreement: SAFTA. This was concluded in December 2003. Its members are the *Mercosur* countries (Argentina, Brazil, Paraguay and Uruguay), plus Bolivia, Chile, Colombia, Ecuador, Peru and Venezuela. It entered into force on 1 July 2004, but liberalization will occur in stages and take up to 15 years in some cases.

South Asian Association for Regional Cooperation: SAARC. It was established on 8 December 1985. Members are Bangladesh, Bhutan, India, Maldives, Nepal,

Pakistan and Sri Lanka. Among the objectives of SAARC are accelerated economic growth in the region and active collaboration in the economic field. As part of this, members signed in 1993 the framework agreement on *SAPTA* (SAARC Preferential Trading Arrangement) which is intended to lead to the formation of *SAFTA* (South Asian Free Trade Area). The Association's secretariat is located at Kathmandu.

South East Europe Free Trade Area: SEEFTA. This was formed in June 2001. Eventually Albania, Bosnia and Herzegovina, Bulgaria, Croatia, Macedonia, Moldova, Romania, and Serbia and Montenegro all became members. SEEFTA was replaced on 1 January by *CEFTA 2006*. At the same time Bulgaria and Romania joined the *European Union*.

Southern African Customs Union: SACU. A *customs union* originally established in 1910 and relaunched in 1969. It consists of Botswana, Lesotho, Namibia, South Africa and Swaziland. It covers the free flow of goods between the partners. Members share customs revenues under an agreed revenue-sharing formula.

Southern African Development Community: SADC. An association of fourteen southern African states (Angola, Botswana, Democratic Republic of Congo, Lesotho, Malawi, Mauritius, Mozambique, Namibia, Seychelles, South Africa, Swaziland, Tanzania, Zambia and Zimbabwe) established in 1992 as the successor to the Southern African Development Co-ordination Conference. Members signed a free-trade protocol in 1996. A *free-trade area* is to be established by 2008. SADC's headquarters is at Gabarone, Botswana.

Southern Common Market: see *Mercosur*.

South Pacific Commission: see *Secretariat of the Pacific Community*.

South Pacific Forum: see *Pacific Islands Forum*.

South Pacific Regional Trade and Economic Cooperation Agreement: see *SPARTECA*.

South-South cooperation: cooperation between developing countries. See also *developing country*, *ECDC*, *GSTP*, *G-15* and *Group of 77*.

South-South trade: trade between developing countries and the attendant *trade policy* issues. See also *ECDC* and *GSTP*.

Sovereign immunity: the principle in *public international law* that a sovereign government cannot be sued without its consent.

Soyabean **case:** see *oilseeds case*.

Spaghetti-bowl effect: a term used by Jagdish Bhagwati to describe the complexity of trade rules resulting from a proliferation of *free-trade areas*. A typical example of this is the existence of different *rules of origin* for each free-trade area. Countries that are members of more than one arrangement of this kind will have to administer different rules for each of them. [in Bhagwati and Panagariya 1996]

SPARTECA: *South Pacific Regional Trade and Economic Cooperation Agreement.* This Agreement, which entered into force on 1 January 1981, gives countries located in the South Pacific preferential non-reciprocal access to Australia and

New Zealand. Access for sugar to the Australian market is excluded. See also *asymmetrical trade agreements*.

Special Agreement on Commodity Arrangements: SACA. A proposal emerging in early 1955 among GATT contracting parties for an agreement to deal outside normal market forces with the disequilibrium between production and consumption of primary commodities, particularly agricultural commodities. The proposal had lapsed by the end of the year. See also *agriculture and the multilateral trading system* and *GATT review session*.

Special agricultural safeguards for developing countries: refers to proposals made by some developing countries in the *Doha Development Agenda* negotiations for the creation of a special safeguards mechanism for agricultural products. It would deal with cases where import volumes of specified agricultural products are rising rapidly and import prices fall below a fixed reference price. The special agricultural safeguards would only be available to developing countries meeting some defined conditions. Increasingly *free-trade agreements* seem to make use of special agricultural safeguards. See also *special safeguards*.

Special and differential treatment: often referred to as S&D or S+D. It is the concept that exports of developing countries should be given preferential access to markets of developed countries, that developing countries participating in trade negotiations need not reciprocate fully the *concessions* they receive, and that they should be able to restrict access to their markets to promote, for example, infant industries. Under S+D developing countries also enjoy longer timeframes for phasing in new rules and lower levels of obligations for adherence to the rules. The term is drawn from the ministerial declaration launching the *Tokyo Round* which raised the possibility of differential measures in favour of developing countries by giving them special and more favourable treatment. See also *developing countries and the multilateral trading system*, *development box*, *enabling clause*, *GSP*, *infant-industry argument*, *least developed countries*, *Part IV of the GATT*, *reciprocity* and *S&D box*. [Keck and Low 2004, Gallagher 2000, OECD/COM/TD/DAFFE/CLP(2001)21/FINAL]

Special Preferential Sugar Agreements: agreements in the form of an exchange of letters between the *European Community* as the importer, some of the *ACP states* and India in which the European Community allocates to them an annual special *tariff quota* for the import of raw cane sugar. The following ACP states are parties to this arrangement: Barbados, Belize, Republic of Congo, Fiji, Guyana, Côte d'Ivoire, Jamaica, Kenya, Madagascar, Malawi, Mauritius, Suriname, St Kitts and Nevis, Swaziland, Tanzania, Trinidad and Tobago, Uganda, Zambia and Zimbabwe. These agreements were first concluded for the years 1995 to 2001. They have been renewed for 2001 to 2006. Sugar quantities from the ACP states enjoying preferential access to the European Community are fixed annually in the light of import needs. For India the special tariff quota is 10,000 tonnes, again in the light of import needs, but it may be higher. The rate of duty within the special quota is zero. Import refineries must pay a minimum purchase price. See also *ACP-EC Sugar Protocol*.

Special products: refers to a proposal in the WTO by developing countries that they should be able to exempt some agricultural products from tariff reductions and liberalization of *tariff rate quotas*. A ceiling would apply to the number of *tariff lines* that could be treated in this way, but developing countries would be able to decide what products would be included. See also *Alliance for Strategic Products and Special Safeguard Mechanism*.

Special protection: seen by some Canadians as a peculiarly American phenomenon. It means that some industries that are especially powerful in a political sense may not have to settle for *trade remedies* to keep foreign competitors at bay. Instead, they are said to be able to secure "special protection" through an executive branch reinforced by powerful congressional pressure.

Special safeguards: a mechanism available under the WTO *Agreement on Agriculture* to members who have converted *non-tariff measures* to *tariff* protection. It allows members to impose additional tariffs on agricultural products if import volumes exceed defined trigger levels or import prices fall below defined *trigger prices*. Special safeguards therefore provide a safety net for importing countries that are also producers in the event of a surge in imports. They are meant to be introduced in a transparent manner. See also *safeguards, selectivity, tariffication* and *transitional safeguards*.

Special-structure countries: a name for Australia, Canada, New Zealand and South Africa in the *Kennedy Round* of *multilateral trade negotiations*. The four claimed, and were accorded, a different status in the *linear tariff cut* negotiations on the basis that their industries had not developed to the point where they would be able to compete with low-tariff imports of manufactures, and that the linear approach would not reduce protection for agriculture in their main export markets. In the event, they followed largely the item-by-item approach in the tariff negotiations.

Specialty air services: defined in *NAFTA* as aerial mapping, aerial surveying, aerial photography, forest fire management, fire fighting, aerial advertising, glider towing, parachute jumping, aerial construction, helilogging, aerial sightseeing, flight training, aerial inspection and surveillance, and aerial spraying services.

Special 301: part of the United States Trade Act of 1974, as amended. It requires *USTR* to make investigations every year of foreign countries that deny adequate and effective protection to United States *intellectual property rights* or that deny fair and equitable market access for persons that rely on intellectual property protection. Countries that have the most onerous or *egregious* conditions and whose conditions have the greatest adverse actual or potential impact on relevant United States products must be designated as *priority foreign countries*. This is done through the priority watch list. Placement on this list results in increased USTR attention. There is also a watch list. Countries on it are thought to pose problems, but not of a sufficient nature to require action. Investigations initiated as a result of Special 301 are fast-track. Unfairness and retaliation determinations must be made within six months of initiating an investigation. A particular feature of Special 301 is that, following amendment through the *Uruguay Round*

Agreements Act, it can be applied to countries denying adequate and effective intellectual property protection even if they are in compliance with their obligations under the WTO *Agreement on Trade-Related Aspects of Intellectual Property Rights*. In contrast to *Super 301*, Special 301 does not have to be renewed at fixed intervals. See also *Section 301*.

Special 301 for agriculture: see *United States Agricultural Products Market Access Act*.

Specific commitments: see *schedules of specific commitments on services*.

Specificity: a concept embodied in Article 2 of the WTO *Agreement on Subsidies and Countervailing Measures*. It is a test to determine whether a *subsidy* is available only to an enterprise or industry, or group of enterprises or industries. A subsidy is considered specific when the granting authority, or the legislation on which it operates, explicitly limits access to it to certain enterprises. A subsidy may also be considered specific when there is use of a subsidy program by a limited number of enterprises, predominant use by certain enterprises, the granting of disproportionately large amounts of subsidy to certain enterprises, and the manner in which discretion has been exercised by the granting authority in the decision to grant a subsidy. Depending on the type of subsidies and the impact they have, they may be *prohibited subsidies*, *actionable subsidies* or *non-actionable subsidies*. Subsidies dependent on export performance are also considered specific. They are always prohibited. See also *but for test*.

Specific process criterion: a concept sometimes used in the administration of *rules of origin* under *preferential trade agreements*. It means that a good has to have been processed in a certain way to qualify for preferential customs tariffs. See also *change in tariff classification*, *substantial transformation* and *value-added criterion*.

Specific reciprocity: see *mirror-image reciprocity*.

Specific rules of origin: a system of *rules of origin* which prescribes the process each product must undergo to qualify as an *originating product*.

Specific subsidy: see *specificity*.

Specific tariff: a *tariff* expressed as a specific charge on the particular item to be imported. A hypothetical example of a specific tariff would be a rate of one dollar per compact disc regardless of its value. See also *ad valorem tariff*.

Specific transitional safeguard mechanism: a mechanism available under the WTO *Agreement on Textiles and Clothing* during the transition period (i.e. the period ending on 1 January 2005 when trade in textiles and clothing had to be liberalized. The agreement has now expired. See also *safeguards*, *selectivity*, *special safeguards* and *Transitional Product-Specific Safeguard Mechanism*.

Specified risk material: SRM. A term used in the administration of *sanitary and phytosanitary measures*. This is a material associated with an identified or defined risk. In the case of *BSE*, for example, SRMs are often defined as the tissues from BSE-affected cattle which have been shown to contain the infective agent and able to transmit the disease. Such tissues cannot be used for producing goods for human consumption.

Split sub-heading: the *Harmonized System* is divided into two-digit entries (chapters), four-digit entries (headings) and six-digit entries (sub-headings). These entries are the same for all economies using this system. They cannot be altered. Countries may, however, divide headings further into split sub-headings. The definitions of split subheadings and the number of digits vary from country to country, though there must be at least seven digits. The following is an example from the Australian tariff. Sub-heading 900130 is contact lenses. This is divided into split sub-headings 900130.10 (ophthalmic powered contact lenses) and 900130.90 (other contact lenses).

Sporadic dumping: a form of *dumping* said to occur when a firm decides from time to time to sell surplus stocks internationally at prices lower than it charges it home. [Carbaugh 2000]

Springboarding: see *generic springboarding*.

SPS regulations: sanitary and phytosanitary regulations. These are government standards to protect human, animal and plant life and health. They help ensure that food is safe for consumption. See also *Agreement on the Application of Sanitary and Phytosanitary Measures*.

Spurious dumping: a term used by Jacob Viner in *Dumping: A Problem in International Trade* to describe situations where differences in price applied to different markets are the result of varying order sizes, length of credit terms and extent of credit risks, method of selling or freight and packaging requirements peculiar to the market, rather than conscious price discrimination. The charge of *dumping* could accordingly not be sustained in these cases. [Viner 1921]

Square brackets: see *bracketed language*.

STABEX: System for the Stabilization of Export Earnings. A scheme established under the *Lomé Convention* which sought to stabilise the export earnings of developing countries associated with the the *European Community* through the Convention. It aimed at compensating them for export earnings shortfalls in their trade with the European Community if they derived a large part of their total earnings from a single commodity. Conditionality was limited and aimed at ensuring that funds were used in the sector causing the difficulties. STABEX was not renewed in the *ACP-EC Partnership Agreement* which replaced the Lomé Convention. See also *Common Fund*, *compensatory financing arrangements* and *SYSMIN*.

Stabilization and Association Agreements: negotiated by the *European Community* with countries in south-eastern Europe (the Balkans). Their emphasis is on fostering respect for key democratic values and to promote the disciplines of the *European Community single market*. The aim of such agreements is to allow partner countries to achieve full association with the *European Union*. See also *association agreements* and *Europe agreements*.

Stacking: the use of two or more trade measures at the same time in respect of one good, e.g. the concurrent imposition of a *non-tariff barrier* and a *tariff*. [United Nations Conference on Trade and Development 2003]

Staging: also known as phasing. The introduction of tariff reductions or other trade-liberalizing measures according to a unilateral or an internationally-agreed timetable. For example, many developed countries phased in their *Uruguay Round* commitments to cut tariffs over five years, starting on 1 January 1995. The tariff eliminations under the *Information Technology Agreement* occurred in four stages, beginning on 1 July 1997 and ending on 1 January 2000. Staging is also a feature of many *free-trade arrangements*. *NAFTA*, for example, has five different staging categories: (a) goods receiving duty-free treatment before entry into force of the Agreement, (b) goods for which tariffs have been eliminated from the day of entry into force, (c) goods on which tariffs are eliminated in five equal annual stages, (d) goods on which tariffs are eliminated in ten equal annual stages, and (e) goods on which tariffs are eliminated in fifteen equal annual stages. In the case of the latter three categories, the first stage occurred on entry into force of the Agreement.

Standard International Trade Classification: see *SITC*.

Standards: methods to ensure uniform specifications or attributes of a product or a service. They are divided broadly into technical standards (e.g. minimum or maximum size, colour, composition, etc.) or performance standards (the product or service must have at least a certain capability). Additionally, standards may be compulsory or voluntary. The WTO *Agreement on Technical Barriers to Trade*, which applies to goods only, defines a standard as a "document approved by a recognized body that provides, for common and repeated use, rules, guidelines or characteristics for products or related processes and production methods, with which compliance is not mandatory. It may also include or deal exclusively with terminology, symbols, packaging, marking or labelling requirements, as they apply to a product, process or production method". See also *conformity assessment*, *International Electrotechnical Commission*, *International Organization for Standardization*, *ISO 9000*, *ISO 14000* and *technical barriers to trade*.

Standards and Trade Development Facility: a mechanism established jointly by the *World Bank*, the World Health Organization and the WTO after the *Hong Kong Ministerial Conference*. It supports developing countries needing help to develop their expertise and capacity to implement sanitary and phytosanitary standards, especially for agricultural products intended for export markets. The World Bank serves as the secretariat for the Facility. See also *sanitary and phytosanitary measures*. [www.standardsfacility.org]

Standards code: see *Tokyo Round agreements* and *Agreement on Technical Barriers to Trade*.

Standards of treatment: the quality of treatment afforded by parties to trade and investment agreements to goods, services, investors and investments from the other parties. Agreements usually provide for *most-favoured-nation treatment* or MFN (non-discrimination between foreign suppliers of goods and services, investors and their investments, as the case may be). Many agreements also provide for *national treatment* (non-discrimination between imported and domestic goods and services, or between foreign and domestic investors and their investments). Both of these standards are variable between countries. One country, for example, may have high agricultural tariffs. Another may have rather low ones. Yet each applies its own standard to all foreign suppliers and their products under the MFN principle. In the case of national treatment, one country may insist on strict product standards in some manufactures, but another may be more flexible. Neither breaches its legal obligations by insisting on its own standards as long as it does not discriminate against imported products. A standard of treatment different to MFN and national treatment is the *minimum standard of treatment* contained in *NAFTA Chapter 11*. According to Article 1105 "each party shall accord to investments of investors of another party treatment in accordance with international law . . .". The minimum standard of treatment is therefore sometimes called an absolute standard. *Fair and equitable treatment* is yet another undefined standard of treatment.

Standing of industry to apply for anti-dumping or countervailing duties investigations: describes the minimum industry participation which is needed for an application for an investigation of alleged *dumping* to be accepted by the relevant authorities. The formula given by the *Anti-Dumping Agreement* and the *Agreement on Subsidies and Countervailing Measures* is this. The agreements assume that domestic producers of the *like product* will either support an application, oppose it or not express a view either way. These producers together make up the total production of the like product produced by the domestic industry. The share of production by the producers not expressing a view is then set aside. This leaves those who support or oppose an application. An application is then considered successful and to have been made "by or on behalf of the industry" if producers representing at least 50% of the production made by this group support the application. However, no investigation may be launched if this group in fact represents less than 25% of the total production of the like product produced by domestic industry. The following example may help. Assume that the domestic industry producing the like product consists of 100 firms each accounting for 1% of the total output of the like product. It now is evident that 20% of these firms (20% of the total output of the like product) have no view on whether alleged dumping should be investigated. That leaves 80 firms accounting for 80% of total production. If 60 of these firms (i.e. three-quarters of them) support the call for an investigation, the application will be successful since they account for 60% of total domestic production of the like product. In practice, calculating industry support for an investigation isn't anywhere near this simple.

Standstill: an undertaking not to impose new or more restrictive trade measures after a certain date, usually the date on which the undertaking was made. Often combined with *rollback*. See also *trade pledge*.

STAR: see *Secure Trade in APEC Region*.

Stare decisis: the principle that a tribunal should follow its own previous decisions and those of other tribunals of equal or greater authority. See also *obiter dictum*. [Brownlie 1990]

State aids: the term for *subsidies* used in the *Treaty of Rome*. According to Article 92 of the Treaty, member states of the *European Economic Community* may not grant any aids to firms that would distort or threaten to distort competition. Exceptions deemed compatible with the provisions of the Treaty include non-discriminatory aids of a social character granted to individual consumers and aids intended to remedy damage caused by natural calamities or other extraordinary events. State aids which may be compatible with the Treaty include those intended to promote regional economic development, important projects or to remedy serious economic disturbances.

State secrets doctrine: also called state secrets privilege. It is the basis for a refusal by a state to disclose documents or information of vital interest to the security of the state.

State trading: there are two basic types of state trading. First, there is international trade conducted by state-owned, state-controlled or state-licensed private enterprises in market economies, sometimes with exclusive rights over certain products. These enterprises trade like normal commercial firms and respond to market signals. Second, state trading is a feature of *non-market economies* where price may not be the only or the dominant consideration in making import or export decisions. In this case, there is significant potential for market distortions and little *transparency*. State trading should be distinguished from *government procurement* which covers purchases by governments for their own use. See also *centrally-planned economies*, *marketing boards* and *single-desk selling*.

State-trading dumping: see *dumping*.

State-trading enterprises: commercial entities usually owned by the state which are authorized to conduct international trade. Often they have a *monopoly* or a near-monopoly on the import or export of a good. See also *marketing boards* and *single-desk selling*.

Statism: theories and policies which stress the importance of the state in the promotion of national economic development. Statism is not synonymous with excessive *regulation*, but it often leads in that direction.

Stockholm Convention on Persistent Organic Pollutants: see *Convention on Persistent Organic Pollutants*.

Stolper-Samuelson theorem: a proposition put forward in 1941 by the economists Wolfgang Stolper and Paul Samuelson. It holds that under certain assumptions (importantly that land and labour are the only factors of production) a move from no trade to free trade results in increasing income going to the factor of production used intensively in the export industry experiencing rising prices. Conversely, such a move would result in decreasing returns for the factor used intensively in the industry subject to falling prices. See also *comparative advantage*, *Heckscher-Ohlin theorem* and *Leontief Paradox*.

Strasbourg Agreement Concerning the International Patent Classification: concluded on 24 March 1971 and amended on 28 September 1979. It establishes the International Patent Classification (IPC). This is a common classification for patents for invention, inventors' certificates, utility models and utility certificates. The eight IPC categories for patents are: (a) human necessities, (b) performing operations; transporting, (c) chemistry; metallurgy, (d) textiles; paper, (e) fixed constructions, (f) mechanical engineering; lighting; heating; weapons; blasting, (g) physics, and (h) electricity. The Agreement is administered by *WIPO*.

Strategic business alliances: SBAs. Cooperative arrangements between firms requiring them to work towards common goals. Typically, partners to such alliances do not invest in the other partner. If they do, they may confine themselves to holding very small stakes. The aim in all cases is to improve the competitive standing of all the partners. The formation of SBAs may be subject to national *competition policy* or *antitrust laws*.

Strategic dumping: see *dumping*.

Strategic exports: goods and services thought to have an actual or potential effect on the military balance in a given region. See also *dual-purpose exports*, *COCOM* and *Wassenaar Arrangement on Export Controls for Conventional Arms and Dual-Use Goods and Technologies*.

Strategic Products and Special Safeguard Mechanism: see *Alliance for Strategic Products and Special Safeguard Mechanism*.

Strategic trade policy: see *strategic trade theory*.

Strategic trade theory: often used interchangeably with strategic trade policy. It is the idea that governments can adopt, or threaten to adopt, domestic policies promoting the emergence and development of industries likely to become significant exporters. The theory appears to take its name from the recognition that actions by government can alter the strategic relationship between firms. The implementation of this theory is almost always based on *subsidies* or *protection* of one kind or another, though its proponents on the whole have not advocated such crude action. The theory shows satisfactorily that in closely defined circumstances such actions could bring net benefits to an economy. It is worth remembering, however, that the constraints and the rigour academic economists bring to their work soon disappears when an attempt is made by governments to translate a theory into a policy. See also *comparative advantage*, *national champions*, *new trade theory* and *picking winners*. [Brander and Spencer 1984, Brander 1995, Dam 2001, Krugman 1986]

Stresa Convention: the *International Convention for the Use of Appellations of Origin and Denominations of Cheeses*, concluded on 1 June 1951 at Stresa, Italy. Founding members were Austria, Denmark, France, Italy, Netherlands and Switzerland. The Convention seeks to reserve the names of certain cheeses for the use of member countries. It distinguishes between *appellations of origin* and denominations. The former refers to cheese made or manufactured in traditional regions and which have special qualities by virtue of long usage, etc. Such names are always reserved for the region giving rise to the name. *Roquefort* (France) is one of them. The characteristics of the latter are defined in terms of shape, weight, size, type and colour of the rind and curd by the party first using the name. Other parties may use these denominations provided that they describe the cheeses in accordance with the terms of the Convention. These cheeses include *Provolone* (Italy) and *Emmental* (Switzerland). [Peaslee 1979]

Structural adjustment: the continuous process experienced by all industries of needing to adjust to new economic and commercial conditions brought about by changes in consumer preferences, technological innovation, tariff reductions, subsidy phase-outs, long-term changes in the cost of components and raw materials, etc. Sometimes this results in the rapid disappearance of a complete sector, such as has occurred in slide-rule production when the electronic calculator appeared. Structural adjustment can be accompanied by government support for the retraining of workers and other measures. Whether governments are prepared to pay up often depends on the political clout of the industry. Since the mid-1980s, the term has also come to refer to a particular set of policy prescriptions requested of developing countries by international financial institutions such as the *World Bank* and the *IMF*. The granting of assistance packages by these institutions is typically conditional on a tightening of fiscal policies and the achievement of macro-economic stability through tough anti-inflationary policies. See also *protectionism*.

Structural impediments: structural features of an economy seen as impeding the emergence of fully competitive markets. These can result from inappropriate or excessive *regulation*, widespread use of *subsidies*, the existence of private or government monopolies, rigid labour markets, inadequate disciplines on *restrictive business practices* and other similar factors.

Structural Impediments Initiative: SII. A 1989 United States initiative aimed at opening the Japanese market to American firms. It was based on the proposition that the removal of traditional barriers to trade was not enough, and that meaningful changes had to be brought about through changes to Japanese domestic policies and practices. Japanese market and distribution systems were a target, as was the relationship between government and business. Few now would claim that the SII had been a success, possibly because the target was not understood well enough. See also *Market-Oriented Specific-Sector talks*, *keiretsu* and *United States-Japan Framework for a New Economic Partnership*.

Structuralism: see *structural trade theory*.

Structural trade theory: a contentious theory emerging in the 1950s which held that structural forces in international trade impeded the development of countries dependent on the production and export of primary commodities and raw materials. Its proponents argued that there was a persistent bias against such producers because of a long-term deterioration in their *terms of trade*. The proposed solutions included the promotion of preferential *South-South trade* (trade among developing countries). It was thought that in this more limited environment developing countries would be relatively more competitive and able to get ready to supply industrialized countries once their industries had developed sufficiently. Preferential access to developed countries for products of export interest to developing countries through a *GSP* was also advocated.

Few of the resulting preferential trade areas became effective enough to make a practical difference, but the structuralists had succeeded in drawing attention to the important issue of trade and development. See also *GSTP* and *UNCTAD*.

Stumbling blocks: a term coined by Jagdish Bhagwati. It is used to describe *free-trade areas* that impede the development of multilateral *trade liberalization*. See also *building blocks*. [Bhagwati 1991]

Sub-heading: a six-digit entry in the *Harmonized System*. Examples are 030110 (ornamental fish), 450310 (corks and stoppers) and 900130 (contact lenses). See also *chapter* and *heading*.

Sub-national obligations: see *second-level obligations*.

Sub-regional economic zones: see *growth triangles*.

Subrogation: a term found in many *investment promotion and protection agreements*. It means that in cases where investors have received payments from their national investment insurance agency against the covered risks, the home country of these investors or its insurance agency takes over the rights or claims of the investors against the home state. [United Nations Centre on Transnational Corporations and International Chamber of Commerce 1992]

Sub-Saharan Africa: a geographic area encompassing 48 countries: Angola, Benin, Botswana, Burkina Faso, Burundi, Cameroon, Cape Verde, Central African Republic, Chad, Comoros, Congo, Côte d'Ivoire, Democratic Republic of Congo, Djibouti, Equatorial Guinea, Eritrea, Ethiopia, Gabon, The Gambia, Ghana, Guinea, Guinea-Bissau, Kenya, Lesotho, Liberia, Madagascar, Malawi, Mali, Mauritania, Mauritius, Mozambique, Namibia, Niger, Nigeria, Rwanda, Sao Tome and Principe, Senegal, Seychelles, Sierra Leone, Somalia, South Africa, Sudan, Swaziland, Tanzania, Togo, Uganda, Zambia and Zimbabwe. See also *African Growth and Opportunity Act*.

Subsidiarity: a concept which postulates that the *European Community* should only take action in areas where it does not have exclusive competence if the envisaged objective cannot be sufficiently achieved by the member states acting alone. The subsidiarity principle appears to have implications for the formulation of European Community policy on aspects of *trade in services*, especially in areas where no fully developed common policy exists as yet. See also *European Community legislation*.

Subsidies: financial or in-kind assistance by governments to producers or exporters of commodities, manufactures and services. There are two general types of subsidies: export and domestic. An export subsidy is a benefit contingent on exports conferred on a firm by the government. A domestic subsidy is a benefit not directly linked to exports. Subsidies are paid for many reasons, including the need to prop up an inefficient production structure, the wish to raise the income of one sector, the wish to promote regional development, the aim to develop export markets, etc. Broadly, the WTO *Agreement on Subsidies and Countervailing Measures* defines subsidies as financial contributions by a government or public body, direct transfer of funds or potential transfer of funds (e.g. grants, loans, equity infusions), government revenue foregone or not collected, government provision of goods and services other than general infrastructure, payments to a funding mechanism or a private body to perform these functions, income or price support if they also confer a benefit. The 2006 *World Trade Report* covers questions related to subsidies in some detail. *Agricultural subsidies* are covered by the *Agreement on Agriculture*. See also *bounty*, *countervailing measures*, *specific subsidy* and *state aids*.

Subsidies Code: see *Tokyo Round agreements* and *Agreement on Subsidies and Countervailing Measures*.

Substantial cause: under some of the trade agreements negotiated by the United States, such as the *free-trade agreement* with Jordan, safeguards action may be taken when increased quantities of imports are a substantial cause of *serious injury*, or *threat of serious injury*, to domestic industries. A substantial cause is defined as "important and not less than any other cause".

Substantial interest: see *interested third parties*.

Substantially-all-discrimination criterion: the *General Agreement on Trade in Services* (GATS) permits the establishment of *free-trade areas* in services under certain conditions. One of these is that the other partners to the arrangement must be given *national treatment* in substantially all the sectors covered by the agreement. The term "substantial" is not defined further in the GATS.

Substantially-all-trade criterion: Article XXIV of the *GATT* sets out the conditions under which *customs unions* and *free-trade areas* may be regarded as consistent with the Agreement. It requires that substantially all trade between the parties to a preferential agreement must be covered as part of qualifying under the rules. The GATT does not say how this is to be understood or calculated. Two schools of thought have emerged on what the criterion means. The first adopts a quantitative approach, and it defines "substantially all trade" in terms of the value of total trade. A broad assumption among WTO members has been that this should be about 80% to 90% of total trade. Under this approach, agriculture or other *sensitive sectors* might not be covered by an agreement, but the remainder of trade might be enough to satisfy the criterion. The second approach is qualitative. It says that all sectors must be covered, and that leaving out agriculture, for example, would automatically violate the criterion. Agreement on which school should prevail is not in sight, even though WTO members have agreed during the *Uruguay Round* that the contribution of a *free-trade agreement* to world trade would be diminished if any major sector of trade was excluded. Article V of the *General Agreement on Trade in Services*, which covers free-trade agreements in services, also has a substantially-all-trade criterion. It is divided into the need for substantial sectoral coverage of services and the absence or elimination of substantially all discrimination in terms of *national treatment*. "Substantial sectoral coverage" is to be understood in terms of number of sectors, volume of trade affected and *modes of services delivery*. Additionally, no mode of supply should be excluded *a priori*.

Substantial New Programme of Action for the 1980s for the Least Developed Countries: see *SNPA* and *Brussels Declaration*.

Substantial sectoral coverage: a criterion preferential *economic integration agreements* in *trade in services* must meet to qualify under Article V of the *General Agreement on Trade in Services* for an exemption from the *most-favoured-nation* requirement. The word "substantial" is not defined in quantitative terms, but a footnote to the Article states that it is to be understood in terms of number of sectors, volume of trade affected and *modes of services delivery*. No mode of supply should be excluded *a priori*.

Substantial supplying interest: under the rules for the negotiation of tariff reductions set out in Article XXVIII of the GATT, negotiations are normally conducted with the party having a *principal supplying interest*. The same Article says that the interests of a party with a substantial interest in trade in that product have to be considered. An explanatory note says that the expression "substantial interest" is not capable of a precise definition, but that it is intended to be construed as a significant market share or the expectation of such a share. See also *renegotiation of tariffs*.

Substantial transformation: a term used by customs authorities in the administration of *rules of origin* to determine what the origin of a good is. In the case of goods originating entirely in the exporting country, so-called *wholly obtained goods*, this is easy. Many goods entering the export trade, however, are made up of imported materials or contain imported components. They may also have undergone *trans-shipment* through a third country. One of the criteria customs officers can use to determine the origin of a good is to ascertain the place where the good acquired its current form through having been substantially reworked from another form. A simple example of a substantial transformation is the case of a stepladder made in China from Canadian aluminium lengths. The ladder would be considered a Chinese product because it acquired its form in China, and that form is substantially different to aluminium lengths. On the other hand, simply repackaging a good or painting it would not be considered a substantial transformation since the good had all of its essential characteristics before it was painted or repackaged. Another way to ascertain whether substantial transformation has occurred is to measure the value added to it in the exporting country. This is the *regional value content*, expressed as a percentage of the total value of the good. See also *preferential rules of origin*, *change in tariff heading* and *last substantial transformation*.

Sufficiently worked or processed: a criterion used in the administration especially of *preferential rules of origin* under *free-trade agreements*. It has a meaning similar to *substantial transformation*. Suppose that economy B imports steel rods from economy A. It then transforms these steel rods into fencing wire. This action makes the imported good into a different good. Hence, when economy B exports the fencing wire to economy C, the customs authority there will consider it a product of economy B. If, however, economy B had done no more than cutting the steel rods into shorter lengths and perhaps painting them, economy C would probably still consider them as products of economy A.

Sugar: see *ACP-EU Sugar Protocol*, *Special Preferential Sugar Agreement* and *Global Sugar Alliance*.

***Sui generis* right:** a type of *intellectual property protection* used often as a form of *copyright* protection. It treats the matter to be protected as unique and requiring specific protection on that basis. *Sui generis* protection is used especially for computer software and related subject matter. See also *lay-out design of integrated circuits* and *plant breeders' rights*.

Sullivan Principles: a set of six principles proposed by the Reverend Leon Sullivan, a director of General Motors, in 1977 for the conduct of the company's operations in South Africa under the apartheid system. The principles quickly gained widespread acceptance. They are concerned especially with equal and fair employment policies for all workers and the improvement of their conditions inside and outside the workplace. See also *trade and environment* and *trade and labour standards*.

Sunrise industries: emerging industries, often with a high *intellectual property* content which, through the use of innovative methods and technological advances, succeed in doing things more efficiently or in creating entirely new classes of products. Information technology in particular has spawned sunrise industries. *Trade policy* interest in sunrise industries partly derives from issues related to the protection of *intellectual property rights* and from the fact that governments sometimes wish to promote them by *picking winners* or through the adoption of actions based on *strategic trade theory*, both of which may have the effect of distorting trade. See also *knowledge-based industry*, *national champions*, *new economy* and *sunset industries*.

Sunset clause: a provision in an agreement under which a measure taken by a government expires automatically once a certain time has elapsed, or unless some specified action has been taken. The WTO agreements dealing with *anti-dumping measures* and *countervailing duties* contain sunset clauses under which relevant measures expire after five years unless a review finds that they should continue. See also *manufacturing clause* for a dispute arising because of a sunset clause in United States legislation.

Sunset industries: industries considered moribund because of technological advances in other sectors of the economy or changes in consumer preferences. Such industries are sometimes exemplified by unprofitable old-style steel mills whose closure would lead to widespread local unemployment. Some new steel mills could of course be classified as *sunrise industries*. Attaining the status of a sunset industry may be a matter of months, as happened among the slide-rule producers when the electronic pocket calculator made its appearance. In other cases, it may be a drawn-out process as industries produce insufficient returns to be able to modernize and are unable to attract new investment, but are earning enough to carry on through cost-saving measures and gradual staff reductions. This is often the time when governments are asked to alleviate an industry's discomfiture through *protection* in the form of *local content requirements*, *import* *restrictions*, measures designed to promote *structural adjustment*, *subsidies*, *voluntary restraint arrangements*, etc.

Sunshine rule: the practice of conducting open hearings to examine proposed or existing governmental policies.

Superfund: a case launched in the GATT in 1987 by Canada, Mexico and the European Community against the United States. It dealt with a tax to be levied under the United States *Superfund Amendments and Reauthorization Act* of 1986. The tax had not become effective at the time the dispute was launched. It imposed, *inter alia*, a new tax on certain imported substances produced or manufactured from taxable feedstock chemicals. The tax to be levied on imported substances equalled in principle the tax that would have been payable on chemical components if these chemicals had been sold in the United States for the same use. A penalty rate could be levied if importers supplied insufficient information regarding the chemical components of the imported substance. The complainants argued that the tax on the imported products was higher than the tax on the like domestic product, and that it therefore contravened the *national-treatment* principle. The *panel* considered that the imported and domestic products were *like products* within the meaning of the GATT, that there was a difference in the prospective treatment of domestic and imported products, and that the tax to be levied by the United States was inconsistent with the obligations the United States had under the GATT. It found at the same time that, as the Act gave the authorities discretion to impose the tax, the existence of penalty rates as such did not constitute a violation of the GATT. [GATT BISD 34S]

Supervised exports: goods which may be exported freely when they are in normal supply, but which may be limited when they are becoming more scarce at home and their price rises.

Super 301: the name commonly given to Section 1302 of the 1988 *Omnibus Trade and Competitiveness Act*. It requires *USTR* (the United States Trade Representative) to prepare a report annually on United States trade expansion priorities which identifies "*priority foreign country* practices, the elimination of which is likely to have the most significant potential to increase United States exports, either directly or through the establishment of a beneficial precedent". This original Super 301 also required the identification of priority foreign countries, but this was changed to priority foreign country practices alone in the *Uruguay Round Agreements Act*. In practice, the effect is the same. At the same time, USTR was authorized to report on foreign country practices that may in the future warrant identification as priority foreign country practices. Super 301 differs from *Section 301* in that it concentrates on systemic unfair trade practices. Super 301 was originally enacted for the years 1989 and 1990. It requires periodic renewal by the President. See also *Special 301*.

Support prices: a device to give producers of primary commodities in particular an assured minimum return. This can be done through, for example, a *floor price*, the *loan rate*, *subsidies* and *variable levies*, sometimes aided by *import restrictions*. Support prices may be related to the market price in that they respond to price signals to some extent. Determining the market price itself becomes problematical under such conditions. Support prices may be unrelated to market prices. Their purpose then simply is to give producers a guaranteed income. The domestic consumer and efficient producers in other countries share the bill between them.

Surrogate country: see *analogue country*.

Surtax: see *import surcharge* and *primage*.

Surveillance: regular monitoring by members of the WTO of national trade policies of other members to ensure that they are in conformity with the rules of the *multilateral trading system* and that they reflect the *commitments* made by individual member states. One mechanism that can be used for this purpose is the *Trade Policy Review Mechanism*, but many of the agreements administered by the WTO contain provisions requiring notification of changes to policies or action taken under the terms of the specific agreement. See also *notification* and *transparency*.

Suspension of concessions or other obligations: if a WTO member fails to act on a recommendation or ruling by a *panel* or the *Appellate Body*, the member bringing the complaint may ask the *Dispute Settlement Body* to suspend the application of *concessions* or other obligations to the member failing to take action. This may be done twenty days after the expiry of *reasonable period of time* (usually no more than fifteen months after the adoption of the origin panel or Appellate Body report). The following main principles apply to the selection of concessions or other obligations to be suspended. First, the suspensions should be in the sector where a violation of the rules occurred. Second, if this is not effective or practicable, other sectors covered by the same agreement may be chosen (i.e. if the matter concerns GATT rules, the suspensions should apply to matters covered by the GATT). Third, if this is not a satisfactory way to proceed, suspensions may made under another agreement covered by the *Dispute Settlement Understanding* (i.e. it would be possible to suspend *commitments* under the *General Agreement on Trade in Services* or the *Agreement on Trade-Related Aspects of Intellectual Property Rights* even though the original matter may have arisen under the GATT). Members suspending concessions are asked to take into account the importance of the trade to the other party and the broader economic consequences of suspending concessions or obligations. See also *Article 21.5 panel*, *Article 22.6 arbitration* and *retaliation*.

Sustainability Impact Assessments: SIA. A mechanism pioneered by the *European Community* to assess the impact of proposed multilateral, regional or bilateral trade measures on *sustainable development*. Assessments take into account matters such as environmental quality, real income, health and equity. Many see SIAs as a main factor in promoting a sustainable environment.

Sustainable development: defined by the *World Commission on Environment and Development* as ensuring that development meets the needs of the present without compromising the ability of future generations to meet their own needs. See also *World Summit on Sustainable Development*.

Sustainable trade policy: a trade policy which seeks to balance the aim of trade liberalisation with the aim of promoting *sustainable development* while at the same time guaranteeing social development.

Sweated labour: describes workers suffering abuse and exploitation through, for example, inadequate working conditions and the payment of wages that are as low as possible. See also *social dumping* and *trade and labour standards*.

Sweatshop-labour argument: see *pauper-labour argument*, *trade and human rights*, *trade and labour standards* and *wage-differential argument*.

Swing mechanism: this refers to an interpretation by some WTO members of the right to use export subsidies for agricultural products. The *Agreement on Agriculture* sets annual limits on the level of export subsidies members may apply. Some now say that if a country does not use up its ceiling level in any year, it should be able to use the unused amount in another year, provided that the total permissible amount is not exceeded. This proposition does not enjoy widespread support. The swing mechanism was an accepted method under the *Agreement on Textiles and Clothing*. The Agreement permitted swing (transfer of part of an export quota for one product to quota for another product), subject to certain established guidelines and practices.

Swiss-Army-knife approach to tariff negotiations: creating a family of modified *Swiss formulas* in which the coefficient is adjusted to increase the reductions in lower tariffs. The standard Swiss formula produces large reductions when tariffs are high and tiny reductions when they are low. [Francois and Martin 2003]

Swiss formula: a compromise formula for achieving *linear tariff cuts* proposed by Switzerland during the *Tokyo Round*. It was intended to reduce higher tariffs by a greater proportion than lower tariffs. The formula reads:
$$Z = AX/(A + X)$$
X represents the initial tariff rate, and A is a coefficient to be agreed on. Z is the resulting lower tariff rate. The *European Economic Community*, the *Nordic countries* and Australia used the coefficient 16, the United States, Japan and Switzerland 14. New Zealand used the item-by-item technique.

Symbolic deals: a term used by Bernard Hoekman in *Trade Laws and Institutions: Good Practices and the World Trade Organization* to describe agreed negotiating outcomes that are apparently or patently not substantive. Such deals can occur in situations where the negotiators realize that agreement on the substantive issues is not possible for the time being, but to leave the table without any agreement at all might be worse presentationally. To do otherwise might also make it more difficult to restart the negotiations. Such deals sometimes are called political outcomes. [Hoekman 1995]

SYSMIN: System for the Promotion of Mineral Production and Exports, or sometimes System for Safeguarding and Developing Mineral Production. A commodity stabilization mechanism established by the *European Economic Community* in 1980 under the umbrella of Lomé-II as an alternative to bringing minerals under *STABEX*. It aimed at protecting *ACP states* against reductions in mine output and consequent export earnings shortfalls. SYSMIN was not renewed in the ***ACP-EC Partnership Agreement*** which replaced the ***Lomé Convention***.

Systemic issues: matters pertaining to the functioning or the broad rules of the ***multilateral trading system***. Issues usually included under this heading include, for example, ***dispute settlement*** provisions, ***safeguards*** mechanisms, ***transparency*** rules, etc.

T

TAFTA: Trans-Atlantic Free Trade Agreement. A proposal for a *free-trade area* between the United States and the *European Community*. It is not on a formal negotiating agenda. See also *New Transatlantic Agenda*.

Tailor-made tariffs: see *made-to-measure tariffs*.

Takeover principle: another name for the *absorption* principle or *"roll-up" principle*. This principle permits the use of *non-originating materials* that have acquired *origin* through processing to retain that status when they are used in a further transformation. See also *rules of origin* and *preferential rules of origin*.

Taking of property: see *expropriation*.

Targeted dumping: dumping concentrated in sales to certain regions, customers, or time periods. See also *anti-dumping measures*. [WTO WT/DS219/AB/R]

Targeting: see *picking winners* and *strategic trade theory*. In United States trade law, targeting by others may give rise to an action under *Section 301*.

TARIC: Tariff Intégré de la Communauté. See *Integrated Tariff of the European Community*.

Tariff: a customs duty on merchandise imports. Levied either as an *ad valorem tariff* (percentage of value) or as a *specific tariff* (e.g. $7 per 100kg). Less often, a *compound tariff* made up of both of these elements applies. Tariffs give a price advantage to similar locally-produced goods and raise revenues for the government. Tariffs are mostly levied on imports, but there are cases of *export tariffs*. For economists, a tariff is the equivalent of the imposition concurrently of a consumption tax and a production subsidy. Although governments often understand this clearly, they may be reluctant to reduce tariffs since this may have important fiscal implications in cases where they rely on *customs duties* as a predictable source of revenue. It is worth noting, however, the view expressed in the *Brigden Report* that the "popularity of a tariff among Treasuries and Governments is due to the fact that it is a means of 'painless extraction', the indirectness of the method acting as an anaesthetic". See also *ad valorem tariff*, *binding*, *Lerner's symmetry theorem*, *seasonal tariff* and *specific tariff*.

Tariff anomaly: used by some to refer to what is commonly known as *tariff escalation*, i.e. the tariff rate on raw materials or semi-finished products is lower than on the finished product made of these materials in order to encourage domestic manufacturing. For others, a tariff anomaly is precisely the opposite, i.e. the tariff rate on raw materials and semi-finished products is higher than the rate levied on the finished product.

Tariff binding: a commitment not to increase a rate of duty beyond an agreed level. Once a rate of duty is bound, it may not be raised without compensating the affected parties.

Tariff classification: a method for listing systematically nearly every good that is traded internationally. Its main purpose is to assist customs authorities in assessing the correct rate of duty, but it can also be used for the presentation of statistics and other purposes. The classification used by WTO members is the *Harmonized System*.

Tariff code: a number assigned to a good or group of goods in a *tariff classification*.

Tariff concession: the same as a *tariff binding*. This is a contractual undertaking, usually as the result of negotiations, not to exceed the tariff level on a good as entered in that country's *tariff schedule*.

Tariff Conference: the formal name for the first four rounds of *multilateral trade negotiations* under the GATT. These were *Geneva 1947, Annecy, Torquay* and *Geneva 1955–56* tariff conferences.

Tariff equivalent: a calculation based on an agreed formula of what the impact of a *non-tariff measure* would be if it were converted into a *tariff*. Such calculations are complex, but they add considerably to the *transparency* of trade regimes. See also *tariffication*.

Tariff escalation: higher import duties on semi-processed products than on raw materials, and higher still on finished products. This practice protects domestic processing industries and discourages the development of processing activity in the countries where the raw materials originate. See also *effective rate of assistance*.

Tariff evasion: the action of avoiding the payment of *customs duties* altogether or of seeking to pay less than should be the case. Main ways of achieving this are seeking to have the goods classified in a category with lower or no tariffs, or having an invoice made out that understates the value of the goods. Sometimes goods are also imported free of duty into *free-trade zones* and then re-exported illegally into the domestic market. Preventing tariff evasion is one of the reasons for adopting *preshipment inspection*. See also *customs valuation* and *smuggling*. [Anson, Cadot and Olarreaga 2003]

Tariff-Free World: a proposal for the elimination of all tariffs on consumer and industrial goods by WTO members by 2015. It was made by the United States in November 2002 in the negotiations under the *Doha Development Agenda*.

Tariffication: procedures relating to the agricultural market-access provision in the *Agreement on Agriculture* under which all non-tariff measures are converted into tariffs. See also *minimum access tariff quotas* and *water in the tariff*.

Tariff-jumping investment: investment in a production facility in another country in order to overcome high tariff barriers or other border measures. Views differ whether trade and investment in such cases are complementary, or whether tariff-jumping replaces trade. A view held by many is that trade and investment are now integrated in nearly all cases, and that the distinction can in practical terms easily be overdrawn. See also *tariff escalation*.

Tariff line: usually, but not always, refers to a six-digit entry in the *Harmonized System*, also known as a *sub-heading*.

Tariff negotiations: a key function of the WTO. From the entry into force of the GATT on 1 January 1948 until the *Dillon Round* of 1960–61, tariffs were negotiated item by item or product by product under the *request-and-offers* system. The principal supplier of a product to another GATT member had the right to request tariff reductions. From the *Kennedy Round* onwards, *linear tariff cuts* became the dominant method. Whole sections of the tariff were thereby reduced uniformly according to an agreed formula. In the *Tokyo Round*, the *Swiss formula* for linear tariff cuts was used as a working hypothesis under which higher tariffs were reduced by a greater proportion than low ones. Tariff negotiations in the *Uruguay Round* were partly of the product-by-product type and partly *zero-for-zero tariff reductions* under which tariffs are reduced to zero for whole classes of products. See also *banded formula*, *blended formula*, *harmonized tariff reductions*, *Information Technology Agreement*, *principal supplier rights*, *renegotiation of tariffs* and *sectoral trade negotiations*.

Tariff-only regime: a trade regime where *tariffs* are the only border measures. Import licences, quotas, etc., are not used. Standards, sanitary and phytosanitary measures and so on would of course still apply.

Tariff peaks: relatively high tariffs, usually on so-called *sensitive products*, amidst generally low tariff levels. For industrialized countries, tariffs of 15% and above are generally recognized as tariff peaks.

Tariff preferences: the fundamental assumption under the agreements administered by the WTO is that countries give each other *most-favoured-nation treatment* in their administration of their *tariff* regimes. It is, however, possible under certain conditions to accord lower tariff rates or zero tariffs to selected trading partners. The principal means are preferential rates by developed countries for developing countries under *GSP* schemes, and zero-tariff rates between members of *customs unions* or *free-trade areas*. Developing countries may also accord each other preferential rates, for example, under *Part IV of the GATT* and the *Enabling Clause*. One occurrence of this is the *GSTP*. See also *imperial preferences arrangement*.

Tariff quota: in common usage this term is a synonym for a *tariff rate quota*, but in its specialized meaning it is a tariff that increases, discreetly, at a certain level or levels of quantity imported. [Deardorff and Stern 1997]

Tariff quota expansion: increases in quantities that may be imported within a *tariff quota*.

Tariff rate quota: TRQ. The application of a reduced *tariff* rate for a specified quantity of imported goods. Imports above this specified quantity face a higher tariff rate. Some claim that tariff quotas liberalize trade since, in contrast to *import quotas*, there is no ceiling on imports under this system. This assumption can be quite erroneous. The difference between the *in-quota tariff* and the *out-of-quota tariff* is often so large as to preclude any trade at the higher rate. See also *current access tariff quotas* and *minmum access tariff quotas*.

Tariff redundancy: that part of a *tariff* which does not have any effect on trade because it is above the point where the tariff would have the desired impact. An example would be where the government decides that a tariff of 10% on a given good would suit its purposes, but for some reason it then sets the tariff at 15%. The difference of 5% would be the redundant tariff. [Corden 1971]

Tariff schedule: the document setting out the tariff rates a country applies to imports and, sometimes, to exports. See also *applied tariff rates*, *bound tariff rates*, *multi-column tariff*, *schedule of concessions* and *single-column tariff*.

Tariff stabilization: a result of the practice in the *GATT* and the WTO of accepting a legally binding obligation not to raise a *bound tariff* except in accordance with the rules. This has made the tariffs of most member countries stable and predictable.

Tariff wall: popularly used for a tariff maintained by an importing country at a sufficiently high level to make importing difficult or even preventing it.

Tariff wedge: under conditions of *tariff escalation*, the difference between the tariff of the more processed product and the tariff on the less processed products that are transformed into the more processed product.

Taxes occultes: literally, hidden taxes. Cumulative indirect taxes a firm incurs in making a product, such as taxes in embodied in capital equipment used in the production process. Taxes on advertising, energy, machinery and transport are the main examples. It does not include taxes on components incorporated in the product. [GATT BISD 18]

TBT agreement: the WTO *Agreement on Technical Barriers to Trade*.

Technical barriers to trade: refers to the impact *standards* and *conformity assessment* systems may have on trade flows. Many of these measures in fact have little impact because of *mutual recognition arrangements* as well as *harmonizations of standards and qualifications*. Some standards are seen as essential, for example, for reasons of health and safety. The WTO *Agreement on Technical Barriers to Trade* contains provisions for the harmonization, reduction and elimination of such barriers. The 2005 *World Trade Report* has a detailed analysis of standards, including *sanitary and phytosanitary measures*, in the multilateral trading system. See also *Code of Good Practice for the Preparation, Adoption and Application of Standards*, *International Electrotechnical Commission* and *International Organization for Standardization*.

Technical Committee on Rules of Origin: established through the WTO *Agreement on Rules of Origin*, but under the auspices of the *World Customs Organization*, to conduct technical work for the harmonization of *non-preferential rules of origin*. See also *rules of origin*.

Technical dumping: occurs when goods are imported under conditions that satisfy the *dumping* criterion (i.e. they are sold for export at a price that is below the price at which they are sold in the exporting market), but the reason for that pricing is meeting the price of the domestic competition in the import market.

Technical regulation: this is defined in Annex 1 of the WTO *Agreement on Technical Barriers to Trade* as a document which lays down product characteristics or their related *processes and production methods*, including the applicable administrative provisions, with which compliance is mandatory. Such a document may also include or deal exclusively with terminology, symbols, packaging, marking or *labelling* requirements as they apply to a product, process or production method.

Technical test method: a method used in the *rules of origin* of some *free-trade agreements* to describe under what conditions goods may receive *tariff preferences*. Such methods usually prescribe that the good must have gone through a defined production process, such as a chemical reaction, or that the materials used must satisfy certain conditions in respect of their origin.

Techno-nationalism: this has two main meanings. First, it is the idea that technological advances are useful only if they are achieved through domestic efforts even if they already exist elsewhere. These advances are normally achieved at much greater cost than if the technology was imported commercially. The results are often inferior to the best available elsewhere. Reasons for this type of techno-nationalism include a shortage of foreign exchange, the need to nurture national self-esteem, defence considerations and the "not-made-here" syndrome. Second, it also refers to policies aimed at keeping technological advances within the originating country in the hope that this will lead to a *competitive advantage*. See also *autarky*, *comparative advantage*, *national champions*, *self-reliance* and *self-sufficiency*.

Telecommunications: defined in the *Annex on Telecommunications* to the *General Agreement on Trade in Services* as "the transmission and reception of signals by any electromagnetic means". See also *Agreement on Basic Telecommunications Services* and *reference paper for telecommunications services*.

Telecommunications termination services: services provided by one telecommunications network to another to allow a caller in one network to talk to a caller in another network. This is done through interconnection. Calls between two networks consist of three stages: (a) transporting the call to the terminating or destination network, (b) providing an entry point or gateway to the terminating network and (c) forwarding the call to its final destination. The latter two make up the termination service. The price charged by the second network for this service is called the *accounting rate*.

Television Without Frontiers: see *broadcasting directive*.

Temporary admission of goods: permission to import goods free of duty on condition that they are re-exported within a certain period. The need for temporary admission arises in the case of trade fairs, exhibitions, trade missions, etc., when an exporter wishes to demonstrate the quality of his products to a prospective buyer in the importing country. See also *Customs Convention on the ATA Carnet for the Temporary Admission of Goods*.

Temporary Exclusion List: these were product lists prepared by *AFTA* members on which member countries were not yet ready to grant full preferential access to the other members. These lists were abolished in 2003. See also *highly sensitive products* and *sensitive products*.

Temporary normal trade relations: a term used by the United States to indicate that giving *most-favoured-nation treatment* to a given country is subject to periodic renewal. See also *normal trade relations* and *permanent normal trade relations*.

Temporary tariff suspension: when a component or finished good is not produced or supplied within the *European Community*, manufacturers or importers may apply for it to enter free of duty. If a temporary tariff suspension is granted, the good may be imported free of duty in unlimited quantities until the tariff suspension is revoked. Other economies employ similar systems. See also *autonomous tariff quota*.

Termination services: see *telecommunications termination services*.

Terms of trade: an expression for the relative price of one good in terms of another, usually originating from different countries. The terms of trade move against country A if it has to offer more of its products for the article produced by country B. The reverse is true if the terms of trade move in favour of country A. See also *commodity terms of trade*.

Textiles and the multilateral trading system: see *Short-Term Arrangement Regarding International Trade in Cotton Textiles* (1961), *Long-Term Arrangement Regarding International Trade in Cotton Textiles* (1962–1973), *Multi-Fibre Arrangement* (1974–94) and *Agreement on Textiles and Clothing* (1995).

Textiles Monitoring Body: TMB. A body established under the WTO *Agreement on Textiles and Clothing* to supervise the implementation of the Agreement. See also *Multi-Fibre Arrangement*.

Textile Surveillance Body: TSB. The body supervising and administering the *Multi-Fibre Arrangement*.

Thai cigarettes: a dispute brought before the GATT in 1990 by the United States over Thailand's import regime for cigarettes. *Background*. Thailand at that time prohibited all imports and exports of tobacco and tobacco products except where a licence had been granted. This had happened only three times since 1966, and then only to the Thai Tobacco Monopoly. Thailand also applied an excise tax, a business tax and municipal taxes to sales of tobacco products. *Claims*. Thailand's main claims were (a) that its restrictions on imports were justified because cigarettes were an agricultural product within the meaning of Article XI, and that Thailand had acted to limit the area in which tobacco could be planted and the production of cigarettes, (b) the restrictions on "imports were also justified under Article XX(b) because measures which could only be effective if cigarette imports were prohibited had been adopted by the government to control smoking and because chemical and other additives contained in United States cigarettes might make them more harmful than Thai cigarettes", (c) the excise, business and municipal taxes on imported cigarettes were no higher than those on domestic ones, and (d) the measures were justified because they predated Thailand's *accession* to the GATT and because they were mandatory in their intent. The United States asked the *panel* to find that (a) the restrictions on imports of cigarettes were inconsistent with Article XI because

417

cigarettes were not an agricultural or fisheries product within the meaning of that Article, and the restriction was therefore an import prohibition not accompanied by domestic supply restrictions, (b) the same restrictions could not be justified under Article XX(b) since, as applied by Thailand, they were not necessary to protect human health, (c) the excise, business and municipal taxes on imported cigarettes were applied at a higher rate than for domestic cigarettes, and (d) that Thailand's *Protocol of Accession* did not apply because the relevant act did not impose mandatory import restrictions. The panel sought advice from the World Health Organization (WHO) on the technical aspects of the case. *Findings*. The panel found that Thailand had acted inconsistently with GATT Article XI (General Elimination of Quantitative Restrictions) in maintaining a virtual import prohibition on cigarettes. It had also acted inconsistently with Article XI:2 which permits import restrictions on agricultural or fisheries products in an early stage of processing when they are still perishable, if this is done to enforce governmental measures to restrict production and selling of the like domestic product. Cigarettes could not be described as "leaf tobacco in an early stage of processing" because they had already undergone extensive processing and were not intended for further processing. The panel further considered that various measures consistent with the GATT were reasonably available to Thailand to control the quality and quantity of cigarettes smoked which could achieve the health policies pursued by the Thai government through import restrictions. The practice of permitting the sale of domestic cigarettes while not permitting the import of foreign cigarettes was an inconsistency with the GATT not "necessary" within the meaning of Article XX(b). Concerning the question of the Protocol of Accession, the panel found that the relevant Thai law did not impose on Thai authorities a requirement to restrict imports that could not be modified by executive action. Indeed, the law explicitly gave the Thai authorities the power to grant import licences. Hence the clause concerning existing legislation in the Protocol did not exempt restrictions on the import of cigarettes. Finally, the panel found that the rates of applicable taxes were broadly consistent with the requirement for *national treatment* (Article III). See also *GATT-consistency of national legislation*. [GATT BISD 37S]

Theory of hegemonic stability: a proposition first developed by Charles Kindleberger and adapted and widened by others since. In his analysis of the reasons for the Great Depression of the 1930s and its persistence, he suggested that the main lesson of the inter-war years could be summed up as: "that for the world economy to be stabilized, there has to a stabilizer, one stabilizer". In the view of those who subscribe to this theory, its correctness was demonstrated by the dominant role the United States assumed in the creation of the *multilateral trading system* exemplified by the *GATT*. [Kindleberger 1973]

Theory of second-best: a theory in international economics which assumes that the first-best solution for optimal trade lies in *free trade* not encumbered by distorting factors such as taxes, monopolies or tariffs. The theory of second-best postulates that it is still possible to aim for the optimality goal in trade by taking certain measures which, however, may not lead to the best possible outcome. What the measures likely to produce the second-best outcome are, assuming the first-best is not possible, depends on a case-by-case analysis. Others see *preferential trade arrangements* as an aspect of second-best. Theories of second-best of course are used in many other areas of economics.

Thin end of the wedge: the first step towards an outcome one wishes to avoid. Much effort is therefore spent in ensuring that the wedge does not gain a hold. See also *slippery slope*.

Third-country dumping: the alleged practice of *dumping* by competitors in third markets in which one also has an interest. The WTO rules on *anti-dumping measures* do not cover so-called third-country dumping.

Third-country problem: a name for a putative trade effect of particular concern during the *Kennedy Round* negotiations on *linear tariff cuts*. The problem is based on the assumption that countries have few export interests in products on which they maintain a high tariff. Hence they are not too concerned if the low-tariff country does not cut its tariffs on these products in the same proportion. This may have the effect, at least in modelling exercises, of shifting the main burden of the resulting trade regime on third countries, forcing them to make adjustments to their tariffs. The problem is therefore concerned with the relative ranking of a country's tariff rate in a given range of products. Any attempt to understand this problem from the perspective of economic sense will be fruitless.

Third-generation free-trade agreements: used by some to describe *free-trade agreements* that include, in addition to trade in goods and services, provisions concerning investment, competition, labour and environmental standards, etc.

Third-line forcing: a term used in the administration of *antitrust laws*. It describes the practice of supplying goods or services only if the buyer at the same time agrees to buy products from a third source. If the buyer does not agree, the supplier in question refuses to deal with him altogether. See also *boycott*.

Third parties: also known as interested third parties. In proceedings under the WTO *Dispute Settlement Understanding* these are members who are not directly involved in the launch of a dispute, but who participate in the proceedings because they have a substantial interest in the matter. A mere interest in the proceedings is not enough. Members wishing to become third parties must show that they have an interest at stake. Third parties may appear before the *panel*. They may also make written submissions. In turn, they receive the submissions to the first panel meeting of the parties in dispute. Third parties may not appeal against panel reports or decisions. In cases where a third party considers that the subject of a dispute has adverse effects on it, it may resort to the normal dispute settlement procedures. Where possible, the original panel will hear this submission also.

Third Protocol to the General Agreement on Trade in Services: the *protocol* giving effect to the new commitments on the *movement of natural persons* which resulted from the 1995 negotiations on this subject. It entered into force on 30 January 1996.

Third Revised Decision on National Treatment: see *national treatment instrument*.

Third United Nations Conference on the Least Developed Countries: see *Brussels Declaration*.

Third-wave free-trade agreements: refers to the *free-trade agreements* concluded since the late 1990s. Some say that what distinguishes them from earlier agreements is that in many cases they are provisions on *competition policy*, protection of *intellectual property rights*, *government procurement*, etc.

Third world: a translation of the French word *tiers-monde* (apparently coined by the French sociologist Maurice Duverger in the 1960s). It is no longer in common use in the English language where it has given way to "developing countries". It generally was understood to include the countries that were not included in the group of industrialized democracies (the first world) or the communist countries (the second world). Like many such umbrella terms, it represents a useful first approach to the subject, but, as the *Harries Report* showed, it masks a considerable diversity of economic progress and political views among the countries included in the group. See also *developing countries and the multilateral trading system*.

Thirty:ten formula: the first proposal for a formula leading to *linear tariff cuts* made by the *European Economic Community* (EEC) during the *Kennedy Round*. The idea initially was that there would be a comparison of the tariff rates of each participant, later modified to mean the EEC, Japan, the United States and the United Kingdom as the largest traders. Whenever the high tariff was more than 30% *ad valorem* and the difference with the low tariff was more than 10 percentage points, it would have been subject to the linear reduction formula yet to be elaborated. The formula was abandoned because it was thought to lead to incongruous results when applied to actual trade flows. It was succeeded by the *double écart formula*. See also *écrêtement* and *peak tariffs*.

Threat of injury: see *injury*.

Threat of serious injury: a term used in the WTO *Agreement on Safeguards* to mean *serious injury* that is clearly imminent. The Agreement states that the existence of a threat of serious injury "shall be based on facts and not merely on allegation, conjecture or remote possibility". See also *injury* and *safeguards*.

Three pillars: in *APEC* this refers to trade and investment liberalization, business facilitation and economic and technical cooperation. The pillars were formed through the *Osaka Action Agenda* and are intended to help implementing the *Bogor Declaration*.

Three pillars of agriculture: the framework for commitments under the WTO *Agreement on Agriculture*. The three pillars are market access, domestic support and export subsidies.

Tied aid: the granting of *official development assistance* in the form of loans to developing countries on condition that some of the funds are used in a certain way, often the purchase of capital goods or services from the donor country. See also *mixed credits* and *trade and aid*.

Tied loan: a loan extended by a government to another country on condition that it is spent in a prescribed way, usually through purchasing goods and services from the lender country.

TMB: see *Textiles Monitoring Body*.

Tokyo Declaration: the declaration adopted by the GATT Ministerial Meeting on 14 September 1973 in Tokyo. It launched what became known as the *Tokyo Round* of *Multilateral Trade Negotiations*.

Tokyo International Conference on African Development: TICAD. A conference initiated by Japan in 1993 and held every three to four years. Its aims are (a) to raise awareness of African development issues, (b) to promote ownership of Africa and partnership in the international community, and (c) to mobilize an expanded partnership.

Tokyo Round: the seventh round of GATT *multilateral trade negotiations* which took place between 1973 and 1979. 102 countries participated in this round. Both from the point of view of participation and the breadth of the negotiating agenda, this was the biggest round up to that time. The Tokyo Round was launched on 14 September 1973 at a Ministerial Meeting in Tokyo, but the negotiations were conducted largely in Geneva. The Ministerial declaration setting out the ambit for the negotiations foresaw work aimed at (a) *tariff* negotiations using the formula method, (b) reducing or eliminating *non-tariff measures*, (c) examining the possibility of reducing or eliminating all barriers in selected sectors, (d) examining the adequacy of the multilateral *safeguard* system, (e) negotiations in agriculture, taking into account the special characteristics and problems in this sector, and (f) treating *tropical products* as a special and priority sector. Ministers intended that the negotiations should be concluded in 1975. The Tokyo Round negotiations were dominated by events within the United States, the European Economic Community (EEC), Japan and the relations between them. The President did not have any negotiating authority until January 1975 when the *Trade Act* of 1974 became law. This negotiating authority was due to expire on 3 January 1980. The situation was complicated by the fact that 1976 was a presidential election year in the United States. The EEC had expanded its membership to nine on 1 January 1973 and was preoccupied with making the enlarged system work. Its internal coordinating system accordingly became much more complex. Japan had achieved its transformation into a first-rate economic and trading power and had become the cause of protectionist pressures in many economies. The various negotiating groups, in which the specialized negotiations would take place, were only established in February 1975. The developing countries were drawn into the negotiating process much more than during the *Kennedy Round*. This was the time of heightened developing-country expectations in that it coincided with preparations for the *New International Economic Order* initiative and the intensification of the *North-South dialogue*. Much necessary preparatory work of a substantive nature was done between 1973 and early 1977, but no real developments in the negotiations were possible until the new United States administration had formulated its policies and appointed its negotiating team.

Negotiations began in earnest in July 1977 following a meeting between the United States and the EEC which ironed out some of their major differences on policy and procedure. The two reached agreement that there should be an accelerated timetable consisting of four phases to be concluded by January 1978. The first phase would consist of a general tariff plan, including a tariff-cutting formula using the *Swiss formula* as a working hypothesis, and specific directives for the treatment of agriculture. The second phase would cover the tabling of requests for tariff cuts and the removal of non-tariff measures. Phase three would see the tabling of draft texts for the codes on *non-tariff measures*, and in the fourth phase participants would respond to the requests by tabling offers. By July 1978 a large group of developed countries was able to put forward a "Framework of Understanding" which set out the principal elements they considered necessary for a balanced outcome to the negotiations. The developing countries objected to this package on substantive and procedural grounds. They objected particularly to what they saw as an attempt to leave them at the periphery of the negotiations. The package nevertheless was an important factor in maintaining momentum as agreement emerged to conclude the negotiations by 15 December 1978. A major obstacle then turned up in the form of a section of the United States *Trade Act* which allowed the President to waive a requirement that *countervailing duties* be imposed on subsidized imports over the four-year period ending on 3 January 1979. If the existing waiver lapsed, *countervailing duties* would become automatic. Congress appeared reluctant to renew the waiver, but it did so once the EEC declared that it could not conclude the negotiations unless the United States first solved its internal problems. This happened in late March 1979, and the Tokyo Round negotiations ended formally on 12 April 1979. The negotiations resulted in average cuts of tariffs by developed countries for industrial products of about 35%, and average tariffs were reduced to about 4.7%, to be phased in over eight years. The Tokyo Round resulted in nine separate agreements (six of which were called "codes") and four understandings on the aims and operation of the GATT. These agreements and understandings added considerably to GATT law. Most of them were adapted further in the *Uruguay Round* and incorporated in the formal overall outcome for that round. Little progress was made on systemic issues in trade in agricultural products. There was agreement that negotiations should be continued after the round on the development of a *Multilateral Agricultural Framework* aimed at avoiding continuing political and commercial confrontations in this highly *sensitive sector*. In reality this was little more than a device enabling the conclusion of the round as a whole and, as many expected, it did not lead anywhere once negotiations resumed. Achievements in the negotiations on tropical products were uneven, but reductions in tariffs and non-tariff measures occurred across the full range of these products. No agreement was reached concerning a multilateral safeguard system. Negotiations were continued after the round, though without much success. One outcome developing countries saw as particularly important for them was the *Enabling Clause*. It was aimed at promoting an increased participation by developing countries in the global trading system, and it allowed developed GATT members to accord differential treatment in favour of developing countries in the tariff and non-tariff areas. See also *linear tariff cuts*, *special and differential treatment* and *Tokyo Round agreements*. [GATT Secretariat 1979, Glick 1984]

Tokyo Round agreements: the collective name for the six codes on *non-tariff measures*, three sectoral agreements and four decisions, sometimes referred to as *framework agreements*, concluded as part of the *Tokyo Round* negotiations. Governments were able to choose to a large extent which of the agreements they would join. The codes are (a) the *Agreement on Technical Barriers to Trade*, usually referred to as the "standards code" which seeks to ensure that technical regulations, standards, testing and certification do not become impediments to trade, (b) the *Agreement on Government Procurement*, aimed at bringing non-discrimination, competition and transparency into purchases made by governments, (c) the *Agreement on Interpretation and Application of Articles VI, XVI and XXIII*, usually known as the "subsidies code", aimed at ensuring that subsidies do not harm the interests of other trading partners, (d) the *Agreement on Implementation of Article VII*, also known as the "customs valuation code" which seeks a fair, uniform and neutral system for the valuation of goods for customs purposes, (e) the *Agreement on Import Licensing Procedures*, aimed at ensuring that import licensing requirements are not in themselves restrictions on trade, and (f) the *Agreement on Implementation of Article VI*, usually known as the "anti-dumping code", a revised version of the anti-dumping code negotiated during the *Kennedy Round*. The three sectoral agreements are (a) the *Agreement Regarding Bovine Meat*, aimed at expanding, liberalizing and stabilizing trade in meat and livestock, (b) the *International Dairy Arrangement* which sought to do the same for world trade in dairy products, and (c) the *Agreement on Trade in Civil Aircraft* under which participants eliminated customs duties on civil aircraft and parts. The four decisions concerned differential treatment for developing countries, trade measures taken for balance-of-payments purposes, greater flexibility for developing countries in taking trade measures for development purposes, and an understanding concerning improved dispute settlement measures. See also *WTO plurilateral agreements* and *WTO Agreement*.

Tokyo Round codes: see *Tokyo Round agreements*.

Tolerance rules: a component of many systems of *rules of origin* used in *free-trade agreements*. Such rules permit the inclusion of some non-*originating materials* that would otherwise not be allowable. The tolerance seldom exceeds 10% of the value of the final product. See also *de minimis*.

Top-down approach: a preference in preparing an agenda for trade negotiations to define the overall shape of the agenda and then to proceed to consider how to deal with individual components. The term is also used to describe the use of *negative lists* for services and investment commitments in *free-trade agreements*. See also *bottom-up approach*.

Torquay Tariff Conference: held at Torquay, United Kingdom, from September 1950 to April 1951. The work program consisted of *accession* negotiations with six countries (Austria, Federal Republic of Germany, Republic of Korea, Peru, Philippines and Turkey) as well as some tariff negotiations among the participants themselves. This is now deemed to have been the third round of *multilateral trade negotiations*. In the end, Korea acceded to the GATT only in 1967 and the Philippines in 1979.

Total Aggregate Measurement of Support: a term used in the WTO *Agreement on Agriculture*. It means the sum of all domestic support provided to agricultural producers. It is the total of all *aggregate measurements of support* for *basic agricultural products*, all aggregate measurements of support not aimed at a specific product and all *equivalent measurements of support* for agricultural products. Formulas like these do a lot to explain why agricultural negotiations consume so much time. See also *amber box*.

TPRB: the *Trade Policy Review Body* is the *General Council* operating under special procedures for meetings to review trade policies and practices of individual WTO members under the *Trade Policy Review Mechanism*.

TPRM: see *Trade Policy Review Mechanism*.

Traceability: the ability to trace, for example, meat sold in retail shops back to an abattoir and thence to the farm where the animal was raised. Traceability has become an important part of efforts to raise and enforce food safety standards. The *European Union* has established a system to trace products containing or produced from *genetically modified organisms* (GMOs). The system permits control and verification of labelling claims, monitoring of potential effects on the environment and withdrawing relevant products in cases of unforeseen health or environment risks.

Trade: usually refers to the sale and distribution of goods and services across international borders. There are many different ways of doing this, but there must be a commercial element for a transaction to qualify as trade. See also *barter*, *commerce*, *compensation trade* and *countertrade*.

Tradeables: goods and services that can be traded on international markets. In the case of services, this includes, for example, air travel, telecommunications and management consulting, but haircutting would not normally be considered a tradeable service. See also *non-tradeables* and *semi-tradeables*.

Trade Act of 2002: the act signed into law by United States President Bush on 6 August 2002 which gives him *Trade Promotion Authority*, previously known as *fast-track*.

Trade adjustment assistance: support, such as training or relocation grants, given by governments to individuals or companies to enable them to adapt more easily to changed circumstances in their area of activity. See also *structural adjustment*.

Trade agreement: see *bilateral trade agreement*.

Trade and aid: this refers to the range of policy issues subsumed in the aim of promoting the economic growth of developing countries through a greater harmonization of trade policies and aid policies of developed countries. Frequently, this is done through the provision of *tied aid* or *mixed credits* for the funding of projects that are not commercially viable in themselves, but which can make a contribution to the export performance of the recipient country. Some point out that there can, however, be an inherent contradiction between the aim of fostering the economic development of developing countries and the willingness of donor countries to open their markets to the newly emerging production and export capacity. There is therefore a view that the concept of trade and aid is no more than a way to subsidize exporters in donor countries. See also *official development assistance*.

Trade and competition: one of the *new trade issues* now under discussion in various international forums, but already a negotiating subject at the time of the *Havana Charter*. As a recent OECD report notes, the liberalization of trade and investment stimulates healthy competition. There are two main reasons for an examination of the relationship between trade and competition. First, there is an increasing recognition that the benefits of international trade liberalization may be negated by domestic measures inimical to an open, competitive market environment. Such barriers may take the form of private anti-competitive behaviour, abuse of monopoly and dominant supplier powers or inappropriate governmental regulatory frameworks. In some countries, the problem is made worse by a weak *competition policy* or its inadequate coverage of domestic economic activity. Sometimes competition laws explicitly allow companies to behave in other markets in ways which would be illegal in the domestic market. Second, there are cases where the use of either *trade policy* or competition policy could lead to differing results, depending on which policy was given priority. A frequently used example is that tests for action under competition laws tend to be harder to satisfy than those applying to *anti-dumping measures*. However, the two sets of laws do not necessarily try to solve the same sets of problems. A bilateral solution found between Australia and New Zealand is that neither country takes anti-dumping action against the other, but each has the right to pursue through the courts anti-competitive behaviour giving rise to dumping. This solution probably is feasible only in cases where each side understands fully the court procedures of the other side and has full confidence in the way they work. Many *free-trade agreements* have chapters on competition, but for the most part these are limited to information and staff exchanges, etc. The WTO *Singapore Ministerial Conference* established in December 1996 a *Working Group on the Interaction between Trade and Competition Policy* to examine this issue. Exploratory work on trade and competition is continuing under the declaration made by the *Doha Ministerial Conference*. A decision was to be made at the fifth *Cancún Ministerial Conference* in 2003 on whether to start negotiations, but no agreement was reached. See also *antitrust laws*, *competition policy*, *international contestability of markets* and *restrictive business practices*. [Hope and Maeleng 1998, OECD 2001]

Trade and corruption: see *trade and illicit payments*.

Trade and culture: one of the possible *new trade issues*, but not yet on any negotiating agenda. It is concerned with the impact international trade has on *cultural identity*. In a narrow sense, the subject covers trade in audio and audiovisual material and the governmental measures, such as *local content rules*, that are applied to it. Some see it as covering in a wider sense the impact of international trade and investment on the cultural identity of a country. A subset of this concern is represented by ideas making up the theory of cultural imperialism which holds that trade and investment threaten to destroy local traditions and to submerge the cultural heritage of other countries. Understood in this way, the issue may provide the excuse for protectionist actions that otherwise would not be available. See also *audiovisual services*, *broadcasting directive*, *Canadian periodicals*, *cultural industries* and *globalization*.

Trade and debt: the question of the relationship between a country's *trade policy*, the impediments it faces to its export aims, and need to service or repay borrowings obtained sometimes a long time ago. Progress on this question is likely to be slow, partly because it would force trade ministries and finance ministries to cooperate more closely than they sometimes seem to like.

Trade and Development Act of 2000: a United States act which includes, among many other provisions, the *African Growth and Opportunity Act*, the *Caribbean Basin Initiative* and the *carousel legislation*.

Trade and Development Board: TDB. The executive body of *UNCTAD* between the quadrennial conferences. It meets once a year in a regular session and deals with the international implications of macro-economic policies, monetary and finance matters, trade issues, trade policies, structural adjustment and economic reform and related matters. There is also provision for up to three one-day executive sessions a year to deal mainly with management and institutional matters.

Trade and Development Report: published annually by *UNCTAD*. It analyses current *trade policy* issues from the perspective of developing countries. That should not stop others from benefiting from the many insights it offers on global economic developments.

Trade and economic agreement: TEA. An imprecise term for an agreement between two or more countries, intended to cover part or all of their trade and economic relations. TEAs frequently have treaty status. The contents and structure of TEAs vary greatly. The simpler ones sometimes contain little more than assurances of *most-favoured-nation treatment* and *best-endeavour undertakings* to promote the expansion of trade and economic relations with the other party or parties or to consider sympathetically any trade issue that may arise between them. More complex TEAs can commit the partners to adopt *trade facilitation* measures, to engage in a regular structured dialogue and to work towards solutions to specific trade issues. TEAs do not normally contain free-trade provisions, but there would be no impediment to including a *free-trade agreement* in the framework of a TEA. See also *Trade and Investment Framework Agreement*.

Trade and employment: one of the items on the agenda of the 1947–48 *United Nations Conference on Trade and Employment* and its preparatory meetings. Its inclusion stemmed from a recognition that pre-war unemployment exacerbated by *beggar-thy-neighbour policies* had been one of the reasons for the outbreak of the war. From the start of the Conference, there was a division between those who wanted to write effective employment provisions into what became the *Havana Charter* and those who were equally desirous of full employment, but who saw *ECOSOC* as the proper organization to deal particularly with cyclical unemployment and the coordination of measures to combat it. The Havana Charter imposed the following principal obligations on its members: (a) to achieve and maintain full employment in their territories, (b) to make measures to sustain employment consistent with other provisions of the Charter, (c) to avoid measures which would create balance-of-payments difficulties in other countries, (d) to take appropriate and feasible action to eliminate unfair labour conditions, (e) to act jointly with others that may be involved to eliminate persistent balance-of-payments problems, and (f) to participate in activities sponsored by ECOSOC to promote employment. The *WTO Agreement* and the *GATT* list the objective of ensuring full employment in their preambles. Some claim that this gives the WTO a mandate for an examination of *trade and labour* issues, but this argument probably goes too far.

Trade and environment: viewed by some as one of the *new trade issues*. It is concerned with the issues arising from the interaction between measures to expand international trade and those aimed at protecting the environment. There is a view that virtually all trade–environment issues fall within one of the following categories: (i) the trade effects of environmental regulation of protection, (ii) the trade effects of environmentally-related product standards, (iii) the use of trade measures to secure international environmental objectives and (iv) the environmental effects of trade and trade liberalization. Hoekman and Kostecki list four main reasons offered by its proponents for the inclusion of this issue in the WTO agenda. First, production and consumption activities in one country may have a detrimental environmental impact on other countries. Second, some environmentalist groups have propounded the view that trade itself is bad for the environment because of its potential to spread pollution. Third, some consider that environmental measures and policies are bad for trade because they might allow countries with low environmental standards to be more competitive than those that have to bear the cost of higher standards. Fourth, environmental policies may unnecessarily restrict trade as shown in the tuna cases. Schoenbaum notes that criticism of the impact of trade on the environment tends to based on the following propositions: (a) free trade is generally bad for the environment, (b) the rules of the *multilateral trading system* can make implementation of *multilateral environment agreements* difficult, (c) the rules of the multilateral trading system impede attempts to protect resources and the environment outside of national jurisdictions, (d) the rules of the multilateral trading system prevent countries from adopting measures to protect their domestic environment, and

(e) the rules of the multilateral trading system obstruct efforts to compel other countries to adopt high environmental standards. These propositions contain in part some misunderstandings about the working of the multilateral trading system. They also contain some deliberate obfuscation of the issues. The multilateral trading system as exemplified by the WTO rules has not prevented any country from instituting environmental measures it deems appropriate. In principle it requires, however, that domestic measures are implemented in the least trade-restrictive manner, that there is no *arbitrary or unjustifiable discrimination* and that the measures must not be a *disguised restriction on international trade*. There is much argument about the possibility that differences in environmental standards might lead to cost differentials which could be exploited by those enjoying lower costs. Extensive academic analysis of this problem has not yielded credible evidence that trade and environment cannot coexist or that trade has a detrimental effect on the environment. The proposition that trade measures ought to be used in support of environmental objectives generally, usually by way of amendment of Article XX (General Exceptions) of the GATT, is not on the whole favoured by trade-policy makers because it might lead to a whole new array of protectionist measures only tenuously connected with the aim of environmental protection. A work program is now under way on these issues in the WTO *Committee on Trade and Environment*. The Committee covers goods and services. See also *Agenda 21*, *Basel Convention*, *CITES*, *environmental goods and services*, *environmental rules under the WTO*, *general exceptions*, *London Guidelines for the Exchange of Information on Chemicals in International Trade*, *Montreal Protocol*, *pollution-haven hypothesis*, *race-to-the-bottom argument*, *Rio Declaration on Environment and Development* and *United Nations Framework Convention on Climate Change*. [Birnie and Boyle 2002, Frankel and Rose 2002, Hoekman and Kostecki 1995, Schoenbaum 2002]

Trade and foreign exchange: suggested by some for consideration in the WTO as a *new trade issue*. It concerns the relationship between international trade and the *exchange rate* system. Proponents tend to subscribe to the view that the system of floating exchange rates is one of the causes of protectionist pressures on the trading system. Others claim that it was the fixed exchange rate system that led to protectionism. Few seem to be keen to start early negotiations.

Trade and gender: refers to international flows of trade and their impact especially on the female population. Often the subject is understood in terms of the existence or otherwise of gender equality. A recent *UNCTAD* study notes that trade can affect gender equality in several ways: (a) a positive or negative impact on growth and employment opportunities, (b) competitive pressures, which may reduce or encourage gender discrimination, in particular wage differentials, (c) facilitating or raising barriers to access by women to resources and services, and (d) multilateral trading rules which may facilitate or constrain governments in applying policies or regulations that address gender inequality. Trade and gender is often seen as an aspect of *trade and poverty* because the burden of coping daily with poverty appears to fall disproportionately on women in many developing countries. Most analysts of this issue accept that income increases and advances in development brought about by trade, and also by implication trade liberalization, will benefit women. It appears, however, that although trade and growth undoubtedly can assist in lessening gender inequality, other factors play a much greater role. Among these are religious and cultural attitudes to the education and employment of women, as well as the economic structures of the countries concerned. [UNCTAD/EDM/2004/2]

Trade and human rights: this expression embraces a set of three broad issues. They have in common the thought that international trade can have an effect on the enjoyment or exercise of *human rights* in all countries. First, there is the pessimistic assumption that *trade liberalization* by developing countries nearly always entails a social cost to them which outweighs its economic benefits. It also assumes that the benefits of trade liberalization go almost exclusively to privileged urban minorities, and that other groups fall further behind in their living standards. Trade liberalization always entails some *structural adjustment*, but it is not of course the only cause of it. Some occupations will be affected adversely by the need for structural adjustment, but the evidence overall points to an improvement in the observance of human rights as economic well-being increases. Second, trade and human rights stands for the proposition that trade measures should be used to promote or enforce human rights. Often this is aimed at a better observance of *core labour standards*. Indeed, some commentators use *human rights* and *labour standards* interchangeably. Holders of this view tend to support the use of *GSP* schemes for this purpose since these are unilateral instruments that can be made conditional on a range of factors. The relationship between the country offering the GSP and a country using it is that of a donor and a beneficiary. The donor can within reason impose conditions on the use of the scheme. A third strand is the thought that non-observance of human rights in the form of core labour standards gives the exporting country an unfair advantage because its exporters supposedly incur fewer costs. This is the *pauper-labour argument* in some other form. Empirical studies cast doubt on the validity of this proposition. Advocates of this view usually argue that importing countries ought to be able to use trade measures to defend themselves against unfair practices of this sort. This is the basis of calls for rules against so-called *social dumping*. Some of the proponents of the view that trade measures should be used to promote the observance of human rights go a step further to argue that the WTO framework of rules could be used for the purpose. They seem to have in mind especially the WTO dispute settlement mechanism which leads to binding decisions on the parties. Several objections have been raised to this proposition. One is that the *Dispute Settlement Understanding* requires *panels* to examine disputed matters in the light of the *covered agreements*, to preserve the rights and obligations of members under these agreements and to clarify "the existing provisions of those agreements in accordance with customary rules of interpretation of public international law". As the WTO framework of rules makes no mention of human rights or any international human rights instrument, panels cannot make their findings against a member's observance of such rights or instruments. Panels examining a case with a human rights aspect could seek advice from competent bodies charged with the promotion of human rights on the nature of these rights. However, one can assume that because of the limit of their jurisdiction to WTO law only, they would seek such advice in an effort to ascertain whether the responding member would have been able to draw on other means to achieve its human rights aims. This, at any rate, is how panels have approached the question of *trade and environment*. Basing one's view on the jurisdictional limitations imposed on panels of course is to some extent a circular argument. WTO members could, if they so wished, decide to amend their rules to introduce a *human rights clause*. The prospects for this appear to be small. Many of them fear, especially developing countries, that a human rights clause in the WTO rules would be open to abuse for protectionist purposes. A further question is what human rights would be protected in this way. Some of the proponents are limiting themselves to the issues covered by *trade and labour standards*. Others see matters in a more expansive way. They see little reason why instruments such as the *Universal Declaration of Human Rights* or the *International Covenant on Economic, Social and Cultural Rights* could not be part of the rules panels routinely consult in their examinations. They argue that, after all, WTO members are already parties to many of these conventions. Moreover, they argue, that the duty of panels to interpret the rules in accordance with the customary rules of international law requires them to go beyond the WTO rules proper. This view is fiercely contested. Opponents point out that the WTO panels and the *Appellate Body* are not international judicial bodies of the kind of the *International Court of Justice* or the *European Court of Justice*. Some also point to a lack of practicality. Panels are not usually composed of jurists, though some members will have had legal training. The Appellate Body, on the other hand, argues its cases with legal rigour. How such a two-tier system would cope with the added burden of human rights law, some of which is far removed from the WTO's role of promoting freer international trade, is difficult to assess. See also *anti-globalization*, *Social Charter*, *social dimension of the liberalization of international trade* and *wage-differential argument*. [Howse 2002, Lim 2001, Marceau 2002, Petersmann 2001, Petersmann 2003]

Trade and illicit payments: one of the *new trade issues*. It is concerned with bribery, corruption and lack of transparency in *government procurement*. The main proponent of negotiations on this issue has been the United States. The aim of such negotiations would be to promote measures to discourage illicit payments in line with its own legislation which makes such payments an offence under the *Foreign Corrupt Practices Act*. The entry into force on 15 February 1999 of the *Convention on Combating Bribery of Foreign Public Officials in International Business Transactions*, negotiated in the *OECD* and the conclusion of the *United Nations Convention Against Corruption* have greatly reduced calls for similar action in the WTO. See also *Draft International Agreement on Illicit Payments*.

Trade and investment: one of the *new trade issues*, even though some rudimentary rules on *investment* formed part of the *Havana Charter*. The issue is concerned with the relationship between trade and investment as factors in *international economic relations* and the emergence of investment as a *market access* issue. Broadly speaking, for a long time trade and investment tended to be regarded as separate policy issues. Today, the two are increasingly regarded as complementing each other. In a situation of declining border protection, investment flows can stimulate new trade patterns and strengthen older ones. In other cases, firms are more or less forced to invest and produce in target markets because high tariffs make importing an unrealistic option. The WTO *Singapore Ministerial Conference* established in December 1996 a *Working Group on the Relationship between Trade and Investment* to examine this issue. The *Doha Ministerial Conference* authorized exploratory work on trade and investment. The *Cancún Ministerial Conference* in 2003 had been expected to make a decision on whether to start negotiations, but agreement was not possible. The *July package* of 2004 means that no negotiations in this area will be undertaken under the *Doha Development Agenda*. See also *globalization*, *Multilateral Agreement on Investment* and *tariff-jumping*.

Trade and Investment Access Facility: a mechanism established by *CHOGM* in October 1997 to assist developing countries with adjusting to, and taking advantage of, the opportunities of *globalization*. The Facility provides technical assistance to help countries identify and manage the potential economic and social impacts of trade in goods and services and investment liberalization, identify new sources of revenue and market opportunities, and help countries fulfil WTO requirements. It operates under the *Commonwealth* umbrella.

Trade and Investment Facilitation Agreement: TIFA. A treaty aimed at promoting trade and investment between the partners through making the existing rules and regulations work more smoothly.

Trade and Investment Framework Agreement: TIFA. A treaty outlining the broad principles and aims for the conduct of trade and investment activities between the parties. It can be accompanied by more detailed subsidiary instruments for issues that require more detailed treatment. In the United States TIFAs also serve to examine whether a trading partner is ready for a *free-trade agreement*.

Trade and labour standards: one of the *new trade issues*. It is concerned with the question whether trade rules should be used to promote minimum labour standards, or *core labour standards*, in exporting countries. Like others of the new trade issues, it has actually been around for some time. Some trace it back to the anti-slavery campaigns of the nineteenth century. The 1919 constitution of the *International Labour Organization* had the adoption and promotion of labour standards as a main objective. Some consider that the concept of "fair labour standards" derives from Article 23(a) of the Covenant of the *League of Nations* in which members endeavoured "to secure and maintain fair and humane conditions of labour for men, women and children both in their own countries and in all the countries to which their commercial and industrial relations extend". The *Atlantic Charter* of 1941 sought to secure "for all, improved labour standards, economic advancement and social security". In 1943, the International Labour Office recommended that "wherever existing conditions are unsatisfactory, there should be arrangements to ensure that labour employed in the production of controlled commodities receive fair remuneration and adequate social security protection and that other conditions of employment are satisfactory". The link between international trade and labour standards was made more explicit in Article 7(1) of the *Havana Charter* which noted that "unfair labour conditions, particularly in production for export, create difficulties in international trade, and, accordingly, each Member shall take whatever action may be appropriate and feasible to eliminate such conditions within its territory". Some of the *international commodity arrangements* also contain provisions exhorting members to promote fair labour standards. The *GSP* scheme of the *European Community* has a special incentive arrangement for countries whose national legislation incorporates *International Labour Organization* conventions covering the abolition of forced labour, the freedom of association and the right to collective bargaining, non-discrimination in respect of employment and occupation, and the abolition of child labour. See also *child labour*, *social clause*, *social dumping*, *social subsidies* and *trade and human rights*. [Addo 2002]

Trade and poverty: this subject is concerned with many aspects not only of economic conditions and activity, but also of related social and political matters. The aspect of this topic of most interest to the trade policy community is the impact of international trade, especially the shock introduced by trade liberalization, on the level and persistence of **poverty**. The *Least Developed Countries Report* for 2004, for example, says that "the field of trade and poverty should be drawn so that it encompasses all issues which are relevant to a proper understanding of trade and poverty". This would include, among others, employment, bargaining power in global production chains, food security, exchange rates, wage inequality, and gender relations and export development. In other words, the entire range of government responsibilities and policies come into play when solutions to poverty are sought. Analysts agree that rapid economic growth is necessary for a sustained alleviation of poverty. The economic evidence over at least the past two decades, moreover, has shown that economic growth and openness are inextricably linked. Some countries have sought to promote growth through systems of *autarky*. These have always ended in failure. Others have sought to rely on *import substitution policies*, though success has on the whole eluded them. Openness means allowing the economy to respond to market forces. This entails an environment receptive to foreign investment, transparency of domestic administrations and absence of excessive protection. The 2004 *Least Developed Countries Report* notes that "the direct impact of trade liberalization varies widely from country to country depending on internal structures, and that domestic factor markets are critically important to the nature of the relationship". Geoffrey J. Bannister and Kamau Thugge have noted that trade liberalization can affect the welfare of the poor in several ways: (i) by changing the prices of tradeable goods (i.e. lowering prices of imports for poor consumers and producers, increasing prices of exports for poor producers), and improving access to new products; (ii) by changing the relative prices of factors (skilled and unskilled labour and capital) used in the production of tradeable goods and affecting the income and employment of the poor; (iii) by affecting government revenue from trade taxes and thus the government's ability to finance programs for the poor; (iv) by changing incentives for investment and innovation and affecting economic growth; and (v) by affecting the vulnerability of an economy (or sub-groups within the economy) to negative external shocks that could affect the poor. They say that these channels of transmission are interdependent and subject to influence from many other types of policies and economic events. They also note that some of these events happen immediately, but others only over a long time. All of this points to a complex relationship between trade liberalization and poverty. In their view, both general and specific studies of this relationship show that "trade liberalization increases economic opportunities and improves incomes for the poor", but they warn that there can be winners and losers among the poor. L. Alan Winters *et al.* also have examined the evidence for any conclusions that might be drawn on the relationship between trade liberalization and poverty. Their analytical framework covers four aspects of this relationship: (a) economic growth and stability, (b) households and markets, (c) wages and employment, and (d) government revenue and spending. They point out that despite the methodological complexities inherent in the study of this subject, some conclusions can be drawn on the basis of the available evidence. First, they note that although there is a good deal of empirical support for the proposition that trade liberalization and openness stimulate long-run growth, the case is not in their view completely proven. At the same time, they could find no evidence that the reverse was true. Second, how poor households are affected by trade liberalization depends very much on the circumstances of a country. They note, however, that most of the causes of vulnerability in developing countries do not seem to be related to trade liberalization. Third, because the poor in developing countries are often not employed in the formal manufacturing sector, trade liberalization in that sector will not affect them directly. However, agricultural trade liberalization is likely to be of great benefit to rural labour because of increased demand for their produce. Fourth, they found no simple link between trade reforms and changes in government revenues. They note that obviously elimination of tariffs will also eliminate the corresponding income streams. More often, however, increased customs collection because of larger trade flows will compensate for any tariff reductions. They also note that simplified tariff structures and greater efficiency in duty collection are likely to outweigh revenues lost through lower tariffs. Bannister and Thugge emphasize that trade reform, if it is to assist the poor, should have certain characteristics. First, trade liberalization should be broad-based to spread both the benefits and the costs of liberalization. Second, exchange rate flexibility is likely to assist trade policy reform. Third, attention has to be paid to effects of reform on urban informal markets and rural agricultural markets. Fourth, complementary reforms, such as infrastructure development, facilitation of markets and labour mobility and training are needed. All of this is a tall order, especially when social safety nets have to be created at the same time. The alternative, however, is to do nothing, and that will almost certainly ensure that poverty remains endemic. Some hold that the main point of interest is the effect of economic growth on incomes. They are concerned that trade liberalization, assuming it increases economic activity, will lead to a growing inequality of incomes. As the experience of China over the last fifty years has shown, it is possible to have a set of economic policies that virtually guarantee poverty (and a great deal of equality) for all, and another set of policies that reduce poverty, at least in the more favoured geographical regions, but that will increase income inequality at the same time. Berg and Krueger say that there are strong reasons to suppose that trade liberalization will benefit the poor at least as much as the average person, partly because trade liberalization tends to reduce monopoly rents and the value of connections to bureaucratic and political power. Nevertheless, it seems difficult to make generalizations about the way poor people are affected by trade liberalization in a given case. See also *globalization*, *Millennium Development ment Goals*, *trade and gender*, *trade and human rights* and *trade and labour standards*. [Bannister and Thugge 2001, Ben-David, Nordström and Winters 1999, Berg and Krueger 2003, Winters, McCulloch and McKay 2004]

Trade and social conditions: see *child labour*, *core labour standards*, *human rights*, *social clause*, *social labelling*, *trade and labour standards* and *workers rights*.

Trade and taxation: an issue proposed by some for inclusion in the agenda of a future round of *multilateral trade negotiations*. It is based on a perception that taxation regimes could be used to distort a country's international trade. The prospective complexities of this issue are such that even most of those who concede a direct relationship between trade and taxation measures have shown little desire to start a discussion of what might be done. See also *new trade issues* and *transfer pricing*.

Trade and transfer of technology: a work program adopted at the *Doha Ministerial Conference* aimed at increasing flows of technology to developing countries.

Trade-balancing requirement: a requirement that an investor use earnings from exports to pay for imports. It is based essentially on *mercantilism*. Such a condition always puts a limit on the growth of the firm concerned, and in this way also on the economic growth of host countries. Trade-balancing requirements contravene the provisions of the WTO *Agreement on Trade-Related Investment Measures*.

Trade Barriers Regulation: a *European Community* instrument which entered into force on 1 January 1995 as the successor to the *New Commercial Policy Instrument*. Its aim is to give a company located in the Community, a Community industry or a member state the right to petition the *European Commission* if it considers that it has suffered adverse trade effects as a result of obstacles to trade in a third country. "Obstacles to trade" is defined as any trade practice adopted or maintained by a third country which is subject to possible action under international trade rules. Importantly, any "adverse trade effects" must have not only an impact on the company making the petition, but also on the economy of the Community, or a region of the Community or on a particular sector of economic activity. The Regulation applies to goods and services within the competence of the Community. It does not apply to allegations of *dumping* or to petitions for *safeguards*. [Council Regulations (EC) No 3286/94 and 356/95]

Trade bloc: used popularly to describe a group of countries that cooperate, often formally, on trade matters, possibly through a *free-trade agreement*.

Trade-chill effect: the result of an action, such as *trade harassment*, which engenders a contraction in the exports of a given product to a defined country.

Trade control measures: an omnibus term for *tariffs*, *para-tariffs* and *non-tariff measures*.

Trade coverage: a term used in *tariff negotiations* to denote how much of a country's trade is liberalized by the tariff reductions under discussion.

Trade creation: a criterion used for the assessment of the impact of *free-trade areas* and *customs unions* on others. Trade theory holds that the reduction or elimination of barriers to trade will lead to increased trade between members and non-members if external barriers are not raised at the same time. The experience of the GATT system and the expansion of trade under it would indicate that this theory is underpinned by evidence. In practice, the validity of the argument is quite difficult to demonstrate for any given area because of the interplay of other factors, particularly secular changes such as technological advances, changing investment patterns, etc. See also *trade diversion*. [Viner 1950]

Trade defence instruments: see *contingent protection*.

Trade deficit: this occurs when the value of one's imports exceeds the value of one's exports over a given period. Often, only merchandise trade is considered for this calculation. Taken in isolation, the existence of a trade deficit does not yield any useful insights about a country's economic health. However, it may be that a persistent trade deficit reflects some deficiencies in prevailing economic settings which need to be corrected. Sometimes the anxiety induced by a trade deficit simply reflects symptoms of *mercantilism*. See also *balance of trade* and *trade surplus*.

Trade deflection: see *trade diversion*.

Trade deviation: a term sometimes used to describe a situation arising from the fact that a country may be a member of two *free-trade areas*. Unless there are appropriate *rules of origin*, goods originating in one of these free-trade areas may in this way circulate freely to the other free-trade area once they have entered the *customs territory* of the first country. See also *hub and spokes*.

Trade diversion: also known as trade deflection. One of the criteria used for the assessment of the impact of *free-trade areas* and *customs unions*. The creation of such bodies normally leads to the expansion of trade between its members, but economic theory postulates that a share of the increased trade experienced by participants is merely due to a redirection of their trade, and not increased trade due to the arrangement. This effect can be demonstrated convincingly in models. In practice, trade diversion has always been very difficult to isolate because of other factors. These include technological innovation, global reduction in tariffs, changes in investment policies, etc. See also *trade creation*. [Viner 1950]

Trade effect: a change in trade flows resulting from a change in laws, regulations, consumer preferences, technological changes, etc.

Trade Efficiency Programme: an *UNCTAD* program aimed at increasing the international awareness and effective application of information technologies to trade, and to promote the use of models capable of reducing procedural costs in international trade. See also *electronic commerce* and *Global Trade Point Network*.

Trade embargo: a ban on trade with a specified country, usually imposed through a United Nations decision, but sometimes based on unilateral or regional action. An example of a justification for a trade embargo can be found in the *security exceptions* written into the GATS and GATT which specifically allow the suspension of obligations under the agreements if this is necessary for conforming with United Nations decisions. See also *United Nations economic sanctions*.

Trade-expanding policies: policies requiring or calling on trading partners to increase their imports from one's economy, often through schemes for *voluntary import expansion*.

Trade Expansion Act: see *Kennedy Round* and *United States trade agreements legislation*.

Trade facilitation: simplification and harmonization of international trade procedures aimed at minimizing obstacles to the movement of goods across borders. Many definitions are available. A definition used by the United Nations *Economic Commission for Europe* is "the systematic rationalization of procedures and documentation for international trade, where trade procedures are the 'activities, practices and formalities involved in collecting, presenting, communicating and processing required for the movement of goods in international trade'". Examples include simplified or standardized customs procedures, electronic transmission and certification of documents, cooperation in quarantine matters, publication of trade directories, cooperation on technical standards, etc. The term "trade facilitation" is often used loosely to mean *behind-the-border issues*. See also *APEC Principles on Trade Facilitation*, *trade liberalization*, *July package* and *trade promotion*. [United Nations Economic Commission for Europe 2003]

Trade Facilitation Alliance: TFA. This is a private-sector organization promoting simplified and harmonized regulation of international trade, including customs procedures. It is located in Geneva. See also *trade facilitation*. [www.tfalliance.org]

Trade facilitation barriers: seen by some as a subset of *non-tariff measures*. They include excessive documentation requirements, refusal to accept electronic versions of documents, lack of administrative transparency, little use of risk assessment procedures by customs authorities which means that they inspect every consignment, customs delays, and many more.

Trade finance: short-term and longer-term funds available to exporters and importers, usually on commercial terms, to facilitate international trade. [Auboin and Meier-Ewert 2003]

Trade – finance – currency linkage: an element of the Ministerial declaration made at Marrakesh in April 1994 at the conclusion of the *Uruguay Round*. It envisages cooperation between the WTO, the *IMF* and the *World Bank* to achieve greater global coherence of policies in the fields of trade, money and finance. See also *trade and foreign exchange* and *trade and taxation*.

Trade harassment: the use of overt and covert domestic measures as a device to make the import of products intentionally difficult. Overt measures include the aggressive use of *anti-dumping measures, safeguards* actions or *countervailing measures*. Sometimes the mere threat of such an action is sufficient to cause importers to reduce or stop purchases from abroad. At other times, the effect of *price undertakings* may make importing less attractive. Trade harassment can also occur through sham litigation. See also *non-price predation*.

Trade in cultural property: see *Beirut Agreement, Convention on the Means of Prohibiting and Preventing the Illicit Import, Export and Transfer of Ownership of Cultural Property, Florence Agreement* and *UNIDROIT Convention on Stolen or Illegally Exported Cultural Objects*. Under Article XX(f) of the GATT, WTO members may take trade measures necessary to protect national treasures of artistic, historic or archaeological significance. See also *trade and culture*.

Trade-induced competition: a situation of enhanced competition on domestic markets caused by imported products. The extent to which trade-induced competition occurs depends on the level of market access foreign firms and their products have. See also *import discipline hypothesis* and *international contestability of markets*.

Trade in services: the supply of *services* on commercial terms to residents of another country, either through *cross-border trade* or through *commercial presence*. See also *data protection in trade in services, General Agreement on Trade in Services, modes of services delivery, services, tradeable services* and *transactions in services*.

Trade in services statistics: in all countries statistics for trade in *services* are much less detailed than they are for trade in goods. Services are intangible. They cannot be counted or inspected at the border in the way goods can be. International financial statistics therefore offer the only reliable way for recording the value of traded services since any service bought from another country eventually has to be paid for through the use of foreign exchange. This approach, however, poses considerable practical difficulties. One is that there is no commonly used definition of what a service or, indeed, an internationally traded service is. Second, services can be bought as part of a good, such as training for a complex piece of equipment, and it may be hard to separate the two. Then there is the challenge of separating capital movements from payments for services rendered or received. The list could go on. Until recently many countries reported their statistics for trade in services according to the fourth edition of the *IMF* Balance of Payments Manual. The IMF Manual defines international trade in services as that occurring between residents and non-residents of an economy. It classifies services transactions into four categories: (a) *shipment:* freight and insurance services provided as part of the transportation of goods, (b) *other transportation services:* passenger services provided by transport operators and measured by way of ticket sales for international journeys and port services, (c) *travel:* goods and services acquired by overseas travellers, and (d) *other services:* insurance, professional, telecommunications, construction, mining, computing, entertainment and others. The last category in fact includes the services showing the fastest trade growth. The fifth edition of the IMF Manual, published in 1993, recognizes this. It offers a greater disaggregation of services, though the classifications remain quite broad. Many national statistical services now publish figures according to the classification contained in the fifth edition or in even greater detail, but in other cases figures based on the earlier versions of the Manual are all that is available. Considerable progress has been made in recent years in developing a framework for the collection of services trade statistics through the efforts of the Inter-Agency Task Force on Statistics of International Trade in Services which was established by the United Nations Statistical Commission. It is convened by the *OECD* and comprises also representatives of EUROSTAT (the *European Community* statistical office), the IMF, *UNCTAD*, the *IMF* and the WTO. The Task Force pursued its work bearing in mind especially the four modes of traded services set out in the *General Agreement on Trade in Services*. In 2002 it issued the *Manual on Statistics of International Trade in Services* which sets out "an internationally agreed framework for the compilation and reporting of statistics of international trade in services in a broad sense". The definition of services trade used in this manual covers trade in services in the conventional sense of transactions between residents and non-residents, but it additionally includes services delivered through locally established enterprises. The Inter-Agency Task Force Manual notes, however, that there is no suggestion that these additional services should be regarded as imports or exports. A framework now exists for producing more detailed statistics for services trade, but it will in all likelihood take some considerable time before such statistics become widely available. See also *Extended Balance of Payments Services Classification*.

Trade Integration Mechanism: TIM. A mechanism established by the *IMF* in 2004 to help member countries in meeting balance of payments shortfalls that might be caused by multilateral trade liberalization. The TIM can only be used to meet shortfalls resulting from trade-liberalizing measures by others. Shortfalls caused by a country's own domestic reforms may be eligible for support under other IMF programs.

Trade intensity: a measure of the importance of trade to a given economy. It is the proportion of imports and exports of goods and services in relation to the total economy.

Trade is good, but imports are bad: see *balance of trade*.

Trade liberalization: a general term for the gradual or complete removal of existing impediments to trade in goods and services. *Free trade* may be its ultimate aim, but more likely it is freer trade. Investment restrictions may also be covered by this term if investment in the target market is necessary for effective market access. See also *trade facilitation*.

Trademark Law Treaty: a treaty negotiated in 1994 under *WIPO* auspices aimed at making national and regional *trademarks* systems easier to use. It seeks to do this through the simplification and harmonization of procedures. The Treaty entered into force on 1 August 1996. See also *Madrid Agreement for the Repression of False or Deceptive Indications of Source, Nice Agreement Concerning the International Classification of Goods and Services for the Purposes of Registration of Marks* and *Singapore Treaty on the Law of Trademarks*.

Trademarks: words, names, symbols, devices or combinations of these, used by manufacturers and merchants to identify their goods and to distinguish them from the products of their competitors. See also *Agreement on Trade-Related Aspects of Intellectual Property Rights, famous mark, intellectual property, service marks, Singapore Treaty on the Law of Trademarks, Trademark Law Treaty* and *well-known mark*.

Trade measures: laws, regulations or rules adopted by a government which influence the way goods are traded across borders. *Tariffs, non-tariff measures* and *trade remedies* are the main ones. However, domestic regulations not framed primarily with foreign trade in mind, such as health, safety and licensing regulations, can also have more or less pronounced effects on trade. See also *sanitary and phytosanitary measures* and *technical barriers to trade*.

Trade negotiations between developing countries: in November 1971 GATT members agreed to a *waiver* from the *most-favoured-nation* rule to permit developing countries to accord each other preferential treatment. Some fifteen developing countries availed themselves of this opportunity. These trade negotiations, conducted under GATT auspices, led to modest results. See also *Asia-Pacific Trade Agreement, developing countries and the multilateral trading system, ECDC* and *GSTP*.

Trade Negotiations Committee: TNC. A committee usually established at the start of a multilateral round of trade negotiations. It consists of all participants and acts mainly as a transparency and stocktake mechanism. Its size makes it unwieldy for actual negotiations. See also *multilateral trade negotiations*.

Trade-neutral measures: measures taken by governments for reasons unrelated to the regulation of international trade which do not have any effect on the flow of trade.

Trade openness: denotes the extent to which a country is receptive to imports and international competition. See also *indicators of market competition*.

Trade pledge: a name sometimes used for the idea of a *standstill*. The term was apparently first used in 1974 by the *OECD*.

Trade Policies for a Better Future: see *Leutwiler Report*.

Trade policy: the complete framework of laws, regulations, international agreements and negotiating stances adopted by government to achieve legally binding market access for domestic firms. Trade policy also seeks to develop rules providing predictability and security for firms. Fundamental components of trade policy are *most-favoured-nation treatment*, *national treatment*, *transparency* and *exchange of concessions*. To be effective, trade policy needs to be supported by domestic policies to foster innovation and international competitiveness, and it needs to be conducted with flexibility and pragmatism. It is worth bearing in mind the observation by Bernard Hoekman and Michael Kostecki in *The Political Economy of the World Trading System* that trade policy is by definition a nationalistic policy in that it discriminates against foreign producers. Put differently, it represents the international dimension of national policies adapted for domestic reasons. See also *commercial policy*, *common commercial policy* and *four pillars of trade liberalization*. [Hoekman and Kostecki 1995]

Trade policy review: a review conducted at fixed intervals in the WTO under the *Trade Policy Review Mechanism*. Its main aim is a smoother functioning of the *multilateral trading system*.

Trade Policy Review Body: TPRB. The WTO *General Council* when it exercises its responsibilities under the *Trade Policy Review Mechanism*.

Trade Policy Review Mechanism: TPRM. A *WTO* review mechanism established in December 1988 at the Montreal Ministerial Meeting which conducted a mid-term review of the *Uruguay Round*. It is managed by the *Trade Policy Review Body*. The TPRM is aimed at a smoother functioning of the *multilateral trading system* through greater domestic and international *transparency* in the trade regime of individual WTO members. Issues may be raised regardless of whether they are covered by WTO rules, though there is an understanding that they should be related to the *trade policy* of the country being examined. Reviews are conducted according to a fixed timetable. The frequency of reviews is related to the share of world trade, with large traders being reviewed more often. The TPRM is not used for the enforcement of specific WTO obligations or for *dispute settlement* procedures. See also *surveillance*.

Trade promotion: activities designed to increase a firm's or a country's export trade. It includes participation in trade fairs, trade missions, publicity campaigns, etc. See also **trade** *facilitation*.

Trade Promotion Agreement: TPA. A term used for a *free-trade agreement* negotiated by the United States under the *Trade Act of 2002* with Colombia, Ecuador, Peru or Bolivia. All four of these countries are beneficiaries under the *Andean Trade Promotion and Drug Eradication Act*. TPAs have so far been concluded with Colombia and Peru.

Trade Promotion Authority: TPA. The name adopted in the Trade Act of 2002 for the negotiating authority given by the United States Congress to the President which had been known as *fast-track*. The TPA applies to all trade agreements negotiated by the United States. It has the following overall trade negotiating objectives: (1) more open, equitable, and reciprocal market access, (2) reduction or elimination of trade barriers, (3) strengthening the international trading system, (4) to achieve faster economic growth, raising living standards and promote full employment, (5) trade and environmental policies to be mutually supportive, (6) promote respect for workers rights and the rights of children, (7) provisions against weakening protections given to environmental and labour laws as an encouragement for trade, (8) benefits for small businesses, and (9) promote universal ratification of and full compliance with the *Convention Concerning the Prohibition and Immediate Action for the Elimination of the Worst Forms of Child Labour* adopted in the *International Labour Organization* (ILO Convention No 182). The TPA expired on 30 June 2005, but the President was authorized by its terms to extend it until 1 July 2007 if neither House of Congress opposed an extension. The President chose that option, and the extension was adopted. A further extension will require the introduction of a new trade law. See also *United States trade agreements legislation*. [Hornbeck and Cooper 2006]

Trade protection: a term sometimes used by the *European Community* instead of *trade remedies*.

Trade-related antitrust principles: the name used by Bernard Hoekman for the *competition policy* issues that might be covered in a future multilateral agreement on *trade and competition*. [Hoekman 1996]

Trade-related aspects of competition law and policy: TRACLAP. A term used by some scholars to denote *trade and competition*. See also *Working Group on the Interaction between Trade and Competition Policy*.

Trade-related aspects of economic development: describes the WTO provisions concerning the participation of developing countries in the world trading system, particularly the *Enabling Clause* and *Part IV of the GATT*.

Trade-related aspects of intellectual property rights: TRIPS. See *Agreement on Trade-Related Aspects of Intellectual Property Rights*.

Trade-related aspects of monetary measures: an expression used by some to refer to the provisions contained in GATT Article XV concerning exchange arrangements.

Trade-related aspects of sustainable development: a subject now under discussion in the *Food and Agricultural Organization*. It deals with the issues arising through a wish to reflect environmental issues fully in *trade policy*, and concern by others that environmental measures should not be used as restrictions on trade. See also *sustainable development* and *trade and environment*.

Trade-related capacity building: see *capacity-building*.

Trade-related human rights: see *trade and human rights* and *trade and labour standards*.

Trade-related investment measures: TRIMS. See *Agreement on Trade-Related Investment Measures*.

Trade-related technical assistance: TRTA. Assistance given to developing countries through bilateral, regional or multilateral schemes to promote their integration into the global system. Such schemes usually aim to improve the competitiveness of receiving countries as well as enabling them to operate more effectively within the multilateral rules. See also *capacity-building* and *Doha Development Agenda Global Trust Fund*.

Trade relief: the easing of competitive pressures on domestic firms through the use of *trade remedies*.

Trade remedies: usually refers to *anti-dumping measures*, *countervailing duties* and *safeguards* to deal with the effects of trade actions by others. The selection of the available trade remedy depends on the section of the trade law applicable to each case. It can include *tariff* increases, *import quotas*, *countervailing measures*, *retaliation*, etc. See also *Section 201*, *Section 301*, *Special 301* and *Super 301*.

Trade-restrictive environmental measures: measures to protect the environment which have a restrictive impact on trade. The impact may be direct and intended, as in the case of United States measures to protect dolphins, or it may be incidental. See also *trade and environment*, *tuna (Canada–United States, 1982)*, *Tuna I* and *Tuna II*.

Trade Restrictiveness Index: TRI. A method devised by Anderson and Neary to measure the restrictiveness of a system of trade protection. It measures the impact of both *tariffs* and *non-tariff measures*. Laird notes that the TRI "is mainly used to measure change in the restrictiveness of trade policy over time for a single economy or sector of an economy, that is, comparing two distorted situations rather than comparing against the free trade benchmark". [Anderson and Neary 1994, Laird 1997]

Trade reversal: used by Max Corden to describe the situation whereby a country has traditionally been an importer of a good and which, through the imposition of an import tariff and an export subsidy, becomes an exporter. [Corden 1971]

Trade secrets: information deriving its value from not being known to the public, competitors or other parties who may gain benefits from its disclosure or use. See also *Agreement on Trade-Related Aspects of Intellectual Property Rights*, *data protection in trade in services* and *material transfer agreement*.

Trade suppression: a term introduced by Jacob Viner and popularized by Max Corden. It describes the replacement, following the formation of a *customs union* or a *free-trade area*, of a cheaper production source outside the union or area by a more expensive source within the newly formed preferential area. The more expensive source could now be more competitive because it could benefit from the absence of tariffs. See also *trade creation* and *trade diversion*. [Corden 1985]

Trade surplus: this comes about when in a given period the value of one's exports exceeds that of one's imports. It is a goal pursued by most governments, but particularly stubbornly and sometimes mindlessly, by adherents of *mercantilism* who tend to look, in any case, at *merchandise trade* only. One should not assume that a trade surplus is intrinsically good and a *trade deficit* automatically bad. A meaningful assessment of the significance of a trade surplus can only be made by looking at the overall state of the economy. See also *balance of trade*.

Trade war: a journalistic exaggeration for periods of major trade disputes between important trading partners. Those involved in attempting to solve these disputes usually seek a negotiated outcome that is acceptable to both sides and that is in conformity with the applicable multilateral trade rules. They seldom see themselves as engaged in warfare. Indeed, as Greg Mastel notes in *American Trade Laws After the Uruguay Round*, "a trade war is only a shade more rational than a nuclear war, harder to launch, and nearly as unpalatable". [Conybeare 1987, Mastel 1996]

Trade-weighted average tariffs: a method of calculating the average impact of a tariff regime through weighting tariffs according to the amount of trade in a given tariff line. Items traded in high volumes therefore have a greater impact on the calculation of the *average tariff* than items less or rarely traded. The major problem with this analytical approach is that high tariffs discourage trade in the first place, and an average tariff calculated in this way is always likely to understate the actual level of tariff protection. Nevertheless, its general usefulness as an indicator of the overall incidence of tariff rates is not in doubt.

Trading rights: the right, accorded to selected firms, to import and export, particularly in *centrally-planned economies* or those in transition to *market economies*. Trading rights may be limited to the export of goods or to trade in certain product categories. Firms need not be owned by the state to enjoy trading rights. See also *state trading*.

Traditional comity: see *negative comity*.

Traditional cultural expressions: used by many with largely the same meaning as expressions of *folklore*, but seen as being more neutral than the term "folklore". They are a subset of *traditional knowledge*. Traditional cultural expressions cover a wide variety of customs, traditions, forms of artistic expression, knowledge, beliefs, products, and so on. [WIPO/GRTKF/IC/5/3]

Traditional expressions: a term used in the administration of *intellectual property rights* as it may relate particularly to the quality, colour or type of wine, spirits and food. Examples of traditional expressions for wine are Spätlese, Qualitätswein, Grand Cru, vin primeur, vino generoso de licor, denominazione di origine controllata, etc. Such expressions may qualify for *intellectual property protection* under bilateral agreements. See also *appellations of origin* and *geographical indications*.

Traditional knowledge: a new subject in discussions concerning the protection of *intellectual property rights*. *WIPO* says that there is no agreed definition, but it is seen as encompassing medicinal, agricultural and ecological knowledge, music and dance, stories and poetry (folklore), the production of artefacts and spiritual expressions. Traditional knowledge is transmitted from generation to generation orally and by example. It is subject to collective responsibility and ownership, and it keeps on evolving. All of these characteristics make the development of a framework of protection a difficult task because intellectual property rights are best suited for codified and documented materials. WIPO also says that protection of intellectual property for traditional knowledge may take three main forms: (a) protection extended to the content, substance or idea of knowledge and culture, (b) protection extended to the form, expression or representation of traditional cultures, and (c) protection extended to the reputation and distinctive character of signs, symbols, indications, patterns and styles associated with traditional cultures. The *Convention on Biological Diversity* enjoins its parties to respect, preserve and maintain knowledge, innovations and practices of indigenous and local communities embodying traditional lifestyles relevant for the conservation and sustainable use of biological diversity. See also *farmers' rights* and *folklore* which raise similar considerations. [WIPO/GRTKF/IC/5/8]

Traffic light approach: a procedural framework adopted during the *Uruguay Round* negotiations on the reduction or elimination of subsidies. Negotiators agreed to a system which ultimately led them to categorize *prohibited subsidies* as red, *actionable subsidies* (i.e. subsidies that may be subject to *countervailing measures* because they are causing to harm to producers in other countries) as amber, and *non-actionable subsidies* (on which no countervailing measures may be taken) as green. Agricultural subsidies did not fall into this framework, and separate rules were negotiated on them as part of the *Agreement on Agriculture*. It uses the *green box*, *blue box* and *amber box*. The traffic light approach had been tried unsuccessfully in the *Tokyo Round* and, indeed, in the early stages of the negotiations for the United States-Canada Free-Trade Agreement. *UNCTAD* has developed the concept of "red light" *host country operational measures* (HCOMs) denoting investment measures explicitly prohibited through multilateral agreements, such as the *Agreement on Trade-Related Investment Measures*. "Yellow light" measures are additionally prohibited, conditioned or discouraged by inter-regional, regional or bilateral agreements. "Green light" HCOMs are the remaining measures not regulated by *international investment agreements*.

Traffic rights: see *freedoms of the air*.

Trafficking: the original meaning of this word was trading or engaging in commerce. It now tends to be used for unsavoury or illegal trading activities, such as the illegal drug trade. See also *smuggling*.

Transaction-based definition of investment: see *investment*.

Transactions in services: preferred by some analysts as an alternative to *trade in services* because they see it as emphasizing that much international activity in services is dependent on foreign direct investment, and that it is not simply cross-border trade. Trade in services, its competitor, appears to have won the day in *trade policy* formulation. See also *cross-border trade in services* and *General Agreement on Trade in Services*.

Transaction value: a method for valuing goods to be imported for the purpose of assessing the *customs duties* payable. Under the WTO *Customs Valuation*

Agreement, it is the price actually paid or payable for the goods when sold under competitive conditions for export to the country of import. This method is based on the **Brussels Definition of Value** developed under the auspices of the Customs Cooperation Council, now the **World Customs Organization**. See also *customs valuation*.

Transaction value method: one of the methods used to establish whether a good imported from another party to a *free-trade agreement* qualifies for the *preferential tariff*. In the free-trade agreement between Canada and Chile the formula is:

$$RVC = \frac{TV - VNM}{TV} \times 100$$

where RVC is the *regional value content*, expressed as a percentage (in this case 35%), TV is the *transaction value* of the good adjusted to an **FOB** (free-on-board) basis, and VNM is the value of *non-originating materials* used by the producer in the production of the good. See also **FOB value method**.

Transatlantic Business Dialogue: a mechanism established in 1995 involving European and United States business leaders to discuss trade and commercial issues of common interest and to propose solutions for the removal of obstacles to trade and investment across the Atlantic. See also *New Transatlantic Agenda* and *New Transatlantic Marketplace*.

Transatlantic Free Trade Agreement: see *TAFTA*.

Transfer of technology: defined in the **Draft International Code of Conduct on the Transfer of Technology** as the transfer of systematic knowledge for the manufacture of a product, for the application of a process or for the rendering of a service. It does not extend to transactions involving the mere sale or mere lease of goods. The WTO **Doha Ministerial Conference** adopted a work program on *trade and transfer of technology*.

Transfer pricing: the practice of using pricing policies that are not based on market prices in order to achieve savings in taxation payments, to optimize the use of foreign exchange or for other reasons. The reference price used to ascertain whether transfer pricing has occurred is the arm's-length price. This is the price that would obtain between completely unrelated parties. Intra-corporate transactions and transactions between related parties are generally thought to be more at risk of exposure to transfer pricing. Articles 33 and 34 of the **Draft United Nations Code of Conduct on Transnational Corporations** seek to minimize its occurrence. See also *arm's-length pricing*.

Transgenic product: a product containing a *genetically modified organism* or made of materials containing such an organism.

Transit fees: fees levied by countries for the handling of goods in transit. Such fees are in addition to freight charges, etc.

Transitional dumping: defined by some as the pricing of products below marginal cost in order to maximize sales and expand market share. There is room for argument that such a practice would be a form of *predatory pricing*, especially if it were to continue for an extended period. See also *dumping* and *anti-dumping measures*.

Transitional measures: measures usually associated with the implementation of a new trade agreement when the old and new systems often exist side by side. Such measures are time-bound. Sometimes transitional measures have the purpose of giving developing countries more time to adjust to the new regime.

Transitional Product-Specific Safeguard Mechanism: a safeguard mechanism established in 2001 under the protocol for China's *accession* to the WTO. It deals with the possibility that Chinese products may cause or threaten to cause market disruption to domestic producers in other WTO members of directly competitive products. In such cases, WTO members may seek consultations aimed at finding a satisfactory solution, including possible recourse to the *Agreement on Safeguards*. The protocol says that disruption shall exist whenever imports of an article, like or directly competitive with an article produced by the domestic industry, are increasing rapidly, either absolutely or relatively, so as to be a significant cause of material injury, or threat of material injury, to the domestic industry. See also *Transitional Review Mechanism*.

Transitional Review Mechanism: a mechanism established in 2001 under the protocol for China's *accession* to the WTO to review annually for eight years progress made by China in bringing its trade regime into conformity with the WTO rules. The final review will be made after ten years. Information to be provided by China includes economic data, economic policies, its framework for making and enforcing policies, policies affecting trade in goods and services, and its trade-related intellectual property regime. See also *Transitional Product-Specific Safeguard Mechanism*.

Transitional safeguards: many *free-trade agreements* permit the use of safeguards when *tariffs* are being phase-out. This mechanism can no longer be used when the tariff for a product reaches zero. See bilateral *transitional safeguards*.

Transition Report: published annually by the European Bank for Reconstruction and Development (EBRD). It contains detailed assessments of the progress made on economic liberalization by the *economies in transition* in central and eastern Europe and the members of the *Commonwealth of Independent States*.

Transit trade: goods passing through at least one other country between manufacture and reaching their final destination. This occurs, for example, when a country is landlocked and needs access to a sea port. See also *trans-shipment*.

Transit zone: a place to which goods may be shipped temporarily pending their departure to their final destination. Usually, no further transformation of the goods takes place in a transit zone, and they are admitted free of duties other than applicable port or handling charges. See also *entrepôt trade*.

Transnational corporations: TNCs. Also called multinational corporations (MNCs) or multinational enterprises (MNEs). They are large and very large corporations and conglomerates with production facilities and sales offices in many countries established as branches, subsidiaries or other units. Individual units usually report to a head office which may be a holding company. It can be quite difficult to establish where effective control over a unit within a TNC in a particular case lies. Their ownership can be diversified, and component units may have much autonomy in the conduct of their business. Units of a TNC may even compete with each other in world markets. Nevertheless, TNCs are often thought of as having a single nationality despite their appearance in many places. In many cases, such companies first rose to prominence in a single market, and their nationality was clear-cut then. In some circles TNCs, because of their **market power** and ability to influence production patterns, have been treated with great suspicion. Calls for greater controls over their activities have led, for example, to a **Draft United Nations Code of Conduct for Transnational Corporations** which, however, remains contentious and is unlikely to enter into force in the near future. More recently, TNCs have met a much more welcoming climate in potential host countries and in international organizations concerned with development issues because of their ability to mobilize investment funds, promote the **transfer of technology** and create employment. A main focus for analysis of issues relating to TNCs is the **Commission on Investment, Technology and Related Financial Services**, located within **UNCTAD**, which also publishes the **World Investment Report**. The **OECD** countries have adopted the **OECD Guidelines for Multinational Enterprises** as one instrument governing their handling of TNCs. See also **dependence theory**, **intra-firm trade** and **multi-domestic corporation**.

Transnationality index: a method developed by **UNCTAD** to measure the degree to which a **transnational corporation** (TNC) or a country (host economy) is actually transnational. In the case of TNCs, it does this by comparing home-country assets, sales and employment of a TNC with its assets, sales and employment abroad. The greater the weight of the foreign numbers, the more transnational a company is thought to be. In the case of countries, the index is calculated as the average of FDI inflows as a share of gross fixed capital formation, FDI inward stock as a percentage of GDP, value-added of foreign affiliates as a percentage of total national value-added, and employment of foreign affiliates as a percentage of total employment. The transnationality index of TNCs and countries is usually published in the **World Investment Report**.

Trans-Pacific Strategic Economic Partnership Agreement: *free-trade agreement* between Brunei, Chile, New Zealand and Singapore. It entered into force on 28 May 2006.

Transparency: the degree to which trade policies and practices, and the process by which they are established, are open and predictable. The transparency obligation is spelt out in Article X of the **GATT**, Article III of the **General Agreement on Trade in Services** and other provisions of the agreements administered by the WTO. Members are required to publish any laws, regulations, judicial decisions, **administrative rulings of general application** and international agreements pertaining to trade in goods and services. They must also administer these instruments reasonably and impartially. See also **APEC transparency principles**, **notification**, **surveillance** and **Trade Policy Review Mechanism**.

Trans-Regional EU-ASEAN Trade Initiative: TREATI. A trade action plan adopted by the *European Union* on 9 July 2003 to expand trade and investment flows. It holds out the possibility of a *free-trade agreement* with *ASEAN* once the negotiations under the *Doha Development Agenda* have been successfully concluded.

Transshipment: the shipment of goods through an intermediary port in another country where they may have to be unloaded and reloaded. This is its main meaning. Another meaning refers to the practice of producing a good in one country, shipping it to another country that is part of a *free-trade area*, attaching a new label to it and then forwarding it to its final destination, also a member of that free-trade area. In this way, the original producer and the importer are able to evade the payment of some *customs duties*. As transshipment entails a cost, the production cost in the producing country would have to be low enough to absorb these and still leave a margin of profit. Opinions differ sharply on how prevalent this practice may be. In any case, *free-trade agreements* usually have detailed provisions to counter it. See also *preferential rules of origin* and *tariff evasion*.

Trans-Tasman Mutual Recognition Arrangement: TTMRA. An arrangement between Australia and New Zealand which enables the sale of goods originating in either country in the other country without the need for further testing or other conformance assessment. The TTMRA also covers skilled personnel. It enables a person registered to practise in either country to seek registration in the other without any need for further testing or the vetting of qualifications. The TTMRA entered into force on 1 January 1997. See also *ANZCERTA*, *mutual recognition arrangements* and *technical barriers to trade*.

Travaux préparatoires: the records produced by preparatory committees, expert groups, negotiating groups, etc., in the negotiations for a treaty or a convention. These records can give valuable guidance to the intentions of the drafters when ambiguous language has to be interpreted later, but this only works properly with consensus documents. Individual members of an agreement may make use of other, not agreed, *travaux préparatoires* to support their case in a dispute, but they still have to demonstrate that their interpretation is to be preferred. Article 32 of the *Vienna Convention on the Law of Treaties* sees *travaux préparatoires* as something to be employed with discretion and in the main only when the treaty text itself is not sufficiently clear to allow a single interpretation or when it would lead to a manifestly absurd or unreasonable result.

Treaties of Friendship, Commerce and Navigation: usually known as FCN treaties. This is a bilateral treaty form favoured in the past by the United States and some European countries. It sets out the terms under which bilateral trade and shipping are conducted, and it describes the rights of persons from one state conducting business in the other state or establishing a commercial presence there, including ownership of property. Main subjects covered by FCN treaties usually are rights of entry for business and residence, protection of individuals and companies, practice of professions, acquisition of property, *patents*, taxes, remittance of earnings and capital, trade measures, expropriation and nationalization, etc. Earlier versions of FCN treaties also contained consular and customs provisions. FCN treaties are considered by some as a form of *preferential trade arrangements*. The FCN treaty form has now been replaced in the United States by *bilateral investment treaties*.

Treaty: defined in the *Vienna Convention on the Law of Treaties* as "an international agreement concluded between States in written form and governed by international law, whether embodied in a single instrument or in two or more related instruments and whatever its particular designation". Other names often used for a treaty are convention, covenant, *protocol* and exchange of letters, the latter two often being concluded as part of a treaty or to supplement a treaty after it has entered into force. Treaties are legal instruments under which the parties establish mutual rights and obligations. Through acceding to a treaty, the parties undertake to become obliged to behave in accordance with it, and to face the possibility of sanction if they do not. Treaties usually have to be ratified, sometimes through a constitutionally defined process, before they enter into effect. See also *good faith* and *pacta sunt servanda*.

Treaty of Abuja: see *African Economic Community*.

Treaty of Amsterdam: a *European Union* treaty which entered into force on 1 May 1999. It supplements the *Treaty of Maastricht* and other treaties, but it does not replace them. It added transparency to European Union decision-making. It also simplified and consolidated the treaties constituting the law of the European Union. In the area of trade policy it brought *services* and *intellectual property* within the *Common Commercial Policy*. See also *Merger Treaty*, *Single European Act*, *Treaty of Nice* and *Treaty of Rome*. [Craig and De Búrca 2003]

Treaty of Maastricht: the treaty, concluded on 7 February 1992 between the then twelve members of the European Communities, which establishes the *European Union*. It entered into force on 1 November 1993. This Treaty goes beyond the *Treaty of Rome* in significant ways to ensure, through a single institutional framework, the consistency of European Union external activities as a whole in the context of external relations, security, economic and development policies. Responsibility for achieving this lies with the *Council of the European Union*, (the Council of Ministers) and the *European Commission*. The Treaty also replaces the term *European Economic Community* with *European Community* which is the principal pillar of the European Union. Only the European Community has a legal personality and can conclude international treaties. The Treaty also establishes a common foreign and security policy and cooperation in the fields of justice and home affairs as the two other pillars of the European Union. See also *European Community and European Union treaties*, *Treaty of Amsterdam* and *Treaty of Nice*. [Corbett 1993]

Treaty of Montevideo: see *ALADI*.

Treaty of Nice: a *European Union* treaty concluded on 11 December 2000 which entered into force on 1 February 2003. The main purpose of the Treaty of Nice was to prepare European Union institutions for the *enlargement* which began on 1 May 2004 with the accession of ten new members. Accordingly it introduces new decision-making procedures for the *Council of the European Union*. A protocol to the Treaty will limit the number of commissioners to one per member in 2005, and the total number of commissioners will be capped at fewer than 27 once the Union reaches 27 members. In the trade policy field the Treaty states that the Community and the member states will have shared *competence* for trade in cultural and audio-visual services, education services, and social and human health services. [Craig and De Búrca 2003]

Treaty of Rome: signed on 25 March 1957 by what became the six original members of the *European Economic Community* (EEC) and entered into force on 1 January 1958. The six were Belgium, Federal Republic of Germany, France, Italy, Luxembourg and the Netherlands. The Treaty has articles dealing with the free movement of goods, establishment of a *customs union*, elimination of *quantitative restrictions*, agriculture, free movement of persons, *services* and capital, a common transport policy, competition and taxation policy, economic and *trade policy*, social policy, establishment of a European Investment Bank, association of overseas countries and territories with the treaty, and institutional measures. Another treaty signed at Rome at the same time was the one establishing the European Atomic Energy Community (Euratom). This Dictionary is not further concerned with Euratom, and "Treaty of Rome" in these pages always refers to the treaty establishing the European Economic Community. See also *Article 133 Committee*, *enlargement*, *European Coal and Steel Community*, *European Community*, *European Community and European Union treaties*, *Common Agricultural Policy* and *four freedoms*.

Treaty on Intellectual Property in Respect of Integrated Circuits: one of the treaties which contains the standards of protection to be applied under the *Agreement on Trade-Related Aspects of Intellectual Property Rights*. It was concluded in Washington, DC, on 26 May 1992 under *WIPO* auspices, but it is not yet in force. Each party must afford intellectual property protection to original *lay-out designs of integrated circuits* (topographies) whether or not the integrated circuit is incorporated in an article. Parties to the Treaty must also accord *national treatment* to natural persons and legal entities of all other parties. Protection of integrated circuits must be for at least eight years. As a minimum, the reproduction of the layout-design, and the import, sale or other distribution for commercial purposes of the lay-out design or its incorporation in an article must be deemed illegal if it is done without the authorization of the holder of the *intellectual property rights*. See also *sui generis right*.

Treble damages: under Section 77 of the Wilson *Tariff Act* of 1894 and Section 4 of the *Clayton Act* of 1914, which are part of the United States framework of *antitrust laws*, the person injured because of a prohibited practice may recover through the courts three times the damages sustained. There is no upper limit on the damages that may be payable. The original antitrust law, the *Sherman Act*, only set maximum fines or prison terms for guilty parties. See also *clawback provisions* and *Anti-Dumping Act of 1916*.

Trends in International Trade: see *Haberler Report*.

Triadization: the recognition, described by the Group of Lisbon, that the process of technological, economic and socio-cultural integration is much more advanced among the three most developed regions of the word. The three regions are Japan plus the Asian *newly industrializing countries*, Western Europe and North America. See also *tripolarization*. [Group of Lisbon 1995]

Trigger price: a price level fixed in domestic support arrangements, particularly for agriculture, or international agreements which, once reached, will automatically authorize, and sometimes make mandatory, the taking of prescribed action. See also *buffer stocks*, *international commodity agreements*, *peril points* and *special safeguards*.

TRIMS: Trade-Related Investment Measures. These include export targets, import limitations, local-purchase requirements or *local-content requirements*, research and development requirements and similar conditions imposed on an enterprise as part of receiving permission to invest in another country. See also *Agreement on Trade-Related Investment Measures* and *export performance requirements*.

Triple transformation: occurs when a good undergoes three *substantial transformations* in succession. An example would be the transformation of bauxite into alumina, then smelting the alumina into aluminium and finally producing intermediate or final goods made of aluminium. Another example would be spinning raw fibres into yarn, then weaving the yarn into a fabric and finally cutting and sewing the fabric into garments. See also *double transformation*.

Tripolarization: a term descriptive of the fact that much international economic activity is caused or influenced by actions originating in Western Europe, East Asia or North America. Every now and then a breathless work appears postulating that the world is about to break up into three trading areas centred around these regions, and this almost certainly will lead to a *trade war*. So far, all of these predictions have been premature. See also *triadization*.

TRIPS: Trade-related aspects of intellectual property rights. See *Agreement on Trade-Related Aspects of Intellectual Property Rights*.

Troika: a consultative or fact-finding body with three members established by some *intergovernmental organizations*. Another of its aims can be ensuring continuity of policy. In the *Black Sea Economic Cooperation Organization*, for example, it consists of the present, past and future chairs of the Council of Ministers. Similarly, in the *Southern African Development Community* the Troika is made up of the Chair, Incoming Chair and the Outgoing Chair of the Community. The *European Union* Troika consists of a representative each of the *European Commission*, the actual presidency and the incoming presidency.

Trophy agreement: a colloquial description of an agreement ostensibly aimed at achieving a defined result, but which in fact is devoid of real obligations. Such agreements are often negotiated quite hastily, sometimes to ensure that ministers visiting other countries can point to an achievement on their return home.

Tropical products: this is not a clearly defined group of products, but in the *Uruguay Round*, where it received priority treatment, it included tropical beverages (coffee, cocoa and tea, and products based on them), spices, cut flowers, tropical plants and plant products, oilseeds, vegetable oils and oilcake, tobacco, rice, manioc and other tropical roots, tropical fruits and nuts, tropical wood and rubber, jute, sisal and other hard fibres. The *Tokyo Round* also treated tropical products as a priority.

TRQ: see *tariff rate quota*.

TSE: transmissible spongiform encephalopathy, a disease related to *BSE*.

Tuna (Canada–United States, 1982): a dispute in the GATT between Canada and the United States. The facts were that on 31 August 1979 the United States prohibited imports from Canada of tuna and tuna products after some United States fishing vessels had been seized by Canadian authorities for fishing without authorization in waters regarded by Canada to be under its jurisdiction. The United States, on the other hand, regarded these waters to be outside the tuna fisheries jurisdiction of any state. The United States action was based on Section 205 (Import Prohibitions) of the *Fishery Conservation and Management Act* of 1976 which required mandatory action in case of violation. The prohibition was lifted one year later following the conclusion of an arrangement with Canada, but before the dispute had been adjudicated in the GATT. The *panel* noted that the dispute was part of a wider disagreement on fisheries matters between the United States and Canada, and that the trade aspects had to be seen in that context. It found that the United States prohibition on the import of tuna from Canada constituted a prohibition in terms of GATT Article XI:1. The panel also found that the requirements of Article XX(g) had not been satisfied in that the alleged conservation measures had not been coupled with restrictions on domestic production or consumption. See also *herring and salmon*, *Tuna I*, *Tuna II* and *general exceptions*.

Tuna I: a dispute brought before the GATT in 1991 by Mexico against the United States. The background to this case was, as noted in the *panel* report, that studies monitoring catch levels had shown that tuna fish and dolphins were found together in a number of areas around the world, and that this could lead to incidental taking of dolphins during fishing operations. This is especially the case in the Eastern Tropical Pacific Ocean where tuna and dolphins often occur together, the former under water, the latter near or on the surface. This association between tuna and dolphins leads fishermen to finding and chasing dolphins on the surface and encircling them with nets to catch the tuna underneath. Once dolphins and tuna are surrounded, it is possible to exclude or eliminate the catch of dolphins through following certain procedures. In 1972 the United States enacted the *Marine Mammal Protection Act* (MMPA) aimed at reducing to insignificant levels approaching zero incidental kill or serious injury of marine mammals during commercial fishing. It imposed a general prohibition of "taking" (harassment, hunting, capture, killing or attempting to do so) and the import into the United States of marine mammals, except where an explicit authorization had been given. The MMPA also required the Secretary of Commerce to require any intermediary nation from which yellowfin tuna or tuna products were to be exported to the United States to certify that it had acted to prohibit the import of such products from countries not meeting the MMPA standards. If satisfactory assurances were not given, imports into the United States of yellowfin tuna and tuna products from intermediary countries were to be prohibited. This is the "intermediary nation embargo". In early 1991 such an embargo went into effect against Mexico. The embargo on imports of yellowfin tuna and tuna products could be strengthened by the use of the "Pelly Amendment", part of the 1967 *Fishermen's Protective Act*, which gave the President discretionary authority to order a prohibition of imports of all fish products from designated countries.The panel, in considering the evidence offered by the parties, noted that the MMPA regulated the domestic harvesting of yellowfin tuna to reduce the incidental taking of dolphins. As these regulations did not apply to tuna products as such, they would not directly regulate the sale of tuna and could not possibly affect tuna as a product. The panel considered that GATT Article III (National Treatment) called for a comparison of the treatment of imported tuna *as a product* with that of domestic tuna *as a product* [emphasis in the original]. The United States was therefore obliged to accord treatment to Mexican tuna no less favourable than that accorded to United States tuna, no matter whether the incidental taking of dolphins differed. The panel also found that the import prohibition was inconsistent with Article XI, and it therefore saw no need to make a finding on the consistency of the United States action with Article XII. The panel then turned to Article XX (General Exceptions). It noted that the broad interpretation of Article XX(b) [measures necessary to protect human, animal or plant life or health] sought by the United States would mean, if accepted, that each GATT member could impose its own policies on other members, and that the GATT would then no longer be a multilateral trade framework for all of its members. The panel noted that Article XX(g) allowed each member to adopt its own conservation policies, subject to the limitation that measures taken under this Article must be related to the conservation of exhaustible natural resources, and this condition had not been satisfied by the United States action. Considering the possible use of the Pelly Amendment, the panel decided to follow previous rulings which held that legislation merely giving executive authorities discretionary power to act inconsistently with the GATT was not, in itself, inconsistent with it. In its concluding remarks, the panel noted that the provisions of the GATT impose few constraints on a member's ability to implement domestic environmental policies. On the other hand, a member may not restrict imports of a product merely because it originates in a country with environmental policies different from its own. See also *herring and salmon*, *tuna (Canada–United States, 1982)*, *Tuna II*, *GATT-consistency of national legislation*, *general exceptions* and *trade and environment*. [GATT BISD 39]

Tuna II: a dispute brought before the GATT in 1992 by the *European Economic Community* (EEC), and separately the Netherlands on behalf of the Netherlands

Antilles, against the United States. The background to this case was that in the Eastern Tropical Pacific Ocean, but not in other waters, schools of tuna often swim below visible herds of dolphin. Fishermen in these waters therefore often use herds of dolphin to locate schools of tuna. The use of purse seine nets (two boats using one net to encircle a school) to catch the tuna then leads to the incidental killing and injury of many dolphins. The United States had long been a leader in promoting international efforts to reduce dolphin mortality from this cause. In 1972 it also passed the *Marine Mammal Protection Act* (MMPA) which, among other things, prohibited the import into the United States of any commercial fish or fish products harvested by a method resulting in the incidental kill or serious injury of marine mammals in excess of United States standards. This was known as the "primary nation embargo". Countries able to demonstrate that they had a regulatory program and a rate of incidental "taking" (harassment, hunting, capture, killing or attempts to do so) of dolphins comparable to that of the United States were not affected by this rule. The MMPA also required proof from countries exporting yellowfin tuna or yellowfin tuna products to the United States that they had not imported yellowfin tuna that would not have been allowed into the United States under conditions of direct export. This was known as the "intermediary nation embargo". In 1991 and 1992 several countries, including some members of the EEC and separately the Netherlands Antilles, were identified as "intermediary nations". This list was, however, shortened later in 1992. The panel did not report on this dispute until May 1994 because of various procedural delays sought by the parties. It found that "Article III calls for a comparison between the treatment accorded to domestic and imported *like products*, not for a comparison of the policies or practices of the country of origin with those of the country of importation". In other words, Article III applied to the product as is, not how it became that product. The panel then said that the embargoes imposed by the United States were "prohibitions or restrictions" in terms of Article XI since the act banned imports of tuna or tuna products from any country not meeting certain policy conditions. The panel found that the policy pursued by the United States to conserve dolphins in the Eastern Tropical Pacific Ocean fell within the range of policies covered by Article XX(g). However, because it was not accompanied by restrictions on domestic production or consumption, the import prohibitions on tuna and tuna products also maintained inconsistently with Article XI were not justified by Article XX(g). The same inconsistency also meant that the import prohibitions were not justified by Article XX(b) [measures necessary to protect human, animal or plant life or health] and Article XX(d) [measures necessary to comply with laws or regulations not inconsistent with the GATT]. In its final observations, the panel noted that the validity of the United States environmental objectives to protect and conserve dolphins was not the issue in this dispute. Rather, it was whether the United States could impose trade embargoes designed to achieve policy changes in other jurisdictions. The panel therefore had to resolve whether the parties to the GATT had given each other the right to impose trade embargoes for this purpose. It considered that Article XX could not be interpreted in this way. See also *extraterritoriality*, *general exceptions*, *tuna (Canada–United States, 1982)* and *Tuna I*.

Two-annex method: a way to schedule commitments for services and investment laws and policies in a *free-trade agreement* when a *negative list* is used. The two annexes to the agreement usually are (a) the list of *non-conforming measures* (i.e. measures that are not in full compliance with the agreement but are expected to be brought into conformity over time) and (b) a *reserved list* containing sectors or activities for which a party may maintain existing restrictions that do not conform to the provisions of the agreement or make them more restrictive. See also *positive list*.

UDEAC: Union douanière et économique de l'Afrique centrale. See *Central African Customs and Economic Union*.

Unbound commitments: commitments under the *General Agreement on Trade in Services* (GATS) which can be changed unilaterally by the country making them. They give the listing country complete flexibility to change its trading regime in the affected activity without the need to offer *compensation*. Unbound commitments are therefore much less valuable than *binding* commitments, though they may in some cases assist *transparency*.

UNCED: United Nations Conference on Environment and Development, held from 3 to 14 January 1992 in Rio de Janeiro. This conference adopted the *United Nations Framework Convention on Climate Change*, the *Convention on Biological Diversity*, *Agenda 21*, the *Rio Declaration* and the Statement on Forest Principles.

UNCITRAL: United Nations Commission on International Trade Law. Established in 1966 for the purpose of reducing or removing legal obstacles to the flow of international trade and the progressive harmonization and unification of the law of international trade. UNCITRAL has 36 members who are selected by the *United Nations General Assembly*. It is the core legal body within the United Nations system in the field of international trade law. UNCITRAL has pursued an extensive work program on subjects covering particularly international commercial arbitration and conciliation and the international transport and sale of goods. It is located in Vienna.

UNCITRAL Arbitration Rules: adopted on 15 December 1976. These rules are aimed at helping to settle disputes arising in the context of international commercial relations. Parties to a contract first have to agree in writing that disputes concerning the contract should be referred to *arbitration* under the UNCITRAL Arbitration Rules. Disputes will then be settled in accordance with these rules. One or three arbitrators may be appointed depending on the circumstances of the case. This instrument also contains a *Model Arbitration Clause*.

UNCITRAL model law on electronic commerce: adopted on 16 December 1996. Its purpose is to give legislators a way to remove legal obstacles to the wider use of electronic messages in the conduct of international transactions. The model law does not define the meaning of *electronic commerce*, but it applies to all kinds of data messages that might be generated, stored or communicated. Chapter II deals with the application of the legal requirements to data messages, such as the treatment of signatures, the admissibility of data messages in evidence and the retention of data messages. Chapter III covers the communication of data messages, especially the formation and validity of contracts. A separate chapter deals with actions related to contracts of carriage of goods.

UNCITRAL model law on procurement of goods, construction and services: a model law adopted by *UNCITRAL* in 1994 for use by national legislatures that are considering adopting new or revised *government procurement* legislation. Its main objectives are economy and efficiency in government purchasing, maximizing participation of bidders and competition among them, fairness in the treatment of bidders, objectivity in decision-making, and transparency of regulations and process.

UN Commodity Trade Statistics Database: see *COMTRADE database*.

UNCPC: see *United Nations Central Product Classification*.

UNCTAD: United Nations Conference on Trade and Development. Established in 1964 through *United Nations General Assembly* resolution (XIX) 1995 to promote a greater participation by developing countries in the global trading system and thereby promote their economic development. In October 2004 it had 192 members. UNCTAD describes itself as the primary forum for analysis, discussion and consensus-building on policies designed to achieve *sustainable development* in all regions to accelerate growth in weaker economies. The reasons leading to the formation of UNCTAD were broadly the difficulties developing countries appeared to experience in furthering their economic development, and the absence of any specialized international organization which might have assisted them in this challenge. Pressure for adequate attention to their problems increased as many colonies became independent in the early 1960s. In 1961, the Second Committee of *ECOSOC* asked the United Nations Secretary-General to consult on the possibility of holding a world conference on international trade problems, and in 1962 the United Nations General Assembly decided to hold the conference in Geneva in 1964. This conference became known as UNCTAD I. One of its early effects was the formation of the *Group of 77* which quickly seized the initiative in formulating the UNCTAD agenda. Many of the issues that would ultimately make up UNCTAD's work program were discussed at this conference, including commodities trade and arrangements, manufactures, transfer of capital and shipping. Later additions to the work program included debt, insurance, *ECDC* (economic cooperation between developing countries), *restrictive business practices*, *transfer of technology*, and the problems of *least developed countries*, among others. Despite the contribution UNCTAD has made to the development of developing countries, it has on the whole not been able to achieve the role its proponents expected it to have. As early as 1968, J G Crawford noted that the question was whether UNCTAD could free itself sufficiently from the political atmosphere and debating practices of the United Nations General Assembly to get down to the realities of securing action on the many trade issues listed in its charter. UNCTAD has been particularly active in the development of the *GSP* and *international commodity arrangements*. The secretariat prepares many high-class reports, particularly the *World Investment Report*, the *International*

Investment Agreement Issues Papers, the *E-Commerce and Development Report*, the *Least Developed Countries Report* and the *Trade Development Report*, which do not always attract adequate discussion by the UNCTAD membership. The executive body of UNCTAD is the *Trade and Development Board* which meets once a year in a regular session. UNCTAD's substantive work is done under the auspices of the *Commission on Trade in Goods and Services, and Commodities*, the *Commission on Investment, Technology and Related Financial Issues* and the *Commission on Enterprise, Business Facilitation and Development*. UNCTAD is also the name used for the ministerial conference held every four years under its auspices. UNCTAD I was held in Geneva. The other conferences were held at New Delhi (UNCTAD II, 1968), Santiago de Chile (UNCTAD III, 1972), Nairobi (UNCTAD IV, 1976), Manila (UNCTAD V, 1979), Belgrade (UNCTAD VI, 1983), Geneva (UNCTAD VII, 1987), Cartagena (UNCTAD VIII, 1992), Midrand (UNCTAD IX, 1996) and Bangkok (UNCTAD X, 2000). UNCTAD XI was held in Sao Paulo in 2004. Ghana will host UNCTAD XII in 2008. See also *ASYCUDA*, *Common Fund for Commodities*, *GSP*, *Integrated Programme for Commodities* and *Trade Efficiency Programme*. [Crawford 1968, United Nations Conference on Trade Development 2004]

UNCTAD BIOTRADE initiative: a mechanism launched in 1996 under *UNCTAD* auspices to support the aims of the *Convention on Biological Diversity*. It seeks to promote the adequate use of economic instruments and strategic partnerships to bring value to biodiversity resources, transfer the appropriate technologies and create export opportunities in these resources. The Initiative consists of seven components: (i) economic and market research on trends in the emerging biochemical prospecting market, described as the possibility of discovering commercially valuable compounds from biological material, (ii) analysis of strategies for the development of biological resource-based industries, (iii) evaluation of conservation and *sustainable development* opportunities, (iv) alternative contractual arrangements for biochemical prospecting activities, (v) training and capacity-building, (vi) private-sector collaboration and (vii) information dissemination and networking.

UNCTAD Coding System for Trade Control Measures: a comprehensive classification system divided into more than 100 different types of trade measures, maintained by the *UNCTAD* Secretariat. Its main components are (a) tariff measures (statutory customs duties, MFN duties, GATT *ceiling duties*, seasonal duties, temporary reduced duties, temporary increased duties and preferential duties under trade agreements, (b) para-tariff measures (customs surcharges, additional charges, internal taxes and charges levied on imports and decreed customs valuation), (c) price control measures (administrative price fixing, voluntary export restraint, anti-dumping measures, anti-dumping investigations, anti-dumping duties, anti-dumping price undertakings, countervailing measures, countervailing investigations, countervailing duties and countervailing undertakings), (d) finance measures (advance payment requirements, multiple exchange rates, restrictive official foreign exchange allocation, regulations concerning terms of payments for imports, transfer delays, queues, etc.), (e) automatic licensing measures and import monitoring, (f) quality control measures (non-automatic licensing, quotas, prohibitions, export restraint arrangements and enterprise-specific restrictions), (g) monopolistic measures (single channel for imports and compulsory national services), and (h) technical measures (technical regulations, pre-shipment inspection, special customs formalities and obligation to return used product). The coding system also lists environmental, sanitary and phytosanitary measures under relevant sub-headings. The *UNCTAD TRAINS* database makes extensive use of this coding system. [www.unctad.org]

UNCTAD Liner Code: see *Convention on a Code of Conduct for Liner Conferences*.

UNCTAD Set of Multilaterally Agreed Equitable Principles and Rules for the Control of Restrictive Business Practices: see *restrictive business practices*.

UNCTAD TRAINS: Trade Analysis and Information System. A database containing trade control measures (tariffs, para-tariffs and non-tariff measures), as well as import flows, for more than 100 countries at the 6-digit level of the *Harmonized System*.

Under-invoicing: preparing or presenting an invoice giving a price for goods or services that is lower than the price actually paid for them. The motivation may be to reduce the amount of customs duties payable in the case of goods, or to reduce the amount of internal taxes payable in the case of goods and services. See also *over-invoicing*.

Understanding on Commitments in Financial Services: an adjunct to the *General Agreement on Trade in Services* (GATS) adopted by developed WTO members only. It defines further how fair trade in *financial services* should be understood in GATS terms. The Understanding forms the basis for *negative listings* in the *schedules of commitments*.

Understanding on Rules and Procedures Governing the Settlement of Disputes: usually known as the *Dispute Settlement Understanding* or simply DSU. It contains the rules WTO members must follow when they become party to a dispute that involves their rights and obligations under the WTO disciplines.

Understanding on the Balance-of-Payments Provisions of the GATT: one of the *Uruguay Round* outcomes. Its purpose is to clarify the rules on the imposition of measures available to WTO members under GATT Articles XII and XVIII:B to improve their balance-of-payments conditions. In particular, it seeks to achieve greater *transparency* through an improved system of *notifications* and *consultations*.

Undertakings: the WTO *Agreement on Subsidies and Countervailing Measures* allows the investigating authority to suspend or terminate its proceedings if it receives a satisfactory voluntary undertaking that would remove the effect of that part of the *subsidy* causing *injury*. Two options are available. First, the exporter's government can agree to eliminate or limit the subsidy or otherwise deal with its effects. Second, the exporter can undertake to raise the price sufficiently to remove the injury caused by the subsidy. Undertakings may only be made or accepted if there has been a *preliminary affirmative determination of subsidization* and injury so caused.

Undisclosed information: the *Agreement on Trade-Related Aspects of Intellectual Property Rights* requires WTO members to protect some types of undisclosed information. This protection is available as long as the information is (a) secret in the sense that it is not, in its entirety or in parts, generally known among or readily accessible to persons who normally deal with this kind of information, (b) has commercial value because it is secret, and (c) and the person lawfully in control of the information has taken reasonable steps to protect it. Members who require testing of new pharmaceuticals or agricultural chemical products before they are put on the market have to protect data supplied against unfair commercial use. See also *in a manner contrary to honest commercial practices* and *trade secrets*.

UNDP: see *United Nations Development Programme*.

UNESCO: see *United Nations Educational, Scientific and Cultural Organization*.

Unfair business practices: see *restrictive business practices*.

Unfair competition: defined in Article 10bis of the *Paris Convention* as any act "contrary to honest practices in industrial or commercial matters". The Convention prohibits (1) all acts of such a nature as to create confusion by any means whatever with the establishment, the goods, or industrial or commercial activities, of a competitor, (2) false allegations in the course of trade of such a nature as to discredit the establishment, the goods, or industrial or commercial activities, of a competitor, and (3) the use of indications or allegations which in the course of trade is liable to mislead the public as to the nature, the manufacturing process, the characteristics, the suitability for their purpose, or the quantity of the goods. Many competition and consumer protection laws also deal with unfair competition. See also *passing off*, *restrictive business practices* and *WIPO Model Provisions on Protection Against Unfair Competition*. [Paris Convention for the Protection of Industrial Property]

Unfair pricing practices: a term used by some to mean *dumping*.

Unfair-trade remedies: see *trade remedies*.

Unfair trading practices: refers to the improper or illegal use of *subsidies* or the export of products at dumped prices. See also *anti-dumping measures*, *countervailing duties* and *dumping*.

Unfavourable balance of trade: see *balance of trade* and *mercantilism*.

Unforeseen developments: GATT Article XIX allows WTO members to impose safeguard action if a "product is being imported in such increased quantities as to cause or threaten serious *injury*" to domestic producers of the *like product*, but only if the increased imports are due to unforeseen developments and the effect of trade liberalization. The article does not define what an unforeseen development might be. In 1950 the Working Party considering *Hatters' fur* noted that ". . . the term 'unforeseen developments' should be interpreted to mean developments occurring after the negotiation of the relevant *concession* which it would not be reasonable to expect that the negotiators of the country seeking the concessions could and should have foreseen at the time when the concession was negotiated". The *Agreement on Safeguards*, which interprets and amplifies Article XIX, does not list "unforeseen developments" among the conditions enabling safeguards action. Many then assumed that this criterion was no longer applicable. They were too hasty. In *Argentina – Safeguard Measures on Imports of Footwear* and *Korea – Definite Safeguard Measure on Imports of certain Dairy Products* the *Appellate Body* held that the two provisions were part of the one treaty, and that they had to be read "harmoniously" and as "an inseparable package of rights and disciplines". [GATT/CP/106, WT/DS/98/AB/R, WT/DS/121/AB/R, Mueller 2003]

Unidroit Convention on Stolen or Illegally Exported Cultural Objects: adopted in Rome on 24 June 1995. The Convention requires the owner of a cultural object which has been stolen, unlawfully excavated or lawfully excavated but unlawfully retained, to return it. A party to the Convention (contracting state) may request the courts of another party to order the return of a cultural object illegally exported from the requesting party. Claims generally have to be made within 50 years from the time of the theft. Compensation may be payable in some circumstances. See also *Convention on the Means of Prohibiting and Preventing the Illicit Import, Export and Transfer of Ownership of Cultural Property*.

Uniform tariff: a tariff schedule in which the rates are the same, or nearly the same, for all products. The best-known example of a uniform tariff is that of Chile which applies a most-favoured-nation rate of 6% for nearly all products. Most of its bound rates were set at 25%. See also *dispersed tariff* and *flat-tariff structure*.

Unilateralism: this term has two quite different meanings in *trade policy*. The first is the policy or action of lowering tariffs or removing other impediments to trade unilaterally without the expectation of reciprocal action by others. The second meaning is the desire to impose one's view of the desirable features of global trade policy or trade in a particular product on others, and have it accepted by them. Unilateralism of this kind only works if one has the advantage of overwhelming economic dominance, but success is not assured even then. It can achieve some of one's objectives, but it usually leads to a prolonged adversarial atmosphere. For most countries, the cost exacted in terms of resources to be used and the likely benefits to be gained would not make it an option anyway. See also *Section 301*, *Special 301*, *Super 301*, *bilateralism*, *multilateralism* and *reciprocity*.

Unilateral preferential agreements: also called *asymmetrical trade agreements*. These are *preferential trade agreements* under which a party receives preferential treatment without being expected to requite this treatment.

Unilateral preferential rules of origin: see *autonomous preferential rules of origin*.

Union Economique et Monétaire Ouest Africaine: UEMOA. See *West African Economic and Monetary Union*.

United Nations: UN. The United Nations Charter, the constituting document of the organization, was signed on 26 June 1945 by 50 countries, and the United Nations came into existence on 24 October 1945 after ratification by the required number of countries. The Charter created six main organs: the General Assembly, the Security Council, the Economic and Social Council (often known as *ECOSOC*), the Trusteeship Council, the *International Court of Justice* and the Secretariat, Its main deliberative organ is the General Assembly (GA or UNGA). The United Nations body most concerned with trade-related matters is *UNCTAD* (United Nations Conference on Trade and Development), but many other agencies and bodies have work programs dealing with various aspects of trade and commodity policies. Among these are the *United Nations regional economic commissions*, and the *United Nations specialized agencies*, such as the *Food and Agricultural Organization* (FAO), the *International Labour Organization, the International Telecommunications Union* and *WIPO* (World Intellectual Property Organization). The *WTO* is not part of the United Nations agencies, but it cooperates closely with them in many areas. See also *United Nations specialized agencies*.

United Nations Central Product Classification: UNCPC. It covers products that are an output of economic activities, including transportable goods, non-transportable goods and services. An earlier version of UNCPC was used as the basis for the original listings in the GATS *schedules of commitments*. Version 2 of 2006 with a much expanded services section is now available in draft. See also *W/120*. [www.unstats.un.org]

United Nations Code of Conduct on Transnational Corporations: see *Draft United Nations Code of Conduct on Transnational Corporations*.

United Nations Conference on Environment and Development: *UNCED*. The Earth Summit. See *Rio Declaration on Environment and Development* and *World Summit on Sustainable Development*.

United Nations Conference on the Least Developed Countries: see *SNPA*.

United Nations Conference on Trade and Development: see *UNCTAD*.

United Nations Conference on Trade and Employment: the conference held in Havana from November 1947 to March 1948 which considered the draft *Havana Charter* and made further amendments to it. The conference was preceded by three preparatory committee meetings. The first meeting, the first preparatory session for the Havana Conference, held in London in 1946, considered a draft of a Charter for an International Trade Organization (ITO). The second, a meeting of the drafting committee, at Lake Success, New York, in January-February 1947, resulted in the first full draft of a *GATT*, with language drawn mainly from the draft Charter. The third meeting, the second preparatory session for the Havana Conference, held in Geneva from April to August 1947, completed a further draft of the Charter for transmission to the Havana Conference. It also completed the GATT, and it conducted some tariff negotiations. See also *GATT 1947*, *ITO* and *trade and employment*.

United Nations Convention Against Corruption: adopted by the United Nations General Assembly on 31 October 2003. The Convention does not attempt to define *corruption* precisely. It leaves that task to the parties. However, the Convention applies to the various forms of corruption now existing, and it aims to be capable of being applied to new forms also. It requires the parties to make corruption a criminal offence. It also enables the recovery of funds. Other parts of the Convention concern prevention of corruption and international cooperation to fight corruption. See also *trade and illicit payments*.

United Nations Convention on a Code of Conduct for Liner Conferences: see *Convention on a Code of Conduct for Liner Conferences*.

United Nations Convention on the Law of the Sea: UNCLOS. Adopted on 10 December 1982 and entered into force on 16 November 1994. The Convention creates a framework for the protection of the sea, the seabed and subsoil as well as the airspace above it. It is intended to promote the peaceful uses of the seas and oceans, the equitable and efficient utilization of their resources, and the study, protection and preservation of the marine environment. Part V of the Convention is of greatest interest to *trade policy*. It creates the Exclusive Economic Zone (EEZ) not extending beyond 200 nautical miles from the baseline, normally the low-water line along the coast. In the EEZ the coastal state has sovereign rights for the purpose of exploring and exploiting, conserving and managing the natural resources of the sea and the seabed. It has the same right for the economic exploitation and exploration of the EEZ, such as the production of energy from the water, current and winds.

United Nations Convention on the Recognition and Enforcement of Foreign Arbitral Awards: see *New York Convention*.

United Nations Development Programme: UNDP. It acquired its present name on 1 January 1966, but many of its aims and functions date back to the establishment of the *United Nations*. UNDP administers and coordinates almost all technical assistance provided to developing countries through the United Nations system. Its main program areas are democratic governance, poverty reduction, crisis prevention and recovery, energy and environment, and HIV/AIDS. It also promotes the achievement of the *Millennium Development Goals*. UNDP publishes annually the *Human Development Report*. [www.undp.org]

United Nations Economic and Social Council: see *ECOSOC*.

United Nations economic sanctions: Under Article 39 of the Charter of the *United Nations*, the *United Nations Security Council* can determine the existence of any threat to the peace, breach of the peace or act of aggression and make recommendations. It may also, under Article 41, decide on measures not involving the use of armed force to give effect to its decisions, and to call upon members of the United Nations to apply these measures. This may include complete or partial interruption of economic relations and of rail, sea, air, postal, telegraphic, radio and other means of communication, as well as the severance of diplomatic relations. The effectiveness of *economic sanctions* as a foreign policy tool has been hotly debated for many years. In nearly all cases, it is impossible to ensure that all United Nations members with a significant interest in the matter participate. This is partly because it can be difficult to convince countries that their exporters will not suffer equally or more than the industry in the country against which sanctions are directed. One of the *security exceptions* listed in each of Article XXI of the GATT, ArticleXIV*bis* of the *General Agreement on Trade in Services* and Article 73 of the *Agreement on Trade-Related Aspects of Intellectual Property Rights* allows WTO members to suspend their obligations under these agreements to the extent necessary to comply with a United Nations decision.

United Nations Educational, Scientific and Cultural Organization: UNESCO. One of the *United Nations specialized agencies*. Several agreements and conventions with an actual or potential trade effect have been negotiated under its auspices. The more important ones include the *Beirut Agreement*, *Convention on the Means of Prohibiting and Preventing the Illicit Import, Export and Transfer of Ownership of Cultural Property*, *Florence Agreement* and the *Universal Copyright Convention*. UNESCO is located in Paris.

United Nations Environment Programme: UNEP. This is the main *United Nations* body responsible for assessing global, regional and national environmental conditions and trends and for developing international and national environmental instruments. It was established in 1972. It hosts, among others, the secretariats for *CITES*, the *Convention on Biological Diversity*, the *Basel Convention* and the *Convention on Persistent Organic Pollutants*. UNEP'S secretariat is Nairobi. See also *multilateral environment agreements*.

United Nations Framework Convention on Climate Change: UNFCC. Adopted on 9 May 1992. Its objective is to achieve the stabilization of greenhouse gas concentrations in the atmosphere at a level that would prevent dangerous anthropogenic interference with the climate system. Such a level should be achieved within a timeframe to allow ecosystems to adapt naturally to *climate change*, to ensure that food production is not threatened and to enable economic development to proceed in a sustainable manner. Parties to the Convention are guided by five principles: (1) protecting the climate system for the benefit of past and future generations, (2) giving full consideration to the special needs of developing countries, (3) taking precautionary measures, (4) to promote *sustainable development*, and (5) measures taken to combat climate change should not constitute a means of arbitrary or unjustifiable discrimination or a disguised restriction on international trade. The Convention divides its members into *Annex I countries* (OECD countries, Russia and some East European countries), *Annex II* countries (OECD members) and the remaining group (mainly developing countries). See also *greenhouse gases*, *Kyoto Protocol*, *precautionary principle* and *trade and environment*.

United Nations General Assembly: UNGA. The main deliberative assembly of the *United Nations*. It usually meets from September to December. Special sessions, abbreviated to UNGASS, are conducted from time to time to discuss particular topics.

United Nations Industrial Development Organization: UNIDO. Established in 1966 as an autonomous organization within the United Nations. It became a specialized agency in 1986. Its mandate is to promote and accelerate industrial development and modernization in developing countries, and to promote cooperation and development at the global, regional and national level as well as in individual industrial sectors. UNIDO also coordinates all activities in the United Nations system relating to industrial development. It is located in Vienna. See also *United Nations specialized agencies*.

United Nations Millennium Declaration: see *Millennium Declaration*.

United Nations Monetary and Financial Conference: see *Bretton Woods agreements*.

United Nations regional economic commissions: bodies established under the United Nations system to promote the economic development of their member countries and to strengthen and improve economic relations between them. Some also have work programs on social issues. They are not usually engaged in the elaboration of binding trade rules. Their immediate parent body is *ECOSOC*. The regional economic commissions are *Economic Commission for Africa* (established in 1958), *Economic Commission for Europe* (1947), *Economic Commission for Latin America and the Caribbean* (1948), *ESCAP* (1947) and *Economic and Social Commission for Western Asia* (1973).

United Nations Security Council: UNSC. One of the principal organs of the *United Nations*. Its main responsibility is maintaining international peace and security. The UNSC has fifteen members. China, France, Russia, United Kingdom and United States are permanent members. The other ten are elected for two years. In some cases, a UNSC decision may result in the invocation of *security exceptions* by WTO members.

United Nations specialized agencies: these are intergovernmental agencies constituted as separate and autonomous organizations related to the *United Nations*. They have their own legislative and executive bodies, membership and budgets. They work with each other and the United Nations through *ECOSOC*. The specialized agencies are the *Food and Agricultural Organization* (FAO), *World Bank* (International Bank for Reconstruction and Development or IBRD), *IMF* (International Monetary Fund), *International Civil Aviation Organization* (ICAO), *International Fund for Agricultural Development* (IFAD), *International Labour Organization* (ILO), *International Maritime Organization* (IMO), *International Telecommunication Union* (ITU), *United Nations Educational, Scientific and Cultural Organization* (UNESCO), *United Nations Industrial Development Organization* (UNIDO), Universal Postal Union (UPU), World Health Organization (WHO), *WIPO* (World Intellectual Property Organization), World Meteorological Organization (WMO) and World Tourism Organization (WTO).

United States Agricultural Products Market Access Act: a bill introduced into Congress in June 2003 modelled on the *Special 301* provisions "to establish procedures for identifying countries that deny market access for agricultural products of the United States". The bill, if adopted, would require *USTR* to identify annually foreign countries that "(a) deny fair and equitable market access to United States agricultural products, or (b) apply standards for the importation of agricultural products from the United States that are not related to pubic health concerns or cannot be substantiated by reliable analytical methods". USTR would then have to prepare a list of *priority foreign countries*. Proposals of this nature have surfaced in United States agricultural politics from time to time.

United States Agricultural Trade and Development Act: see *PL 480*.

United States–Andean Free Trade Agreement: under negotiation since May 2004. The Andean Partners are Colombia, Ecuador and Peru. Bolivia may decide to join later.

United States Anti-Dumping Act of 1916: see *Anti-Dumping Act of 1916*.

United States–Caribbean Basin Trade Partnership Act: see *Caribbean Basin Initiative*.

United States–Central America Free Trade Agreement: CAFTA. It consists of Costa Rica, Dominican Republic, El Salvador, Guatemala, Honduras, Nicaragua and the United States.

United States–Japan financial services agreement: Concluded in February 1995 following United States complaints about closed financial markets in Japan. The main components of the Agreement are that Japan will (a) provide unrestricted access to its public pension fund market by investment advisory companies, (b) eliminate balanced funds requirements, thus enabling more firms to compete, (c) move towards market value accounting for pension liabilities, (d) permit dual licensing of investment trust businesses and discretionary investment management businesses, (e) liberalize restrictions on the introduction of new financial instruments, (f) introduce a domestic asset-backed securities market in Japan, and (g) eliminate restrictions on the offshore securitization of Japanese assets.

United States–Japan Framework for a New Economic Partnership: concluded in July 1993 to create more avenues of entry for United States firms into Japan. Japan committed itself to address five major areas: (a) *government procurement*, (b) regulatory reform and competitiveness, (c) other major sectors, including cars and car parts, (d) economic harmonization, aimed at correcting macroeconomic imbalances in the Japanese market, and especially its low inflow of foreign investment, and (e) implementation of existing arrangements and measures. See also *Market-Oriented Specific-Sector talks*, *Structural Impediments Initiative* and *United States–Japan financial services agreement*.

United States–Jordan free-trade agreement: entered into force on 17 December 2001. In most respects this is a standard bilateral *free-trade agreement*, but it has strong provisions on labour and environment. In Articles 5 and 6 the parties recognize that it is inappropriate to encourage trade by relaxing domestic environmental and labour laws. Each party may establish its own level of domestic environmental protection and labour standards, though these are expected to be high. The parties agree to enforce their environmental and labour laws effectively. In Article 6 the parties also reaffirm their obligations under the ILO *Declaration on Fundamental Principles and Rights at Work*. Environmental laws are defined as statutes or regulations with the primary purpose to protect the environment, or to prevent danger to human, animal, or plant life or health, through (a) the prevention, abatement or control of the release, discharge or emission of pollutants or environmental contaminants; (b) the control of environmentally hazardous or toxic chemicals, substances, materials and wastes, and the dissemination of information related to this; or (c) the protection or conservation of wild flora or fauna, including endangered species, their habitat, and specially protected natural areas. Labour laws are defined as (a) the right of association, (b) the right to organize and bargain collectively, (c) a prohibition on the use of any form of forced or compulsory labour, (d) a minimum age for the employment of children, and (e) acceptable conditions of work with respect to minimum wages, hours of work, and occupational safety and health. See also *core labour standards*.

United States Marine Mammal Protection Act: see *Tuna I* and *Tuna II*.

United States Merchant Marine Act: see *Jones Act*.

United States–Middle East Free-Trade Area: proposed by President Bush on 9 May 2003 for completion within a decade. It consists of bilateral *free-trade agreements* between Middle Eastern countries and the United States. As of December 2006, agreements were in force with Israel, Jordan, Morocco and Bahrein.

United States prohibition of imports of tuna and tuna products from Canada: see *tuna (Canada–United States, 1982)*.

United States Reciprocal Trade Agreements Program: established by the *Reciprocal Trade Agreements Act* of 1934 which is an amendment to the *Tariff Act* of 1930, known also as the *Smoot-Hawley Tariff Act*. It authorized the President to enter into trade agreements with foreign governments and to modify existing duties, *import restrictions* and customs or excise treatment as necessary to carry out the agreements made with them. There was no sense, however, that tariffs on agricultural products would be included in the program of prospective reciprocal tariff reductions. It should be noted that some of the earlier tariff acts had contained provisions permitting reciprocal tariff reductions, but these were not used, either because the conditions were too strict, or because there was no inclination anyway to reduce tariffs. Until the passing of the *Reciprocal Trade Agreements Act*, the tariff levels prescribed by the 1930 *Tariff Act* were mandatory, and they could only be changed with the consent of Congress. The Reciprocal Trade Agreements Program's importance for the *multilateral trading system* partly stems from the language included in some of the 32 bilateral agreements negotiated under it between 1934 and 1945. For example, all of the seventeen general clauses contained in the United States–Mexico bilateral trade agreement of December 1942 are reflected to a greater or lesser extent in the GATT. These include a *most-favoured-nation* clause, *national treatment*, agreed rules for the non-discriminatory application of *quantitative* *restrictions*, *customs valuation*, *transparency*, *safeguards*, etc. The tenor of the safeguards clause was changed considerably by a strengthened element of consultation. Other GATT articles drawing on this agreement contain additional principles reflecting the views of other trading countries. The 1934 *Reciprocal Trade Agreements Act*, as amended, was superseded by the *Trade Expansion Act* of 1962. See also *United States trade agreements legislation*.

United States – restrictions on imports of tuna: see *Tuna I*.

United States – Standards for Reformulated and Conventional Gasoline: see .

United States Tariff Act of 1930: see *Smoot-Hawley Tariff Act*.

United States – taxes on petroleum and certain imported substances: see *Superfund*.

United States trade agreements legislation: like other countries, the United States has a range of legislation covering its import and export trade, but the influence of the United States in the world economy, the GATT and the WTO, and the role Congress has in the formulation of external economic relations have always meant that its trade legislation is viewed as particularly important by other countries. This entry mainly deals with the legislation enabling the United States to participate in *multilateral trade negotiations*. The starting point for such legislation is the *Reciprocal Trade Agreements Act* of 1934 which authorized the President to enter into trade agreements with other governments and to modify the United States tariff regime for the entry of goods. This Act was extended with minor changes in 1937, 1940, 1943 and 1945. On the expiry of the 1945 extension on 1 June 1948, it was extended for one year with the significant inclusion of *peril points*. The 1949 extension, to 30 June 1951, repealed this change. The *Trade Agreements Extension Act* of 1955 permitted the President to make limited tariff reductions which, with some minor changes, was carried forward into the 1958 extension, due to expire in 1962. It reintroduced the idea of peril points. This limited negotiating authority was a major reason for the meagre results of the *Dillon Round*. Until 1962 the President did not have the authority to deal with *systemic issues*. The passage of the *Trade Expansion Act* of 1962 extended the presidential authority considerably, largely because of a realization of what the economic and trade potential of the *European Economic Community* (EEC), now that Europe had fully recovered from the damage caused by the war, might mean to United States trading interests. The Act allowed a reduction of existing tariffs by 50% and even to zero if they were less than 5%, but leaving it to the President how this might be achieved. This allowed experimentation with the *linear tariff cut* formula. Some prospective reductions to zero were conditional on an agreement with the EEC. There was provision in the Act for retaliatory action if foreign governments harmed the trade of the United States. Industries and workers injured by increased imports became eligible for direct assistance. Finally, this Act also created the Office of the Special Representative for Trade Negotiations, the forerunner of the *USTR*. When the 1962 negotiating authority expired in 1967, it was not renewed until the *Trade Act* of 1974 which gave the President authority to participate in the *Tokyo Round* negotiations until 5 January

1980. This was the first appearance of *fast-track*. This Act also formalized the retaliatory power of the United States Government in cases of illegal or unfair action by foreign governments through *Section 301*. This section became part, in amended form, of all subsequent trade legislation. The *Trade Agreements Act* of 1979 adopted the Tokyo Round outcomes. The next act, the *Trade and Tariffs Act* of 1984, did not give the President new negotiating authority. That had to wait until 1988 with the passing of the *Omnibus Trade and Competitiveness Act*. This was also the first time since the end of World War II that a major trade act did not emanate from the executive. President Clinton failed to obtain fast-track authority when the *Uruguay Round Agreements Act* became law in December 1994. He appeared to have regained the initiative when he tabled the *Export Expansion and Reciprocal Trade Agreements Act* in September 1997. There appears to be some intended symbolism in the choice of the title in that it harks back to the great trade acts passed during the presidencies of Franklin Delano Roosevelt and John F Kennedy. In the end, Congress did not act on the bill. When in early 2001 the new administration again sought fast-track authority, it renamed it the *Trade Promotion Authority*. On 6 August 2002 President Bush was able to sign it into law through the *Bipartisan Trade Promotion Authority Act of 2002*. See also *Smoot-Hawley Tariff Act*, *Jackson-Vanik Amendment* and *United States Reciprocal Trade Agreements Program*. [U.S. International Trade Commission 2003]

United States Trade Representative: see *USTR*.

Universal Copyright Convention: administered by the *United Nations Educational, Scientific and Cultural Organization* (UNESCO). Many of its basic principles are the same as those contained in the *Berne Convention*, except for the requirement of a copyright notice on the copyright work itself. See also *copyright*.

Universal Declaration of Human Rights: adopted by the *United Nations General Assembly* on 10 December 1948. It has established a framework for all discussion of, and progress in, *human rights* since the end of World War II. Some parts of it are directly relevant to the debate on *trade and labour standards*. Article 23 states everyone has the right to work, to free choice of employment, just and favourable conditions of work and to protection against unemployment, the right to equal pay for equal work, the right to just and favourable remuneration and the right to form and join trade unions for the protection of his interests. Article 24 grants everyone the right to rest and leisure, including reasonable limitation of working hours and periodic holidays with pay. See also *International Covenant on Economic, Social and Cultural Rights*.

Universal service: a term used for services, such as telecommunications or postal services, which are available to all prospective users at a guaranteed level of quality and at affordable prices. See also *basic telecommunications*.

Unrecorded trade: trade flows not recorded in statistical summaries prepared by the customs or revenue authorities. No duties are paid on unrecorded trade, and the country therefore suffers a revenue shortfall. See also *smuggling*.

UPOV: Union internationale pour la protection des obtentions végétales. See *International Convention for the Protection of New Varieties of Plants*.

Upper-middle-income economies: a group of 40 economies classified in this way by the *World Bank* and the 2007 *World Development Report*. In 2005 these countries have a per-capita GNI (gross national income) ranging from $3,466 to $10,725. See also *high-income economies*, *low-income economies* and *lower-middle-income economies*.

Upstream subsidy: a *subsidy* paid to a producer of a product that is incorporated into the final product.

Upward harmonization: harmonization of standards on the principle that participants in a harmonization arrangement will meet the highest standard prevailing among them. See also *harmonization of standards and qualifications*.

Uruguay Round: the eighth round of *multilateral trade negotiations*. It was launched at Punta del Este, Uruguay, on 25 September 1986. Negotiations concluded in Geneva on 15 December 1993, and it was signed by Ministers in Marrakesh, Morocco, on 15 April 1994. The objectives of the negotiations were (i) further liberalization and expansion of world trade, (ii) strengthening the role of the GATT and improving the *multilateral trading system*, (iii) increasing the responsiveness of the GATT to the international economic environment and (iv) foster international cooperative economic action. Participants agreed to a *standstill* on trade-restrictive measures during the negotiations and a *rollback* provision. The subjects for negotiations, the widest of any GATT round, were *tariffs*, *non-tariff measures*, *tropical products* as a priority area, *natural resource-based products*, textiles and clothing, agriculture, review of GATT articles, *safeguards*, *Tokyo Round* agreements and arrangements, subsidies and countervailing measures, *dispute settlement*, *trade-related aspects of intellectual property rights*, *trade-related investment measures* and the Functioning of the GATT System (FOGS). Each of these subjects was managed by a negotiating group established for the purpose. Negotiations on *trade in services* were to be held on a legally separate track at the insistence of a group of developing countries who did not accept that services should be covered by the GATT. Ministers agreed that negotiations would conclude within four years. The negotiations can be divided into three stages: (a) from the launch at Punta del Este to the Montreal mid-term review in December 1988, (b) the period from then on up the Brussels Ministerial Meeting in December 1990 which was supposed to mark the end of the negotiations, and (c) the events leading up to the Marrakesh Ministerial Meeting in April 1994. Substantive negotiations ended on 15 December 1993 when the second extension to the United States negotiating authority, the *fast-track* authority, expired. The Uruguay Round was therefore by far the longest round of *multilateral trade negotiations*. It would be wrong, however, to view it as a continuous set of negotiations. Long stretches of its seven-and-a-half years were spent waiting for this or that participant or group of participants to come to terms with the need for a change in its negotiating position. This was the case especially in the third period when the *Blair House Accord* was negotiated and then renegotiated. The text of the "first approximation to the Final Act" of the Uruguay Round, submitted by the Director-General of the GATT to the Brussels Ministerial Meeting in December 1990, was in fact very close to the agreement finally adopted at Marrakesh in April 1994. The main achievements of the Uruguay Round included a *trade-weighted average tariff* cut of 38%, conclusion of the *Agreement on Agriculture* which brought agricultural trade for the first time under full *GATT* disciplines, adoption of the *General Agreement on Trade in Services*, the *Agreement on Trade-Related Aspects of Intellectual Property Rights* and the *Agreement on Trade-Related Investment Measures*, the creation of a unified and predictable *dispute settlement* mechanism, adoption of the *Trade Policy Review Mechanism*, and the establishment of the *World Trade Organization* (WTO) which administers 15 multilateral and four plurilateral trade agreements. Other results of the round were strengthened provisions on anti-dumping, subsidies and safeguards. The new *Agreement on Textiles and Clothing* brought this sector under the GATT rules by replacing the *Multi-Fibre Arrangement*. See also *Cairns Group*, *Leutwiler Report* and *WTO Agreement*. [Bourgeois, Berrod and Fournier]

Uruguay Round *acquis*: a term used particularly by the *European Community* for the agreements and decisions that make up the *Uruguay Round* outcome. See also *acquis communautaire* and *WTO Agreement*.

US–EU aircraft agreement: see *EU–US aircraft agreement*.

USTR: refers both to the Office of the United States Trade Representative and the person of cabinet rank in charge of it. First created in 1962 as Special Representative for Trade Negotiations and upgraded to cabinet rank in 1974. It was renamed USTR in 1980. USTR is the principal United States locus for *trade policy* coordination and negotiations, including commodity negotiations. In *financial services*, USTR has responsibility for insurance, but Treasury handles banking, funds management and securities. USTR publishes annually the *National Trade Estimate Report on Foreign Trade Barriers*, an inventory of the perceived most important barriers affecting United States exports of goods and services, *foreign direct investment* by United States persons, and protection of *intellectual property* rights. See also *Monitoring and Enforcement Unit*, *Section 301*, *Section-306 monitoring*, *Special 301*, *Super 301* and *United States trade agreements legislation*. [Dryden 1995]

Vaduz Convention: see *EFTA Convention 2001*.

Value-added criterion: a concept used in the administration of *rules of origin* under *preferential trade agreements*. It means that a specified amount of transformation or processing, usually expressed as a percentage of the total value of the good, has to have occurred in the country exporting the good if the good is to benefit from preferential tariff treatment. See also *change in tariff classification* and *substantial transformation*.

Value-added tax: a *consumption tax* levied *ad valorem* on goods and services at the point of retail sale.

Value-added telecommunications: also called enhanced services. It includes services such as electronic mail, voice mail, enhanced facsimile services, including store-and-forward services. See also *basic telecommunications*.

Variable geometry: another way to describe matters concerning *special and differential treatment* for developing countries in the *multilateral trading system*. It appears to have been taken from the *European Union* practice of sometimes allowing separate paths to integration for less developed member states. It seems that the term has been drawn from the shape and function of swing-wing aircraft which are equally versatile at high and low speeds.

Variable levies: customs duty rates which vary in response to domestic criteria. They are intended to ensure that the price of a product on the domestic market remains unchanged regardless of price fluctuations in world markets and always well above world prices. Variable levies are a feature of the *Common Agricultural Policy*. See also *Chicken War* and *oilseeds case* for examples of trade tension caused by the introduction of variable levies.

Variable tariff: a *tariff* that is adjusted according to the relationship between the domestic price and the *world market* price for a *commodity*. It is lowered when the domestic price is high compared to the world price and raised when the domestic price is low. The purpose of a variable tariff therefore is partly to bring stability to a market and partly to protect domestic producers.

VAT: see *value-added tax*.

VER: voluntary export restraint. See *voluntary restraint arrangement*.

Vertical arrangements: see *competition policy*.

Vertical foreign direct investment: this refers to *foreign direct investment* by a firm either upstream or downstream of its own production activity. For example, a cloth manufacturer might invest in a wool processing plant or in a garment factory.

Vertical *keiretsu*: see *keiretsu relationships*.

Vestigial thought: the term used by Robert Reich in his *Work of Nations* to describe economic analysis based on conditions that no longer apply, or that now apply to a limited extent only. It follows that vestigial thinking offers a fair prospect of leading to the wrong conclusions. See also *conventional wisdom* and *QWERTY principle*. [Reich 1991]

VIE: see *voluntary import expansion*.

Vienna Convention on the Law of Treaties: entered into force on 27 January 1980. It applies to treaties between states. Part II of the Convention contains provisions concerning the conclusion of treaties, the formulation of reservations, and the entry into force and provisional application of treaties. Part III is concerned with the observance, application and interpretation of treaties, Part IV with amendments and modifications, and Part V with invalidity, termination and suspension of the operation of treaties. Part VI deals with problems arising from the succession of states, hostilities and severance of diplomatic and consular relations. Part VII covers depositaries, modifications, corrections and registration of treaties. An annex deals with procedures for conciliation. The Convention is drafted in unusually clear language, and it is in fact an excellent introduction to the main elements and principles of international treaties law. See also *pacta sunt servanda* and *treaty*.

Violation cases: dispute settlement proceedings in the WTO in which a party alleges that another party is in direct breach of its obligations under one or more of the agreements administered by the WTO. See also *non-violation*.

Virtual Institute on Trade and Development: a cooperative undertaking between *UNCTAD* and several academic institutions. It was established at UNCTAD XI in June 2004. The Institute aims to assist through an interactive website the development of a global network of institutions of higher learning that have a strong focus on issues of trade development.

Virtuous circle: used in many policy areas to describe a beneficial sequence of events. One frequently mentioned in *trade policy* consists of economic development, the growth of trade and social progress. See also *social dimension of the liberalization of international trade*.

Visegrád countries: Czech Republic, Hungary, Poland and Slovakia. The name for these countries had its origin in the Declaration of Visegrád, made on 15 February 1991 by Hungary, Poland and the then Czechoslovakia. This declaration marked the first sign that these countries would seek closer cooperation with the *European Community*. Visegrád is a small town on the Danube not far from Budapest. See also *CEFTA* and *enlargement*.

Vitamin B12: a case brought by the *European Economic Community* (EEC) against the United States in 1981 on the grounds that the United States was not honouring one of its *Tokyo Round* commitments. The United States had agreed to abolish the *American Selling Price* (ASP) as part of the Tokyo Round outcome. Imports of both Vitamin B12 feedgrade and pharmaceutical quality were subject to the ASP at a *bound rate* negotiated in the *Kennedy Round*. At the time of the binding, the United States had reserved the right the change the tariff rate for goods in the event that the ASP was abolished, as seemed possible at the time. Between 1976 and 1980 Vitamin B12 of pharmaceutical quality entered the United States at a higher rate than Vitamin B12 of feedgrade quality. When the Customs Valuation Code, one of the *Tokyo Round agreements*, entered into force on 1 July 1980, the two rates were combined at the weighted average of the actual charges collected for both rates, which meant that Vitamin B12 feedgrade was now subject to a higher duty. In an understanding dated 2 March 1979 the EEC and the United States had agreed to consult on differences arising from the conversion of ASP rates. The *panel* held that the United States had no obligation to maintain a tariff rate differentiation for feedgrade quality and pharmaceutical quality Vitamin B12. The EEC could have foreseen that the ASP conversion would in some cases result in higher tariff rates, but not to the extent that it actually affected its trade. The panel therefore felt that the United States should be invited to advance the tariff reductions envisaged in the implementation of the Tokyo Round commitment on feedgrade Vitamin B12 at a rate that would allow imported vitamins to regain their traditional competitive position in the United States. [GATT BISD 29S]

Voluntarism: one of the principles pervading the activities of *APEC*. By and large, participation in many APEC sub-programs and working groups is voluntary, as long as the end-dates for full trade liberalization expressed in the *Bogor Declaration* are met. In practice, however, member economies find that it can be quite difficult to opt out of an activity when most of the others are willing to pursue it. See also *pathfinder approach*.

Voluntary export restraint: VER. See *voluntary restraint arrangement*.

Voluntary import expansion: VIE. A mechanism under a bilateral arrangement under which a country agrees, ostensibly voluntarily, to adopt measures promoting the use of imported products of particular export interest to the other country. Some fear that such arrangements could be taking the place of the *grey-area measures* which are now illegal under WTO rules.

Voluntary restraint arrangement: VRA. A bilateral arrangement whereby an exporting country (government or industry) agrees to reduce or restrict exports so that the importing country does not have to use quotas, raise tariffs or impose other import controls. VRAs have been used for steel, cars, semi-conductors and other products in so-called *sensitive sectors*. These arrangements are voluntary only to the extent that the exporting country wishes to avert an even greater threat to its trade and therefore chooses the lesser of two evils. VRAs not only deny the benefits of *comparative advantage* to efficient suppliers. They can also lead to an inefficient allocation of resources because industries affected by them may be forced to invest in less efficient markets to retain access to them. Another possible outcome is that they give exporters and importers windfall profits because of lessened competition. Michael Kostecki has proposed a useful three-part framework for considering the reasons underlying the imposition of *export quotas* under VRAs. First, there is the home-industry approach under which a certain minimum level of projected domestic demand is allocated to producers in the importing country. Second, under the exporters-first approach a certain maximum level of exports is fixed and the rest of the market left to producers in the importing country. Third, the risk of demand fluctuation in the importing country is shared equally between domestic producers and foreign suppliers. The WTO *Agreement on Safeguards* makes new VRAs illegal, and all those in existence on 1 January 1995, when the WTO was established, had to be phased out within five years. [Kostecki 1987]

Voting rights in the WTO: each WTO member is entitled to one vote regardless of its ranking as a trading nation. The *European Communities* are entitled to a number of votes equalling the number of their member states, but the member states themselves do not vote. See also *amendments to WTO agreements*, *common commercial policy*, *consensus* and *decision-making in the WTO*.

VRA: see *voluntary restraint arrangement*.

Vulnerability: the extent to which a country, household or person is likely to suffer harm from adverse developments, or the extent to which it is exposed to the risk of such events occurring. This is a concept sometimes used in the study of problems facing *least developed countries*. See also *small and vulnerable economies*, *trade and poverty*, *vulnerability index* and *weak and vulnerable countries*.

Vulnerability index: a concept currently under discussion in *United Nations* forums to permit a more objective assessment of the needs of *least developed countries* and their eligibility for treatment as a least-developed country. Various proposals have been put forward for the construction of a vulnerability index, but none enjoy widespread support.

Wage-differential argument: the proposition that countries with low wages are able to undercut countries with high wages, and that they therefore enjoy a competitive advantage. Economists have been satisfied for 150 years that this is not the case, and that the difference in wages can be accounted for by a gap in productivity. In *trade policy* the argument lives on, and it underlies part of the debate on *trade and labour standards* and the alleged need for a *social clause*. See also *pauper-labour argument* and *race-to-the-bottom argument*.

Waiver: a dispensation granted by WTO members to another member freeing it from the obligation to apply a particular provision to a defined aspect of its international trade. Under WTO rules, waivers must be approved by three-quarters of WTO members. Once granted, they are subject to periodic review. See also *Section 22 waiver*.

Washington Consensus: a much-misunderstood term coined by John Williamson proposed in 1990. He uses it for a set of eleven principles that he considered embodied the "lowest common denominator" of reforms the Washington-based financial institutions, including the *IMF* and the *World Bank*, could agree on in 1989 as suitable for Latin America. The principles were: fiscal discipline, redirection of public expenditure towards high economic returns and better income distribution, tax reform, interest rate liberalization, competitive exchange rate, trade liberalization, liberalization of inward direct investment, privatization, deregulation and secure property rights. Though Williamson saw merit in many of these principles individually, he was critical of what he saw as a tendency by the Washington-based institutions to apply this set of principles as a universal remedy. He later became particularly displeased that the term "Washington Consensus" had been appropriated by those who advocated "market fundamentalism". [Williamson 1990, Williamson 2000]

Washington Treaty on Intellectual Property in Respect of Integrated Circuits: see *Treaty on Intellectual Property in Respect of Integrated Circuits*.

Wassenaar Arrangement on Export Controls for Conventional Arms and Dual-Use Goods and Technologies: this arrangement entered into force on 1 November 1996 as the successor to *COCOM*. Its purpose is to promote transparency, exchange of views and information and greater responsibility in transfers of conventional arms and dual-use goods and technologies. The Arrangement is not directed against any state or group of states. Each member country enforces its own export control laws. Members are Argentina, Australia, Austria, Belgium, Bulgaria, Canada, Croatia, Czech Republic, Denmark,

Estonia, Finland, France, Germany, Greece, Hungary, Ireland, Italy, Japan, Latvia, Lithuania, Luxembourg, Malta, Netherlands, New Zealand, Norway, Poland, Portugal, Republic of Korea, Romania, Russia, Slovakia, Slovenia, South Africa, Spain, Sweden, Switzerland, Turkey, Ukraine, United Kingdom and the United States. See also *dual purpose exports*. [www.wassenaar.org]

Watch list: see *priority foreign countries* and *Special 301*.

Water in the tariff: an expression used in the *Uruguay Round* negotiations on *tariffication* (the conversion of *non-tariff measures* into *tariff equivalents*), but of much earlier origin. Negotiators accept that such conversions can never be completely accurate because of legitimate differences about the impact of these measures and the methods to be adopted. There were cases, however, where countries offered tariff equivalents that were obviously inflated. The difference between what would be seen as a defensible tariff conversion and the one actually offered was described as "water in the tariff" or "dirty tariffication".

WCO: see *World Customs Organization*.

Weak and vulnerable countries: in 2004 the *European Commission* proposed in the *Doha Development Agenda* negotiations that this group of countries should not be required to open its markets further, and that it should be able to benefit from increased market access in developed and developing countries. The group was described as consisting "essentially of the *G-90*", i.e. the *ACP states* and the *least developed countries*. See also *small and vulnerable economies*.

Webb-Pomerene Act: a United States law adopted in 1918 which permits American companies to combine within certain limits for the purpose of engaging in export trade. Firms may not, as a result of combining, restrain trade in the United States or restrain the export trade of competitors. That would still be illegal under the *Sherman Act* and other *antitrust laws*. See also *competition policy*.

Well-known mark: a *trademark* registered in one country which, under Article 6bis of the *Paris Convention*, may qualify for protection in another by virtue of having a reputation as such even though it is not registered there. Using a confusingly similar mark would often be considered *unfair competition*. The *WIPO Joint Recommendations Concerning Provisions on the Protection of Well-Known Marks*, adopted in September 1999, list the following criteria which may assist in determining whether a mark is well known: (a) the degree of knowledge or recognition in the relevant sector of the public (i.e. not the public at large), (b) duration, extent and geographical area of any use of the mark, (c) duration, extent and geographical area of any promotion of the mark, (d) duration and geographical area of any registration and/or applications for registration of the mark, (e) record of successful enforcement of rights in the mark and (f) the value associated with the mark. [WIPO 833(E); Abbott *et al.* 1999]

West African Economic and Monetary Union: WAEMU. Established in 1994 with the aim of achieving full economic integration with a *common external tariff*, a common *commercial policy* and harmonized economic policies. Work is under way towards a *common market*. WAEMU's members are Benin, Burkina

Faso, Côte d'Ivoire, Guinea Bissau, Mali, Niger, Senegal and Togo. Its secretariat is located at Ouagadougou, Burkina Faso. [www.uemoa.int]

West African Economic Community: established in 1967. Its membership included Benin, Côte d'Ivoire, Dahomey (now Burkina Faso), Liberia, Mali, Mauritania, Niger, Senegal and Sierra Leone. It was succeeded in 1975 by *ECOWAS*.

Western European Union: established in 1948 as the Western Union under the *Treaty of Economic, Social and Cultural Cooperation and Collective Self-Defence* and renamed Western European Union in 1954. It is mainly concerned with political and security matters and organizationally distinct from the *European Union*. It is located in Brussels.

Western Hemisphere Free Trade Agreement: see *FTAA*.

Westinghouse Uranium: a case brought in the mid-1970s by Westinghouse, a manufacturer of nuclear power stations, under United States *antitrust laws* against 29 domestic and foreign uranium suppliers. Much of the case against the foreign companies had to be conducted under *extraterritoriality* provisions. The matters raised by this case were eventually settled, partly because the foreign companies were loath to lose their access to the United States market. One of its longer-term effects was, however, the emergence of *blocking statutes* and *clawback provisions*.

Wheat flour: a case brought in 1982 by the United States before the GATT against the *European Economic Community* (EEC) on the grounds the EEC did not honour its commitments under the *Tokyo Round* Subsidies Code, one of the *Tokyo Round agreements*. Much of the case was concerned with the meaning of *equitable share of the market*, and whether the EEC had acquired more than it should have. The *panel* concluded that (a) EEC export refunds for wheat flour were a subsidy in terms of Article XVI (Subsidies) of the GATT, (b) the EEC share of world exports of wheat flour had increased considerably, and that the share of the United States and others had decreased, (c) in the light of the many factors to be considered, a ruling on whether this had resulted in "more than an equitable share" was not possible, (d) market displacement in the sense of Article 10:2(a) of the Subsidies Code, under which the effect of an export subsidy has to be taken into account, was not evident, (e) there was insufficient evidence concerning price undercutting, (f) the EEC export refunds had caused undue disturbance to the normal commercial interests of the United States, and (g) the EEC should make greater efforts to limit the use of subsidies on the exports of wheat flour. The panel also expressed concern, from a broader economic and trade policy perspective, about the effectiveness of the legal provisions regarding export subsidies and other aspects of trade in wheat flour. It found it anomalous that the EEC, which would not be able to export substantial quantities of wheat flour without subsidies, had become the world's largest exporter. It suggested that a clearer understanding of the concept of "more than an equitable share" was needed to make the concept more operational. It also questioned whether international understandings on sales on non-commercial terms adequately complemented the intended disciplines on export subsidies. [GATT SCM/42]

White Paper: a public document, originally with a white cover, which sets out actual or proposed government policy. The practice of governments in their use varies considerably. The annual White Papers issued by Japanese ministries and agencies are rather like annual reports, though they often examine in detail new policies adopted by the Government. *European Union* White Papers contain proposals for Community action in a specific area which, if received favourably, may in time be adopted as policy. Many governments issue White Papers infrequently, and then to indicate their broad policy aims in a given area. See also *Green Paper*. [www.europa.eu.int]

Wholly obtained goods: the *rules of origin* under *free-trade agreements* always distinguish between goods that were made or produced (obtained wholly) in the territories of the partners to the agreement and those that were made partly in them. Goods made or obtained wholly within these territories always enjoy *preferential tariff treatment*, but those made there partly have to undergo some test to ascertain their eligibility for preferential treatment. This is to ensure that preferences do not leak to third countries. The definition of wholly obtained goods varies between arrangements. The *United States – Singapore Free Trade Agreement*, for example, defines them as; (a) a mineral extracted from the soil, waters, seabed, or beneath the seabed; (b) a vegetable good harvested or gathered there [i.e. the party exporting the good]; (c) a live animal born and raised there; (d) a good obtained from live animals born and raised there, (e) a good obtained from hunting, trapping, fishing or aquaculture conducted there; (f) a good of sea fishing and other marine goods taken outside its waters by vessels registered or recorded there; (g) a good processed and/or made on board factory ships registered or recorded there exclusively from products taken by vessels registered there; (h) a good taken by a Party, or a person of a Party, from the seabed or beneath the seabed outside territorial waters, provided that the Party has the right to exploit that seabed; (i) waste and scrap derived from production there; (j) waste and scrap derived from used articles, provided that the articles are fit only for the recovery of raw materials; (k) recovered goods, parts left over after cleaning, inspecting, testing, etc., of the goods; and (l) a good produced exclusively from the goods listed above. See also *non-originating goods*, *originating goods* and *preferential rules of origin*.

Wider competition policy: this deals with the approach of governments to the promotion of competition in sectors currently benefiting from regulation now seen as inappropriate or the opening of so-called natural monopolies to competition. See also *antitrust laws*, *competition policy*, *deregulation*, *narrow competition policy* and *re-regulation*.

Wine: see *Agreement on Mutual Acceptance of Oenological Practices*, *Agreement on Trade-Related Aspects of Intellectual Property Rights*, *appellations of origin*, *appellation d'origine contrôlée* and *World Wine Trade Group*.

Wine gallon assessment: the United States practice, now terminated, of assessing spirits imported at less than 100 proof as though they were 100 proof since they same rule would have applied to domestic spirits of less than 100 proof if withdrawn from bond. The importer could get around this by purchasing spirits at 100 proof or more and diluting them later. This meant importing in bulk and bottling in the United States. Customers, however, generally preferred spirits bottled in the country of origin. This rule therefore disadvantaged foreign products even though there was no difference with the treatment of similar domestic products. The wine gallon assessment is often used to show how formally identical *national treatment* can in fact be discriminatory. See also *implicit discrimination*.

Wine lake: the name given in popular parlance to the wine surplus created in Europe through the *Common Agricultural Policy*. See also *butter mountain*.

Wingspread Declaration: a version of the *precautionary principle*, adopted by participants in an environmental seminar at the Wingspread Conference Center, University of Wisconsin, in January 1998. It states in part that "when an activity raises threats of harm to human health or the environment, precautionary measures should be taken even if some cause and effect relationships are not established scientifically. In this context the proponent of the activity, rather than the public, should bear the burden of proof. The process of applying the Precautionary Principle must be open, informed and democratic and must include potentially affected parties. It must also involve an examination of the full range of alternatives, including no action."

WIPO: World Intellectual Property Organization, one of the *United Nations' specialized agencies*. It is the main *intergovernmental organization* responsible for the protection of *intellectual property rights* and, through it, the encouragement of innovation and economic development. The two most important agreements administered by WIPO are the *Paris Convention for the Protection of Industrial Property* and the *Berne Convention for the Protection of Literary and Artistic Works*. The WIPO secretariat is located in Geneva. See also *Budapest Treaty on the International Recognition of the Deposit of Microorganisms for the Purposes of Patent Procedure*, *Copyright Treaty*, *folklore*, *Geneva Convention*, *Joint Recommendation Concerning Provisions on the Protection of Well-Known Marks*, *Lisbon Agreement*, *Locarno Agreement Establishing an International Classification for Industrial Designs*, *Madrid Agreement Concerning the International Registration of Marks*, *Madrid Agreement for the Repression of False or Deceptive Indications of Source on Goods*, *moral rights*, *Patent Cooperation Treaty*, *Rome Convention*, *Singapore Treaty on the Law of Trademarks*, *Strasbourg Agreement Concerning the International Patent Classification*, *Trademark Law Treaty*, *WIPO Copyright Treaty* and *WIPO Performances and Phonograms Treaty*.

WIPO Copyright Treaty: entered into force on 6 March 2002. It updates the *Berne Convention* by, for example, giving *copyright* protection to computer programs and databases (but not the material making up the database). It also covers rental rights and legal protection against the circumvention of effective technological measures used by authors. See also *Agreement on Trade-Related Aspects of Intellectual Property Rights* and *parallel import*.

WIPO Internet treaties: a name sometimes given to the *WIPO Copyright Treaty* and the *WIPO Performances and Phonogram Treaty* because they offer some *copyright* protection for digital products delivered electronically, for example, through the Internet.

WIPO Model Provisions on Protection Against Unfair Competition: produced by the International Bureau of WIPO in 1996. They represent an effort to show how Article 10bis of the *Paris Convention* could be given effect. This Article prohibits acts of *unfair competition* in matters covered by the Convention.

WIPO Performances and Phonograms Treaty: entered into force on 20 May 2002. It gives performers (actors, singers, musicians, dancers and others who perform literary or artistic works or expressions of folklore) *moral rights* (the right to claim to be identified as the performer of performances), economic rights in unfixed performances (the right to authorize the broadcasting, etc., of unrecorded performances), right of reproduction (the right to authorise direct and indirect reproduction of recordings) right of distribution and the right to make available to the public recordings of performances. These rights are balanced by rights to producers of phonograms (the person responsible for the first recording of a performance), including the right of reproduction, right of distribution, right of rental, and the right of making available phonograms. See also *neighbouring rights* and *WIPO*.

Withdrawal of trade benefits: an expression meaning the imposition of trade sanctions or resort to *retaliation*. See also *suspension of concessions or other obligations*.

Without prejudice: used to signify in negotiations that although one is willing to examine a proposition made by the other side, or that one is prepared to propose a course of action, this is done on the understanding that one's options remain open. That is, one declares that although one may be ready to consider or propose something, this is done without commitment to a specific outcome. See *ad referendum agreement* and *bracketed language*.

Worker rights: an issue identified by sections of the United States Congress as relevant to the emergence of more equitable trade practices and policies. It is partly based on the view that some governments gain a competitive advantage by denying their workforces the conditions considered normal in the United States. The issue also has a more general human rights dimension. In practice the two strands are difficult to disentangle, but for many the human rights aspect is more important. The *Trade Promotion Authority* seeks to promote respect for worker rights defined as (a) the right of association, (b) the right to organize and bargain collectively, (c) a prohibition on the use of any form of forced or compulsory labour, (d) a minimum age for the employment of children, and (e) acceptable conditions of work with respect to minimum wages, hours of work, and occupational health and safety. *Section 301* requires *USTR* to take action if a foreign country shows a persistent pattern of conduct of denying worker rights. See also *core labour standards*, *social clause*, *trade and human rights*, and *trade and labour standards*.

Working Group on the Relationship between Trade and Investment: established in December 1996 at the WTO *Singapore Ministerial Conference* to examine the relationship between *trade and investment*.

Working Group on the Interaction between Trade and Competition Policy: established in December 1996 at the WTO *Singapore Ministerial Conference* to study issues related to the interaction between *trade policy* and *competition policy*, including anti-competitive practices. Its task is to identify any areas that need to be considered further in the WTO framework. See also *trade and competition*.

Working Group on Transparency in Government Procurement: established at the December 1996 WTO *Singapore Ministerial Conference* to conduct a study on *transparency* in *government procurement* practices. It has developed elements for inclusion in an appropriate agreement, but it does not have a negotiating mandate.

Working Party on Domestic Regulation: established by the WTO on 26 April 1999 to develop disciplines aimed at ensuring that licensing requirements, technical standards and qualification requirements do not become unnecessary barriers to trade in services. The mandate for this Working Party also reflects to a large extent Article VI:4 of the *General Agreement on Trade in Services*. See also *Working Party on Professional Services*.

Working Party on Professional Services: WPPS. A WTO working party established in 1995 to examine the extent to which qualifications, licensing and standards requirements are impediments to trade in professional services, and to develop appropriate multilateral disciplines. It produced the *Guidelines for Mutual Recognition Agreements or Arrangements in the Accountancy Sector*. The WPPS was abolished on 26 April 1999 and the *Working Party on Domestic Regulation* established instead. See also *mutual recognition arrangements*.

Working Party on the Social Dimension of Globalization: established in March 2002 by the *International Labour Organization* to continue and broaden its work on the *social dimension of trade liberalization*. See also *World Commission on the Social Dimension of Globalization*.

Workshop economies: refers to economies which produce large quantities of labour-intensive products for export. [Trade and Development Report 2003]

World Association of Investment Promotion Agencies: established in April 1995 under the auspices of *UNCTAD*. Its objectives are (a) to promote and develop understanding and cooperation among investment promotion agencies, (b) to strengthen information-gathering systems and information exchange amongst investment promotion agencies, (c) to share country and regional experiences in attracting investment, (d) to help investment promotion agencies gain access to technical assistance and training through referrals to relevant agencies, (e) to facilitate access to funding and other assistance through referrals to relevant bilateral and multilateral agencies for the development and implementation of investment promotion programs, and (f) to assist investment promotion agencies in advising their respective governments in the formulation of appropriate investment promotion policies and strategies. Its secretariat is located in Geneva.

World Bank: the International Bank for Reconstruction and Development (IBRD). One of the organizations established at the 1944 United Nations Monetary and Financial Conference held at Bretton Woods. One of its main functions is to promote the development of economically less advanced member countries. It does this through the financing of projects for which private capital is not available on reasonable terms. It obtains most of its capital on international bond markets. The *World Bank* publishes annually the *World Development Report* which always contains trade policy analysis of topical interest. Among its operating agencies are the *International Development Association*, *International Finance Corporation* and the *Multilateral Investment Guarantee Agency*. See also *Bretton Woods Agreements*, *Foreign Investment Advisory Service*, *ICSID*, *high-income economies*, *lower middle-income economies*, *low-income economies*, *Poverty Reduction and Growth Facility*, *upper-middle-income economies* and *World Bank Guidelines on the Treatment of Foreign Direct Investment*.

World Bank Guidelines on the Treatment of Foreign Direct Investment: a set of voluntary principles adopted in September 1992 to address governmental treatment of good-faith foreign investors. The Guidelines do not deal with the conduct of foreign investors. The broad aim of the Guidelines is to encourage foreign investment because of its benefits in terms of improving the long-term efficiency of the host country through greater competition, transfer of capital, technology and managerial skills, enhancement of market access and expansion of international trade. Article I states that the Guidelines are based on the general premise that equal treatment of investors in similar circumstances and free competition among them are prerequisites of a positive investment environment, and that there is no suggestion that foreign investors should receive better treatment than national investors. Article II seeks an open environment for the admission of investment. Article III exhorts states to extend to investments by nationals of any other state fair and equitable treatment. Article IV deals with expropriation and unilateral alterations or terminations of contract. Article V seeks to promote the orderly settlement of disputes, either through national courts or through other agreed mechanisms. See also *investment* and *Multilateral Investment Guarantee Agency*.

World Commission on Environment and Development: established in 1983 by the *United Nations General Assembly* to work out an action plan for long-term environmental strategies and to strike a balance between the aims of development and the protection of natural resources. It was chaired by Gro Harlem Brundtland, Prime Minister of Norway. The Commission's report, *Our Common Future*, was completed in 1987. The final chapter of the report called for an international conference to review progress and to create a follow-up structure. This became the *United Nations Conference on Environment and Development*.

World Commission on the Social Dimension of Globalization: established by the *International Labour Organization* in February 2002 to examine and report on all major aspects of *globalization*. It was chaired jointly by Ms Tarja Halonen, President of Finland, and Mr Benjamin Mkapa, President of Tanzania. Its report was issued in February 2004 under the title *A Fair Globalization: Creating Opportunities for All*. The report makes many detailed recommendations, but in essence it seeks (a) a process of globalization based on universally shared values which require all actors to assume their individual responsibilities, (b) an international commitment to ensure the basic material and other requirements of human dignity for all, (c) a sustainable path of development which provides opportunities for all, expands sustainable livelihoods and employment, promotes gender equality, and reduces disparities between countries and people, and (d) a more democratic governance of globalization, which allows for greater participation, ensures accountability while fully respecting the authority of institutions of representative democracy and the rule of law. See also *social dimension of globalization*.

World Customs Organization: WCO. Previously known as the Customs Co-operation Council (CCC). Based in Brussels. It is the principal body for international cooperation to simplify and rationalize customs procedures. It developed and administers the *Harmonized System*, and it administers the *Istanbul Convention* and the *Kyoto Convention*.

World Development Report: a report published annually by the *World Bank* on issues of particular relevance to the development process. It often contains analysis on trade policy issues.

World Economic Forum: an independent non-profit organization founded in 1971 and located in Geneva. It aims to bring together people in politics, business, academia and other circles to explore current political, social and economic issues.

World Food Programme: WFP. A body established in 1961 by the United Nations. It began operations on 1 January 1963. Its mission is to manage food aid to low-income food-deficit countries as well as to victims of natural disasters. The WFP also runs programs aimed at economic and social development of these countries. It cooperates closely with the *Food and Agricultural Organization*. Its administration is located in Rome.

World Integrated Trade Solution: WITS. A database trade measures and tariffs developed jointly by *UNCTAD* and the *World Bank*. It contains data on many countries contributed by several international agencies. The database aims to help policy-makers engaged in identifying trade and negotiating options through, for example, letting them do simulations.

World Investment Report: an annual report issued by the *Commission on Investment, Technology and Related Financial Services* of *UNCTAD* on global investment trends and issues related to them. It contains much useful analysis, and its recent issues have become very readable. At times it still tends to ascribe some of the problems experienced by developing countries to actions taken, or not taken, by *transnational corporations*, but on the whole it now sees foreign investment by these corporations as a good thing, as indeed do many developing countries.

World market: an imprecise term denoting more or less the largest possible market for a good or a service. In some cases, this may well be something close to the world. In practice, however, consumer tastes, licensing agreements, distribution arrangements, levels of development, etc., mean that the actual market is rather smaller.

World Organisation for Animal Health: see *International Office of Epizootics*.

World Summit for Social Development: see *Copenhagen Declaration and Programme of Action*.

World Summit on Sustainable Development: WSSD. This summit was held in Johannesburg, South Africa, from 26 August to 4 September 2002. Its purpose was to review progress in the implementation of the work program of the *United Nations Conference on Environment and Development* of 1992, now renamed WSSD. The summit produced the Johannesburg Declaration on Sustainable Development, a political statement. It commits participants to the Johannesburg Plan of Implementation, an unusually long action plan which, partly because of its many checks and balances, defies easy summing-up. Its chapters deal with poverty eradication, changing unsustainable patterns of consumption and production, protecting and managing the natural resource base of economic and social development, sustainable development in a globalizing world, health and sustainable development, sustainable development of small island developing states, and sustainable development for Africa and other regions. See also *Agenda 21* and *Rio Declaration*.

World Trade Organization: see *WTO*.

World Trade Point Federation: see *Global Trade Point Network*.

World Trade Report: published annually by the WTO Secretariat to explore trends in world trade and highlight major issues in the world trading system. See also *Trade and Development Report*, *World Development Report* and *World Investment Report*.

World Wine Trade Group: WWTG. An association of new-world wine-producing countries. It consists of Argentina, Australia, Canada, Chile, Mexico, New Zealand, South Africa and the United States. They have adopted an agreement on mutual recognition of wine-making practices and another one on labelling.

Worst forms of child labour: defined in the *Convention Concerning the Prohibition and Immediate Action for the Elimination of the Worst Forms of Child Labour* (known as ILO Convention No 182) adopted by the *International Labour Organization* as (a) all forms of slavery or practices similar to slavery, such as the sale and trafficking of children, debt bondage and serfdom and forced or compulsory labour, including forced or compulsory recruitment of children for use in armed conflict, (b) the use, procuring or offering of a child for prostitution, for the production of pornography or for pornographic performances, (c) the use, procuring or offering of a child for illicit activities, in particular for the production and trafficking of drugs as defined in the relevant international treaties, and (d) work which, by its nature or the circumstances in which it is carried out, is likely to harm the health, safety or morals of children. The promotion of ratification and full compliance with this Convention is one of the objectives of the United States *Trade Promotion Authority*.

WTO: World Trade Organization, established on 1 January 1995 as the successor to the *GATT (General Agreement on Tariffs and Trade)* and its secretariat. Among the agreements it manages are the *General Agreement on Trade in Services* (GATS) and the *Agreement on Trade-Related Aspects of Intellectual Property Rights*. In January 2007 the WTO had 150 members. The WTO is an organization for the discussion, negotiation and resolution of trade issues covering goods, services and intellectual property. Its essential functions are administering and implementing the multilateral and plurilateral trade agreements that constitute it, acting as a forum for *multilateral trade negotiations*, seeking to resolve trade disputes, overseeing national trade policies and cooperating with other international institutions involved in global economic policy-making. *Understanding the WTO*, available on www.wto.org, offers the best description of how the WTO works. See also *WTO Agreement*. [Gallagher 2005]

WTO Agreement: formally the *Marrakesh Agreement Establishing the World Trade Organization.* Adopted on 15 April 1994 at the Marrakesh Ministerial Meeting. It established the *World Trade Organization*. It also sets out, in four annexes, the multilateral and plurilateral agreements under its jurisdiction. These are described at the end of this entry. The WTO Agreement entered into force on 1 January 1995. Article I establishes the WTO. Article II makes all of the agreements contained in Annexes 1, 2 and 3 binding on all members. The agreements listed in Annex 4 are binding only on those that have accepted them. Article III outlines the functions of the WTO. These are administering and operating the multilateral and plurilateral trade agreements, providing a forum for negotiations among members and to administer the dispute settlement mechanism. Article IV requires the *WTO Ministerial Conference* to meet at least once every two years. In the intervals the *General Council* carries out these functions. The General Council also convenes as the *Dispute Settlement Body* and the *Trade Policy Review Body*. Below the General Council are the *Council for Trade in Goods*, the *Council for Trade in Services* and the *Council for Trade-Related Aspects of Intellectual Property Rights*. Article V charges the General Council with making arrangements for effective cooperation and consultation with intergovernmental and non-governmental organizations with related responsibilities. Article VI establishes the WTO Secretariat headed by the Director-General. Article VII sets out broadly the procedures to be followed for the establishment of the budget and the financial contributions to be paid by members. Article VIII gives the WTO legal personalitywith privileges and immunities as necessary. Article IX states that the WTO follows the practice of making decisions by *consensus* as was done under the GATT. Where a decision by consensus is not possible, the matter is decided by voting as outlined in this Article. Article

X deals with amendments to the agreements administered by the WTO. Under Article XI all contracting parties of the GATT become original members of the WTO. Accession is possible under Article XII for any state or separate customs territory having full autonomy to conduct its external economic relations. Terms of the accession have to be negotiated between the applicant and existing members. Article XIII states the Agreement does not apply between two members only in the case where one member, at the time the other becomes a member, does not consent to the accession. Article XIV sets out the procedures to be followed for accepting the terms of accession to this Agreement either as an original member of the WTO or through a later accession. Article XV says that withdrawal from the Agreement becomes effective six months after the Director-General has received written notice of the intention to withdraw. Article XVI contains some miscellaneous provisions. Among these are that the WTO is to be guided by the decisions, procedures and practices followed by the GATT. If there is a conflict between the provisions of this Agreement and a provision in any of the multilateral agreements, this Agreement prevails. No reservations are possible in respect of any provision of this Agreement. Annex 1 contains the following multilateral agreements: *General Agreement on Tariffs and Trade 1994*, *Agreement on Agriculture*, *Agreement on the Application of Sanitary and Phytosanitary Measures*, *Agreement on Technical Barriers to Trade*, *Agreement on Textiles and Clothing*, *Agreement on Trade-Related Investment Measures*, *Agreement on Implementation of Article VI of the General Agreement on Tariffs and Trade 1994*, *Agreement on Implementation of Article VII of the General Agreement on Tariffs and Trade [Customs Valuation] 1994*, *Agreement on Preshipment Inspection*, *Agreement on Rules of Origin*, *Agreement on Import Licensing Procedures*, *Agreement on Subsidies and Countervailing Measures* and the *Agreement on Safeguards*. Annex 2 consists of the *General Agreement on Trade in Services*. Annex 3 is the *Agreement on Trade-Related Aspects of Intellectual Property Rights*. Annex 4 consists of the *Understanding on Rules and Procedures Governing the Settlement of Disputes*, the *Trade Policy Review Mechanism* and the *WTO plurilateral trade agreements*. [Gallagher 2005]

WTO Analytical Index: a guide to the interpretation of the agreements administered by the WTO It reflects the decisions taken by the various WTO bodies, the *panels* and the *Appellate Body*. Like its predecessor, the *GATT Analytical Index*, it is indispensable for the study and analysis of WTO law.

WTO Basic Instruments and Selected Documents: the successor to the *GATT Basic Instruments and Selected Documents*. It is the official collection of legal documents, protocols and reports adopted by the WTO, including the *Protocols of Accession* to the WTO since 1995.

WTO built-in agenda: see *built-in agenda*.

WTO-consistency: being in conformity with the rules and disciplines of the WTO. All members of the WTO have to ensure that their laws, regulations, practices, etc., meet this criterion. See also *GATT-consistency of national legislation*.

WTO Enabling Regulation: a *regulation* adopted by the *European Community* on 23 July 2001 following a finding by the *Appellate Body* that the administration of its *anti-dumping* measures in a contested case was inconsistent with the relevant WTO rules. The regulation allows the Community, whenever the *Dispute Settlement Body* adopts a report concerning anti-dumping or anti-subsidy measures taken by the Community, to "(a) repeal or amend the disputed measure; or (b) adopt any other special measures which are deemed to be appropriate in the circumstances". In other words, the regulation allows the Community to depart from its fixed framework of anti-dumping and anti-subsidy rules to provide remedies for points at issue. [Council Regulation (EC) No 1515/2001; Zonnekeyn 2002]

WTO Ministerial Conference: a conference composed of the representatives of all WTO members at ministerial level which is to meet at least once very two years. It has authority to take decisions on all matters under any of the multilateral trade agreements under its jurisdiction. The five ministerial conferences so far have been held in Singapore (9–13 December 1996), Geneva (18–20 May 1998), Seattle (30 November–3 December 1999), Doha (9–13 November 2001) and Cancún (10–14 September 2003). The sixth ministerial conference was held in Hong Kong from 13 to 18 December 2005. See also *Doha Ministerial Conference*, *Seattle Ministerial Conference* and *Singapore Ministerial Conference*.

WTO plurilateral trade agreements: these are the: *Agreement on Trade in Civil Aircraft*, *Agreement on Government Procurement*, *International Dairy Agreement* and *International Bovine Meat Agreement*. They are included in Annex 4 to the *WTO Agreement*. These agreements were originally negotiated as so-called "codes" during the *Tokyo Round*. They contain additional disciplines for each of the sector they cover. Membership of these agreements is not a precondition of WTO membership. The *International Bovine Meat Agreement* and the *International Dairy Agreement* were terminated on 31 December 1997, and they have been deleted from Annex 4. See also *Tokyo Round agreements*.

WTO plus: used especially for provisions in *free-trade agreements* and other economic cooperation agreements that go beyond the WTO framework of rules. For example, an agreement may contain provisions on competition policy. Although this expression is often used with great conviction, one may wonder whether a free-trade agreement is worth doing if does not go beyond the WTO framework of rules.

W/120: a services sectoral classification list prepared by the GATT Secretariat in 1991 to support the *Uruguay Round* negotiations on trade in services. It was issued as document MTN.GNS/W/120.

X-ing out: this can mean either a *carve-out* or a decision to leave an aspect of negotiations aside until some other problems have been solved.

Yaoundé Convention: an agreement of association between the *European Economic Community* and eighteen African developing countries giving them a range of trade and economic benefits. It was concluded on 20 July 1963 and superseded in 1975 by the *Lomé Convention*. See also *ACP–EC Partnership Agreement*.

Yarn forward rule: a *rule of origin* in *NAFTA* and other *free-trade agreements* (FTAs) concluded by the United States. It says that yarns, threads, cordage, twine and similar products are deemed to originate in the country where they are spun from their constituent fibres, or, in the case of synthetic filaments produced by extrusion, in the country where they are extruded. This means, in the case of free-trade agreements, that the yarns for the component conferring the essential character of a garment must originate within one of the FTA partners to qualify for preferential treatment. See also *fabric forward rule* and *fibre-forward rule*.

$$\boxed{Z}$$

Zanzibar Declaration: a statement adopted at a meeting in Zanzibar in July 2001 of trade ministers representing *least developed countries* in preparation for the *Doha Ministerial Conference*. It calls on WTO members to make a range of greater efforts to promote increased integration of least developed countries into the multilateral trading system. Among these are cancellation of debts, increased *official development assistance* and duty-free and quota-free access for products from these countries.

Zero binding: a legally binding undertaking in the WTO to eliminate *customs duties* altogether on defined products.

Zero-for-zero tariff reductions: a request/offer system for the achievement of *tariff* reductions in which the parties involved aim at reducing tariffs to zero (i.e. at eliminating tariffs) on a reciprocal basis in complete sectors, such as pharmaceuticals or wood products. The *Information Technology Agreement* is a recent example of this approach. See also *requests and offers* and *sectoral trade negotiations*.

Zeroing negative margins of dumping: when a group of closely related products is subject to a single anti-dumping investigation, some of the individual products may show a *positive margin of dumping* (i.e. they are deemed to have been dumped). Others may show a *negative margin of dumping* (i.e. they are deemed not to have been dumped). Once the pricing of the individual products in the group has been investigated, the relevant authority has to make an assessment for the group of products as a whole. Some of the positive and negative margins will then cancel each other out. Some investigating authorities have, however, adopted the practice of allocating any negative value a zero value. This means that only positive margins count for the assessment of the extent of dumping. Obviously, the result will always err in favour of a finding of dumping. The *Appellate Body* found in *EC – Bed Linen* that zeroing violates the WTO Anti-dumping Agreement. [WTO/DS141/AB/R; Lindsey and Ikenson 2002; Durling and Nicely 2002]

Zero-margin harmonization: a situation in which there is complete harmonization of laws, regulations, standards, etc., in one or more areas of economic activity.

Zero option: this usually refers to a United States proposal early in the *Uruguay Round* negotiations on agriculture to the effect that all subsidies distorting agricultural trade or production should be eliminated within ten years.

Zero-price knowledge: a concept used as part of the justification of protection for *intellectual property*. If knowledge always is free, i.e. available at a zero price, there will be less incentive to add to the stock of knowledge since adding will not be rewarded. Granting the originator of knowledge the right to profit from it through the protection of *intellectual property rights* provides this incentive.

Zero rating: said to be attracted by goods that enter a country free of any *customs duties*.

Zero risk: in the use of *sanitary and phytosanitary measures*, a judgment made in identifying the *appropriate level of risk* for a given product that not taking any risk is justified by the facts. In practice this usually means a complete ban on imports of that product.

Zero-sum nationalism: the view that in the conduct of international trade and economic relations countries only have a choice between winning or not winning. A win by another country, however temporary, is considered a loss by the country making the comparison. This is essentially a broader, more political, restatement of the idea underpinning *mercantilism* which sees the aim of trade as the accumulation of specie and foreign exchange, the maximization of manufacturing exports and the minimization of manufacturing imports. It completely ignores the benefits available through the *international division of labour* and the effect of *globalization* on the international economy.

Zero tolerance: used in the same sense as *zero risk*.

Zollverein: (*Ger.* customs union). Established under Prussian leadership in 1834 through unifying several local customs unions. Its growth continued through the adhesion of other German states until 1871 when it was subsumed in the newly formed German Empire. The Zollverein is given credit for much of Germany's economic progress in the first half of the nineteenth century. However, as its early years coincided with the industrial revolution in Germany, its exact contribution to economic development, though clearly substantial, is difficult to assess. See also *customs union*.

ACRONYMS USED IN INTERNATIONAL TRADE RELATIONS

AA	Association Agreement
AACP	Alleged Anti-Competitive Practice
ABAC	APEC Business Advisory Council
ABTC	APEC Business Travel Card
ACDS	APEC Communications and Database System
ACP	African, Caribbean and Pacific [States]
ACV	Agreement on Customs Valuation
ACWL	Advisory Centre on WTO Law
AD	Anti-Dumping
ADP	Anti-Dumping Practices
ADR	Alternative Dispute Resolution
AEC	African Economic Community
AEC	ASEAN Economic Community
AECF	Asia-Europe Cooperation Framework 2000
AEM	ASEAN Economic Ministers
AFL-CIO	American Federation of Labor–Congress of Industrial Organizations
AFTA	ASEAN Free Trade Area
AGOA	African Growth and Opportunity Act
AGP	Agreement on Government Procurement
AIA	Advance Informed Agreement
AIA	ASEAN Investment Area
AICO	ASEAN Industrial Cooperation [Scheme]
AIJV	ASEAN Industrial Joint Venture [Scheme]
AIS	Andean Integration System
AISP	ASEAN Integration System of Preferences
AITIC	Agency for International Trade Information and Cooperation
AJCEP	ASEAN-Japan Comprehensive Economic Partnership
ALADI	Asociación Latinoamericana de Integración (Latin American Integration Association)
ALOP	Acceptable Level [of Sanitary or Phytosanitary] Protection
AMAD	Agricultural Market Access Database
AMS	Aggregate Measure of Support
AMU	Arab Maghreb Union
ANZCERTA	Australia New Zealand Closer Economic Relations Trade Agreement

AOC	Appellation d'Origine Contrôlée
AOSIS	Alliance of Small Island States
AP	Administrative Protection
APEC	Asia Pacific Economic Cooperation
ARMS	Actions Reporting and Monitoring System (APEC)
ARO	Agreement on Rules of Origin
ASEAN	Association of South East Asian Nations
ASEM	Asia-Europe Meeting
ASP	American Selling Price
ASYCUDA	Automated System for Customs Data (UNCTAD)
ATC	Agreement on Textiles and Clothing
ATCA	Agreement on Trade in Civil Aircraft
ATL	Accelerated Tariff Liberalization
ATPA	Andean Trade Preference Act
ATPC	Association of Tin Producing Countries
ATPDEA	Andean Trade Promotion and Drug Eradication Act
AV	Adjusted Value
AV	Audiovisual [Services]
AVE	*Ad Valorem* Equivalent
BAA	Buy American Act
BDV	Brussels Definition of Value
BEM	Big Emerging Market
BFTA	Bilateral Free-Trade Agreement
BIA	Built-In Agenda (World Trade Organization)
BIMP-EAGA	Brunei-Indonesia-Malaysia East ASEAN Growth Area
BIMST-EC	Bangladesh India Myanmar Sri Lanka Thailand Economic Cooperation
BISD	Basic Instruments and Selected Documents
BIT	Bilateral Investment Treaty
BOB	Balance of Benefits
BOP	Balance of Payments
BOT	Balance of Trade
BPO	Business Process Outsourcing
BSEC	Black Sea Economic Cooperation Organization
BTA	Bilateral Trade Agreement
BTA	Border Tax Adjustment
BTN	Brussels Tariff Nomenclature
BTS	Basic Telecommunications Services
CAA	Clean Air Act (United States)
CACEU	Central African Customs and Economic Union
CACM	Central American Common Market
CACO	Central Asian Cooperation Organization
CAFTA	China-ASEAN Free-Trade Agreement

CAFTA	[United States–] Central American Free Trade Agreement
CAP	Collective Action Plan (APEC)
CAP	Common Agricultural Policy
CARICOM	Caribbean Community and Common Market
CARIFTA	Caribbean Free Trade Association
CBD	Convention on Biodiversity
CBERA	Caribbean Basin Economic Recovery Act
CBI	Caribbean Basin Initiative
CBTPA	[United States]-Caribbean Basin Trade Partnership Act
CBTS	Cross-Border Trade in Services
CCC	Commodity Credit Corporation (United States)
CCC	Customs Cooperation Council
CCFF	[IMF] Compensatory and Contingency Financing Facility
CCP	Common Commercial Policy
CCT	Common Customs Tariff
CDSOA	Continued Dumping and Subsidy Offset Act [United States]
CE	Council of Europe
CEAO	West African Economic Community
CEC	Commission of the European Community
CECA	Comprehensive Economic Cooperation Agreement
CEEC	Central and East European Countries
CEFTA	Central European Free Trade Agreement
CEMAC	Communauté Économique et Monétaire de l'Afrique Centrale
CEP	Comprehensive Economic Partnership
CEPAL	Comisión Económica de las Naciones Unidas para América Latina y el Caribe [ECLAC]
CEPT	Common Effective Preferential Tariff (ASEAN)
CER	[Australia New Zealand] Closer Economic Relations
CERDS	Charter of Economic Rights and Duties of States
CET	Common External Tariff
CF	Common Fund
CFC	Chlorofluorocarbons
CFF	Compensatory Financing Facility
CG-18	Consultative Group of Eighteen (GATT)
CGIAR	Consultative Group on International Agricultural Research
CHOGM	Commonwealth Heads of Government Meeting
CHOGRM	Commonwealth Heads of Government Regional Meeting
CI	Consular Invoice
CIEC	Conference on International Economic Cooperation
CIF	Cost, Insurance and Freight
CIS	Commonwealth of Independent States
CITES	Convention on International Trade in Endangered Species of Wild Fauna and Flora

CLMV	Cambodia, Laos, Myanmar and Vietnam
CM	Common Market
CMEA	Council for Mutual Economic Assistance
CNUCED	Conférence des Nations Unies sur le Commerce et le Développement (UNCTAD)
COCOM	Co-ordinating Committee for Multilateral Export Controls
COMESA	Common Market for Eastern and Southern Africa
COREPER	Committee of Permanent Representatives (EC)
CP	Contracting Party (GATT)
CPE	Centrally Planned Economy
CRTA	Committee on Regional Trade Agreements (WTO)
CSD	Commission on Sustainable Development
CSE	Consumer Subsidy Equivalent
CSI	Container Security Initiative
CSME	CARICOM Single Market and Economy
CSSD	Consultative Sub-Committee on Surplus Disposal
CTD	Committee on Trade and Development (WTO)
CTE	[WTO] Committee on Trade and Environment
CTH	Change in Tariff Heading
CTI	[APEC] Committee on Trade and Investment
CTS	Consolidated Tariff Schedule
CU	Customs Union
CUSTA	Canada-United States Trade Agreement
CVD	Countervailing Duties
CXT	Common External Tariff
DA	Development Assistance
DAE	Dynamic Asian Economy
DDA	Doha Development Agenda
DDAGTF	Doha Development Agenda Global Trust Fund
DEIP	Dairy Export Incentive Program
DG	Directorate-General (European Commission)
DIAC	Draft International Antitrust Code
DISC	Domestic International Sales Corporation (United States)
DME	Developed Market Economy
DPG	Domestically Prohibited Goods
DSB	Dispute Settlement Body
DSM	Dispute Settlement Mechanism
DSP	Dispute Settlement Procedures
EAC	East African Cooperation
EADB	East African Development Bank
EAEC	East Asia Economic Caucus
EAFTA	East Asia Free Trade Agreement
EAGA	East ASEAN Growth Area

EAGGF	European Agricultural Guidance and Guarantee Fund
EAI	Enterprise for ASEAN Initiative
EAI	Enterprise for the Americas Initiative
EALAF	East Asia Latin America Forum
EAS	East Asia Summit
EBA	Everything But Arms
EBOPS	Extended Balance of Payments Services Classification [IMF]
EBRD	European Bank for Reconstruction and Development
EC	European Community
ECA	Economic Cooperation Agreement
ECABS	Economic Cooperation Area of Black Sea Countries
ECAFE	[United Nations] Economic Commission for Asia and the Far East
ECDC	Economic Cooperation between Developing Countries
ECE	[United Nations] Economic Commission for Europe
ECJ	European Court of Justice
ECLAC	[United Nations] Economic Commission for Latin America and the Caribbean
ECO	Economic Cooperation Organization
ECOSOC	[United Nations] Economic and Social Council
ECOTECH	[APEC] Economic and Technical Cooperation
ECOWAS	Economic Community of West African States
ECSC	European Coal and Steel Community
ECT	Energy Charter Treaty
EDI	Electronic Data Interchange
EDIFACT	Electronic Data Interchange for Administration, Commerce and Transport
EEA	European Economic Area
EEC	European Economic Community
EEP	Export Enhancement Program
EEZ	Exclusive Economic Zone
EFTA	European Free Trade Association
EIA	Economic Integration Agreement
e-IAP	Electronic Individual Action Plan
EIT	Economies in Transition
ELS	Eco-Labelling Scheme
EME	Emerging Market Economy
EMEA	Euro-Mediterranean Economic Area
EMR	Exclusive Marketing Right
EMS	Equivalent Measure of Support
EPA	Economic Partnership Agreement
EPC	European Political Cooperation
EPG	Eminent Persons Group

EPR	Export Performance Requirement
EPZ	Export Processing Zone
ERA	Effective Rate of Assistance
ERA	Export Restraint Arrangement
ERP	Effective Rate of Protection
ESCAP	[United Nations] Economic and Social Commission for Asia and the Pacific
ESCWA	[United Nations] Economic and Social Commission for Western Asia
ESM	Emergency Safeguard Mechanism (or Measures)
EU	European Union
EURASEC	Eurasian Economic Community
EUROSTAT	Statistical Office of the European Communities
EVSL	Early Voluntary Sectoral Liberalization
FAC	Food Aid Convention
FAO	[United Nations] Food and Agricultural Organization
FCCC	[United Nations] Framework Convention on Climate Change
FCN	[Treaties of] Friendship, Commerce and Navigation
FCPA	Foreign Corrupt Practices Act (United States)
FDI	Foreign Direct Investment
FEALAC	Forum for East Asia and Latin American Cooperation
FEOGA	Fonds Européen d'Orientation et de Garantie Agricole
FIAS	Foreign Investment Advisory Service (World Bank)
FIG	Food-Importing Group
FIPA	Foreign Investment [Promotion and] Protection Agreement
FIPs	Five Interested Parties
FIRA	Foreign Investment Review Act [or Agency] (Canada)
FMO	Framework of Mutual Obligations
FOB	Free on Board
FOGS	Functioning of the GATT System
FPTA	Full Preferential Trade Agreement
FSC	Foreign Sales Corporation (United States)
FTA	Free-Trade Area, Free-Trade Agreement, Free-Trade Arrangement
FTAA	Free Trade Area of the Americas
FTAAP	Free Trade Area of the Asia-Pacific
FTZ	Free-Trade Zone
GAAP	Generally Accepted Accounting Principles
GAFTA	Greater Arab Free Trade Area
GATS	General Agreement on Trade in Services
GATT	General Agreement on Tariffs and Trade
GBT	Group on Basic Telecommunications
GCC	Gulf Cooperation Council

GDP	Gross Domestic Product
GEF	Global Environment Facility
GHS	Global Classification and Labelling System for Chemicals
GI	Geographical Indication
GII	Global Information Infrastructure
GLP	Good Laboratory Practice
GMM	Genetically Modified Micro-Organism
GMO	Genetically Modified Organism
GMP	Good Manufacturing Practice
GNG	Group of Negotiations on Goods
GNI	Gross National Income
GNS	Group of Negotiations on Services
GPA	Government Procurement Agreement
GRULAC	Group of Latin American and Caribbean Countries
GSA	Global Sugar Alliance
GSP	Generalized System of Preferences
GSTP	Global System of Trade Preferences
GTC	Grains Trade Convention
GTPN	Global Trade Point Network (UNCTAD)
HACCP	Hazard Analysis and Critical Control Points [Program]
HCOM	Host Country Operational Measures
HGP	Hormone Growth Promotant
HIC	High-Income Country
HLM	High-Level Meeting
HS	Harmonized [Commodity Description and Coding] System
HST	Hegemonic Stability Theory
HTS	Harmonized Tariff Schedule
IAC	Industrially Advanced Country
IAJJP	International Agreement on Jute and Jute Products
IAS	International Accounting Standards
IASC	International Accounting Standards Committee
IATTC	Inter-American Tropical Tuna Commission
IBA	International Bauxite Association
IBMA	International Bovine Meat Agreement
IBRD	International Bank for Reconstruction and Development
ICA	International Commodity Agreement
ICAC	International Cotton Advisory Council
ICAO	International Civil Aviation Organization
ICB	International Commodity Body
ICC	International Chamber of Commerce
ICCA	International Cocoa Agreement
ICCEC	Intergovernmental Council of Copper Exporting Countries

ICCICA	Interim Co-ordinating Committee for International Commodity Arrangements (ECOSOC)
ICCO	International Cocoa Organization
ICDR	International Commercial Dispute Resolution
ICFA	International Coffee Agreement
ICFO	International Coffee Organization
ICIDI	Independent Commission on International Development Issues
ICJ	International Court of Justice
ICPM	Interim Commission on Phytosanitary Measures
ICREA	International Commodity-Related Environment Agreement
ICSG	International Copper Study Group
ICSID	International Centre for Settlement of Investment Disputes
ICT	Information and Communication(s) Technology
ICTSD	International Centre for Trade and Sustainable Development
IDA	International Development Association
IDL	International Division of Labour
IEA	International Energy Agency
IEC	International Electrotechnical Commission
IFA	Interregional Framework Agreement
IFAD	International Fund for Agricultural Development
IFC	International Finance Corporation
IFDI	Inward Foreign Direct Investment
IFI	International Financial Institution
IGC	Intergovernmental Conference (European Union)
IGC	International Grains Council
IGO	Indication of Geographical Origin
IIA	International Investment Agreement
IIT	Intra-Industry Trade
IJO	International Jute Organization
IJSG	International Jute Study Group
ILO	International Labour Organization
ILP	[Agreement on] Import Licensing Procedures
ILSA	Iran–Libya Sanctions Act (United States)
ILZSG	International Lead and Zinc Study Group
IMC	International Meat Council
IMF	International Monetary Fund
IMO	International Maritime Organization
INR	Initial Negotiating Right
INRA	International Natural Rubber Agreement
INRO	International Natural Rubber Organization
INSG	International Nickel Study Group
IOOA	International Olive Oil Agreement

IOOC	International Olive Oil Council
IOR	Indian Ocean Rim
IOR-ARC	Indian Ocean Rim Association for Regional Cooperation
IORI	Indian Ocean Regional Initiative
IOSCO	International Organization of Securities Commissions
IP	Intellectual Property
IPC	Integrated Programme for Commodities
IPC	International Patent Classification
IPE	International Political Economy
IPEC	International Program for the Elimination of Child Labour
IPIC	Treaty on Intellectual Property in Respect of Integrated Circuits
IPPA	Investment Promotion and Protection Arrangement
IPPC	International Plant Protection Convention
IPR	Intellectual Property Right
IPR	Investment Policy Review
IRA	Import Risk Assessment
IRE	Independent Review Entity
IRSG	International Rubber Study Group
IRTM	Investment-Related Trade Measure
ISA	International Sugar Agreement
ISD	Investment Services Directive (European Community)
ISIC	International Standard Industrial Classification
ISO	International Organization for Standardization
ISO	International Sugar Organization
ISONET	International Organization for Standardization Information Network
ISPM	International Standard for Phytosanitary Measures
ITA	Information Technology Agreement
ITA	International Tea Agreement
ITA	International Tin Agreement
ITC	International Trade Centre (UNCTAD/WTO)
ITC	International Trade Commission (United States)
ITCB	International Textiles and Clothing Bureau
ITO	International Trade Organization
ITSG	International Tin Study Group
ITTA	International Tropical Timber Agreement
ITTO	International Tropical Timber Organization
ITU	International Telecommunications Union
IUCN	International Union for the Conservation of Nature and Natural Resources
IVANS	International Value-Added Network Services
IWA	International Wheat Agreement

IWC	International Wheat Council
JITAP	Joint Integrated Technical Assistance Programme
JTC	Joint Trade Committee
JUSCANZ	Japan, United States, Canada, Australia, New Zealand [plus Switzerland, Norway and Turkey]
JV	Joint Venture
KPCS	Kimberley Process Certification Scheme
LAC	Latin America(n) and Caribbean
LAC	Less-Advantaged Countries
LAFTA	Latin American Free Trade Association
LAIA	Latin American Integration Association
LASU	Large Aircraft Sector Understanding
LCA	Life Cycle Assessment
LCR	Local Content Requirement
LDC	Least Developed Country [now used in preference to LLDC]
LDC	Less-Developed Country
LLDC	Least Developed Country [obsolete use]
LMG	Like-Minded Group
LMICs	Low and Middle-Income Countries
LMO	Living Modified Organism
LTA	Long-Term Arrangement Regarding International Trade in Cotton Textiles
LTFV	Less than Fair Value
MAC	Multilateral Agreement on Competition
MAI	Multilateral Agreement on Investment
MALIAT	Multilateral Agreement on the Liberalization of International Air Transportation
MAPA	Manila Action Plan for APEC
MAV	Minimum Access Volume
MCA	Monetary Compensation Amount
MCF	Multilateral Competition Policy Framework
MCM	Ministerial Council Meeting (OECD)
MDB	Multilateral Development Bank
MEA	Multilateral Environment Agreement
METI	Ministry of Economy, Trade and Industry (Japan)
MFA	Multi-Fibre Arrangement
MFN	Most-Favoured-Nation [Treatment]
MIGA	Multilateral Investment Guarantee Agency
MIP	Minimum Import Price
MITI	Ministry of International Trade and Industry (Japan)
MMPA	Marine Mammal Protection Act (United States)
MNC	Multinational Corporation
MNE	Multinational Enterprise

MOP	Margin of Preference
MOSS	Market-Oriented Sector-Selective [talks]
MOU	Memorandum of Understanding
MRA	Mutual Recognition Agreement
MRU	Mano River Union
MSA	Multilateral Steel Agreement
MSSA	Multilateral Specialty Steel Arrangement
MTA	Material Transfer Agreement
MTA	Mini-Trading Area
MTA	Multilateral Trade Agreement
MTN	Multilateral Trade Negotiations
MTO	Multilateral Trade Organization
MTS	Multilateral Trading System
NAALC	North American Agreement on Labour Cooperation
NAFTA	New Zealand-Australia Free Trade Agreement
NAFTA	North American Free Trade Agreement
NAM	Non-Aligned Movement
NAMA	Non-Agricultural Market Access
NBIP	Non-Binding Investment Principles (APEC)
NCPI	New Commercial Policy Instrument
NEAFTA	North East Asia Free-Trade Area
NEPAD	New Partnership for Africa's Development
NFIC	Net Food-Importing Country
NFIDC	Net Food-Importing Developing Country
NGBT	Negotiating Group on Basic Telecommunications
NGMTS	Negotiating Group on Maritime Transport Services
NGO	Non-Governmental Organization
NIC	Newly-Industrializing Country
NIDL	New International Division of Labour
NIE	Newly-Industrializing Economy
NIEO	New International Economic Order
NIP	New Industrial Policy
NIS	Newly Independent States
NLC	Newly Liberalizing Country
NRA	Nominal Rate of Assistance
NRBP	Natural Resource-Based Product
NRP	Nominal Rate of Protection
NT	National Treatment
NTA	New Trade Agenda
NTA	New Transatlantic Agenda
NTB	Non-Tariff Barrier
NTE	National Trade Estimate [Report] (United States)
NTI	National Treatment Instrument

NTM	New Transatlantic Marketplace
NTM	Non-Tariff Measure
NTR	Normal Trade Relations
NTT	New Trade Theory
NWO	New World Order
OAA	Osaka Action Agenda (APEC)
OAS	Organization of American States
OAU	Organization of African Unity
ODA	Official Development Assistance
OECD	Organisation for Economic Cooperation and Development
OECS	Organization of Eastern Caribbean States
OEEC	Organisation for European Economic Cooperation
OFDI	Outward Foreign Direct Investment
OIE	Office International des Epizooties
OIF	Organisation Internationale de la Francophonie
OIV	Office international de la Vigne et du vin
OMA	Orderly Marketing Arrangement
OMC	Organisation Mondiale du Commerce [WTO]
OPEC	Organization of Petroleum Exporting Countries
OPTAD	Organization of Pacific Trade and Development
ORIGIN	Organisation for an International Geographical Indications Network
ORRC	Other Restrictive Regulations of Commerce
OTC	Organization for Trade Cooperation
OTCA	Omnibus Trade and Competitiveness Act
OVOP	One Village, One Product
PACER	Pacific Agreement on Closer Economic Relations
PAFTA	Pacific Free Trade Area
PBEC	Pacific Basin Economic Conference
PBR	Plant Breeders' Right
PDO	Protected Designation of Origin [European Community]
PECC	Pacific Economic Cooperation Council
PFC	Priority Foreign Country
PFP	Partners for Progress (APEC)
PGE	Permanent Group of Experts
PGI	Protected Geographical Indication [European Community]
PIC	Prior Informed Consent
PICTA	Pacific Island Countries Trade Agreement
PIF	Pacific Islands Forum
PITs	Partners in Transition (OECD)
PL	Public Law 480 (United States)
PMD	Processing, Marketing and Distribution [of Commodities]
PMV	Passenger Motor Vehicle

PNTR	Permanent Normal Trade Relations
PPA	Protocol of Provisional Application
PPM	Processes and Production Methods
PPTA	Partial Preferential Trade Agreement
PRA	Pest Risk Assessment
PRGF	Poverty Reduction and Growth Facility
PSE	Production Subsidy Equivalent
PSI	Pre-Shipment Inspection
PTA	Preferential Trade Agreement (or Area)
PTA	Preferential Trade Area for Eastern and Southern African States
QR	Quantitative Restriction
RA	Risk Assessment
RBPs	Restrictive Business Practices
REI	Regional Economic Integration
REIO	Regional Economic Integration Organization
REPA	Regional Economic Partnership Agreement
RHQ	Regional Headquarters
RIA	Regional Integration Arrangement
ROOs	Rules of Origin
RTA	Regional Trade Agreement
RTAA	Reciprocal Trade Agreements Act (United States)
RTIA	Regional Trade and Investment Agreement
RVC	Regional Value Content
S+D	Special and Differential [Treatment]
SAARC	South Asian Association for Regional Cooperation
SACA	Special Agreement on Commodity Arrangements
SACU	Southern African Customs Union
SADC	Southern African Development Community
SAFTA	South American Free Trade Agreement
SAP	Structural Adjustment Program
SAPTA	South Asian Preferential Trade Area
SBA	Strategic Business Alliance
SBCD	Second Banking Coordination Directive (European Community)
SCM	Subsidies and Countervailing Measures
SCU	Sectoral Customs Union
SEA	Single European Act
SEE	State Economic Enterprise
SEEFTA	Southeast European Free Trade Agreement
SELA	Sistema Económico Latinoamericano (Latin American Economic System)
SEM	Single European Market

SFTA	Sectoral Free-Trade Area
SIA	Sustainability Impact Assessment
SICA	Sistema de la Integración Centroamericana
SIDS	Small Island Developing States
SIECA	Secretaría de Integración Económica Centroamericana ([Permanent] Secretariat of the General Treaty on Central American Economic Integration)
SII	Structural Impediments Initiative
SITC	Standard International Trade Classification
SMC	Singapore Ministerial Conference
SNPA	Substantial New Programme of Action [for the 1980s for the Least Developed Countries]
SOM	Senior Officials' Meeting
SPARTECA	South Pacific Regional Trade and Economic Cooperation Agreement
SPF	South Pacific Forum
SPM	Sanitary and Phytosanitary Measures
SPS	Sanitary and Phytosanitary [Measures]
SPS	Single Payment Scheme
SPS	Special Preferential Sugar Agreement (ACP-EC)
SREZ	Sub-Regional Economic Zone
SRM	Specified Risk Material
SSG	Special Safeguard
SSP	Special Safeguard Provisions
STA	Semiconductor Trade Arrangement
STA	Short-Term Arrangement Regarding International Trade in Cotton Textiles
STABEX	[System for the] Stabilization of Export Earnings (European Community)
STDF	Standards and Trade Development Facility
STE	State-Trading Enterprise
STO	State Trading Organization
STR	Special Trade Representative
SYSMIN	System for the Promotion of Mineral Production and Exports (European Community)
TABD	Trans-Atlantic Business Dialogue
TAFTA	Trans-Atlantic Free Trade Area
TARIC	Tarif Intégré de la Communauté (Integrated Tariff of the European Community)
TBT	Technical Barriers to Trade
TCDC	Technical Cooperation between Developing Countries
TCF	Textiles, Clothing and Footwear
TDB	Trade and Development Board

TDR	Trade and Development Report
TE	Traditional Expression
TEA	Trade and Economic Agreement
TEA	Trade Expansion Act (United States)
TECA	Trade and Economic Cooperation Agreement
TEL	Temporary Exclusion List (AFTA)
TEU	[Maastricht] Treaty of European Union
TFA	Trade Facilitation Alliance
TICAD	Tokyo International Conference on African Development
TIDDB	Trade and Investment Data Database (APEC)
TIFA	Trade and Investment Facilitation Agreement
TIFA	Trade and Investment Framework Agreement
TILF	Trade and Investment Liberalization and Facilitation (APEC)
TIS	Trade in Services
TLT	Trademark Law Treaty (WIPO)
TMB	Textiles Monitoring Body
TNC	Trade Negotiations Committee
TNC	Trans-national Corporation
TOT	Transfer of Technology
TPA	Trade Promotion Agreement
TPA	Trade Promotion Authority
TPM	Trigger Price Mechanism
TPRB	Trade Policy Review Body
TPRM	Trade Policy Review Mechanism
TPSEPA	Trans-Pacific Strategic Economic Partnership Agreement
TQ	Tariff Quota
TRACLAP	Trade-Related Aspects of Competition Law and Policy
TRAINS	[UNCTAD] Trade Analysis and Information System
TRAPs	Trade-Related Antitrust Principles
TREATI	Trans-Regional EU-ASEAN Trade Initiative
TREM	Trade-Restrictive Environmental Measure
TREPS	Trade-Related Aspects of Environmental Policies
TRIMS	Trade-Related Investment Measures
TRIPS	Trade-Related Aspects of Intellectual Property Rights
TRQ	Tariff Rate Quota
TRTA	Trade-Related Technical Assistance
TSB	Textile Surveillance Body
TSSC	Textiles-Specific Safeguard Clause
TSUS	Tariff Schedule of the United States
TTMRA	Trans-Tasman Mutual Recognition Arrangement
UAP	Unprocessed Agricultural Products
UDEAC	Union Douanière et Économique de l'Afrique Centrale (*see* CACEU)

UN	United Nations
UNCAC	United Nations Convention Against Corruption
UNCED	United Nations Conference on Environment and Development
UNCITRAL	United Nations Commission on International Trade Law
UNCLOS	United Nations Convention on the Law of the Sea
UNCPC	United Nations Central Product Classification
UNCTAD	United Nations Conference on Trade and Development
UNEP	United Nations Environment Program
UNESCO	United Nations Educational, Scientific and Cultural Organization
UNFCCC	United Nations Framework Convention on Climate Change
UNGA	United Nations General Assembly
UNGASS	United Nations General Assembly Special Session
UNIDO	United Nations Industrial Development Organization
UNISTE	United Nations International Symposium on Trade Efficiency
UNSC	United Nations Security Council
UPOV	International Union for the Protection of New Varieties of Plants (*Fr.* Union Internationale Pour la Protection des Obtentions Végétales)
UR	Uruguay Round
URAA	Uruguay Round Agreements Act (United States)
USITC	United States International Trade Commission
USTR	United States Trade Representative
UTL	Unilateral Trade Liberalization
VCLT	Vienna Convention on the Law of Treaties
VER	Voluntary Export Restraint
VIE	Voluntary Import Expansion [Program]
VNM	Value of Non-originating Materials
VOM	Value of Originating Materials
VRA	Voluntary Restraint Agreement
WAEMU	West African Economic and Monetary Union
WAIPA	World Association of Investment Promotion Agencies
WCED	World Commission on Environment and Development
WCO	World Customs Organization
WDR	World Development Report
WEF	World Economic Forum
WEU	Western European Union
WFP	World Food Programme
WHFTA	Western Hemisphere Free Trade Agreement
WIPO	World Intellectual Property Organization
WIR	World Investment Report
WITS	World Integrated Trade Solution
WPPS	Working Party on Professional Services

WPPT	WIPO Performances and Phonograms Treaty
WSSD	World Summit on Sustainable Development
WTO	World Trade Organization
WWTG	World Wine Trade Group
ZFZ	Zero-for-Zero [Tariff Reductions]

BIBLIOGRAPHY

Abbott, Frederick, Thomas Cottier and Francis Gurry, 1999, *The International Intellectual Property System: Commentary and Materials*, Kluwer Law International, The Hague

Adams, R., P. Dee, J. Gali and G. McGuire, 2003, *The Trade and Investment Effects of Preferential Trading Arrangements – Old and New Evidence*, Productivity Commission Staff Working Paper, Canberra

Addo, Kofi, 2002, "The Correlation Between Labour Standards and International Trade: Which Way Forward?", *Journal of World Trade*, **36(2)**: 285–303

Addor, Felix, and Alexandra Grazioli, 2002, "Geographical Indications beyond Wines and Spirits: A Roadmap for a Better Protection for Geographical Indications in the WTO TRIPs Agreement", in *Journal of World Intellectual Property*, **5(6)**: 865–897

Adhikari, Ramesh, and Prema-chandra Athukorala, 2002, *Developing Countries in the World Trading System*, Edward Elgar, Cheltenham, UK, and Northampton MA, USA

Aho, C. Michael, 1990, "A Recipe for RIBS – Resentment, Inefficiency, Bureaucracy and Stupid Signals", in Belous, Richard S. and Rebecca S. Hartley, eds., *The Growth of Regional Trading Blocs in the Global Economy*, National Planning Association, Washington DC

American Economic Association, 1950, *Readings in the Theory of International Trade*, George Allen and Unwin Ltd, London

1968, *Readings in International Economics*, George Allen and Unwin Ltd, London

American Law Institute, 1986, *Restatement (Third) of the Foreign Relations Law of the United States*, American Law Institute Publishers, St Paul, Minn.

Anderson, James E., and J. Peter Neary, 1994, "Measuring the Restrictiveness of Trade Policy", *The World Bank Economic Review*, **8(2)**: 151–169

Anderson, Kym, 1999, *Globalization, WTO and development strategies for poorer countries*, Centre for International Economics, University of Adelaide, Adelaide

Anderson, Kym, and Bernard Hoekman, eds., 2002, *The Global Trading System*. Volume 1: Genesis of the GATT, Volume 2: Core Rules and Procedures, Volume 3: Exceptions to the Core Rules, and Volume 4: 'New' issues for the WTO, I. B. Tauris, London and New York

Anderson, Kym, Cheryl McRae and David Wilson, 2001, *The Economics of Quarantine and the SPS Agreement*, Centre for International Economic Studies, Adelaide, and AFFA Biosecurity Australia, Canberra

Anson, José, Oliver Cadot and Marcelo Olarreaga, 2003, *Tariff Evasion and Customs Corruption: Does Pre-Shipment Inspection Help?*, World Bank Policy Research Paper No. 3156, Washington DC

APEC, 2000, *Towards Knowledge-based Economies in APEC*, APEC Secretariat, Singapore

Areeda, Phillip and Donald F. Turner, 1975, "Predatory pricing and related practices under Section 2 of the Sherman Act", *Harvard Law Review*, **88(4)**: 697–733

Arnau, Juan C. Sánchez, 2002, *The Generalised System of Preferences and the World Trade Organisation*, Cameron May, London

Arrowsmith, Sue, 2003, *Government Procurement in the WTO*, Kluwer Law International, The Hague

Asian Development Bank, 2002, *Asian Development Outlook 2002*, Manila

Ataman, Aksoy, and John C. Beghin, eds., 2004, *Global Agricultural Trade and Developing Countries*, World Bank, Washington DC

Atlantic Council of the United States, 1976, *GATT-plus – Proposal for Trade Reform*, Praeger Publishers, New York

Aubion, Marc, and Moritz Meier-Ewert, 2003, *Improving the Availability of Trade Finance During Financial Crises*, WTO Discussion Paper, World Trade Organization, Geneva

Audier, J., 2000, *TRIPs Agreement: Geographical Indications*, Office for Official Publications, European Communities, Luxembourg

Aust, Anthony, 2000, *Modern Treaty Law and Practice*, Cambridge University Press, Cambridge

Bal, Salman, 2001, "International Free Trade Agreements and Human Rights: Reinterpreting Article XX of the GATT", *Minnesota Journal of Global Trade*, **10** (1): 62–108

Baldwin, Richard, 1993, *A Domino Theory of Regionalism*, NBER Working Paper No. 4465, Cambridge, MA

Bannister, Geoffrey J., and Kaman Thugge, 2001, *International Trade and Poverty Alleviation*, IMF Working Paper WP/01/54, International Monetary Fund, Washington DC

Barfield, Claude E., 2001, *Free Trade, Sovereignty, Democracy: The Future of the World Trade Organization*, American Enterprise Institute, Washington DC

Bartels, Lorand, and Federico Ortini, eds., 2006, *Regional Trade Agreements and the WTO Legal System*, Oxford University Press, Oxford

Bayard, Thomas O, and Elliott, Kimberley Ann, 1994, *Reciprocity and Realisation in U.S. Trade Policy*, Institute for International Economics, Washington DC

Bayne, Nicholas, and Stephen Woolcock, 2003, *The New Economic Diplomacy: Decision-making and negotiation in international economic relations*, Ashgate Publishing Limited, Aldershot

Belous, Richard S. and Rebecca S. Hartley, eds., 1990, *The Growth of Regional Trading Blocs in the Global Economy*, National Planning Association, Washington DC

Ben-David, Dan, Håkon Nordström and L. Alan Winters, 1999, *Trade, Income Disparity and Poverty*, WTO Special Studies 5, World Trade Organization, Geneva

Bergsten, C. Fred, 1996, *Competitive Liberalization and Global Free Trade: A Vision for the Early 20th Century*, Working Paper 96–15, Institute for International Economics, Washington DC

Bertrand, Trent, J., and Jaroslav Vanek, 1971, "The Theory of Tariffs, Taxes, and Subsidies: Some Aspects of the Second Best", *American Economic Review*, **61**: 925–931

Bhagwati, Jagdish N., 1988, *Protectionism*, MIT Press, Cambridge, MA
  1991, *The World Trading System at Risk*, Harvester Wheatsheaf, London
  1993, "Regionalism and Multilateralism: An Overview". In Jaime de Melo and Arvind Panagariya, eds., *New Dimensions in Regional Integration*, Cambridge University Press
  1995, "The Demands to Reduce Domestic Diversity among Trading Nations". In Bhagwati, Jagdish, and Robert E. Hudec, eds., *Fair Trade and Harmonization*, vol. 1, MIT Press, Cambridge, MA

2002, *Free trade today*, Princeton University Press, Princeton, NJ

ed., 1977, *The New International Economic Order: The North-South Debate*, MIT Press, Cambridge, MA

2002, *Going Alone: The Case For Relaxed Reciprocity in Freeing Trade*, The MIT Press, Cambridge, Massachusetts

Bhagwati, Jagdish N., and Hudec, Robert E., eds., 1995, *Fair Trade and Harmonization: Prerequisites for Free Trade*, 2 vols., MIT Press, Cambridge, MA

Bhagwati, Jagdish, and Arvind Panagariya, eds., 1996, *The Economics of Preferential Trade Agreements*, AEI Press, Washington, DC

Bhagwati, Jagdish N., Arvind Panagariya and T. N. Srinivasan, 1998, *Lectures on International Trade*, MIT Press, Cambridge, MA

Bhalla, A. S., and P. Bhalla, 1997, *Regional Blocks: Building Blocks or Stumbling Blocks?*, Macmillan Press Ltd, London

Birnie, P. W., and A. E Boyle, 2002, *International Law and the Environment*, 2nd edn., Oxford University Press, Oxford

Blakeslee, Merrit R. and Carlos A Garcia, 1999, *The Language of Trade*, updated edition, United States Department of State, Office of International Information Programs, Washington DC (also available on *http://usinfo.state.gov/products/pubs/trade/*

Bora, Bijit, Aki Kuwahara and Sam Laird (2002), *Quantification of Non-Tariff Measures*, UNCTAD Policy Issues in International Trade and Commodities Study Series No. 18, New York and Geneva

Bourgeois, Jacques H. J., Frédérique Berrod and Eric Gippini Fournier, eds. (no date), *The Uruguay Round Results: A European Lawyers' Perspective*, European Inter University Press, Brussels

Brack, Duncan, 1999, "Environmental Treaties and Trade: Multilateral Environmental Agreements and the Multilateral Trading System". In Sampson, Gary P., and W. Bradnee Chambers, *Trade, Environment, and the Millennium*, United Nations University Press, Tokyo

Brander, James A., 1995, *Strategic Trade Policy*, NBER Working Paper No. 5020, National Bureau of Economic Research, Cambridge, MA

Brandt Commission, 1980, *North-South: A Programme for Survival*, Pan Books, London
   1983, *Common Crisis: North-South: Cooperation for World Recovery*, Pan Books, London

Brenton, Paul, Henry Scott and Peter Sinclair, 1997, *International Trade: A European Text*, Oxford University Press, Oxford

Brown, William Adams, 1950, *The United States and the Restoration of World Trade*, Brookings Institution, Washington DC

Brownlie, Ian, 1990, *Principles of Public International Law*, 4th edn., Clarendon Press, Oxford

Butler, Nicholas, 1983, "The Ploughshares War Between Europe and America", *Foreign Affairs*, **62(1)**: 105–122

Cameron, James, 1999, "The Precautionary Principle". In Sampson, Gary P., and W. Bradnee Chambers, *Trade, Environment, and the Millennium*, United Nations University Press, Tokyo

Carbaugh, Robert J., 2000, *International Economics*, 7th edn., South-Western College Publishing, Cincinnati

Centre for Human Rights, 1988, *Human Rights: A Compilation of International Instruments*, United Nations, New York

Chang, Sea-Jin, 2003, *Financial Crisis and Transformation of Korean Business Groups: The Rise and Fall of Chaebols*, Cambridge University Press, Cambridge

Cheng, Chia-Jui, ed., 1999, *Basic Documents on International Trade Law*, 3rd edn., Kluwer Law International, The Hague

Cho, Sungjoon, 1998, *GATT Non-Violation Issues in the WTO Framework: Are they the Achilles Heel of the Dispute Settlement Process?*, Jean Monnet Working Paper No. 9/98, New York University School of Law, New York

Chowdhury, Subrata Ray, Erik M. G. Denters and Paul J. M. de Wart, 1992, *The Right to Development in International Law*, Martinus Nijhoff Publishers, Dordrecht

Cline, William R., ed., 1983, *Trade Policy in the 1980s*, Institute for International Economics, Washington DC

Coats, A.W, 1987, *Mercantilism: Economic Ideas, History, Policy*, University of Newcastle, Australia

Cohn, Theodore H., 2002, *Governing Global Trade: International Institutions in Conflict and Convergence*, Ashgate Publishing Limited, Aldershot

Cohn, Theodore H., 2003, *Global Political Economy: Theory and Practice*, 2nd edn., Longman, New York

Commission of the European Communities, 2003, *Green Paper on the Future of Rules of Origin in Preferential Trade Arrangements*, Brussels

Commission on Intellectual Property Rights, 2002, *Integrating Intellectual Property Rights and Development Policy*, CIPR, London

Conybeare, John A. C., 1987, *Trade Wars: The Theory and Practice of International Commercial Rivalry*, Columbia University Press, New York

Cook, Gary, ed., 1998, *The Economics and Politics of International Trade*, Freedom and Trade, vol. II, Routledge, London and New York

Corden, W. Max, 1971, *The Theory of Protection*, Clarendon Press, Oxford
1974, *Trade Policy and Economic Welfare*, Clarendon Press, Oxford
1985, *Protection, Growth and Trade*, Basil Blackwell, London

Corbett, Richard, 1993, *The Treaty of Maastricht*, Longman Current Affairs, London

Cossy, Mireille, 2006, *Determining likeness under the GATS: Squaring the circle*, Staff Working Paper ERSD-2006-08, World Trade Organization, Geneva

Cottier, Thomas, and Petros C. Mavroidis, 2003, *Intellectual Property: Trade, Competition and Sustainable Development*, University of Michigan Press, Ann Arbor

Cowhey, Peter F., and Jonathan D. Aronson, 1993, "A new trade order", *Foreign Affairs*, **72(1)**: 183–195

Craig, Paul, and Grainne de Búrca, 2003, *EU Law: Text, Cases and materials*, 3rd edn., Oxford University Press, Oxford

Crawford, James, 2000, *Third report on State responsibility*, International Law Commission, United Nations General Assembly document A/CN.4/507

Crawford, J. G., 1968, *Australian Trade Policy 1942–1966: A Documentary History*, Australian National University, Canberra

Crawford, Jo-Anne, and Roberto V. Fiorentino, 2005, *The Changing Landscape of Regional Trade Agreements*, WTO Staff Discussion Paper No. 8, World Trade Organization, Geneva

Croome, John, 1995, *Reshaping the World Trading System*, World Trade Organization, Geneva
1999, *Guide to the Uruguay Agreements*, Kluwer Law International, The Hague

Cuddington, John T., Rodney Ludema and Shamila A. Jayasuria, 2002, *Prebisch-Singer Redux*, Central Bank of Chile Working Papers, No. 140, Santiago

Curzon, Gerard, 1965, *Multilateral Commercial Diplomacy*, Michael Joseph, London

Dabbah, Maher, M., 2003, *The Internationalisation of Antitrust Policy*, Cambridge University Press, Cambridge

Dam, Kenneth W., 1970, *The GATT: Law and International Economic Organisation*, University of Chicago Press

2001, *The Rules of the Global Game: A New Look at US International Policymaking*, University of Chicago Press, Chicago and London

Das, Bhagirath Lal, 1999, *The World Trade Organization: A Guide to the Framework of International Trade*, Zed Books Ltd., London and New York

Davidow, Joel, and Hal Shapiro, 2003, "The Feasibility and Worth of a World Trade Organization Competition Agreement", *Journal of World Trade*, **37(1)**: 49–68

Deardorff, Alan V., 1990, "Economic Perspectives in Anti-Dumping Law", in Jackson, John H. and E. A. Vermulst, eds., *Antidumping Law and Practice: A Comparative Study*, HarvesterWheatsheaf, London

The Terms of Trade and Other Wonders: Deardorff's Glossary of International Economics, *http://www-personal.umich.edu/~alandear/glossary*

2003, "What Might Globalisation's Critics Believe", *World Economy*, **26(5)**: 639–658

Deardorff, Alan V., and Robert M. Stern, 1997, *Measurement of Non-Tariff Barriers*, Economics Department Working Papers No. 179, OECD, Paris

De la Torre, Augusto, and Margaret R. Kelly, 1992, *Regional Trade Arrangements*, International Monetary Fund, Washington DC

De Melo, Jaime, and Arvind Panagariya, eds., 1993, *New Dimensions in Regional Integration*, Cambridge University Press, Cambridge

Dent, Christopher M., 2006, *New Free Trade Agreements in the Asia-Pacific*, Palgrave Macmillan, Houndmills

Department of Foreign Affairs and Trade (Australia) and Ministry of Foreign Trade and Economic Cooperation (China), 2001, *Paperless Trading: Benefits to APEC*, Canberra

Desker, Barry, 2004, "In defence of FTAs: from purity to pragmatism in East Asia", *The Pacific Review*, **17(1)**: 3–26

Destler, I. M., 1993, *American Trade Politics*, 3rd edn., Institute for International Economics, Washington DC

Didier, Pierre, 2001, "The WTO Anti-Dumping Code and EC Practice: Issues for Review in Trade Negotiations", *Journal of World Trade*, **35(1)**: 33–54

Dollar, David, 2002, "Global Economic Integration and Global Inequality". In Gruen, David, Terry O'Brien and Jeremy Lawson, eds., *Globalisation, Living Standards and Inequality: Recent Progress and Continuing Challenges*, Reserve Bank of Australia and Australian Treasury, Canberra

Dryden, S., 1995, *Trade Warriors: USTR and the American Crusade for Free Trade*, Oxford University Press, Oxford and New York

Durling, James P., and Matthew R. Nicely, 2002, *Understanding The WTO Anti-Dumping Agreement: Negotiating History and Subsequent Interpretation*, Cameron May, London

Eeckhout, Piet, 2004, *External Relations of the European Union: Legal and Constitutional Foundations*, Oxford University Press, Oxford

Estevadeordal, Antoni, and Kati Suominen, 2003, *Rules of Origin in the World Trading System*, Paper Prepared for the Seminar on Regional Trade Agreements and the WTO, 14 November 2003, World Trade Organization, Geneva

Esty, Daniel C., 1994, *Greening the GATT: Trade, Environment and the Future*, Institute for International Economics, Washington DC

Evans, Gail E., 2000, *Lawmaking under the Trade Constitution: A Study in Legislating by the World Trade Organization*, Kluwer Law International, The Hague, London, Boston

Evans, John W., 1972, *The Kennedy Round in American Trade Policy*, Harvard University Press

Fieldhouse, D. K., 1999, *The West and the Third World*, Blackwell Publishers, Oxford

Fikentscher, Wolfgang, and Ulrich Immenga, 1995, *Draft International Antitrust Code: Kommentierter Entwurf eines internationalen Wettbewerbsrechts*, Nomos, Baden-Baden

Finger, J. Michael, 1998, *GATT Experience with Safeguards: Making Economic and Political Sense of the Possibilities that the GATT Allows to Restrict Imports*, World Bank Policy Research Working Papers WPS2000, Washington DC

    ed., 1993, *Antidumping: How it Works and Who Gets Hurt*, The University of Michigan Press, Ann Arbor

    ed., 2002, *Institutions and Trade Policy*, Edward Elgar, Cheltenham, UK

Francois, Joseph F., and Kenneth A. Reinert, 1997, *Applied Methods for Trade Policy Analysis: A Handbook*, Cambridge University Press, Cambridge

Francois, Joseph, and Will Martin, 2003, "Formula Approaches for Market Access Negotiations", *The World Economy*, vol. 26, number 1, pp. 1–23

Frankel Jeffrey A. and Andrew K. Rose, 2002, *Is Trade Good or Bad for the Environment? Sorting out the Causality*, Working Paper 9201, National Bureau of Economic Research, Cambridge, MA

Gadrey, Jean, 2003, *New Economy, New Myth*, Routledge, London and New York

Galbraith, John Kenneth, 1958, *The Affluent Society*, Hamish Hamilton, London

    1981, *A Life in Our Times*, Houghton Mifflin Company, Boston

Gallagher, Peter, 2000, *Guide to the WTO and Developing Countries*, Kluwer Law International, The Hague, and World Trade Organization, Geneva

    2005, *The First Ten Years of the WTO*, Cambridge University Press, Cambridge, and World Trade Organization, Geneva

Garner, Richard N., 1969, *Sterling-Dollar Diplomacy*, new, expanded edition, Oxford University Press

GATT documents:

    GATT/CP/106, Report of the Intersessional Working Party on the Complaint of Czechoslovakia Concerning the Withdrawal by the United States of a Tariff Concession under the Terms of Article XIX

    SCM/42, European Economic Community – Subsidies on Exports of Wheat Flour

    SCM/43, European Economic Community – Subsidies on Export of Pasta Products

GATT Secretariat, 1979, *The Tokyo Round of Multilateral Trade Negotiations*, Geneva

    1952–1994, *General Agreement on Tariffs and Trade: Basic Instruments and Selected Documents*, GATT, Geneva

Gervais, Daniel, 2003, *The TRIPS Agreement: Drafting History and Analysis*, 2nd edn., Sweet & Maxwell, London

Ghatak, Subrata, 2003, *Introduction to Development Economics*, 4th edn., Routledge, London and New York

Gillingham, John, 2003, *European Integration, 1950–2003: Superstate or New Market Economy*, Cambridge University Press, Cambridge

Gilpin, Robert, 1987, *The Political Economy of International Relations*, Princeton University Press

Glick, Leslie Alan, 1984, *Multilateral Trade Negotiations: World Trade After the Tokyo Round*, Rowman & Allanheld, Totowa, NJ

Godek, Paul E., 1986, "The Politically Optimal Tariff: Tariff Levels of Trade Restrictions across Developed Countries", *Economic Inquiry*, vol. 24, no. 4, pp. 587–593

Goklany, Indur M., 2001, *The Precautionary Principle: A Critical Appraisal of Environment Risk Assessment*, Cato Institute, Washington DC

Goode, Walter, 2005, *Negotiating free-trade agreements: a guide*, Department of Foreign Affairs and Trade, Canberra

Green, Roy E., ed., 2003, *The Enterprise for the Americas Initiative*, Praeger Publishers, Westport

Group of Lisbon, 1995, *Limits to Competition*, MIT Press, Cambridge MA

Gruen, David, Terry O'Brien and Jeremy Lawson, eds., 2002, *Globalisation, Living Standards and Inequality: Recent Progress and Continuing Challenges*, Reserve Bank of Australia and Australian Treasury, Canberra

Hansson, Göte, ed., 1992, *Trade, Growth and Development: The Role of Politics and Institutions*, Routledge, London and New York

Harrison, Mark, 2001, *"Pop mercantilism"? Staff and student attitudes in economics at Warwick*, www.warwick.ac.uk/economics/harrison/comment/mercantilism.pdf

Hart, Michael M. and William A. Dymond, 2002, *NAFTA Chapter 11: Precedents, Principles and Prospects*, paper given at NAFTA Chapter 11 Conference, Carleton University, 18 January

Heyne, Paul, 1991, *The Economic Way of Thinking*, 6th edn., Macmillan Publishing Company, New York

Hill, T. P., 1977, "On Goods and Services", *Review of Income and Wealth*, **23**, 315–338

Hoekman, Bernard, 1995, *Trade Laws and Institutions: Good Practices and the World Trade Organization*, World Bank Discussion Papers No. 282, World Bank, Washington DC
    1996, *Trade and Competition Policy in the WTO System*, Centre for Economic Policy Research Discussion Paper No. 1501, London

Hoekman, Bernard and Michael Kostecki, 1995, *The Political Economy of the World Trading System: From GATT to WTO*, Oxford University Press, Oxford

Hoekman, Bernard, Aaditya Mattoo and Philip English, eds., 2002, *Development, Trade and the WTO*, The World Bank, Washington DC

Hope, Einar, and Per Maeleng, eds., 1998, *Competition and Trade Policies: coherence or conflict?*, Routledge, London and New York

Horlick, Gary N., and Steven A. Sugarman, 1999, "Antidumping Policy as a System of Law". In Mendoza, Miguel Rodríguez, Patrick Low and Barbara Kotschwar, eds., *Trade Rules in the Making: Challenges in Regional and Multilateral Negotiations*, Organization of American States, Brookings Institution Press, Washington DC

Hornbeck, J. F., and William H. Cooper, 2006, *Trade Promotion Authority (TPA): Issues, Options and Prospects for Renewal*, Congressional Research Service, Washington, DC

Howse, Robert, 2002, "Human Rights in the WTO: Whose Rights, What Humanity? Comment on Petersmann, *European Journal of International Law*, **13(3)**: 651–660

Hudec, Robert E., 1999, *Essays on the Nature of International Trade Law*, Cameron May, London

Hudec, Robert E., Daniel L. M. Kennedy and Mark Sgarbossa, 1993, "A Statistical Profile of GATT Dispute Settlement Cases: 1948–1989", *Minnesota Journal of Global Trade*, **2(1)**: 1–113

Hufbauer, Gary Clyde, Jeffrey J. Schott and Kimberley Ann Elliott, 1990, *Economic Sanctions Reconsidered: History and Current Policy*, Institute for International Economics, Washington DC

Inama, Stefano, 2000, "Non-Preferential Rules of Origin". In *A Positive Agenda for Developing Countries: Issues for Future Trade Negotiations*, United Nations Conference on Trade and Development, New York and Geneva

Ingco, Merlinda D., John D. Nash and Kevin M. Cleaver, 2004, *Agriculture and the WTO: Creating a Trading System for Development*, World Bank, Washington DC

International Labour Office, 2003, *Fundamental rights at work and international labour standards*, International Labour Organization, Geneva

International Trademark Association, 2000, *Issue Brief: Lisbon Agreement for the Protection of Appellations of Origin: Violation of the TRIPS Agreement*, New York

Irwin, Douglas A., 1996, *Against the Tide: An Intellectual History of Free Trade*, Princeton University Press, Princeton, New Jersey

   2002, *Free trade under fire*, Princeton University Press, Princeton, NJ

Israel, Fred L., ed., 1967, *Major Peace Treaties of Modern History, 1648–1967*, Chelsea House Publishers, New York

Jackson, John H., 1969, *World Trade and the Law of the GATT*, The Bobs-Merril Company, Indianapolis, Kansas City, New York

   1997, *The World Trading System: Law and Policy of International Economic Relations*, MIT Press, Cambridge MA

   2000, *The Jurisprudence of the GATT and the WTO*, Cambridge University Press, Cambridge

Jackson, John H. and Alan O. Sykes, eds., 1997, *Implementing the Uruguay Round*, Clarendon Press, Oxford

Jackson, John H. and E. A. Vermulst, eds., 1990, *Antidumping Law and Practice: A Comparative Study*, HarvesterWheatsheaf, London

Jackson, John H. and William A. Davey, 1986, *Legal Problems of International Economic Relations*, 2nd edn., West Publishing, St Paul

Johnson, Harry G., 1968, "Tariffs and Economic Development: Some Theoretical Issues". In Theberge, J. D., ed., *Economics of Trade and Development*, John Wiley & Sons, New York

Josling, Timothy E., Stefan Tangermann and T. K. Warley, 1996, *Agriculture in the GATT*, St. Martin's Press, New York

Jung, Youngjin, and Sun Hyeong Lee, 2003, "The Legacy of the Byrd Amendment Controversies: Rethinking the Principle of Good Faith", *Journal of World Trade*, **37(5)**: 921–958

Kahnemann, D. and A. Tversky, 1979 "Prospect Theory: an analysis of decision under risk", *Econometrica*, 263–291

Kasahara, Shigehisa, 2004, *The Flying Geese Paradigm: A Critical Study of its Application to East Asian Regional Development*, Discussion Paper No. 169, United Nations Conference on Trade and Development, Geneva

Keck, Alexander, and Patrick Low, 2004, *Special and Differential Treatment in the WTO: Why, When and How?*, Staff Working Paper ERSD-2004-03, World Trade Organization, Geneva

Kindleberger, Charles P., 1973, *The World in Depression 1929–1939*, Allen Lane, The Penguin Press, Harmondsworth

Kirton, John J., and Maclaren, Virginia W., 2002, *Linking Trade, Environment and Social Cohesion: NAFTA experiences, global challenges*, Ashgate Publishing Company, Aldershot

Kjeldsen-Kragh, Søren, 2001, *International Trade Policy*, Copenhagen Business School Press, Copenhagen

Klabbers, Jan, 1992, "Jurisprudence in International Law: Article XX of GATT", *Journal of World Trade*, **26(2)**: 63–94

Kohl, Richard, ed., 2003, *Globalization, Poverty and Inequality*, OECD, Paris

Komuro, Norio, 1998, "*Kodak-Fuji Film* Dispute and the WTO Panel Ruling", *Journal of World Trade*, **32(5)**: 161–217

Kostecki, Michael (1987), "Export restraint arrangements and trade liberalisation", *The World Economy*, **10(4)**: 425–454

Kreinin, Mordechai E., 1998, *International Economics: A Policy Approach*, The Dryden Press, Fort Worth, TX

Krugman, Paul R., 1986, *Strategic Trade Policy and the New International Economics*, MIT Press, Cambridge, MA

1990, *Rethinking International Trade*, MIT Press, Cambridge, MA

1991, "The Move Toward Free Trade Zones". In *Symposium sponsored by the Federal Reserve Board of Kansas City on Policy Implications of Free Trade and Currency Zones*

1994, *Peddling Prosperity*, W. W. Norton & Company, New York and London

1998, "Ricardo's difficult idea: why intellectuals don't understand comparative advantage". In Gary Cook, ed., *The Economics and Politics of International Trade*, Freedom and Trade, vol. II, Routledge, London and New York

Krugman, Paul R., and James Brander, 1983, "A Reciprocal Dumping" Model of International Trade", *Journal of International Economics*, **15**: 313–321. Reprinted in Krugman, Paul R., 1990, *Rethinking International Trade*, MIT Press, Cambridge, MA

Laird, Samuel, 1997, "Quantifying Commercial Policies". In Francois, Joseph E., and Kenneth A. Reinert, *Applied Methods for Trade Policy Analysis: A Handbook*, Cambridge University Press, Cambridge

1999, "Regional Trade Agreements: Dangerous Liaisons?", *World Economy*, **22(9)**: 1179–1200

Laird, S., and Vossenar, R., 1991, "Porqué nos preocupan las bareras no arancelarias?", *Informacion Comercial Española*, pp. 31–54

LaNasa III, Joseph A., 1995, *An Evaluation of the Uses and Importance of Rules of Origin, and the Effectiveness of the Uruguay Round's Agreement on Rules of Origin in Harmonizing and Regulating Them*, Jean Monnet Working Paper 1/96, New York University School of Law, New York

Lane, Timothy, and Steven Phillips, 2000, *Does IMF Financing Result in Moral Hazard?*, IMF Working Paper 00/68, International Monetary Fund, Washington DC

Lawrence Robert Z., ed., 1998, *Brookings Trade Forum 1998*, Brookings Institution Press, Washington, DC

Leclerc, Jean-Marc, 1999, "Reforming Anti-Dumping Law: Balancing the Interests of Consumers and Domestic Industries", *McGill Law Journal*, **44**, 111–140.

Lee, Shi Young, and Sung Hee Jun, 2004, "On the Investigation Effects of United States Anti-dumping Petitions", *Journal of World Trade*, **38(3)**: 425–439

Lee Yong-shik, 2003, *Safeguard Measures in World Trade: The Legal Analysis*, Kluwer Law International, The Hague

Lerner, A. P., 1936, "The Symmetry between Import and Export Taxes", *Economica*, **III(11)**: 306–313. In American Economic Association, *Readings in International Economics*, vol. XI, George Allen and Unwin Ltd, London

Lim, Hoe, 2001, "Trade and Human Rights: What's at Issue?", *Journal of World Trade*, **35(2)**: 275–300

Lindsey, Brink, and Dan Ikenson, 2002, *Antidumping 101: The Devilish Details of "Unfair Trade" Law*, Trade Policy Analysis Paper No. 20, Cato Institute, Washington DC

López, Ramó, and Arvind Panagaryia, 1992, "On the Theory of Piecemeal Tariff Reform: The Case of Pure Imported Intermediate Inputs", *American Economic Review*, **82(3)**: 615–625

Magnusson, Lars, 1994, *Mercantilism: The Shaping of an Economic Language*, Routledge, London and New York

Maneschi, Andrea, 1998, *Comparative Advantage in International Trade*, Elgar, Cheltenham

Marceau, Gabrielle, 1994, *Anti-Dumping and Anti-Trust Issues in Free Trade Areas*, Clarendon Press, Oxford

2002, "WTO Dispute Settlement and Human Rights", *European Journal of International Law*, **13(4)**: 753–814

Marceau, Gabrielle, and Joel P. Trachtman, 2002, "The Technical Barriers to Trade Agreement, the Sanitary and Phytosanitary Measures Agreement, and the General Agreement on Tariffs and Trade: A Map of the World Trade Organization Law of Domestic Regulation of Goods", *Journal of World Trade*, **36(5)**: 811–881

Marconini, Mario, 2005, *Emergency safeguard measures in the GATS: Beyond feasible and desirable*, United Nations Conference on Trade and Development, Geneva

Martin, Will, and Winters, Alan L., eds., 1995, *The Uruguay Round and the Developing Countries*, World Bank Discussion Papers No. 307, World Bank, Washington DC

Maskus, Keith E., 2000, "Parallel Imports", *The World Economy*, **23(9)**: 1269–1284

Mastel, Greg, 1996, *American Trade Laws after the Uruguay Round*, M. E. Sharpe, Armonk, New York

Mathis, James H., 2002, *Regional Trade Agreements in the GATT/WTO: Article XXIV and the Internal Trade Requirement*, T M C Asser Press, The Hague

Matsushita, Mitsuo, Thomas J. Schoenbaum and Petros C. Mavroidis, 2003, *The World Trade Organization: Law, Practice and Policy*, Oxford University Press, Oxford

Mavroidis, Petros C., 2000, "Remedies in the WTO Legal System: Between a Rock and a Hard Place", *European Journal of International Law*, **11(4)**: 763–813

2001, *Amicus Curiae Briefs Before the WTO: Much Ado About Nothing*, Jean Monnet Working Paper 2/01, New York University School of Law, New York

Mayer, Jörg (2002), "The Fallacy of Composition: A Review of the Literature", *The World Economy*, **25(6)**: 875–894

McCulloch, Neil, L. Alan Winters and Xavier Cirera, 2002?, *Trade Liberalization and Poverty: A Handbook*, Centre for Economic Policy Research, London

McDonald, Brian, 1998, *The World Trading System: The Uruguay Round and Beyond,* Macmillan Press Ltd, London

McKeough, Jill, 1992, *Blakeney & McKeough: Intellectual Property: Commentary and Materials*, 2nd edn., The Law Book Company, Melbourne

McTaggart, Douglas, Christopher Findlay and Michael Parkin, 1996, *Economics*, 2nd edn., Addison-Wesley Publishing Company, Sydney

Meade, J. E., 1955, *Trade and Welfare*, Oxford University Press, London

Melaku Geboye Desta, 2002, *The Law of International Trade in Agricultural Products: From the GATT 1947 to the WTO Agreement on Agriculture*, Kluwer Law International, The Hague, London, New York

Mendoza, Rodríguez Miguel, Patrick Low and Barbara Kotschwar, eds., 1999, *Trade Rules in the Making: Challenges in Regional and Multilateral Negotiations*, Organization of American States, Brookings Institution Press, Washington, DC

Ministry of Economic Development, 2002, *Bioprospecting in New Zealand: Discussing the options*, Wellington

Ministry of Foreign Affairs and Trade, 2001, *United Nations Handbook 2001*, Wellington

Moon, Bruce E., 2000, *Dilemmas of International Trade*, Westview Press, Boulder, Colorado

Moore, Mike, ed., 2004, *Doha and Beyond: The Future of the Multilateral Trading System*, Cambridge University Press, Cambridge

Mueller, Felix, 2003, "Is the General Agreement on Tariffs and Trade Article XIX 'Unforeseen Developments Clause' Still Effective under the Agreement on Safeguards?", *Journal of World Trade*, **37(6)**: 1119–1151

Murinde, Victor, ed., 2001, *The Free Trade Area of the Common Market for Eastern and Southern Africa*, Ashgate, Aldershot

Nagai, Fumio, 2003, "Thailand's FTA Policy: Continuity and Change between the Chuan and Thaksin Governments, in Okamoto, Jiro, ed., *Whither Free Trade Agreements? Proliferation, Evaluation and Multilateralization*, Institute of Developing Economies, Chiba

Naiki, Yoshiko, 2004, "The Mandatory/Discretionary Doctrine in WTO Law: The *US – Section 301* Case and its Aftermath", *Journal of International Economic Law*, **7(1)**: 23–72

Ndlela, Daniel B., 1992, "Regional economic integration and intra-Africa trade: Issues for development". In Hansson, Göte, ed., *Trade, Growth and Development: The Role of Politics and Institutions*, Routledge, London and New York

Neufeld, Inge Nora, 2001, *Anti-Dumping and Countervailing procedures – Use or Abuse? Implications for Developing Countries*, Policy Issues in International Trade and Commodities Study Series No. 9, United Nations Conference on Trade and Development, New York and Geneva

Nicolaïdis, Kalypso, 1997, "Managed Mutual Recognition: The New Approach to the Liberalization of Professional Services". In OECD, *Liberalization of Trade in Services*, Paris

OECD, 1997, *Liberalization of Trade in Services*, OECD Secretariat, Paris
   Economic Outlook (twice a year)
   2000, *International Trade and Core Labour Standards*, OECD, Paris
   2001, *DAC Guidelines on Strengthening Trade Capacity for Development,* Paris
   2001, *Trade and Competition: Options for a Greater Coherence*, OECD, Paris

2002, *The Size of Government Procurement Markets*, OECD, Paris

2003, *Multifunctionality: the Policy Implications*, OECD, Paris

OECD documents:

C(98)35/FINAL, *Recommendation of the Council Concerning Effective Action Against Hard Core Cartels*

SG/EC(98)9REV5 *OECD Ministerial Conference "A Borderless World: Realising the Potential of Global Electronic Commerce", OECD Action Plan for Electronic Commerce*

COM/AGR/APM/TD/WP(2000)15/FINAL, *Appellations of Origin and Geographical Indications in OECD Member Countries: Economic and Legal Implications*

COM/TD/DAFFE/CLP(2001)21/FINAL, *The Role of "Special and Differential Treatment" at the Trade, Competition and Development Interface*

CCNM/GF/TR/M(2001)3, *Trade Policy Issues: The Labour, Environment and Competition Dimensions*

TD/TC(2002)8/FINAL, *Regional Trade Agreements and the Multilateral Trading System*

Office of the United States Trade Representative, 2003, *2003 Comprehensive Report on U.S. Trade and Investment Policy Toward Sub-Saharan Africa and Implementation of the African Growth and Opportunity Act*, Washington

First Report to the Congress on the Operation of the Andean Trade Preferences Act as Amended, Washington

Ohmae, Kenichi, 1991, *The Borderless World: Power and Strategy in the International Economy*, Fontana, London

Okamoto, Jiro, ed., 2003, *Whither Free Trade Agreements: Proliferation, Evaluation and Multilateralization*, Institute of Development Economics, Chiba

ed., 2004, *Trade Liberalization and APEC*, Routledge, London

Okigbo, P. N.C., 1967, *Africa and the Common Market*, Longman, London

Oxfam, 2002, *Rigged Rules and Double standards: trade, globalisation and the fight against poverty*, www.maketradefair.com

Paemen, Hugo, "The Significance of the Uruguay Round". In Bourgeois, Jacques H. J., Frédérique Berrod and Eric Gippini Fournier, eds. (no date), *The Uruguay Round Results: A European Lawyers' Perspective*, European Interuniversity Press, Brussels

Palmeter, David, and Mavroidis, Petros C., 1999, *Dispute Settlement in the World Trade Organization: Policy and Practice*, Kluwer Law International, The Hague

Parry, Clive, and Grant, John P., 1988, *The Encyclopaedic Dictionary of International Law*, Oceania Publications, New York

Pauwelyn, Joost, 2002, *The Nature of WTO Obligations*, Jean Monnet Working Paper 1/02, New York University School of Law, New York

2004, "The Puzzle of WTO Safeguards and Regional Trade Agreements", *Journal of International Economic Law*, **7(1)**: 109–1142

Peaslee, Amos J., 1979, *International Governmental Organizations: Constitutional Documents*, revised 3rd ed., Martinus Nijhoff Publishers, The Hague

Peel, Jacqueline, 2004, *Risk Regulation Under the WTO SPS Agreement: Science as an International Normative Yardstick?*, Jean Monnet Working Paper 02/04, New York University School of Law, New York

Petersmann, Ernst-Ulrich, 2001, *Time for Integrating Human Rights into the Law of Worldwide Organizations: Lessons from European Integration Law for Global Integration Law*, Jean Monnet Working Paper 7/01, New York University School of Law, New York

Pierce, Richard J. Jr, 2000, "Antidumping Law as a Means of Facilitating Cartelization", *Antitrust Law*, 7.

Pomfret, Richard, 1997, *The Economics of Regional Trading Arrangements*, Clarendon Press, Oxford

Porter, Michael E., 1990, *The Competitive Advantage of Nations*, Free Press, New York

Porter, Roger B., Pierre Sauvé, Arvind Subramanian and Americo Beviglia Zampetti, eds., 2001, *Efficiency, Equity, and Legitimacy: The Multilateral Trading System at the Millennium*, Brookings Institution Press, Washington DC

Prebisch, Raúl, 1950, "The Economic Development of Latin America", reprinted in *Economic Bulletin for Latin America*, **7(1)**: (1962), 1–22

1963, "Development Problems of the Peripheral Countries and the Terms of Trade", reprinted in Theberge, J. D., ed., 1968, *Economics of Trade and Development*, John Wiley & Sons, New York (published originally in *Towards a Dynamic Development Policy for Latin America*, United Nations, New York, 1963)

Preeg, Ernest H., 1970, *Traders and Diplomats: An Analysis of the Kennedy Round of Negotiations under the General Agreement on Tariffs and Trade*, The Brookings Institution, Washington DC

1995, *Trade Policy Ahead: Three Tracks and One Question*, Center for Strategic and International Studies, Washington DC

1995, *Traders in a Brave New World: The Uruguay Round and the Future of the International Trading System*, University of Chicago Press

Productivity Commission, 2002, *Review of Australia's General Tariff Arrangements*, Report No. 12, AusInfo, Canberra

2003, *Rules of Origin under the Australia–New Zealand Closer Economic Relations Trade Agreement: Interim Research Report*, Canberra

Rangnekar, Dwijen, 2003, *Geographical Indications: A Review of Proposals at the TRIPS Council: Extending Article 23 to Products other than Wines and Spirits*, UNCTAD/ICTSD, Geneva

Reich, Robert R., 1991, *The Work of Nations*, Simon & Schuster, London

Ricardo, David, 1960 *[1817]*, *The Principles of Political Economy and Taxation*, Everyman Library, London

Robertson, David, 2000, "Civil Society and the WTO", *World Economy*, **23(9)**: 1119–1134

Robinson, Joan, 1947, "Beggar-my-neighbour Remedies for Unemployment". Reprinted in American Economic Association, *Readings in the Theory of International Trade*, vol. IV, George Allen and Unwin Ltd, London

Robson, Peter, 1968, *Economic Integration in Africa*, George Allen and Unwin Ltd, London

Rome, Emily, 1998, "The Background, Requirements, and Future of the GATT/WTO Preshipment Inspection Agreement", *Minnesota Journal of Global Trade*, **7(2)**: 469–507

Ruggie, John Gerard (1982), "International Regimes, Transactions, and Change: Embedded Liberalism in Postwar Economic Order", *International Organization*, **36(2)**: 379–415

Russell, Brian R., 1999, "How Long Can You Tread Water? The Anti-Economics of Trade Remedy Law". In Mendoza, Miguel Rodríguez, Patrick Low and Barbara Kotschwar, eds., *Trade Rules in the Making: Challenges in Regional and Multilateral Negotiations*, Organization of American States, Brookings Institution Press, Washington DC

Ruttley, Philip, MacVay, Iain, and Masa'deh, Ahmad, 1999, *Liberalisation and Protectionism in the World Trading System*, Cameron May, London

Sacerdoti, Giorgio, Alan Yanovich and Jan Bohanes, eds., 2006, *The WTO at Ten: The Contribution of the Dispute Settlement System*, Cambridge University Press, Cambridge, and World Trade Organization, Geneva

Salvatore, Dominick, 1987, *The New Protectionist Threat to World Welfare*, North-Holland, New York

Sampson, Gary P., and W. Bradnee Chambers, 1999, *Trade, Environment, and the Millennium*, United Nations University Press, Tokyo

Sands, Philippe, 2003, *Principles of International Environmental Law*, 2nd edn., Cambridge University Press, Cambridge

Sauvant, Karl P., and Hajo Hasenpflug, eds., 1977, *The New International Economic Order: Confrontation or Cooperation between North and South*, Westview Press, Boulder, Colorado

Sauvé, Pierre, 1995, "Assessing the General Agreement on Trade in Services: Half-Full or Half-Empty?", *Journal of World Trade*, **29(4)**: 125–145

Sauvé, Pierre and Robert M. Stern, eds., 2000, *GATS 2000: New Directions in Services Trade Liberalization*, The Brookings Institution, Washington DC

Schiff, Maurice, and L. Alan Winters, 2003, *Regional Integration and Development*, The International Bank for Reconstruction and Development / World Bank, Washington, DC

Schoenbaum, Thomas J., 2002, "International Trade and Environmental Protection". In Birnie, P. W., and A. E. Boyle, *International Law and the Environment*

Schott, Jeffrey J., ed., 2000, *The WTO After Seattle*, Institute for International Economics, Washington, DC

Schroeder, Werner, 2003, *European Union and European Communities*, Jean Monnet Working Paper 9/03, New York University School of Law, New York

Schumpeter, Joesph A., 1982 [1954], *History of Economic Analysis*, Allen & Unwin, London

Seid, Sherif H., 2002, *Global Regulation of Foreign Direct Investment*, Ashgate Publishing Limited, Aldershot

Shaw, Malcolm N., 1997, *International Law*, 4th edn., Grotius Publications, Cambridge

Sim, Kwan Kiat, 2003, "Rethinking the Mandatory/Discretionary Legislation Distinction in WTO Jurisprudence", *World Trade Review*, **2(1)**: 33–64

Singer, H. W., 1950, "U.S. Foreign Investment in Underdeveloped Areas: The Distribution of Gains Between Investing and Borrowing Countries", *American Economic Review*, **40**: 473–485

Singh, Jyoti Shankar, 1977, *A New International Economic Order: Towards a Redistribution of the World's Resources*, Praeger Publishers, New York

Smith, Adam, 1991 [1776], *The Wealth of Nations*, Everyman Library, London

Starke, J. G., 1989, *Introduction to International Law*, Butterworths, London

Steele, Keith, ed., 1996, *Anti-Dumping under the WTO: A Comparative Review*, Kluwer Law International and International Bar Association, London

Sterling, J. A. L., 2000, *TRIPs Agreement: Copyright and related rights*, Office for Official Publications, European Communities, Luxembourg

Stiglitz, Joseph E., 2002, *Globalization and its Discontents*, W. W. Norton & Company, New York

Stoever, William A., 2002, "Attempting to Resolve the Attraction-Aversion dilemma: A Study of the FDI Policy of the Republic of Korea", *Transnational Corporations*, **11(1)**: 49–76

Sykes, Alan O., 1998, "Antidumping and Antitrust: What Problems Does each Address?" In Robert Z. Lawrence, ed., *Brookings Trade Forum 1998*

Tanzi, Vito, 1998, *Corruption Around the World: Causes, Consequences, Scope and Cures*, IMF Working Paper WP/98/63, Washington, DC

The American Society of International Law, *International Legal Materials*, (bi-monthly), Washington DC

The International Trade Law Reports, Cameron May, London

Theberge, J. D., ed., 1968, *Economics of Trade and Development*, John Wiley & Sons, New York

Toye, John, and Richard Toye (2003), "The Origins and Interpretation of the Prebisch-Singer Thesis", *History of Political Economy*, **35(3)**: 437–467

Toye, Richard (2003), "Developing Multilateralism: The Havana Charter and the Fight for the International Trade Organization, 1947–1948", *The International History Review*, **XXV(2)**: 282–305

Trade Policies for a Better Future: Proposals for Action, 1985, GATT Secretariat, Geneva

Transparency International, 2004, *Global Corruption Report 2004*, Pluto Press, London

Trebilcock, Michael J., and Howse, Robert, 1999, *The Regulation of International Trade*, 2nd edn., Routledge, London and New York

Trends in International Trade: Report by a Panel of Experts, 1959, GATT Secretariat, Geneva

U.S. International Trade Commission, 2003, *The Impact of Trade Agreements: Effects of the Tokyo Round, U.S.–Israel FTA, U.S.–Canada FTA, NAFTA and the Uruguay Round on the U.S. Economy*, Washington, DC

United Mexican States v. Metalclad, 2001, British Columbia Supreme Court (Tysoe J.), 2001 B.C.D. Civ. J. 1708

United Nations Centre on Transnational Corporations and International Chamber of Commerce, 1992, *Bilateral Investment Treaties 1959–1991*, United Nations, New York

United Nations Conference on Trade and Development, 1985, *The History of UNCTAD*, United Nations, New York and Geneva

1996–, *International Investment Instruments: A Compendium*, United Nations, New York and Geneva

1999, *Fair and Equitable Treatment*, UNCTAD Series on issues in international investment agreements, United Nations, New York and Geneva

1999a, *Trends in international investment agreements: an overview*, United Nations, New York and Geneva

2000, *Positive Agenda and Future Trade Negotiations*, New York and Geneva

2001, *Host Country Operational Measures*, UNCTAD Series on Issues in International Investment Agreements, Geneva

2003, *Back to Basics: Market Access Issues in the Doha Agenda*, United Nations, New York and Geneva

2003, *Can Developing Countries Benefit from WTO Negotiations on Binding Disciplines for Hardcore Cartels?*, United Nations, New York and Geneva

2004, *Beyond Conventional Wisdom in Development Policy: An Intellectual History of UNCTAD 1964–2004*, United Nations, New York and Geneva

2004a, *Protecting and Promoting Traditional Knowledge: Systems, National Experience and International Dimensions,* United Nations, New York and Geneva

2004b, *Key Terms and Concepts in IIAs: A Glossary*, United Nations, New York and Geneva

2005, *Investor-State Disputes Arising from Investment Treaties: A Review*, New York and Geneva

2006a, *Developments in International Investment Agreements in 2005*, New York and Geneva

2006b, *Preserving Flexibility in IIAs: The Use of Reservations*, New York and Geneva

E-Commerce and Development Report, annual, United Nations, New York and Geneva

The Least Developed Countries Report, annual, United Nations, New York and Geneva

Trade and Development Report, annual, United Nations, Geneva

World Investment Report, annual, United Nations, Geneva

United Nations Conference on Trade and Development (UNCTAD) documents

UNCTAD/DITC/COM/2003/6, *An Analysis of the Agricultural Domestic Support under the Uruguay Agreement on Agriculture: the Blue Box*

UNCTAD/EDM/2004/2, *Trade and Gender: Opportunities and Challenges for Developing Countries*

UNCTAD/ITCD/TSB/2, 24 March 1998, *Globalization and the International Trading System: Issues Relating to Rules of Origin*

UNCTAD/TD(XI)/BP/13, *Creative Industries and Development*

United Nations Conference on Trade and Development and World Bank, 1994, *Liberalizing International Transactions in Services: A Handbook*, United Nations, New York and Geneva

United Nations Development Programme, 2003, *Human Development Report 2003: Millennium Development Goals: A Compact among Nations to end Human Poverty*, Oxford University Press, New York and Oxford

United Nations Economic Commission for Europe, 2003, *Trade Facilitation: The Challenges for Growth and Development* (Carol Cosgrove-Sacks and Mario Apostolov, eds.), United Nations, New York and Geneva

United States House of Representatives Committee on the Judiciary, 1994, *Compilation of Selected Antitrust Laws: As Amended Through December 31, 1994*, United States Government Printing Office, Washington

Valdés, Alberto, and William Foster (2003), "Special Safeguards for Developing Country Agriculture: A Proposal for WTO Negotiations", *World Trade Review*, 2(1): 5–31

Vermulst, Edwin A., 1990, "The Antidumping Systems of Australia, Canada, the EEC and the USA: Have Antidumping Laws Become a Problem in International Trade?", in Jackson, John H., and Edwin A. Vermulst, *Antidumping Law and Practice*, Harvester Wheatsheaf, London

Vermulst, Edwin, and Folkert Graafsma, 2002, *WTO Disputes: Anti-Dumping, Subsidies and Safeguards*, Cameron May, London

Vermulst, Edwin, Paul Waer and Jacques Bourgeois, 1994, *Rules of Origin in International Trade: A Comparative Study*, The University of Michigan Press, Ann Arbor

Vernon, Raymond, 1966, "International Investment and International Trade in the Product Cycle", *Quarterly Journal of Economics*, **80**: 190–207

Viner, Jacob, 1921, *Dumping: A Problem in International Trade*, reprinted in A. M. Kelley, *Reprints of Economic Classics*, New York, 1966

1950 [1923], *The Customs Union Issue*, Stevens & Sons, London

Walters, F. P., 1952, *A History of the League of Nations*, Oxford University Press, London

Weiler, J.H.H., ed., 2000, *The EU, the WTO and the NAFTA*, Oxford University Press, Oxford

Wessel, Ramses A., 2003, *The Constitutional Relationship between the European Union and the European Community: Consequences for the Relationship with the Member States*, Jean Monnet Working Paper 9/03, New York University School of Law, New York

Whalley, John, 1996 *Why do Countries seek Regional Trade Agreements?*, NBER working paper 5552, National Bureau of Economic Research, Cambridge, MA

Wilcox, Clair, 1949, *A Charter for World Trade*, Macmillan Company, New York

Williamson, John, 1990, "What Washington Means by Policy Reform". In John Williamson, ed., *Latin American Adjustment: How Much Has Happened?*, Institute for International Economics, Washington, DC

2000, "What Should the World Bank Think about the Washington Consensus", *The World Bank Research Observer*, **15(2)**: 251–264

Willig, Robert D., 1998, *Economic Effects of Antidumping Policy*. In Robert Z. Lawrence, ed., *Brookings Trade Forum 1998*

Winham, Gilbert R., 1986, *International Trade and the Tokyo Round Negotiations*, Princeton University Press

Winters, L. Alan, Neil McCulloch and Andrew McKay, 2004, "Trade Liberalization and Poverty: The Evidence So Far", *Journal of Economic Literature*, **XLII**: 72–115

WIPO, 2000, *Joint Recommendations Concerning Provisions on the Protection of Well-Known Marks, adopted at the Thirty-Fourth Series of Meetings of the Assemblies of Member States of WIPO, September 20 to 29, 1999*, Geneva

WIPO documents:

SCT/9/4, Standing Committee on the Law of Trademarks, Industrial Designs and Geographical Indications, Geneva, November 11 to 15, 2002, *The Definition of Geographical Indications*

SCT/8/4, Standing Committee on the Law of Trademarks, Industrial Designs and Geographical Indications, Geneva, May 27 to 31, 2002, *Geographical Indications: Historical Background, Nature of Rights, Existing Systems for Protection and Obtaining Protection in Other Countries*

SCT/5/3, Standing Committee on the Law of Trademarks, Industrial Designs and Geographical Indications, Geneva, September 11 to 15, 2000, *Possible Solutions for Conflicts Between Trade and Geographical Indications and for Conflicts Between Homonymous Geographical Indications*

WIPO/GRTKF/IC/5/3, Intergovernmental Committee on Intellectual Property and Genetic Resources, Traditional Knowledge and Folklore, Geneva, July 7 to 15, 2003, *Consolidated Analysis of the Legal Protection of Traditional Cultural Expressions*

WIPO/GRTKF/IC/5/8, Intergovernmental Committee on Intellectual Property and Genetic Resources, Traditional Knowledge and Folklore, Geneva, July 7 to 15, 2003, *Composite Study on the Protection of Traditional Knowledge*

WIPO/IPTK/MCT/02/INF.4, WIPO International Forum on "Intellectual Property and Traditional Knowledge: Our Identity, Our Future", Muscat, January 21 and 22, 2002, *The Protection of Traditional Knowledge, Including Expressions of Folklore*

Wolf, Martin, 2004, *Why Globalization Works*, Yale University Press, New Haven

World Bank, 2004, *Global Economic Prospects 2005: Trade, Regionalism and Development*, World Bank, Washington DC

World Commission on the Social Dimension of Globalization, 2004, *A Fair Globalization: Creating Opportunities for All*, International Labour Office, Geneva

World Health Organization and World Trade Organization, 2002, *WTO Agreements and Public Health*, Geneva

World Trade Organization, 1995, *Analytical Index: A Guide to GATT Law and Practice*, updated 6th edn., Geneva

1995, *Regionalism and the World Trading System*, Geneva

1996–, *Dispute Settlement Reports*, Cambridge University Press, Cambridge

1999, *The Legal Texts: Results of the Uruguay Round of Multilateral Trade Negotiations*, Cambridge University Press, Cambridge

1999a, *Guide to the Uruguay Round Agreements*, Kluwer Law International, The Hague

2001, *Guide to the GATS: An Overview of Issues for Further Liberalization of Trade in Services*, Kluwer Law International, The Hague

2001a, *The WTO Dispute Settlement Procedures: a collection of the relevant legal texts*, 2nd edn., Cambridge University Press, Cambridge

2001b, *Trading into the Future*, 2nd edn., revised, Geneva (also available on *http://www.wto.org*)

2003a, *World Trade Report 2003*, Geneva

2003b, *Understanding the WTO*, Geneva

2006, *WTO Dispute Settlement: One-Page Summaries, 1995-September 2006*, Geneva (also available on *www.wto.org*)

WTO documents:

TN/MA/S/2, Data Availability and Software Tools for Tariff Negotiations

WT/DS2/R, United States – Standards for Reformulated and Conventional Gasoline

WT/DS6/AB/R, Japan – Taxes on Alcoholic Beverages

WT/DS26ARB, European Communities – Measures Concerning Meat and Meat Products (Hormones) – Original Complaint by the United States – Recourse to Arbitration by the European Communities under Article 22.6 of the DSU

WT/DS27/AB/R, European Communities – Regime for the Importation, Sale and Distribution of Bananas

WT/DS44/R, Japan – Measures Affecting Consumer Photographic Film and Paper

WT/DS58/R, United States – Import Prohibition of Certain Shrimp and Shrimp Products

WT/DS75/AB/R, WT/DS84/AB/R, Korea – Taxes on Alcoholic Beverages

WT/DS98/R, Korea – Definitive Safeguard Measure on Imports of Certain Dairy Products

WT/DS/98/AB/R, Korea – Definitive Safeguard Measure on Imports of Certain Dairy Products

WT/DS/121/AB/R, Argentina – Safeguard Measures on Imports of Footwear

WT/DS135/R, European Communities – Measures Affecting Asbestos and Asbestos-Related Components

WT/DS136/R, United States – Anti-Dumping Act of 1916

WT/DS136/AB/R, United States – Anti-Dumping Act of 1916

WT/DS136/ARB, United States – Anti-Dumping Act of 1916 – Original Complaint by the European Communities – Recourse to Arbitration by the United States under Article 22.6 of the DSU

WT/DS160/R, United States – Section 110(5) of the US Copyright Act

WT/DS161/AB/R, WT/DS169/AB/R, Korea – Measures Affecting Imports of Fresh, Chilled or Frozen Beef

WT/DS/217/AB/R, WT/DS234/AB/R, United States – Continued Dumping and Subsidy Offset Act of 2000

WT/DS219/AB/R, European Communities – Anti-Dumping Duties on Malleable Cast Iron Tube or Pipe Fittings from Brazil

WT/DS243/R, United States – Rules of Origin for Textiles and Apparel Products: Report of the Panel

WT/DS257/R, United States – Final Countervailing Duty Determination with Respect to Certain Softwood Lumber from Canada

WT/REG/W/45, Rules of Origin Regimes in Regional Trade Agreements (5 April 2002)

Wyatt, Derrick, ed., 2002, *Rudden & Wyatt's EU Treaties & Legislation*, 8th edn., Oxford University Press, Oxford

Zeiler, Thomas W., 1999, *Free Trade, Free World: the advent of GATT*, University of North Carolina Press, Chapel Hill

Zonnekeyn, Geert A., 2002, "The *Bed Linen* Case and its Aftermath: Some Comments on the European Community's World Trade Organization Enabling Regulation", *Journal of World Trade*, **36(5)**: 993–1003